EIGHTH EDITION

Including Students with Special Needs

A Practical Guide for Classroom Teachers

MARILYN FRIEND
The University of North Carolina at Greensboro

WILLIAM D. BURSUCK
The University of North Carolina at Greensboro

Director and Publisher: Kevin M. Davis
Content Producer: Janelle Rogers
Sr. Development Editor: Alicia Reilly
Media Producer: Lauren Carlson
Portfolio Management Assistant: Casey Coriell
Executive Field Marketing Manager: Krista Clark
Executive Product Marketing Manager: Christopher Barry

Procurement Specialist: Carol Melville
Full Service Project Management: Thistle Hill Publishing Services
Cover Designer: Cenveo® Publisher Services
Cover Image: PM Images/Digitalvision/ Getty Images
Composition: Cenveo Publisher Services
Printer/Binder: LSC Communications
Cover Printer: LSC Communications
Text Font: ITC Garamond Std

Credits and acknowledgments for materials borrowed from other sources and reproduced, with permission, in this textbook appear on the appropriate page within the text.

Every effort has been made to provide accurate and current Internet information in this book. However, the Internet and information posted on it are constantly changing, so it is inevitable that some of the Internet addresses listed in this textbook will change.

The photo credits appear on p. xxiv and constitute a continuation of this copyright page.

Library of Congress Cataloging-in-Publication Data
Names: Friend, Marilyn Penovich, author. | Bursuck, William D., author.
Title: Including students with special needs : a practical guide for classroom teachers / Marilyn Friend, The University of North Carolina at Greensboro, William D. Bursuck, The University of North Carolina at Greensboro.
Description: Eighth edition. | New York, NY : Pearson, [2019] | Includes bibliographical references and index.
Identifiers: LCCN 2017055896| ISBN 9780134801674 (pbk.) | ISBN 0134801679 (pbk.)
Subjects: LCSH: Inclusive education—United States. | Mainstreaming in Education—United States. | Special education—United States. | Children with disabilities—Education—United States.
Classification: LCC LC1201 .F75 2019 | DDC 371.9/046—dc23
LC record available at https://lccn.loc.gov/2017055896

 **Pearson**

ISBN 10:   0-13-480167-9
ISBN 13: 978-0-13-480167-4

TO BETH AND BRUCE

our infinitely patient and supportive spouses—we are grateful for all you do for us.

With over 40 years of experience in the field of education, **MARILYN FRIEND** has been both a special education teacher and a general education teacher as well as a teacher educator, consultant, and staff developer. She currently is professor emerita in the Department of Specialized Education Services at The University of North Carolina at Greensboro and works extensively with local schools, school districts, and other education agencies to ensure that students with disabilities or other special needs reach their potential. Her particular areas of expertise—the focus of her research, teaching, writing, and consultation—include inclusive schooling, co-teaching and other collaborative school practices, systems change, urban education, and family–school partnerships.

WILLIAM D. BURSUCK began his career as a general education teacher, and as a special education teacher and university teacher educator he has maintained an active interest in inclusive practices. Dr. Bursuck continues to take particular pleasure in providing classroom and future teachers with practical, research-based strategies to improve educational outcomes for students with special needs in this age of school reform and teacher accountability. He is a professor emeritus in the Department of Specialized Education Services at The University of North Carolina at Greensboro.

Education in the first two decades of the twenty-first century undoubtedly will be remembered for the ongoing clamor for reform. From the mandates of the Elementary and Secondary Education Act (ESEA), currently referred to as the Every Student Succeeds Act (ESSA), through those of the Individuals with Disabilities Education Act (IDEA) to the increasingly higher standards adopted at the state level, relentless efforts are underway to improve the academic outcomes of U.S. students. And like all students, those who struggle to learn because of intellectual, physical, sensory, emotional, communication, learning disabilities, or other special needs must be taught using research-based practices and are expected to reach the same high academic standards as other learners. Further, teachers, administrators, and other professionals are being held directly accountable for the achievement of all of their students.

In many ways, the current educational climate is consonant with the beliefs on which *Including Students with Special Needs: A Practical Guide for Classroom Teachers* is based. In this eighth edition, we have continued our efforts to integrate today's expectations for students with our own continued strong commitment to inclusive practices, a commitment tempered by our knowledge and experience of the realities of day-to-day teaching. We know that teachers cannot do the job themselves; they rely on strong and sustained administrative support and adequate resources. We cannot guarantee that such key supports will always be in place, but we can provide teachers with a firm grounding in critical special education concepts, an understanding of the professionals who support these students and the procedures followed to ensure their rights are upheld, and a wealth of research-based strategies and interventions to foster their success.

The textbook is divided into four main sections. The first section provides fundamental background knowledge about the field of special education as well as current information on how students with disabilities are served within inclusive school environments. This is information that readers will find essential as they move from being students to teachers. The second section of the book provides a framework for thinking about effective instructional practices for students who struggle to learn. It provides a foundation for the remainder of the book. The third section introduces readers to students with specific disabilities and other special needs. Although each student is unique, this material provides readers with examples of students they may teach and summaries of their most typical characteristics. The material in the fourth section of the text represents the heart of any course on inclusive practices: instructional approaches that emphasize teaching students effectively in the academic, social, and behavior domains. Our emphasis is on reality-based techniques that can be implemented for many students with a range of special needs and that are consistent with today's instructional expectations and the knowledge base on effective practices.

We have brought to this project our own diversity: Marilyn with expertise in elementary and secondary education, especially in urban settings, and in collaboration, inclusive practices, and co-teaching; Bill with expertise in secondary education, literacy, instructional strategies, assessment, and grading practices. Our collective perspective on educating students with disabilities and other special needs is reflected in the organization and substance of the book; our ultimate goal is for general educators to be well prepared to effectively teach all of their students. Our approach to preparing this book is based on our research; our analysis of the scholarly literature on instruction, teacher preparation, and professional development; and our experiences teaching undergraduate and graduate educators. Our understanding, though, ultimately is grounded in our many observations of and conversations with general education and special education teachers who are diligently working, often in difficult circumstances, to make a difference in the lives of their students. We truly hope that we have managed to find the right blend of reader-friendly and research-based information. Above all, we hope this eighth edition is responsive to the many instructional dilemmas confronting today's teachers.

New to the Eighth Edition

Each time we revise *Including Students with Special Needs*, we carefully consider feedback from reviewers and users who contact us to offer their perspectives, and we also analyze the current trends, issues, policies, and practices influencing schools. The following are several of the key revisions made for each chapter in the eighth edition:

- CHAPTER 1 introduces in a straightforward way the complex concepts that characterize special education. In addition, readers are provided with an overview of several of the most critical issues that are shaping education for students with disabilities and other special needs as well as a discussion of inclusive practices as they occur in this second decade of the twenty-first century. This chapter also overviews the most recent relevant education legislation, that is, the *Every Student Succeeds Act* (ESSA) and the *Individuals with Disabilities Education Act* (IDEA), as well as the landmark special education 2017 Supreme Court decision *Endrew F. v. Douglas County School District*.

- CHAPTER 2 reflects the recent shift in the field of education from response to intervention (RtI) as an alternative to traditional approaches for determining whether students have learning disabilities to the broader preventive approach for both learning and behavior concerns represented by multi-tiered systems of support (MTSS). The chapter also outlines details that general education teachers must understand about parents' rights in making decisions regarding their children who may have disabilities. This chapter's discussion of the professionals in special education emphasizes those with whom elementary and secondary teachers most typically work.

- CHAPTER 3 explores the well-established importance of professional collaboration in the delivery of special education and other school services, including those related to RtI and MTSS. It directly addresses the complexity of collaboration when disagreements occur, especially those between school professionals and parents. Updated information is provided on co-teaching, teaming, and consultation, with attention also given to teacher–paraprofessional partnerships.

- CHAPTER 4 provides the latest information on the use of universal screening and progress-monitoring assessments in MTSS as well as high-stakes testing, including the testing requirements of the ESSA of 2015. The chapter also has a new Technology Notes feature on the use of computer-based standardized testing with students with disabilities.

- CHAPTER 5's already comprehensive coverage of foundational teaching practices has been updated and expanded by providing more in-depth, nuanced information on the use of research-based practices. The update also includes expanded coverage of computer-assisted instruction.

- CHAPTER 6 includes updated details about the characteristics and needs of students with autism spectrum disorders and other low-incidence disabilities, including physical, health, and sensory disorders. Strong emphasis is placed on the use of technology to meet the needs of students with these special needs, but attention also is paid to practical ideas for supporting these students in general education classrooms.

- CHAPTER 7 includes important updates on dyslexia research, the use of assistive technology in reading, and controversial therapies in special education. The latest information on practices for identifying students with learning disabilities using MTSS has also been added.

- CHAPTER 8 is intended to alert educators to the many students they will teach who have special needs, but not necessarily disabilities. It includes updated data related to these students (e.g., students who live in poverty, students who are abused or neglected) and also focuses on students with attention deficit–hyperactivity disorder (ADHD) and the best ways to accommodate them. In addition, this chapter addresses students who have special gifts and talents, and it examines the role of RtI and MTSS in preventing the need for special education for some at-risk students.

- CHAPTER 9's practical, research-based coverage of ways to adjust instruction for students with special needs now includes thoroughly updated sections on Tier 2 and 3 instructions in MTSS/RtI, expanded coverage of vocabulary instruction, and a new Technology Notes feature on virtual manipulatives.

- The already extensive focus in CHAPTER 10 on strategies for fostering student independence has been expanded by adding new strategies in the areas of reading and writing as well as a thoroughly updated Technology Notes feature on web-based programs to improve writing.

- In addition to the already strong, now updated section on classroom testing accommodations, CHAPTER 11 includes the most current information available on grading strategies that benefit all students, including those with special needs. The chapter has also added a Technology Notes feature on the use of electronic portfolios.

- CHAPTER 12 covers a dimension of education that can truly shape students' lives and determine educator effectiveness: strategies for addressing students' social, emotional, and behavioral needs. Emphasis is placed on preventing behavior problems, addressing serious problems with behavior intervention plans, and fostering positive social interactions among students with disabilities and their classmates.

RESOURCES AND TOOLS

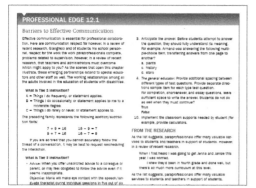

PROFESSIONAL EDGE features describe conceptual material, cutting-edge trends, and contemporary issues relevant to today's teachers. Included are new and sometimes controversial topics that experts in the field are talking about right now.

TECHNOLOGY NOTES features illustrate the use of technology to support students with disabilities in inclusive schools. For example, Chapter 3 explores options for electronic collaboration. In Chapter 10, research on the effectiveness of the latest computer software for improving the writing skills of students with disabilities provides teachers with the most current information.

WORKING TOGETHER features present cases in which professional family collaboration is needed and provide tips for optimizing collaborative efforts. For example, Chapter 5 presents two teachers learning to work together to accommodate a student in their shared class. Chapter 12 includes an example of what may occur when parents and professionals disagree.

DIMENSIONS OF DIVERSITY

Diversity has many faces. It includes ethnic, cultural, economic, linguistic, religious, ability, gender, and racial differences among the students you may teach.

WWW RESOURCES

The Family Village School website (www.familyvillage.wisc.edu/education/inclusion.html) provides a wide variety of information about associations, instructional resources, legal issues, projects, and research related to inclusion.

FYI

A primary disability is one that most adversely affects a student's educational. A secondary disability is an additional disability that also affects a student's education but to a lesser degree. For example, a student identified with a learning disability as a primary disability could have an emotional disability or health.

RESEARCH BASED PRACTICES

Dunn, Chambers, and Rabren (2004) found that students with learning disabilities are less likely to drop out of school if they perceive that (1) a connection exists between what they are learning and life after high school, (2) someone in school is trying to help them, and (3) at least one class in high school is helpful to them.

MARGINAL ANNOTATIONS are designed to extend readers' thinking and provide additional information on cultural and linguistic diversity, information related to the topic at hand, and useful websites. They provide readers access to the most current research related to teaching students with disabilities.

INSTRUCTIONAL PRACTICE

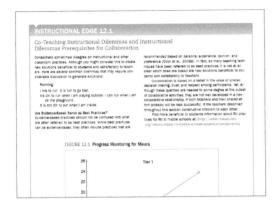

INSTRUCTIONAL EDGE features provide numerous research–based practices for teachers to use. For example, Chapter 8 provides strategies for teaching students with ADHD and, in Chapter 10, a model high school RtI program is discussed.

CASE IN PRACTICE features clarify key principles by providing brief case studies related to chapter concepts and teaching scripts as models. Chapter 8, for example, provides a case about meeting the needs of twice-exceptional students.

CHAPTER-OPENING VIGNETTES open each chapter, describing the experiences of elementary, middle school, and high school students as they relate to the topics discussed in each chapter. These individuals' experiences are referenced at key points in the chapter as well. The vignettes can form the basis for applying information and strategies from the chapter, and they can be a launching point for discussions of issues influencing the field, including inclusive practices, collaboration, and response to intervention. They are revisited at the ends of the chapters in the *Back to the Cases* features.

BACK TO THE CASES features conclude each chapter, offering readers the opportunity to visit MyLab Education to apply what they have learned in the chapter to these opening cases and receive immediate feedback. In some instances, questions are asked that require readers to analyze student characteristics and discuss how their success could be fostered. In others, situations educators are likely to encounter are outlined, and readers are asked how they would respond. In yet others, readers are asked to integrate learning across chapters to consider educational strategies for the highlighted students. This feature provides instructors with an effective summative activity for each chapter—one that can be completed by individual students or as a collaborative effort.

APPLICATIONS IN TEACHING PRACTICE cases at the end of each chapter are designed to encourage students to apply the chapter contents to real-life classroom situations.

AIDS TO UNDERSTANDING

MyLab Education

One of the most visible changes in the new edition, and one of the most significant, is the expansion of the digital learning and assessment resources embedded in the etext through the inclusion of MyLab Education in the work. MyLab Education is an online homework, tutorial, and assessment program designed to work with the text to engage learners and to improve learning. Within its structured environment, learners see key concepts demonstrated through real classroom video footage, are given opportunities to practice what they learn, and can test their understanding and receive feedback to guide their learning and to ensure their mastery of key learning outcomes. Designed to bring learners more directly into the worlds of students with special needs and the educators who work with them, the online resources in MyLab Education with the Enhanced Etext include:

Video Examples

In all chapters, embedded videos provide illustrations of special education principles or concepts in action. These video examples show students, teachers, and families working in classrooms and/or providing their perspectives about real life situations.

Self-Checks

In each chapter, self-check quizzes help assess how well learners have mastered the content. The self-checks are made up of self-grading multiple-choice items that not only provide feedback on whether questions are answered correctly or incorrectly, but also provide rationales for both correct and incorrect answers.

Application Exercises

These scaffolded analysis exercises are built around the scenarios that open each chapter, describing the experiences of elementary, middle school, and high school students as they relate to the topics discussed in each chapter. In the *Back to the Cases* feature at the end of each chapter, readers are challenged to apply what they have learned to the students they met at the beginning of the chapter. The questions in these exercises are usually constructed-response. Once learners provide their own answers to the questions, they receive feedback in the form of model answers written by experts.

Video Analysis Tool

The Video Analysis Tool is also available in the left-hand navigation bar of MyLab Education. This tool uses video case-based exercises to help students build their skills in analyzing teaching. Exercises provide classroom videos and rubrics to scaffold analysis. Timestamp and commenting tools allow users to easily annotate the video and connect their observations to concepts they learned in the text.

Support Materials for Instructors

The following resources are available for instructors to download on www .pearsonhighered.com/educators. Instructors enter the author or title of this book, select this particular edition of the book, and then click on the "Resources" tab to log in and download textbook supplements.

Instructor's Resource Manual (0-13-475414-x)

The Instructor's Resource Manual provides a multitude of activities and ideas to help instructors teach their courses, whether traditional or online. Each chapter provides a teaching outline, learning activities, and handouts.

Test Bank (0-13-475416-6)

The Test Bank provides hundreds of test items, with answer keys, organized by chapter and ready for use in creating tests based on the associated textbook material.

PowerPoint™ Slides (0-13-480173-3)

The PowerPoint™ slides include key concept summarizations, diagrams, and other graphic aids to enhance learning. They are designed to help students understand, organize, and remember core concepts and theories.

TestGen (0-13-475412-3)

TestGen is a powerful test generator that instructors install on a computer and use in conjunction with the TestGen test bank file for the text. Assessments, including equations, graphs, and scientific notation, may be created for both print and online testing.

TestGen is available exclusively from Pearson Education publishers. Instructors install TestGen on a personal computer (Windows or Macintosh) and create tests for classroom testing and for other specialized delivery options, such as over a local area network or on the web. A test bank, which is also called a Test Item File (TIF), typically contains a large set of test items, organized by chapter and ready for use in creating a test, based on the associated textbook material.

The tests can be downloaded in the following formats:

TestGen Testbank file—PC

TestGen Testbank file—MAC

TestGen Testbank—Blackboard 9 TIF

TestGen Testbank—Blackboard CE/Vista (WebCT) TIF

Angel Test Bank (zip)

D2L Test Bank (zip)

Moodle Test Bank

Sakai Test Bank (zip)

Acknowledgments

Many individuals helped us during the preparation of the eighth edition of *Including Students with Special Needs*, and without their assistance and encouragement the project undoubtedly would have stalled. First and most important, we express our gratitude to our families. They have listened to us worry about how to respond to reviewer comments and suggestions, meet the deadlines that sometimes seemed impossibly near, analyze aloud whether particular video clips accurately represented the concept at hand, and fret about what material to add or keep in the book and what material had to be dropped. They helped us sort through the conundrums, offered suggestions with the perspective of outsiders who deeply cared, and tolerated our need to hide in our offices as we wrote and rewrote. We cannot possibly say thank you in enough ways for their support.

We also thank the individuals who helped us with all the innumerable details of revising a textbook. Tammy Baron from Western Carolina University was instrumental in developing the Back to the Cases and MyLab activities. Tammy also assisted us in finding just the right videos to help bring our text to life, and she made suggestions and corrections that helped improve our final product. Sonia Martin, an invaluable colleague at The University of North Carolina at Greensboro, helped with the myriad formatting tasks that accompany textbook revision. We especially thank her for lending a sympathetic ear and for her inimitable sense of humor. Courtney Barron's contribution likewise is greatly appreciated: She created the new icon for the INCLUDE process that is a centerpiece concept for *Including Students with Special Needs*.

The professionals at Pearson also have supported this effort with both words and actions. Director and Publisher Kevin Davis has steered this eighth edition through the many steps of its creation, offering guidance and insights with encouragement, clarification, and patience. Developmental Editor Alicia Reilly was, as always, diligent in her efforts to help us keep the book clear, responsive to the needs of the field, and on target with the many components of the book, from the main manuscript to the features to the videos—and she demonstrated once again that nagging about deadlines and tasks still awaiting attention can be accomplished in a way that is neither overly intrusive nor offensive. Alicia also helped us navigate the increasingly complex waters encountered in seeking permissions for reproduced material. Thanks so much, Alicia.

Special thanks go to the reviewers for this edition: Glennda McKeithan—North Carolina State University; Genevieve Hay—College of Charleston; and Dennis Attick—Clayton State University. We were impressed with their meticulous approach to reviewing the manuscript and their perceptive suggestions. We tried to incorporate as many of their recommendations as we could, and they definitely contributed to the development of a better textbook.

Finally, we continue to be grateful to all of our university colleagues, students, and professionals in schools who influence our thinking about educating students with special needs in general education settings. Their questions about best practices, their challenges to our thinking, and their ideas for better communicating our message have been invaluable.

BRIEF CONTENTS

CONTENTS

CHAPTER 4
Assessing Student Needs 106

CHAPTER 5
Planning Instruction by Analyzing Classroom and Student Needs 136

FEATURES AT A GLANCE

	Professional Edge	Instructional Edge
CHAPTER 1 The Foundation for Educating Students with Special Needs	• Characteristics of Inclusive Schools, 19 • Promoting Cultural Competence: A Self-Assessment, 30	Understanding Multi-Tiered Systems of Support (MTSS), 15
CHAPTER 2 Special Education Procedures and Services	• Working with Paraprofessionals, 42 • Self-Determination for Students with Disabilities, 43 • Sample IEP Goals and Objectives, 59	RtI and Intensity, 50
CHAPTER 3 Building Partnerships Through Collaboration	• Who Is Responsible for What?, 74 • Barriers to Effective Communication, 77 • Professional Interactions that Extend Beyond School, 89 • Collaborating with Families from Asian/Pacific Islander Cultures, 95	Co-Teaching Instructional Dilemmas, 92
CHAPTER 4 Assessing Student Needs	• Accommodations for Students with Disabilities on Standardized Tests, 117 • Assessing Student Fluency in Basic Academic Skills, 121	• Using Universal Screening in RtI/MTSS to Identify Students at Risk, 110 • Strategies for Fair Assessment of Diverse Students, 116 • Using Progress Monitoring to Evaluate Student Performance in RtI/MTSS, 132
CHAPTER 5 Planning Instruction by Analyzing Classroom and Student Needs	• Using "Sponges" to Increase Academic Learning Time, 157 • Guidelines for Evaluating Basic Skills Materials, 162	• Common Questions About Evidence-Based Practices, 151 • Delivering Effective Instruction in the Tier 1 Core Curriculum, 158 • Strategies for Teaching Science to English-Learners (ELs), 166
CHAPTER 6 Students with Low-Incidence Disabilities	• Warning Signs That Students May Have Vision or Hearing Loss, 195 • What to Do When a Student Has a Seizure, 205	• Teaching Students with Autism Spectrum Disorders, 186 • Teaching Students with Traumatic Brain Injury (TBI), 208
CHAPTER 7 Students with High-Incidence Disabilities	• Understanding Dyslexia, 224 • Controversial Therapies in Learning and Behavioral Disabilities: What Does the Research Say?, 232	Accommodating Learners in Math Who Are Linguistically and Culturally Diverse, 229
CHAPTER 8 Students with Special Needs Other Than Disabilities	• Section 504 Accommodations, 248 • Gifted Underachievers, 262 • Levels of Language Proficiency, 268	• Strategies for Teaching Students with ADHD, 257 • English Learners and Reading, 266

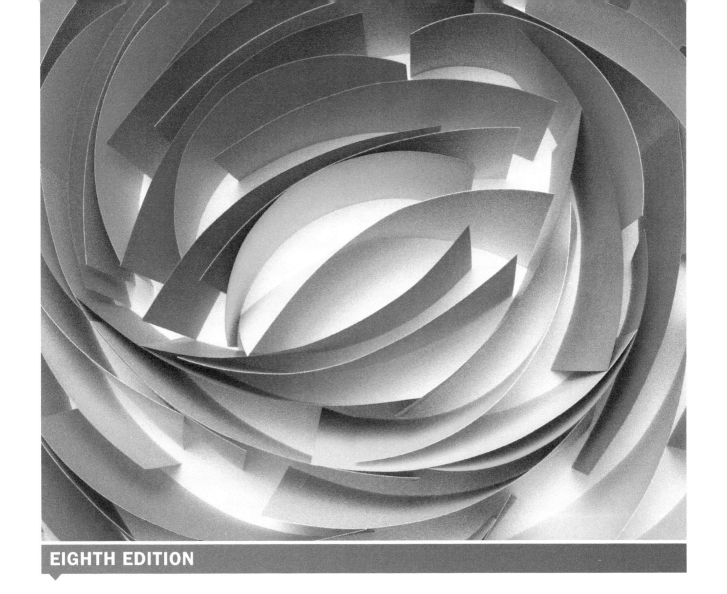

EIGHTH EDITION

Including Students with Special Needs

A Practical Guide for Classroom Teachers

CHAPTER 1

The Foundation for Educating Students with Special Needs

LEARNING OUTCOMES

After you read this chapter, you will be able to:

1-1 Explain fundamental terms and concepts that describe special education, including those in federal law.

1-2 Explore significant factors that have shaped contemporary special education services.

1-3 Analyze key themes that characterize today's educational priorities for students with disabilities,

including prevention, high expectations and accountability, evidence-based practices, and inclusiveness.

1-4 Describe the categories of disabilities addressed in federal law and note other special needs your students may have.

LUCAS was diagnosed as having autism when he was just three years old. His parents, worried about his delayed language development and extreme sensitivity to noise, took him to the pediatrician. After his diagnosis, Lucas was enrolled in an early childhood special education program, and his parents attribute his remarkable progress to that early intervention. Now in middle school, Lucas spends most of each day in general education, seeing a special education teacher three times each week for academic and social support that is grounded in research-based approaches. He has an assigned seat in each academic class; he becomes upset if someone else sits where he prefers to be. He sometimes participates in the many small-group activities his teachers arrange, but when he is having a difficult day, he works by himself in an isolated corner of the classroom. Lucas's classmates have known him for so long that they are patient with his social awkwardness, and they often are in awe of his knowledge of favorite topics, currently music groups from the 1960s. Lucas generally does well in school, and he says that he would like to be a musician when he grows up. However, Lucas's mother reports that school is extremely stressful. She notes that when Lucas arrives home each afternoon, he heads straight for his bedroom where he rocks in a favorite chair, usually for about 20 minutes. She explains that this is Lucas's "decompression" routine and that he needs this time and procedure to recover from the stress of school's demands.

What is special education and how did it come to be? How does special education meet the needs of students with autism or other disabilities? Why is it so important for Lucas to be educated as much as possible with his peers?

MONIKA is a second-grade student who has an inherited disorder called Fragile X syndrome, diagnosed when she was just a year old. She has received special education and related services since that time, including speech/language therapy because of her delayed language development and occupational therapy to help her with fine motor skills such as grasping a pencil and cutting with scissors. Because Monika has a moderate intellectual disability and has significant delays in learning academic skills, she spends about half of her day in a special education classroom for instruction in language arts and math, but she joins her peers without disabilities for science, social studies, art, physical education, lunch, and recess. The goal is for her to learn as many academic skills as possible while also working on her skills for interacting with peers and adults and her ability to function in the larger environment of general education. Ms. Shriner, Monika's teacher, describes her as eager-to-please and "sweet," noting that she works best on days when a clear routine is followed. Ms. Shriner also knows that Monika is easily overwhelmed, and so she sometimes permits her to work quietly wearing headphones or with just one or two classmates. One reward that is very effective when encouraging Monika to complete difficult tasks is music; she listens to her favorites for as long as permitted.

How likely are you to teach a student like Monika? What is an intellectual disability? What factors have led to students like Monika being welcomed members of their school communities, working to reach the highest learning standards possible, instead of being relegated to separate classrooms and schools?

AARON has a learning disability that was identified when he was in third grade after intensive academic remediation failed to accelerate his learning progress. He also takes medication for attention deficit–hyperactivity disorder (ADHD). Now in 11th grade, Aaron is continuing to learn how to compensate for the academic difficulties he experiences. Although he is a bright and personable young man, he reads at about a seventh-grade level, and his writing is much like that of a student in second grade. He doesn't like to talk about his learning disabilities (LD); he doesn't want other students

3

to make fun of him or treat him differently because he has LD. He is even more sensitive when asked to talk about why he takes medication. Even though his doctor has cautioned him to take the medication exactly as prescribed, he sometimes secretly skips taking it to see if he can get along without it. In his U.S. history class, Aaron is most successful on tests when he answers questions orally; he understands the concepts even if he cannot efficiently write down or type his thoughts. Because he doesn't like to be singled out, however, he sometimes refuses to take tests in that manner or get additional assistance during study period, and so his grades are lower than they could be. Aaron is an excellent athlete, and on the basketball court he feels equal to his friends. However, his parents are concerned that his interest in sports is distracting him from schoolwork.

How do educators try to prevent the need for special education for students like Aaron? What is a learning disability? What types of supports and services do Aaron and other students with LD and other disabilities need to succeed in school?

Students like Lucas, Monika, and Aaron are just three of the nearly 6.1 million school-age students in the United States who have disabilities that make them eligible for special education (U.S. Department of Education, 2016). But their disabilities do not tell you who they are: They are children or young adults and students first. Like all students, they have positive characteristics and negative ones, they have great days and not-so-great days, and they have likes and dislikes about school and learning. As a teacher, you probably will instruct students like Lucas, Monika, and Aaron along with other students with disabilities or other special needs.

The purpose of this textbook is to help you understand these students and learn strategies for effectively teaching them. Ultimately, you can be the teacher who makes a profound positive difference in the life of a student with a disability or other exceptional needs. With the knowledge and skills you acquire for instructing these learners, you will be prepared for both the challenges and the rewards of helping them achieve their education goals.

What Is Special Education?

As you begin your study of special education and think about your responsibility for teaching students with disabilities, it is important that you understand that the field is guided by several critical concepts, many of them deriving directly from federal special education law. These key concepts illustrate clearly contemporary expectations for the education of students with disabilities as well as the importance of your role as a general educator in contributing to their success.

Special Education Components

When teachers refer to students with *disabilities*, they mean students who are eligible to receive special education services according to federal and state guidelines. Special education includes three types of services, each briefly described next, intended to enable these students to reach their potential.

SPECIALLY DESIGNED INSTRUCTION All students who are eligible for special education services must receive specially designed instruction (SDI) (Kauffman, 2015a). SDI is tailored to meet the individual needs of the student with a disability, it is monitored closely, and students' progress related to it must be documented. Further, this specialized instruction usually pertains to students' academic skills, but it also may address students' communication skills, behavior challenges, social interaction skills, vocational or functional skills, or any other areas related to education affected by the disability, as would be the case for Lucas, Monika, and Aaron, whom you met in the introduction to this chapter. Special educators are the professionals primarily responsible for delivering SDI, but in some states general education teachers share this responsibility. Even when this is not the case, when special educators work with general education teachers in their classrooms, an increasingly common arrangement, both professionals participate in SDI delivery.

RELATED SERVICES Students with disabilities also may receive related services, that is, assistance beyond academic instruction that enables students to benefit from special education. Monika, whom you met at the beginning of the chapter, is an example of a student receiving related services, both speech/language therapy and occupational therapy. However, many other related services are available to students with disabilities, including physical therapy, counseling, adapted physical education, and transportation to and from school in a specialized van or school bus (NICHCY, 2013a; Teasley, 2016). Some related services are offered in a separate setting such as an office or specially equipped classroom, but sometimes these services are delivered in the general education classroom and integrated with the other instruction occurring there. Some students eligible for special education do not need related services, some receive them for just a relatively brief period (e.g., speech therapy in kindergarten and first grade), and others require them throughout their school years.

SUPPLEMENTARY AIDS AND SERVICES The third part of special education is termed supplementary aids and services (SAS). This is a broad array of supports that enable students with disabilities to participate in general education, extracurricular activities, and other school settings so that they can be educated with peers who do not have disabilities (NICHCY, 2013b). SAS may include, as needed, supports such as preferential seating, access to computer technology, and instructional adjustments (e.g., more time to complete tests, simplified assignments, alternative but equivalent instructional materials).

You may encounter one additional set of terms related to supplementary aids and services. Students with disabilities are entitled to receive accommodations and modifications as part of their instruction. Accommodations are changes in *how* the student learns key curriculum. For example, a student may be learning the same math as classmates, but he may be assigned fewer math problems because he takes longer than other students to complete each one. Another student may respond to an essay question on a history test by writing bullet points instead of paragraphs, because it reduces the writing task and the goal is to determine what she has learned about history rather than to assess paragraph-writing ability. In each case, the curriculum has remained the same. Modifications refer to *what* the student learns and usually imply that some curriculum is removed. For example, a student with a significant intellectual disability may not learn all the vocabulary in a science unit, focusing instead on words that he is likely to encounter in day-to-day life. As you might surmise, many students with disabilities need accommodations, but only those with significant intellectual disabilities usually require modifications.

As a general education teacher, your most common responsibilities as part of special education will be to provide students with their supplementary aids and services, especially their accommodations and, for a few students, modifications (e.g., Baker & Scanlon, 2016). That is, you will be informed of changes such as those outlined in this section needed by each student with a disability whom you teach, and you will be expected to make those changes so that the student can succeed. If you have questions about the changes, a special educator will clarify what is expected, but it will be your responsibility to be sure that the required supports are part of your instruction.

MyLab Education

Video Example 1.1: Five Steps to an Inclusive Classroom

This video offers many suggestions on effectively teaching students with disabilities, and it's a succinct preview of many topics addressed in this textbook. https://www.youtube.com/watch?v=MGPDqzhjtj0

DIMENSIONS OF DIVERSITY

Diversity has many faces. In addition to ability and disability, it includes ethnic, cultural, economic, linguistic, religious, gender, and racial differences among the students you may teach.

Federal Special Education Law

The three components of special education just outlined are spelled out in federal special education law, called the **Individuals with Disabilities Education Act (IDEA)**. This law was originally passed as the **Education for All Handicapped Children Act, (EHCA) Public Law 94–142**, in 1975. It describes categories of disabilities that make students eligible to receive special education and specifies the related services and supplementary aids and services to which students might be entitled. In addition, it establishes procedures for identifying a student as needing special education and outlines the rights of parents who disagree with the educational services offered to their children (Johns, 2016).

CORE PRINCIPLES OF IDEA Over the four decades since IDEA was enacted, it has been revised several times to increase the range of services students with disabilities must receive, expand the groups of students who are eligible for special education, and clarify procedures for addressing particular types of issues (e.g., serious student behavior incidents). However, the following six core principles have remained its foundation (Zirkel, 2015):

MyLab Education

Video Example 1.2: What Does the Least Restrictive Environment Look and Sound Like?

Watch a video that connects the history of special education and specific examples of LRE in action.

- *Free appropriate public education (FAPE)*. Students with disabilities are entitled to attend public schools and receive the educational services that have been designed specifically to address their special needs, possibly including specialized materials, settings, and technology. This education is provided at no cost to parents.
- *Least restrictive environment (LRE)*. Students with disabilities must be educated in the educational setting most like that for students without disabilities in which they can succeed with appropriate supports provided. That is, the law clearly sets an expectation that students with disabilities should not be assigned to separate special classes or schools without access to typical peers, except to the extent it is the only option for them to be appropriately educated. For most students with disabilities, the LRE is the general education classroom for much or all of the school day. For some students, it is a combination of a general education and a special education setting. For a few students with the most complex needs, a special education setting for most or all of the school day is required.
- *Individualized education*. The instructional services and other assistance for a student with disabilities must be tailored to meet his assessed needs according to a prepared **individualized education program (IEP)** that is reviewed and updated annually. IEPs are written by a team of professionals and the student's parents, and they are a sort of roadmap for educating the student. You will learn much more detail about IEPs in Chapter 2.
- *Nondiscriminatory evaluation*. Students must be assessed using instruments that do not discriminate on the basis of race, culture, or disability. Here is a simple example of this concept: If a math test item was based on football, American students might conjure up their favorite teams and think about touchdowns and the gridiron. Students from many other cultures would immediately assume the question was about soccer and might thus interpret it incorrectly. Further, in considering eligibility for special education services, a student must be assessed by a multidisciplinary team in her native language using tests that are valid for assessing the areas of concern (e.g., reading or math, social skills). Students' eligibility for special education cannot be decided on the basis of only one test.
- *Due process*. If a disagreement occurs concerning a student's eligibility for special education, the student's educational placement, or the services the student receives, a specific set of informal and formal procedures must be followed to resolve the dispute. Generally, no changes can be made regarding the student's education until the issue has been resolved at a formal hearing and, if necessary, the appropriate court. Collectively, these procedures are referred to as due process.
- *Zero reject/child find*. No student may be excluded from receiving a public education because of having a disability. That is, school district representatives

may not tell the parents of a child with a disability that the child has so many needs that they cannot be met through the public school system. If children have extraordinary needs, the school district is obligated to find a way to appropriately educate them. This provision also prohibits schools from excluding children who have communicable diseases, such as AIDS, or from expelling students and ceasing the provision of special education services. The child find part of this principle mandates that each state must be proactive in locating children who may be entitled to special education services (e.g., through public service announcements or highway billboards).

ADDITIONAL PROVISIONS OF IDEA As you continue your study of the field of special education, you will become familiar with many additional parts of IDEA that will guide your practices as an education professional. Some of the most important additional provisions in the current law include these:

- On most teams writing the IEP for a student, at least one general education teacher must be a participating member.
- Students with disabilities must be taught by teachers who are highly qualified in the core academic content being taught. This implies that students either should be in general education with the classroom teacher or in a special education setting with a teacher who has met state requirements to demonstrate proficiency to teach the core curriculum.
- Students with disabilities must be included in the assessment program that exists for all students. However, they may be entitled to accommodations so that they can demonstrate their learning (e.g., longer time to take the test, shorter test sessions, assistance with instructions). You are very likely to have students with disabilities who receive these special provisions during both classroom assessments and annual high-stakes assessments.

Further IDEA provisions are summarized in Figure 1.1. Keep in mind that IDEA is not static. It is interpreted through court cases and periodically revised based on research and trends in education (e.g., Bailey & Bauer-Jones, 2015; Yell,

WWW RESOURCES

https://sites.ed.gov/idea/topic-areas
At the *Topic Areas* page of the U.S. Department of Education IDEA website, you can learn more detail about the requirements of federal special education law. Click on any topic to find specifics on many aspects of IDEA.

FIGURE 1.1 **Provisions of the Individuals with Disabilities Education Act (IDEA)**

In addition to the core principles that have characterized special education law since its 1975 passage, this list summarizes several major provisions in the current authorization of IDEA. You will learn more about these and other provisions as you continue your study of special education.

- Parent participation
  - Parents must be part of the decision-making team for determining special education eligibility and the appropriate education placement.
  - School professionals must report to parents on their children's progress at least as often as other parents receive such information.
- Placement justification
  - A clear justification must be provided whenever a student is assigned to a setting other than general education.
- Discipline
  - As needed, strategies for addressing a student's behavior must be included as part of the IEP.
  - Even if a student commits a serious offense (e.g., bringing a weapon to school), special education services must be continued.
- Transition services
  - By the time a student with a disability reaches age 16, a plan must be implemented to prepare the student for life after school (e.g., college, vocational training, a job).
  - The transition plan must be updated annually and have specific and measurable goals.
- Disproportionate representation
  - School districts must take specific steps to ensure that students from minority groups are not overidentified as being eligible for special education.
  - If disproportionality has occurred, school districts are required to take steps to correct the problem.

Katsiyannis, Losinski, & Marshall, 2016). In fact, what you learn about special education now may change over the next several years. However, the core principles of IDEA are unlikely to be modified, nor are its most essential provisions that ensure students with disabilities can receive an education equivalent to that of their typical peers.

MyLab Education Self-Check 1.1:

What Influences Have Shaped Special Education?

Special education as it exists today has been shaped by a number of different factors. Although people with disabilities have been identified and treated for centuries, special education grew rapidly only in the twentieth century (Kode, 2002; Winzer, 1993). As special education has evolved, it has been influenced by the social and political context in which it emerged, parent advocacy, the civil rights movement, several precedent-setting court cases, current civil rights law, and current general education legislation. These factors are highlighted in Figure 1.2 and explained in the following sections.

FIGURE 1.2 Influences on Current Special Education Practices

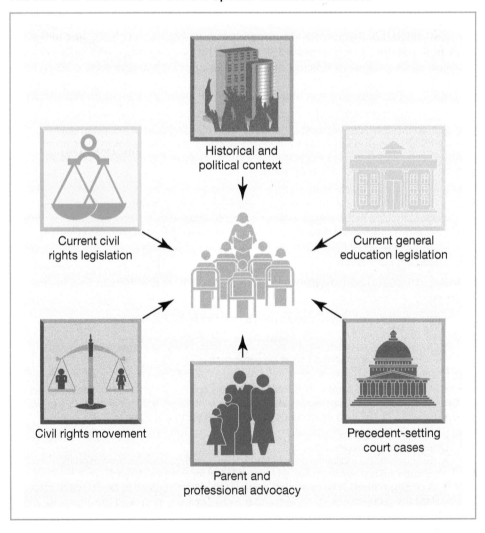

The Context for the Development of Special Education

When compulsory public education began near the turn of the twentieth century, almost no school programs existed for students with disabilities (Kode, 2002; Scheerenberger, 1983). Students whose disabilities were relatively mild—that is, learning or behavior problems or minor physical impairments—were educated along with other students because their needs were not considered extraordinary. Many children with significant intellectual or physical disabilities did not attend school at all, and others were educated by private agencies or lived in institutions. In fact, for the first half of the twentieth century, many states explicitly permitted school districts to prohibit some students with disabilities from attending (Yell, Rogers, & Rogers, 1998).

However, as compulsory education became widespread during the 1920s and 1930s, the number of special classes in public schools grew. Schools were expected to be like efficient assembly lines, with each class of students moving from grade to grade and eventually graduating from high school as productive citizens prepared to enter the workforce (Patton, Payne, & Beirne-Smith, 1986; Scheerenberger, 1983). Special classes were developed as a place for students who could not keep up with their classmates. Because many students with disabilities still were not in school, most of the students sent to special classes probably had mild or moderate learning or intellectual disabilities. Educators at the time believed that such students would learn better in a protected setting and that segregating them would preserve the efficiency of the overall educational system (Bennett, 1932; Pertsch, 1936).

By the 1950s, special education programs were available in many school districts, but some undesirable outcomes were becoming apparent. For example, students in special classes often were considered incapable of learning academic skills. They spent their school time practicing what were called "manual skills" such as weaving and bead stringing. Researchers began questioning this practice and conducted studies to explore the effectiveness of special education. When they compared students with disabilities who were in special education classes to similar students who had remained in general education, they found the latter group often had learned more than the former (Goldstein, Moss, & Jordan, 1965). By the late 1960s, many authorities in the field questioned whether segregated special classes were the most appropriate educational setting for many students with disabilities (Blatt, 1958; Christopolos & Renz, 1969; Dunn, 1968; Lilly, 1971).

Parent Advocacy

During the same time period that the number of special education classrooms was growing and professionals were beginning to question their value, parents of children with significant disabilities began to organize (Blatt, 1987). These early advocates usually were reacting to the then-common practice of institutionalizing children with significant disabilities; they wanted their children to live at home and to receive appropriate services in their communities. Several organizations whose names you may know were founded during this era:

- United Cerebral Palsy (UCP) was founded in 1949 by two sets of parents whose children had cerebral palsy (a disability affecting motor skills, discussed in more detail in Chapter 6). They advertised in the newspaper for parents of other children with disabilities to join them to advocate for community integration and services. These parents were the first to call media attention to the needs of this group of children (UCP, 2015).

- The ARC (originally called the National Association for Retarded Children) was founded in 1950 by a group of parents committed to helping others understand their children's potential and to gaining access for them to preschool programs, education, and jobs. This organization was the first to call attention to the connection between lead-based paint and intellectual disabilities in children (The ARC, 2016).

MyLab Education

Video Example 1.3: Inclusive Practices
Think about how this teacher's comments about inclusive practices might pertain to the students that you will teach.

DIMENSIONS OF DIVERSITY

As you prepare to be an educator, you will learn about the importance of developing *cultural competence* by increasing your awareness of your own worldview, understanding and valuing worldwide cultural differences, and developing effective cross-cultural communication skills so that you can interact effectively with students, parents, and colleagues from diverse backgrounds. That concept is extended with *cultural proficiency*, that is, your skill for teaching about differences in a way that conveys respect for all cultures.

- The National Association for Down Syndrome (NADS) began in 1960 when a young girl's parents ignored their physician's advice to institutionalize their daughter and decided to raise her at home. They joined with other parents of children with Down syndrome (a condition explained in more detail in Chapter 6), organized educational and recreational programs for them, and provided supports for families (NADS, 2016).

These and other parent groups became a strong voice for the rights of children with disabilities (Osgood, 2008; Winzer 2012), a voice that continues in the present day. They questioned traditional practices and insisted that children with disabilities were entitled to the same educational experiences as other children. Such groups focused public attention on these children's needs, lobbied for increased research to address their children's disorders, and sought assistance through legislation and litigation.

The Civil Rights Movement

During the 1950s and 1960s, another powerful force began contributing to the development of new approaches for special education, and it still has an impact today (U.S. Department of Education, 2010; Winzer, 2012). The civil rights movement, although initially focused on the rights of African Americans, expanded and began to influence thinking about people with disabilities (Chaffin, 1975; Fleischer & Zames, 2001). In the *Brown v. Board of Education* decision in 1954, the U.S. Supreme Court ruled that it was unlawful under the Fourteenth Amendment to discriminate arbitrarily against any group of people. The Court then applied this concept to the education of children, ruling that the state-mandated separate education for African American students could not be an equal education. This court decision introduced the concept of *integration* into public education, the notion that the only way to protect students' constitutional right to equal opportunity was to ensure that diverse student groups learned together. Soon people with disabilities were recognized as another group whose rights often had been violated because of arbitrary discrimination. For children, the discrimination occurred when they were denied access to schools because of their disabilities. Parents and advocates soon began arguing that the education of children with disabilities was not just a moral obligation of public schools, it was a civil right to which all children, regardless of disabilities or other special needs, were entitled.

Precedent-Setting Court Cases

The combination of the civil rights movement and parents' (and professionals') advocacy for children with disabilities led to several precedent-setting court cases (e.g., Rueda, Klingner, Sager, & Velasco, 2008; Yell, 2012). The following cases are especially important to your understanding of today's special education. Several other landmark cases are presented in Figure 1.3.

PENNSYLVANIA ASSOCIATION FOR RETARDED CHILDREN V. COMMONWEALTH OF PENNSYLVANIA (343 F. SUPP. 279) (1972) This decision, issued by the U.S. District Court of the Eastern District of Pennsylvania, is considered the basis for most of the key principles of IDEA. The Court ruled that schools may not refuse to educate students with intellectual disabilities and that a free public education must be provided to all students, not just those school officials decided they were prepared to serve.

OBERTI V. BOARD OF EDUCATION OF CLEMENTON SCHOOL DISTRICT (995 F.2D 204) (1993) This decision about a child with Down syndrome by the U.S. Court of Appeals for the Third Circuit established that school districts must make available in the general education setting a full range of supports and services in order to accommodate students with disabilities. The fact that a student learns differently from other students does not necessarily warrant that student's exclusion from the general education classroom.

FYI

The *Council for Exceptional Children* (CEC), founded in 1922 by Elizabeth Farrell, is a professional organization for teachers, administrators, parents, and other advocates for the rights of students with disabilities. Explore its many resources at http://www.cec.sped.org.

FIGURE 1.3 **Court Cases Affecting Special Education**

Since the passage of federal special education law, numerous legal decisions have clarified the rights of students with disabilities and the responsibilities of schools for educating them (e.g., Alquraini, 2013; Yell, Ryan, Rozalski, & Katsiyannis, 2009). Several cases that have significantly affected special education include these:

- *Larry P. v. Wilson Riles* (793 F.2d 969) (1986)
  The U.S. District Court for the Northern District of California ruled that intelligence (IQ) tests—because of their racial and cultural bias—cannot be used to determine whether African American students have intellectual disabilities or any other disability.
- *Board of Education of Hendrick School District v. Rowley* (632 F.2d 945) (1982)
  The U.S. Supreme Court ruled that although special education services must provide an appropriate education, the law does not require optimum services. The result was that the parents' request for a sign-language interpreter for their daughter was denied because she was achieving at an average level without this support.
- *Daniel R. R. v. State Board of Education* (874 F.2d 1036) (1989)
  The U.S. Court of Appeals for the Fifth Circuit ruled that appropriate placement for students with disabilities depends on whether:
  (1) a student can be satisfactorily educated in the general education setting with supplementary supports provided and
  (2) the student is included to the maximum extent appropriate in cases in which the general education setting is not successful.
  The school district did not violate the rights of Daniel, a student with Down syndrome, when he was moved to a special education setting after an unsuccessful attempt to include him in general education.
- *Schaffer v. Weast* (126 S. Ct. 528) (2005)
  The U.S. Supreme Court ruled that the burden of proof in any disagreement about a student's individualized education program lies with the party bringing suit—in this case, the Schaffer family. Until this case, it typically had been assumed that a school district had to prove that its position in a lawsuit was correct, even if the district had not filed the lawsuit.

DOE V. WITHERS (20 IDELR 422, 426-427) (1993) As a high school history teacher, Mr. Withers refused to make the accommodations needed by a student with a learning disability, resulting in a failing grade and athletic ineligibility. The West Virginia Circuit Court ruled that Mr. Withers was personally liable for failing to make a good-faith effort to provide required accommodations; the family was awarded $5,000 in compensatory damages and $30,000 in punitive damages.

ENDREW F. v. DOUGLAS COUNTY SCHOOL DISTRICT (2017) Because Drew was making very little educational progress in public school, his parents enrolled him in a private school where he was much more successful, and the school district was asked to reimburse the parents for the tuition. The school district refused, saying that because Drew had made some progress, the mandate of IDEA had been met. The Supreme Court ruled that *de mimimus* progress, a standard set in an earlier lower court decision, was not the intent of the law. School districts must educate students so that they have ambitious goals and make meaningful educational progress. This case is considered the most significant special education decision in 30 years.

Current Civil Rights Legislation

Based on events of the civil rights movement and court cases such as those just outlined as well as many others, two civil rights laws currently protect individuals with disabilities against discrimination. These laws are broader than the education-focused IDEA, but they are complementary to it.

SECTION 504 OF THE VOCATIONAL REHABILITATION ACT OF 1973 Section 504 prevents discrimination against all individuals with disabilities in programs that receive federal funds, as do all public schools. For children of school age, Section 504 ensures equal opportunity for participation in the full range of school activities (Zirkel, 2015). Through Section 504, some students not eligible for services

RESEARCH-BASED PRACTICES

In a qualitative study, Cameron and Cook (2013) reported that general education teachers' goals for students with mild disabilities in their classrooms related to academics and behavior. For students with severe disabilities, goals were focused primarily on social development, with academics viewed, unfortunately, as largely irrelevant.

The rights of individuals with disabilities were established in part through the influence of the civil rights movement of the 1950s and 1960s.

through special education may be entitled to receive specific types of assistance to help them succeed in school (Zirkel & Weathers, 2015).

For example, Sondra is a student with a severe attention problem. She cannot follow a lesson for more than a few minutes at a time; she is distracted by every noise in the hallway and every car that goes by her classroom window. Her teacher describes her as a student who "acts first and thinks later." Sondra does not have a disability as established in special education law, but she does need extra assistance and is considered disabled according to Section 504 because her significant attention problem negatively affects her ability to function in school. The professionals at her school are required to create and carry out a plan to help Sondra access education. Special education teachers may assist other teachers in their work with Sondra because they know techniques that will help her, but Sondra does not receive special education services, and responsibility for the plan lies with the principal and teachers. Some other students who might receive assistance through Section 504 include those with health problems such as asthma and extreme allergies and those with physical disabilities who do not need special education (Zirkel, 2009b). More detail on Section 504 is presented in Chapter 8.

AMERICANS WITH DISABILITIES ACT In July 1990, President George H. W. Bush signed into law the Americans with Disabilities Act (ADA). This law was based on the Rehabilitation Act of 1973, but it further extended the rights of individuals with disabilities. This law, amended and updated through the Americans with Disabilities Act Amendments (ADAA) in 2008, is the most significant disability legislation ever passed (Bowman, 2011). It protects all individuals with disabilities from discrimination, and it requires most employers, whether in the public or private sector, to make reasonable accommodations for them. Although ADA does not deal directly with the education of students with disabilities, it does clarify the civil rights of all individuals with disabilities and thus has an impact on special education. This law also ensures that transportation, buildings, the workplace, and many places open to the public are accessible to people with disabilities. It also mandates that telecommunications companies make available options so that individuals with hearing loss and those with speech impairments can communicate with others. If you are a teacher with a disability, you might be influenced by ADA in the same way that it affects you in other situations. For example, if your school is not accessible to wheelchairs and undergoes renovation, then ramps, elevators, and wide entries with automatic doors may have to be installed. If you have a disability, this law also protects you from discrimination when you look for a teaching position.

Current General Education Legislation

One additional significant influence on special education has been legislation passed to govern the education of all students, including those with disabilities. The most far-reaching law is the Elementary and Secondary Education Act of 1965 (ESEA). Most recently reauthorized in 2016 and also referred to as the Every Student Succeeds Act (ESSA), it is the law that has the goal of ensuring that all students, including those who live in poverty, have equal access to a high-quality education (Chenoweth, 2016). It generally mandates the highest academic standards and increased accountability for all students, including those with disabilities. Think of how the following sample of key provisions in the law and its related regulations affect the expectations and educational practices for Lucas, Monika, and Aaron, whose stories began this chapter:

- All states must adopt rigorous standards in math, English/language arts, science, and other subjects as selected. These standards must apply to all students, except for 1 percent (with significant intellectual disabilities) who are eligible to meet alternate achievement standards. The standards for the latter group must be aligned with the typical standards.
- States must assess student math and reading achievement annually in grades 3–8 and at least once in grades 9–12. Science achievement must be assessed at least once in grades 3–5, 6–9, and 10–12. Eligible students must be provided with appropriate accommodations (including the use of technology).
- Students with significant intellectual disabilities may take alternate assessment that aligns with the established alternate curriculum.
- States must establish a way to look at the achievement data of four subgroups: students who are economically disadvantaged, students from racial and ethnic groups, students with disabilities, and English learners. If achievement gaps exist for these groups, states must require that schools take steps to close the gaps.
- Schools must establish programs to identify students at-risk for school failure and provide intervention to accelerate their learning.

These provisions and the many others of ESEA/ESSA reinforce the notion that students with disabilities can and should achieve at a level comparable to that of most students. Although flexibility exists in how that goal is achieved, this education law has made it clear that to expect anything less is unacceptable.

Special education has evolved on the basis of many factors. When special education began, essentially no services were offered in public schools. Today comprehensive services in a wide variety of settings are supplied, and both very young children and young adults, as well as students in elementary and secondary schools, benefit from them. As the rights and needs of students with disabilities have been better understood and federal legislation has set higher standards for their education, general education teachers—in traditional core academic areas as well as in the essential related areas such as art, music, and physical education—have become increasingly involved in their education, a trend that surely will continue (e.g., Brownell, Smith, Crockett, & Griffin, 2012; Kauffman & Badar, 2014).

WWW RESOURCES

http://www2.ed.gov/teachers/needs/speced/list.jhtml
The U.S. Department of Education's website for helping students with disabilities includes more than 1,000 resources. These materials include legal and technical information, as well as information for teachers, parents, families, and school administrators.

MyLab Education Self-Check 1.2

What Are the Key Themes of Contemporary Special Education Practice?

Now that you have learned about the core concepts that guide special education, the development of the field, and the range of factors that have shaped special education services, you have a strong foundation for understanding the context for contemporary practices for students with disabilities. In the following sections, several of the most central themes that characterize special education are outlined, including prevention through response to intervention (RtI) and multi-tiered systems of support (MTSS), high expectations and accountability, evidence-based practices, and inclusive schooling. The purpose of this discussion is to demonstrate that special education no longer is a set of services isolated from the rest of education and that, increasingly, general educators are expected to play a critical role in all students' education.

Prevention of the Need for Special Education

Some students have disabilities because of physical or medical conditions, including those who have sensory disabilities (that is, hearing or vision loss), those with physical or health disabilities, and those with significant intellectual disabilities. These students often are identified at a very young age and receive special education services throughout their school careers. However, most students who receive special education do so because of gaps between their academic achievement and that of their peers or because of serious problems in the behavior, social, or emotional domains. These disabilities most often are identified when students face the demands of formal schooling, and although these problems are real and are verified through specific assessment procedures (outlined in Chapter 4), students' school experiences and professional judgments also play a role in determining their presence. Over the past decade, attention has increasingly focused on this latter group of students and the options that might help some of them succeed so that they never need special education services.

RESPONSE TO INTERVENTION One prevention strategy is a procedure called response to intervention (RtI). Introduced for the first time in the 2004 reauthorization of IDEA, RtI is an approach for exploring whether students have learning disabilities (Zirkel, 2013). Rather than relying just on test scores, such as tests of ability and achievement, RtI permits school professionals to base that decision on whether increasingly intensive instructional interventions, most often in reading and math, implemented to address the student's academic problems have a positive impact on learning. If they do, no disability exists, and the need for special education can be prevented. If little or no improvement occurs after carefully selected strategies and programs are used more frequently and for longer periods of time, the student may be found to have a learning disability. You will learn more about this concept in Chapter 2 and the rest of this text, including its broader application as a means for carefully monitoring and assisting all struggling learners (e.g., Castro-Villarreal, Villarreal, & Sullivan, 2016; Fisher & Frey, 2013). For now, what is essential to remember is that RtI is implemented primarily by general education teachers, reading specialists, and others. It is not a special education service, even though special educators sometimes participate in delivering interventions. This means that it is very likely you will have a role in an RtI process, and this is the case whether you plan a career in elementary, middle, or high school.

POSITIVE BEHAVIOR SUPPORTS Response to intervention was designed to address students' academic learning needs but, for many students, problems related to behavior also may lead to a need for special education. Although not specifically addressed in IDEA, professionals across many states and school districts have applied principles similar to those of RtI to the behavior domain. That is, when a student displays problematic behavior, professionals implement increasingly intensive interventions to try to clearly identify the reason for the behavior and to help the student to learn alternative behaviors that are acceptable in the school setting, an approach termed positive behavior supports (PBS) (Childs, Kincaid, George, & Gage, 2016; Freeman, Simonsen, McCoach, Sugai, Lombardi, & Horner, 2016). Just as for RtI, the goal is to intervene before the problem is so serious that special education is viewed as necessary. Also similar to RtI, general education teachers usually are responsible for implementing many of the behavior interventions effective in re-directing and re-shaping students' behavior. You will learn more about positive behavior supports in Chapter 12.

MULTI-TIERED SYSTEM OF SUPPORT RtI and PBS both have value, but professionals increasingly have noted that it is logical to create a single system for responding to student academic and behavior needs and to coordinate resources, policies, personnel, and services for struggling learners. This makes sense, particularly because the procedures implemented for RtI and PBS are similar and because in some cases an individual student may have both academic and behavior challenges. Further, in a single system, it is easier to ensure that clear communication occurs among professionals serving students and to allocate the resources needed to provide intensive supports. This blended system, termed **multi-tiered systems of support (MTSS)**, enables educators to coordinate their work and focus their efforts to help all their students to succeed (Jimerson, Burns, & VanDerHeyden, 2016). This model recently gained prominence when it was included in ESEA/ESSA, described earlier in this chapter.

MTSS approaches also are appealing because they may extend beyond the school, drawing on district supports, community outreach, and other resources to improve learner outcomes. And as with RtI and PBS, general educators have primary responsibility for implementing an MTSS, both as team members who contribute to decision making about students and as the implementers of interventions for groups of students and individual students. The Instructional Edge feature highlights the critical components of MTSS.

DISPROPORTIONATE REPRESENTATION One additional topic must be mentioned in any discussion of preventing the need for special education. *Disproportionate representation* refers to the fact that students from some racial and cultural groups, especially African American males, historically have been identified as needing special education in greater numbers than would be expected, given the overall composition of the student population. For example, African American students are 2.22 times more likely than would be expected to be identified as intellectually disabled and 2.08 times as likely to be identified as having emotional or behavioral disabilities (U.S. Department of Education, 2016). Many reasons have been proposed to explain this unacceptable situation, including the influence of poverty and the impact of cultural and linguistic differences between students and their teachers. Eliminating disproportionate representation is a top priority nationwide (e.g., Skiba, Albrecht, & Losen, 2013; Sullivan, Artiles, & Hernandez-Saca, 2015), one that partly is being addressed through the

WWW RESOURCES

http://www.rtinetwork.org
If you visit the website of the RtI Action Network and type "MTSS" in the search bar, you will find many helpful resources as well as links to teacher blogs, research articles, and other postings about this important process.

DIMENSIONS OF DIVERSITY

Among all racial and ethnic groups tracked in federal special education data, students in the Native American/Other Pacific Islander group are most disproportionately represented: They are 2.35 times more likely than expected to be identified as disabled (U.S. Department of Education, 2016).

INSTRUCTIONAL EDGE 1.1

Understanding Multi-Tiered Systems of Support (MTSS)

Multi-tiered systems of support (MTSS) are rapidly becoming central to schools' efforts to reach learners struggling academically or behaviorally, and general education teachers, literacy and math specialists, administrators, and many other professionals share responsibility for implementing this model. These are the key elements of MTSS:

- *Universal screening.* The academic, behavior, and social functioning of all students must be periodically assessed to determine which learners are at risk for failure so that interventions can be implemented at the earliest indications of problems.

- *Evidence-based instruction.* Academic, behavioral, and other supports are only those demonstrated through research to be effective. Further, careful attention is paid to fidelity of implementation—that is, consistently and precisely carrying out such evidence-based interventions.

- *Tiered interventions with increasing intensity.* Increasingly specific interventions are used when student functioning does not adequately improve; intensity may pertain to the type of intervention selected as well as the frequency of its use, with most systems having three tiers of levels of intensity.

- *Data-based decision making.* A clear procedure is in place to determine appropriate next steps for assisting learners, grounded in data gathered about the student's performance and progress. When students are struggling, data collection and interpretation are frequent so that intervention effectiveness can be closely monitored.

- *Collaboration.* MTSS is premised on clear communication and a highly collaborative problem solving process established at the school level. Educators come together, with support from their site and district leadership, to consider individual student needs and to enhance their school's capacity to effectively educate all its students.

use of RtI, PBS, and MTSS. As a general education teacher, your understanding of your own culture and your ability to be responsive to the cultures of your students, including their language, will be essential for fostering student learning (Kahn, Lindstrom, & Murray, 2014). If you are employed in a district in which disproportionate representation is still occurring, you are likely to participate in specific professional development, data collection, and other activities designed to address this issue.

High Expectations and Accountability

A second major theme for the field of special education concerns holding students with disabilities to the same high expectations established for all students and professional accountability for reaching that goal. In fact, the priority for educating students with disabilities is not just raising their achievement scores; it also includes reducing the gap between their achievement and that of typical peers.

CURRICULUM ACCESS The first critical component of setting high expectations for students with disabilities, reflected in both ESEA/ESSA and IDEA, relates to ensuring that they have access to the same learning opportunities as other students. Access to the general curriculum was added as a specific requirement to special education law in 1997 and is still in effect. Specifically, students must have access to the general curriculum, be directly involved in it, and make progress in it. This is true for all students with disabilities, including those with significant intellectual disabilities. For the latter group of students, access may be defined as learning related to the curriculum while focused on life and practical skills. For most (but not all) students, curriculum access occurs through instruction in the general education setting, the practice implemented for Lucas, introduced in the chapter-opening vignette. Some students access curriculum in a special education setting, either by participating in electronic instruction (for example, an online course) or by learning from a special educator who is qualified to deliver that curriculum.

A relatively recent development in curriculum access pertains to the Common Core State Standards (CCSS) and similar state initiatives to increase academic rigor and better prepare students for postsecondary education and life (McLaughlin, 2012). These contemporary standards address English/language arts and math from kindergarten to 12th grade and are intended to focus education on the knowledge and skills that students need to succeed in the twenty-first century. Professionals know that for many students with disabilities, the increased rigor of the standards necessitates use of a variety of learning supports, from additional or more intensive practice to electronic options (e.g., digitally recorded instructional materials). General education teachers play a key role in ensuring that students have the tools that make access possible, especially when they use the principles of *universal design for learning* (UDL), that is, careful planning so that instruction is designed prior to delivery to be accessible by all learners (e.g., Al-Azawei, Serenelli, & Lundqvist, 2016). Specific examples of UDL will be introduced throughout this textbook.

ASSESSMENT OF STUDENTS WITH DISABILITIES As noted earlier, ESEA/ESSA mandates that all students, including those with disabilities, be assessed in order to evaluate their learning progress; clearly, this is an important aspect of ensuring rigor. Further, because a large majority of students with disabilities do not have intellectual disabilities, nearly all of them take the same standardized assessments as their peers without disabilities. However, many students receive special accommodations related to completing these assessments. They may take the tests in the special education classroom so that distractions can be minimized, and they may receive other supports.

Students with significant intellectual disabilities take alternate assessments designed to measure their learning in the selective general and functional curriculum in which they participate. That is, unlike past practices when many students with such disabilities were exempt from the academic assessment process because of a belief that it was not applicable to their education, the clear expectation now is that the progress of all students is a priority. You will learn more about assessment as it pertains to students with disabilities in Chapters 4 and 11.

PROFESSIONAL ACCOUNTABILITY One additional component of high expectations and accountability concerns the responsibilities of educators for their students' learning outcomes. Increasingly, teachers' performance evaluations (and sometimes their pay and continued employment) rely in part on the achievement gains of their students (Martínez, Schweig, & Goldschmidt, 2016). The scores of students with disabilities and other special needs (for example, those who live in poverty, those whose native language is not English) are part of this calculation. Further, at the school level, this means that if students with disabilities are not improving enough in terms of achievement, the school is identified as needing improvement, and corrective actions may be required.

Many issues are being raised about holding teachers directly accountable for student achievement. Some professionals note that many influences contribute to student learning, including the home and neighborhood environment, culture, background experiences, and even the effectiveness of earlier instruction, and that a teacher's instruction may not be powerful enough to overcome negative influences in students' lives. Some educators question whether general education teachers should be accountable for the learning of students known to have disabilities. Yet others see the current teacher-accountability trend as a strong positive, affirming that it will, like never before, focus a positive spotlight on maximizing achievement for students with disabilities. Whatever your view of this accountability issue, it reinforces the importance of all teachers knowing the most effective ways to reach all their students.

> **FYI**
>
> Although this text focuses on special education for students in kindergarten through 12th grade, young children—those birth to age five—also may be determined to be eligible for special education. IDEA includes specific provisions for their services.

Evidence-Based Practice

Yet another strong trend that has directly affected special education is the expectation for evidence-based practice. Begun in the field of medicine in the 1990s and adopted in many professions, including education, evidence-based practice (EBP) is an approach that relies on these principles (Hughes, Powell, Lembke, & Riley-Tillman, 2016; Smith, Doabler, & Kame'enui, 2016):

1. Interventions, strategies, techniques, policies, and programs implemented as part of students' education should be grounded in research that has demonstrated their effectiveness.

2. The studies used to determine intervention effectiveness should be of high quality as defined by the profession.

3. EBP is intended to close what is frequently a gap between what researchers know is effective and the practices teachers actually use in their classrooms.

4. EBP is designed to eliminate the use of interventions without demonstrated effectiveness that may still be common practice because of teacher preference and familiarity, tradition, anecdotes about their value, or popularity resulting from advertising or celebrity endorsement.

Evidence-based practices are mandated in both ESEA/ESSA and IDEA, and the importance of this priority is obvious: How can it be justified to spend the limited precious minutes of any child's education using interventions that have not been demonstrated to improve learner outcomes? For example, you probably have heard about student learning styles; many educators believe that teaching to students' learning styles is an effective practice. Yet, little research directly supports this view (Fleischman, 2012; Hale, 2016). In contrast, some professionals are reluctant to group students and provide instruction through peer-mediated strategies such as peer tutoring and cooperative learning, but these approaches have consistently been demonstrated to improve student learning (e.g., Wexler, Reed, Pyle, Mitchell, & Barton, 2015).

MyLab Education

Video Example 1.4: Access to Public Education

The concept of inclusion evolved as part of efforts to effectively educate students with disabilities.

Consistent with EBP, you will find as you read this textbook that the strategies presented for improving learning for students with disabilities are strongly grounded in research. If you're curious about EBP and would like to learn more about it, you can find further details and examples of EBP resources in Chapter 5.

Inclusiveness

A final major theme characterizing contemporary special education is inclusiveness. Although IDEA stipulates that a range of settings (e.g., separate special education classrooms and schools) must be made available to meet the needs of students with disabilities, many professionals now seriously question the assumption that students who need more intensive services should routinely receive them in such restrictive settings (e.g., Sailor, 2015; Theoharis & Causton, 2016). The concept of *inclusive practices* implies that students are more alike than different and that all students should be welcomed members of their learning communities (e.g., Antia, Jones, Luckner, Kreimeyer, & Reed, 2011; Artiles & Kozleski, 2016), just as all individuals should have those rights in the larger society (Sharma, 2015). Inclusiveness is not directly addressed in ESEA or IDEA, but many provisions in those laws (e.g., least restrictive environment, curriculum access, participation in assessment) as well as other education and civil rights legislation you have already read about in this chapter provide a strong foundation for inclusive practices.

Keep in mind that in the not-too-distant past, many students with disabilities were only temporary guests in general education classrooms, and few efforts were made to provide assistance so they could be successfully educated with their nondisabled peers. Although some professionals still express concerns about inclusive practices (e.g., Kauffman, 2015b), many educators now find that most supports for students with disabilities can be provided effectively in general education classrooms when teachers are prepared to work with such students and related concerns are addressed (Causton-Theoharis, Theoharis, Bull, Cosier, & Dempf-Aldrich, 2011; Dieker, 2013). They further maintain that if students cannot meet traditional academic expectations, preference should be given to changing the expectations instead of routinely presuming that a different setting is necessary. The increased use of inclusive practices in today's schools can be demonstrated through recent data: During the 2014–2015 school year, approximately 62.6 percent of all school-age students with disabilities received more than 80 percent of their education in general education classrooms (U.S. Department of Education, 2016). The Professional Edge feature includes a summary of critical characteristics of inclusive schools.

UNDERSTANDING INCLUSIVE PRACTICES **Inclusive practices** represent a philosophy based on three dimensions (Friend, 2013):

1. *Physical integration:* Placing students in the same classroom as nondisabled peers should be a strong priority, and removing them from that setting should be done only when absolutely necessary. However, it is important to understand that inclusiveness does not imply that all students should be in a general education setting at all times, as is true for Monika, introduced at the beginning of the chapter (McLeskey & Waldron, 2011). Such a practice would be detrimental to some students and would violate IDEA.

2. *Social integration:* Relationships should be nurtured between students with disabilities and their classmates, other peers, and adults (e.g., Carter et al., 2015). As you might suspect, the preferred location for accomplishing this goal is the general education setting, but in some instances typical peers may interact with students with disabilities in the special education classroom.

3. *Instructional integration:* Most students should be taught in the same curriculum used for students without disabilities and helped to succeed by adjusting how teaching and learning are designed (that is, providing specially designed instruction and accommodations) and measured. For some

PROFESSIONAL EDGE 1.1

Characteristics of Inclusive Schools

As you learn about your responsibilities as a teacher for students with disabilities, this list of characteristics can help you understand in a real-world way what an inclusive school is like.

- Every person who works in the school is committed to the goal of helping all students achieve their potential; inclusiveness is a school-level belief system.
- The principal is a strong and vocal advocate for all students, adamant that they access the general curriculum with a system of supports around them.
- Professionals and other staff routinely use respectful, person-first language (for example, *student with a disability* rather than *disabled student*).
- Emphasis is on abilities rather than disabilities.
- Special education and other services are seamless—their benefit to students is maximized and their cost to students (e.g., time out of a general education classroom) is minimized.
- Special education and other services do not exist as separate entities (e.g., "we have inclusion, resource, and self-contained programs; speech and ESL are pullout programs"); they are integrated and always addressed as part of a whole.

- Specially designed instruction required for students with disabilities can be offered in a general education setting as well as in a special education setting.
- Differentiation is considered the rule for all students, not the exception.
- Assistive technology enhances access to the general curriculum.
- Parents are not just welcomed partners in the schools; their participation and collaboration are actively sought.
- Multiple locations for instruction are available to students, including service in a separate setting—but only when it is the last choice and only for as long as data indicate it is effective.
- Inclusiveness is communicated in many ways—materials displayed, books and other media available, adult interactions with students and each other, schedules, room assignments, and so on.
- The term *inclusion* is rarely needed because it is such an integral part of the school culture.

students with significant intellectual disabilities, instructional integration means anchoring instruction in the standard general curriculum but appropriately adjusting expectations (that is, making modifications). Ultimately, the concept of inclusive practices as used in this text means that all learners are viewed as the responsibility of all educators (Dessemontet, Bless, & Morin, 2012), giving general educators a major responsibility for them, supported by special educators (e.g., Schifter, 2016; Walsh, 2012). It further implies that educators' strong preference is for these students to be educated with their peers without disabilities.

We also would like to note that we prefer the phrase *inclusive practices* to the term *inclusion* because the latter can imply that there is a single model or program that can serve all students' needs, whereas the former more accurately conveys that inclusiveness is made up of many strategies and options that are discussed throughout this textbook.

One more term should be mentioned in this discussion of inclusiveness. When the LRE concept became part of special education laws during the 1970s, the LRE for most students with disabilities was usually a part-time or full-time special education class. When such students were permitted to participate in general education, it was called mainstreaming. **Mainstreaming** involves placing students with disabilities in general education settings only when they can meet traditional academic expectations with minimal assistance or when those expectations are not relevant (e.g., participation only in recess or school assemblies for access to social interactions with peers). In most locales, *mainstreaming* now is considered a dated term and has been replaced with the phrase *inclusion* or *inclusive practices*. However, as you participate in field experiences and speak to experienced educators, you may find that in some schools, the vocabulary of inclusion is used, but the practices implemented seem more like mainstreaming. That is, teachers may say that their school is inclusive but then explain that students like Aaron, featured in the beginning of the chapter, need to be in separate classes because of their below-grade reading levels. This practice is more accurately called mainstreaming.

RESEARCH-BASED PRACTICES

Ryndak, Ward, Alper, Storch, and Montgomery (2012) compared long-term outcomes for two brothers with intellectual disabilities, one who was educated in self-contained settings and one who received an inclusive education. Outcomes (for example, social behavior, tolerance for change) were more positive for the latter brother.

General education teachers are accountable for the education of all the students in their classrooms, including those with disabilities.

The vocabulary terms introduced in this section and elsewhere in this chapter may be a bit overwhelming. Special education is a field with many dimensions and extensive terminology, and understanding its technical language will assist you in carrying out your responsibilities for students with disabilities. Many terms will be explained further in subsequent chapters; additionally, a glossary is provided at the back of this textbook. Keep in mind, though, that knowing the terms used in special education is not nearly as important as learning about your students, developing skills for addressing their needs, and celebrating your role in enabling them to achieve success.

THE EFFECTIVENESS OF INCLUSIVE PRACTICES As you might imagine, inclusiveness is influenced by many factors, from the characteristics of the students being educated to the preparation and skill of their teachers to the amount of administrative support available (e.g., Causton & Theoharis, 2013; Hoppey & McLeskey, 2013; Litvack, Ritchie, & Shore, 2011; Solis, Vaughn, Swanson, & McCulley, 2012). Because of this complexity, research regarding inclusive practices has been difficult to conduct, and the results have been mixed. However, especially with the understanding that inclusiveness provides for separate instruction when needed, compelling positive results have been reported.

For example, any discussion of inclusive practices must consider the impact on student outcomes (Huberman, Navo, & Parrish, 2012). That is, if students with disabilities in inclusive settings do not progress in their learning, then inclusion is not in their best interests. Generally, academic and other outcomes in inclusive schools have been found to be positive (Hang & Rabren, 2009; Kurth & Mastergeorge, 2012). For example, one recent large-scale analysis found a positive correlation between students' access to and participation in general education classes and their post-school success (e.g., employment, higher education) (Mazzotti, Rowe, Sinclair, Poppen, Woods, & Shearer, 2016). In a statewide study, researchers found that students with disabilities who spent more time in general education passed the eighth-grade assessment at a higher rate than similar students with disabilities who were educated in special education settings. Students comparable in ability educated in general education settings also have been found to graduate from high school at a higher rate than those educated in special education settings (Gonzalez & Cramer, 2013; Luster & Durrett, 2003). Two other studies examined the policies and practices in school districts achieving higher-than-expected academic outcomes for students with disabilities. In both studies, the districts were characterized as having strong leaders, highly collaborative cultures, firm and sustained commitment to inclusiveness, and programs and instructional practices demonstrated to be effective with students with disabilities (Huberman et al., 2012; Silverman, Hazelwood, & Cronin, 2009). Inclusive practices also have been found to have a positive impact on students' math achievement (Kunsch, Jitendra, & Sood, 2007), problem-solving skills (Ryndak, Ward, Alper, Storch, & Montgomery, 2012), and discipline referrals (Cawley, Hayden, Cade, & Baker-Kroczynski, 2002). Keep in mind, though, that some students—whether their disabilities are considered mild or significant—receive part of their instruction in a special education setting for at least a small part of the day in order to achieve such success (e.g., McLeskey & Waldron, 2011).

FYI

Using *person-first language* is a way to ensure that you focus on students and not their labels. For example, say "students with disabilities" instead of "disabled students," and "my student who has autism" instead of "my autistic student." Never say "special education students" or "IEP students."

A second way to determine the effectiveness of inclusive practices is to consider parent perceptions. Parents generally are positive about special education services, and they often prefer that their children be educated with peers in general education classrooms (Lalvani, 2012; Leach & Duffy, 2009). They believe that inclusive practices are beneficial for academic achievement, and, especially for children with intellectual disabilities, they also strongly believe that their children learn critical social skills when they spend most or all of the school day with their typical peers (Bennett & Gallagher, 2013). One parent commented that when her fourth-grade son with autism was integrated into a general education classroom for most of the day, his behavior improved both at school and at home. She also noted that the other students in the class were clearly kind to her son, and she was grateful that they sought him out on the playground and chose him as a lunch partner. Not surprisingly, parents' perceptions of inclusive practices are more positive when they participate in collaborative decision making concerning their children's educational services; their views also are influenced by the age of their child and the nature of the child's disability (Falkmer, Anderson, Joosten, & Falkmer, 2015; Matuszny, Banda, & Coleman, 2007).

You might wonder about teachers' perceptions of inclusive practices. In the past, research suggested a continuum of responses, from strongly positive to somewhat equivocal (e.g., Crouch, Keys, & McMahon, 2014; King & Youngs, 2003; Sze, 2009), often related to the nature of students' disabilities and educators' sense of their skills for effectively teaching these students. Although a similar situation might exist today (e.g., Soleas, 2015), questions about inclusive practices and teacher perception have rapidly become outdated. Simply put, nearly every general educator, whether at the elementary school, middle school, or high school level, teaches students with disabilities. Focus has shifted from whether teachers are supportive of inclusion to instructional, behavioral, social, and other strategies that can enhance their skills for educating diverse learners (e.g., Able, Sreckovic, Schultz, Garwood, & Sherman, 2015; Hartzell, Liaupsin, Gann, & Clem, 2015).

MyLab Education

Video Example 1.5: Students' Perspectives on Disabilities
These fifth-grade students share their perspectives on classmates with different abilities. What lessons do they and their teacher share that could guide your approach to teaching students with disabilities?

PUTTING THE PIECES TOGETHER In some ways, inclusive practices are like puzzle pieces. In today's schools, some of the pieces may be missing and others difficult to fit into place; yet others may be readily addressed and fit easily into the larger picture. Even in your own course, you and your classmates may come across studies on inclusive practices that present contradictory results. In your field experiences, you are likely to discover that in some schools inclusive practices are the norm, whereas in others very traditional approaches are still in place. You may find yourself struggling to reconcile all these views.

One way that you can put the puzzle together is to learn to teach in a way that is responsive to a wide range of student needs (Clarke, Haydon, Bauer, & Epperly, 2016; Lane, Royer, Messenger, Common, Ennis, & Swogger, 2015; O'Keeffe & Medina, 2016) and to use collaboration with colleagues and parents (e.g., Edwards & Da Fonte, 2012), as described in the Working Together feature, as a means for extending your expertise. As you will learn in the chapters that follow, much is known about effective ways to instruct students with disabilities, and many of those strategies will help other students learn as well. By welcoming all your students and making these strategies an integral part of your instruction, your pieces of the inclusive practices puzzle will fit right into place.

MyLab Education Self-Check 1.3

WORKING TOGETHER 1.1
The Importance of Collaboration for Meeting Student Needs

As you read this textbook and learn about your responsibilities for educating students with disabilities, you will find that *collaboration*—working together with others—is one of the keys to successful inclusive practices. It is a topic so critical that a feature on collaboration appears in every chapter. To introduce how important collaboration is for educators, here are just a few examples of how you will work with others on behalf of students with disabilities:

- *Meeting with special education teachers:* You will meet frequently with special education teachers, both formally and informally. A special educator may contact you to see how a student is doing in your class, or you may contact a special educator to ask for new ideas for responding to a student's behavior. You and the special educator may share responsibility for meeting with parents during open houses or parent conferences.
- *Co-teaching:* Depending on local programs and services, you may co-teach with a special education teacher or related services professional such as a speech/language therapist. In co-teaching, you share teaching responsibilities, with both educators working with all students in the general education classroom. This topic is addressed in detail in Chapter 3.
- *Working with paraprofessionals:* If your class includes a student with a significant disability or several students who need

support (but not co-teaching), you may collaborate with a paraprofessional. You will guide the work of that individual in your class to ensure that student support is appropriately provided, even while you retain primary teaching responsibility for all the students.

- *Meeting on teams:* Various school teams support inclusive practices. Your grade-level or middle or high school department team likely will spend part of its time discussing students with disabilities and problem solving to address their needs. You also may be part of a team that tries to address student learning and behavior problems prior to any consideration of the need for special education. If a student in your class is being assessed to determine whether special education is needed, you will be part of that team. The latter two teams are discussed in Chapter 2.
- *Interacting with parents:* Perhaps the most important part of collaborating on behalf of students with disabilities is working with parents. You may communicate with parents through notes sent home and through e-mail; meet with them occasionally as they express concerns about their children; confer with them at formal team meetings; and work with them as they volunteer at school, help with field trips, and participate in other school activities and initiatives.

Who Receives Special Education and Other Special Services?

Throughout this chapter, we have used the phrase *students with disabilities*. At this point, we will introduce you to the specific categories of disabilities that may entitle students to receive special education services, as well as other special needs that may require specialized assistance. As you read the following definitions, keep in mind that additional information about these disability categories, including the federal eligibility criteria for each, are included in Chapters 6 and 7. Most important, remember that a disability label can only provide general guidelines about a student. Labels are a form of shorthand that professionals use, but no label can accurately describe a student. Your responsibility is to understand your students with disabilities in ways that extend beyond what any label communicates so you can help them reach their goals.

Categories of Disability in Federal Law

When we say that students have disabilities, we are referring to the specific categories of exceptionality prescribed by federal special education law. Each state has additional laws that clarify special education practices and procedures, and the terms used to refer to disabilities in state laws may differ from those found in federal law. For example, although federal law specifies the label *emotional disturbance* for some students, the term *behavior disorder* or *emotional and behavior disability* may be used in your state. Similarly, although IDEA uses the term *intellectual disability*, some states use *cognitive disability* or *intellectual impairment*; a few may still use the outdated term *mental retardation*. Check with your instructor or your state department of education website for the terms used in your state.

According to IDEA, students with one or more of the following 13 disabilities that negatively affect their educational performance are eligible for special education services. These disabilities also are summarized in Figure 1.4.

LEARNING DISABILITY Students with a *learning disability (LD)* have dysfunctions in processing information typically found in language-based activities. They

FIGURE 1.4 **IDEA Disability Categories**

Federal Disability Term[1]	Brief Description[3]
Learning disability (LD) (39.2%)[2]	A disorder related to processing information that leads to difficulties in reading, writing, and computing; the most common disability, accounting for more than one-third of all students receiving special education.
Speech or language impairment (SLI) (17.6%)	A disorder related to accurately producing the sounds of language or meaningfully using language to communicate.
Intellectual disability (ID) (7.0%)	Significant limitations in intellectual ability and adaptive behavior; this disability has a range of severity.
Emotional disturbance (ED) (5.9%)	Significant problems in the social-emotional area to a degree that learning is negatively affected.
Autism (8.6%)	A disorder characterized by extraordinary difficulty in social responsiveness; this disability occurs in many different forms and may be mild or significant.
Hearing impairment (deaf or hard-of-hearing) (HI) (1.1%)	A partial or complete loss of hearing.
Visual impairment (VI) (0.4%)	A partial or complete loss of vision.
Deaf-blindness (<.05%)	A simultaneous significant hearing loss and significant vision loss.
Orthopedic impairment (OI) (0.8%)	A significant physical limitation that impairs the ability to move or complete motor activities.
Traumatic brain injury (TBI) (0.4%)	A medical condition denoting a serious brain injury that occurs as a result of accident or injury; potentially affecting learning, behavior, social skills, and language.
Other health impairment (OHI) (14.4%)	A disease or health disorder so significant that it negatively affects learning; examples include cancer, sickle-cell anemia, and diabetes. Students with severe ADHD may be included in this category.
Multiple disabilities (2.1%)	The simultaneous presence of two or more disabilities such that none can be identified as primary; the most common is the combination of intellectual and physical disabilities.
Developmental delay (DD) (2.4%)	A nonspecific disability category that states may choose to use as an alternative to specific disability labels for students up to age nine.

[1] The terms used in your state may vary from those specified in federal special education law.
[2] Percent of students with disabilities ages 6 through 21 served through IDEA (Fall 2014).
[3] More complete federal definitions of each category are presented in Chapters 6 and 7.

Video Example from

MyLab Education

Video Example 1.6: Dear Teacher . . .

Watch this video about students with learning and attention disabilities. They offer great advice to their teachers. https://www.youtube.com/watch?v=lTMLzXzgB_s

generally have average or above-average intelligence, but they often encounter significant problems in learning how to read, write, and compute. They may not see letters and words in the way others do, they may not be able to pick out important features in a picture they are looking at, and they may take longer to process a question or comment directed to them. They also may have difficulty following directions, attending to tasks, organizing assignments, and managing time. Sometimes these students appear to be unmotivated or lazy when in fact they are trying their best. Aaron, described at the beginning of this chapter, has one type of learning disability, but many other types also exist, and no single description characterizes all students with LD. Learning disabilities are by far the most common special need: Approximately 39.2 percent of all students receiving special education services in public schools in 2014–2015 had a learning disability (U.S. Department of Education, 2016).

SPEECH OR LANGUAGE IMPAIRMENT When a student has extraordinary difficulties communicating with others for reasons other than maturation, a *speech or language impairment* is involved. Students with this disability may have trouble with *articulation*, or the production of speech sounds. They may omit words or mispronounce common words when they speak. They also may experience difficulty in *fluency*, such as a significant stuttering problem. Some students have far-reaching speech or language disorders, in which they have significant problems receiving and producing language. They may communicate through pictures or sign language. Some students' primary disability is a speech or language disorder, and they may receive services for this. For other students with disabilities, speech/language services supplement their other educational services. For example, a student with a learning disability also might receive speech/language services, as might a student with autism or traumatic brain injury. In these instances, speech/language services are usually considered a related service, as defined earlier in this chapter.

INTELLECTUAL DISABILITY Students with an *intellectual disability* (ID) have significant limitations in intellectual ability and adaptive behaviors. They learn at a slower pace than do other students, and they may reach a point at which their learning levels off. Although the federal description of disability categories does not distinguish between students with mild intellectual disabilities and those with more significant intellectual disabilities, some state descriptions do. Most individuals with this disability lead independent lives after they leave school, holding jobs and fully participating as community members. A few individuals need lifelong support, whether minimum or extensive. Monika, one of the students you met in the introduction to this chapter, has an intellectual disability.

EMOTIONAL DISTURBANCE When a student has significant difficulty in the social-emotional domain—serious enough to interfere with the student's learning—*emotional disturbance (ED)*, also sometimes called an *emotional and behavior disorder (EBD)* or an *emotional disability*, exists. Students with this disability may have difficulty with interpersonal relationships and may respond inappropriately in emotional situations. That is, they may have extraordinary trouble making and keeping friends; they may get extremely angry when peers tease or play jokes on them; and they may repeatedly and significantly show little or inappropriate emotion when it is expected, such as when a family pet dies. Some students with ED are depressed; others are aggressive. Students with ED display these impairments over a long period of time, across different settings, and to a degree significantly different from their peers. Students with emotional disabilities are not just students whose behavior in a classroom is challenging to address; rather, they have chronic and extremely serious emotional or behavioral problems.

AUTISM Students with *autism*, sometimes referred to as *autism spectrum disorder* (ASD) because of its many variations, usually lack appropriate social responsiveness from a very early age. They generally avoid physical contact (e.g., cuddling and holding), and they may not make eye contact. Problems with social interactions persist as these children grow; they appear unaware of others' feelings and may not seek interactions with peers or adults. They may have unusual language patterns, such as speaking without inflection, repeating what others say, or repeating something heard on television over and over. To feel comfortable, they may need highly routinized behavior, such as a precise procedure, followed every single day, for entering the classroom and preparing for the start of the day's instruction. Some students with autism have above-average intelligence; others have intellectual disabilities. The causes of autism are still being researched, and the best approaches for working with students with autism are still emerging. Lucas, one of the students you met at the beginning of the chapter, has autism. You can learn a little more about autism by reading the Case in Practice

CASE IN PRACTICE 1.1

Problem Solving in Inclusive Schools: The General Education Teacher's Role

At Adams Middle School, staff members are meeting to discuss John, a seventh-grade student who has a formal diagnosis of autism from a pediatric psychologist. Ms. Diaz is John's English teacher, and Ms. Horton is the special educator who provides his specially designed instruction and other needed support. Mr. Powell, the school psychologist, also is present.

Ms. Diaz: John is a student with many dimensions. He usually does fairly well in class, and his behavior is much less disruptive than it was at the beginning of the school year, but whenever we transition from one activity to another, there is a strong chance that John will refuse to change. If I insist, even using the strategies you've given me, Ms. Horton, John often starts rocking and singing in a loud voice and essentially shutting me out. I've had two calls from other parents who said their children reported that John takes up too much of my time in class. It was difficult to respond because I think that perception is accurate. I hope we can come up with some ideas to improve the whole situation.

Ms. Horton: I know you also discussed John at your last team meeting. What did his other teachers have to say?

Ms. Diaz: Everyone except Mr. Bryant is experiencing the same problems. Mr. Bryant said that John really likes science and that his behavior problems might not be as pronounced there because John really wants to do the labs. He also said that sometimes he can tell by watching John's facial expression that John is trying very hard to transition between activities without a problem—and that it's very difficult for him. He tries to give John extra time to finish what he is doing to avoid the rocking and singing problem.

Mr. Powell: You've mentioned the problem of transitioning between activities as one concern. Before we start addressing that, are there any other problems we should be aware of?

Ms. Diaz: No. Right now, it's the behavior during transitions—and I want to be clear that all of us on the team know John is quite capable of learning what we're teaching, and our data tell us he is making very strong gains academically. We are committed to finding more solutions before the problem becomes more serious.

Ms. Horton: One contribution I can make is to get into your classroom—and also into the classrooms of other teachers on your team—to gather some additional information. It will help

to gather data on the sequence of events in class that seem to prevent or lead to his behavior. For example, I'd like to observe John during rapid and slower transitions, and it will be valuable to gather data on how other students respond when he has a problem during a transition.

Ms. Diaz: That would be helpful, but I hope you can observe him within the next couple of days so we can come up with new strategies. There is no time to waste. I've been cuing him as you suggested—it's not working now (she shows Ms. Horton her data charts). I also tried to ignore him, but that made it worse.

Mr. Powell: Maybe we should focus for a minute or two on what is going well for John in your class.

Ms. Diaz: Let's see . . . he usually is attentive, begins work when assigned, and makes a good contribution when we're talking about assignments that are very concrete or literal. For example, he knows the nuances of parts of speech better than nearly any of the other students and always knows the answers and wants to share when an objective like that is the focus.

Mr. Powell: Our meeting time is nearly up—the bell is about to ring. Are we all clear on next steps? Ms. Horton, will you be able to observe in Ms. Diaz's class by the end of the week? I know you need answers right away, but I hope we can get a clearer sense of the pattern of John's behavior and the context in which it is occurring so we can find the right strategy for addressing it. If we can get in to observe this week, could we meet next Tuesday to try to generate some strategies?

Ms. Diaz: That would be great. Let's work out the details on observing.

REFLECTION

Why was this meeting a positive example of teachers addressing a student problem in an inclusive school? What did they do that has set them up for success? If you were trying to understand John better, what other questions would you ask about him? What would you like others to observe in the classroom in relation to him? In relation to you as the teacher? What do you think will happen at the next meeting? Based on this case, how would you describe the role of general education teachers in addressing the challenges of inclusion?

The labels given to students may give a general description of their disabilities, but they do not convey students' abilities and potential.

feature, in which teachers meet to problem solve regarding another student with this disability.

HEARING IMPAIRMENT Disabilities that concern inability or limited ability to receive auditory signals are called *hearing impairments (HI)*. When students are hard of hearing, they have a significant hearing loss but can capitalize on residual hearing by using hearing aids and other amplifying systems. Students who are deaf have little or no residual hearing and therefore do not benefit from traditional devices that aid hearing. Some students with hearing loss may be assisted through the use of advanced technology such as a cochlear implant, which is a small, complex electronic device implanted near the ear that can provide a sense of sound. Depending on the extent of the disability, students with hearing impairments may use sign language, speech reading, or other strategies to communicate with others.

VISUAL IMPAIRMENT Disabilities that concern the inability or limited ability to receive information visually are called *visual impairments (VI)*. Some students have partial sight and can learn successfully using magnification devices and other adaptive materials; students who are *blind* do not use vision as a means of learning and instead rely primarily on touch and hearing. Depending on need, students with visual impairments may use braille, computers adapted for their use, and other aids to assist in learning. In addition, some students with vision loss need specialized training to help them learn to move successfully in their environment.

DEAF-BLINDNESS Students who have both significant vision and hearing loss sometimes are eligible for services as deaf-blind. These students have extraordinarily unique learning needs, particularly in the domain of communication, and they require highly specialized services to access their education. The degree of the vision and hearing loss may vary from moderate to severe and may be accompanied by other disabilities. Students in this category are likely to receive special education services beginning at birth or very soon thereafter.

ORTHOPEDIC IMPAIRMENT Students with *orthopedic impairments (OI)* have physical conditions that seriously limit their ability to move about or complete motor activities. Students who have cerebral palsy are included in this group, as are those with other diseases that affect the skeleton or muscles. Students with physical limitations resulting from accidents also may be orthopedically impaired. Students with orthopedic impairments are difficult to describe as a group because their strengths and needs vary tremendously. For example, some students with this disability are unable to move about without a wheelchair and may need special transportation to get to school and a ramp to enter the school building. Others may lack the fine motor skills needed to write and may require extra time or adapted equipment to complete assignments.

TRAUMATIC BRAIN INJURY Students with *traumatic brain injury (TBI)* have a wide range of characteristics and special needs, including limited strength or alertness, developmental delays, short-term memory problems, hearing or vision loss that may be temporary or permanent, irritability, and sudden mood swings. Their characteristics depend on the specific injuries they experienced, and their

WWW RESOURCES

https://www.dol.gov/odep
Managed by the U.S. Department of Labor, the Office of Disability Employment Policy (ODEP) website includes numerous resources related to disabilities across the lifespan, including youth with disabilities and those transitioning from school to work.

needs often change over time. Because TBI is a medical condition that affects education, diagnosis by a physician is required along with an educational assessment of students' learning, behavior, and social skills. Students who experience serious head trauma and resulting TBI from automobile accidents, falls, and sports injuries are among those who might be eligible for services.

OTHER HEALTH IMPAIRMENT Some students have a disease or disorder so significant that it affects their ability to learn in school. The category of disability addressing their needs is called *other health impairment (OHI)*. Students who have chronic heart conditions necessitating frequent and prolonged absences from school might be eligible for special education in this category, as might those with severe and chronic asthma. Students with diseases such as acquired immune deficiency syndrome (AIDS) and sickle cell anemia also may be categorized as having other health impairments, depending on the impact of their illnesses on learning. Some students—but not all—with attention deficit–hyperactivity disorder (ADHD) also receive special education services in this category.

MULTIPLE DISABILITIES The category used when students have two or more significant disabilities is called **multiple disabilities**. Students in this group often have an intellectual disability as well as a physical disability, but this category also may be used to describe any student with two or more disability types (with the exception of deaf-blindness). However, this classification is used only when the student's disabilities are so serious and interrelated that none can be identified as a primary disability. Students with multiple disabilities often benefit from *assistive technology*, that is, simple or complex devices that facilitate their learning, as explained in the Technology Notes feature.

TECHNOLOGY NOTES 1.1

The Opportunities of Assistive Technology

Whether the students you teach have mild or significant disabilities, they can use technology to help them to communicate, access learning, complete assignments, and fully participate in school and in the community. *Assistive technology*, which students with disabilities are entitled to use as needed, refers to any device (that is, piece of equipment, product, or other item) used to increase, maintain, or improve the functional capabilities of an individual with a disability. These are examples of the levels of assistive technology students might use.

NO TECHNOLOGY OR LOW TECHNOLOGY

No technology (no-tech) or *low technology (low-tech)* refers to items that do not include any type of electronics. Examples:

- A rubber pencil grip that enables a student with a disability to better grasp a pencil or pen
- A nonslip placemat on a student's desk that makes it easier for her to pick up items because it stops them from sliding
- A study carrel that helps a student pay closer attention to the schoolwork at hand

MID-TECHNOLOGY

Devices in the *mid-technology (mid-tech)* category use simple electronics. Examples:

- A digital audio recorder that a student uses to record lectures or dictate test responses
- A calculator that assists a student in completing math computations
- A timer that lets a student know it is time to change from one activity to another

HIGH TECHNOLOGY

Items considered *high technology (high-tech)* incorporate more sophisticated, sometimes costly technology. Examples:

- Voice-recognition software that allows a student to use a microphone to dictate information that then appears in print on the computer
- Electronic communication boards on which a student can touch a picture and a prerecorded voice communicates for him. For example, a student touches a picture of himself and a voice says "Hello. My name is Danny. What is your name?"

Technology in Action

Are you interested in assistive technology such as the examples just noted? The following students demonstrate using these tools, and they are students you might teach.

- Mason is a first grader who uses several types of technology to help him learn. Watch him in action in this video: https://www.youtube.com/watch?v=IcUNnnwFm4g
- Brody, a sixth grader, has a learning disability. To help him with writing, he uses two technology tools, Co-Writer and a spelling pen. You can watch him use these tools and learn more about them at this site: https://www.youtube.com/watch?v=D6i5CtPoGh0
- Elle, a 14-year-old student with cerebral palsy, communicates using a Dynavox, an assistive communication device. Her mom explains the process for accessing this type of technology in this video: https://www.youtube.com/watch?v=g95TO2Ohnmo

DEVELOPMENTAL DELAY The category *developmental delay (DD)* is somewhat different than the other disabilities recognized in IDEA. It is an option that states may use for children ages three through nine. This category includes youngsters who have significant delays in physical, cognitive, communication, social-emotional, or adaptive development, but it is applied instead of one of the more specific disability categories. This option has two advantages: First, it avoids the use of more stigmatizing labels for young children, and second, it acknowledges the difficulty of determining the nature of a specific disability when children are rapidly growing and changing.

Categories versus Understanding Student Needs

Federal and state education agencies and local school districts use the categories of disability described in the previous section for counting the number of students receiving special education, allocating money to educate them, and designing educational service options. When you prepare to teach a student, however, you probably will find that the specific category of disability does not guide you in discovering that student's strengths and devising appropriate teaching strategies. Further, students labeled in different categories often benefit from the same instructional adjustments (Gage, Lierheimer, & Goran, 2012; Rojewski, Lee, & Gregg, 2015; Yakimowski, Faggella-Luby, Kim, & Wei, 2016). Therefore, throughout this text, students generally are discussed in terms of only the following two groups:

1. *High-incidence disabilities* are those that traditionally have been most commonly identified, including learning disabilities, speech or language impairments, mild intellectual disabilities, and emotional disturbance. Together these disabilities account for more than two-thirds of the disabilities reported in 2015–2016, the most recent year for which official data are available (U.S. Department of Education, 2016). It should be noted, though, that this pattern gradually is changing. Specifically, as the number of students with ADHD served in the category of other health impairments grows and the number of students identified as having autism increases, the students considered to be in "high-incidence" groups may change.

2. *Low-incidence disabilities* are those that are less common and include all the other categories: moderate to severe intellectual disabilities, multiple disabilities, hearing impairments, orthopedic impairments, other health impairments, visual impairments, deaf-blindness, autism, traumatic brain injury, and developmental delays.

Consistent with this textbook's contemporary approach to understanding students and effectively educating them, characteristics of students with disabilities are discussed in more detail in Chapters 6 and 7, but more attention is paid to students' learning needs than to their specific labels. In addition, although some strategies specific to categorical groups are outlined in those chapters (for example, the use of large-print books for students with visual impairments), it is critical to keep in mind that many of the strategies presented throughout this textbook can be used effectively with a wide range of students with disabilities. If you adopt this approach in your own thinking about teaching students with disabilities, you will see that many options are available for helping all students succeed.

Other Students with Special Needs

Not all students who have special learning and behavior needs are protected by special education laws. The instructional strategies you learn in this textbook also sometimes can assist you in teaching many other students who may struggle in school, including those described in the following sections.

STUDENTS WHO ARE GIFTED OR TALENTED Students who demonstrate ability far above average in one or several areas—including overall intellectual ability, leadership, specific academic subjects, creativity, athletics, and the visual or performing arts—are considered *gifted* or *talented.* Erin is included in this group; she seems to learn without effort, and she also is eager to learn about almost everything. Evan is considered talented; still in elementary school, he has participated in state and national piano recitals, and his parents have requested that he have access to the music room during recess so he can practice. Students who are gifted or talented are not addressed in federal special education law, but some states have separate laws that provide guidelines for identifying and educating students with special talents. Adequate funds are not always provided to implement these laws, however, and so the availability and scope of services for students with particular talents vary across the country and even within each state.

STUDENTS PROTECTED BY SECTION 504 Some students not eligible to receive special education services are entitled to protection through Section 504 and receive specialized assistance because of their functional disabilities, as described earlier in this chapter. Among those likely to be included in this group are some students with attention deficit–hyperactivity disorder (ADHD). These students have a medical condition often characterized by an inability to attend to complex tasks for long periods of time, excessive motor activity, and/or impulsivity. The impact of this disorder on students' schoolwork can be significant. Students with ADHD may take medication, such as Ritalin or Strattera, that helps them focus their attention. Many students with learning disabilities or emotional disturbance also have ADHD, but these students receive assistance through IDEA, as do students with ADHD whose disorder is so significant that they are determined to be eligible for special education. In addition to those mentioned earlier in the chapter, other students who may be protected by Section 504 include those with dwarfism, those who have spina bifida, or those with a medical disorder such as Crohn's disease.

STUDENTS AT RISK The general term *at risk* often refers to students whose characteristics, environment, or experiences make them more likely than others to fail in school. Students whose primary language is not English—sometimes referred to as *English learners (ELs)* or students who have *limited English proficiency (LEP)*—sometimes are considered at risk, and they may need assistance in learning at school. They receive bilingual education or English as a second language (ESL) services to have opportunities to learn English while also learning the standard curriculum. These services may occur in a separate classroom or within the general education setting. Some ELs also have disabilities; when this is the case, both English-language instruction and special education may be provided. The checklist presented in the Professional Edge feature is a tool you can use to analyze your readiness to work with students and families from diverse backgrounds, including those who are English language learners.

A second group of at-risk students includes struggling learners whose educational progress is below average but who do not have a disability. These students are learning to the best of their abilities, but they often cannot keep pace with the instruction in most general education classrooms without assistance. They are sometimes described as "falling between the cracks" of the educational system, because although most professionals agree they need special assistance, they are not eligible for special education. They are likely to access and benefit from response to intervention (RtI) or similar services described earlier in this chapter.

Other students who might be considered at risk include those who are homeless, those who live in poverty or move frequently, those who are born to mothers abusing drugs or alcohol or who abuse drugs or alcohol themselves, and those who are victims of physical or psychological abuse. Students in these groups are at risk for school failure because of the environment or circumstances in which they live.

You may find it challenging to find effective strategies to reach your students who have special needs but who do not have disabilities as defined in special education law. However, current trends in education can help you. First, you

PROFESSIONAL EDGE 1.2

Promoting Cultural Competence: A Self-Assessment

Cultural competence refers to your understanding of and responses to diversity. Here is an excerpt from a tool designed to help professionals reflect on their awareness of a variety of factors that contribute to cultural competence. You can find the complete self-assessment checklist at the National Center for Cultural Competence: http://nccc.georgetown.edu/documents/ChecklistCSHN.pdf

Directions: Please select A, B, or C for each item listed below.

A = Things I do frequently, or statement applies to me a great deal.

B = Things I do occasionally, or statement applies to me to a moderate degree.

C = Things I do rarely or never, or statement applies to me to a minimal degree or not at all.

- For children who speak languages or dialects other than English, I attempt to learn and use key words in their language so that I am better able to communicate with them during assessment, treatment, or other interventions.
- I use visual aids, gestures, and physical prompts in my interactions with children who have limited English proficiency.
- When interacting with parents who have limited English proficiency, I always keep in mind that:
  - Limitation in English proficiency is in no way a reflection of their level of intellectual functioning.
  - Their limited ability to speak the language of the dominant culture has no bearing on their ability to communicate effectively in their language of origin.
  - They may or may not be literate either in their language of origin or English.
- I use alternative formats and varied approaches to communicate and share information with children and/or their family members who experience disability.
- I avoid imposing values that may conflict or be inconsistent with those of cultures or ethnic groups other than my own.

- I recognize and accept that individuals from culturally diverse backgrounds may desire varying degrees of acculturation into the dominant culture.
- I accept and respect that male–female roles in families may vary significantly among different cultures (e.g., who makes major decisions for the family, play and social interactions expected of male and female children).
- I recognize and understand that beliefs and concepts of emotional well-being vary significantly from culture to culture.
- I accept that religion and other beliefs may influence how families respond to illnesses, disease, disability, and death.
- I recognize and accept that folk and religious beliefs may influence a family's reaction and approach to a child born with a disability or later diagnosed with a physical/emotional disability or special health care needs.
- I understand that traditional approaches to disciplining children are influenced by culture.
- I understand that families from different cultures will have different expectations of their children for acquiring toileting, dressing, feeding, and other self-help skills.
- I accept and respect that customs and beliefs about food and its value, preparation, and use are different from culture to culture.

Note: This checklist is intended to heighten the awareness and sensitivity of personnel to the importance of cultural diversity and cultural competence in human service settings. There is no answer key with correct responses. However, if you frequently responded "C," you may not necessarily demonstrate values and engage in practices that promote a culturally diverse and culturally competent service-delivery system for children with disabilities or special health care needs and their families.

Source: From *Promoting Cultural Competence: A Self-Assessment, Promoting cultural diversity and cultural competency: Self-assessment checklist for personnel providing services and supports to children with disabilities & special health needs and their families* by Tawara D. Goode. Copyright © 2009. Reprinted by permission of the National Center for Cultural Competence.

can access RtI or MTSS procedures, already introduced, for research-based interventions for your struggling learners. In addition, as students with disabilities spend increasing amounts of time in general education classes, special education teachers and other special services providers often informally assist teachers in planning and adapting educational activities for at-risk students. Thus, other students with special needs often benefit from inclusive education for students with disabilities.

MyLab Education Self-Check 1.4

WRAPPING IT UP

Back to the Cases

Now that you have read about the foundations for educating students with special needs, look back at the student stories at the beginning of the chapter. Then go to MyLab Education to apply the knowledge you've gained in this chapter to each case.

MyLab Education Application Exercise 1.1: Case Study 1.1

LUCAS is a middle school student with autism. Although he is succeeding in his general education classes, the demands of that setting cause him a great deal of stress.

MyLab Education Application Exercise 1.2: Case Study 1.2

MONIKA, the elementary student with fragile X syndrome and an intellectual disability, receives some of her education in a general education setting and some in a special education setting.

MyLab Education Application Exercise 1.3: Case Study 1.3

AARON, as you may recall, is an excellent athlete, but he does not like to have attention called to his learning disability. When he refuses the support of teachers, he hurts his performance on assignments and tests.

Summary

LO 1.1 *Special education* refers to the specially designed instruction, related services, and supplementary aids and services received by the millions of students in the United States who have disabilities. The requirements for special education services are specified in federal special education law, the Individuals with Disabilities Education Act, and its regulations.

LO 1.2 Current special education practices have been influenced by a number of critical factors, including the context in which it began early in the twentieth century, parent advocacy, the civil rights movement that began in the mid-twentieth century, significant court cases, and current civil rights and education legislation.

LO 1.3 Contemporary special education practice is characterized by several themes that affect nearly all general education teachers. These include prevention of the need for special education whenever possible, high academic expectations and accountability for ensuring all students meet those expectations, implementation of evidence-based practices, and the concept of inclusiveness.

LO 1.4 Federal law identifies 13 categories of disability that may entitle students to special education services: learning disability, speech or language impairment, intellectual disability, emotional disturbance, autism, hearing impairment, visual impairment, deaf-blindness, orthopedic impairment, traumatic brain injury, other health impairment, multiple disabilities, and developmental delay. However, many students have special needs not addressed through special education, including those who are gifted or talented; who have ADHD; who are at risk, including English learners and struggling learners; and students whose life situations comprise high risk for school failure. Students with disabilities also may have these additional special needs.

APPLICATIONS IN TEACHING PRACTICE
Understanding Contemporary Special Education

It is a new school year—your first as a teacher in the Danville School District. You are excited about your new job but worried about following the district curriculum and making sure your students succeed on high-stakes tests. Then you learn that you will be responsible for the following students, and you find that you need all the skills for reaching diverse groups of students that you learned in your professional preparation program:

- Cassie is a bright student who has a visual impairment. To read, she uses a computer that greatly magnifies materials. She also needs to work in bright light, and she gets fatigued from the effort required to use what little vision she has. If a teacher points at the whiteboard and says, "Everyone, look at this . . . ," Cassie will not know what the teacher is referring to; the information must be stated out loud for her to follow the instruction.

- Ramon is identified as having a learning disability. His reading ability is significantly below grade level. He also seems disorganized. He often forgets to bring materials and assignments to school, and he frequently asks for help immediately after directions for an assignment have been given and without trying on his own to follow them.

- Tory lives in a foster home. He was removed from his mother's care because of several incidents of abuse. Tory's responses to teachers and classmates often change suddenly: Although he sometimes follows directions, at other times he refuses to work, and he sometimes loses his temper and throws a book or crumples a paper. He frequently is absent from school.

QUESTIONS

1. What are the possible strengths that Cassie, Ramon, and Tory might bring to your classroom? How can you emphasize these strengths instead of their difficulties? What is the rationale for assigning these students to a general education classroom like yours? How do the provisions of IDEA and ESEA/ESSA affect these students' educational rights and responsibilities? What are appropriate goals that you as a teacher should have as you begin to instruct them? Discuss with your classmates how Cassie, Ramon, and Tory's special needs might be demonstrated in an elementary school, middle school, or high school classroom.

2. What are some of the benefits and opportunities of educating these students in your classroom? What positive outcomes should you expect? How can you ensure these positive outcomes?

3. What are some of the risks and concerns related to educating these students in your classroom? What types of supports could prevent or significantly reduce

these risks and concerns? How might your own beliefs be either a benefit or a risk for these students?

4. If you spoke with the parents of Cassie, Ramon, and Tory, what might you expect them to say? What unique views might each student's parents have? How might their views be influenced by their family cultures and experiences?

5. What are your concerns and questions when you think about your responsibilities for educating students with disabilities and other special needs in your classroom—whether in the elementary grades, middle school, or high school? In what ways do you think you can make a contribution to your students' education? What types of support might you need? If you write your responses to these questions, keep them at hand and use them as a basis for discussion as you read and consider the information in each following chapter.

CHAPTER 2

Special Education Procedures and Services

LEARNING OUTCOMES

After you read this chapter, you will be able to:

2-1 Analyze the roles and responsibilities of the individuals who may participate in educating students with disabilities.

2-2 Apply to your planned teaching role the steps teachers should take in deciding whether an identified student need might indicate the presence of a disability.

2-3 Describe the process through which a student may become eligible to receive special education services,

including the role that parents play throughout that process.

2-4 Name the components of individualized education programs (IEPs) and provide examples of them.

2-5 Outline the types of services that students with disabilities may receive and the settings in which they may receive them.

MS. KUCHTA continues to worry about Christopher, one of her first-grade students, and she is preparing for a meeting with her school's multi-tiered systems of support (MTSS) team to discuss his slow learning progress. Christopher was identified as being at risk for school failure early in kindergarten. With intensive instruction and frequent monitoring of his progress, his learning accelerated. But now in first grade, problems are occurring again. Ms. Kuchta has been implementing what are referred to as Tier 1 interventions, research-based reading strategies, but Ms. Kuchta's data indicate they are not having enough of an impact to help Christopher catch up to his peers. In addition, he recently has been refusing to do his reading assignments, and concern is growing about his behavior. At today's meeting, Ms. Kuchta anticipates that the team—which includes the school psychologist, the assistant principal, the literacy coach, and another teacher—will decide to move Christopher to Tier 2. This means he will receive additional reading instruction three times each week for 40 minutes. She also anticipates receiving assistance related to Christopher's behavior. If, after 10 weeks, the academic and behavior interventions are not increasing his learning rate, he will receive even more intensive interventions at Tier 3. The goal, if possible, is to improve Christopher's classroom behavior and address his academic deficits before they become so significant that special education might be needed.

What actions do Ms. Kuchta and other teachers take when their students are struggling? How do educators decide whether Christopher's (and other students') learning challenges are so significant that they may constitute a disability and require special education services? Why should a single team address both academic and behavior problems instead of having a different team for each domain?

MS. LEE, a high school English teacher, has just pulled from her mailbox a document titled "IEP at a Glance." As she reads through it, she realizes that it is a summary of the individualized education program (IEP) for Jennifer, one of her students. The summary includes a list of tools Jennifer should receive as part of instruction (including shorter assignments, preferential seating, and longer timelines for assignments) as well as specification of test accommodations Jennifer should receive. For example, Jennifer needs to complete unit tests in a small, structured environment. That means she will go to the special education classroom on test days instead of reporting to Ms. Lee's room. The form also mentions steps being taken to help Jennifer prepare for a vocational program she will attend after high school. Ms. Lee notes that the speech/language therapist, the transition specialist, and the social worker are mentioned in the document, but the special education teacher is listed as the person to contact to answer questions.

What roles do general education teachers play in writing and implementing IEPs? How are they responsible for ensuring that IEP accommodations and modifications are available in the classroom? Who are the other service providers that teachers may work with as they educate students with disabilities?

MR. BLONCOURT teaches science to eighth-grade students, and he works diligently to design lessons that engage his students and foster their understanding of key concepts. However, in a recent meeting with his science colleagues he learned that a significant proportion of his students—as well as other eighth graders—did not reach proficiency last year on the high-stakes science test. Further, the data suggest that students with disabilities and those who are English learners fared particularly poorly. Mr. Bloncourt is surprised by these negative results, and his first reaction is to be somewhat defensive, noting that some students do not do their homework, that some are frequently absent, that some students who are not identified as having disabilities should be, and that some parents do not provide adequate support for his efforts. His principal acknowledges these challenges, but she quickly moves the conversation toward problem solving, asking Mr. Bloncourt how he tracks student progress, what he does when some students do not master critical concepts, and how he communicates regularly with the special education teacher regarding the eight students in his class who have IEPs to be sure they are receiving their accommodations and other supports. Mr. Bloncourt suddenly feels pressured to change what he thought were great teaching techniques, and he decides to seek input from his mentor, another science teacher. He is realizing that he may have been basing his teaching on beliefs about instructional effectiveness rather than data. But he still wonders about the students with IEPs: If they cannot do the work shouldn't they go to a separate class that is tailored to their needs?

How are decisions made about the most appropriate place for a student with a disability to be educated? What happens if a teacher believes that a different setting would be most appropriate, for example, moving a student from a general education class to a separate special class? What happens if parents disagree with professionals' decisions about placement?

Whether you teach young children, those approaching adolescence, or those about to leave school for post-secondary education or vocational preparation, you will encounter students who struggle to learn. Some may appear to do everything they can *not* to learn. Others may try their best but still not be successful. Yet other students may have challenging behaviors that interfere with their learning, and you may find that the strategies effective with most students do not work with them. You may wonder whether some of these students should receive special education services, how a student becomes eligible for those services, and who provides them.

This chapter introduces you to people who specialize in working with students with disabilities and procedures for deciding whether a student is eligible for special education services. You also will learn how students' individualized education programs (IEPs) are designed and monitored and to which services students with disabilities are entitled. You will discover that parents play a crucial role in special education procedures and that when they or students disagree with school professionals about special services, procedures exist to help them resolve these differences. Most important, you will learn about your role in working with other professionals and parents to prevent the need for special education by using effective instructional strategies, determine student eligibility for special education, carry out students' educational programs, and monitor student learning.

Who Are the Professionals in Special Education?

Students with disabilities are entitled to a wide range of supports and programs. Not surprisingly, many different individuals can be involved in the delivery of these services. You probably will interact with some of these professionals, such as special education teachers, almost every day. Others you might work with only occasionally. Some of these professionals serve students indirectly or work only with the few students who have the most challenging disabilities. Together, however, these educators create, implement, and evaluate the special education that students with disabilities receive.

DIMENSIONS OF DIVERSITY

African American students are more likely than Caucasian students to be referred for discipline issues, but recent research suggests this unfortunate occurrence is more likely to happen in a classroom setting than other school settings (e.g., playground, cafeteria) and is more likely during the early part of the school day as opposed to the later part of the day (Smolkowski, Girvan, McIntosh, Nese, & Horner, 2016).

General Education Teachers

As the *general education teacher*, you are the first professional discussed in this section because for many students with suspected or documented disabilities, you are the person who has the most detailed knowledge of their day-to-day strengths and needs in your classroom. Your responsibilities span several areas. You are the person most likely to bring to the attention of other professionals a student whom you suspect may have a disability (e.g., Kurz, Elliott, & Roach, 2015). That is, you may encounter a student who is reading significantly below grade level despite your use of instructional strategies demonstrated to be successful; a student whose behavior is so different from that of other students that you suspect an emotional disorder; or a student who has extraordinary difficulty focusing on learning. When you suspect a disability, you document the student's characteristics and behaviors that led to your concern by gathering samples of the student's work, compiling descriptions of his or her behavior, and keeping notes of how you have attempted to address the problem (Walker-Dalhouse et al., 2009). You work with teacher colleagues and other professionals to systematically implement interventions in your classroom to clarify whether the student's problems need further exploration, gathering data to document the impact of those interventions (e.g., Vujnovic, Fabiano, Morris, Norman, Hallmark, & Hartley, 2014; Lee, Vostal, Lylo, & Hua, 2011).

If the student is referred for assessment for special education, you contribute information about his or her academic and social functioning in your classroom and help identify the student's strengths, needs, and educational program components. For example, you might help others understand the curricular expectations in your classroom and the types of accommodations that may be necessary for the student to succeed there. If special education services are deemed necessary, you participate in deciding appropriate goals and, for some students, objectives. You also might assist special services staff members in updating parents on their child's quarterly and yearly progress. Most important, you are expected in many instances to effectively teach the student as well as to work with special services staff members to provide appropriate instruction within your classroom (Friend, 2014; Olson, Leko, & Roberts, 2016; Pearl, Dieker, & Kirkpatrick, 2012). Several of the key responsibilities of a general education teacher are summarized in Figure 2.1.

When all your responsibilities are listed, your role in planning and providing special services to students may seem overwhelming. However, studies of general education teachers typically indicate that they positively contribute to the education of students with disabilities, especially when they receive support in doing so. The supports most often mentioned as critical include administrative leadership, staff preparation and professional development, sufficient time for collaborative planning, and adequate funding and other resources for program support (Conderman & Johnston-Rodriguez, 2009; Hoppey & McLeskey, 2013).

Special Education Teachers

Special education teachers are the professionals with whom you are most likely to have ongoing contact in teaching students with disabilities, and these professionals have increasingly complex roles (Mitchell, Deshler, & Lenz, 2012; Shepherd, Fowler, McCormick, Wilson, & Morgan, 2016). They are responsible for managing and coordinating the services a student receives, including writing and implementing the individualized education program (IEP). They typically also provide direct and indirect instruction to students who are assigned to them. In addition, they may consult with you regarding a student suspected of having a disability and work with you to determine whether a referral for assessment for possible special education is warranted, a process explained later in this chapter.

Depending on the state in which you teach and the disabilities of the students in your classroom, you may work with several types of special education

> **FYI**
>
> The most recent data available indicate that there are 378,614 special education teachers in the United States for students ages 6–21 (U.S. Department of Education, 2016).

FIGURE 2.1　**General Education Teacher Responsibilities Related to Implementing IDEA**

Identify students with learning, behavior, or other needs serious enough to seek input from colleagues.

Provide evidence-based and appropriately differentiated day-to-day instruction.

Implement strategies and gather data as part of a response-to-intervention (RtI) procedure.

Collaborate with colleagues regarding students with disabilities.

Participate in writing IEPs as a member of the multidisciplinary team.

teachers. Sometimes special education teachers are assigned to work with all the students with disabilities in your class. For example, a special education teacher may support a student with a learning disability and also a student with a moderate intellectual disability or a speech or language impairment. That professional may work indirectly with other special education professionals to ensure that each student's educational plan is being implemented and monitored. Sometimes, special education teachers work only with specific groups of students. For example, a teacher for students with visual impairments or hearing loss generally will be responsible only for students with those disabilities. In states that do not use categorical labels for students, some teachers work with students with high-incidence disabilities or low-incidence disabilities, as introduced in Chapter 1.

In other situations, special education teachers may be designated by the type of services they provide. For example, for some students with high-incidence disabilities in your class, you may work with a *consulting teacher* or perhaps an *inclusion facilitator* (Friend & Cook, 2017). This professional might meet with you regularly to monitor students' progress, problem solve with you about student concerns, and coordinate students' services, in some cases working directly with students but in other situations working indirectly by supporting teachers. You also might work with a *resource teacher* who divides time among directly instructing students, working with teachers regarding student needs, and co-teaching, a topic addressed in Chapter 3 (Friend, 2016; Ketterlin-Geller, Baumer, & Lichon, 2015; Swanson & Vaughn, 2010). In some high schools, special education teachers now are assigned to work with a particular department, attending department meetings and providing supports for all students with disabilities enrolled in that department's courses.

For some groups of students, the special educator with whom you interact might be an *itinerant teacher*. Itinerant teachers often have roles like the professionals just described, but they travel between two or more school sites to provide services to students. Teachers for students with vision or hearing loss often are itinerant. However, if you work in a school district where each school has only a few students with disabilities, even the special educator for students with high-incidence disabilities may deliver services this way.

One other type of special education teacher is a *transition specialist*. This professional typically works in a high school setting and helps prepare students to leave school for vocational training, employment, or post-secondary education (Balcazar et al., 2012; Plotner, Mazzotti, Rose, & Carlson-Britting, 2016). No matter what subject you teach in high school, you might work very closely with a transition specialist, but this is especially likely in career and technical education, consumer sciences, industrial arts, and similar areas. This professional also spends time working directly with students to assess their skills and interests related to life after school. A transition specialist works with local businesses to arrange student job sites and resolve problems related to student workers. This professional also may serve as a *job coach*, accompanying a student to a job site and helping her master the skills needed to do the job successfully.

As the nature of special education services changes, so also do the job responsibilities and titles of special educators. For example, you might find that the professionals in your school who used to be called *special education teachers* are now referred to as *intervention specialists (IS)* or *exceptional educators*. This change in title represents an effort to de-label teachers and parallels the effort to de-emphasize students' labels—that is, to focus on student strengths and needs rather than the language of disability. Regardless of the type of special education teachers with whom you work, you will find that they are important instructional partners who are no longer relegated to teaching just in the special education classroom. They support students by creating adapted materials, teaching with you in the general education classroom, working directly and separately with students who have disabilities, and often serving as coordinators for all the services any single student may receive.

Related Service Providers and Other Specialists

In addition to working with special education teachers, you will have contact with a variety of other service providers. They, too, play important roles in educating students with disabilities. The following list includes the individuals with whom you are most likely to work.

SCHOOL PSYCHOLOGISTS *School psychologists* offer at least two types of expertise related to educating students with disabilities (Barringer & Dixon, 2017; Merrell, Ervin, & Gimpel, 2012). First, school psychologists often have a major responsibility for determining a student's intellectual, academic, social, emotional, and/or behavioral functioning. They typically contribute a detailed written analysis of the student's strengths and areas of need; in many school districts, this document is referred to as a "psych report" (that is, a psychological report). In a related role, school psychologists sometimes chair the multidisciplinary team that meets to decide whether a student has a disability and, if so, what types of services are needed.

DIMENSIONS OF DIVERSITY

When middle school teachers were shown videos of students displaying "traditional walking" or stylized "strolling," they concluded the latter students had lower achievement, were more aggressive, and were more likely to need special education than the former students (Neal, McCray, Webb-Johnson, & Bridgest, 2003). The race or ethnicity of the student did not make a difference in the results.

A second major task for school psychologists is designing strategies to address students' academic and social or behavior problems, whether students have been identified as having a disability or not (Bennett, Erchul, Young, & Bartel, 2012; McCurdy, Thomas, Truckenmiller, Rich, Hillis-Clark, & Lopez, 2016). For example, these professionals typically are part of the team that designs and implements interventions prior to a decision about referral for possible special education services. Sometimes they serve as behavior consultants. Occasionally, they assist a teacher by working with an entire class group on social skills. They also might provide individual assistance to students with emotional or behavioral problems who are not eligible for special education.

COUNSELORS Although *counselors* most often advise high school students and assist students with disabilities as they transition from school to post-school options (Milsom & Hartley, 2005), they also work at other school levels and contribute to the education of students with disabilities (Quigney & Studer, 2016; Serres & Nelson, 2011). For example, counselors in some school districts assess students' social and emotional functioning, including areas such as self-concept; motivation; attitude toward school, peers, and teachers; and social skills. Counselors also can provide services to both teachers and students. For teachers, they might suggest ways to draw out a student who is excessively shy, to incorporate activities designed to enhance students' self-concept into day-to-day classroom instruction, or to create an emotionally safe classroom environment. For students, counselors might provide individual assistance to a student struggling to understand a parent's death or unexplained departure from the family or other stressful events, arrange group sessions with several students who share specific needs, or work with an entire class on how to interact with a peer who has a disability.

SPEECH/LANGUAGE THERAPISTS Many students with disabilities have communication needs. Some have mild problems in pronouncing words or speaking clearly. Others have an extremely limited vocabulary. Yet others rely on alternative means of communication, such as communication boards. The professionals who specialize in meeting students' communication needs are *speech/language therapists*, and they have a tremendously diverse range of school responsibilities (Adams, Gaile, Lockton, & Freed, 2015; McConnellogue, 2011). At the early elementary level, they might work with an entire class on language development or with an individual student on pronouncing sounds. At the intermediate elementary level, they might work on vocabulary with a group of students and might also help a student with a moderate cognitive disability pronounce some words more clearly or combine words into sentences. At the middle or high school level, they often focus on functional vocabulary and work mostly with students with low-incidence disabilities. For example, they might help a student with an intellectual disability learn to read common signs and complete tasks such as ordering in a restaurant or asking for assistance.

SOCIAL WORKERS *Social workers'* expertise is similar to that of counselors in terms of being able to help teachers and students address social and emotional issues (e.g., Sherman, 2016). Thus, social workers may serve as consultants to teachers and also may provide individual or group assistance to students. However, social workers have additional expertise (Kelly, Constable, Capio, Swanlund, Thomas, & Leyba, 2016; Massat, 2013). They often are liaisons between schools and families. For example, they can create a family history by interviewing parents and visiting a student's home; this information may be critical in determining whether a student needs special education

Video Example from

You Tube

MyLab Education
Video Example 2.1: What I Love About Working in a School Setting!
This SLP provides insight into the roles of related services professionals in elementary, middle, and high school. https://www.youtube.com/watch?v=4Ac0-NAxDSs

Speech/language therapists may work with students individually or in small groups in a separate setting, but they also may integrate these services into the instruction of your general education classroom.

services. Similarly, they may help other school professionals work with families on matters such as gaining access to community health services. The school social worker often follows up on teacher reports about the suspected abuse or neglect of students.

ADMINISTRATORS　The school principal, assistant principal, and sometimes a department chairperson or team leader are the *administrators* most likely to participate actively in the education of students with disabilities. Their role is to offer knowledge about the entire school community and provide perspective on school district policies regarding special education and also to help address parents' concerns (e.g., Burdette, 2012; Theoharis & Causton, 2016). Every team that determines whether a student is eligible for special education must have administrative representation. In one school, the mother of Marisha, a student with severe language delays, requested that her daughter receive speech/language therapy for 40 minutes daily. School professionals agreed that this amount of therapy was not appropriate. Dr. Wade, the principal, worked with the team and the parent to negotiate the amount of speech therapy needed to accomplish Marisha's goals.

In some locales, especially large urban and suburban districts where it is difficult to ensure that all required special education procedures are followed, a *special education coordinator* or *supervisor* is part of the district's administration. This professional specializes in understanding the sometimes complex procedures of special education. Coordinators help alleviate the pressure on principals and assistant principals to accurately interpret and follow guidelines. They also explain services and options to parents, problem solve with teachers when issues arise, and assist in monitoring to ensure that students with disabilities receive needed supports.

PARAPROFESSIONALS　Individuals who assist teachers and others in the provision of services to students with disabilities are *paraprofessionals* (Biggs, Gilson, & Carter, 2016; Fisher & Pleasants, 2012). These individuals usually have a certificate based on completing a community college or similar training program; some are licensed teachers. Regardless, these service providers generally complete their work under the direction of teachers and other professional staff members. Paraprofessionals also might be called *paraeducators, instructional assistants, teaching assistants, aides*, or other titles, depending on local practices.

School districts use paraprofessionals in many different ways (Azad, Locke, Downey, Xie, & Mandell, 2015; Carter et al., 2016), but two roles are especially common. Some paraprofessionals are assigned to specific students who need ongoing individual assistance. For example, a student with no ability to move his arms may have a paraprofessional who takes notes for him and completes other tasks such as feeding. A few students have medical conditions that require a specially trained paraprofessional be present to monitor their status. Paraprofessionals in this role may be referred to as *personal assistants* or *one-to-one assistants*.

A second and more common role for paraprofessionals is to assist in the delivery of special services for many students. These paraprofessionals often work in both general education classrooms and special education classrooms as well as on the playground, at assemblies, and during bus duty. These paraprofessionals' primary responsibility is to work with students with disabilities, but they sometimes also help other students and the teacher as the need arises and time permits. The Professional Edge feature contains more information about recommended responsibilities for paraprofessionals.

OTHER SPECIALISTS　Depending on student needs and state and local practices, other professionals also may participate in the education of students with disabilities. Here is a list of these individuals and a brief description of their roles:

- *Physical therapist.* Assesses and intervenes with regard to gross motor skills, that is, large muscle activity such as gait.

PROFESSIONAL EDGE 2.1

Working with Paraprofessionals

No matter what grade level you teach, you will likely find yourself at some point working closely with paraprofessionals, also called *paraeducators*. These individuals are employed by school districts to provide support to students with disabilities, either by working with specific students one-to-one or by working in general or special education classrooms on behalf of several students.

Generally, paraprofessionals work under the direction of teachers or other professionals, and they do not have sole responsibility for any aspect of a student's educational program. These are some of the responsibilities a paraprofessional could have in your classroom:

- Locate, arrange, or construct instructional materials.
- Assist students with eating, dressing, personal care, and bathroom use.
- Help prepare the classroom for students and keep work areas neat.
- Instruct students with disabilities individually, in small or large groups, and/or with typical peers, supervised by licensed educators and as specified in students' IEPs or by professionals on the service delivery team. Such instruction generally is review or reteaching rather than initial core instruction.
- Collect data for professional team members regarding student progress toward IEP goals.
- Score tests and certain papers using a key or rubric.
- Maintain files or records about students.
- Assist with routine school–home communication (e.g., sending a reminder to a parent about a needed permission form).

- Supervise playgrounds, halls, lunchrooms, buses, and loading zones.
- Address students' specific health needs (e.g., suction tracheotomy tubes as assigned and trained by a school nurse).
- Facilitate appropriate interactions between students with disabilities and typical peers.
- Assist students using adaptive equipment or assistive technology (e.g., a communication board).
- Support student behavior and social needs according to plans and under teacher supervision.
- Communicate with professionals about their work and students' progress on assigned tasks.
- Move or accompany students from one place to another, assisting students with mobility and transition.

FROM THE RESEARCH

As the list suggests, paraprofessionals offer many valuable services to students and teachers in support of students. However, Giangreco and his colleagues (e.g., Giangreco, 2013; Giangreco, Suter, & Doyle, 2010; Giangreco, Doyle, & Suter, 2012) have found persistent issues in the roles and responsibilities of these school personnel, including practices for hiring, assigning, and retaining them; their preparation for their jobs; specific job expectations; respect for the work paraprofessionals complete; problems related to supervision; and student perceptions of these support personnel.

- *Occupational therapist.* Assesses and intervenes with regard to fine motor skills, that is, small muscle activity such as grasping a pencil.
- *Adaptive physical educator.* Designs physical education activities for students with physical, health, or other special needs that affect participation in traditional programs.
- *Nurse.* Gathers needed medical information about students with disabilities and interprets such information from physicians and other medical personnel.
- *Bilingual special educator.* Specializes in serving students from diverse cultural and linguistic backgrounds because of expertise in both special education and bilingual education.
- *Mobility specialist.* Helps students with visual impairments learn how to become familiar with their environments and how to safely travel from place to place.
- *Sign language interpreter.* Listens to classroom instruction and relays it to students who are deaf or hard of hearing using sign language.
- *Professional from outside agencies.* Provides services away from school (for example, private school, hospital, juvenile justice system) and serves as the liaison between such services and school personnel, especially during transitions from such services back to school.
- *Advocate.* Serves as an advisor and sometimes represents parents at meetings related to their children with disabilities, especially when parents believe they are not knowledgeable enough about the legal and educational requirements of special education.

Parents and Students

When decisions are being made concerning a student with a suspected or documented disability, the best interests of the student and her family must be represented. The parents—or a person serving in the role of a parent, such as a guardian or foster parent—have the right to participate in virtually all aspects of their child's educational program (Lalvani, 2012), a topic addressed in more detail later in this chapter.

Often parents are strong allies for general education teachers. They can assist teachers by reviewing at home what is taught in school, rewarding their child for school accomplishments, and working with school professionals to resolve behavior and academic problems (Cianca & Wischnowski, 2012; Francis, Blue-Banning, Turnbull, Hill, Haines, & Gross, 2016).

Whenever appropriate, students with disabilities also should be active participants in decision making about their own education. Increasingly, educators are involving students so they can directly state their needs and goals and learn to advocate for themselves, a concept referred to as self-determination (Hart & Brehm, 2013; Van Laarhoven-Myers, Van Laarhoven, Smith, Johnson, & Olson, 2016).

The extent of student participation on the team depends on the age of the student, the type and impact of the disability, and the professionals' and parents' commitment. In general, the older the student, the greater her ability to contribute, and the higher the value placed on her contribution, the greater the participation. Thus, first-grade students with disabilities usually are not expected to participate in making most decisions about their education. However, high school students with disabilities usually attend and participate in their team meetings, and their priorities and preferences are central to decision making (Martin & Williams-Diehm, 2013; Seong, Wehmeyer, Palmer, & Little, 2015). These students often have strong opinions about what they would like to do after high school, and they also take on more responsibility for monitoring their progress in reaching their goals. You can learn more about student participation on teams in the Professional Edge feature and in Chapter 10.

MyLab Education

Video Example 2.2: Olivia, Parent Teacher Conference

What does this mother's experiences with teacher conferences tell you about working with parents and families of students with disabilities?

MyLab Education Self-Check 2.1

PROFESSIONAL EDGE 2.2

Self-Determination for Students with Disabilities

Think how you would react if other people constantly controlled your life, deciding what you should wear, where you should go, what career you should pursue, and what type of housing and roommates you should have. Beginning at a very young age, children typically begin to express their wishes, and they learn that they have a right to act on those wishes. (For example, have you ever tried to convince a three-year-old that the two articles of clothing she selected to wear do not match?) But despite good intentions by professionals and parents, many students and adults with disabilities have been denied opportunities to make their own life decisions. Reversing this situation has become a goal for the field (e.g., Van Laarhoven-Myers, Van Laarhoven, Smith, Johnson, & Olson, 2016; Wehmeyer, Palmer, Shogren, Williams-Diehm, & Soukup, 2013).

STUDENT-LED IEPS

When students lead their IEP meetings, they learn to think and advocate for themselves (Griffin, 2011; Nolan-Spohn, 2016).

They can learn to do this beginning at a very early age and gradually develop their skills as they progress through school:

- Elementary students might have the role of introducing their parents to the team and describing to team members what they have been learning in school.
- Students in middle school might explain their disabilities and the impact of those disabilities, share their strengths, and discuss accommodations needed.
- High school students might lead the entire IEP meeting, working to ensure that the IEP and transition plan reflect their preferences and aspirations for the future.

General education teachers find that students who actively participate in their IEP meetings have better skills for interacting with adults, better understanding of their special needs, greater awareness of resources available to help them, and more willingness to accept responsibility for themselves (Test et al., 2004).

(continued)

PERSON-CENTERED PLANNING

Another method of self-determination called *person-centered planning* (e.g., Luft, 2015) was developed by professionals from both the United States and Canada and usually is related to IEP planning. It emphasizes these dimensions:

- *Community presence.* Identify the community settings that the student uses and the ones that would benefit him. The intent is to incorporate these settings into the educational planning process.
- *Choice.* Identify decisions made *by* the student and decisions made *for* the student. The goal of person-centered planning is to transfer as many choices to the student as possible.
- *Competence.* Identify the skills that will best assist the student to participate fully in the school and community and the strategies that will be most effective for teaching those skills.

- *Respect.* Clarify roles the student has in the school and local community. The goal is to strengthen and expand those roles and decrease or eliminate personal characteristics that might cause the student to be perceived by others in a stereotypical way.
- *Community participation.* Specify people with whom the student spends time at school and in other settings. The goal is to identify individuals who can advocate for the student and to foster friendships with age-appropriate peers.

Several person-centered planning approaches have been developed, including Making Action Plans (MAPs), Planning Alternative Tomorrows with Hope (PATH), and Circle of Friends. You can learn more about this topic by visiting the PACER Center website at http://www.pacer.org/ and typing *person-centered planning* into the site search option.

WWW RESOURCES

http://www.beachcenter.org
The Beach Center on Disability, affiliated with the University of Kansas, has as its goal helping families of individuals with disabilities and the individuals themselves through research, teaching, technical assistance, and community service. The website has many resources on a wide array of topics to help teachers work effectively with families.

How Do You Decide Whether a Student Need Might Be a Disability?

You will play a key role in deciding whether a student in your class should be evaluated for the presence of a disability, as is true of Ms. Kuchta, introduced at the beginning of this chapter. Although youngsters with obvious intellectual, sensory, and physical impairments usually are identified when they are infants or toddlers, learning, language, attentional, and behavioral disabilities—such as those displayed by Christopher, introduced at the beginning of the chapter—often are not diagnosed until children experience difficulty in school. Because you are the professional in daily contact with the student, you are the person most likely to notice an unmet need. Combined with data gathered to measure all students' progress, called **universal screening**, your judgment is essential for initiating the process of increasingly intensive interventions and, potentially, the special education decision-making process.

Analyze Unmet Needs

As you teach, you sometimes will discover that you have a nagging concern about a student. This concern might begin early in the school year, or it might take several months to emerge. For example, when you review a student's records of academic progress and consider your own impressions and evaluation of student work, you may decide that the student's achievement is not within the typical range, given the standards of your school district, community expectations, and state achievement standards. Should you propose that the student receive intensive interventions and eventually, if needed, be assessed for eligibility for special education? Perhaps. But first, you need to ask yourself some questions.

WHAT ARE SPECIFIC EXAMPLES OF UNMET NEEDS? Having a vague worry about a student is far different from specifically stating a concern. For example, sensing that a student is unmotivated is not a clear concern. What does the student do that leads you to conclude that motivation is a problem? Is it that the student doesn't make eye contact when speaking to you or that the rewards and consequences that other students enjoy seem to have no effect, positive or negative, on this student? If you are thinking that the student is not making enough academic progress, what does that mean? Is it that classmates have mastered letters, sounds, and blends, but this student knows only about half the letters? Is it that other students easily use basic math procedures in solving multiple-step equations, but this student makes computational errors in 8 out of 10 problems?

Vague concerns and hunches must be supported by specific information. Phrases such as "slow in learning," "poor attitude toward school," "unmotivated," "doesn't pay attention," and "never gets work completed" might have very different meanings to different professionals. To prepare to share your concern with others, your first step is to ask yourself "When I say the student . . ., what examples, supported with data, clarify what I mean?"

IS THERE A CHRONIC PATTERN NEGATIVELY AFFECTING LEARNING? Nearly all students go through periods when they struggle to learn, behave inappropriately, or otherwise cause you concern. Sometimes a situation outside school affects a student. For example, parents divorcing, the family being evicted from its apartment, elderly grandparents moving in with the family, or a family member being injured or arrested might negatively affect student learning or behavior. However, the impact of these traumatic events should not be permanent, and the student should gradually return to previous levels of functioning.

Students with disabilities also may be affected by specific situations and events, but their learning and behavior needs form a chronic pattern. In other words, they struggle over a long period of time regardless of the circumstances. For example, Betsy, who has a learning disability, has difficulty remembering sight words no matter what level they are or how creatively they are introduced. Jared, a high school student with an emotional disability, is withdrawn whether sitting in a large class or interacting in a small group. Julianna, an eighth grader who experienced a severe head injury last year, usually seems to grasp abstract concepts as they are taught, but she struggles to describe or apply them after instruction.

ARE THE UNMET NEEDS BECOMING MORE SERIOUS AS TIME PASSES? Sometimes a student's needs appear to become greater over time. For example, Ben, who seemed to see well at the beginning of the school year, now holds books closer and closer to his face, squints when he tries to read, and complains about headaches. Karen, who began the school year reluctant but willing to complete assignments, by November refuses to do any work during class. Indications that a student's needs are increasing are a signal to ask for input from others.

IS THE STUDENT'S LEARNING OR BEHAVIOR SIGNIFICANTLY DIFFERENT FROM THAT OF CLASSMATES? As you think about your concerns about a student, ask yourself how he or she compares to other students. For example, it has been demonstrated that students at risk for special education referral achieve at a significantly lower level than other students and are more likely to have serious behavior problems (Hosp & Reschly, 2003; Oldfield, Hebron, & Humphrey, 2016). However, if you have eight students who are all struggling, the reason might be that the information or skills are beyond the reach of the entire group or that your teaching approach is not accomplishing what you had planned. Even though self-reflection is sometimes difficult, when many students are experiencing problems, it is important to analyze how the curriculum or teaching might be contributing to the situation. In such instances, you should make adjustments in those two areas before seeking other assistance.

Keep in mind that many students have needs that *do* signal the presence of disabilities. Perhaps you are an elementary teacher who cannot seem to find enough books at the right level for one student in your fourth-grade class who is almost a nonreader. Perhaps you are an eighth-grade social studies teacher who is worried about two students' apparent inability to read the e-textbook or understand the themes of history integral to your curriculum. Maybe you are an algebra teacher who finds that one student seems to lack many prerequisite skills for succeeding in the course. Students with disabilities have needs that are significantly different from those of most other students.

DO YOU DISCOVER THAT YOU CANNOT FIND A PATTERN? In some instances, the absence of a pattern in students' learning or behavior is as much an indicator that you should request assistance as is a distinct pattern. Perhaps Curtis has tremendous mood swings, and you arrive at school each day wondering whether he will have a good day or a bad day. However, you cannot find a way to predict which it will be. Or consider Becka, who learns science with ease but is failing English, according to a colleague on your seventh-grade team. You are not sure why her learning is so different in the two subjects. In a third example, in physical education, Tyrone seems to have average motor skills on some days but on other days frequently stumbles and cannot participate fully in the learning stations you have created.

Communicate Your Observations and Try Your Own Interventions

Your analysis of your students' unmet needs is the basis for further action. Although you eventually may decide to formally seek assistance for a student, part of your responsibility in attempting to help the student is gathering other information and trying to resolve the problem first.

CONTACT THE PARENTS One of your first strategies should be to contact the student's family (Neuman, 2016; O'Connor, 2010). Parents or other family members often can inform you about changes in the student's life that could be affecting school performance. Family members also can help you understand how the student's activities outside school might influence schoolwork, including clubs, gang involvement, employment, and responsibilities at home. Further, by contacting the family, you might learn that what you perceive as a problem is mostly a reflection of a cultural difference. For example, a student whose family emigrated from Thailand is extremely quiet because silence signals respect in her native culture, not because she is unable to participate.

Parents also are your partners in working to resolve some student learning problems (e.g., McKenna & Millen, 2013). They can assist you in monitoring whether homework is completed and returned to school, whether behavior problems are occurring on the walk home, or whether a physician is concerned about a child's medical condition. If you have students whose homes do not have a telephone or e-mail, Internet, or text messaging access and whose parents do not have transportation to come to school, your social worker or principal often can help you make needed contact.

CONTACT COLLEAGUES Especially as a new teacher, you will want to informally discuss your concerns with other professionals to gain additional perspectives on the student's needs. In many schools, a special education teacher, assistant principal, department chairperson, literacy coach, or another professional can arrange to observe the student in your class and then discuss the observation. If your school psychologist is available, you might ask for consultation assistance. In schools where grade-level teams or other types of teams or departments meet, you can raise your concerns in that context. Hallmarks of today's schools include an array of professionals with expertise in many areas and a strong emphasis on the use of data. With a little exploration, you will likely find that your school has an in-house resource you can access to check your perceptions against a broader perspective including data about the student's performance.

TRY SIMPLE INTERVENTIONS Part of your responsibility as a teacher is to create a classroom where students can succeed. To cultivate such a setting, you can make simple changes as part of your efforts to address a student's unmet needs. Here are some examples:

- Have you tried moving the student's seat?
- Have you incorporated teaching strategies that help the student actively participate in lessons (for example, using choral responding, in which all students together repeat answers aloud)?
- Have you thought about ways to make your tests easier for the student to follow (for example, using more white space between items or sections)?

- Have you given the student only part of an assignment at one time to prevent him from becoming overwhelmed?
- Have you observed the student closely to determine whether helping her work one problem is enough to get her to work on the rest?

These are just a few instructional adjustments that many teachers make; many others are presented throughout this textbook. Sometimes these small adjustments are sufficient to help a student learn. In any case, you should try common interventions before deciding a student might need the far more intensive service of formal interventions or special education.

DOCUMENT THE UNMET NEED If you anticipate requesting assistance for a student, you need to demonstrate the seriousness of your concern and your systematic attempts to help meet the student's needs. If you have implemented a plan to improve student behavior, keep a record of how effective it has been. If you have contacted parents several times, keep a log of your conversations. If you have tried strategies to improve student learning, be prepared to describe those strategies and share the data you have gathered related to their impact. Documenting student needs serves two main purposes. First, it helps you do a reality check on whether the problem is as serious as you think it is. If you gather data from other students as a comparison, you can judge whether the unmet needs of one student are significantly different from those of typical students. Second, the information you collect will help you communicate with other professionals. Special service providers cannot possibly meet every need in every classroom. Their work is reserved in large part for extraordinary student needs, and your documentation will help in decision making about the amount and intensity of support a student may require.

REFLECT ON YOUR UNDERSTANDING OF AND RESPONSES TO THE STUDENT One final consideration, and a tremendously important one, concerns your perceptions of the student. As introduced in Chapter 1, some students are identified as disabled, especially in the learning or behavior domains, at a rate that is significantly higher than expected (e.g., Cartledge, Kea, Watson, & Oif, 2016; Sullivan & Bal, 2013). This problem of disproportionate representation begins long before formal special education procedures are triggered. In fact, as a general education teacher, your perceptions of particular students, especially those whose backgrounds and cultures are different from yours, may affect your assessment of their strengths and struggles, a point illustrated by Mr. Bloncourt in the chapter opening vignette. It is your professional obligation to recognize this possibility, including how your interactions with these students could affect their performance on academic tasks and their classroom behavior. Further, it is your responsibility to find effective ways to reach your students so as to avoid, even inadvertently, contributing to a student's learning or behavior challenges.

> **DIMENSIONS OF DIVERSITY**
>
> Latina mothers report that they have an important role to play in their children's education; they are most likely to continue to help their children with homework when directions are clear and they are informed that their efforts have a positive impact (Gillanders, McKinney, & Ritchie, 2012).

MyLab Education Self-Check 2.2

How Do Students Obtain Special Services?

Most students who receive special education have high-incidence disabilities (such as learning disabilities) that you may be the first to recognize. If you teach at the elementary level, you probably will have students nearly every year whom you refer for possible special services. If you teach in middle school, junior high, or high school, you will find that many students with disabilities already have been identified before they reach your classes. However, there are exceptions; students may be found eligible for special education at any time during their

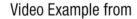

MyLab Education

Video Example 2.3: As the Expert: Multi-Tiered System of Supports—MTSS vs. RtI

Watch a video that provides a succinct explanation of MTSS and how systems such as RtI and PBIS are incorporated into it. https://www.youtube.com/watch?v=xfP_o6m47P4&t=13s

school years. As a teacher, you always have the option of asking a team of professionals to consider whether one of your students should be considered for special education services.

Having a serious and documented concern about a student is only the first step in considering whether a disability may be present. Your concern brings the student to the attention of other school professionals so that further information can be gathered and decisions made. The specific, formal procedures that must be followed to determine student eligibility for special education services are designed to ensure that only students who truly need these services receive them. These procedures are described in the following sections and summarized in Figure 2.2, which illustrates the flow of the procedures from beginning to end.

Initial Consideration of Student Problems

General education teachers, principals, special services personnel, parents, physicians, and social service agency personnel all may initiate the process of determining whether a student's needs constitute a disability. Most often, however, a general education teacher notices a pattern of academic underachievement, inconsistent learning, serious behavior problems, difficulties in social skills, or a persistent physical or sensory problem. When such problems occur, the teacher, having considered the questions posed in the preceding section, brings the student to the attention of others who help decide whether special education services might be warranted.

Depending on the policies of your state and local district, there are two primary ways that the process of formally addressing student learning and behavior concerns can begin: (1) accessing a prereferral team or (2) using response-to-intervention procedures, possibly as embedded in a broader multi-tiered systems of support (MTSS) framework.

PREREFERRAL TEAM The traditional way to begin the process of helping a student suspected of having a disability is to bring the problem to the attention of a team (Friend & Cook, 2017). This team, sometimes called a prereferral team but also referred to as an intervention assistance team or teacher assistance team, usually includes general education teachers, special services personnel, and an administrator. Teachers who want to "bring a student to the team" complete an information form on which they outline the student's strengths and problems and describe efforts they have made to assist the student. The teacher then meets with the team to discuss the written information, consider alternative strategies for assisting the student, and determine whether the student should have a detailed assessment for potential special education services (Capio, Swanlund, & Kelly, 2016). The unifying characteristic of this type of team is an emphasis on problem solving among all members.

RESPONSE TO INTERVENTION A more clearly data-driven and structured procedure for analyzing students' learning problems is response to intervention (RtI), introduced in Chapter 1 and illustrated in Ms. Kuchta's story at the beginning of this chapter. Currently authorized in federal law just for students who may have learning disabilities but established now in many states as a strategy to address a wide variety of student academic and behavior needs across all school levels (e.g., Dulaney, 2013; Jimerson, Burns, & VanDerHeyden, 2016), response to intervention calls for the systematic use of increasingly intensive, research-based interventions as a means for deciding whether a disability exists (Skinner, Mccleary, Skolits, Poncy, & Cates, 2013). It is based on the assumption that approximately 75 to 80 percent of students will be able to learn if they receive high-quality instruction, that approximately 15 to 20 percent will benefit from moderately intensive instruction, and that the remaining 5 to 10 percent will need highly intensive instruction and possibly special education services. The Instructional Edge feature provides examples of interventions and how they vary by intensity.

RESEARCH-BASED PRACTICES

Fisher and Frey (2013) report on the successful implementation of RtI in a high school. Results included improved achievement and decreased special education referrals. Challenges included fostering high-quality core instruction.

FIGURE 2.2 The Decision-Making Process for Special Education

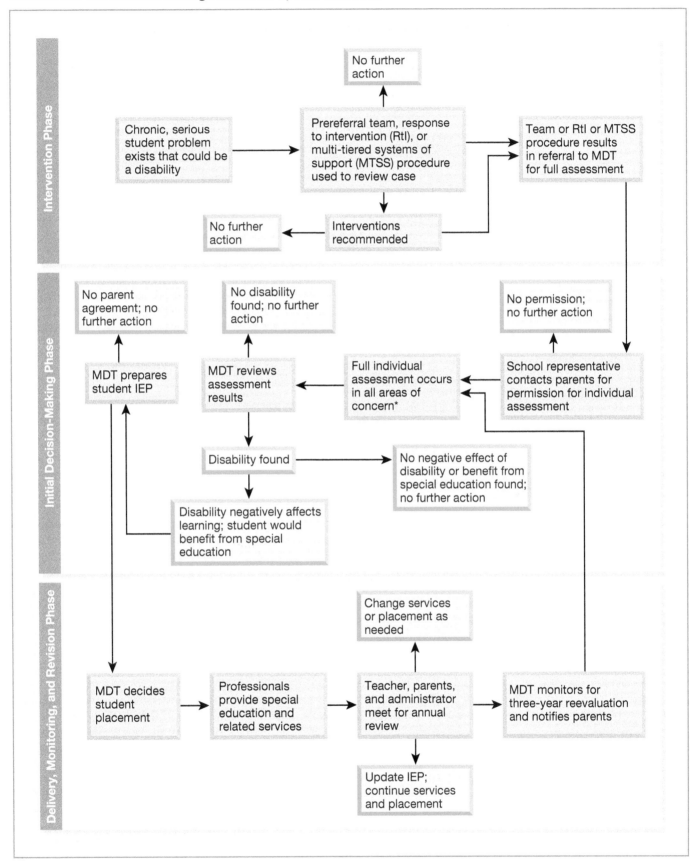

INSTRUCTIONAL EDGE 2.1

RtI and Intensity

Response to intervention is based on increasingly intensive interventions designed to avoid, if possible, the need for special education. Here are several dimensions that contribute to intensity:

- *Frequency of intervention.* In Tier 2 (sometimes called targeted intervention), an intervention may be offered three or four times each week. In Tier 3 (sometimes called intensive intervention), interventions typically occur five times per week.
- *Duration of intervention sessions.* In Tier 2, the intervention might be implemented for 30 minutes per session. In Tier 3, the intervention might be implemented for 45 minutes per session.
- *Location of the intervention.* In Tier 2, the intervention may be implemented in the general education setting. For example, three fourth-grade teachers skill group all their students and provide interventions in homogeneous groups to students in need while other students complete practice or enrichment activities. In Tier 3, intervention typically occurs in a setting away from the general education classroom.
- *Group size.* Although specific group guidelines do not exist, Tier 2 interventions tend to be delivered in larger groups in middle or high school (for example, 6–10 students) and smaller groups in elementary school (for example, 3–4 students). Tier 3 interventions often require a small group size—usually fewer than four—and sometimes involve one-to-one instruction.

- *Individual implementing the intervention.* In Tier 2, the general education teacher often is responsible for implementing the intervention, and in some cases paraprofessionals may assist with this instruction. At Tier 3, a reading specialist, psychologist, special educator, or other specialist may be assigned to instruct the targeted students.
- *Type of intervention.* Tier 2 includes research-based programs and strategies that supplement, enhance, and support Tier 1 instruction (e.g., Jenkins, Schiller, Blackorby, Thayer, & Tilly, 2013). Tier 2 instruction is systematic and explicit, and it provides students with multiple opportunities to practice skills essential for success in Tier 1. Two examples in reading at the elementary level are peer-mediated instruction (such as peer tutoring) and repeated readings (reading the same story or material several times to improve reading fluency and comprehension). In Tier 3, students receive highly intensive interventions that are more tailored to their individual needs (e.g., Jimerson et al., 2016; Vaughn & Fletcher, 2012). Examples of these interventions include teaching specific strategies such as those to improve vocabulary, comprehension, or pre-algebraic math skills.

As you might imagine, several of these dimensions can be changed at one time. Further, students may move up and down through the tiers, depending on what data indicate about their learning.

Here is an example of an RtI procedure. Ms. Petersen is a first-grade teacher. She uses a district-adopted reading program in her class that has been demonstrated through research to be effective with students. This is called a *Tier 1 intervention.* The most recent screening assessment showed that one of Ms. Petersen's students, Jorgé, has not made much progress in reading; his skills are still at a kindergarten level. A team agreed that Jorgé's problems are significant and decided that he should participate in a supplemental reading program in a small group led by the school's reading specialist. This service occurred four times each week for 30 minutes and was considered a Tier 2 intervention. After 12 weeks, the team reviewed the data gathered weekly about Jorgé's progress and noted that he still was not making adequate progress to catch up to his peers. The team enrolled Jorgé in an even more intensive skills-based reading program delivered five days a week for 50 minutes. If data indicate that the Tier 3 intervention does not work, the team may review the data, gather additional assessment information, and make a decision about Jorgé's eligibility for special education. If it is effective, he will continue in that program so his reading skills continue to develop until they are comparable to those of peers.

Key to understanding RtI is the importance of data as the basis for making decisions about students' functioning within the curriculum, the gap between their achievement and that of peers, and the effectiveness of the interventions implemented to facilitate student learning. In the Technology Notes feature you can learn about resources that can assist you in gathering such student data.

Although RtI is most likely to be implemented at the elementary level, it can occur whenever professionals determine a student is experiencing learning

TECHNOLOGY NOTES 2.1

Implementing Response to Intervention Using Technology

Effectively implementing response to intervention requires familiarity with research-based interventions, frequent and valid monitoring of student learning progress, and analysis of the gathered data so that next steps can be identified. Fortunately, many websites are providing free materials to teachers so that they can implement RtI without having to develop interventions, assessments, and graphing tools on their own. Here are two of the most comprehensive sites to help you with RtI.

INTERVENTION CENTRAL (http://interventioncentral.org)

This website has so many ideas and options for RtI that you may need several visits to explore all the information available. Here are highlights:

- Under "Academic Interventions," you will find research-based interventions for reading comprehension, reading fluency, math, writing, and other skill areas.
- Under "Behavior Interventions" you will find many positive ideas for addressing behavior problems, including bullying and unmotivated students. Strategies include the use of behavior contracts and "mystery motivators."
- In the "Tools" section, you will find a variety of templates for graphing data. Other tools include random-item generators so that you can easily create assessments on skills such as reading comprehension, writing, and math computation.

- The RtI blog discusses issues and topics in RtI, including the importance of principal leadership in implementing RtI and the dilemma of sustaining RtI when budget cuts limit staff members available to assist in implementing intensive interventions.

RTI WIRE (http://www.jimwrightonline.com/php/rti/rti_wire.php)

This website includes many free RtI resources for teachers. Examples of the materials and information you can find at the site include these:

- In "understand the model," you will find descriptions of various approaches to RtI as implemented across the United States.
- In "use teams to problem solve," you will find descriptions of the various team models being used across the states to make RtI a reality.
- In "select the right intervention," links are provided to many sites with academic interventions that span topics and skills areas as well as grade levels.
- In "monitor student progress," links are provided to sites with data templates using a variety of recording strategies, from simple tallies of behaviors to more complex approaches such as time sampling.
- In "graph data for visual analysis," the tools include several Excel® spreadsheets preformatted so that you can easily enter and graph your student data.

---

problems that are significant and interfering with achievement (Smith, Dombek, Foorman, Hook, Lee, & Cote, 2016). For example, Dana is a ninth-grade student whose assessed skills in written language are far below those of her peers. As a Tier 2 intervention she is enrolled in a composition class with nine other students; in this one-semester class the teacher focuses on key elements of written language. The goal is for Dana to complete the course and improve her skills so that she can take a more traditional elective next semester. If her skills do not improve, she will probably be enrolled in a Tier 3 elective with a smaller group of students with a teacher as well as a literacy coach.

It is important to note that IDEA permits RtI but does not mandate it, and so although it is a common practice, you should check locally to see whether an RtI procedure is in place and the specifics of the procedure. You might find that it is being utilized as a means of addressing the problem of disproportionality, or that it is a strategy when a school has many students from diverse backgrounds, as in Mr. Bloncourt's schools, discussed in the chapter opening. Further, the specific number of tiers of intervention, the length of time that interventions are implemented, and the exact nature of the interventions vary depending on state and local policies (e.g., Bohanon, Gilman, Parker, Amell, & Sortino, 2016). The Case in Practice shows an example of how an RtI procedure might be implemented.

MULTI-TIERED SYSTEMS OF SUPPORT (MTSS) MTSS does not have a formal role in the procedures for determining whether a student should receive special education services. However, that does not mean it is irrelevant. If you remember that MTSS is the broad framework for tiered interventions related to both academics and behavior, you will understand that in some locales, the RtI information just presented is incorporated into an MTSS process. Further, it is increasingly

> **FYI**
>
> Although most RtI models have three tiers, after which students are considered for special education services, in some cases there are four tiers. In other models, Tier 3 consists of special education services rather than highly intensive interventions without special education eligibility.

CASE IN PRACTICE 2.1

Response to Intervention: Looking at the Data

Mr. Thomas is a fourth-grade teacher attending a meeting to discuss Samuel, one of his students who is a struggling reader. Here is a brief segment of the conversation among Mr. Thomas, the school psychologist, and the reading specialist:

Mr. Thomas: With assistance from Ms. Jefferson [a paraprofessional], I completed the reading fluency measure for all my students last week. Overall, the students are just a little below average for this point in the school year, reading at 85 words per minute with fewer than five errors. But Sam is reading at only 50 words per minute, making an average of eight errors.

School psychologist: With these data and the other information you've provided, we should discuss whether Sam should start receiving more intensive instruction.

Reading specialist: Looking at his data, I can add that I already have a group that he could join, if we can work out the schedule. There are four other students with similar levels of skills, and I'm using the supplemental fluency materials from our reading program. But I would need you to do a quick curriculum-based check twice each week to see if his fluency is improving.

Mr. Thomas: We can work on the schedule. It's important to do something so we can see that Sam is making progress. And we need to talk a little bit about the data collection.

School psychologist: I'd also like to suggest that Sam participate in the peer-tutoring program with the sixth graders. I think he would benefit from repeated reading with one of the older students.

Mr. Thomas: That's a good idea. I do have some questions, though. For how long will we try these two interventions? What will happen if Sam's reading fluency does not improve? I'm a little concerned that we should refer him for an assessment for special education. I spoke with his mother on Monday, and she commented that Sam is talking about hating school and being embarrassed about his problems with reading. She is very worried about keeping his attitude positive, and she is in favor of special education testing.

School psychologist: The guideline is to intervene for 12 weeks, but if we don't see any change in six weeks, we can meet to decide if we should make a different decision either for a more intensive intervention or even to refer Sam for assessment for special education. Will Sam's mother agree to assist by reading with him at home each evening? That would provide both her and us with an ongoing basis for communicating.

REFLECTIONS

Why are you, as an elementary, middle school, or high school teacher, responsible for implementing increasingly intensive interventions for your students who struggle to learn? Why do professionals consider data-based decision making so important in planning interventions for students? If you were Mr. Thomas, what additional questions would you have about the planned intervention?

RESEARCH-BASED PRACTICES

Interventions address behavior problems as well as academic concerns. Flannery, Fenning, Kato, and McIntosh (2014) tracked for three years the implementation of positive behavior interventions and supports (PBIS) at eight high schools, with an additional four high schools serving as a control group. The schools implementing PBIS had a significant decrease in office discipline referrals, especially when fidelity of implementation was high.

common that data gathered as part of MTSS are considered when a team decides if assessment for special education services is warranted.

Regardless of the specific model used in a school—RtI, MTSS, or some combination of them—one element is consistent: These prereferral activities are largely carried out by general educators (Castillo et al., 2016; Hazelkorn, Bucholz, Goodman, Duffy, & Brady, 2011). That is, as a general education teacher, you may be asked to work with a small group of students in your grade level during scheduled reading and language arts time, or you may be asked to gather data concerning student skill acquisition or comprehension of key concepts in a math or English course. Ultimately, the goal of RtI is to prevent some students from ever needing special education. At the same time, following RtI procedures will help ensure that students who need specialized instruction will receive it as soon as a problem is identified.

Note, too, that parent participation has not been mentioned as a required part of any of the prereferral procedures outlined in this section. This is because a parent is not legally required to be involved at this stage. However, educators should notify parents of their concerns and enlist parental assistance in trying to solve the problem. In some schools, parents are routinely invited to team meetings and are active participants in the prereferral or RtI/MTSS process (Byrd, 2011). Parents should never be surprised when the possibility of providing special education is raised. They should be made aware of the existence of any serious problems as soon as they are noticed.

The Special Education Referral and Assessment Process

If a student does not respond to increasingly intensive interventions or the intervention assistance team believes the student's needs are serious enough to consider special education as an option, the student's parents are formally contacted and the assessment process begins. At this point, a multidisciplinary team (MDT)—consisting of parents, educators, and others as appropriate—assumes responsibility for making educational decisions regarding the student. No student may receive special education unless the steps discussed in the upcoming sections are followed.

PARENTS' RIGHTS Before any discussion of how a student comes to receive special education services can proceed, it is essential that you understand how central parents are in all aspects of the referral, assessment, eligibility, planning, and placement process (Mueller, 2015; Yell, Ryan, Rozalski, & Katsiyannis, 2009). As summarized in Figure 2.3, parents are key participants in all decision making related to their child's suspected or documented disability. They must be

FIGURE 2.3 **Parents' Rights in Special Education**

Rights

IDEA provides extensive procedural safeguards to parents to guarantee that they are active participants in decisions about their children. Parents' rights include these:

1. To give consent before their child is evaluated to determine whether a disability exists and before any special education services are provided to that child.

2. To receive prior written notice before school professionals initiate, change, or refuse to initiate or change the identification, evaluation, or educational placement of their child.

3. To have their child independently evaluated, that is, assessed by professionals outside the school district. In some cases (but not all), the school district may be responsible for paying for this independent evaluation.

4. To access and review any records pertaining to their child's education, to obtain copies of records for a reasonable fee, to expect that their child's records will be kept confidential, and to know who has accessed records related to their child (that is, through a log of each person accessing those records).

5. To be reimbursed for fees related to enrolling their child in a private school, but only if it is determined that the school district could not adequately provide the educational services needed by the student.

6. To participate in a voluntary mediation process, led by an impartial facilitator, as a means for resolving conflict with the school district concerning their child with a disability. Mediation must be made available to parents prior to a due process hearing, but it may not delay a hearing.

7. To file a formal complaint with the appropriate state agency and request an investigation if they believe the school district is not adhering to special education law.

8. To file a request for an impartial due process hearing regarding the evaluation, identification, education appropriateness, or education placement of their child. Specific timelines must be adhered to in addressing such a request.

9. To appeal for review any decision made as part of a due process hearing to the state education agency's special education department.

10. To file a lawsuit in civil court if the decisions reached through the IDEA due process and appeals procedures are determined to be unsatisfactory.

11. To be reimbursed for reasonable attorney's fees if they prevail in their due process hearing or court proceeding. However, parents' attorneys or even parents may have to pay a school district's attorney's fees if the case is determined to be trivial or unreasonable.

12. To access protective procedures related to discipline incidents. For example, these procedures generally include limiting to 10 the number of days their child may be suspended from school, unless a formal meeting is held related to the issue and an agreement is reached concerning changing the child's placement.

FYI

Although current emphasis is on avoiding, if possible, the need for special education by implementing RtI or MTSS procedures, parents have the option of requesting that those procedures be skipped and that individualized assessment be completed instead.

informed of their rights in their own language and in a manner they can understand. If you teach older students, you also should know that beginning at least one year before reaching 18 years of age, students also must be informed directly of their rights, and at age 18, most students assume the rights that parents have held for them (National Center on Secondary Education and Transition, 2012).

The very first application of parents' rights comes before any assessment process begins. That is, parents must give written permission for their child to be individually assessed. Although it is not common for parents to deny permission, if they do, the process must stop unless the school district asks for a hearing to compel parents to comply. As you read about the rest of the procedures related to special education, you will notice many references to the rights parents have.

COMPONENTS OF ASSESSMENT Although the specific requirements regarding the types of data gathered vary somewhat by state and by the type of initial intervention processes used, assessment generally involves gathering information about a student's strengths and needs in all areas of concern. Typically, if the student has not had a vision and hearing screening and you have reason to suspect a sensory impairment, these tests precede other assessments. If this screening raises concerns, the parents are notified of the need for a more complete assessment by a physician or appropriate specialist.

Assessments completed by school professionals may address any aspect of a student's educational functioning. Often, for example, the student's intellectual ability is assessed. An individual intelligence test (often referred to as an *IQ test*) is administered and scored by a school psychologist or another qualified school professional. The student also usually completes an individual academic achievement test administered by a psychologist, special education teacher, educational diagnostician, or other professional. A third area often evaluated is social and behavior skills. This evaluation might involve a checklist that you and parents complete concerning a student's behavior, a test given by the school psychologist, or a series of questions asked of the student.

Another domain for assessment is the student's social and developmental history. A school social worker may meet with the parents to learn about the student's family life and major events in his or her development that could be affecting education. For example, parents might be asked about any traumatic events in the family's past, their child's friends and favorite out-of-school activities, their expectations for their child as an adult, and their child's strengths. Parents also might be asked whether their child has had any serious physical injuries, medical problems, or recurring social or behavior problems.

As another assessment component, a psychologist, counselor, or special education teacher often observes the student in the classroom and other settings to learn how he or she responds to teachers and peers in various school situations. For example, a psychologist may observe Scott, who usually plays with younger students during recess and gets confused when playground games are too complex. Scott also watches other students carefully and often seems to take cues for how to act from how they are acting. Similarly, a special educator may observe D. J., a sixth-grade student, in the cafeteria to try to understand what is triggering his many behavior incidents there. Such observations are helpful for understanding students' social strengths and needs.

If a potential need exists for speech, occupational or physical therapy, or other related services, another component is added to the assessment. The professionals in those areas complete assessments in their respective areas of expertise. A speech/language therapist might use a screening instrument that includes having the student use certain words, tell stories, and identify objects. The therapist also might check for atypical use of the muscles of the mouth, tongue, and throat that permit speech and for unusual speech habits such as breathiness in speaking or noticeable voice strain. Similarly, an occupational or physical therapist might assess a student's gait, strength and agility, range of motion, or ability to perform fine motor tasks such as buttoning and lacing.

Throughout the entire assessment process, IDEA specifically gives parents the right to provide information to be used as part of the evaluation. In addition, as the general education teacher, you typically provide details on the student's performance in class, patterns of behavior, and discrepancies between expectations and achievement. Your informal and formal observations play an important role in assessment.

Assessment Procedures The exact procedures for assessing a student's needs vary according to the areas of concern that initiated the assessment process. The assessment must be completed by individuals trained to administer the tests and other assessment tools used; the instruments must be free of cultural bias; the student's performance must be evaluated in a way that takes into account the potential disability; and the assessment must provide data that are useful for designing an appropriate education for the student. School professionals are responsible for ensuring that these obligations are met.

RtI and Assessment It should be noted that, for students being assessed to determine whether a learning disability exists, the data gathered as part of RtI procedures may be the basis for making that decision. Grounded in IDEA and based on state and local policies, RtI data may be used in lieu of other assessments of ability and achievement, or, as is more common, these data may be used in addition to other assessment data.

Before a team can make a decision about a student's eligibility to receive special education, a comprehensive and individual assessment of strengths and needs must be completed.

Decision Making for Special Services

After a comprehensive assessment of the student has been completed, the multidisciplinary team (MDT) meets to discuss its results and make several decisions. The first decision the MDT must make is whether the student is eligible under the law to be categorized as having a disability. If team members decide that a disability exists, they then determine whether the disability is affecting the student's education, and from that they decide whether the student is eligible to receive services through special education. In most school districts, these decisions are made at a single meeting, and parents must agree with the decisions being made or the student cannot receive special education services. Most school districts have specific guidelines to direct team decision making about the presence of a disability and the need for special education services. However, the decisions ultimately belong to the team. For example, most states specify that students identified as having a mild intellectual disability generally should have an IQ less than 70 as measured on an individual intelligence test and should have serious limitations in adaptive behaviors. However, if a student's score is slightly above 70 and her adaptive skills are particularly limited, a team can still decide that she has a mild intellectual disability. Likewise, if a student has a measured IQ lower than 70 but seems to have many adaptive skills, the team might decide that she does not have an intellectual disability.

If the MDT determines the student has a disability affecting her education and is eligible for services according to federal, state, and local guidelines, the stage is set for detailed planning of the student's education and related services. This planning is recorded in the student's individualized education program, or IEP, the document that outlines all the special education services the student is to receive. More details about IEPs and their preparation are provided later in this chapter.

The final decision made by the MDT concerns the student's placement. *Placement* refers to the location of the student's education. For most students (but not all), the placement is the general education classroom, often with some type of support offered, either there or part time in a special education setting such as a resource room. According to IDEA, when a placement is a location

RESEARCH-BASED PRACTICES

In a qualitative study of a high school IEP meeting attended by an African American mother and her son, Angelov and Anderson (2012) reported that some decisions had been made prior to the meeting, that the special educator viewed the student from a deficit perspective, and that the parents' rights material was written significantly above the mother's reading level.

other than general education, justification must be provided for that decision. Later in this chapter, special education services are discussed and placement options are outlined in more detail.

In your school district, the essentials of the procedures described in the preceding sections must be followed, but the specific steps, paperwork required, and names for the various parts of the process may vary. Nonetheless, all school district procedures are designed to ensure that students with disabilities are systematically assessed and that a deliberate and careful process is followed to provide for their education needs, and you are a critical participant throughout that process. You are likely to participate on MDTs; you will contribute data related to student academic, social, physical, and behavior functioning; and you will contribute to analyzing students' strengths and needs and the types of services that should be provided. You offer a perspective that is critical, the understanding of the student's performance in a typical classroom.

Monitoring Special Education Services

In addition to specifying the procedures that must be followed to identify a student as needing special education services, federal and state laws also establish guidelines for monitoring student progress. The monitoring process ensures that a student's educational program remains appropriate and that procedures exist for resolving disputes between school district personnel and parents.

ANNUAL REVIEWS The first strategy for monitoring special services is the annual review. At least once each year, a student's progress toward his or her annual goals must be reviewed and the IEP changed or updated as needed. Not all multidisciplinary team members who participated in the initial decisions about the student's disability and educational needs are required to contribute to the annual review. However, a teacher instructing the student and an administrator or other professional representing the school district must meet with the student's parents to discuss whether goals and objectives (as required) have been met and what the next steps in the student's education should be. In practical terms, if you work in your classroom with a special educator, that person is likely to sometimes be called away because of her responsibility to attend such reviews. Depending on local practices, you will likely be asked to attend annual reviews for some students, because a general education teacher is most knowledgeable about their day-to-day functioning. This concept was highlighted with the mandate in IDEA that a general education teacher participate in the development of most students' IEPs, not necessarily by writing them but by contributing a classroom perspective.

THREE-YEAR REEVALUATIONS A second monitoring procedure required by law is the three-year reevaluation. At least every three years, and more often if deemed necessary by the MDT, students receiving special education services must be reassessed to determine whether their needs have changed. This safeguard is designed to prevent students with disabilities from remaining in services or programs that may no longer be appropriate for them. Parents are informed of this reevaluation but do not have to give permission for it to occur. In some cases, the reevaluation includes administering all the tests and other instruments that were used initially to identify the student as needing special education. However, in some cases IDEA permits existing information to be used for reevaluation instead of requiring new assessments. In fact, with parent and team agreement, the reevaluation may not involve any new assessment at all. Based on the three-year reevaluation, the MDT meets again to develop an appropriate IEP.

ADDITIONAL REVIEWS In addition to annual reviews and three-year reevaluations, IDEA stipulates that an IEP must be revised whenever a lack of expected progress toward achieving goals is noted, reevaluation information is gathered, or parents bring to the attention of the MDT information that affects the IEP.

This suggests that an IEP may need to be revised more frequently than the once per year mandated by the basic requirements of the law. In some cases, necessary changes can be made with parent approval and without reconvening the team.

Parents have one more formal mechanism for obtaining information about their child's learning. IDEA specifies that the parents of students with disabilities have the right to receive progress reports about their children as often as do parents of typical learners. In many school districts, this means that formal communication about student learning progress occurs every six or nine weeks during the school year, that is, at the end of each grading period.

DUE PROCESS Yet another strategy for monitoring students receiving special education services is due process, the set of procedures outlined in the law for resolving disagreements between school district personnel and parents regarding students with disabilities (Center for Appropriate Dispute Resolution in Special Education, 2014). Due process rights begin when a student is first brought to the attention of a team as potentially having a disability. Both the school district and parents are entitled to protection through due process, but parents typically exercise their due process rights when they fear the school district is not acting in the best interests of their child (Ong-Dean, Daly, & Park, 2011). For example, if parents have their child independently evaluated because they believe the assessment for special education did not accurately portray his needs and if the school district does not agree with the findings of the independent evaluator, the parents may request a due process hearing. Parents also may request a hearing if they disagree with the goals and objectives listed on the IEP and with the way services are being provided to meet those goals and objectives.

Due process hearings seldom address blatant errors on the part of the school or parents regarding special education; most often, they reflect the fact that many decisions made about students with disabilities are judgment calls in which a best course of action is not always clear. For example, Mr. and Mrs. Dotson filed a due process complaint in a dispute about the services their son Jeremiah would receive when he transitioned from middle school to high school. They wanted him to spend much of the day in general education classes with assistance from a paraprofessional and other supports. School district personnel maintained that Jeremiah's behavior outbursts when faced with frustrating tasks as well as his tendency to become overwhelmed in unfamiliar situations indicated the need for most of his education to occur in a separate setting. When discussion reached an impasse, a hearing officer was assigned by the state department of education to hear the case and issue a decision.

In practice, most school districts and parents want to avoid due process hearings, which tend to be adversarial and can damage the parent–school working relationship to the detriment of the student. To foster a positive working relationship, IDEA requires that all states have a system in place to offer no-cost mediation to parents as an initial means for resolving conflicts with schools (Osborne & Russo, 2014). In mediation, a neutral professional skilled in conflict resolution meets with both parties to help them resolve their differences informally. Mediation, however, is not allowed to cause delay in the parents' right to a due process hearing. A hearing is preceded by mediation—a less formal dispute resolution strategy—unless parents decline this option.

Whether or not mediation occurs, IDEA also mandates a dispute resolution session, a sort of last chance for reaching agreement (Center for Appropriate Dispute Resolution in Special Education, 2013; Zirkel & McGuire, 2010). If neither mediation nor a dispute resolution session is successful, a hearing is conducted by an independent and objective third party selected from a list provided by the state, but the school district bears the expense. If either party disagrees with the outcome of a due process hearing, the decision can be appealed to a state-level review hearing officer. If disagreement still exists, either party can then take the matter to court.

If a due process hearing occurs concerning a student you teach, you may be called to testify. In such a case, you would be asked to describe the student's level of functioning in your classroom, the supports you provided, and your efforts with other special service providers to ensure the student was successful. An administrator and an attorney might help you prepare for the hearing, and they would answer any questions you might have about your role in it.

> **MyLab Education** Self-Check 2.3

What Is an Individualized Education Program?

As introduced earlier, the document that the multidisciplinary team, including the child's parents, uses to decide the best placement for a student with an identified disability and that serves as a blueprint for a student's education is called an *individualized education program* (IEP) (e.g., Cheatham, Hart, Malian, & McDonald, 2012; Darden, 2013). The IEP addresses all areas of student need, including accommodations to be made in the general education setting and the services and supports to be provided there. The IEP also is the means through which student progress is documented (Wright, Wright, & O'Connor, 2010; Yell, Katsiyannis, Ennis, Losinski, & Christle, 2016). General education teachers typically are involved as team participants in preparing an IEP if a student has any participation in the general education setting (Diliberto & Breaver, 2012). Whether or not you are the teacher who serves in this role for particular students, if you have students with disabilities in your classroom, you will have opportunities to examine their IEPs or to meet with special educators to review highlights of these important plans, just as Ms. Lee, introduced at the beginning of the chapter, learned.

Required Components of an IEP

The essential components of the IEP were established by Public Law 94–142 in 1975, and they have been updated through the years. Although specific state requirements for IEPs vary somewhat, the federally required elements of IEPs, which all states must adopt, are described in the following sections.

PRESENT LEVEL OF PERFORMANCE Information about a student's current level of academic achievement, social skills, behavior, communication skills, and other areas of concern must be included on an IEP. This information serves as a baseline and makes it possible to judge student progress from year to year. Often, highlights of the information collected from the individual assessment of the student or MTSS/RtI data are recorded on the IEP to partially meet this requirement. Individual achievement test scores, teacher ratings, and summaries of assessments by specialists such as speech therapists and occupational therapists also can be used to report the present level of performance. Another component of this assessment is information about how the student's disabilities affect involvement in the general education curriculum.

ANNUAL GOALS AND SHORT-TERM OBJECTIVES Annual goals are the MDT's estimate of what a student should be able to accomplish within a year, related to meeting his measured needs resulting from the disability. For some students, annual goals may refer primarily to academic areas and may include growth in reading, math problem solving, and other curricular areas. Specifically, a student with a learning disability might have an annual goal to read and comprehend books at a particular grade level or demonstrate skills for finding and keeping a job. For other students, annual goals address desired changes in classroom behavior, social skills, or other adaptive skills. An annual goal for a student with a moderate intellectual disability, for example, may be to order a meal at a fast-food restaurant. A student with autism might have participating in conversation as a goal. Annual goals also may encompass speech therapy, occupational and physical therapy, and other areas in which a student has specialized needs. There is no right number of annual goals. Some students have as few as 2 or 3, and others as many as 8 or 10. However, IDEA specifies that annual goals must be measurable, and increased emphasis is placed on annual goals that enable a student to progress in the general education curriculum.

Short-term objectives are descriptions of the steps needed to achieve an annual goal, and they may or may not be required for all students, depending on state policies. Federal law requires that short-term objectives be written only for the IEPs of students with significant intellectual disabilities. For example, for a student with multiple disabilities whose annual goal is to feed herself, short-term objectives might include grasping a spoon, picking up food with the spoon, and using the spoon to transport food from plate to mouth. The number of short-term objectives for each annual goal relates to the type and severity of the disability, its impact on student learning, and the complexity of the goal. Examples of IEP goals and objectives are included in the Professional Edge feature.

MyLab Education

Video Example 2.4: Josie and Brandon

These students describe their participation in their IEP meetings.

PROFESSIONAL EDGE 2.3

Sample IEP Goals and Objectives

The goals and objectives on IEPs are related to assessed student needs, and they are written in specific ways (Courtade & Browder, 2011; Heitin, 2017). They must:

- Be aligned with the curriculum for the grade level of the student, regardless of the severity of the student's disability.
- Be measurable and specify the conditions under which the student should be able to carry out an activity (such as the reading level of print material or the people with whom a student should communicate).
- Indicate the level of mastery needed (such as a level of accuracy in an assignment).

Goals usually outline progress expected for approximately one school year. For all students with significant intellectual disabilities who take alternate assessments and, in some states, for all students with disabilities, goals are supplemented by short-term objectives or benchmarks that measure progress toward achieving the annual goal. The following are sample IEP goals and objectives:

STUDENTS WITH MILD/MODERATE DISABILITIES

- *Goal:* When assigned to write an essay of three paragraphs, Jerome will use complete sentences, capital letters, and punctuation with 80 percent accuracy.
  Objective: When assigned to write one paragraph, Jerome will use periods, commas, question marks, and exclamation points with 90 percent accuracy.

- *Goal:* Susan will complete at least 80 percent of her homework assignments in English, algebra, and U.S. history.
  Objective: Susan will write down homework assignments 90 percent of the time with 90 percent accuracy.

STUDENTS WITH SIGNIFICANT INTELLECTUAL DISABILITIES

- *Goal:* Maria will make eye contact when communicating with adults in school in at least five out of six trials.
  Objective: Maria will make eye contact with the speech/language therapist during individual sessions in five out of six interactions initiated by the therapist.
  Objective: Maria will make eye contact when the special education teacher calls her name and looks at her in at least five out of six interactions.
  Objective: Maria will make eye contact when a classroom teacher calls her name and looks at her in at least five out of six interactions.

Would you like to see an entire completed IEP? Options include asking if this is possible as part of a field experience in a local school, checking your state department of education's website, or accessing this example by Holbrook (2007) (see p. 12): http://www.nasdse.org/portals/0/standards-basediep-examples.pdf.

EXTENT OF PARTICIPATION IN GENERAL EDUCATION In keeping with the trend toward inclusive practices, the IEP must include a clear statement of justification for placing a student anywhere but in a general education classroom for all or part of the school day. Even for extracurricular and other nonacademic activities, if the team excludes the student from the setting for typical peers, a specific, evidence-based explanation of why that student cannot participate in such activities must be part of the IEP.

SERVICES AND MODIFICATIONS NEEDED The IEP contains a complete outline of the specialized services the student needs; that is, the document includes all the special education instruction to be provided and any other related services needed. Thus, a student receiving adaptive physical education has an IEP indicating that such a service is needed. A student's need for special transportation is noted in the IEP, too. A student who is entitled to transition or vocational assistance has an IEP that clarifies these services. Perhaps most important, the statement of services must include information about the supplementary aids and services, described in Chapter 1, to be provided so that the student can access and progress in the general education curriculum.

One additional element of this IEP component concerns assessment. IDEA stipulates that if a student needs accommodations (for example, extended time) on district or state assessments, including high-stakes assessments, these should be specified on the IEP and implemented throughout the school year, not just for high-stakes tests. If a student is to be exempt from such assessments, the team must ensure the student will complete an alternate assessment that takes into account her functioning levels and needs. The Every Student Succeeds Act (ESSA) affirmed the need to hold students with IEPs to high standards. It sets specific limits on which students are exempt from high-stakes testing and eligible for alternate assessments, limits consistent with those in IDEA. Most of the students with disabilities you teach will be required to complete mandated assessments, and their scores will be part of the data for evaluating teacher and school effectiveness.

Part of identifying services is indicating who is responsible for providing them. Any of the professionals introduced earlier in this chapter could be listed on the IEP to deliver special services. As a general education teacher, you may be included, too, as was true of Ms. Lee in the chapter-opening vignette. For some students, you will be the teacher who completes most of the required instruction; for others, you will assist but not be primarily responsible. For example, a student with a mild intellectual or learning disability probably will be able to complete many class tasks with minor accommodations that you can make. However, if your student has significant intellectual and physical disabilities, other professionals undoubtedly will help develop the materials and activities you will use when the student is in your classroom.

WWW RESOURCES

https://www.youtube.com/watch?v=92F_MFzMXp4
Would you like help in remembering what is included in an IEP? This rap summarizes the most critical components of an IEP.

BEHAVIOR INTERVENTION PLAN Every student with significant behavior problems, not just those students labeled as having emotional disabilities, must have as part of the IEP an intervention plan based on a functional assessment of the student's behavior (e.g., Oram, Owens, & Maras, 2016). This requirement reflects the increasing pressure for students to be supported in general education settings and the acknowledged difficulty of accomplishing that goal without fostering appropriate student behavior.

DATE OF INITIATION AND FREQUENCY AND DURATION OF SERVICE AND ANTICIPATED MODIFICATIONS Each IEP must include specific dates when services begin, the frequency of the services, the types of accommodations and modifications that are part of the services, and the period of time during which services are offered. Because the law generally requires that student progress in special education be monitored at least once each year, the most typical duration for a service is a maximum of one year. If during the year an MDT member sees a need to reconsider the student's educational plan, additional IEP meetings can be convened or amendments made by phone with parent approval.

STRATEGIES FOR EVALUATION When a team develops an IEP, the members must clarify how to measure student progress toward achieving the annual goals and how to regularly inform parents about this progress (Yell et al., 2016). For example, when short-term objectives are written, the team indicates the criteria and procedures to be used to judge whether each objective has been met. For a student learning to move around the school without assistance, the criteria might include specific point-to-point independent movement, and a checklist might be used to judge student progress toward reaching the goal.

TRANSITION PLAN For each student who is 16 years of age or older, part of the IEP is an outcomes-oriented description of strategies and services for ensuring that the student will be prepared to leave school for adult life. This part of the IEP is called a transition plan (Seong, Wehmeyer, Palmer, & Little, 2015). Students with disabilities who are college bound might have a transition plan that includes improvement of study skills, exploration of different universities and their services for students with disabilities, and completion of high school course requirements necessary to obtain admission to a university. For students who plan to work immediately after graduation, the transition plan might include developing skills such as reading employment ads and filling out job applications, as well as developing important job skills such as punctuality and respect toward people in authority and customers. This plan must be tailored to match the assessed strengths and needs of the student (Martin & Williams-Diehm, 2013). It is updated annually, with participation by professionals from agencies outside the school typically increasing as the student nears graduation or school departure at age 21 or 22.

MyLab Education

Video Example 2.5: Interview: Logan: Logan's Plans for the Future

In this video you will observe how one student provides input on his transition plan.

In addition to the basic components, IEPs have several other requirements. For example, they are signed by the individuals who participate in their development, including the student's parent or guardian. In addition, if a student has highly specialized needs, they must be addressed in the IEP. Examples of such needs are behavior, communication, braille (unless specifically excluded in the IEP), and assistive technology. In such cases, appropriate supports, services, and strategies must be specified (Wright et al., 2010).

The Value of IEPs

Although technical and potentially time consuming, IEPs guide the education of students with disabilities. An IEP helps you clarify your expectations for a student and provides a means for you to understand the student's educational needs. The document also informs you about the types of services the student receives and when the student's educational plan will next be reviewed.

Your job is to make a good-faith effort to accomplish the goals and/or short-term objectives in the IEP as they relate to your instruction. If you do that, you will have carried out your responsibility; if you do not do that, you are accountable for that failure. For example, suppose an IEP indicates that a student should learn the concept of freedom of speech. You can demonstrate that you are helping the student learn this by providing class discussion, role-play activities, and access to appropriate resources on the Internet, even if the student does not master this concept. If you state that the student is expected merely to read about the concept in the textbook chapter and you refuse to create opportunities for supported learning in this area, you may be violating the IEP.

Do you have questions about your role in the prereferral, referral, or IEP process? Additional considerations related to your role are presented in the Working Together feature.

DIMENSIONS OF DIVERSITY

When queried about their goals for their children with significant disabilities, Hispanic mothers stressed their children's (a) ability to protect themselves and (b) inclusion in the community with a strong social network (Shogren, 2012).

WORKING TOGETHER 2.1
Understanding the Intervention, Assessment, and Decision-Making Process

Even experienced teachers sometimes have questions about their roles and responsibilities related to prereferral or intervention assistance teams, RtI and MTSS procedures, the eligibility process, and the design of special education services. Here are a few common questions and their answers:

- I work in a high school, and most students already have been identified by the time they get to this level. Do high schools still need to have prereferral teams and procedures in place for RtI or MTSS?

  Federal law requires that across all levels of schools, including high schools, a system must be in place to identify students who are not making expected academic progress. However, recent research indicates that RtI in high school must take into account significant context factors, including impact on graduation requirements, student choice in selecting interventions, involvement of parents, and staff members' perceptions of their roles (National High School Center et al., 2010).

- Do all the teachers on the middle school team need to attend the intervention assistance, RtI or MTSS, and/or IEP team meetings for their students who have been referred or assessed?

  In most cases, it is not reasonable to expect all the teachers on the middle school team to attend a meeting about a student with a suspected or identified disability. The composition of the prereferral team is a school's decision. In some

cases, *the middle school team might serve as the intervention assistance team and hold meetings during scheduled common planning time. In others, a representative from the team might work with the team in monitoring a student's response to intervention. When an initial IEP is written, one general education teacher usually can provide a representative perspective for the team.*

- Are general education teachers responsible for writing parts of the IEP?

  Federal law requires participation of general education teachers in most IEP meetings because they bring an important viewpoint to them. However, those teachers generally do not write sections of the IEP. No matter what your role (e.g., elementary, middle school, or high school teacher; related arts teacher; technology specialist), you are obligated to carry out any IEP provisions that pertain to you, including participating in services offered in the general education classroom and making adjustments to assignments and strategies as specified.

Keep in mind that the education of each student, including those struggling to learn and those with a disability, is a collaborative effort. Further, all decisions made about these students must be grounded in data. When you attend any type of meeting about students with special needs you should be prepared to share data you have gathered and participate in a thoughtful and analytical review of this information as well as that brought by others.

MyLab Education Self-Check 2.4

What Services Do Students with Disabilities Receive?

The services that a student with disabilities can receive are comprehensive, limited only by the stipulation that they must be necessary as part of that student's education. These services are provided in a variety of placements. Both the services and placements are determined by the multidisciplinary team.

Special Education and Other Services

As noted in Chapter 1, the types of services students receive can be grouped into three categories: special education, related services, and supplementary aids and services. *Special education* refers to the specially designed instructional services students receive. For example, these services may include a curriculum aligned with the standard curriculum but significantly simplified, access to a special education teacher qualified to teach students with a particular disability, and individualized instruction using specialized approaches. When a student's special education teacher comes to the classroom and teaches with the general education teacher, that is special education. When a student leaves a classroom for 30 minutes three times each week for intensive tutoring, that is special education. When a middle school or high school offers a life or study skills class only for students with disabilities, that is special education, too.

Related services are all the supports students may need in order to benefit from special education. Examples of related services are speech therapy, transportation, physical and occupational therapy, adapted physical education, counseling, psychological services, and social work. A student's need to ride a special bus equipped with a wheelchair lift is a related service, as is a student's need for assistance with personal care such as toileting.

Supplementary aids and services are all means used to enable students to succeed in a general education setting. They include materials that are written at a different level or reformatted to make them easier for students to read, peer or paraprofessional support, assistive and other technology, and even special professional development for general education teachers so they know how to address students' instructional needs.

As you might guess, the range of possibilities for special education, related services, and supplementary aids and services is immense. Some students, particularly those with high-incidence disabilities, receive a limited number of special education services and perhaps no related services at all. For example, T.J., a high school student with a learning disability in math, attends a geometry class in which a special education teacher teams with a math teacher. T.J.'s assignments are sometimes shortened, and he is allowed extra time to complete tests. He already is looking into colleges that are recognized for their support of students with his special needs. Students with more complex or severe disabilities may have a more highly specialized special education as well as numerous related services. For example, Charmon, a student with physical and intellectual disabilities, receives the services of both a physical and an occupational therapist and a speech/language therapist, as well as a special education teacher.

Student Placement and Educational Environments

Where students receive their educational services is guided by the principle of least restrictive environment (LRE), that is, the setting in which they can succeed that is most like the setting for other students. In today's schools, the LRE for most students is general education for more than 80 percent of the school day. Nearly all school districts appropriately have some separate special education classrooms, but the requirement that teachers delivering core academic instruction be specifically qualified for that role and the increasing recognition that students with disabilities can, with supports, succeed when educated with typical peers has caused educators to rethink such classrooms for all except students with extraordinary needs. As in Ms. Turner's school, which you read about at the beginning of the chapter, emphasis now is on designing systems of support in general education settings. Figure 2.4 shows the IDEA continuum of placements, referred to as *educational environments*, that must exist for students with disabilities; it also provides recent national data on the percentage of students with disabilities in each of those placements.

As discussed earlier, the MDT makes student placement decisions and reviews them along with the IEP at least annually. Placement can be changed as often as appropriate, with parental permission. Generally, if the parents and school district representatives disagree about placement, the student remains in the current placement until the disagreement is resolved. Exceptions to this occur when discipline issues arise. Administrators may unilaterally change a student's placement (for example, through suspension) for up to 10 days in a school year, provided such methods are used with other students, too. If students with disabilities bring a weapon or drugs to school, they can be placed in an alternative educational setting for up to 45 school days while a decision is made concerning long-term placement (Yell, 2006).

RESEARCH-BASED PRACTICES

In a qualitative study, Cummings and Hardin (2017) found that immigrant families vary in their acceptance of their child's disability, and this in turn may affect their understanding of and access to special education and related services. Struggles are greater for refugee families than for those who immigrated directly from their native country.

FIGURE 2.4 **IDEA Educational Environments for Students with Disabilities**

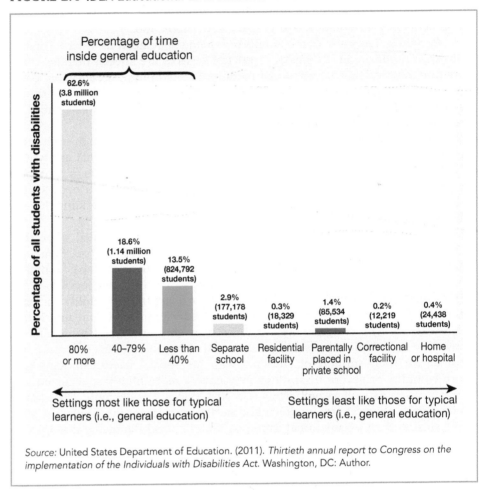

Percentage of time inside general education

62.6% (3.8 million students) — 80% or more		
18.6% (1.14 million students) — 40–79%		
13.5% (824,792 students) — Less than 40%		
2.9% (177,178 students) — Separate school		
0.3% (18,329 students) — Residential facility		
1.4% (85,534 students) — Parentally placed in private school		
0.2% (12,219 students) — Correctional facility		
0.4% (24,438 students) — Home or hospital		

Percentage of all students with disabilities

Settings most like those for typical learners (i.e., general education) ← → Settings least like those for typical learners (i.e., general education)

Source: United States Department of Education. (2011). *Thirtieth annual report to Congress on the implementation of the Individuals with Disabilities Act.* Washington, DC: Author.

MyLab Education

Video Example 2.6: IEP Meeting: Present Levels of Performance

This brief segment of an IEP meeting demonstrates the importance of your input as a general educator and the likelihood that a student's preferred educational setting will be a general education classroom.

REGULAR (GENERAL EDUCATION) CLASSES More than 62 percent of students with disabilities spend more than 80 percent of the school day in a general education setting (U.S. Department of Education, 2016), like Jennifer, introduced as one of Ms. Lee's students at the beginning of the chapter. In another example, a kindergartener with a communication disorder might be served by a speech/language therapist who comes to the classroom and teaches language lessons with the general education teacher. For a middle school student with intellectual and physical disabilities, an inclusion specialist might adjust a lesson on fractions by helping the student learn how to cut simple shapes into halves. For a high school student with a learning disability, a paraprofessional might provide assistance in biology class for carrying out lab directions and recording and completing assignments. This student also might have one special education class for instruction in study skills and learning strategies, or the student might have an English class that is co-taught by a general educator and a special educator.

RESOURCE PROGRAMS Another group of students with disabilities attends school mostly in general education settings, that is, from 40 to 79 percent of the school day. However, they also receive assistance in a special education classroom, often called a resource room, for the remaining 21 to 60 percent of the day (U.S. Department of Education, 2016). In elementary schools, resource programs sometimes are organized by the skills being taught. For instance, from 10:00 am until 10:45 am, basic math skills may be taught, and all the second- and third-grade students needing math assistance may come to the resource room at that time. Alternatively, some resource rooms are arranged by same-age groups. For example, all fifth graders with disabilities needing some separate service may go to the resource room together.

In middle schools and high schools, students are scheduled to have resource classes in the same way the rest of their classes are scheduled. For example, a student may attend a resource class that provides study strategies or reviews the curriculum being taught in general education classes. In some instances, core academic instruction is taught in the resource room by a special educator qualified to teach in the academic area; this class might be called, for example, resource English or resource algebra.

SEPARATE CLASSES Some students with disabilities spend less than 40 percent of the day in general education, attending *separate classes* the rest of the time (U.S. Department of Education, 2016). In this placement, a special education teacher has the primary instructional responsibility for the students who receive grades from the special educator for the subjects taught there. However, a separate class placement does not mean that students remain in a single classroom or that they do not interact with typical peers. They may receive instruction in different classrooms from several special educators, particularly in high school. They may attend general education classes for part of the day or a certain class period such as an elective course, and they also may participate with peers in related arts, assemblies, and other school activities.

For example, although Kurt is in a separate class most of the day at his high school, he takes a horticulture class with students without disabilities. A paraprofessional accompanies him because he has limited ability to understand directions and needs close guidance from an adult to participate appropriately. At Kyle's elementary school, 30 minutes each day is called *community time*, during which students read and write together, share major events from their lives, and learn about their neighborhood and community. For community time, Kyle goes to Mr. Ballinger's fifth-grade class. The students are about Kyle's age and assist him with the community activities and learning. Kyle's special education teacher helps Mr. Ballinger plan appropriate activities for him during that time.

SEPARATE SCHOOLS A small number of students with disabilities attend public or private *separate schools* (U.S. Department of Education, 2016). Some separate schools exist for students with moderate or severe intellectual and physical disabilities, although such schools are, for the most part, considered obsolete. Other separate schools serve students with multiple disabilities who need high levels of specialized services. For example, in a suburban community, approximately 25 students are educated at a separate school adjacent to a middle school. These students all need the services of a physical and occupational therapist; most have complex medical problems that must be closely monitored; and most cannot move unless someone assists them. These students have opportunities for contact with typical peers who come to the school through a special program to function as "learning buddies." Some students with serious emotional disabilities also attend separate schools. These students might harm themselves or others. They are not able to cope with the complexity and social stress of a typical school, and so the least restrictive environment for them is a school where their highly specialized needs, including therapeutic supports, can be addressed.

RESIDENTIAL FACILITIES A few students have needs that cannot be met at a school that is in session only during the day. If students in separate settings have even greater needs, they might attend school as well as live in a public or private *residential facility*. Few students with disabilities are educated in this manner (U.S. Department of Education, 2016). The students for whom this placement is the LRE often are those with severe emotional problems or severe and multiple intellectual, sensory, and physical disabilities. In some states, students who are blind or deaf also might receive their instruction in a residential facility, an approach that is supported by some professionals and parents and opposed by others.

A somewhat different, also small, group of students likewise can be considered under the residential placement option. According to IDEA, children and young adults with disabilities who are incarcerated in the juvenile justice system must receive special education services. Further, children and young adults who are convicted of crimes and incarcerated as adults also may be entitled to special education services, unless the IEP team determines there is a compelling reason to discontinue services.

HOME AND HOSPITAL SETTINGS Some students with disabilities receive their education in a home or hospital setting (U.S. Department of Education, 2016). This placement often is appropriate for students who are medically fragile, who are undergoing surgery or another medical treatment, or who have experienced an emotional crisis. For a few students with limited stamina, school comes to their homes because they do not have the strength to come to school. That is, a special education teacher comes to the home for a specified amount of time each week to deliver instruction. Home instruction also might be used for a student with serious behavior problems or for a student for whom there is disagreement about the appropriate school placement, pending resolution of the dispute.

One more point should be made about placement. For some students, the team may decide that their learning will suffer significantly if schooling stops during the summer. For these students, any of the services in any of the placements just described can be extended into school breaks and summer vacations through extended-school-year (ESY) programs.

Placements in separate classes and schools are far less preferred than those that support the education of students with disabilities in general education classrooms and schools. When placement includes a specialized setting, it often is appropriate for a specific skill or service and for a specific and limited period of time. The appropriate and required educational setting for most students with disabilities is the same classroom they would attend if they did not have a disability. This means that you, as a general education teacher, will play a key role in the education of students with disabilities. Thus, it is important for you to understand the kinds of special services your students receive and your role in assisting to deliver them.

MyLab Education Self-Check 2.5

WRAPPING IT UP

Back to the Cases

Now that you have read about the procedures and services for educating students with special needs, look back at the teacher stories at the beginning of the chapter. Then go to MyLab Education to apply the knowledge you've gained in this chapter to each case.

MyLab Education Application Exercise 2.1: Case Study 2.1

MS. KUCHTA will report information about the Tier 1 interventions she has used with Christopher at the meeting with the SIT. Although some school districts have selected research-based Tier I interventions, other school districts may not have adopted specific strategies.

917- 744- 7935

MyLab Education Application Exercise 2.2: Case Study 2.2

MS. LEE is looking forward to working with the special educator and the speech/language therapist, but she is unsure of what to expect.

MyLab Education Application Exercise 2.3: Case Study 2.3

MR. BLONCOURT has learned that a significant proportion of his eighth grade students did not reach profi-ciency last year on the high-stakes science test, and that his students with disabilities and those who were Eng-lish learners fared particularly poorly. He realizes that he may have been basing his teaching on beliefs about instructional effectiveness rather than data, but he also wonders about the students with IEPs: If they cannot do the work, shouldn't they go to a separate class that is tailored to their needs?

Summary

LO 2.1 The individuals who work to ensure that students with disabilities receive an appropriate education include general education teachers; special edu-cation teachers; related service providers such as school psychologists, counselors, speech/language therapists, social workers, administrators, para-professionals, and other specialists; and parents and students.

LO 2.2 To determine whether special education services are needed, general education teachers usually begin a process of deciding whether to request that a student be assessed for the presence of a disability by analyzing the nature and extent of the student's unmet needs; clarifying those needs by describing them through examples; determin-ing that the needs are chronic and possibly wors-ening over time; comparing the student's needs to those of comparable students; possibly recog-nizing that no pattern seems to exist for the stu-dent's performance; and intervening to address the unmet needs and documenting those efforts.

LO 2.3 If concerns persist, the student's needs may be assessed by a prereferral or intervention assis-tance team (IAT), or response-to-intervention (RtI) or multi-tiered systems of support (MTSS) pro-cedures. If not successful in improving student performance, a multidisciplinary team (MDT) fol-lows federally established special education refer-ral and assessment steps, including completing an individualized assessment with parental permis-sion, making decisions about the need for special education, developing an individualized education program (IEP), and monitoring special education services. Procedures exist to resolve disagreement that may arise as part of these procedures.

LO 2.4 When an IEP is developed, it includes the stu-dent's present level of functioning, goals (and sometimes objectives), justification for any place-ment outside general education, needed services, the person(s) responsible for the services, begin-ning and ending dates for service delivery, and criteria for evaluation. The IEP also may include a behavior intervention plan and a transition plan and generally must be reviewed at least annually.

LO 2.5 The services a student may receive, as outlined by the IEP, include special education, related ser-vices, and supplementary aids and services. The educational environments in which these services are offered include a general education classroom, resource program, separate special education classroom, a separate school, or other separate set-ting (e.g., home, hospital, residential setting).

APPLICATIONS IN TEACHING PRACTICE
A Visit to an MDT Meeting

Ms. Young teaches language arts to sixth graders. Begin-ning in the fall, she and her team members will be work-ing with Natasha, a student newly identified as having a learning disability. Natasha has many friends and enjoys extracurricular activities such as track and basketball, but she has extraordinary difficulties with reading flu-ency, reading comprehension, and written expression. She also has significant problems organizing her work and remembering to complete and turn in assignments. To help set appropriate goals for the coming year, Ms. Young is participating in an MDT meeting to create an IEP for Natasha. Although it would be ideal for all the sixth-grade team members to attend the meeting, that is not feasible, and so Ms. Richards, with expertise in grade-level expectations related to reading and other skills, is representing her colleagues.

General education (sixth-grade) language arts teacher: Ms. Young

General education (fifth-grade) teacher: Mr. Tucker

Special education middle school teacher: Ms. Hill

Principal: Ms. Hubbert

Psychologist: Ms. Freund

Speech/language therapist: Mr. Colt

Parent: Ms. Wright

Ms. Hubbert: Our next task is to develop goals for Natasha. I'd like to suggest that we discuss academics first, then social areas, and wrap up with related services needed. Let's look at Natasha's strengths first—in all those areas.

Mr. Colt: Natasha has a very strong speaking vocabulary. Reviewing her scores, she is considerably above average in that realm.

Ms. Freund: Along with that, according to the assessment data, Natasha's general knowledge is very good. She also is near grade level in math skills.

Mr. Tucker: It's not academics, but one strength I see that Natasha has is her willingness to help classmates. She really wants to assist everyone in class to learn even when she herself is struggling. She also was very active in extracurricular sports this year. She also participated in the service learning program and volunteered to read to the kindergarten class.

Ms. Hill: As we write academic goals, then, we need to remember that Natasha has strong vocabulary skills and general knowledge and that she does not need services in math. Perhaps we can use her social skills and other interests to help in the academic arena. Ms. Wright, what strengths do you see in Natasha?

Ms. Wright: Hmmm. She minds me, that's for sure. And she helps around the house with chores. She likes to help me watch her baby brother, and she likes to cook. She makes up her own recipes.

Ms. Hill: Helping really seems to be Natasha's priority—let's keep that in mind.

Ms. Hubbert: Let's focus for a minute on academic areas of need.

Ms. Freund: Reading comprehension and written expression are by far the areas that need the most work. Natasha's comprehension is just at a beginning third-grade level, and her written expression is about a year below that. The assessment data completed for this meeting are very consistent with classroom data.

Ms. Wright: She says she doesn't like reading because the other kids make fun of her when she can't read the words, and they tease her when you give her a "baby book," Mr. Tucker.

Ms. Young: In middle school, that could be even more of a problem. We need to be sure that she uses the same textbooks as the other students next year; let's be sure we get the technology in place, too, so that she can use audio books. I'm sure we can also arrange to get some supplemental materials for her to use at home. Before we finish today, let's be sure that we talk about that some more.

Ms. Freund: Ms. Young and Ms. Hill, given what you know and have heard about Natasha, what might be priorities for next year?

Ms. Hill: I agree that comprehension is the key. Given the data and the other information we're discussing, I think a goal should be for her to improve her comprehension to a fourth-grade level on reading tasks that include stories, textbooks, and other materials such as children's magazines.

Ms. Hubbert: Ms. Wright, how does that sound to you? [*Ms. Wright nods.*]

The conversation continues.

Before the meeting ends, the MDT has generated the following additional goals in reading comprehension, using materials at her instructional level:

- Natasha will identify with 90-percent accuracy the main characters and the problem and solution in literature that she reads at a third-grade level.
- Natasha will comprehend 80 percent of both narrative and expository material she reads aloud (third- to fourth-grade level) and 80 percent of material she reads to herself.

QUESTIONS

1. What are the responsibilities of the professionals present at the MDT meeting? Which of the professionals are required to attend? How would your responses be different if this were an annual review?

2. What role does Ms. Young take at the meeting? Why is her presence helpful in creating an educational program for Natasha? How else might she contribute during this meeting? Now apply what you said about Ms. Young to your own teaching role. What contributions should you make when plans are being made for the educational services for a student with a disability?

3. What is the purpose of having both the fifth-grade teacher and a sixth-grade teacher attend the meeting? How might this improve the quality of the IEP? What problems might it cause?

4. What steps likely were completed prior to this meeting? How did the general education teacher prepare? What other team responsibilities were met?

5. What part of the IEP is the team addressing? What other parts have to be completed before the meeting ends? What must occur for the IEP to be valid? Given what you know, in what setting would you predict Natasha will be served? What is the justification for your answer?

6. How might this meeting be different (with adjusted achievement levels) if Natasha was a kindergartener going to first grade? A 10th grader going to 11th grade?

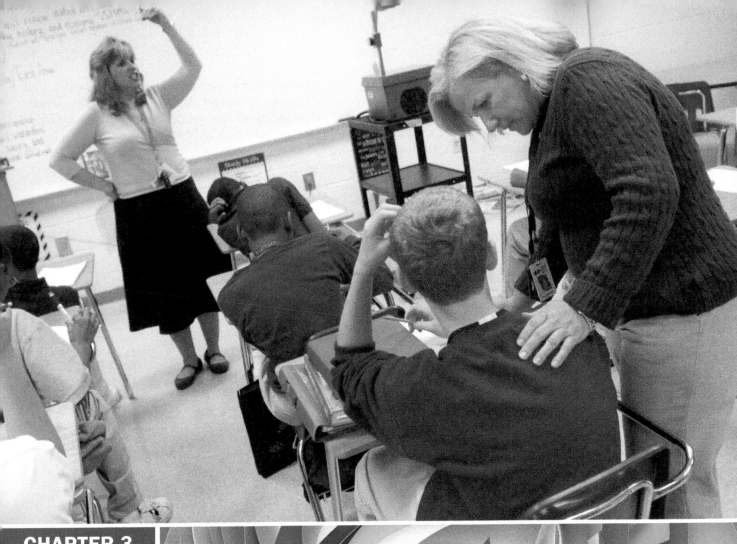

CHAPTER 3

Building Partnerships Through Collaboration

LEARNING OUTCOMES

After you read this chapter, you will be able to:

3-1 Explain the technical meaning of the term *collaboration*, analyze the role of collaboration in providing services to students with disabilities, and clarify how it is influencing the roles and responsibilities that you have as a general education teacher.

3-2 Describe common collaboration-based applications for students with disabilities and other special needs, including shared problem solving, co-teaching, teaming, and consulting, and consider your role in each of them.

3-3 Identify ways you can work effectively with parents to successfully educate students with special needs, even if their views about their child differ from yours.

3-4 Explain your responsibilities when working with paraprofessionals, and explore ways you can enhance collaboration with them.

70

MS. RANDELMAN and Ms. Pickett have nine students who have individualized education programs (IEPs) in their co-taught biology class of 36. Four of the students with disabilities have only math goals, and they generally do not need extensive assistance in this course. James and Louis receive services for emotional disabilities; they are fully capable of completing the work, but they each have an extensive plan for addressing their behavior needs. Rebecca has a learning disability; she reads several years below grade level and has significant short-term memory problems. Courtney has autism spectrum disorder, and the teachers have created comic-strip-like stories with pictures to help her understand classroom expectations and to deal with social situations with her peers. Janet, who has a physical disability and limited vision, comes to class on a motorized scooter but moves around the classroom using a walker. She is an average student, and most of her accommodations concern making sure she has large-print materials and assistance with handling lab equipment. Ms. Randleman and Ms. Pickett recognize that they each bring different strengths to the instruction, and they blend their expertise to reach every student, usually through grouping and occasionally through whole-group instruction. Ms. Randleman is an expert in the science curriculum; Ms. Pickett is an expert in identifying and using specialized techniques that enable the students with disabilities—and others who struggle—to learn. Their goal is to have every student pass the high-stakes biology test at the end of the semester, a requirement for graduation. They met this goal with last year's students, and so they are optimistic about reaching it again.

What happens when two teachers share instructional responsibilities in a classroom? How can two professionals create a classroom partnership that maximizes each one's strengths? What topics might Ms. Randleman and Ms. Pickett need to discuss to ensure that their shared teaching is effective?

MR. HERNANDEZ, a third-grade teacher, has requested that Mr. Moore, a behavior specialist who consults in all the district's elementary schools, observe Kenneth and meet regarding what to do about his increasingly troubling behavior. Kenneth has autism spectrum disorder (ASD) and, although he is capable of learning similarly to his peers, he is falling behind. Part of the reason relates to his special needs. For example, he is currently obsessively interested in Disney characters, and he frequently fails to complete his work as he talks about them and looks for Disney books and other Disney-related items. He also is distracted by even small sounds, sometimes pointing out to Mr. Hernandez that there is a chirping bird outside or that the computer (in sleep mode) is making loud noise. An autism consultant and the special educator responsible for Kenneth's IEP have helped Mr. Hernandez find effective strategies for Kenneth, but a new concern has arisen: At least three or four times per week during reading and writing instruction, Kenneth is becoming increasingly aggressive, throwing books on the floor, crumpling papers, pushing over his desk, and making a fist as though he wants to hit Mr. Hernandez or a peer. Principal Dr. Taylor casually suggested that perhaps Kenneth should be placed in a special education classroom full time, but Mr. Hernandez is committed to finding out what Kenneth's behavior means and how to help Kenneth express himself without the current worrisome behaviors. He knows that Mr. Moore will first observe Kenneth in class and other settings and review his records; it is most likely that he will then schedule a meeting with Mr. Hernandez, the special educators, and anyone else who might contribute to devising a plan to address Kenneth's behaviors.

What options do general education teachers have when one of their students with disabilities is experiencing extraordinary challenges? Why is it important to find solutions to such challenges instead of deciding prematurely that the student should be placed in a separate special education setting? What is the place of consultation in services for students with disabilities?

MS. REYES, the eighth-grade English teacher and team leader, is meeting with Mr. Barnes, the special education teacher; Ms. Whitmore, a school district special education administrator; and Ms. Jordan, Annie's mother. Annie has struggled in school since kindergarten, when she was identified as having an intellectual disability. In third grade she was still learning her letters and numbers, and she still is a beginning reader. She also has had increasing difficulty interacting with her peers; they usually ignore her because her interests are very different from theirs. Ms. Jordan, however, has always maintained that Annie could improve significantly if the school professionals were better meeting her needs and maintains that Annie will go to college. In addition, Ms. Jordan refuses to allow Annie to receive any educational services in a separate special education setting, which is what the teachers and other IEP team members firmly believe she needs because of her level of academic functioning. Last year Ms. Jordan threatened to file a complaint against the school district regarding her daughter's education, and this meeting concludes with Ms. Jordan angrily asking for the information on how to do just that. The professionals left the meeting feeling attacked and frustrated with Ms. Jordan's lack of understanding of her daughter's functioning in school and her refusal to acknowledge their attempts to effectively educate her.

What is your role as a general educator when interactions with parents become contentious? What factors are likely to contribute to parent dissatisfaction with special education services? How should educators communicate with parents in order to reduce the likelihood of such difficult situations occurring?

Although teaching used to be characterized as a profession of isolation (e.g., Dussault, Deaudelin, Royer, & Loiselle, 1999; Lortie, 1975), over the past two decades expectations gradually have changed (e.g., Evans, 2012; Ostovar-Nameghi & Sheikhahmadi, 2016; Sgouros & Walsh, 2012). Elementary school teachers are meeting with their grade-level colleagues to share ideas and problem solve, and middle school and high school teachers are creating interdisciplinary teams to redesign curriculum and share instructional responsibility for smaller groups of students. Response to intervention (RtI) and multi-tiered systems of support (MTSS), data-based approaches to remediating students' skills when they are struggling, are premised on a structured but collaborative problem-solving process. School reform efforts also are characterized by partnerships. For example, entire schools are stressing the need to build collaborative professional learning communities to implement their state's high curricular standards, meet the current expectations of accountability for student learning, and address all the challenges of twenty-first-century schooling (Liou, 2016; Nicholson, Capitelli, Richert, Bauer, & Bonetti, 2016).

As the scenes that open this chapter illustrate, these emerging partnerships extend to special educators and other support staff as well. Particularly as school personnel increase their use of inclusive practices, the working relationships among all the adults involved in the education of students with disabilities become critical (e.g., Asher & Nichols, 2016; Friend & Barron, 2015; Kellems, Springer, Wilkins, & Anderson, 2016). For example, as a general education teacher, you may find that your grade-level or department team periodically meets to discuss the progress of students with disabilities. The goal is to share ideas and concerns in order to collectively ensure that these students are reaching their academic potential. Similarly, you might find that some of your students cannot complete the grade-level work you are accustomed to assigning. To assist you, a special education teacher might meet with you to design the necessary accommodations.

WWW RESOURCES

Are you interested in learning more about the scope of collaboration related to students with disabilities? Go to CalSTAT (http://calstat.org/) and then click on the hyperlink for collaboration in the left column. You will find an array of practical information on the whats, whys, and hows of general education–special education collaboration, including articles, videos, and websites.

At first glance, these interactions seem like logical, straightforward approaches to optimizing education. And often they are. However, because of the lingering tradition of professionals working alone and the still-limited preparation many teachers have had to work effectively with other adults, problems sometimes occur (Friend & Cook, 2017). In some instances, special educators and other support professionals are reluctant to make suggestions for fear they will sound as if they are interfering with a general education teacher's instruction. In other cases, a general education teacher insists that no change in classroom activities or assignments is possible, even though a special educator is available to collaborate during instruction. And when professionals in schools disagree, they may be uncomfortable discussing issues directly and may struggle to find shared solutions.

Research indicates that collaboration is a universal characteristic of successful inclusive schools, that is, schools that improve outcomes for all students, including those with disabilities and other special needs (e.g., Huberman, Navo, & Parrish, 2012; Olson, Leko, & Roberts, 2016; Walsh, 2012). The purpose of this chapter is to introduce you to the principles of collaboration and the school situations in which professionals are most likely to collaborate to meet the needs of students with disabilities. You also will learn how to develop strong working relationships with parents, an essential part of every teacher's responsibilities and an especially important one when educating students with special needs. The special partnerships that are formed when teachers work with paraprofessionals also are considered. Finally, you will find out how to respond when disagreements arise as part of collaboration.

MyLab Education

Video Example 3.1: How Collaboration Leads to Great Ideas

This explanation of the importance of collaboration across professions and activities offers a strong rationale for the importance of collaboration among school professionals. https://www.youtube.com/watch?v=ga1_a4qw-As

What Are the Basics of Collaboration?

As a teacher, you will hear colleagues refer to many of their activities as collaboration. Sometimes they are referring to a team meeting to propose ideas to help a student; sometimes they mean sharing a classroom to teach a particular subject; and sometimes they use the term to describe required professional meetings at which data are discussed and grade-level, team, or course standardized lessons are planned. How can all these things be collaboration? Actually, they are not. Collaboration is how people work together, not what they do. As Friend and Cook (2017) have stated, collaboration is a *style* professionals choose to accomplish a goal they share. Professionals often use the term *collaboration* to describe any activity in which they interact with someone else. But the mere fact of working in the same room with another person does not ensure that collaboration occurs. For example, in some team meetings, one or two members tend to monopolize the conversation and repeatedly insist that others agree with their points of view. The team is seated together at a table, but being together is not sufficient to ensure collaboration (Hartmann, 2016).

True collaboration exists only when all members of a team or participants in a shared activity feel their contributions are valued and the goal is clear, when they share decision making, and when they sense they are respected (Conoley & Conoley, 2010). It is how individuals work with each other that defines whether collaboration is occurring. In the Professional Edge feature, you can complete an activity designed to help you reflect on your thinking about the responsibilities of special education teachers and general education teachers when they collaborate.

FYI

Along with teachers, you will collaborate with related services professionals such as speech/language therapists, counselors, and social workers. These professionals sometimes work in more than one school, and so challenges can include scheduling meetings and keeping communication consistent and clear.

Characteristics of Collaboration

Collaboration in schools has a number of defining characteristics that clarify its requirements. Friend and Cook (2017) have outlined these key attributes, described in the following sections.

COLLABORATION IS VOLUNTARY Teachers may be assigned to work in close proximity, but they cannot be forced to collaborate. They must make a personal choice

PROFESSIONAL EDGE 3.1

Who Is Responsible for What?

This activity is designed to help you think about collaborating with special educators. First, working by yourself, review the list of responsibilities for general and special educators. Then decide which professional is responsible for each of them. List each item in the appropriate section of a Venn diagram. Then compare your responses with those of classmates. If possible, ask individuals preparing to be special educators to complete the task as well. Discuss areas of agreement and disagreement and the implications for working together, whether in the class-room or at other times.

TEACHER RESPONSIBILITIES RELATED TO STUDENTS WITH DISABILITIES

1. Plan for instruction.
2. Write the IEP.
3. Complete student assessments.
4. Communicate with parents regarding day-to-day school matters.
5. Provide report card grades.
6. Evaluate student work (e.g., assignments, tests).
7. Supervise the work of paraprofessionals.
8. Implement classroom supports needed by the student (e.g., provide calculators, allow student to work on a computer).
9. Teach the student social skills for interactions with peers and adults.
10. Provide specially designed instruction to students, that is, learning methods or instructional delivery specified on the IEP.
11. Reteach instruction that the student does not understand.
12. Gather data about student learning and behavior.
13. Prepare materials that take student needs into account (e.g., create a word bank; rearrange test items for clarity).
14. Serve as a member of the student's special education team, as appropriate.
15. Deliver interventions as part of RtI or a multi-tiered system of support.
16. Respond to student behavior issues.
17. Raise concerns about student achievement or behavior.
18. Place the student's achievement in the context of the cur-riculum standards.
19. Facilitate social interactions between students with and without disabilities.
20. Assist students to identify post-school goals and arrange instruction to help them achieve those goals.

to use this style. For example, your principal may tell you and another teacher that you are expected to be part of the RtI or MTSS team. You could choose to keep your ideas to yourself instead of readily participating. Or you could con-clude that even though you did not plan to volunteer for this activity, as long as you are a team member, you will contribute. Your principal assigned the activity; you decided to collaborate. Because collaboration is voluntary, teachers often form close but informal collaborative partnerships with colleagues, regardless of whether collaboration is a schoolwide ethic.

COLLABORATION IS BASED ON PARITY Teachers who collaborate must believe that each individual's contributions are equally valued. The number and nature of professionals' contributions may vary greatly, but all those contributions are integral to the collaborative effort. If you are at a meeting concerning a student's highly complex needs, you might feel you have no background for addressing the situation. However, you have valuable information about how the student responds in your class and the progress he has made in developing peer relationships. The technical discussion of the student's disabilities is not your area of expertise, nor should it be; your ideas are valued because of your knowl-edge and skills related to teaching in your classroom. This is an illustration of the collaboration concept of *parity*.

COLLABORATION REQUIRES A SHARED GOAL Teachers truly collaborate only when they share a goal. For example, if a fifth-grade teacher and a special educa-tor want to design a behavior intervention to help support a student with an emo-tional disability, their goal is clear. They can pool their knowledge and resources and jointly plan the intervention. However, if one teacher wants the student to spend more time in a special education setting and the other opposes that solu-tion, they are unlikely to work collaboratively on this matter. The teachers might even think at the outset that they share a goal—supporting the student—but that broad statement does not capture their differing views of how the student can best be assisted. They need to resolve this difference for collaboration to proceed.

COLLABORATION INCLUDES SHARED RESPONSIBILITY FOR KEY DECISIONS Although teachers may divide the work necessary to complete a collaborative teaching or teaming project, they should share as equal partners the fundamental decision making about the activities they are undertaking. This shared responsibility reinforces the sense of parity that exists among the teachers. In the behavior intervention example outlined in the preceding discussion of shared goals, the teachers together decide what the key problems are, what strategies might work, how long to try an intervention, and how the intervention may affect the student. However, if they assign many tasks to just one person, they are not collaborating. Instead, one may ask the school psychologists for ideas, review a book of behavior intervention ideas, and talk to last year's teacher. The other may call the parents to seek their input, interview the student, and prepare any needed materials, such as a behavior chart. Without collaboration, their activities may be redundant and lead to miscommunication and misunderstanding.

COLLABORATION INCLUDES SHARED ACCOUNTABILITY FOR OUTCOMES Shared accountability follows directly from shared responsibility: That is, if teachers share key decisions, they also must share accountability for the results of the decisions, whether those results are positive or negative. If both teachers carry out their assigned tasks, the behavior intervention they design will have a high probability of success. If one teacher fails to carry out a responsibility, valuable time will be lost and their shared effort probably will be less successful. If something happens that is exceptionally positive (for example, the student's behavior changes dramatically in a positive direction), the teachers will share the success. If something happens that is not so positive (for example, the intervention appears to have no impact on the behaviors of concern), they will share the need to change their plans. The word *fault* generally is not associated with collaboration.

COLLABORATION IS BASED ON SHARED RESOURCES Each teacher participating in a collaborative effort contributes some type of resource. This contribution increases commitment and reinforces each professional's sense of parity. Resources may include time, expertise, space, equipment, and other assets. The teachers working on the behavior intervention contribute the time needed to make necessary plans, but they also pool their knowledge of working with students with behavior difficulties, share information about other professionals who might assist them, and contribute student access to the computer and other rewards they design.

COLLABORATION IS EMERGENT Collaboration is based on a belief in the value of shared decision making, trust, and respect among participants. However, although these qualities are needed to some degree at the outset of collaborative activities, they are not well developed in a new collaborative relationship. As teachers become more experienced at collaboration, their interactions become characterized by the trust and respect that grow within successful professional relationships. If the teachers described throughout this section have worked together for several years, they may share freely, including offering constructive criticism to each other. If this is their first collaborative effort, they are much more likely to be a bit cautious and polite, because each is unsure how the other person will respond.

Collaboration is a means for achieving a goal, and it is most effective when all participants understand its characteristics and believe in its potential.

Prerequisites for Collaboration

Creating collaborative relationships requires effort on everyone's part (e.g., Rose & Norwich, 2014; Solis, Vaughn, Swanson, & McCulley, 2012). Most professionals who have close collegial working relationships note that it is challenging work to collaborate—but worth every minute of the effort. They also emphasize that collaboration gets better with experience. When colleagues are novices at co-teaching or participating on teams, their work seems to take longer and everyone has to be especially careful to respect others' points of view. However, with additional collaboration, everyone's comfort level increases, honesty and trust grow, and a sense of community develops. The following sections discuss some essential ingredients that foster the growth of collaboration.

REFLECTING ON YOUR PERSONAL BELIEF SYSTEM The first ingredient for collaboration is your personal beliefs. How much do you value sharing ideas with others? Would you prefer to work with someone to complete a project, even if it takes more time that way, or do you prefer to work alone? If your professor in this course offered the option of a small-group exam, would you be willing to receive a shared grade with your classmates? If your responses to these questions suggest that you prefer working with others, you probably will find professional collaboration exciting and rewarding. If your responses are just the opposite, you might find collaboration somewhat frustrating. For collaboration to occur, all the people participating need to believe that their shared effort will result in a better outcome than could be accomplished by any one participant, even if the outcome is somewhat different from what each person envisioned at the outset (Sayeski, 2009; Tucker & Schwartz, 2013).

Part of examining your belief system also concerns your understanding of and respect for others' belief systems (Yoon, 2016). This tolerance is especially important for your collaborative efforts with special educators in inclusive schools. For example, what are your beliefs about changing your teaching practices so that a student with disabilities can achieve the standards for your curriculum? At first, you might say that changing your teaching practices is no problem, but when you reflect on the consequences of that belief, you might have second thoughts. For example, changing your practices may mean that you must give alternative assignments to students who need them, that you must deliberately change the way you present information and the way you expect students to learn that information, and that, if needed, you must evaluate the work of students with disabilities differently from the work of other students.

The special educators with whom you work are likely to believe strongly not only that alternative teaching practices are helpful in inclusive settings but that they are a requirement. How will you respond when you meet a colleague with this belief? If some general education teachers at your school oppose making accommodations for students with disabilities, will you feel pressured to compromise your beliefs and agree with them? In schools that value collaboration, professionals value others' opinions and know they can respectfully disagree while maintaining positive working relationships.

REFINING YOUR INTERACTION SKILLS The second ingredient you should bring to school collaboration is effective skills for interacting (e.g., Beebe, Beebe, & Redmond, 2014; Friend & Cook, 2017). In many ways, interaction skills are the fundamental building blocks on which collaboration is based, because collaboration occurs through interactions with others. There are two major types of interaction skills: communication skills and steps to productive interactions. You already may have learned about the first type, communication skills, in a public speaking or communication course. These skills include listening, attending to nonverbal signals, and asking questions and making statements in clear and nonthreatening ways (Beebe & Masterson, 2012). They also include paralanguage, such as your tone of voice and your use of comments like "uh-huh" and "OK." Additional information about communication skills is included in the Professional Edge feature.

RESEARCH-BASED PRACTICES

Huberman, Naro, and Parrish (2012) studied four California districts with unusually strong academic performance for students with disabilities when compared to other districts, finding that the districts shared a strong commitment to inclusive education as well as in-class and out-of-class collaboration between general and special educators.

PROFESSIONAL EDGE 3.2

Barriers to Effective Communication

Effective communication is essential for professional collaboration. Here are some barriers to communication that teachers and administrators may have to overcome. Which might apply to you?

- *Advice:* When you offer unsolicited advice to a colleague or parent, that person may be confused by your intent, may reject the advice and form an unfavorable opinion of you, or may feel obligated to follow the advice even if it seems inappropriate. In general, you should offer advice only when it is sought.

- *False reassurances:* If you offer parents or colleagues false reassurances about student achievement, behavior issues, or social skills, you may damage your own credibility and set the stage for future issues. Being truthful—but constructive—is the best strategy, even if you are concerned that an awkward situation may result.

- *Wandering interactions:* When another person communicates with you, it sometimes happens that you conversationally drift to peripheral topics that waste valuable time. For example, discussing a student's participation in varsity athletics when the concern is academic performance is a distraction that may reflect avoidance of the key issues.

- *Interruptions:* When you interact with others, they are entitled to your full attention. Responding to a teacher who comes to your classroom door or answering a text message while you are speaking with a colleague harms the interaction. During an interaction, it also is important to avoid interrupting others. If the person speaking has a language pattern that is slower than yours, you may have to make an especially concerted effort to wait until the person finishes speaking before responding.

- *Being judgmental:* If you tend to speak in absolute terms (e.g., "The only way to resolve this is to . . ." or "I don't see any way for him to complete the work. . . ."), you may be perceived as a professional who sees only one right answer. This may lead others to conclude that attempting to collaborate with you is futile.

- *One-way communication:* Communication is most effective when it involves all participants. If one person monopolizes the interaction, the others' points of view are not represented and any decisions made will likely be questioned later. Likewise, if a participant seldom offers ideas during the interaction, others may wonder what that individual really thinks or believes.

- *Fatigue:* If you are so tired that you cannot accurately follow the thread of a conversation, your communication may be impaired and you may misspeak or misunderstand others' messages. In such a case, it may be best to request a rescheduling of the interaction.

- *"Hot" words and phrases:* In some communities and in some schools, certain words are "hot" and prompt emotional responses. For example, even the term *inclusion* sometimes is considered controversial, as is *response to intervention*. To facilitate productive interactions, such words (or even suspected words and phrases) are best avoided.

Do any of these barriers sound familiar? What examples of each can you and your classmates provide relating to your own professional communication experiences? Are you interested in learning more? Many videos are available on effective communication. This TEDTalk is an example of ways to listen better: http://www.youtube.com/watch?v=cSohjlYQI2A.

The other type of interaction skill comprises the steps that make interactions productive. Have you ever been in a meeting and realized a single topic was being discussed repeatedly? Perhaps you wished someone would say, "I think we've covered this; let's move on." Or have you ever tried to problem solve with classmates or friends, only to realize that every time someone generated an idea, someone else began explaining why the idea would not work? In both instances, your frustration occurred because of a problem in the interaction process, that is, the steps that characterize an interaction. The most commonly needed interaction process for you as a teacher is shared problem solving (e.g., Azad, Kim, Marcus, Sheridan, & Mandell, 2016; Newton, Horner, Todd, Algozzine, & Algozzine, 2012), a topic addressed later in this chapter. Other interaction process skills include conducting effective meetings, responding to resistance, resolving conflict, and persuading others.

You need both types of interaction skills to collaborate. If you are highly skilled in communicating effectively but cannot contribute to get an interaction from its beginning to its end, others may be frustrated. Likewise, even though you may know the steps in shared problem solving, if you speak to others carelessly or ineffectively, they may withdraw from the interaction.

CONTRIBUTING TO A SUPPORTIVE ENVIRONMENT The third ingredient for successful collaboration is a supportive environment (Compton, Appenzeller, Kemmery, & Gardiner-Walsh, 2015; Murawski & Bernhardt, 2016; Waldron & McLeskey, 2010). As a teacher, you will contribute to this atmosphere through your personal

MyLab Education

Video Example 3.2: Collaborating

These professionals' comments about collaboration demonstrate its potential but also its complexity.

belief system and interaction skills, but this environment is influenced by other factors as well. For example, most professionals working in schools that value collaboration comment on the importance of administrative support. Principals play an important role in fostering collaboration (Shen, Leslie, Spybrook, & Ma, 2012; Stosich, 2016). They can raise staff awareness of collaboration by making it a school goal and distributing information about it to staff. They can reward teachers for their collaborative efforts. They can urge teachers who are uncomfortable with collaboration to learn more about it and experiment in small-scale collaborative projects, and they can include collaboration as part of staff evaluation procedures. When principals do not actively nurture collaboration among staff members, collaborative activities are more limited, more informal, and less a part of the school culture.

Another component of a supportive environment is having time available for collaboration (Wilson, 2016). It is not enough that each teacher has a preparation period; shared planning time also needs to be arranged. In many middle schools, shared planning occurs as part of the middle school team planning period. In other schools, substitute teachers are employed periodically so that general education teachers and special services staff can meet. In yet other schools, quarterly workdays are scheduled for teachers and part of this time is for collaborative planning. If you need common planning time, these are ideas you might raise with your administrator.

As a teacher, you will find that time is a critical issue (Bauml, 2016; Bettini, Crockett, Brownell, & Merrill, 2016). The number of tasks you need to complete during scheduled preparation time will be greater than the number of minutes available. The time before and after school will be filled with faculty meetings, conferences with parents, preparation, bus duty, and other assignments. You can help yourself maximize time for collaboration if you keep several things in mind. First, it may be tempting to spend the beginning of a shared planning time discussing the day's events or catching up on personal news. But if you engage in lengthy social conversations, you are taking time away from your planning. You should have as a priority to finish the business at hand first and then to chat about personal and school events if time is left. Second, because you never truly have enough time to accomplish all that you would like to as a teacher, you must learn to prioritize. You have to choose whether collaborating about a certain student or teaching a certain lesson is justified based on the needs of students and the time available. Not everything can be collaborative, but when collaboration seems appropriate, time should be allocated for it.

MyLab Education Self-Check 3.1

What Applications of Collaboration Foster Inclusion?

The basic principles of collaboration should be your guide to many types of partnerships in schools. These partnerships may involve other general education teachers, special education teachers, support staff such as speech therapists and counselors, paraprofessionals, parents, and others. Four of the most common collaborative applications concerning students with disabilities are formal or informal shared problem solving, co-teaching, teaming, and consultation. As you read about these activities, keep in mind that the face-to-face interactions that characterize them can be extended with electronic collaboration using technology now readily available. This is the topic of the Technology Notes feature.

TECHNOLOGY NOTES 3.1

Electronic Collaboration

Professional collaboration in education traditionally has relied on face-to-face interactions, but electronic options are rapidly re-shaping how professionals communicate, plan their shared work, and problem solve. Although in-person conversations still are valuable and necessary, the following options for asynchronous (that is, not in real time) collaboration (with free basic versions and subscription plans for accessing additional features) are a valuable companion to them:

- Many schools now use Google for Education (e.g., Google Apps for Education [GAFE], recently renamed GSuite). If you work in a district using these tools, you likely will collaborate with others using Google Docs (https://docs.google.com). The procedure is simple: After opening the web page, you start a new document and use the sharing option in the upper right hand corner of the screen to invite others to contribute to the document, entering their g-mail addresses. If using Docs for co-planning, consider using or adapting one of the available templates designed for that purpose.

- If you tend to prefer visual options for planning, Trello (trello .com) might suit your needs. This planning tool is designed to manage projects, and it works well for co-planning as well as team discussion and other tasks teachers may collaboratively address. It is based on "boards" that can be used to capture projects, and within the boards, teachers can create cards to stand for subtasks or elements of their projects. Trello enables professionals to add comments and questions, have discussion about their shared work, and to upload attachments. It is available on several platforms and so can be accessed through computer, tablet, and phone.

- Planbook (planbook.com) is a cloud planning platform designed by teachers for teachers. Many teachers subscribe to it individually (approximately $1.00/month) because it includes provisions for dragging-and-dropping into lesson plans each state's curriculum standards, adding attachments, moving lessons forward or backward a day as needed, and even transferring lesson plans from one year to the next. For co-teachers, Planbook is attractive because it allows two teachers with accounts to make lesson plans viewable and editable, thus enabling special educators to annotate a general educator's plans with needed specialized instruction and accommodations.

- Slack (slack.com) is another example of a team collaboration option teachers have discovered can make their work more effective and efficient. Operating in a way similar to Twitter with @mentions and #hastags to organize conversations (but without the 280-character limit), Slack users can choose to follow conversations among educators around the world or to create their own team. They can discuss ideas (bypassing the drawbacks of traditional e-mail), upload documents, and search messages. One particularly helpful feature is that slack is highly compatible with Google products and Dropbox (Dropbox .com), another tool some educators use extensively to share files.

With some Internet searching or conversations with colleagues, you undoubtedly will find other electronic collaboration options. The goal is to find an option that you find useful and become adept at navigating it with colleagues, collaborating in order to make a difference in the lives of students with disabilities. One caution should be mentioned, however. If your electronic collaboration includes posting student information, you should check local policies regarding preserving confidentiality.

Electronic collaboration is a valuable companion to face-to-face interactions. It enables today's busy educators to discuss ideas, problem solve about teaching dilemmas, and jointly plan lessons.

Shared Problem Solving

Shared problem solving is the basis for many of the collaborative activities that school professionals undertake on behalf of students with disabilities and other special needs (Bennett, Erchul, Young, & Bartel, 2012; Musti-Rao, Hawkins, &

FYI

One currently popular type of school collaboration is the *professional learning community* (PLC) (De Neve & Devos, 2017), in which teachers regularly meet to share data and design instruction to ensure that all learners meet today's high academic standards. Although this application of collaboration is not specific to students with disabilities, they often benefit from educators' PLC work.

WWW RESOURCES

Harvard University's Project Zero (http://www.pz.harvard.edu/resources/the-good-collaboration-toolkit) offers a checklist that can be applied across many types of collaboration in professional and other environments. It incorporates many essential elements of collaborative interactions.

Tan, 2011). Although shared problem solving sometimes occurs informally when a general education teacher and a special education teacher meet to decide on appropriate accommodations or other instructional adjustments for a student, it also occurs in many other contexts. For example, as you read the applications that follow, you will find that some variation of shared problem solving exists in each. This happens because one way of thinking about co-teaching, teaming, and consultation is as specialized problem-solving approaches.

You might be wondering why problem solving is such a critical topic for professional partnerships. In fact, you may consider yourself already adept at problem solving because it is an ongoing responsibility of educators. However, as many authors have noted (for example, Newton et al., 2012; Friend & Cook, 2017), when professionals share a problem-solving process, outlined in the following sections, it is much more complex than when educators problem solve alone, because the needs, expectations, and ideas of all the participants must be blended into shared understandings and mutually agreed-on solutions. Successful shared problem solving requires skilled participants.

DISCOVER A SHARED NEED The starting point for problem solving is discovering a shared need, which demonstrates the complexity of shared problem solving. If you face a problem that concerns only you, you try to resolve it by yourself. When you problem solve with colleagues and parents, all the participants need to perceive that a problem exists. Further, it is important that all participants believe they can have an impact on the problem, that they feel accountable for the results of problem solving, and that they can contribute constructively to resolving the problem. When these conditions exist, shared problem solving results in a high level of commitment. When these conditions do not exist, the problem solving is not shared at all and may appear one sided, with some participants trying to convince others to contribute. For example, many teachers report they have been unable to enlist parents' help in resolving discipline problems. They then go on to describe meetings with parents in which school personnel describe the problem, and the parents respond that they do not see such behavior occurring at home. Too often, instead of all parties working to come to a shared understanding of the problem behavior, this type of meeting ends with the parents superficially agreeing to assist in solving a problem they do not believe exists and the school professionals perceiving the parents as only marginally supportive. This dilemma can be avoided if more effort is made to identify a shared need to problem solve (Olivos, Gallagher, & Aguilar, 2010).

IDENTIFY THE PROBLEM The most critical step in the problem-solving process is problem identification. However, when educators meet to share problem solving, they often feel pressured because of time constraints, and they may rush through this essential stage. Problem identification includes gathering information, compiling it, analyzing it, and reaching consensus about the nature of a student's problem.

In a shared-problem-solving situation, you can help emphasize the importance of problem identification by asking whether everyone has agreed on the problem. You also may ask someone else to restate the problem to check your grasp of it and encourage participants who have not spoken to share their understanding of the problem.

Consider the following situation, which shows what can happen when problem identification is not effectively addressed: A teacher in a shared-problem-solving session says to the parent of a student whose attendance is irregular and who consistently comes to school without assignments or basic supplies, "We really need your help in making sure Demitrious gets up when his alarm goes off so he can catch the bus. And we'd like to establish a system in which you sign off on his written assignments." The parent replies, "It's so hard. I work until midnight, and I don't get up when it's time for the kids to go to school. I don't think he sees any point in the homework he's getting—that's why he doesn't bring it back." In this situation, the educator has identified the problem before the meeting has even started: Demitrious needs to assume responsibility, and his parents need to provide more guidance for school activities. Further, the teacher is proposing a solution to the problem and not exploring the problem itself. The parent's response suggests that she does not see the same problem; in fact, the parent is implying that perhaps the problem is not with Demitrious at all but with the school staff.

Consider how this interaction could have been handled differently: The teacher says to the parent, "Ms. Trenton, thanks so much for taking time off work to meet with us. We appreciate your concern for Demitrious. Lately, we've seen a problem with his attendance. We asked you to come to school so we can learn about your perspective on this situation and to let Demitrious know that we're working together to help him." When the parent replies with the comment about her working hours and Demitrious's perception of the homework, the teacher replies, "That's valuable information for us. We're hoping we can find ways to motivate Demitrious to come to school—and that includes assigning homework that he sees as valuable." In this situation, the school professionals are working with the parent to identify the problem, not presenting the problem to her.

PROPOSE SOLUTIONS Once a problem has been clearly identified, the next step is to create a wide range of options for solving the problem. One of the most common ways to come up with solutions is to brainstorm.

Brainstorming is based on two important principles. First, judgment is deferred; that is, to free the mind to be creative, people must suspend their predisposition to judge ideas. Second, quantity leads to quality; the more ideas that are generated for solving a problem, the more likely it is that novel and effective solutions can be found. Brainstorming requires openness and creativity. When implemented effectively, it often leads to several ideas that are highly likely to resolve the problem being addressed.

EVALUATE IDEAS With a list of ideas, the next step in shared problem solving is to evaluate the ideas by considering whether they seem likely to resolve the problem and are feasible. One way to evaluate ideas is to use a decision sheet like that illustrated in Figure 3.1. On this decision sheet, the participants stated the problem—to find ways of encouraging Angela to work independently on classroom tasks—and generated ideas for achieving this goal. They then selected criteria by which to judge the merits of each idea. They considered the following:

- The likelihood the idea would increase the amount of time Angela spends on her independent assignments
- The extent to which the idea has a reasonable time cost
- The "fit" between the idea and existing classroom routines

Ideas that were not seriously considered were crossed out, and the criteria for decision making were applied to those remaining, with each idea being rated against each criterion. In Figure 3.1, the two ideas with the highest ratings were assigning a study buddy and using picture directions.

PLAN SPECIFICS Once one or two ideas have been chosen using a process such as the one just described, more detailed planning needs to occur. For example, suppose you and others have decided you would like to try having a high school service club provide volunteer tutoring in an after-school program. Some of the tasks to assign include asking club members about their interest in the project, arranging a place for the program, ensuring that needed supplies are available, obtaining permission to operate the program, establishing a schedule for students, determining who will provide adult supervision and scheduling it, advertising the program, and creating and conducting training sessions for the tutors.

Typically, at this step of shared problem solving, not only do participants list the major tasks that need to be completed to implement the solution, but they also decide who will take responsibility for each task. In addition, they specify a

---

DIMENSIONS OF DIVERSITY

Based on a case-study analysis of a conference between a teacher and a Hispanic parent, Cheatham and Jimenez-Silva (2012) recommended that teachers be positive but realistic about students' progress, stop talking so that parents can share their perspectives, and provide clear explanations for their recommendations regarding next steps in the student's education.

FIGURE 3.1 A Sample Decision-Making Sheet for Problem Solving

Problem Statement: How can we encourage Angela to work independently on assigned classroom tasks?

Ideas:

Digitally record instructions.	Don't give independent work.
Have an assigned "study buddy."	Let her choose the assignment.
Make the work easier.	Make her stay in from recess to complete work.
Use pictures for directions.	Give her frequent breaks.
Ask a parent volunteer to help.	

Decision Making: (3 = high, 2 = medium, 1 = low)

Idea	Criteria			Total	Rank
	Time commitment is reasonable for teacher	Idea does not disrupt class routine	Angela will work for at least 5 minutes		
1. Recorded instructions	3	1	2	6	
2. Study buddy	3	3	3	9	1
3. Easier work	2	2	2	6	
4. Picture directions	3	2	3	8	2
5. Parent volunteer	3	2	1	6	
6. Choose assignment	1	2	1	4	
7. Frequent breaks	2	2	2	6	

timeline for completing all the tasks and usually decide how long to implement the solution before meeting to evaluate its effectiveness.

IMPLEMENT THE SOLUTION If all the steps in the shared-problem-solving process have been carefully followed, then implementing the selected idea(s) may be the most straightforward part of the process. When problem solving occurs concerning a student with a disability in an inclusive school, each team member may have some obligation to implement the solution. Occasionally, you will have much of the immediate responsibility. In other cases, parents will have a major role to play. Each person involved must do his or her part for the solution to have a high probability of success. During implementation, it is essential to keep some type of record documenting your efforts and how the intervention affects the student.

EVALUATE OUTCOMES After a period of time—anywhere from just a few days to two weeks or longer—the professionals who are implementing the solution meet to evaluate its effectiveness. Now, three possibilities exist:

1. If the solution has been especially effective, it may be judged a success. It then will be continued to maintain the results, discontinued if no longer needed, or gradually phased out.

2. If the solution seems to be having a positive effect but is not ideal for some other reason, it may be modified. For example, suppose a behavior management plan is helping a student attend class rather than skip it, but the general education teacher notes that the system is too time consuming. The

problem-solving group may then try to streamline the plan to make it more feasible.

3. Even when the steps in problem solving are carefully completed, a solution occasionally is judged ineffective. The team then must decide what to do next: Select a different solution, find additional solutions, or possibly reconsider whether the problem has been accurately identified. The team needs to consider all these possibilities before proceeding with additional problem solving.

Professionals who regularly employ the strategies of shared problem solving are quick to acknowledge that the steps do not automatically lead to a simple solution that always works. However, they report that when they problem solve in this fashion, they perceive that their professional time is well spent and that the problem-solving process is truly a collaborative endeavor (Newton et al., 2012).

RESPONSE TO INTERVENTION, MULTI-TIERED SYSTEMS OF SUPPORT, AND SHARED PROBLEM SOLVING Because response to intervention (RtI) and multi-tiered systems of support (MTSS) are common problem-solving applications used in schools, special mention is needed regarding how they relate to the procedures just described. In most locales, RtI and MTSS are implemented using a somewhat different problem-solving process, what is considered a *technical* approach (Friend & Cook, 2017; King & Coughlin, 2016). It follows a prescribed format, and the intervention options are already specified. The team selects interventions from a prepared list. That is, elements of the problem solving process just outlined may be included with RtI or MTSS problem solving (and in some schools such an exact problem solving approach is used), but more often it has a somewhat different character and outcomes.

Finally, remember that the INCLUDE process, described in chapter 4 and used throughout this book as a way to effectively meet students' needs, also is a problem solving process that you may complete by yourself or with colleagues. It illustrates how important a constructive problem solving mindset is for today's educators.

Co-Teaching

Co-teaching occurs when two or more educators—a general education teacher and a special education teacher or other specialist—share the instruction for a single group of students, typically in a single classroom setting (Friend, 2014a). Although any two teachers can teach together (and this sometimes occurs at elementary, middle, and high schools for a variety of reasons, including interdisciplinary units or courses), we focus here on the unique arrangement of two professionals with potentially very different points of view and areas of expertise working together on behalf of all the students in a class, the type of arrangement that Ms. Randleman and Ms. Pickett, introduced at the beginning of the chapter, have in their classroom.

Co-teaching is a widely used service-delivery option in inclusive schools (Friend, 2014a; Friend, Cook, Hurley-Chamberlain, & Shamberger, 2010). In a classroom with several students with disabilities, combining the strengths of the general education teacher and a special educator can create options for all students (Friend & Cook, 2017; Murdock, Finneran, & Theve, 2016). Co-teaching typically occurs for a set period of time either every day (e.g., every morning from 9:30 until 10:15, or during second-period seventh-grade math) or on certain days of the week (e.g., on Mondays, Tuesdays, and Wednesdays during third period or second block). Other options for scheduling may be used, depending on student needs and the availability of special education teachers.

As effective as co-teaching is when carefully implemented, it is not the answer for every student with a disability or for every classroom in an inclusive school. Co-teaching is only one option for meeting the needs of students. It should be implemented when the number of students with disabilities in a class and the nature of their needs justify the presence of two teachers, or the class is one in which all students with disabilities must enroll (for example, a high school U.S. history class).

Many approaches are available to teachers who decide to co-teach. Friend (2014a) has outlined some of the common ones, and they are depicted in Figure 3.2.

ONE TEACH, ONE OBSERVE In this approach, one teacher leads the lesson and the other gathers data on one student, a small group of students, or even the whole class to better understand student learning needs and make instructional decisions. For instance, while Ms. Tran, the general education teacher, leads a lesson in which students work in cooperative groups to answer questions about a map, Ms. Firestone, the special education teacher, systematically observes three students who are known to struggle with social skills. Ms. Firestone notes on a chart the number of times those students initiate interactions with peers, as well as how often other students direct comments or questions to them. How can this information be helpful to the teachers? Teachers can observe many relevant student behaviors, including their attention to the lesson, their ability to work independently, their grasp of academic standards or competencies, their participation during instruction, and their willingness to seek assistance when they have questions. However this approach is applied, it is essential that *each* educator sometimes takes the primary teaching role in the class while the other observes. In this way, both teachers have the opportunity to watch the class in action, and both have credibility with students as a result of leading instruction.

STATION TEACHING In *station teaching,* three groups of students are arranged. Two stations include teacher-facilitated instruction; in the third station, students, alone or with a partner or in a small group, complete a review activity or a project.

MyLab Education

Video Example 3.3: Co-Teaching at Revere High School

What characteristics of collaboration do these teachers illustrate as they describe their co-teaching experience? https://www.youtube.com/watch?v=wb-ax4vyX9U

FIGURE 3.2 **Co-Teaching Approaches**

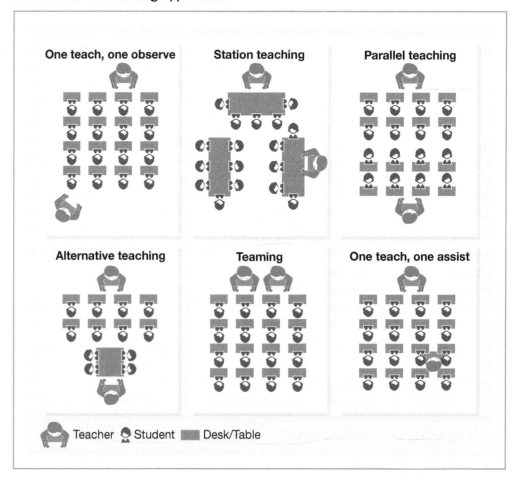

If students cannot work independently, the last group can be eliminated. During the lesson, students move to each station. In an elementary school, an entire lesson based on stations may be completed in a single day; in a secondary school, a single station may take an entire class period or more. For example, in a ninth-grade math class, some of the students are working with the general education teacher to learn one method for solving quadratic equations. A second group is meeting with the special education teacher to learn an alternative method, one that students who struggle may find easier to comprehend. A third group of students is working in pairs on an assignment. Each station lasts an entire class period.

PARALLEL TEACHING Sometimes when two teachers are present, they find it advantageous simply to divide a heterogeneous class group and have each teacher instruct half the class. In this format, called *parallel teaching*, every student has twice as many opportunities to participate in a discussion or respond to teacher questions. A teacher particularly skilled in presenting information through pictures can use this approach while the other teacher emphasizes learning through listening. Students who prefer one method to the other can be placed with the appropriate teacher. In an elementary classroom, this approach may be used to enable students to read different books based on their interests or skill levels. In a secondary classroom, this approach may give students more opportunities to respond during a discussion of a current events topic or enable teachers to present different points of view on a topic, which students then can present to each other when the large group comes back together.

ALTERNATIVE TEACHING In many classrooms, having one teacher work with most of the class while the other teacher focuses attention on a small group is sometimes appropriate. This co-teaching option is referred to as *alternative teaching*. Traditionally, the small group has been used for remediation, but many other options are recommended. For example, some students may benefit from *preteaching*, in which one teacher works with a small group of students who may struggle to learn (whether or not they have IEPs), who are shy, or who are learning to speak English. Information to be presented the next day or later in the same day or class—an example is key vocabulary words—is taught to these students to give them a jump start on learning (Munk, Gibb, & Caldarella, 2010).

WWW RESOURCES

At the Co-Teaching Connection (http://coteach.com), you can find resources related to co-teaching, sample co-teaching lesson plans, and answers to common questions concerning this highly inclusive service-delivery option for students with disabilities and other special needs.

Co-teaching blends the expertise of the educators, including the general educator's knowledge of the curriculum and the special educator's understanding of individual student needs and specialized instructional techniques.

Enrichment also works well in small groups. For example, as a unit of instruction on global warming is concluding, several students may have a strong interest in the topic. As the other students review and complete assigned tasks, this group may meet to discuss career opportunities related to environmental issues, write letters to obtain more information about research on global warming, or explore websites on related topics. The members in this group could include high-achieving students, students who have average academic achievement but strong interest in this topic, a student with a behavior disorder who would benefit more from this activity than from the assigned work, and a student with a moderate intellectual disability for whom the written task is not appropriate.

Grouping students for remediation is appropriate, but only when it is one of many grouping options and is used only occasionally for a specific instructional purpose. Otherwise, such an arrangement becomes the equivalent of running a special education program in the back of a general education classroom—an arrangement that completely undermines the purpose and principles of inclusive schooling.

TEAMING In the co-teaching option of *teaming*, the teachers share leadership in the classroom; both are equally engaged in the instructional activities. For example, one teacher may begin a lesson by introducing vocabulary while the other provides examples to place the words in context. Two teachers may role-play an important event from history or demonstrate how to complete a lab activity. Two teachers may model how to address conflict by staging a debate about a current event. You reach the limits of teaming only when you run out of exciting ideas for creating instruction with two teachers instead of one. Co-teachers who use this approach find it the most energizing of all the co-teaching options, but you should also be aware that you and a co-teacher might not be compatible enough in terms of teaching style to use it. If that is the case, using several of the other approaches might be more effective.

ONE TEACH, ONE ASSIST Occasionally during instruction, one teacher is appropriately leading the lesson while the other is quietly assisting individual students. For example, while the special education teacher leads a lesson that is a test review, the general education teacher helps students individually as they have questions about the vocabulary. Alternatively, while the general education teacher leads a lesson on the causes of World War II, the special education teacher helps keep students on task and responds quietly to student questions. The key to implementing this approach successfully is to use it carefully and only occasionally. With overuse, one of the teachers, often the special educator, may perceive that she has no legitimate role in the class and is mostly functioning as a teaching assistant (Legutko, 2015). In addition, if this approach to co-teaching is used too frequently, students may become overly dependent on the extra help that always seems to be available. Further, they may miss valuable instruction while interacting with the teacher in the assisting role.

CO-TEACHING PRAGMATICS As you consider these co-teaching approaches, you might notice that, in addition to how the teachers arrange themselves and the students, several other factors need to be taken into account (Fitzell, 2013; Friend, 2014a; Kluth & Causton, 2016). First, in a co-taught class, students are grouped so that those with disabilities are integrated appropriately with their peers without disabilities. Thus, in a station teaching arrangement, students with special needs are likely to be in each of the three groups, although at times they may be placed together to meet a specific instructional need. When alternative teaching occurs, the smaller group may or may not contain students with disabilities. Second, both teachers take on teaching and supportive roles. Sometimes those roles are similar, but often they are different because the teachers are in the classroom for distinct reasons, the general education teacher prioritizing the curriculum to be addressed and overall classroom management and the special education teacher prioritizing individual students' specialized instructional needs. Third, the best

RESEARCH-BASED PRACTICES

Tremblay (2013) compared the academic achievement of elementary (grades 1 and 2) students in inclusive environments with co-teaching versus solo-taught separate special education classes. Students were comparable on several key demographic variables, but those in inclusive settings outperformed those who were educated away from their peers.

approaches to use depend on student needs, the subject being taught, the teachers' experience, and practical considerations such as space and time for planning. Novice co-teachers may prefer station teaching or parallel teaching over teaming, especially in a class that includes several students with attention problems who would benefit from a smaller group structure. Finally, the type of curriculum sometimes dictates the approach. For example, a topic that is sequential obviously cannot be taught in stations; it may be presented best through teaming followed by parallel-taught study groups.

Working on a Team

In Chapter 2, you learned that you have responsibility as a member of an intervention assistance, MTSS, or RtI team to problem solve about students before they are considered for special education (e.g., Chard, 2013; White, Polly, & Audette, 2012). You also learned that you may be a member of the multidisciplinary team (MDT) that determines whether a student is eligible to receive special education services and then writes the student's IEP. These teams rely on collaboration among members, and it is important that you understand the characteristics they and other school teams have that make them effective. The Working Together feature captures a few moments of an MTSS team meeting illustrating these team traits.

When you think about highly successful teams, what comes to mind? Your favorite athletic team? A surgical team? An orchestra? What is it about these teams that makes them successful? Teams are formal work groups that have certain

> **FYI**
>
> In some cases, students who need intensive remedial services should receive them in a separate setting. This may occur as part of Tier 2 or 3 in RtI or MTSS, or as an option for students with disabilities, for example, for reading instruction. When this practice occurs, collaboration focuses on communication between those providing the remedial instruction and general education teachers.

WORKING TOGETHER 3.1
An MTSS Problem-Solving Meeting

At Triton Middle School, the multi-tiered systems of support procedure is the responsibility of each team. Today, a sixth-grade team is meeting to review data on student progress. Present are the four core content-area teachers (Mr. Land, science; Mr. Graf, math; Ms. Fitzgerald, English; Ms. Lincoln, social studies); Mr. Lashley, the assistant principal who helps the team members analyze their data; Ms. Gardner, the reading specialist; and Ms. Dunn, the special educator assigned to the team. One student the team is discussing is Scott.

Ms. Gardner: Scott has been participating in the Tigers Reading Club during intervention time for the past 12 weeks. His attendance is nearly perfect, and he is completing all the reading activities. I think our Tier 2 intervention is really working well for many students, but Scott still is not making enough progress in comprehension—it's still at a mid-fourth-grade level, and our criteria indicate he should be approaching an early-fifth-grade level by now.

Ms. Dunn: I did some checking with Scott's fifth-grade teacher. She told me that Scott had gone back and forth between Tier 2 and Tier 3 interventions last year, but that their team decided he was making adequate progress. His records do not indicate he has ever been referred for special education services.

Ms. Buchanan: I see the comprehension problems in English. Scott tries, and he's a nice kid, but he misses a lot because he hasn't understood what he has read.

Mr. Land: I can say that exact same thing about science. I try to discuss almost everything—not have the students just read in their books—partly because I know Scott has difficulty with the reading, even with a highlighted text and shortened assignments.

Ms. Lincoln: Same thing happens in social studies. I brought several samples of his work and his weekly quiz scores since the beginning of the year.

Mr. Graf: In math, he's doing well—his average on tests and assignments is slightly above the class average.

[Additional data on Scott's comprehension skills are discussed by team members.]

Mr. Lashley: Based on the data we have from progress monitoring and the information all of you have contributed, it seems like we're saying he needs a more intensive intervention. Does everyone agree?

[Head nods from everyone.]

Ms. Gardner: I think our best option is to have him enroll in the reading class for the next grading quarter. That would give him a daily computer-based, highly structured reading program with me as the teacher, and it would provide twice as much intervention time as he receives now.

The meeting continues. . . .

REFLECTION

What collaborative roles do general education teachers play during MTSS meetings? Why is it important that each teacher bring data to such a meeting and share the information with colleagues? What parts of a problem-solving process did this meeting include? What role do you think parents should have in such a process? How is this type of collaboration an improvement over past practices for addressing student learning or behavior problems?

characteristics. They have clear goals, active and committed members, and competent leaders; they follow clear procedures to achieve their results; and they do not let personal issues interfere with accomplishment of their goals. What are other characteristics of effective teams? Their success depends on the commitment of every member and the clarity of their goals. On effective school teams, members keep in mind why they are a team, setting aside personal differences to reach a goal that often is to design the best educational strategies possible for students with disabilities or other special needs.

TEAM PARTICIPANT ROLES As a team member, you must assume multiple roles (e.g., Mathieu, Hollenbeck, van Knippenberg, & Ilgen, 2017). First, in your professional role as a general education teacher, you bring a particular perspective to a team interaction, as do the special education teacher, counselor, adaptive physical educator, principal, and other team members (Shapiro & Sayers, 2003). You contribute an understanding of what students without disabilities are accomplishing in your grade or course, knowledge of the curriculum and its pace, and a sense of the prerequisites of what you are teaching and the expectations for students likely to follow the next segment of instruction.

The second contribution you make is through your personal role; that is, the characteristics that define you as a person. For example, are you a person who sees the positive aspects of almost any situation? If so, you will probably be the person who keeps up the team's morale. Are you a detail-oriented person who is skilled at organizing? If so, you will probably be the team member who ensures that all the tasks get completed and all the paperwork is filed.

Third, you have a team role to fulfill as well, whether informal or formal. You may be the individual who makes sure the agenda is being followed or who watches the time so team meetings do not last too long. Or you may have the role of suggesting ways to combine what seem to be contradictory points of view into integrated solutions to student problems. As an effective member, you will recognize your strengths and use them to enhance the team; you also will be vigilant so your weaknesses do not interfere with the team's completing its tasks. Common formal team roles include team facilitator, recorder, and timekeeper. These roles might rotate so that every team member has the opportunity to experience each one. Informal team roles include being a compromiser, information seeker, and reality checker.

TEAM GOALS One of the keys to effective teams is attention to goals (Friend & Cook, 2017). Being clear and explicit about goals is particularly important in educational settings because team goals often are assumed or too limited. For example, on some RtI teams, teachers perceive the team goal to be to document interventions so that the special education identification procedures can begin. Others believe the team functions to help teachers address student learning problems so that any consideration of special education can be avoided, if at all possible. Note how crucial this difference in perception of team purpose is. Without clear and specific goals, teams often flounder.

Another aspect of team goals is especially important. The goals just discussed are commonly referred to as *task goals*; that is, they are the business of the team. But teams have another set of goals called *maintenance goals*. Maintenance goals refer to the team's status and functioning as a team. Maintenance goals may include beginning and ending meetings on time, finishing all agenda items during a single meeting, and taking time to check on team members' perceptions of team effectiveness. These and other maintenance goals enable effective teams to reach the task goals they set.

Consultation

In some cases, you may not have direct support for a student in your classroom. Perhaps the student does not have an identified disability, or perhaps the student's needs can be met with occasional supports. For example, you might have an outgoing student who suddenly begins acting very withdrawn. Or you may learn that for the next school year, you will have a student who has a significant physical disability; you would like to know how to assist the student and whether you should seek special training. As illustrated in the chapter-opening vignette about Kenneth, if you have a student with autism in your class, you might find that both you and the special education teacher need assistance from someone else to help the student learn the best ways to transition from activity to activity. These are examples of situations in which you might seek support through consultation.

Consultation is a specialized problem-solving process in which one professional who has particular expertise assists another professional (or parent) who needs the benefit of that expertise (Sheridan et al., 2017). For example, you may contact a behavior consultant for assistance when a student in your class is aggressive or has extraordinary difficulty with social interactions (e.g., Garbacz & McIntyre, 2016; MacSuga & Simonsen, 2011). You might meet with a vision or hearing consultant when a student with a disability in one of those areas is included in your class. If you have a student who has received medical or other services outside school, you may consult with someone from the agency that has been providing those services. Examples of consultative interactions with professionals who are not employees of a school district are presented in the Professional Edge feature.

Consultation is most effective when it is based on the principles of collaboration already presented, but its purpose is not reciprocal (Kampwirth & Powers, 2016). That is, in consultation, the goal is for someone with specific expertise to assist you (or another professional); the other person may learn from you, but that is not the goal. The process of consulting generally begins when you as the teacher complete a request form or otherwise indicate you have a concern about a student (Knackendoffel, Dettmer, & Thurston, 2018). The consultant then

> **FYI**
>
> Although many special education teachers occasionally act as consultants, this role is more often filled by school psychologists, counselors, and specialists for concerns such as student behavior or a specific disability such as autism. Both general educators and special educators seek guidance from such specialists.

PROFESSIONAL EDGE 3.3

Professional Interactions that Extend Beyond School

Although this chapter focuses on the most common applications of school collaborative interactions in which you are likely to be a participant, you should be aware that many other situations arise that may require you to contribute as a team member, follow instructions given in a directive way, or contribute to problem solving. Here are several examples:

Experts for Unique Student Problems. Students sometimes receive significant services outside of school because of their unique needs. For example, a student with autism may participate in a private therapeutic program. A student with a neurologic disorder could be working with a specialist. It is possible that professionals in such situations will need to interact with you as a student's teacher. You may be asked to offer your observations of a student's behavior or changes in it, or you may be asked to complete a brief questionnaire about the student. Occasionally a staff member from agencies providing outside services may need to observe the student in your class.

Drug, Juvenile Justice, Police, and Related Agency Personnel. If one of your students is involved in any type of activity that has come to the attention of law enforcement, you may interact with professionals such as a case worker, a police representative, or a social worker assigned to manage the student's case.

Hospital or Rehabilitation Personnel. When students have been hospitalized (e.g., after an accident) and possibly spent time in a rehabilitation facility, you may interact with professionals whose job is to facilitate the transition from the medical setting to the school setting. The same may be true if one of your students has been hospitalized because of a mental health or emotional crisis.

Child Protective Services. If one of your students is in foster care or the family is involved with child protective services, you may attend a meeting related to these services so that you understand, within the parameters of information you are entitled to know, who is legally responsible for the student and can speak for/give permission on behalf of the student in school-related activities (e.g., field trips).

Keep in mind that interactions with professionals in situations like those just described generally will also include a school administrator, possibly a school psychologist or counselor, possibly a special educator, and others. If you have questions about your roles related to any potential interaction with experts from outside the school district, you should ask your principal or another administrator for guidance concerning expectations for your participation.

contacts you to arrange an initial meeting. At that meeting, the problem is further clarified, your expectations are discussed, and often arrangements are made for the consultant to observe in your room. Once the observation phase has been completed, you and the consultant meet again to finalize your understanding of the problem, generate and select options for addressing it, and plan how to implement whatever strategies seem needed. A timeline for putting the strategies into effect is also established. Typically, you then carry out the strategies. Following this phase, you and the consultant meet once again to determine whether the problem has been resolved. If it has, the strategy is either continued to maintain the success or eliminated as no longer needed. If the problem continues to exist, the consultant may suggest that you begin a new consulting process, or together you may decide that some other action is needed. When appropriate, the consultant closes the case. In the Working Together feature, you can learn more about what it's like to work with a consultant.

For consulting to be effective, both the consultant and the consultee (that is, you as the teacher) need to participate responsibly (Kampwirth & Powers, 2016). Your role includes preparing for meetings, using data to describe your concern

WORKING TOGETHER 3.2
Consultation with an Autism Specialist

When teachers cannot find solutions for student issues, they sometimes call on the expertise of a consultant. Consultants usually have specialized knowledge and skills in a particular area (e.g., autism, behavior, reading), and they are employed to help teachers and other professionals find strategies to help students. Here is an example of what might occur in a consultation session regarding a high school student with autism who is a high achiever but whose teachers are very concerned because of his social anxiety.

Mr. Riordan is meeting with Ms. Moller, the district autism specialist, concerning Liam, a student identified as having autism spectrum disorder (ASD). Ms. Constantino, the special educator, also is present. Ms. Constantino asked for this meeting after Mr. Riordan raised his serious concerns about Liam's behaviors in his advanced placement (AP) calculus class, confirming her own observations. Liam used to participate in group discussions and ask questions, but now he almost always refuses to interact with classmates, becomes upset when asked to respond to a teacher-posed question, and ignores other students' efforts to include him in their conversations. Ms. Constantino has noticed that Liam stands too far away from other students when in a group, and they often treat him as though he is not there. Liam also has mentioned that he does not want to go to college because of all the different people, classes, and related expectations.

Mr. Riordan: Thanks for meeting with us. I've been trying to do everything Ms. Constantino has suggested to help Liam, but I'm not seeing any improvement. If anything, things are worse. Ms. Constantino, you asked me to keep some data about what's occurring, and I did that. In the past week, my students have been working on a group project. Three different times, Liam refused to join his group, and one additional time he joined only after I threatened to call his mother. I also observed during transitions that Liam never talked to anyone else; instead he put his head down on his desk. With other students, it's often difficult to get them to stop talking. Liam has so much potential, but this situation is deteriorating, and knowing that he has autism, I thought someone should be aware of what is occurring.

Ms. Moller: Ms. Constantino, what are you seeing?

Ms. Constantino: Social situations are becoming more and more difficult for Liam. He seems hyperaware of everything that occurs, and he is mortified when he has made a social mistake, no matter how small, or frozen into inaction over fear he will make a mistake. When I see him with no one else around, he expresses his fears—in fact, it has occurred to me that he is seeking me out in the resource room so that he does not have to be around other students.

Ms. Moller: These details are helpful. I'm thinking that I should have a private conversation with Liam to better understand his perspective, and Mr. Davidson, could I come to your room a couple of times this week to observe Liam? Sometimes an outside observer can pick up on other patterns of what is happening. I'll also arrange to observe him at lunch and will check with his other teachers to see if they have noticed what both of you have. I'll try to get back in touch within a week to decide if we should meet again, contact his parents, or perhaps create a specific intervention to help him.

Mr. Riordan: That sounds fine with me. I'd prefer you observe later in the week when there will be more group work.

Ms. Constantino: If you'd like to observe Liam working in the resource room, please do—he is there for half of third block, primarily to give him a break from the classroom social demands. We really need some new solutions.

Ms. Moller: I'm confident we'll come up with some novel ideas. I just want to be sure that we address the real problem and not just a symptom of it.

After a few minutes, the meeting breaks up, to be continued the following Monday.

When might it be appropriate to seek input from a consultant such as Ms. Moller? What are your obligations as a general education teacher to identify extraordinary difficulties being experienced by students with disabilities? To arrange for an in-class observation? To implement an intervention and report on its effectiveness?

about the student, being open to the consultant's suggestions, implementing the agreed-upon strategies systematically, and documenting the effectiveness of ideas you try. The consultant's role includes listening carefully to your concerns; assisting to analyze data that can inform decision making; and working with you to design, implement, and evaluate feasible strategies. Together, your partnership can provide supports for many students whose needs do not require direct specialized services.

The Complexity of Professional Collaboration

As you have read the information about collaborative services for students with disabilities, you probably have realized that they are based on caring and committed professionals who believe in the power of shared efforts and are open to the ideas of colleagues. However, even when all the conditions essential for collaboration are in place, disagreements can occur. And occasionally, you may find yourself working with a colleague or group of colleagues with whom you have deep disagreements (e.g., Conderman, 2011; Webb, Coleman, Rossignac-Milon, Tomasulo, & Higgins, 2017). What happens then? Is collaboration possible?

Although most professionals would prefer that all interactions be pleasant and based on agreements, that, of course, is not a real-world expectation. You may find that you believe that the special educator who reads tests to the students with disabilities in your class is providing so much assistance that they are getting higher scores than you think accurately represent their learning. Perhaps your principal has said that she expects you to co-teach next year, and you are not sure you want to participate—but you have not been given a choice. Or perhaps you and one team member tend to have different points of view on everything from making changes in grading policies for students with disabilities to classroom behavior expectations for them.

Disagreement is an inevitable by-product of collaboration. Disagreements can be minor or major, and the people involved can be committed to resolving them or maintaining their own viewpoints. Regardless, here are a few ideas for responding to disagreements:

- Try to understand the situation from the perspective of the other person, using the concept of frame of reference—that is, the totality of the other person's viewpoint that is based on her background, experiences, education, and even work history in schools. Using frame of reference can help you see things as the other individual sees them, a valuable first step in resolving a disagreement. For example, if you are anticipating that a new special educator will function as an equal partner in your co-taught class, you might be disappointed that he seems very reluctant. However, this could be because in his last position, he was relegated to being a classroom helper and so is uncertain about your expectations. Understanding that helps you to be patient and to have a meaningful conversation about creating an instructional partnership.

- See if you can get agreement by trying a solution that can be reevaluated at a later time. For example, if you think the special educator is creating dependence by providing too much assistance to students, perhaps the test could be read by a paraprofessional, or perhaps you could read the test while the special educator supervises the other students taking it. After trying one of these (or other) options two or three times, you and your colleague should review them for effectiveness. Sometimes a solution can be reached if everyone knows it can be changed later as needed.

- Examine your own part in the disagreement. If you tend to be a person for whom every issue is a major concern, a straightforward way to address the disagreement is to work diligently to reflect on your behavior. If you tend to insist on your solution, you might want to deliberately work to sometimes acquiesce to others' preferences. For honest input on this difficult possibility, you might want to seek input from a colleague, mentor, or administrator.

WWW RESOURCES

New Conversations (http://www.newconversations.net/) is a website dedicated to fostering collaboration by providing free materials to those interested. If you'd like to enhance your communication skills, the posted *Seven Challenges Workbook* has many practical ideas.

In the Instructional Edge feature you will find examples of topics that sometimes are sources of disagreements between general and special educators, particularly when they work together through co-teaching. Ultimately, the most important message related to disagreements with colleagues is this: Conflict provides opportunities to create new and better options for students. Disagreements may be stressful, but you can turn them into solutions by thinking carefully about your views and the basis for them, engaging in constructive conversations with other professionals, and keeping in mind that any resolution ultimately has as its goal helping students with disabilities.

MyLab Education Self-Check 3.2

How Can You Work Effectively with Parents?

The partnerships presented thus far in this chapter have focused primarily on your interactions with special education teachers and other professionals who will support you in meeting the needs of students with disabilities in your classroom. In this section, we emphasize your working relationship with parents.

Having quality interactions with the parents of all your students is important, but it is vital with the parents of students with disabilities (Elbaum, Blatz, & Rodriguez, 2016). Parents may be able to help you better understand the strengths and needs of their child in your classroom. They also act as advocates for their child, so they can help you ensure that adequate supports are provided for the child's needs. Parents often see their child's experiences in your classroom in a way that you cannot; when they share this information, it helps both you

---

INSTRUCTIONAL EDGE 3.1

Co-Teaching Instructional Dilemmas

Co-teachers sometimes disagree on instructional and other classroom practices. Although you might consider this a negative, it really is not. Instead, disagreements on such matters present opportunities to create fresh solutions beneficial to students and satisfactory to teachers. Here are several common dilemmas that may require considerable discussion to generate solutions:

- The special educator believes that students need her support during instruction, and she often assists students with their assignments, quickly answers their questions, and provides structured guidance as they work. The general educator believes students need support, but that they also need to be challenged. She thinks students should attempt their work, try to find answers to their questions, and learn to follow directions independently.

- The general educator has a policy that students who are late turning in assignments should receive a grade penalty. The special educator argues that if the work was submitted, it should be given full value, even if the student's IEP did not specify extended timelines as an accommodation.

- The special educator believes that his students work very hard and that the grading scale should be adjusted for them. The general educator is very supportive of students with disabilities, but he believes that if many changes are made as supports, the highest grade that can be earned should be a B. (Note that this issue is addressed in detail in Chapter 11.)

- The general educator has, in her opinion, appropriate classroom management. However, she perceives that some students with disabilities misbehave a great deal. The special educator finds the classroom expectations unclear, and she observes that students (not just those with disabilities) sometimes misbehave because they are often told what they do that is wrong but seldom told what they do that is right. She believes there should be a clearer system of rewards for appropriate behavior.

What is your role in resolving disagreements on topics such as these? What would you do if you and your co-teachers could not agree at all? How might your reaction be different if issues like those above were raised at a grade level, team, or department meeting?

and the student achieve more success. Finally, parents are your educational allies (Edwards & DaFonte, 2012). When you enlist their assistance to practice skills at home, to reward their child for accomplishments at school, and to communicate to their child messages consistent with yours, then you and the parents can multiply the student's educational opportunities and provide a consistency that is essential for maximizing student learning.

Understanding the Perspective of Family Members

You might be tempted to assume that because you work with a student with a disability in your classroom on a daily basis, you understand what it would be like to be the student's parent. This assumption could not be further from the truth. The parent of a high school student with a moderate intellectual disability as well as multiple physical disorders made this comment at a meeting of parents and teachers:

> You see my child in a wheelchair and worry about getting her around the building and keeping her changed. But remember, before you ever see her in the morning, I have gotten her out of bed, bathed her, brushed her teeth, washed her hair and fixed it, fed her, and dressed her. I have made sure that extra clothes are packed in case she has an accident, and I have written notes to teachers about her upcoming surgery. When she's at school, I worry about whether she is safe, about whether kids fighting in the hall will care for her or injure her, and whether they are kind. And when she comes home, I clean up the soiled clothes, work with her on all the skills she is still learning, make sure that she has companionship and things to do, and then help her get ready for bed. And I wonder what will be the best option for her when she graduates in three years. You can't possibly know what it's like to be the parent of a child like my daughter.

What this parent so eloquently demonstrated is that you do not understand what it is like to be the parent of a child with a disability unless you, too, are the parent of such a child. This means you should strive to recognize that the range of interactions you have with parents is influenced in part by the stresses they are experiencing, their prior dealings with school personnel, and their own beliefs about their child and her future. How should this idea apply to teachers and other professionals as they work with Annie's parent, Ms. Jordan, who was introduced at the beginning of the chapter?

Parents' Reactions to Their Child's Disability

Parents of children with disabilities have many reactions to their children's special needs, and these reactions may focus on positive or negative factors (Hallberg, 2014). Some parents go through several emotions roughly in a sequence; others may experience only one or several discrete reactions. For some, the reactions may be minor and their approach pragmatic. For others, their child's disability might affect their entire family structure and life. Part of your work with parents includes recognizing that the way they respond to you may be influenced by any of the following reactions to their children's disabilities (Ferguson, 2002):

1. *Grief:* Some parents feel grief about their child's disability (Douglas, 2014). Sometimes this is a sorrow for the pain or discomfort their child may have to experience, sometimes it is sadness for themselves because of the added stress on the family when a child has a disability, and sometimes it is a sense of loss for what the child may not become. Grief may be temporary or it may

MyLab Education

Video Example 3.4: Patrick O'Hearn School, Boston, Massachusetts

Parent communication is an essential component of your work with students. Watch this video to learn what happened when a school staff made increasing parent engagement a specific goal.

DIMENSIONS OF DIVERSITY

One way to convey to parents that you welcome them and sincerely want to collaborate with them is to learn a few key phrases in their language, perhaps words of greeting, a few educational expressions, and key special education terms.

be chronic (Ray, Pewitt-Kinder, & George, 2009), a realization nearly every day of how their lives are different from those of families with children who do not have disabilities. Parents have a right to grieve about their child—a right that educators should respect.

2. *Ambivalence:* Another reaction parents may have toward their child is ambivalence. This feeling may occur as parents attempt to confirm that the child's disability is not temporary or fixable, as they try to determine what the best educational options are for their child, and as they ponder how their child will live as an adult. The decisions that parents of children with disabilities must make are often difficult, and they continue throughout childhood and adolescence and sometimes throughout adulthood. Parents often attend meetings with school personnel at which tremendous amounts of information are shared with little time for explanation, and they often meet with representatives from many different disciplines. It is no wonder they may feel ambivalent.

3. *Optimism:* At a recent well-attended event to celebrate the achievements of children and young adults with a variety of disabilities, a high school student with a moderate intellectual disability and autism was recognized for her art. As the audience enthusiastically applauded her accomplishment, a beaming man leaned over and proudly whispered to one of the authors of this textbook, "That's MY daughter!" For this parent, his child's special needs are just part of the configuration of needs that any child in any family might have; the emphasis is on the person and her abilities rather than the disabilities. There are many families like this one, in which the special needs of the child are met without an extraordinary reaction. Parents may work diligently to optimize their child's education, and they are hopeful about their child's future. They work closely with educators and others to ensure that the child's life, whatever it may be, is the best one possible.

How parents respond when they have a child with a disability depends on many factors. One is the intensity and complexity of the disability. The reaction of parents whose child is diagnosed with a learning disability in third grade will likely be somewhat different from that of parents who learn two months after their child is born that she cannot see.

Another factor affecting the way parents respond is how the information about the disability is shared with them. When such information is presented in a coldly clinical manner, without adequate sensitivity to the parents' emotions, their response can be quite negative. This is true even for children with relatively mild disabilities. When one parent was told about her son's learning disability, she said, "Wait a minute. Stop and let me think. Do you realize what you've just said? You've just unraveled my whole way of thinking about my son. What do you mean a *learning disability?* What does that mean? Will it ever change? How can you sit there and keep talking as though it's no big thing?" A father related how he learned about his daughter's moderate intellectual disability. A physician simply said, "She's retarded. There's nothing we can do." The father left the office crying, partly because of the information and partly because of the insensitive way it had been communicated.

Yet another factor influencing a family's response to having a child with a disability is culture (Cummings & Hardin, 2017; Palawat & May, 2012). In some cultures, disability is a spiritual phenomenon that may reflect a loss of the soul or evidence of transgressions in a previous life. In other families, a child with a disability is considered a reflection on the entire family. In some families, a disability is accepted as just part of who the child is. In others, it is believed that a cure should be sought. It is important to listen to family members as they discuss their child to better understand their perspective on him as well as their response to ideas and suggestions that you and the rest of the team make (Olivos, 2009).

One other factor that affects the parents' response concerns resources, including financial support (Bahr, 2015; Gannotti, Oshio, & Handwerker, 2012). When parents have the resources necessary to provide what they believe is the

FYI

Individualized family service plans (IFSPs) are the documents that guide services for young children with disabilities. Strongly based on collaboration, IFSPs set the expectation that professionals and families are partners in the education of infants and toddlers with disabilities.

best set of services for their child, they are less likely to experience strong negative emotions. However, when parents know that their child would benefit from some intervention, such as surgery, a piece of computer equipment, or tutoring, they are invariably frustrated if they cannot provide that needed support and have difficulty accessing it from school and community resources. Another valuable resource is people. In large families, families with many supportive relatives living in the same community, families with a strong network of neighbors and friends, or families with strong support from their faith, the stresses of having a child with a disability are greatly reduced (e.g., Gannotti et al., 2012). When parents are isolated or when friends and family are uncomfortable with the child, the parents are likely to experience far more difficulties.

FAMILY-CENTERED PRACTICES The recommended approach for working with families of students with disabilities is referred to as family-centered practices (Fox, Nordquist, Billen, & Savoca, 2015; Sewell, 2012). **Family-centered practices** are based on the notion that outcomes are best for students when their families' perspectives are respected, their families' input is sincerely sought, and school professionals view their job as helping families get the information they need to make the best decisions for their children. Do you agree with this approach? Most professionals do, but implementing it means setting aside preconceived notions about parents and families and sometimes respecting the fact that a family's goals for their child may not be the ones you would choose.

Your understanding of parents' and families' point of view is critical (Cummings & Hardin, 2017; Olivos et al., 2010). For example, some parents find school an unpleasant or intimidating place. They may have had negative experiences when they were students, or if they are from another country, they may be unfamiliar with the expectations for parental involvement in U.S. public schools. If the parents' primary language is not English, they may be uncomfortable because of the need for an interpreter, or they may misunderstand information communicated by school personnel, whether in face-to-face interactions or in writing. If parents are from a culture that views teachers as experts, they may wonder why you keep asking for their input. Some ideas for reflecting on and responding to parents from diverse cultures are included in the Professional Edge feature.

> **DIMENSIONS OF DIVERSITY**
>
> Many parents, especially those from cultural or linguistic minority groups, can find school an intimidating place. You can promote participation by encouraging parents to come to school meetings with a friend or another family member and by asking them positive questions early during meetings (for example, "What does your child say about school at home?" "What is your child's favorite out-of-school activity?").

PROFESSIONAL EDGE 3.4

Collaborating with Families from Asian/Pacific Islander Cultures

Even with the best intentions, building collaborative relationships with families of diverse learners is sometimes challenging, especially when students have disabilities. Several of the dilemmas that must be considered in working with Asian/Pacific Islander families should be considered in working with families from any nondominant culture (Palawat & May, 2012; Pinquart & Kauser, 2017):

- *Language differences:* At the most basic level, when school professionals and families do not speak a common language, misunderstandings are much more likely to occur. Even with an interpreter, the subtleties of language may not be adequately communicated.

- *Communication context:* In some Asian cultures, communication relies on the social context and subtle movements, gestures, and other nonverbal signals as much as on words. Communication patterns in the United States generally are direct and far less reliant on contextual variables. As you might expect, a tremendous risk exists for miscommunication and misunderstandings.

- *Cultural values:* In many Asian cultures, family unity is central and emphasized throughout children's lives. In contrast, the U.S. education system tends to stress the development of independence. When families and professionals interact, they may—even without realizing it—be focused on conflicting life goals for children.

- *Academic, social, and behavioral expectations:* In some Asian families, academic expectations, tolerance for child behaviors, and social mores may be somewhat different from those in dominant culture families. These factors may have a direct impact on family–school communication.

Consider what you have learned about families from various cultures. What other differences might affect collaboration with family members of your diverse students with disabilities? Frame your answer around the key characteristics of collaboration that you have learned. How could you as a professional educator prepare for interactions with families so as to maximize understanding and clear communication?

Some parents may not be visibly involved in their children's education because of pragmatic barriers. Parents who work at jobs that are far from school may not be able to take time off to participate in activities at school and may not be able to afford the lost work time. For some parents, involvement is largely a matter of economics: The costs of child care and transportation may prevent them from being able to work with you. These parents, however, may be involved through their work with their child at home.

In general, your attitude toward parents and their perceptions of their children greatly affect how you interact with them (Tucker & Schwartz, 2013). If you telegraph through your choice of words, your question-asking skills, and your body posture that parents should see their children as you do and accept your input without question, then you are violating the principles of family-centered practice, and you probably will find that parents will not communicate with you readily. However, if you make parents feel welcome in your classroom or by phone or e-mail, listen carefully to their perceptions and concerns, treat them as important, and work with them to address student needs, then many benefits will accrue for the student, the family, and you (Olivos et al., 2010).

Collaborating with Parents

As a school professional, you can make family-centered practices a reality when you find ways to effectively collaborate with parents (Aceves, 2014; Wellner, 2012). Some examples of positive ways to partner with parents include home–school communication, parent conferences, parent education, and direct parent involvement in volunteer programs and similar activities.

HOME–SCHOOL COMMUNICATION One straightforward way to build a positive working relationship with parents is by using informal and formal home–school communication strategies (e.g., Buchanan, Nese, & Clark, 2016; Semke, Garbacz, Kwon, Sheridan, & Woods, 2010). For example, at the beginning of the school year, you can send home a letter to parents that introduces you and explains your classroom goals for the year. You can follow this up with a positive phone call to parents sometime during the first weeks of the school year. A positive call is particularly important for parents of students with disabilities because they often hear from educators only when a problem occurs.

You can continue a system of communication with parents throughout the school year. For example, some teachers send home weekly or periodic updates or newsletters to the parents of all their students, or they post information for parents on their websites. Others send progress reports midway through a grading period. For a student who is struggling, the IEP might require you to exchange a notebook in which you briefly list accomplishments of the day and a parent writes back with information from home (Turnbull, Turnbull, Erwin, Soodak, & Shogren, 2011). A time-saving alternative is to have a checklist that describes the positive behaviors expected of your student (for example, "Raises hand to ask a question"; "Comes to class with all needed materials"). You can then check the items that were successfully completed for that day. For a student with severe disabilities in your class, a paraprofessional might assist by preparing under your direction daily communication to parents (Chopra et al., 2004). Whenever you use a daily communication system, you should encourage parents to respond so you are aware of their perspectives and concerns.

Many teachers use electronic communication with parents. For example, if most families of your students have access to e-mail, you can send a group communication or electronic newsletter on a regular schedule, and you can send information about a specific student more frequently as needed. Some teachers also use e-mail or a class website or district learning platform (e.g., Google Classroom) to ensure that communication about homework is clear. Remember, though, that some families cannot readily access a computer, so you should use an alternative means of communication with them. Remember, too, that

---

DIMENSIONS OF DIVERSITY

Families from traditional American Indian culture sometimes define disability in terms of a relationship between individuals with unequal abilities, not a status assigned based on medical diagnosis (Begay, Brown, & Bounds, 2015; Pewewardy & Fitzpatrick, 2009). This is an example of why cultural competence is so important in your work with families.

communication through electronic means holds risks. Your district may have policies about using electronic communication because of concerns about privacy and security. In addition, anything that you write becomes a permanent record that may be requested at a future time; professionals must learn to keep such correspondence objective and free of comments that could be misinterpreted.

Finally, your strategies for home–school communication may be influenced by culture (Finkbeiner & Lazar, 2015). With some families, indirect communication through print or electronic media will not be effective. In such cases, your responsibility is to ensure that you reach out to parents through a phone call or an invitation to come to school to meet. Depending on local policy and parent preference, you might even suggest meeting the parents at a local library or another setting that might be perceived as more parent-friendly than school. In general, you should remember that if your goal is to enhance collaboration with parents, the communication approaches you select should clearly help you achieve that purpose.

PARENT CONFERENCES In addition to the informal, day-to-day communication in which you engage with parents, you also can collaborate with them through conferences. Preparing for, conducting, and following up on parent conferences helps ensure that this communication vehicle is valuable for the parents of all your students, including those with disabilities (Harvard Family Research Project, 2010; Pillet-Shore, 2016).

Before a conference, you should clarify the purpose of the meeting. Is it to speak to a group of parents about your overall goals for the year? Is it to meet individually with parents to discuss their child's progress? You can help parents prepare for the latter type of meeting by sending a list of questions and suggestions home in advance of the conference (e.g., What does your child say about school? What questions do you have about your child's work in my class?). As you prepare questions for parents, you also should think about the questions you wish to address with them during the conference and make a list. Finally, you will communicate more effectively if you have samples of student work, your grade and plan books, and other pertinent student data and records easily available.

During the conference, your goal is to create a two-way exchange of information. Whether meeting with parents by yourself or with a special educator, you can accomplish this goal when you greet parents positively, arrange to meet with them at a table instead of at your desk, set a purpose for the conference, and actively involve them in discussion. In addition, you should use language respectful of the parents, their child, and their culture. Avoid using jargon (for example, acronyms such as RtI, MTSS, and MDT). In addition, you should work to understand that parents might interpret the meaning of disability and educators' response to it in ways that differ from educators. For example, some African American parents may distrust school professionals and the decisions made about their children because of past segregation and discriminatory special education practices (Lofton & Davis, 2015; Salend & Duhaney, 2005).

After a parent conference, you should complete several tasks. First, you should write a few notes to remind yourself of the important points discussed. These notes will help you improve the accuracy of your recollections. Second, if you made any major decisions regarding strategies that you and the parents will implement, you should write a brief note to the parents to confirm those decisions. Third, if you agreed to any action (for example, sending information to parents or asking a counselor to call parents), it is best to carry it out as soon as possible. Finally, if the special education teacher did not attend the conference, he may appreciate receiving a brief note from you with an update on the conference outcomes.

PARENT EDUCATION Another type of communication with parents can be accomplished through a variety of parent education activities (e.g., Gyamfi et al., 2010). Although you probably would not undertake this type of activity without your

MyLab Education
Video Example 3.5: Effective Strategies for Parent-Teacher Communication
This teacher highlights the importance of clear and frequent communication with parents.
https://www.youtube.com/watch?v=MWNUM-XGpnU

colleagues, you may find parent education programs helpful for informing parents and giving them an opportunity to discuss important matters concerning their children. For example, if your school decides to emphasize inclusive practices, an information session for the parents of all students might be very helpful. One school invited the parent of a student with disabilities to present on this topic to other parents at the beginning of the school year; the result was increased understanding and a positive start. Some schools offer parent programs related to understanding children's behavior, preparing for transitions from one school level to the next, and other topics of common interest, including ADHD and autism.

PARENT INVOLVEMENT One additional type of collaboration with parents occurs through their involvement in their children's schools (Fishman & Nickerson, 2015; Zablotsky, Boswell, & Smith, 2012). Some parents, especially at the elementary level, make time to volunteer at school, tutoring students, assisting with clerical chores, and helping to supervise students on field trips. Other parents cannot make such commitments, but they might be willing to help design a newsletter by working at their convenience or to come to school on a Saturday to help set up for a special event. Alternatively, some schools help parents get involved by making school facilities more available. For example, some schools regularly hold evening sessions during which parents can bring their children to school to work on computers, read, or participate in discussion groups. Some schools find space in the building to set up a parent center, a comfortable gathering place designed for and operated by parents where books can be borrowed and important school district and community information is readily available.

THE COMPLEXITY OF PARENT COLLABORATION Just as with your interactions with colleagues, your interactions with parents sometimes will be successful and satisfying and sometimes will be challenging and perplexing. The notion of frame of reference applies as well. The more you can understand what is behind a parent's thinking, the better prepared you will be to try to work for a solution. Keep in mind that some parents of students with disabilities feel they have had to fight to get for their children the services to which they are entitled, and so they may come across as aggressive, even if you approach an interaction with the intent of collaboration. Occasionally, a parent will ask you for something that truly is not reasonable, and in such a case, you should enlist the assistance of the special education teacher and possibly an administrator in responding. If a disagreement with a parent occurs, avoid making unilateral statements such as "We don't offer any services in a special education classroom" or "I won't permit that type of assistance in my classroom." Remember that because students with disabilities have special rights, you run the risk of speaking in error and causing further difficulties. One strategy usually recommended is to defer: Let the parent know that you will be back in touch after checking on options. This provides you with the time needed to seek additional information, enlist assistance, and formulate options for resolving the matter. You can read about an example of a meeting in which a parent and professionals disagree in the Case in Practice feature.

MyLab Education Self-Check 3.3

CASE IN PRACTICE 3.1

Everyone Wants What Is Best . . . Teachers and a Parent in Conflict

Mitchell has been experiencing a variety of difficulties in his eighth-grade classes. The greatest concern expressed by his teachers is that he refuses to use any of the materials that have been specially prepared for him by the special educator, Ms. Antovich. This definitely is affecting his grades. His teachers believe he is quite capable of learning the material and have asked Mitchell's parents to come to school to discuss what to do. Along with Ms. Cox, Mitchell's mother, the meeting is being attended by Ms. Antovich; Mr. Roscoe, the team's math teacher; and Mr. Crain, the assistant principal. The school professionals have explained their concerns, and they are ready to seek Ms. Cox's assistance.

Mr. Crain: Given what we've described, Ms. Cox, I'm wondering what your reaction is.

Ms. Cox: I didn't realize letting Mitchell receive special education meant he was going to be singled out in class. No wonder he won't use the things Ms. Antovich is preparing. I'm sure he's embarrassed. He said something at home about that the other day, and I wasn't sure what he was referring to. Now I know. Just stop singling him out!

Ms. Antovich: I should clarify the types of adjusted materials I've been providing, Ms. Cox. My goal is to make anything that is used in class as much like the other kids' materials as possible. Most of the time, several students are using them. I'm not sure it's the materials themselves that are the issue. I think Mitchell has decided that he doesn't want any type of assistance in class.

Mr. Roscoe: That is the impression I have. For example, it really helps Mitchell to use a calculator for computation, and calculators are available for all the students who want to use them. But Mitchell refuses. As a result, he makes avoidable errors and hurts his scores.

Ms. Cox: How many other kids use calculators?

Mr. Roscoe: Several do. It's just an accepted part of my class.

Ms. Cox: All I know is that he feels stupid in his classes. He's proud, just like his father. He doesn't want anyone to know that school is so hard for him, and I know he doesn't want people helping him.

Mr. Crain: You've added the information that Mitchell is embarrassed by any assistance received in the classroom, and that's helpful. We still have to address two key issues. First, Mitchell is unlikely to succeed in his classes without supports. With supports, he seems to do well, and so we shouldn't even think about pulling him out of his classes to a special education setting. Second, he sees supports as embarrassing. Perhaps we should focus on how to integrate those supports better into the instruction so they are not seen by Mitchell as singling him out.

Mr. Roscoe: I'm open to any ideas we can come up with. This is such a critical year in math instruction, and I know the other teachers feel the same way about their subjects.

Ms. Antovich: Ms. Cox, how would it be if I had a private conversation with Mitchell to raise the issue of embarrassment with him? I could then give you a call to discuss options we might try. But I'll really need your assistance in convincing Mitchell to do whatever we plan.

The meeting continued for another few minutes while details of the plan were outlined.

REFLECTION

What parts of a problem-solving process did this meeting include? How effective were the professionals in exploring Ms. Cox's perspective on her son's problem? What was the role of each professional attending the meeting? Could any of them have been excused? Should others have been invited? What did the professionals say that might have lessened Ms. Cox's concern? That could have increased it? Mitchell was not present at this meeting. Why not? How could Mitchell's input be included without his presence at the meeting? How might the meeting have been different with him present? What are your responsibilities as a professional educator when parents disagree with your perceptions of their child with a disability? What types of assistance might you seek to help address the matter?

How Can You Work Effectively with Paraprofessionals?

Throughout this chapter, the assumption has been made that all the individuals involved in forming school partnerships have equal status; that is, a general education teacher has approximately the same level of authority and equivalent responsibilities as a special education teacher, speech/language therapist, school psychologist, reading teacher, and so on. In many school districts, individuals in these types of positions are referred to as *licensed, certificated,* or *professional staff.*

One other partnership you may form involves another category of staff. As mentioned in Chapter 2, **paraprofessionals**, or paraeducators, are school personnel employed to assist professional staff in carrying out educational programs

As inclusive education becomes a norm across the country, general education teachers increasingly must learn the roles and responsibilities of paraprofessionals who may be assigned to assist them in meeting the needs of students with disabilities.

and otherwise assisting in the instruction of students with disabilities. Although some school districts also employ other types of paraprofessionals, for this discussion we refer only to paraprofessionals who are part of special education services. Paraprofessionals usually have completed two years of college or have passed an examination related to their responsibilities, but they generally are not required to have a four-year college degree (although some do). When students with disabilities are members of your class, a special educator may not have adequate time or opportunity to assist them frequently, or the students might not need the direct services of that professional. Instead, a paraprofessional might be assigned to you for a class period or subject or, depending on the intensity of student needs and grade level, for much of the school day (Douglas, Chapin, & Nolan, 2016; Giangreco, Suter, & Doyle, 2010).

Understanding Your Working Relationship with Paraprofessionals

The partnerships you form with paraprofessionals are slightly different from those you form with professional staff members because you have some supervisory responsibility for a paraprofessional's work, a situation that would not exist in your work with other colleagues (Carnahan, Williamson, Clarke, & Sorensen, 2009; Wasburn-Moses, Chun, & Kaldenberg, 2013). For example, you may be expected to prepare materials for the paraprofessional to use in working with a group of students, you may have the responsibility of assigning tasks to this person on a daily basis, and you may need to provide informal training to the paraprofessional regarding your classroom expectations.

Many general education teachers have never been supervisors, and they worry about what types of tasks to assign to a paraprofessional and how to set expectations. Adding to the complexity of the situation is the fact that some paraprofessionals have extensive professional preparation, a teaching license, and years of classroom experience, which makes them prepared to do nearly everything you do; others meet only the minimum requirements and have little experience working with students. In Chapter 2 you learned about the types of responsibilities paraprofessionals may have in your classroom. If you will be working with a paraprofessional, you should receive a written description of that person's job responsibilities, specifying the types of activities that individual is to complete. You also can arrange to meet with the special education teacher or another professional who has overall responsibility for the paraprofessional's job performance.

Two general guidelines for working effectively with paraprofessionals are these: First, paraprofessionals generally enjoy working with students and want to participate actively in that process, and they should have the opportunity to do so. However, they also are expected to help teachers accomplish some of the chores of teaching, such as record-keeping and instructional preparation tasks. Second, paraprofessionals complete their instructional assignments under the direction of a teacher who either has already taught the information or has decided what basic work needs to be completed; that is, paraprofessionals should not engage in initial teaching, nor should they make instructional decisions without input from a professional staff member.

You have a key role in setting expectations for a paraprofessional who may work in your classroom, for ensuring that you and the paraprofessional are satisfied with your working relationship, and for resolving any problems that arise (e.g., Causton-Theoharis, 2014; Fisher & Pleasants, 2012). At the beginning of the school year, you can orient the paraprofessional to your classroom by providing a place for him to keep personal belongings and instructional materials, explaining essential rules and policies for your classroom, clarifying where in the classroom you want him to work, and asking him to voice questions and concerns (Fitzell, 2013). It is particularly important to touch base with the paraprofessional frequently early in the school year to be certain that expectations are clear. The paraprofessional may be working in several classrooms and trying to remember several sets of directions from different teachers, all with their own styles. You might even find that discussing these topics is best accomplished in a meeting that includes the special education teacher, you, any other general education teachers involved, and the paraprofessional. Figure 3.3 offers additional tips for working with a paraprofessional.

To continue nurturing the working relationship you have with a paraprofessional, you should communicate clearly and directly all activities you would like him to complete (e.g., Bryan, McCubbin, & van der Mars, 2013; McGrath, Johns, & Mathur, 2010). Some paraprofessionals report that they enter a classroom only to find that the teacher is already working with students and expects the paraprofessional to know what to do with the students with special needs, assuming that the special education teacher has provided this direction. Meanwhile, the special educator is assuming that the general education teacher is guiding the paraprofessional. Unfortunately, in this situation the paraprofessional may be left frustrated and wondering how to proceed.

Collaborating with Paraprofessionals

An often-asked teacher question regarding paraprofessionals is this: Given the supervisory nature of teacher–paraprofessional work, is it possible to collaborate with this group of staff members? The answer is yes. Paraprofessionals can collaboratively participate in shared problem solving about student needs, planning field trip and class activity details, and making decisions regarding how best to adapt information for a specific student (Giangreco et al., 2010; Friend & Barron, in press). Your responsibility as a teacher is to encourage this type of collaboration. At the same time, you should clearly inform the paraprofessional when a matter being discussed is not one in which the principles of collaboration are appropriate. It also is important that you tell paraprofessionals when they are meeting your expectations and that you promptly address any issues of concern as soon as you become aware of them. For example, Ms. Fulton is a paraprofessional in the seventh-grade math class. At a recent brief meeting, the math teacher

MyLab Education

Video Example 3.6: Collaboration and Communication with Paraprofessionals and General Educators

Paraprofessionals often play a critical role as collaborative partners with general and special educators in students' education.

FIGURE 3.3 **Tips for Working Effectively with Paraprofessionals in General Education Classrooms**

DO This	AVOID This
1. Explain basic classroom procedures, behavior expectations, and other key information to the paraprofessional.	1. Presume that the paraprofessional will figure out what you expect simply by being in the classroom.
2. Discuss your understanding of the needs of the students with disabilities in the class and the role of the paraprofessional in meeting those needs.	2. Assume that the paraprofessional knows what she or he is supposed to do in relation to students with disabilities.
3. Distinguish your responsibility to provide initial instruction from the paraprofessional's responsibility to support students through follow-up instruction.	3. Ask the paraprofessional to take responsibility for initial instruction of students with disabilities in the general education class.
4. Include the paraprofessional in planning meetings.	4. Avoid asking the paraprofessional to participate in planning.
5. Have the paraprofessional manage *routine* information sharing with students' parents (e.g., notices of field trips).	5. Permit the paraprofessional to communicate with parents based on his or her preference, including events that happened at school and concerns about the student.
6. Frequently communicate to the paraprofessional what is being done correctly or in an exemplary manner.	6. Presume the paraprofessional knows that you appreciate his or her efforts on behalf of students with disabilities.
7. Address concerns or issues as soon as you are aware of them, involving the special education teacher and/or principal as appropriate.	7. Avoid directly addressing your concerns, perhaps because doing so is uncomfortable or because the paraprofessional is more experienced than you.
8. Take into account that the paraprofessional may be working with multiple teachers and students and may occasionally confuse directions or experience stress in moving from classroom to classroom.	8. Treat the paraprofessional as though your expectations and concerns are the only ones that matter, possibly becoming impatient when other priorities must be addressed by that individual.

FYI

Depending on the students you teach and local policies, a paraprofessional may be assigned to just one student in your class. An individual in this role sometimes is informally referred to as a *one-to-one paraprofessional*. In the guide available at Wikispaces Classroom (http://paraprofessionalsguide .wikispaces.com/), you will find tips for working effectively with such paraprofessionals.

thanked her for quietly answering students' questions about directions and providing assistance in reading items in the textbook. However, he also directed Ms. Fulton to avoid assisting students in answering the problems being worked. His judgment, based on student assessment data, is that her help is approaching the level of providing students with answers on work that they should complete independently. He illustrated his point by talking through with her an example of how to respond to a student who asks for assistance. His directions to Ms. Fulton were direct and clear but also respectful of her many years of experience in working with students with disabilities.

The Complexity of Working with Paraprofessionals

Most of your interactions with paraprofessionals will be positive, and you will realize how valuable these school personnel are in inclusive classrooms (Ashbaker & Morgan, 2013; Fisher & Pleasants, 2012). Although most paraprofessionals work diligently, have a tremendous commitment to working with students with disabilities, and manage their roles superbly, problems occasionally arise.

If you teach older students, you might find that the paraprofessional does not have enough knowledge of the content being presented to reinforce student learning. A few paraprofessionals violate principles of confidentiality by discussing classroom or student matters away from school. Some paraprofessionals are disruptive in classrooms—for example, their speech is too loud or their interactions with students are too casual. If problems such as these occur and cannot be resolved directly between you and the paraprofessional, you should ask the special educator with whom you work to meet with you and the paraprofessional to problem solve. If further action is needed, an administrator such as a principal or special education coordinator can assist. Ultimately, you are directing the day-to-day work of the paraprofessionals in your class. If problems arise, it is your responsibility to follow up until they are resolved and students' support is being provided appropriately.

An entirely different type of problem can occur, but it is equally serious. Some paraprofessionals tend to hover over students with disabilities, preventing them from establishing social relationships with peers and fostering dependence instead of independence (Giangreco et al., 2010). You should discuss this well-intentioned but inappropriate activity with such paraprofessionals and give clear, alternative directions for their interactions with students. By offering encouragement and addressing concerns, you can establish an environment that will make your collaboration with paraprofessionals invaluable.

MyLab Education Self-Check 3.4

WRAPPING IT UP

Back to the Cases

Now that you have read about building partnerships through collaboration, look back at the teacher stories at the beginning of the chapter. Then go to MyLab Education to apply the knowledge you've gained in this chapter to each case.

MyLab Education Application Exercise 3.1: Case Study 3.1

MS. RANDLEMAN and Ms. Pickett have nine students who have individualized education programs (IEPs) in their co-taught biology class of 36 students, representing a broad range of special needs. Ms. Randleman and Ms. Pickett blend their expertise to reach every student, usually through grouping and occasionally through whole-group instruction. Their goal is to have every student pass the high-stakes biology test at the end of the semester, a requirement for graduation. They met this goal with last year's students, and so they are optimistic about reaching it again.

MyLab Education Application Exercise 3.2: Case Study 3.2

MR. HERNANDEZ, a third-grade teacher, has a student in his class named Kenneth who has autism spectrum disorder (ASD) and, although he is capable of learning similarly to his peers, he is falling behind and also becoming increasingly aggressive. The school principal suggests that perhaps Kenneth should be placed in a special education classroom full-time, but Mr. Hernandez is committed to finding out what Kenneth's behavior means and how to help Kenneth express himself without the current worrisome behaviors.

MyLab Education Application Exercise 3.3: Case Study 3.3

MS. REYES, an eighth-grade English teacher and team leader, is meeting with Mr. Barnes, the special education teacher; Ms. Whitmore, a school district special education administrator; and Ms. Jordan, Annie's mother. Annie has struggled in school since kindergarten, when she was identified as having an intellectual disability. Annie's mother refuses to allow Annie to receive any educational services in a separate special education setting and has threatened to file a complaint against the school district regarding her daughter's education.

Summary

LO 3.1 Collaboration has become an important job responsibility for all educators and is especially central in educating students with special needs. It is a style professionals use in interacting with others, and it includes voluntary participation, parity, shared goals, shared responsibility for key decisions, shared accountability for outcomes, shared resources, and the emergence of trust, respect, and a collaborative belief system. Collaboration is more effective when educators have a strong commitment to it and refine their skills for interacting with others.

LO 3.2 Collaboration has many special education applications, including shared problem solving, co-teaching, working in teams, and consulting. General educators participate in all of these applications.

LO 3.3 When working with parents, you should use *family-centered practices*, including striving to understand parents' perspectives on having a child with a disability, collaborating with them based on your understanding of their perspective, interacting respectfully with them, and responding professionally when disagreements occur.

LO 3.4 Understanding the roles and responsibilities of paraprofessionals and your obligation to direct their work is essential. Basing your collaboration on this understanding leads to positive working relationships, particularly if you directly and appropriately address problems that occur as paraprofessionals work with you on behalf of the students with disabilities.

APPLICATIONS IN TEACHING PRACTICE

Collaboration in the Washington School District

Although the administrators in the Washington School District would tell you that staff members have always worked together well, when increasing the use of inclusive practices was made part of the district's strategic plan, it became clear that collaboration also needed to be a priority. Each principal was asked to work with staff members to incorporate collaboration into the school's improvement plan. Each school created a committee to study collaboration and its application in inclusive schools, set priorities, and plan staff development. Committee members also created a plan for evaluating the impact of increased collaboration on student outcomes.

In every elementary, middle, and high school, the teachers reviewed their school mission statements as a starting point for discussions of their beliefs about how students learn, how teachers teach, and how schools can be learning communities. In most of the schools, the teachers quickly realized that their mission statements did not explicitly say that teachers in the school were expected to work together to meet the needs of all their students. During after-school meetings, the mission statements were revised.

Next, teachers began to discuss various forms their collaboration might take. In one elementary school, Carole, a first-grade teacher anticipating a class group with many special needs, argued strongly for co-teaching. She stated that she needed someone to help her for at least a couple of hours each day. Peggy, another teacher, reminded her that with only two special education teachers and one paraprofessional available for everyone from kindergarten through fifth grade, she was asking for far too much, especially because these professionals also had other responsibilities. Jim, the special education teacher who works with students

with moderate and severe disabilities, agreed. He noted that he had to reserve time to work individually with some of his students in a special education setting.

Co-teaching was a popular topic in other schools, too. In the middle school, one special education teacher was assigned to each team, and the teachers learned that they had the responsibility for deciding how to co-teach while making sure that students' IEP goals were addressed. Most teams decided that co-teaching should occur mostly in English and math classes. In the high school, the teachers approached their investigations with caution. First, they decided that special education teachers should be assigned to academic departments. Then they decided that co-teaching would occur only in English and math for the upcoming year; other services would remain the same while everyone became accustomed to working together, even though teachers in science and social studies objected because of their need to improve student outcomes, especially those of students with disabilities. These teachers also decided that they wanted to learn more about collaboration skills as they applied to their MTSS process, and they arranged with a local consultant for professional development as well as for observations of and feedback related to their interactions during MTSS meetings.

Principals decided to survey teachers, paraprofessionals, and parents at the halfway point of the school year and again at the end of the year in order to gauge perceptions of these efforts to enhance collaboration. They also worked with the district's data manager to develop several strategies to measure impact on student learning and behavior.

With much excitement and some anxiety, the district's administrators and teachers finished their detailed planning. They were a little concerned about new teachers who might be hired during the summer and how to help them become oriented quickly to the collaborative initiative. They recognized that additional topics would need to be addressed. For example, the new teacher evaluation system was designed only for teachers working solo; its application in a co-teaching setting would have to be clarified for teachers and administrators. They also were concerned about whether they could demonstrate that collaboration improved student achievement, the ultimate goal. However, they felt they had worked closely to develop the plan and were eager to implement it.

QUESTIONS

1. Which characteristics of collaboration can you identify in the teachers' interactions and plans? Which are not evident?

2. How were the teachers working to ensure their collaborative efforts would be successful? What is the role of the principal in fostering collaboration?

3. How would you respond to Carole? What do you recommend she do? What do you recommend that her colleagues do in their interactions with her?

4. Why would it be important to incorporate a statement about collaboration into a school mission statement? Check the websites of your local schools. If their mission statements are posted, do they address collaboration, either directly or indirectly?

5. How could the teachers communicate with parents about their plans? What reactions might they expect from parents? Why? How could they involve parents in their programs?

6. How might collaboration among professionals be similar and different in the elementary schools, middle schools, and high schools? What opportunities and constraints might exist for each group?

7. How could the teacher evaluation system lead to disagreements among the teachers? If you were asked to chair a work group to address this topic, what resources would you seek? What do you think the key question to address would be?

CHAPTER 4

Assessing Student Needs

LEARNING OUTCOMES

After you read this chapter, you will be able to:

4-1 Explain how general education teachers can contribute significantly to the assessment process.

4-2 Describe the use of high stakes, standardized achievement, psychological tests, and alternate assessment in making education decisions for students with special needs.

4-3 Provide accommodations and modifications for students with disabilities on standardized tests.

4-4 Define curriculum-based assessment; explain its benefits; construct types in basic academic skills, content-area knowledge and independent learning skills; and use to make decisions involving special education.

MS. LYONS is concerned that Rob, a student in her second-grade class, is not keeping up with the rest of the class in math. On this fall's RtI universal screening assessment, Rob's results indicated that he was at the at-risk level in math computation, concepts, and applications. Ms. Lyons knows that he will be taking the state math test in third grade, and she is afraid that if he continues to fall behind, he won't meet state standards. She plans to assign Rob to a Tier 2 math group to provide him with extra help. Mr. Blair, the special education teacher, suggests that Ms. Lyons do some informal assessment herself to make sure she is providing him with help in the right areas of need and can monitor his progress adequately.

What kinds of assessments can Ms. Lyons use to clarify Rob's problems in math? How might these assessments help her make changes in Rob's Tier 2 math instruction? Under what circumstances should she consider Rob for Tier 3 instruction, special education, or other services?

MR. BLOUNT teaches a high school U.S. history class. He has learned that three students with disabilities will be in his class this fall. Mr. Blount was told that these students have some reading problems and may have trouble reading the textbook. He decides to make up a test to give at the beginning of the year to see how well all of his students are able to use the textbook. Using a section of a chapter from the text, he writes questions to test how well students can figure out the meanings of key vocabulary words, use parts of the book (e.g., the table of contents, glossary, and index), read maps, and read for information (e.g., note main ideas and draw conclusions). When Mr. Blount gives the test, he finds that the three identified students have trouble reading the text, but many other students also have difficulty.

How could Mr. Blount use the information from this assessment to adjust his instruction for his students with and without disabilities?

ROBERTO is a student with moderate to severe intellectual disabilities who is in Ms. Benis's sixth-grade social studies class. As a result of Roberto's cerebral palsy, he has significant cognitive, language, and motor deficits. Roberto can read his name, as well as some high-frequency sight words. He uses a wheelchair, and he has trouble with fine motor movements such as cutting and handwriting. Roberto speaks with the aid of an assistive technology device called a Communicator.

How can Roberto meet the state standards for sixth grade in social studies? What kinds of assessments can Ms. Benis use to determine whether Roberto is meeting standards in social studies?

As an increasing number of students with disabilities is being served in general education classes, teachers need to make many important decisions that can greatly affect these students' success. This is particularly important in view of federal requirements in the Individuals with Disabilities Education Act (IDEA) that students with disabilities participate in district testing programs, have access to the general education curriculum, and make meaningful progress toward meeting general curriculum goals. For example, in the preceding vignettes, Ms. Lyons wanted to help Rob before he failed the state math test in grade 3, which will be based on state standards. Mr. Blount wanted to find out whether his students could read the textbook for his history class to help him decide which students would benefit from adjustments in his instruction such as oral or highlighted text. Ms. Benis needed to include Roberto, who had significant disabilities, in her social studies class but had to figure out how he would meet state standards. To respond effectively in situations such as these, teachers need accurate, relevant information. Thus, they need to develop informal measures to help them make instructional decisions, as well as participate in special education decision making. This chapter explores assessment strategies that help general education teachers contribute to the process of decision making for students with special needs. This process involves determining whether a student needs special education services; when a student is ready to learn in inclusive settings; when an alternative to state testing is required; and what classroom accommodations and modifications to try, continue to use, or change. The assessment strategies described are also helpful if your school is implementing RtI/MTSS.

How Do Your Student Assessments Contribute to Special Education Decisions?

As a general education teacher, you make an important contribution to the process of identifying and meeting the needs of students with special needs. A major part of that contribution involves assessing student needs. Assessment has been defined as the process of gathering information to monitor progress and to make educational decisions when necessary (Overton, 2015). The most common ways of collecting information are through standardized, commercially produced tests, high-stakes state accountability tests, and informal tests devised by the teacher. Much of the information in this chapter is about ways in which these measures can be used to make decisions about students with special needs. General education teachers contribute assessment information in six important decision-making areas for students with special needs: screening, diagnosis, program placement, curriculum placement, instructional evaluation, and program evaluation.

Screening

> **FYI**
>
> In RtI, screening is referred to as *universal screening* because it involves assessing all students.

In Chapter 2 you learned that screening involves the decision about whether a student's performance differs enough from that of his or her peers to merit changes in instruction, or, eventually, more in-depth assessments to determine the presence of a disability.

For example, to clarify Rob's problems in math, Ms. Lyons from the chapter-opening vignette examined the most recent RtI universal screening assessment results for her class in math and found that Rob was at risk in a number of areas. Ms. Lyons then gave Rob some mini-tests on various math computation skills, concepts, and word problems she had taught to see with which skills in particular Rob was struggling. Ms. Lyons found that a number of other students were performing similarly to Rob. In consultation with her colleagues on the Rti team, she decided to form a small Tier 2 group with Rob and these students.

Classroom teachers are in an ideal position to assess students with special needs and monitor their progress.

Screening assessments are at the heart of prevention-based systems such as the MTSS approach used in Ms. Lyons's school. An explanation of universal screening for academic skills, including how to select and use universal screening measures, is presented in the Instructional Edge feature. Screening measures for student behavior are covered in Chapter 12.

Diagnosis

The major decision related to **diagnosis** concerns eligibility for special education services, a decision you first learned about in Chapter 2. Does a student meet established federal guidelines for being classified as having a disability? If so, what are the nature and extent of the student's disability? For example, Paula was a student in Ms. Clark's class. In September, when Paula appeared to be struggling to keep up with the class in reading, Ms. Clark paired her up with a classmate for 15 minutes before reading each day to go over key words and vocabulary. When Paula's reading accuracy and fluency problems persisted even after four weeks of this extra help, Ms. Clark arranged for her to have 30 minutes more practice later in the day with the reading teacher. After a month of this extra help, Paula still showed no improvement. Ms. Clark suspected Paula had a learning disability and referred her for a case study evaluation. The school psychologist gave Paula a test on cognitive functioning—including a test of memory, attention, and verbal reasoning—and an individual achievement test. She found that Paula was slow in processing visual information (that is, letters, numbers, and shapes) and that her achievement in reading was significantly lower than that of other students her age. However, her achievement in math was at grade level. Ms. Clark evaluated Paula's classroom reading performance by having her read orally and answer questions from a grade-level trade book that was part of the classroom literature program. Paula's oral reading fluency was well below norms for her grade level, and she was able to answer only 40 percent of the comprehension questions correctly. In the end, Paula was declared eligible to receive services for learning disabilities because she did not respond favorably to two levels of extra classroom help, she showed problems processing visual information quickly enough, and her achievement was significantly below grade level as measured by both a standardized achievement test and informal classroom reading tests. The Working Together feature highlights effective ways to communicate to parents the results of diagnostic tests, as well as resulting decisions about placement.

Program Placement

The major **program placement** decision involves the setting in which a student's special education services take place—for example, in a general education classroom, resource room, or separate special education classroom. The individualized education program (IEP) team must make this decision carefully. In the past, the tendency was to pull students out of general education classrooms without considering whether they could be supported within the general education setting instead. In today's schools, the emphasis is on doing all that can be done within the general education class first. This approach is consistent with guidelines for accessing the general education curriculum outlined in IDEA and RtI, in which students with learning disabilities are identified by monitoring how they respond to evidence-based instruction of varying intensity. Still, students have different needs, and some may require specially designed instruction that cannot be delivered in the general education classroom. That is why it is important to make placement decisions based on measures that accurately reflect student performance in class. For example, Carlos was eligible to receive services for learning disabilities in math. His IEP team needed to decide whether his learning needs could be met by adjusting the math methods and materials in the general education classroom or whether he should be provided more intensive, specially designed math instruction in a resource room setting. Carlos's general education teacher gave Carlos and his classmates a series of informal math tests. She found that Carlos was significantly behind his peers on some but not all of the tests; his

MyLab Education

Video Example 4.1: Screening Decisions and the Referral Process

Screening decisions are also an important part of the referral process in special education and pre-referral interventions explained in this video.

INSTRUCTIONAL EDGE 4.1

Using Universal Screening in RtI/MTSS to Identify Students at Risk

What Is Universal Screening?

A key feature of RtI /MTSS is identifying and intervening with students at risk early to prevent problems before they become insurmountable. The process of assessing all students to identify those who are having difficulty learning despite an evidence-based Tier 1 program is called universal screening.

What Are the Qualities of Effective Universal Screening Measures?

- Universal screening measures must accurately classify students who are at risk or not at risk for academic failure. This means that only students who need extra support get it, and that students who need support are not overlooked (Crawford, 2014).
- Universal screening measures must be brief, easy to give, reflect the school's core curriculum, and not interfere with teaching (VanDerHyden et al., 2016).
- Screening should be conducted at a minimum of twice per year (beginning and end of year) and ideally three times per year (beginning, middle, and end of year) (Crawford, 2016). Screening more than once per year allows you to detect students who may no longer be at risk or have become at risk.
- Effective universal screening measures should do no harm to the student. This means they should avoid leading to inequitable treatment and be linked to effective interventions (Hughes & Dexter, 2010; Jenkins, 2009).

How Should a Universal Screening Measure Be Chosen?

- A screening battery that measures multiple aspects of an academic area is more accurate than a test that measures only one (Salinger, 2016). For example, if you are doing universal screening in reading, you would want to measure phonemic awareness, phonics, fluency, and comprehension. In math, you would want to assess math computation, concepts and problem solving.
- There is a research base that shows which universal screening measures are the most accurate. Consult that research base before you select a universal screening measure for your school (See link later in this feature). Not all universal screening measures are created equal (Jenkins, 2009; Salinger, 2016).

How Are At-Risk Students Identified?

- Screening decisions can be based on one score or one score plus a measure that shows how the student responds to instruction. Having a two-stage universal screening process can reduce the number of false positives and allow for more support for students who truly need it (Fuchs, Fuchs, & Compton, 2012).
- Currently, there is no agreement as to what criteria should be used to identify students who are at risk in Tier 1 (Hughes & Dexter, 2010). Some programs use a percentile approach whereby students performing below a certain percentile are considered at risk (Crawford, 2014; Silberglitt & Hintze, 2007). For example, all children scoring below the 25th percentile may be considered at risk. Others may use benchmark performance levels that predict future reading performance. Those using a two-stage approach consider rates of progress toward meeting benchmark goals (Fuchs et al., 2012).
- A potential drawback of an RtI approach is that it can delay the provision of supports for students who need them (Rosenthal & Barned-Smith, 2016). For example, there may be low-performing students who may be better served by going right into Tier 3 rather than having to first experience 10 weeks of Tier 2. Although more research is needed to solve this particular problem, there is some evidence to suggest that using an initial screening score plus additional achievement and cognitive tests can accurately identify those students and place them into a more intensive tier right away (Fuchs et al., 2012; Al Otaiba et al, 2014).

What Measures Are Commonly Used for Universal Screening?

- A list of commonly used universal screening assessments for math and literacy, including an evaluation of their technical adequacy, can be found at (http://www .rti4success.org). Click on "screening" and then "screening tools chart."
- Universal screening is still necessary at the secondary level in order to identify students who (a) have learning problems that did not emerge until later, (b) are in schools with weak or newly-developed prevention programs, (c) are newly arrived English-language learners, and (d) have problems that require long-term interventions (Johnson, Pool, & Carter, 2013). A likely source in addition to assessments available in the elementary years is student performance on high-stakes assessments and/or end-of-grade or end-of-course tests (Johnson, Smith, & Harris, 2009).

FYI

Program placement decisions for students with moderate to severe intellectual disabilities should be based on the supports needed to meet the curricular goals outlined in their IEPs.

math problem solving was very deficient compared to that of his classmates, but his math computational skills were fine. The IEP team decided to keep Carlos in his general education class and to support his instruction in problem solving by providing him extra teacher-guided practice whenever a new problem-solving skill was introduced. The team also decided to carefully monitor Carlos's problem-solving skills; if those skills showed little improvement, they would consider other options.

WORKING TOGETHER 4.1
Communicating Effectively with Parents

Mrs. Perez has just attended a multidisciplinary committee meeting for her son Jorgè and is distraught. First, being in the same room with all those professionals made Mrs. Perez nervous; she felt like an outsider who was there because she had done something wrong. Second, she was embarrassed that her English wasn't very good, so she was afraid to say anything. She had hoped the meeting would result in Jorgè getting extra help, but that was not what happened at all.

The school psychologist, Mr. Tanner, talked too fast and used a lot of technical language Mrs. Perez didn't understand, such as "performance-based," "verbal IQ," and "age- and grade-level expectations." He said Jorge was in the slow-learner range. Mrs. Perez was afraid that he meant her Jorgè was stupid. She thought that Jorgè was unable to understand tests because his English skills weren't very good, but she was afraid to say so.

When the special education teacher said that Jorgè was two to three years below grade level in reading and writing and about a year below level in math, Mrs. Perez wondered whether that meant there was no hope for Jorgè. His teacher said that Jorgè was having trouble keeping up in class and that last year he had failed to pass the state tests in reading and writing. Mrs. Perez wanted to hear more about what the class was doing and how Jorgè was coping with the material, but she was afraid she would offend Jorgè's teacher. Mr. Tanner finished by saying that Jorgè was behind in his skills but achieving as expected given his ability. He said that Jorgè wasn't eligible for special education services and asked Mrs. Perez if she had any questions.

Mrs. Perez knew that Jorgè's English skills were holding him back, but now the committee members were telling her he couldn't get any extra help. Having a million questions but not knowing how to ask them, she nodded her head and left the meeting, afraid that there was no hope for her Jorgè in school.

ADDRESSING THE DILEMMA

Chapter 3 presented communication barriers that can exist between parents and teachers, and this interaction illustrates many of those barriers. How could you address each of the following issues?

- Few attempts were made to make Mrs. Perez feel comfortable.
- Mrs. Perez has difficulty expressing herself in English.
- The team explained the testing and eligibility process using highly technical language that Mrs. Perez did not understand.
- The standardized tests were hastily explained.
- The team did not clearly ensure that Mrs. Perez agreed with its decisions.
- The team did not address Mrs. Perez's primary concern: Getting help for her son.

Curriculum Placement

Curriculum placement involves deciding at what level to begin instruction for students. For an elementary school teacher, such a decision may mean choosing which reading or math book a student should use. For example, Ms. Tolhurst has her students read orally and answer questions to find the appropriate trade books for them to read. That is, she determines the level of difficulty at which the books in her classroom reading program are neither too easy nor too hard for them. At the secondary level, curriculum placement decisions are likely to determine which class in a sequence of classes a student should take. For example, Mr. Nowicki, the guidance counselor, was trying to decide whether to place Scott in Algebra 1. He gave Scott a screening test developed by his state that identifies students at risk for not passing algebra in ninth grade.

Of course, information about curriculum placement also provides teachers with a good measure of the extent to which students with disabilities are accessing the general education curriculum, an explicit goal of IDEA. In the examples just mentioned, a student with a disability in Ms. Tolhurst's class who can read only books that are two levels below grade level could be seen as having difficulty accessing the general education reading curriculum. In contrast, a student who enters Mr. Nowicki's algebra class with all of the necessary prerequisite skills is fully accessing the district math curriculum.

Instructional Evaluation

Decisions in instructional evaluation involve whether to continue or change instructional procedures that have been initiated with students. These decisions are made by carefully monitoring student progress. For example, Ms. Bridgewater is starting a peer-tutoring program to help Cecily, a student with severe intellectual disabilities, read her name and the names of her family members. Each week,

Ms. Bridgewater tests Cecily to see how many of the names she has learned. She uses the results of the tests to find out whether the peer-tutoring program is helping Cecily make progress. In another example, Mr. Jackson decides to accompany each of his history lectures with a graphic organizer of the material. He gives weekly quizzes to find out whether the graphic organizer is helping his students better learn the material. Schools implementing RtI use information collected from progress-monitoring assessments to assign students to instructional tiers.

Program Evaluation

Program evaluation decisions involve whether a student's special education program should be terminated, continued as is, or modified. One consideration is whether or not the student is accessing the general education curriculum by meeting standards, as evidenced by reaching goals or attaining benchmark levels on assessments. For example, when Addie, a student with a reading disability, attained benchmark levels in reading fluency and comprehension for her grade level, her program was changed. She was integrated into general education for the entire reading block, and her progress was carefully monitored to ensure that her gains were maintained.

Another way to evaluate the success of special education programming is by monitoring the attainment of IEP goals. For example, Amanda is receiving social work services twice per week. Her IEP goal is to decrease the number of times she has a verbal confrontation with Mr. Alvarez, her English teacher. Mr. Alvarez is keeping track of the number of times daily that Amanda refuses to comply with his requests to see whether sessions with the social worker are improving Amanda's behavior.

MyLab Education Self-Check 4.1

How Are Standardized Achievement Tests and Psychological Tests Used in Decision Making for Students with Special Needs?

Numerous information sources are used in programming for students with special needs. The use of multiple assessment sources is consistent with the principle of nondiscriminatory testing, discussed in Chapter 2, which says that no single measure should be used to establish eligibility for special education services or make other important educational decisions such as those just discussed. The measures described in this section include high-stakes achievement tests, standardized achievement tests, and psychological tests.

High-Stakes Achievement Tests

A key requirement of IDEA is that students with disabilities have maximum access to the general education curriculum. Unlike in the past, however, access today is defined not as spending a certain amount of time in general education but as making meaningful progress toward meeting general curriculum goals (Nolet & McLaughlin, 2005). In general education today, that means meeting educational standards. Standards, which are set by individual states, comprise what students should be able to know or do as a result of their public education. For the past three decades, general dissatisfaction with public education has dramatically raised learning standards and has led to increased accountability for schools as they teach students to attain those standards. Despite recent efforts to establish national standards such as the Common Core State Standards (CCSS), the primary responsibility for setting learning standards remains at the state level.

As you probably know, high-stakes tests are assessments designed to measure whether students have attained learning standards. These tests are a type of assessment referred to as *criterion referenced* because they involve comparing student performance to a specific level of performance, or benchmark, rather than to a norm, or average, as with traditional standardized achievement tests. Most states have created their own high-stakes tests based on an agreed-on set of learning outcomes. For each identified outcome, standards or benchmarks are set that represent an acceptable level of knowledge or competence. Schools are then evaluated on the basis of the percentage of students meeting standards on each of the learning outcomes identified. For example, State A wanted all of its fifth graders to be able to comprehend the key elements of short stories, such as character, setting, problem identification, problem resolution, and moral. Reading experts were chosen by the state to create an item that would test student competence in comprehending short stories. The experts chose a short story written at the fifth-grade level and developed a series of multiple-choice questions about the story elements. They then tried out the test on a diverse sample of students and through careful analysis determined that students who could answer at least 90 percent of the story-element questions were competent at identifying story elements. State A then tested all its fifth-grade students on this item to determine the percentage able to identify key elements in short stories. These tests are referred to as *high-stakes* because their results carry consequences for teachers and administrators. When students perform well, teachers and administrators are rewarded; when students don't meet standards, schools are criticized.

How do high-stakes tests relate to students meeting educational standards? What are the implications for students with special needs?

IDEA requires that most students with disabilities take their states' high-stakes tests. This is how districts can show the degree of access to the general education curriculum attained by students with disabilities. These IDEA requirements were reinforced by the reauthorization of the Elementary and Secondary Education Act (ESEA), the Every Student Succeeds Act (ESSA) of 2015, which, with the exception of up to 1 percent of students who need alternate assessments, requires that all children in each of grades 3 through 8 and at least once in grades 10 through 12 take high-stakes tests to show whether they are meeting state standards or making adequate progress toward them. Both IDEA and ESEA/ESSA require that the results for students with disabilities be aggregated with the results of the other students and reported publicly. Results for students with disabilities, along with ELs, students who are economically disadvantaged, and students from racial and ethnic groups must also be disaggregated and reported separately; students with disabilities who are tested are held to the same standards as their classmates without disabilities. Research has shown that holding school leaders accountable for the performance of students with disabilities makes leaders more likely to pay attention to their learning (Thurlow & Thompson, 2002). An increased focus on the learning of students with disabilities can lead to greater involvement for them in the general education program and, ultimately, to higher achievement (Ysseldyke, Dennison, & Nelson, 2003).

FYI

In a national survey of public school teachers of grades K–12, Rentner, Kobel, and Frizzell (2016) found that 68 percent of teachers of math and 71 percent of teachers of English/language arts said that the information from high-stakes tests caused them to modify their teaching at least somewhat.

MyLab Education

Video Example 4.2: Preparing Students for High Stakes Testing

This video explains how high stakes tests are standardized. What are the potential advantages and disadvantages of high stakes tests for students with disabilities? Why is it important to prepare students on how to take your state's high stakes tests?

WWW RESOURCES

Learn about the National Assessment of Educational Progress (NAEP), the only ongoing national test of academic progress, at https://nces.ed.gov/nationsreportcard/about/.

Why is the issue of high-stakes for students with disabilities important for you? The answer is that high stakes tests reflect state standards and students with disabilities in all states are required to meet those standards. Therefore, it is critical for you to carefully monitor the progress of your students with disabilities and, if needed, to provide extra supports or resources to ensure that the standards are met. Part of effective monitoring requires paying close attention to the policies of your particular state as well as the results of high-stakes tests. More important, effective monitoring requires you to keep track of student performance on a daily basis using assessments such as the ones described in this chapter. To find out your state policies regarding students with disabilities and high stakes test and graduation requirements, go to nceo.umn.edu; click "Graduation Requirements" under "Standards and Accountability," and click relevant tiles under "Related Publications."

Standardized Achievement Tests

Another common source of information for making educational decisions is standardized achievement tests. These tests are designed to measure academic progress, or what students have retained from the curriculum. Unlike the high-stakes tests just described, standardized achievement tests are *norm referenced*. In a norm-referenced test, the performance of one student is compared to the average performance of other students in the country who are the same age or at the same grade level. Student performance is often summarized using grade equivalents and/or percentile ranks.

GROUP-ADMINISTERED TESTS Two major types of standardized achievement tests are group-administered and individually administered diagnostic tests. As the name implies, group-administered standardized achievement tests are completed by large groups of students at one time; this usually means that the general education teacher gives the test to the entire class. These tests assess skills across many areas of the curriculum, none in much depth. For this reason, they are intended to be used solely as screening measures. Nonetheless, caution is advised in using these scores, even if only for screening. As with any test, the general education teacher should be sure that students with disabilities receive appropriate accommodations when taking the test. Otherwise, the resulting score may be a measure more of the disability than of the ability. For example, Alicia has a learning disability in reading and has problems comprehending written directions. When Alicia obtained a low score on a group-administered standardized test in writing, it was hard to determine whether her low score was due to a lack of knowledge or her inability to follow the directions. Specific testing accommodations are described in the next section.

Another potential problem with group-administered standardized achievement tests is that the norms used to interpret scores are of little use when evaluating students with disabilities; these students are often excluded from the norming group because they have taken the test with accommodations. Also, all students may be affected by the fact that the content of the test might not match what is taught in a particular classroom (Ysseldyke, Burns, Scholin, & Parker, 2010). For example, one teacher stressed problem solving in his science class, whereas the standardized achievement test given in his district stressed the memorization of facts. Therefore, the teacher had to give his own tests to determine whether students were learning the material.

Whereas in the past group-administered standardized achievement tests were used to make administrative and policy decisions on a school-district or even national level, it appears that today, high-stakes tests are being used more often for these purposes. Given the time and effort it takes to test an entire school, as well as the value of instructional time to children's learning, many schools have found it more prudent to use only their state's high-stakes accountability test.

INDIVIDUALLY ADMINISTERED TESTS A special education teacher or the school psychologist usually gives **individually administered diagnostic tests** as part of a student's case study evaluation. Although these tests may screen student performance in several curricular areas, they tend to be more diagnostic in nature. For example, an individually administered diagnostic reading test may include test components in the areas of letter identification, word recognition, oral reading, comprehension, and phonetic skills; a diagnostic test in math might include math computation, fractions, geometry, word problems, measurement, and time. Because individually administered diagnostic tests provide information on a range of specific skills, they can be useful as an information source in making educational decisions. For example, Tamara scored two years below grade level on the vocabulary subtest of an individually administered diagnostic test in reading. On the basis of this finding, the teacher of her Tier 2 RtI group added instruction in vocabulary taken from her American history text. Individually administered diagnostic tests may also be useful within RtI frameworks for helping identify students with learning disabilities without having to wait for them to fail (Adlof, Catts, & Lee, 2012; Fuchs, Fuchs, & Compton, 2012).

Although individually administered diagnostic tests may be more helpful than group-administered achievement tests, they are still subject to many of the same problems. Again, you should always verify findings from these tests using more informal measures based on the content you teach.

Psychological Tests

Psychological tests are used as part of the process of evaluating students with special needs, particularly to determine whether a student has intellectual or learning disabilities. Reports of the results of these tests are often written by school psychologists and consist of a summary of the findings and the implications for instruction. Psychological tests can include intelligence tests and tests related to learning disabilities (Overton, 2015; Salvia, Ysseldyke, & Whitmer, 2016).

The overall purpose of psychological tests is to measure abilities that affect how efficiently students learn in an instructional situation. These abilities are inferred based on student responses to items that the test author believes represent that particular ability. For example, comprehension, an important learning ability, is often assessed on psychological tests (Salvia et al., 2016). To test comprehension, students may be asked to read and answer questions about a series of directions or other tasks described in printed material. Student scores are then compared to a norm group of other same-age students, with an average score being 100. Other abilities commonly assessed by psychological tests include generalization (the ability to recognize similarities across objects, events, or vocabulary), general or background information, vocabulary, induction (the ability to figure out a rule or principle based on a series of situations), abstract reasoning, and memory (Salvia et al., 2016).

Psychological tests can be helpful if they clarify why students may not be learning in class and lead to effective changes in instruction. For example, the results of Tiffany's test showed that she had difficulty with visual memory. Her biology teacher, Ms. Fasbacher, felt that this was related to her poor performance in labeling parts of the human body on her tests. As a result, Ms. Fasbacher provided Tiffany with extra tutoring prior to each test. Interpreting the results of psychological reports seems less daunting if you follow these five general guidelines:

1. Do not be intimidated by the sometimes generous quantity of technical terms and jargon. You have the right to expect that reports be translated into instructionally relevant language.

2. In the event of discrepancies between psychological reports and your experience, do not automatically discount your experience. The results of psychological tests are most valid when corroborated by classroom experience.

> **FYI**
>
> Standardized tests can be biased against students from diverse backgrounds. Use them only in conjunction with other formal and informal measures.

INSTRUCTIONAL EDGE 4.2

Strategies for Fair Assessment of Diverse Students

Although today's teachers are much more aware of the possibility of bias in assessing students who live in poverty and students from culturally diverse backgrounds, bias and discrimination continue to exist. The following two lists identify areas that can be problematic when assessing diverse students and provide strategies for assessing and interpreting their performance more accurately, respectively.

PROBLEM

1. Students may exhibit test anxiety due to lack of familiarity with the assessment process.
2. Students may lack motivation to perform well on tests because of differing cultural expectations.
3. Students may not respond to traditional motivators.
4. Students' test scores may be depressed because the assessor is unfamiliar or speaks a different language.
5. Students may have different communication styles; for example, they may not feel comfortable asking for help with directions or may respond using fewer words.
6. Students may be unwilling to take risks; for example, they may be reluctant to guess on a test even though it is to their benefit.
7. Students may be accustomed to working at a slower pace.
8. Students may lack exposure to test content.
9. Students may not be proficient in the language used for a test.
10. Students may speak with a dialect that differs from that of the assessor.

RECOMMENDATION

1. Give students practice tests.
2. Qualify test performance with class performance.
3. Allow more time to establish rapport and gain trust.
4. Check for understanding of directions; avoid automatically penalizing students for not saying enough or not giving details.
5. Teach test-taking skills. For example, teach students strategies for when and how to make a best guess on a test.
6. Extend test-taking time to accommodate students' pace.
7. Eliminate unfamiliar content or do not give the test.
8. Assess students using both English and students' native language.
9. Do not count dialectical differences as errors; examine your attitudes about nonstandard dialects for potential bias.

RESEARCH-BASED PRACTICES

Two testing accommodations are especially helpful for ELs:

- Modifying the language (but not the content) of the test items by reducing low-frequency vocabulary and complex language structures
- Providing students with definitions or simple paraphrases of potentially unfamiliar or difficult words on the test (Abedi, Hofstetter, & Lord, 2004)

WWW RESOURCES

The home page for the National Council on Measurement in Education (NCME), http://www.ncme.org, provides information on the organization and links to other relevant measurement-related websites.

Keep in mind that your impressions are the result of many more hours of classroom observation than are psychological evaluations, which are based on fewer samples of student behavior and on samples that represent behavior that takes place outside the classroom.

3. Be sure to check the technical adequacy of the psychological tests included in your report. You may be surprised to find that many of these tests are not acceptable. The recent emphasis in RtI/MTSS of using students' responses to instruction to identify learning disabilities further reinforces the importance of not relying solely on standardized tests.

4. Be sure to check for possible cultural bias. The various ways in which psychological and other tests can be biased, along with suggestions for making them more fair, are presented in the Instructional Edge feature.

5. Keep in mind that the primary purpose of psychological tests is to establish possible explanations for particular learning, behavioral, or social and emotional problems. Such explanations should be springboards for helping students overcome these problems, not excuses for students' lack of achievement.

For a wealth of information on understanding psychological tests, go to http://www.apa.org. Click "Publications and Data Bases," search "Psychological Tests," and click "FAQ/Finding Information About Psychological Tests."

How Can I Provide Accommodations and Modifications for Students with Disabilities on Standardized Tests?

To ensure that the scores obtained are accurate, students with disabilities are entitled to a range of testing accommodations and modifications on standardized tests.

Testing Accommodations

Common accommodations include changing the setting of the test (e.g., allowing students to take tests in special education classrooms), changing the timing of the test (e.g., providing extended time or more frequent breaks), changing the response format (e.g., allowing students to mark responses in test booklets rather than on Scantron sheets), and changing the presentation format (e.g., using a braille edition of a test or giving directions in sign language) (Roeber, 2002; Thurlow, Elliott, & Ysseldyke, 2003). A more complete description of the accommodations available and a process for finding the right accommodations for individual students is provided in the Professional Edge feature. The advantages and challenges of using computer-based testing with students with disabilities is in Technology Notes.

> **RESEARCH-BASED PRACTICES**
>
> Feldman, Kim, and Elliott (2011) found that testing accommodations boosted the test-related self-efficacy and motivation of eighth-grade students with disabilities.

Alternate Assessments

As you have learned, IDEA and ESEA/ESSA require states to include students with disabilities in statewide and district-wide educational assessments. Although most students with disabilities are able to participate when given appropriate accommodations, up to 1 percent of students with disabilities are entitled to

---

PROFESSIONAL EDGE 4.1

Accommodations for Students with Disabilities on Standardized Tests

Under guidelines from IDEA and ESEA/ESSA, most students with disabilities are required to take district and state standardized tests, including state high-stakes tests. A list of standard accommodations provided is shown here. Keep in mind that research on effective strategies for determining which students get which accommodations is still being done. Given the range of abilities within all disability groups, it is recommended that teachers avoid using students' labels to make these decisions and instead base them on individual student characteristics.

UNIVERSAL DESIGN

As applied to assessment, universal design is the idea that tests designed with built-in supports minimize the need for accommodations (Lazarus, Thurlow, Lail, & Christensen, 2009). Lazarus and colleagues (2009) assert that universally designed assessments should have the following qualities:

- Accessible, nonbiased items
- Simple, clear, and intuitive instructions and procedures
- Maximum readability and comprehensibility
- Maximum legibility
- Precise definition of what is being measured (p. 78)

TYPES OF TESTING ACCOMMODATIONS

Scheduling/Timing

- Providing extended time
- Providing unlimited time
- Testing over multiple days
- Adjusting the testing order
- Giving breaks as needed

Setting

- Testing in separate location
- Testing individually or in small groups
- Providing preferential seating such as carrels
- Providing adaptive furniture/equipment
- Making environment arrangements in lighting, acoustics, and sound
- Eliminating distractions

Method of Presentation

- Using Braille or large print
- Increasing spacing between items
- Increasing size of answer spaces/bubbles
- Decreasing number of items per page
- Testing orally
- Simplifying/clarifying/presenting orally, test directions
- Providing cues (e.g., arrows and stop signs) on answer form
- Presenting only one sentence per line

Method of Response

- Writing answers on the test booklet
- Using additional paper for math calculations
- Dictating answers to a recorder or scribe
- Responding using technology (e.g., assistive technology, word processing)
- Receiving help with copying between drafts

Finally, Thurlow, Elliott, and Ysseldyke (2003) suggest making any accommodations that are needed but don't fit under the common categories listed here.

TECHNOLOGY NOTES 4.1
Using High-Stakes Computer-Based Testing with Students with Disabilities

High-stakes paper and pencil tests are increasingly being replaced by computer-based testing (CBT). Computer-based tests have the potential to be dramatically more accessible for students with disabilities because accommodations can be built right into the software. While the use of CBT with students with disabilities has many potential advantages, its usage poses important challenges as well. Advantages and challenges of using CBT with students with disabilities as they relate to the testing areas of timing/scheduling, setting, presentation, and student responding are summarized below.

	Advantages	Challenges
Timing/Scheduling	Makes individualization easier (e.g., allows breaks, multiple test sessions and individual timings).	Multiple test sessions raise potential security issues, scheduling problems, and issues related to saving responses.
Setting	Aids accommodation anonymity and reduces class disruptions such as those caused by read-alouds and speech recognition systems.	Requires computer and location availability and comparability of results; occasionally need to reduce distractions from peripherals and glare from windows and lights.
Presentation	Tests can be adapted for font size, graphics, screen size, read-aloud capabilities, headphones, highlighting text, speech-to-text capabilities, spell checking, the option to self-select alternative directions, signed instructions and/or screen readers, and capacity for multiple screen and text colors.	Requires up-to-date technology; digital voice may be difficult to understand; technical terminology may differ from instruction (e.g. H_2O and water); Braille/large print magnification difficult to create in some formats; need clarity of directions and navigational scheme between items and pages.
Responding	Multiple options for selecting responses; access to online calculators and spell checkers can increase student confidence	Requires preparation of students and teachers in computer skills needed to access accommodations; operation of online calculators can be difficult; working memory can be taxed; speech recognition software may not work for some; need paper and pencil options for some.
Other Benefit Areas	Improved test security; potential for more universally-designed assessments; increased chance of correct, consistent test delivery	

Sources: "Students with Learning Disabilities and Computer-Based High Stakes Testing," by W. R. Gelbart, 2016, *Intervention in School and Clinic*, retrieved from http://journals.sagepub.com/doi/abs/10.1177/1053451216676706; "Using Computer-Based Tests with Students with Disabilities: NCEO Policy Directions," by S. Thompson, M. Thurlow, & M. Moore, 2003, Synthesis Report No. 15, Minneapolis: University of Minnesota, National Center on Educational Outcomes; "Computer-Based Testing: Practices and Considerations," by M. Thurlow, S.S. Lazarus, D. Albus, & J. Hodgson, 2010, Synthesis Report No. 78, Minneapolis: University of Minnesota, National Center on Educational Outcomes.

testing modifications in the form of alternate assessments geared to their individual needs as specified on their IEPs. The most common group of students taking **alternate assessments** are students with disabilities who typically work on a more individualized curriculum and do not have to meet the same requirements as those students graduating with a standard diploma. In other words, they are required to meet the same broad standards as your other students, but they meet them in different, more basic ways. For example, Damon met the standard of completing a search for post-secondary opportunities by compiling a list of his work preferences and specific jobs aligned with his preferences. Sibilie demonstrated her effective use of technology by using an augmentative communication device across a range of school and community settings. Carolyn, a student with multiple disabilities, demonstrated achievement in skills and values related to physical activity by participating in a volleyball game in physical education class. Linus demonstrated his ability to use patterns to understand events by recognizing that

Students with more severe disabilities participate in alternate assessments that stress authentic skills and experiences in real-life environments. What skills do you think are being assessed here?

on days when his paraprofessional wasn't in school he had less time to get ready for recess.

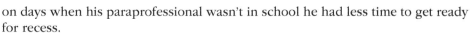

Alternate assessment information can be collected in a number of ways, including: (1) a portfolio or collection of student work gathered to demonstrate student performance on specific skills and knowledge; (2) an IEP-linked body of evidence or collection of work, similar to a portfolio, demonstrating student performance on standards-based IEP goals and objectives; (3) performance assessments or direct measures of a student's skill, usually in a one-on-one assessment; (4) a checklist of skills reviewed by persons familiar with the student; and (5) a traditional test requiring student responses, typically with a correct and incorrect forced-choice answer format (Browder, Wakeman, & Flowers, 2006; Towles-Reeves et al., 2009).

The IEP team considers these three questions when deciding whether a student should take an alternate assessment and how the assessment should be designed.

1. *What are the district's eligibility requirements for alternate assessments?* Keep in mind that only small numbers of students have disabilities so severe that they are eligible. The decision to give an alternate assessment should not be based on whether the student is expected to do poorly on the general education assessment.

2. *Is the focus of the assessment on authentic skills and on assessing experiences in community or real-life environments?* For a younger child, the community might mean the school, playground, or home; for a high school senior, the community might mean the store, bank, or other commercial or public sites.

3. *Is the assessment aligned with state standards?* The skills assessed should have a meaningful relationship to content areas covered by the standards, such as reading and math. For example, one of Clifford's IEP goals in language is to communicate by pointing to pictures on a communication board. Chatrice is learning to give correct coins to the bus driver as a way to meet the math standards. As the general education teacher who is responsible for students meeting the regular state standards, you may be in the best position to answer this question of standards alignment.

RESEARCH-BASED PRACTICES

Alternate assessments need to be highly individualized in order to meaningfully measure progress (Goldstein and Behuniak, 2012).

WWW RESOURCES

For information on the use of technology in *alternate* assessments, go to www .electronicportfolios.com; click on *electronic portfolio development*.

The United States Office of Special Education Programs has published a tool kit containing research-based ideas on large-scale assessments, alternate assessments, progress monitoring, and RtI. You can access this toolkit using the link: https://www.osepideasthatwork.org/federal-resources-stakeholders/tool-kits/tool-kit-teaching-and-assessing-students-disabilities.

MyLab Education Self-Check 4.2

What Are Curriculum-Based Assessments and How Can I Use Them to Make Special Education Decisions?

Because of the limited utility of standardized achievement tests and psychological reports for making day-to-day instructional decisions, you need other tools in order to be a partner in the evaluation process. Curriculum-based assessment (CBA) is an effective option that in many instances can be an alternative to standardized tests. CBA has been defined as a method of measuring students' levels of achievement in terms of what they are taught in the classroom (Deno, 2003; Hosp, 2008). In CBA, student performance also is measured repeatedly over time, and the results are used to guide instruction (Hintze, Christ, & Methe, 2006; Hosp & Hosp, 2003). CBA has a number of attractive features. When using CBA, you select the skills that are assessed based on what you teach in class, thus ensuring a match between what is taught and what is tested. This match makes CBA measures accurate indicators of student access to the general education curriculum and ideal for use in prereferral or RtI systems. Curriculum-based measurement (CBM) is a particular kind of curriculum-based assessment. CBM is characterized by an emphasis on general indicators in basic skills, an extensive research base establishing its technical adequacy, and standardized measurement tasks and scoring procedures that are fluency-based (Deno, 2003; Fuchs, 2017).

In the chapter-opening vignette, before placing Rob in an RtI Tier 2 group, Ms. Lyons gave him some curriculum-based assessments in math to determine the specific kinds of problems he was having. She then implemented a peer-tutoring program and used these same tests to measure its effectiveness. Mr. Blount used an informal reading assessment based on his U.S. history textbook to see how well his students were able to read the text. Research shows that when teachers use CBA to evaluate student progress and adjust their instruction accordingly, student achievement increases significantly (Deno, 2003; Stecker, Fuchs, & Fuchs, 2005).

Two major kinds of CBAs are commonly used: probes of basic academic skills (for example, reading, math, and writing) and probes of content-area knowledge and learning strategies (for example, vocabulary knowledge, prerequisite skills, textbook reading, and note taking). Although probes of basic academic skills relate more directly to elementary school teachers and probes of content-area knowledge and learning strategies to middle and high school teachers, each of these measures is relevant for both groups. For example, high school students need to perform basic skills fluently if they are to have ready access to curriculum content; elementary school students need early instruction in subject-matter knowledge and learning strategies to make the difficult transition to middle and high school instruction easier.

Probes of Basic Academic Skills

Probes are quick and easy measures of student performance in the basic skill areas of reading, math, and written expression. They consist of timed samples

PROFESSIONAL EDGE 4.2

Assessing Student Fluency in Basic Academic Skills

When basic skills or other academic content is assessed informally in the classroom, *student accuracy* is usually stressed. For example, we say that Jill formed 85 percent of her cursive letters correctly, John was 90 percent accurate on his addition facts, or Al identified key pieces of lab equipment with 100 percent accuracy. Although accuracy is important because it tells us whether a student has acquired a skill or section of content, accuracy is not the only useful index of pupil performance. *Student fluency*, or how quickly a student is able to perform a skill or recall academic material, is also relevant. Before you consider the reasons for assessing student fluency provided here, consider this: If your car needed service and you had your choice between two mechanics, both of whom did accurate work and charged $85 an hour but one of whom worked twice as fast as the other, which mechanic would you choose?

THE RATE RATIONALE

- Students who are proficient in a skill are more likely to remember the skill, even if they do not need to use it very often. If they forget the skill, they need less time to relearn it.

- Students who are proficient in a basic skill are better able to master more advanced skills. For example, students who can perform addition problems fluently often acquire advanced multiplication skills more easily.
- Performance of basic skills at an automatic level frees students to perform higher-level skills more readily. For example, students who can read fluently with understanding are more likely to be successful in high school classes that require reading lengthy textbook assignments in little time. Students who know their math facts without counting on their fingers can solve word problems more efficiently.
- Students with special needs are often so labeled because they work more slowly than their peers. Fluency scores allow teachers to compare these students directly with their classmates on this important dimension of speed; they also provide a useful index of student progress, including, for some students, the extent to which supports are needed to access the general education curriculum.

---

of academic behaviors and are designed to assess skill accuracy and fluency. Probes, like in CBM, can sample a range of skills in a particular area, as in a mixed probe of fifth-grade math computation problems in addition, subtraction, multiplication, and division; or they can sample one skill area, such as letter identification or writing lowercase manuscript letters.

Typically, students work on probe sheets for one minute. The teacher then records the rate of correct and incorrect responses as well as any error patterns. Student performance rates have been shown to be useful for making many of the important evaluation decisions described earlier in the chapter: screening, diagnosis, program placement, curriculum placement, instructional evaluation, and program evaluation (Bursuck & Damer, 2015; Deno, 2003; Fuchs, 2017). The Professional Edge feature describes the importance of considering both student accuracy and student fluency when assessing basic academic skills.

Probes are classified according to how students take in task information (for example, seeing or hearing) and how they respond (for example, writing or speaking). They include four major types: see-say, see-write, hear-write, and think-write. For example, when reading orally from a textbook, students *see* the text and *say* the words. Hence, oral reading is referred to as a see-say probe. Similarly, in a spelling probe, students *hear* the teacher dictate words and *write* the words as they are dictated. This is a hear-write probe. As you develop CBAs, keep in mind the following suggestions:

1. Identify academic skills that are essential in your particular course or grade. In the elementary grades, include skills in handwriting, spelling, written expression, reading (e.g., letter identification, letter sounds, oral reading accuracy, and comprehension), and math (e.g., number identification, computation, problem solving, time, and money). In secondary courses these could include key vocabulary, prerequisite skills, and independent learning skills.

2. Select skills representing a *sample* of skills that are taught, not necessarily every skill. Performance on these skills then acts as a checkpoint for

MyLab Education

Video Example 4.3: Assessing Reading Fluency

Watch a teacher give a probe in oral passage reading fluency. Why was it important for the teacher to also have the student retell the story? https://www.youtube.com/watch?v=M2N5-IBkt4o&index=3&list=PLITdZVDqRAMaqU5u7Yl0VjPFx_9T4tLCg

MyLab Education

Video Example 4.4: Curriculum Based Assessments in Early Reading

Watch this video of a curriculum-based assessment in word identification. Why is the teacher measuring accuracy and fluency?

WWW RESOURCES

For assistance in finding already constructed CBMs, generating your own curriculum-based measures, and finding CBM norms, go to www.interventioncentral.org; click on "cbm/downloads" and then "cbm warehouse."

identifying students in trouble or measuring student progress. For example, in assessing reading performance, having students read a passage aloud from their reading or literature book and then answer comprehension questions may not represent all the reading skills you have taught (such as words in isolation), but it will include a representative sample of many of these skills.

3. Even though CBA is considered informal assessment, its utility in helping to make instructional decisions depends on the teacher's keeping the difficulty level of the assessment items, as well as the administration and scoring procedures, consistent over time (Deno, 2003; Deno et al., 2009; Fuchs, 2017). For example, Ms. Solomon was concerned because her students were using the same words over and over in their writing. After showing them various strategies for increasing their variety of words used, she monitored their progress by taking a writing sample every month and measuring the percentage of different words they used.

4. Remember, curriculum-based assessment has been used successfully by teachers for many years. Therefore, assessments as well as norms or benchmarks may already exist for many of the skills you are teaching. See the WWW Resources margin note on this page for benchmarks in essential beginning reading skills.

PROBES OF READING SKILLS The critical reading skills in the elementary years include phonemic awareness, letter sounds, word recognition, vocabulary, and comprehension. Phonemic awareness can be measured using a hear-say probe. Student ability to identify letter names and sounds can be assessed using a see-say probe. Word recognition and comprehension can be assessed using a see-say oral passage reading probe, such as the one in Figure 4.1.

Maze assessments (Shin, Deno, & Espin, 2000) are curriculum-based measures for assessing reading comprehension that can be given either in groups or using a computer. Maze assessments are graded passages in which every seventh word is deleted; in place of each deleted word are three choices. One of the choices is the correct choice and the other two are distracters. Students read the passage silently and circle the answers they think are correct. The number or percentage of correct responses is scored. Research has shown that maze assessments are an effective, time-saving way of monitoring student progress in reading comprehension (Deno et al., 2009; Shinn et al., 2000), though they are not a substitute for asking questions to more specifically diagnose student reading comprehension needs.

If you are having your students read trade books, you may need to design your own questions, which can be a difficult task. Carnine, Silbert, Kame'enui, and Tarver (2010) have suggested one practical model for designing comprehension questions for narrative text, based on story grammar. *Story grammar* is simply the description of the typical elements found frequently in stories. These include theme, setting, character, initiating events, conflict, attempts at resolution, resolution, and reactions. These elements can be used to create comprehension questions that may be more appropriate than traditional main idea and detail questions, because story grammar describes the organization of most stories that elementary school students are likely to read. The Case in Practice feature shows how a teacher uses story grammar with one of her second-grade students.

At times, you might not wish to ask questions about a story. Specific questions can give students clues to the answers, and they especially help students identify the information you think is important to remember or the way you organize this information. One way to solve this problem is to have students retell stories after they read them. Students themselves then must organize the information they think is important, and you can evaluate the completeness of their recall. Such a situation has two requirements for effective evaluation to occur: a standard set of criteria to evaluate the completeness of the retelling, and

FIGURE 4.1 See-Say Probe: Oral Passage Reading

Time	1 minute
Materials	*Student*—Stimulus passage
Directions to Student	*Examiner*—Duplicate copy of stimulus passage, pencil, timer "When I say 'Please begin,' read this story out loud to me. Start here [examiner points] and read as quickly and carefully as you can. Try to say each word. Ready? Please begin."
Scoring	As the student reads, place a mark (/) on your copy over any errors (mispronunciations, words skipped, and words given). (If student hesitates for three seconds, give her the word and mark it as an error.) If student inserts words, self-corrects, sounds out, or repeats, do not count as errors. When the student has read for one minute, place a bracket ( ]) on your copy to indicate how far the student read in one minute. (It is usually good practice to let students finish the paragraph or page they are reading rather than stopping them immediately when one minute is over.) Count the total number of words read during the one-minute sample. Tally the total number of errors (words mispronounced, words skipped, and words given) made during the sample. Subtract the total number of errors from the total words covered to get number correct (total words − errors = correct words per minute). If students complete the passage before the minute is up, compute student rate using this formula: $$\frac{\text{\# correct words}}{\text{seconds}} \times \frac{60}{1} = \text{correct words per minute}$$
Note:	Probe is administered individually. If you use the optional comprehension questions, be sure to have students finish the passage first.

Billy decided to go down by the river and	(9)
demonstrate his fishing ability. He always could deceive	(17)
the fish with his special secret lure. He had his best	(28)
luck in his own place, a wooded shady spot downstream	(38)
that no one knew about. Today he was going to try	(49)
to catch a catfish all the boys called Old Gray. Old Gray	(61)
was a legend in this town, because even though many boys	(72)
had hooked him, he always managed to get away.	(81)
This time Billy knew that if he sat long enough, he could	(93)
catch his dream fish!	(97)

1. Who is the main character in this story?
2. Where does the story take place?
3. What problem is Billy trying to solve?
4. How is Billy going to try to solve the problem?
5. What do you think is going to happen?

Source: From *Curriculum-Based Assessment and Instructional Design*, by E. Lessen, M. Sommers, and W. D. Bursuck, 1987, DeKalb, IL: DeKalb County Special Education Association. Reprinted with permission from DeKalb Special Education Association.

the opportunity to evaluate each student's retelling individually. Finally, it is also important to assess students' ability to comprehend informational text. Suggestions for assessing student comprehension of informational text are described later in the chapter.

PROBES OF WRITTEN EXPRESSION Written expression can be assessed using a think-write probe (Dombeck & Al Otaiba, 2016). In this probe, the teacher reads the students a story starter. A picture or photo prompt can be used instead of a

CASE IN PRACTICE 4.1

Using Story Grammars

Ms. Padilla's second-grade students have just read the story "The Funny Farola," by Ann Miranda and Maria Guerrero. The story is about a girl and her family participating in an ethnic festival in their city. The girl, Dora, makes a *farola*, which is a type of lantern people carry while marching in a parade. Dora's family laughs at her farola, because it is in the shape of a frog. However, her unusual farola saves the day when it helps Dora and her parents find Dora's lost brother and sister. Ms. Padilla is assessing Chantille's comprehension of the story using the story-grammar retelling format.

Ms. Padilla: Chantille, you have just read "The Funny Farola." Would you tell me in your own words what the story is about?

Chantille: The story is about a girl named Dora who made this funny frog that she carried in a parade. You see, her brother and sister got lost at the parade 'cause they were having such a good time, but they got found again 'cause they could see Dora's frog.

Ms. Padilla: Chantille, where does this story take place?

Chantille: It took place in a city and the people were having a big festival. That's why they were having the parade.

Ms. Padilla: Chantille, what was the problem with Dora's frog?

Chantille: Well, it was called a *farola,* which is a kind of lantern. Everyone was making them for the parade. Dora's family laughed at her farola 'cause they had never seen a frog farola before.

Ms. Padilla: You said that Dora's sister and brother got lost. What did they do to solve that problem?

Chantille: Well, they saw Dora's frog, so they knew where to find them.

Ms. Padilla: How did you feel at the end of the story?

Chantille: I felt happy.

Ms. Padilla: Why did you feel happy?

Chantille: Well, 'cause Dora's brother and sister found their mom and dad.

Ms. Padilla: Chantille, what lesson do you think this story teaches us?

Chantille: Not to get lost from your mom and dad.

A score sheet that Ms. Padilla completed for Chantille is shown in the accompanying figure. A plus (+) means that Chantille responded accurately to that element without any prompting or questioning; a checkmark (✓) means that Chantille mentioned the element after she was questioned or prompted; a minus (−) means that she failed to refer to the element even after questioning or prompts. Look at Chantille's scores. As you can see, she had a good idea of who the main characters were and received a + for this component (Characters). Chantille named two problems in the story: Dora making a farola that her family laughed at, and Dora's brother and sister getting lost. Chantille identified the problem of the lost kids without being prompted, and the problem of the funny farola with prompts; thus, a + and a ✓ were scored for Goal/Problem.

Story-Grammar Retelling Checklist

Student Name	Story Elements Evaluated												
	Theme		Setting		Characters		Goal/Problem		Attempts		Resolution		Reactions
Chantille	−		✓		+		+	✓	−		+		+

+ Responded correctly without prompting
✓ Responded correctly after prompting
− Did not identify relevant story component

It was unclear from Chantille's response exactly how the characters tried to solve their problem, so she received a − for Attempts. Chantille did say the problem was solved when Dora's brother and sister saw the frog; she received a + for this element of Resolution. However, she did not say how this resolved the problem of her family laughing at the farola, so she received a −. Chantille's reaction to the story was appropriate, so a + was scored. For Setting, Chantille received a ✓; she identified the setting after Ms. Padilla prompted her. Finally, Chantille received a − for Theme. This response was lacking, even after prompting.

Notice that Ms. Padilla's prompts included explicit references to the various story-grammar components. For example, she asked, "You said that Dora's sister and brother got lost. What did they do to solve that problem?" as opposed to asking a more general question, such as "What happened to Dora's sister and brother?" This use of specific language makes the story-grammar components clearer, a necessary structure for younger, more naïve learners. How could this use of language and other features of story retellings be incorporated into a classroom literature-based program? How do you think these results will be helpful to Ms. Padilla in working with her included students with disabilities?

story starter (McMaster, Du, & Petursdottit, 2009). The students then have one minute to plan a story and three minutes to write it. This probe can be scored in a number of different ways depending on the decisions you will be making. If you are merely interested in screening students for serious writing difficulty, use the number of intelligible words the student is able to write per minute (total words written, or TWW; Powell-Smith & Shinn, 2004). Intelligible words are those that make sense in the story.

You can modify this measure to make it more appropriate for students in kindergarten and first grade by having them write only one or two sentences in response to the story starter (Coker & Ritchey, 2010). For students in high school, extending the length of time for writing to 7–10 minutes improves the accuracy and usefulness of the results (Espin, Wallace, Campbell, Lembke, Long, & Ticha, 2008). If you are interested in measuring the overall quality of the writing as well as collecting other diagnostic information, such as grammar usage, spelling, handwriting, punctuation, vocabulary, organization, or ideas, you can score this probe differently or give another probe designed to measure these areas specifically (see Romig, Therrien, Lloyd, & Lloyd, 2017; Hessler, Conrad, & Alber-Morgan, 2009; Howell & Morehead, 1993; Mercer, Mercer, & Pullen, 2010; and Vaughn & Bos, 2014 for sample informal assessments in these areas).

PROBES OF MATH SKILLS Teachers need to measure student math skills in two general areas: computation and concepts. Math computation includes operations in addition, subtraction, multiplication, and division, including math facts in each of these areas. Essential math concepts include money, measurement, word problems, graphs/charts, and geometry. See-write probes for both computation and problem solving have been developed and can be used for making the key special education decisions you have been learning about in this chapter (see Fuchs, Hamlett, & Fuchs, 1998; Fuchs, Hamlett, & Fuchs, 1999; and Howell & Morehead, 1993, as well as the WWW Resources note on page 122). Of course, other types of probes might be needed, such as think-write probes to measure number-writing skills, and see-say probes for skills such as the identification of numbers, coins, and geometric figures. For those teaching middle and high school math, Foegen has developed see-write probes to monitor progress in algebra (Foegen, 2008; Foegen et al, 2016). You can create your own math probes at these websites: www.aplusmath.com; http://themathworksheetsite.com/; and http://www.superkids.com/aweb/tools/math/.

Curriculum-Based Assessments in Content Areas

Although content-area teachers can use CBA probes to test student knowledge of subject matter (see Figure 4.2 for an example of an assessment of key content-area vocabulary), they may need to take a somewhat different approach to student assessment.

Content-area classrooms are characterized by high curricular demands with fewer opportunities for individualization; students are also expected to take responsibility for learning much of the material on their own. Although ESEA/ESSA clearly state that the curricular expectations for most students with disabilities are the same as for their classmates without disabilities, students who enter a class significantly behind their classmates in either background knowledge or independent learning skills are likely to struggle. Thus, it is important to identify these students early so that they can be better prepared when they enter a content-area class. For example, at the beginning of this chapter, Mr. Blount assessed his U.S. history students' ability to read the class textbook independently because students in his class were expected to read much of the material on their own.

ASSESSMENTS OF PREREQUISITE SKILLS Teachers can find out whether their students possess the knowledge and skills needed to be successful in their classes by using assessments of prerequisite skills. For example, a high school English department developed a test of prerequisite skills for ninth-grade English. All

FIGURE 4.2 Using Curriculum-Based Assessment (CBA) Probes to Measure Vocabulary in Content Areas

5. biome	1. A community of organisms interacting within a given physical environment
3. ecology	2. The total of all of the surroundings that affect an organism or group of organisms
1. ecosystem	3. The branch of biology dealing with the interrelationships between living things and their environment
2. environment	4. A group of organisms involved in the transfer of energy from its primary source
4. food chain	5. Large areas classified by the types of plants and animals living there, the climate, and the soil
6. natural history	6. General study of a specific group of animals, plants, and minerals focusing on classification, life cycle, and geographic distribution

Source: Based on Espin, Christine et al. (2001). "Curriculum Based Measurement in the Content Areas: Validity of Vocabulary-Matching as an Indicator of Performance in Social Studies." *Learning Disabilities Research & Practice, 16* (3), Council for Exceptional Children (CEC).

students were given this test at the beginning of the year to see what material needed to be reviewed in the first month of school.

The process of developing assessments of prerequisite skills is similar to the process of developing curriculum-based probes described previously in this chapter. This process consists of the following four steps:

1. Identify critical content learning or skills for your class.
2. Identify entry-level content or skills needed. Be certain these are not skills for which a bypass strategy is possible.
3. Develop a measure to assess the identified skills.
4. Administer the measure to your current class. If most of the class is unable to pass the test, you will need to teach and/or review the prerequisite skills or knowledge to the entire class prior to introducing new course material. If only a few students lack the prerequisites this extra help could take place in a Tier 2 or Tier 3 instructional group. The Texas Education Agency has developed a screening assessment to identify students who might be at risk for not passing algebra in ninth grade. Go to **MSTAR** at http://www.txmstar.org.

MEASURES OF INDEPENDENT LEARNING SKILLS When students enter high school, they find an environment often not as supportive as the smaller elementary and junior high or middle school environments they left. The student body is often larger and more diverse. Daily routines change and curriculum is more difficult (Sabornie & deBettencourt, 2009). High schools also demand a much higher level of student independence through the application of a range of independent learning skills. These skills, often referred to as *learning strategies,* include note taking, textbook reading, test taking, written expression, and time management. A student's ability to perform these various skills independently can make the difference between passing or failing a class. For example, at the beginning of the chapter, Mr. Blount decided to assess textbook-reading skills because these were important for success in his class.

As with the basic and prerequisite skills mentioned previously, probes can be developed to assess independent learning. A key consideration is that the tasks used for assessment should parallel the tasks students are faced with in your classroom: If you are evaluating textbook reading, the reading task should come from the textbook you are using in class; if you are measuring a student's ability to take lecture notes, the task should involve elements similar to a typical lecture delivered in your class.

Once the task has been selected, next decide what kind of measure to use. Three possible choices are direct observation checklists, analysis of student products, and student self-evaluation. With *direct observation checklists*, the teacher develops a list of observable steps necessary to perform a given strategy. Next, the teacher has a student perform a classroom task that requires her to use the strategy and records which behaviors the student performed on the checklist.

Although direct observation of student behavior can provide much more useful information, it is time consuming, particularly when you are a high school teacher who teaches many students each day. For most students, you can use analysis of student products or student self-evaluations. Nonetheless, if you have the luxury of a free moment with an individual student, such as before or after school or during a study hall, the time spent directly observing a student perform a task is very worthwhile.

Analysis of student products involves looking at student notebooks, tests, papers, and other assignments or written activities to find evidence of effective or ineffective strategy performance. In most cases, you can evaluate your whole classroom at once, and you do not have to score the products while you are teaching. For example, Mr. James assessed his students' ability to take notes from the textbook by having them take notes from a sample passage and then answer questions about the passage using only their notes.

In *student self-evaluations*, students perform a task such as taking a test, are given a checklist of strategy steps, and are then asked to tell which of these steps they used (Mercer et al., 2010; Miller, 1996). Student self-reports are useful for several reasons. They can provide information about strategy behaviors that cannot be directly observed. Student evaluations also stimulate student self-monitoring, a behavior critical for independent learning. Self-report measures can also include interview questions that further clarify strategy usage. For example, one teacher asked, "What was the first thing you did when you received your test?" As with all measures, student self-evaluations need to be corroborated by information from other sources (for example, direct observation checklists and student products). Such corroboration may be particularly important for students with special needs, many of whom have difficulty evaluating their own behavior.

WWW RESOURCES

To learn more about identifying students for RtI in high school, go to https://air.org. Search "National High School Center"; click "National High School Center"; click "Special Education"; and click "RtI" under "Related Topics."

MyLab Education Self-Check 4.3

FYI

Student self-evaluations and other independent learning strategies are described in Chapter 10.

Using Curriculum-Based Probes to Make Special Education Decisions

Academic probes can help teachers make many of the assessment decisions discussed previously in this chapter. Several examples are discussed in the following sections.

PEER COMPARISON IN SCREENING You have learned that the key question involved in screening is whether a student is different enough from his peers on important skills in a given academic area (or areas) to indicate that some form of instructional adjustment is necessary. In an MTSS school this may mean providing more intensive instruction for a student in a small Tier 2 group. If the difference between a student and his peers continues or worsens despite repeated attempts in the classroom to remediate, placement in a more intensive tier or referral to special education and a more comprehensive assessment may be necessary.

WWW RESOURCES

For benchmarks in early literacy skills, go to: https://dibels.org; click "Dibels Next"; and click on "Dibels Next Benchmark Goals."

When screening, first select probes in the area(s) of suspected difficulty. Next, give the assessment to the student in question and compare his or her performance to benchmark or norm levels to find out the extent of the achievement gap. Benchmarks or norms are available for probes in most basic skill areas (see the WWW Resources note on page 122 and this page). You might also want to assess your entire class to identify other students at risk and obtain valuable feedback about the overall effectiveness of your teaching.

Note the results of an oral reading fluency probe given by a third-grade teacher to his entire class in April, shown in Figure 4.3. Each score represents the number of correct words read orally per minute from a grade-level passage in the classroom reading program. The teacher was particularly interested in the performance of the student who ended up scoring 50 words correct per minute. According to oral reading fluency norms (Hasbrouck & Tindal, 2006), this student is well below the 25th percentile score for this time of year of 78 words correct per minute, a definite sign of being at risk. Although this student may need extra support from the general education teacher or even a referral for a special education eligibility determination, other factors should also be considered, including how he performs across other academic skills assessed such as reading comprehension, and whether other students in the class are having similar problems. This low score did prompt the teacher to seek pre-referral consultation to get ideas for improving the student's reading performance. The teacher also planned to regularly monitor the student's progress in oral reading fluency and comprehension to help guide future decision making about his program.

Note that three other students in the class scored 10 or more words below 97, the 50th percentile. According to Hasbrouck and Tindal (2006), this puts them at some risk in reading. The teacher decided to monitor the progress of these students more regularly while also providing them with a peer-tutoring program to give them extra practice in reading fluency. Finally, the teacher learned from this experience that 19 of his 23 students were achieving at acceptable levels on an important indicator of reading ability, though, as indicated previously, the teacher should examine these students' performance

FIGURE 4.3 **Classroom Performance on Academic Skill Probe in Reading**

Grade 3, Reading Orally in Context, April 2006

Number of correct words per minute read orally

190	136	103
189	128	99
172	125	97
160	123	86
159	120	84
151	119	80
139	119	50*
136	117	

Median 123
Median/2 61.5
*Denotes score of median/2 or lower

in reading comprehension as well before declaring they are making adequate progress.

If benchmarks do not exist for the assessment selected, compare the performance of the student in question to half the median of the entire class, a subsample of the class (for example, five average performers), or even an entire grade level. The median, or middlemost score, is used to summarize the scores because it is affected less by extreme scores than is the mean, or average, which could over- or underestimate the performance of the group as a whole. The teacher in Figure 4.3 used a score equal to one-half the median as a cutoff for identifying students who are having trouble with that particular skill (Shinn & Hubbard, 1992). Such a cutoff point typically identifies 6 to 12 percent of a class or grade level that may be experiencing difficulty with a particular skill (Bursuck & Lessen, 1987; Marston, Tindal, & Deno, 1984). As shown, the class scores range from a high of 190 words read correctly per minute to a low of 50 words read correctly per minute. The median, or middlemost, score for the class is 123 words read correctly per minute. A score of 61.5 words read correctly per minute is half the median. Our student in question was the only student scoring below this point. Deno and colleagues (2002) have shown that using the bottom 20 percent of a class can also be helpful in identifying students who are at risk. Whether you use half the median or the bottom 20 percent of the class, caution is advised when using these formulas in schools with a high percentage of low-achieving students, as they can seriously underidentify learners at risk in such settings. Finally, if this teacher were in an MTSS school, the students at risk would have been identified earlier as part of schoolwide universal screening. The teacher would have also had the option of placing students into more intensive instructional tiers if needed.

FLUENCY AND ACCURACY IN DIAGNOSIS CBA probes also can help teachers diagnose specific skills deficits. For example, a student who performs poorly on a math facts probe may not know the math facts or may simply be unable to write numbers fast enough. You can figure out which situation exists by examining the student's rate, or *fluency*, of think-write number writing. Likewise, keeping track of the number of errors per minute, or *accuracy*, in oral reading, as well as the number of story elements that can be identified in a retell of a story can help you more precisely detect students' reading problems. Figures 4.4–4.7 show the results of several reading probes for two seventh-grade students. As shown in Figure 4.4, the correct rate for both students is 75 words correct per minute. However, the results reveal very different reading problems. Jalisha has a problem with reading fluency. Looking at Figure 4.5, when she reads, she reads accurately; the problem is that 75 words correct per minute is slow for a seventh-grade student. In addition, the results of her story retells, shown in Figure 4.6, indicate that when she reads the story herself, she is only able to identify half of the story elements in her retell. However, Figure 4.7 shows that when the story is read to her, she is able to identify all of the story elements. It appears that Jalisha's lack

FIGURE 4.4 **Reading Fluency Information for Jalisha and Simone**

Jalisha		Simone	
Number of words correct per minute	Number of words incorrect per minute	Number of words correct per minute	Number of words incorrect per minute
75	2	75	16

FIGURE 4.5 **Percentage of Accuracy in Passage Reading for Jalisha and Simone**

Jalisha	Simone
Percentage of accuracy	Percentage of accuracy
96	70

FIGURE 4.6 **Story Retelling Information for Jalisha and Simone**

Jalisha	Simone
Percent story elements identified:	Percent story elements identified:
57% (4/7)	14% (1/7)

FIGURE 4.7 **Listening Comprehension Information for Jalisha and Simone**

Jalisha	Simone
Percent story elements identified:	Percent story elements identified:
100% (7/7)	28% (2/7)

of fluency is primarily responsible for her problems with comprehension. She will need help in fluency building, maybe as part of a Tier 2 RtI group. According to Figure 4.5, Simone is less accurate in her reading than Jalisha; she is making many word identification errors. Figure 4.6 shows that she is unable to identify key story elements in her retell, even, as shown in Figure 4.7, when the story is read to her. First, Simone needs to be assessed further to ascertain whether her word identification errors are a pattern or due to carelessness. Second, she was unable to comprehend the story whether it was read to her or not. She may require extra support with listening and reading comprehension as well. Simone's support will be more extensive and will likely take place either in a resource room or as part of a Tier 3 RtI group.

SKILL MASTERY AND CURRICULUM PLACEMENT Inclusive education involves the use of a variety of instructional grouping arrangements. Sometimes students are grouped based on their skill levels; at other times a broader range of student skills is desired in a group. Students with special needs benefit from both types of instructional arrangements. You can use CBA probes to group your students by rank ordering and then visually inspect your students' probe scores. For example, Mr. Glass wanted to form cooperative groups in math. He used scores on a problem-solving task probe, picking one lower performer, two middle performers, and one higher performer for each group. Ms. Robins, in contrast, found that three of her students were having difficulty with capitalization but the rest of the students were not. She formed a small group of those having difficulty to review capitalization rules. The small groups used in RtI are formed based on students' skill levels.

MONITORING STUDENT PROGRESS AND INSTRUCTIONAL EVALUATION Although education has come a long way in terms of establishing a profession based on evidence-based practices, predicting whether a given practice will work for a given student in a particular situation is still difficult. Thus, it is important that you carefully monitor the results of your teaching. This monitoring is particularly relevant for students with special needs who by definition are less likely to respond favorably to commonly used instructional methods.

CBA probes, because they are time efficient, easy to give, and match what is taught in the classroom, are ideal for monitoring student progress in class. For example, Mr. Harris was interested in whether Maria, a student with learning disabilities, was retaining any of the words featured on weekly spelling lists. She had scored 90 and above on her weekly tests, but Mr. Harris was unsure whether she was remembering the words from week to week. He developed a spelling probe using words from previous spelling lists. He gave the probe to his entire class and found that Maria and 10 other students were retaining only 20 percent of the words. As a result, he started a peer-tutoring program to help students review their words. Mr. Harris also set up group competitions and awards for groups scoring the highest on the review probes. Implementing these two activities improved Maria's and the other students' retention significantly.

Teaching approaches, no matter how well they are carried out, can affect students differently. By monitoring the progress of all of your students using CBA probes, you can better meet your students' individual needs. Ways that student progress is monitored within an RtI program are described in the Instructional Edge feature.

MyLab Education

Video Example 4.5: Helping Teachers Use Progress Monitoring

How is progress monitoring used to gauge the amount of support students need? How do you think progress monitoring could be used at the middle and high school levels? https://www.youtube.com/watch?v=3EPVJDne8Vo

---

INSTRUCTIONAL EDGE 4.3

Using Progress Monitoring to Evaluate Student Performance in RtI/MTSS

WHAT ARE PROGRESS-MONITORING ASSESSMENTS?

Progress-monitoring assessments are brief assessments given during the school year that inform teachers whether students are making adequate progress toward meeting grade-level performance benchmarks so support can be provided if they aren't (Bursuck & Damer, 2015; Jenkins, 2009).

WHAT IS THE PURPOSE OF USING PROGRESS-MONITORING ASSESSMENTS IN RTI/MTSS?

The RtI/MTSS process begins with effective instruction in Tier 1 in the general education classroom using evidence-based practices. However, as much as we know about evidence-based instruction, we still cannot predict how each student will respond to any given instructional practice. That is why monitoring student progress is such an important part of RtI/MTSS. Progress monitoring can help make important instructional decisions in RtI, such as whether a student should remain in a tier, enter a more intensive tier, exit into a less-intensive tier, or be further evaluated for having a disability. A sample progress-monitoring graph is shown in Figure 4.8.

WHAT ARE THE QUALITIES OF EFFECTIVE PROGRESS-MONITORING MEASURES?

Progress-monitoring measures must be able to forecast later achievement, be given by real teachers in real classrooms, and provide results in a timely fashion so that appropriate support can be provided before too much time is lost (Jenkins, 2009). Progress-monitoring assessments also must directly reflect the curriculum, and, because they are given repeatedly over time, must be of approximately equal difficulty. That is why curriculum-based assessments such as CBMs are ideally suited for progress monitoring.

WHAT IS THE PROCESS FOR USING PROGRESS MONITORING TO MAKE DECISIONS IN RTI/MTSS?

The process of progress monitoring involves these steps: Set student goals, select progress-monitoring assessments of approximately equal difficulty, assess regularly to determine growth rates, and adjust instruction when growth is unsatisfactory (Jenkins, 2009). Generally, students in Tier 1 are assessed a minimum of three times per year, whereas Tier 2 and Tier 3 students can be assessed every 3–4 weeks, or more often if

(continued)

FIGURE 4.8 **Progress Monitoring for Maura**

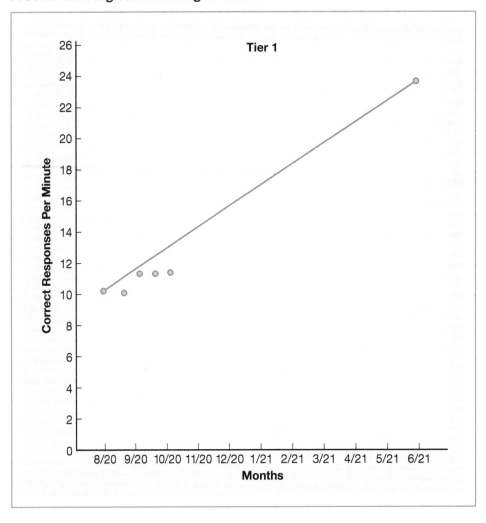

desired (Jenkins, 2009). Progress monitoring uses research-based decision rules to interpret progress-monitoring data and determine whether instruction is sufficient (Hamilton, Halverson, Jackson, Mandinach, Supovitz, & Wayman, 2009; Mellard & McKnight, 2008). A commonly used decision rule is the "four and above" rule. According to this rule:

- If the last four data points are above the aimline, keep the current program and consider raising the goal if appropriate.
- If the last four data points are below the line, make a change in intervention, tier, or both.
- If some data points are above the line and some are below, keep the current program and goal in place (Fuchs, Fuchs, Hintze, & Lembke, 2007).

To see progress monitoring in action, consider this case. Mr. Henley, a fifth-grade general education teacher, is monitoring Maura's progress in reading comprehension. Mr. Henley is using the maze (Parker, Hasbrouck, & Tindal, 1992), a CBM measure described on page 122.

As shown in Figure 4.8, Maura's score at the beginning of the year was 10 Responses Correct (RC). Although this score is at the 25th percentile, Mr. Henley didn't want to place Maura into Tier 2 until he first saw how well she performed in his Tier 1 reading instruction. Mr. Henley set an end-of-the-year goal for Maura of

24 RC, the 50th percentile for grade 5, and drew an aimline from Maura's beginning score of 10 RC to her annual goal of 24 RC. Mr. Henley decided to monitor Maura's performance in Tier 1 twice per month using a different fifth-grade maze passage of equal difficulty each time. He used the recommended "four and below" rule to decide whether Maura would stay in Tier 1 or move to Tier 2 for additional support. As shown in the figure, Maura made some progress, but all four of her data points were below the line. At this rate, she is unlikely to meet her goal of 24 RC by the end of the year. Mr. Henley decided to form a Tier 2 group with Maura and three other students in the class who were also struggling with reading comprehension. He assessed them further using a curriculum-based assessment to see what type of comprehension questions he needed to cover in the group. He planned to continue monitoring Maura's progress twice monthly to evaluate the effectiveness of the Tier 2 instruction.

The National Center on Intensive Intervention has published a table providing information about the quality of commonly used progress-monitoring assessment tools. Go to https:// intensiveintervention.org. Under "Tools Charts," click "Academic Progress Monitoring." This center has also created a helpful EXCEL tool for data collection and graphing. When at http://www .intensiveintervention.org, search for "student progress monitoring tool for data collection and graphing."

WRAPPING IT UP
Back to the Cases

Now that you have read about assessing student needs, look back at the teacher stories at the beginning of the chapter. Then go to MyLab Education to apply the knowledge you've gained in this chapter to each case.

MyLab Education Application Exercise 4.1: Case Study 4.1

MS. LYONS is concerned that Rob, a student in her second-grade class, is not keeping up with the rest of the class in math. On this fall's universal screening assessment, he was performing at the at-risk level in math computation concepts and applications. Ms. Lyons knows Rob needs to be ready to take the state's high stakes math test next year in third grade. She plans to assign Rob to a Tier 2 math group to provide him with extra help. Mr. Blair, the special education teacher, suggests that Ms. Lyons also do some informal assessments herself to make sure she is providing him with help in the right areas of need and can monitor his progress adequately.

MyLab Education Application Exercise 4.2: Case Study 4.2

MR. BLOUNT has been proactive in assessing how well his students can use the assigned text in his class and has used the information gathered from those assessments to teach the prerequisite skills needed to learn from the text. However, he is aware that if his students with disabilities have difficulty reading textbooks, they may also have difficulty reading the texts of high-stakes, end-of-grade tests required in his school system. He wants to use appropriate accommodations during these tests.

MyLab Education Application Exercise 4.3: Case Study 4.3

ROBERTO will most likely have difficulty participating in the standardized assessments given in his state. Ms. Benis and Roberto's special education teacher met after school yesterday to discuss what assessment methods they will use to demonstrate Roberto's progress toward meeting state standards. At this meeting, the two teachers reviewed the full range of options available and prepared a list of pros and cons for each option.

Summary

LO 4.1 General education teachers can use assessments that contribute to six decision-making areas of special education: screening, diagnosis, program placement, curriculum placement, instructional evaluation, and program evaluation.

LO 4.2 Numerous information sources are used in programming for students with special needs, including high-stakes tests, group-administered standardized achievement tests, individually administered diagnostic tests, and psychological tests. All of these assessments are helpful in making instructional decisions for students with special needs, but there is no substitute for observing and measuring how students respond to instruction in class, a key component of MTSS/RtI.

LO 4.3 To ensure that test scores obtained are accurate, students with disabilities are entitled to a range of accommodations and modifications on standardized tests. Accommodations include changing the setting, timing, response format, and presentation format of the test. A small percentage of students who are typically working on a more individualized curriculum do not have to meet the same requirements as those students graduating with a standard diploma. These students are eligible for a modification called an alternate assessment whereby they are required to meet the same broad standards as your other students, but they meet them in different, more basic ways.

LO 4.4 Curriculum-based assessment (CBA) measures student achievement in terms of what they are taught in the classroom. There are two major kinds of CBA: probes of basic academic skills and measures of content-area knowledge and independent learning strategies. CBA is helpful in making a range of special education decisions, particularly those involving day-to-day instruction. CBA norms and peer-comparison methods can help screen for students in academic difficulty. Probes can also be used to help teachers diagnose specific skill deficits to help form instructional groups and allow teachers to monitor the progress of students in class by measuring student performance over time.

APPLICATIONS IN TEACHING PRACTICE
Collecting and Using Assessment Information

Yolanda is a student with a learning disability in your class who has been receiving indirect support or consultation in one area. You are interested in knowing how she is doing relative to the rest of the class. Select the subject area in which Yolanda has been receiving indirect support (reading, math, or written expression). Then select a particular skill in that subject matter that you have been working on in your class (for example, in reading: word identification, passage reading, comprehension, letter or letter–sound identification; in math: any math computation skill, word problems, money, geometry; in written expression: writing mechanics, writing productivity, quality of ideas). Next, describe a curriculum-based assessment strategy you would use to judge how well Yolanda is doing on that skill as compared with her classmates. Respond to the following questions in your description.

QUESTIONS

1. How will you use curriculum-based norms to measure the extent of Yolanda's problem?
2. What additional information will you collect to clarify Yolanda's problem?
3. How will you use probe information to measure the effectiveness of classroom supports for Yolanda?
4. How will you use probe information to help you instruct the rest of the class?

If you are teaching a class for which student success depends on prerequisite knowledge and/or skills, develop a prerequisite skills/knowledge assessment using the steps described on page 126.

CHAPTER 5

Planning Instruction by Analyzing Classroom and Student Needs

LEARNING OUTCOMES

After you read this chapter, you will be able to:

5-1 Describe how to apply the steps of the INCLUDE decision-making process to adjust instruction for students with disabilities and other special needs in your classroom.

5-2 Analyze the major components of classroom organization with respect to how they can have an impact on students with disabilities.

5-3 Describe the various ways students can be grouped for instruction in an inclusive classroom, and analyze the impact they may have on students with special needs.

5-4 Analyze classroom materials and instructional methods with respect to their potential impact on students with disabilities.

MR. RODRIGUEZ teaches world history at a large urban high school. When he introduces new content related to the state standards, he teaches to the whole class. First, he reviews material that has already been covered, pointing out how that material relates to the new content being presented. Next, he provides any additional background information that he thinks will help students understand the new material better. Before Mr. Rodriguez actually presents new material, he hands out a partially completed outline of the major points he will make. This outline helps students identify the most important information. Every 10 minutes or so, he stops his lecture and allows students to discuss and modify the outline and ask questions. When Mr. Rodriguez completes his lecture, he organizes students into cooperative learning groups of four to answer a series of questions on the lecture. Manuel is a student with ADHD in Mr. Rodriguez's class. He has a history of difficulty staying on task during lectures and figuring out what information to write down. He also has trouble remembering information from one day to the next. Mr. Rodriguez has noticed that Manuel has a particular interest in soccer and loves to perform for his classmates.

How well do you think Manuel will perform in Mr. Rodriguez's class? What changes in the classroom environment might help Manuel succeed? How might Mr. Rodriguez capitalize on Manuel's interests and strengths?

JOSH has cerebral palsy. He is in the normal range in ability; in fact, he excels in math. However, he has a lot of trouble with muscle movements, has little use of his lower body and legs, and also has problems with fine muscle coordination. As a result, Josh struggles to write quickly and correctly. Josh also has trouble with his speech; he speaks haltingly and is difficult to understand. Josh is included in Ms. Stewart's middle school English class.

How can Ms. Stewart set up her classroom to make it easier for Josh to fully participate? What aspects of the classroom environment will Ms. Stewart need to adjust for Josh? How can she use technology to facilitate Josh's inclusion?

CHARLENE is a student with autism in Mr. Rowen's fourth-grade general education class. She is considered high functioning and is on grade level in math and science but struggles with reading comprehension. Like many students with autism, she has difficulties initiating and sustaining relationships with her peers and teachers. Charlene has difficulty coping with transitions and can become very upset if she is unsure of the routine for the day. Charlene enjoys activities that utilize repetitive movements, so she often wants to swing the entire time during recess. She enjoys playing games such as Minecraft that allow her to focus on building items in a virtual world with 3-D blocks. Listening to music seems to calm Charlene when she becomes upset, especially if she can listen to her music selection on her device using her "ear buds."

How can Mr. Rowen create a classroom climate and routines that support Charlene's need for structure? What instructional materials may be most beneficial for Charlene? How can Charlene's interests help her learn how to communicate with her peers?

D isabilities and other special needs arise when characteristics of individual students and various features of students' home and school environments interact. Effective teachers analyze the classroom environment in relation to students' academic and social needs and make adjustments to ensure students' success in the classroom. For example, Manuel has difficulty staying on task and retaining new information. However, Mr. Rodriguez's partially completed lecture outlines help him focus his attention on specific information as he tries to listen and stay on task; the pauses help him catch any lecture information he might have missed. Josh has some serious motor problems, but he may be able to function quite independently if Ms. Stewart makes her classroom accessible to a wheelchair and works with special educators to use assistive technology to meet Josh's needs in handwriting and oral communication. Mr. Rowen can make Charlene feel more comfortable in his class by establishing regular routines and can use her love of 3-D blocks as a way of getting to know her likes and dislikes and stimulating social interactions with her classmates.

This chapter introduces you to a systematic approach for helping all students with special needs gain access to the general education curriculum, a requirement of the Individuals with Disabilities Education Act (IDEA). Part of that approach is for you to be the best teacher you can be so that fewer of your students require special education in the first place. Many of the teaching strategies recommended in this text are what exemplary teachers would do that are particularly important to be in place for students with disabilities. Despite your best efforts, however, there will always be students who require a more individualized approach. Discussion of the INCLUDE strategy, introduced below, is provided for use with these students. While there are times when teachers need to seek input from special education teachers, either through consultation or as part of co-teaching, INCLUDE gives teachers a systematic process for supporting students based on their individual needs and the classroom demands on, or expectations of, the teacher.

The rest of this textbook expands and elaborates on this approach. Later chapters present a more in-depth look at the relationship between your classroom environment and the diverse needs of learners. An important assumption throughout this text is that the more effective your classroom structure and practices are, the greater the diversity you will be able to accommodate and the fewer individualized classroom changes you will need to make. This idea is incorporated into current MTSS/RtI models, which focus on problem prevention by establishing a strong base of research-based practices (RBP) in Tier 1.

How Can the INCLUDE Strategy Help You Make Instructional Adjustments for Students with Special Needs?

At a recent conference presentation that included both general education teachers and special education teachers, one of the authors of this text asked the audience how many of those present worked with students with disabilities. A music teacher at the back of the room called out, "Everyone in schools works with students with disabilities!" He is right. As you have learned in the previous chapters, IDEA entitles students with disabilities to "access," "participation," and "progress" in the general education curriculum. These entitlements were reinforced by the ESSA (formerly No Child Left Behind), which requires that most students with disabilities meet the same standards as their classmates without disabilities. Therefore, although the professionals who specialize in meeting the needs of students with disabilities are valuable and provide critical instructional and support systems for students, ultimately you and your peers will be the primary teachers for many students with disabilities and other special needs, and you will form partnerships with special educators to meet the needs of others. That makes it critical for you to feel comfortable making accommodations, modifications, and other classroom adjustments for students in order for them to have fair access to your curriculum.

The INCLUDE strategy is based on two key assumptions. First, student performance in school is the result of an interaction between the student and the

MyLab Education

Video Example 5.1: Universal Design for Special Needs

As explained in this video, assistive technology is grounded in the concept of universal design for learning.

instructional environment (Gaurdino & Fullerton, 2010; Gilbertson, Duhon, Wi, & Dufrene, 2008; Pisha & Coyne, 2001; Shamaki, 2015; Treptow, Burns, & McComas, 2007). Consequently, what happens in a classroom can either minimize the impact of students' special needs on their learning or magnify it, making adjustments necessary. In the first chapter-opening example, Mr. Rodriguez engaged in a number of teaching practices that minimized the impact of Manuel's attention deficits, such as starting each class with a review of material covered the day before, providing the students with lecture outlines to help them identify important ideas, and engaging his students in regular discussions of the material presented. Nevertheless, if part of Manuel's special need is in reading and the classroom text used in Mr. Rodriguez's class is too difficult for Manuel to read independently, Mr. Rodriguez will need to alleviate Manuel's problems in reading. This aspect of the INCLUDE approach is consistent with the idea behind RtI/MTSS. If all students receive effectively delivered, evidence-based instruction, then fewer will be identified as needing more supports. Further, those eventually identified for special education—the most intensive level of support—will be only those truly in need.

The second key assumption of INCLUDE is that by carefully analyzing students' learning needs and the specific demands of the classroom environment, teachers can reasonably include most students with special needs in their classrooms. You can maximize student success without taking a disproportionate amount of teacher time or diminishing the education of the other students in the class. For example, with the help of the special education teacher, Mr. Rodriguez provided Manuel with a digital text with a built-in speech-to-print component and study guide. Soon Mr. Rodriguez discovered that other students in the class could also benefit from using the digital text and made it available to them. In this way, reasonable accommodations often assist many students in the class.

The INCLUDE strategy contains elements of both universal design and differentiated instruction, two widely recognized approaches to addressing classroom diversity in general and inclusion in particular. The idea of universal design originated in the field of architecture, where it was learned that designing buildings for persons with diverse needs from the beginning makes them more accessible and saves money spent on costly retrofits of ramps and automatic doors. As applied to classrooms, the idea is that instructional materials, methods, and assessments designed with built-in supports are more likely to be compatible with learners with special needs than those without such supports (Pisha & Stahl, 2005; Rao, OK, & Bryant, 2014), and they minimize the need for labor-intensive accommodations later on. For example, print alternatives such as graphics, video, and digital text allow students with reading problems to more readily access subject content. The use of templates with partially filled-in sections and links to more information can help students construct a better essay. The use of student choice in the selection of classroom activities can maximize individual student engagement. Universal design is consistent with RtI/MTSS's prevention emphasis; when effective practices are in place, many learning problems can be prevented.

The idea behind differentiated instruction is that a variety of teaching and learning strategies are necessary to meet the range of needs evident in any given classroom. Students' diverse needs are met by differentiating the content being taught, the process by which it is taught, and the ways students demonstrate what they have learned and their level of knowledge through varied products (Huebner, 2010; Tomlinson, 2014). Differentiation is achieved by providing materials and tasks at varied levels of difficulty, and with varying levels of instructional support, through the use of multiple grouping arrangements, student choice, and varied evaluation strategies (Rock, Gregg, Ellis, & Gable, 2008; Tomlinson, 2014).

Differentiated instruction is consistent with the approach taken in this text for adjusting instruction for students with disabilities and other special needs. In fact, the INCLUDE process of determining student supports based on student needs and classroom demands is an ideal vehicle for differentiating instruction in your classroom. The way instruction is addressed in INCLUDE also is consistent

WWW RESOURCES

A universal design tool kit describing lots of ideas for using universal design for learning (UDL) in the classroom can be found at http://www.osepideasthatwork .org. Click on "Toolkits," then click on "Toolkit for Universal Design for Learning," and last, click on "Instructional Practices."

How does the concept of universal design relate from building access to teaching? How does this concept simplify the job of a general education teacher?

with the RtI/MTSS principle that when it comes to providing effective instruction, one size does not fit all.

The INCLUDE strategy for adjusting instruction for students with special needs in the general education classroom is displayed in Figure 5.1 and follows seven steps:

Step 1 Identify classroom demands.
Step 2 Note student learning strengths and needs.
Step 3 Check for potential paths to student success.
Step 4 Look for possible problem areas.
Step 5 Use information to brainstorm ways to adjust instruction.
Step 6 Decide which adjustments to make.
Step 7 Evaluate student progress.

INCLUDE

These steps are designed to apply to a broad range of student needs and classroom environments. Throughout this text, the INCLUDE icon will denote suggestions for adjusting instruction according to this strategy, with an emphasis on the appropriate step.

Step 1: Identify Classroom Demands

Because the classroom environment significantly influences what students learn, identifying and analyzing classroom requirements allows teachers to anticipate or explain problems that a given student might experience (Deshler et al., 2004; Shamaki, 2015). Then, by modifying the environment, teachers can solve or reduce the impact of these learning problems. Common classroom demands relate to classroom management, classroom grouping, instructional materials, and instructional methods.

CLASSROOM MANAGEMENT The ways in which a teacher promotes order and engages students in learning in a classroom are referred to as *classroom management* (Doyle, 2006; Korpershoek, Harms, deBoer, vanKujik, & Doolaard, 2014; Miller & Hall, 2005). Classroom management includes a number of factors:

- *Physical organization,* such as the use of wall and floor space and lighting
- *Classroom routines* for academic and nonacademic activities

FIGURE 5.1 **Steps in the INCLUDE Strategy**

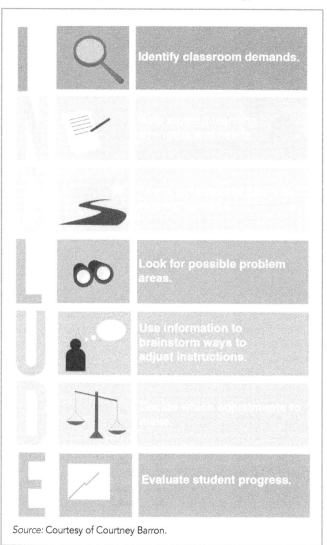

Identify classroom demands.

Look for possible problem areas.

Use information to brainstorm ways to adjust instructions.

Decide which adjustments to make.

Evaluate student progress.

Source: Courtesy of Courtney Barron.

- *Classroom climate,* or attitudes toward individual differences
- *Behavior management,* such as classroom rules and monitoring
- *The use of time* for instructional and noninstructional activities

Classroom management strategies can have real benefits for students with disabilities. For example, LaVerna is a student who needs accommodations in physical organization; she uses a wheelchair and requires wide aisles in the classroom and a ramp for the step leading to her classroom. Shawn has behavioral difficulties and thus would benefit from a behavior management system: He might go to his next class prior to the end of each period to eliminate potential opportunities to fight with classmates. He would also benefit from an efficient use of time: Minimizing transition times or the amount of time between activities would eliminate further opportunities for inappropriate interactions with his classmates.

CLASSROOM GROUPING Teachers use a variety of *classroom grouping* arrangements. Although extensive or exclusive use of this approach is no longer recommended (Friend, 2018), sometimes teachers teach the whole class at once, as when they lecture in a content area such as American history. At other times, they may employ small-group or one-to-one instruction. For example, they may teach a small group of students who have similar instructional needs, such as a group

What classroom demands might this student have difficulty meeting? What bypass strategies or other accommodations might help her demonstrate that she has learned her assignment as well as her classmates have?

of students who all require extra help on multiplication facts or an individual student who needs extra help with an English assignment. Teachers also may group students of differing interests and abilities in an effort to foster cooperative problem solving and/or peer tutoring. Students respond differently to these types of groupings. For example, Mike needs adjustments to classroom grouping in order to succeed; he might do better in a small group in which other students read assignments aloud so that he can participate in responding to them. Using a variety of grouping strategies based on student need is sometimes referred to as *flexible grouping* (Vaughn, Hughes, Moody, & Elbaum, 2001), an essential part of meeting the diverse needs of students in your classroom.

INSTRUCTIONAL MATERIALS The types of *instructional materials* teachers use can have a major impact on the academic success of students with special needs. Although many teachers choose to develop or collect their own materials, published textbooks are still most commonly used (Berkeley, King-Sears, Hott, & Bradley-Black, 2014; Davilla & Talanquer, 2010; Dewitz, Jones, & Leahy, 2009; Reutzel, Child, Jones, & Clark, 2014). Published textbooks include basic skills texts used in reading and mathematics, and texts that stress subject-matter content in areas such as history and biology. Other materials commonly used by teachers include concrete representational items such as manipulatives and technological devices, including audiovisual aids, telecommunication systems, and computers. These materials would prove beneficial for a student like Charlene in the opening vignettes, who already shows great interest and familiarity in using such items. Roberta's use of large-print materials to assist her in seeing her work and Carmen's use of a study guide to help her identify important information in her world history text are also examples of adjusting instruction by making changes to instructional materials.

INSTRUCTIONAL METHODS The ways in which teachers present content or skills to students and evaluate whether learning has occurred are the essence of teaching and are crucial for teaching students with special needs effectively. These are their *instructional methods*. Teachers use a number of different approaches to teach content and skills. Sometimes they teach skills directly, whereas at other times they assume the role of a facilitator and encourage students to learn on their own, providing support only as needed. Instructional methods also involve student practice that occurs either in class, through independent seatwork activities or learning centers, or out of class through homework. Ms. Correli's decision to use a PowerPoint presentation in class and then give Lon a copy of the slides to help his learning is an example of an adjustment in presenting subject matter. Using the help of a paraprofessional to write a student's words is an example of an accommodation in student practice.

Student evaluation, or determining the extent to which students have mastered academic skills or instructional content, is an important aspect of instructional methods. Grades frequently are used to communicate student evaluation. For some students, grading is an appropriate evaluation strategy. But for others, such as Anita, a fifth-grade student who has a moderate intellectual disability and is learning to recognize her name, a narrative report might be a better evaluation tool. When evaluating students with disabilities, teachers must focus on measuring what a student knows rather than the extent of his disability. For example, Alex, who has a severe learning disability in writing, may need to answer test questions orally to convey all he knows; if he gives written answers, only his writing disability may be measured.

Step 2: Note Student Learning Strengths and Needs

Once instructional demands are specified, the *N* step of INCLUDE calls for noting student strengths and needs. Remember that students with disabilities are a very heterogeneous group; a disability label cannot communicate a student's complete learning profile. For example, some students with intellectual disabilities can learn many life skills and live independently, whereas others will continually need daily assistance. Also keep in mind that students with disabilities are more like their peers without disabilities than different from them. Like their nondisabled peers, they have patterns of learning strengths and weaknesses. Focusing on strengths is essential (Farmer, Farmer, & Brooks, 2010; Hurley, Lambert, Epstein, & Stevens, 2015; Shaywitz, 2003). Teachers who see the strengths in students teach positively, helping students to see themselves and others positively, to see learning positively, and to overcome their weaknesses (Tomlinson & Jarvis, 2006). Three areas describe student learning strengths and needs: academics, social-emotional development, and physical development. Problems in any one of these areas may prevent students from meeting classroom requirements, resulting in a need for instruction being adjusted. Strengths in any of these areas can help students overcome these problems. For example, a student with good listening skills may be able to compensate for her reading problem by using a digital recording of her civics and government textbook.

ACADEMICS The first part of academics is *basic skills*, including reading, math, and oral and written language. Although these skills might sometimes be bypassed (for example, through the use of a calculator in math), their importance in both elementary and secondary education suggests teachers should consider them carefully. For example, a student with a severe reading problem is likely to have trouble in any subject area that requires reading—including math, social studies, and science—and on any assignment with written directions.

Cognitive and learning strategies make up the second part of academics. These strategies involve skills for "learning how to learn," such as memorization, textbook reading, note taking, test taking, and general problem solving. Such skills give students independence that helps them in adult life. Students with problems in these areas experience increasing difficulty as they proceed through the grades. For example, students who have difficulty memorizing basic math facts likely will have trouble learning to multiply fractions, and students who cannot take notes may fall behind in a civics course based on a lecture format.

Survival skills, the third area of academics, are skills practiced by successful students, such as attending school regularly, being organized, completing

RESEARCH-BASED PRACTICES

Structure (e.g., communicating clear expectations, providing explicit directions and guidance) and support for student autonomy (students' needs, preferences, personal goals) are both important to stimulate student engagement in the classroom (Jang, Reeve, & Deci, 2010).

tasks in and out of school, being independent, taking an interest in school, and displaying positive interpersonal skills (Kerr & Nelson, 2009). Students lacking in these areas usually have difficulty at school. For example, disorganized students are not likely to have work done on time, nor are they likely to deliver parent permission forms for field trips to their parents or return them to school. Survival skills also help some students compensate for their other problems. For example, given two students with identical reading problems, teachers sometimes offer more help to the student who has good attendance and tries hard.

SOCIAL-EMOTIONAL DEVELOPMENT Students' social-emotional development involves classroom conduct, interpersonal skills, and personal-psychological adjustment. Classroom conduct problems include a number of aggressive and disruptive behaviors, such as hitting, fighting, teasing, hyperactivity, yelling, refusing to comply with requests, crying, and destructiveness. Although most of these behaviors may be exhibited by all children at one time or another, students with special needs may engage in them more frequently and with greater intensity.

Conduct problems seriously interfere with student learning and can lead to problems in interpersonal relations and personal-psychological adjustment. For example, students who are disruptive in class are less likely to learn academic skills and content. Their outbursts also may be resented by their peers and may lead to peer rejection, social isolation, and a poor self-image. Interpersonal skills include but are not limited to initiating and carrying on conversations, coping with conflict, and establishing and maintaining friendships. Although these skills are not ordinarily part of the explicit school curriculum, their overall impact on school adjustment makes them important. For example, students lacking in peer support may have difficulty completing group projects (an example of student practice) or finding someone to help with a difficult assignment (an example of homework).

Personal-psychological adjustment involves the key motivational areas of self-image, frustration tolerance, and proactive learning. For example, students with a poor self-image and low tolerance for frustration may do poorly on tests (an example of student evaluation); students who are inactive learners may have difficulty pursuing an independent science project (an example of student practice).

PHYSICAL DEVELOPMENT Physical development includes vision and hearing levels, motor skills, and neurological functioning. Students with vision problems need adapted educational materials. Students with poor fine motor skills may need a computer to do their homework, an accommodation in student practice. Finally, students with attention deficits may need a wider range of approaches for instruction, including lecture, discussion, small-group work, and independent work. It is important to remember that students potentially have a wide range of physical needs, some minor and some significant. Anytime you are unsure of what to do, you should seek input from others.

MyLab Education

Video Example 5.2: Fifth Graders Discuss Different Abilities

In this video, fifth grade students discuss how they feel about differences in abilities.

Step 3: Check for Potential Paths to Student Success

The next INCLUDE step is *C*, analyzing student strengths in view of the instructional demands identified in Step 1 and checking for activities or tasks students can do successfully. Success enhances student self-image and motivation. Look for strengths in both academic and social-emotional areas. Reading the "Current Levels of Performance" section of the individualized education program (IEP) is a good way to begin identifying a student's strengths. For example, Jerry does not read but can draw skillfully using his computer. In social studies, his teacher asks him to be the class cartographer, creating maps for each region of the world as it is studied. Kareem has a moderate intellectual disability and learns very slowly, but he always comes to school on time. His second-grade teacher appoints him attendance monitor. Dwayne has attention deficit–hyperactivity disorder (ADHD), is failing all his classes in school, and is beginning to become difficult to handle at home. His parents and teachers have noticed, however, that he is able to identify personal strengths, has a good sense of humor, and can enjoy a hobby. They support Dwayne's positive interests by enrolling him in the school band.

Step 4: Look for Potential Problem Areas

In the *L* step of the INCLUDE strategy, student learning needs are reviewed within a particular instructional context, and potential mismatches are identified. For example, Susan has a learning need in the area of expressive writing; she is unable to identify spelling errors in her work. This is an academic learning need. When evaluating students' work, her world cultures teacher, who believes that writing skills should be reinforced in every class, deducts one letter grade from papers that contain one or more spelling errors. Susan also cannot read the history text accurately and fluently enough to understand it. For Susan to succeed in history class, these mismatches need to be addressed. Similarly, Sam has a severe problem that prevents him from speaking fluently. This physical problem creates a learning need. His fourth-grade teacher requires that students present book reports to the class. Again, a potential mismatch exists that could prevent Sam from succeeding. Mismatches such as those experienced by Susan and Sam can be resolved by adjusting your instruction, the topic of the next two INCLUDE steps.

Step 5: Use Information to Brainstorm Ways to Adjust Instruction

Once potential mismatches have been identified, the *U* step of INCLUDE is to use this information to identify possible ways to eliminate or minimize their effects, allowing students to gain full access to class content and instruction and demonstrate accurately what they know (Byrnes, 2008a; Warren et al., 2011). These supports can be implemented as part of supplementary aids and services based on students' IEPs or simply as adjustments made in the normal course of instruction.

It is important to remember that with accommodations or adjustments, school expectations that students meet learning standards remain unchanged. This means that students with disabilities receiving them are expected to learn everything their classmates without disabilities are supposed to learn (Nolet & McLaughlin, 2005). Instructional modifications, described in more detail below, are different; they are always made by the IEP team and involve altering the content expectations and performance outcomes expected of students (Giangreco, 2007; Nolet & McLaughlin, 2005).

This is a teacher-centered grouping arrangement for large-group instruction. What are some advantages and disadvantages of this strategy for students with special needs? What other ways of grouping students should be part of a teacher's instructional repertoire?

MyLab Education

Video Example 5.3: Tyler Talks about His Progress in the General Education Classroom

In this video Tyler and his teachers discuss the expectations in his general education classroom and some of the support that aids in his success.

ACCOMMODATIONS, ADJUSTMENTS, AND INTENSIVE INSTRUCTION Accommodations, classroom adjustments, and intensive instruction encompass three areas: bypassing students' learning needs by allowing them to employ compensatory learning strategies; making changes in classroom teaching materials, group organization, and classroom management; and providing specially designed instruction in basic or independent learning skills.

Bypass or compensatory strategies allow students to gain access to or demonstrate mastery of the school curriculum in alternative ways. For example, Susan, the student with problems in spelling and reading, could benefit from several bypass strategies. For spelling, having a computerized spell-checker could help. Alternatively, she could enlist the help of a peer to proofread her work. To help Susan access content in her government text, she could use an electronic reader. She also could be allowed to have her exams read to her so she could demonstrate her knowledge without her reading disability being an obstacle. Bypassing cannot be used in a primary area of instruction, however. For instance, Susan cannot spell-check her spelling test, but she can spell-check her science homework. Similarly, she cannot have a reading test read to her, but it would be appropriate to have a history test read to her. Also, bypassing a skill does not necessarily mean that the skill should not be remediated. Susan may need both spelling and reading instruction, either as part of her English class or in a more intensive pull-out type of setting. Finally, bypass strategies should encourage student independence. For example, Susan might be better off learning to use a spell-checker rather than relying on a peer proofreader.

Teachers can also adjust their *instructional methods, materials, grouping, and classroom management* to help students succeed. For example, if Ramos has attention problems, he might be seated near the front of the room, and he might benefit from a special system of rewards and consequences as well as a classroom from which "busy" bulletin board displays are removed. All these are classroom management adjustments. A change in classroom instruction would be to call on Ramos frequently during class discussions and to allow him to earn points toward his grade for appropriate participation. Ramos might pay better attention in a small group—a grouping change—and he might be better able to comprehend his textbooks if the key ideas are highlighted—a materials adjustment. These types of changes can be provided as supports in Tiers 1 and 2 in schools implementing RtI/MTSS.

A third option for supporting students with special needs is to provide *intensive, specially designed instruction on basic skills and learning strategies*. This option is for students who require more structure than is normally provided in a given subject, but who, after careful consideration, it is felt do not yet qualify for a case study evaluation to establish eligibility for disability services under IDEA (Chard, 2013). Often this more intensive instruction is provided as part of Tiers 2 or 3 in RtI. It can be delivered within the general education classroom or outside of the classroom using a pull-out model and can be provided by a general education, Title 1 or in some cases, a special education teacher.

While it is sometimes more feasible for some students to receive more intensive instruction support outside of their general education classroom, caution is advised when using such a pull-out approach, as the results of research on whether skills taught in pull-out programs transfer to the general education class are mixed (Fernandez & Hynes, 2016; Kavale & Forness, 2000). Some studies show positive results (Freeman & Alkin, 2000; Rea, McLaughlin, & Walther-Thomas, 2002), whereas others show minimal effects (Baker & Zigmond, 1995; Richmond, Aberasturi, Abernathy, Aberasturi, & Del Vecchio, 2009). Studies do suggest that teachers play an important role in determining whether skills taught in a separate setting transfer to their classrooms (Sabornie & deBettencourt, 2009). For example, Ms. Henry had Jamie in her English literature class; Jamie was receiving pull-out Tier 2 support on taking effective lecture notes. First, Ms. Henry found out what strategy for note taking Jamie was learning. Then she reminded Jamie to perform the strategy before she delivered a lecture and sometimes even during a lecture. Finally, Ms. Henry collected Jamie's notes on a weekly basis to see whether she was performing the strategy correctly, giving specific feedback to her as needed, and reporting her progress to the pull-out teacher.

It is feasible for the general education teacher to provide more intensive instruction when many students have similar instructional needs and he or she can easily monitor skill development. For example, Mr. Higgins, a seventh-grade science teacher, lectures frequently. As a result, students need to be proficient note takers. At the beginning of the school year, Mr. Higgins noticed during a routine check of student notebooks that many students were not taking adequate notes. With assistance from the special education teacher, he taught note taking as part of science. Three students for whom note taking was especially difficult handed in their notes each day so Mr. Higgins could monitor their progress. Establishing a productive relationship like this between co-teachers takes effort and commitment on your part, as shown in the Working Together feature.

INSTRUCTIONAL OR CURRICULAR MODIFICATIONS. Instruction or curricular modifications are made by the IEP team when students have behavioral and/or intellectual disabilities that are so significant that the curricular expectations in general education are inappropriate. These are usually the same students described in Chapter 4 as being eligible for alternate assessments. Instructional or curricular modifications are generally of two types: teaching less content and teaching different content (Nolet & McLaughlin, 2005). For example, in order to meet district grade-level science standards, Ms. Lamb's class was learning to label the parts of the human digestive system and state the purpose for each. Manny, a student with a significant intellectual disability included in Ms. Lamb's class, met the same learning standard by pointing to his stomach when asked where food goes when it is eaten. This is an example of teaching less content. In contrast, teaching different content means that the curricular outcomes are different from those of the rest of the class. For example, an instructional goal for Tony, a student with autism, is to remain calm when there is a change in the classroom schedule.

It is important to reserve instructional modifications for students with only the most significant disabilities. Otherwise, instructional modifications reduce a student's opportunity to learn critical knowledge, skills, and concepts in a given subject, leaving gaps in learning that can interfere with meeting school standards and that can be a disadvantage in later school years and beyond. For example, when one class was learning four reasons for the worldwide spread of AIDS, Steven, a student with a learning disability, was required to learn only two reasons, because he had difficulty remembering information. However, when Steven was required to take the state high-stakes science test, he was held responsible for learning the same information about AIDS as everyone else. It would have been more effective for the school to help Steven better remember science content by using a memory-enhancing device rather than reducing the amount of information. In short, reducing or simplifying content inappropriately can lead to watering down the curriculum.

Step 6: Decide Which Adjustments to Make

After you have brainstormed possible adjustments, you can carry out the *D* step in INCLUDE, which involves deciding which strategies to try. Many guidelines are suggested here to help you with this decision.

- *Select Age-Appropriate Strategies:* Students' adjustments should match their age. For example, using a third-grade book as a supplement for an eighth-grade science student who reads at the third-grade level would embarrass the student. In such a situation, a bypass strategy such as a digitally recorded textbook would be preferable if the student has the necessary background knowledge and attentional and intellectual skills to listen to the book with understanding. A good rule of thumb is to remember that no students, whether in 1st or 12th grade and regardless of their special needs, want to use what they perceive as "baby" books or materials. Of course, material for

FYI

Byrnes (2008a) found that written descriptions of accommodations on student IEPs were often ambiguous and led to considerable confusion on the part of teachers as to how to implement them. For suggestions on how to write and interpret IEP descriptions of accommodations, see Byrnes (2008b).

WORKING TOGETHER 5.1
The Reluctant Co-Teacher

Juanita Kirk is the special education teacher assigned to the high school math department. Initially, Juanita was excited about being assigned to be a co-teacher with Susan Harris, the ninth-grade algebra teacher. As part of her preparation as a special education teacher, Juanita learned that co-teachers worked as a team, sharing instructional leadership, with both being engaged equally in instruction. Juanita was comfortable with the idea of being a co-teacher in math because she was dually certified to teach both special education and math. Juanita's special education training emphasized universal design for learning, so she recognized the importance of providing instruction to the group as a whole that minimized the need for individualization. At the same time, she recognized that some students required instruction that was more highly structured. Now, though, two weeks into the semester, she is becoming disillusioned. Instead of being equally engaged in the classroom instruction, Susan prefers that Juanita circulate around the class while Susan is teaching, reminding students what to do, correcting their behavior, and redirecting their attention. Whatever academic support she provides is brief and situation specific, involving immediate assistance with immediate academic problems. Although Juanita comments from time to time when Susan is teaching, she has yet to be the lead instructor. Juanita realizes that the one teach, one assist option is one co-teaching arrangement, but she wonders why that is the only one Susan wants to use and why she is always the one who assumes the supportive role. Juanita became a teacher because she wanted to teach, not just "help out." She also feels that several of the students with and without disabilities in the class are struggling and could benefit from some of the more intensive teaching strategies she learned in her teacher preparation program. Because this is happening in math, an area in which she is certified, Juanita wonders what is going to happen when she co-teaches in English, an area in which she isn't certified!

ADDRESSING THE DILEMMA

What are the instructional drawbacks to a co-teaching relationship such as this one between Juanita and Susan? Using ideas from Chapter 3, as well as this chapter, what might you do as a co-teacher to prevent such a situation from happening?

younger students can provide you with ideas for how to present more complex content in a way that students understand.

- *Select the Easiest Approach First:* Adjustments need to be feasible. Although making changes often means some additional work for you, it should not require so much time and effort that it interferes with teaching the entire class. For instance, it is easier to circle the 6 out of 12 math problems you want Maria to complete than to create a separate worksheet just for her.

- *Select Adjustments You Are Comfortable With:* You are more likely to implement an approach successfully if you believe in it (Kleinhenz & Ingarvson, 2004), especially in the area of behavior management (Polloway, Bursuck, Jayanthi, Epstein, & Nelson, 1996). For example, in selecting rewards for good behavior, if you are uncomfortable with giving students phone time, try giving time for desirable activities such as playing learning games on the computer. However, adjustments should not be considered only in light of teacher beliefs. IDEA is clear that the unique needs of students take precedence over the convenience of schools and professionals; the IEP is a legal document and accommodations and modifications that appear on a student's IEP need to be honored. With imagination and some input from special educators, you will undoubtedly find strategies that match your teaching approach while maximizing your students' learning.

- *Determine Whether You Are Dealing with a "Can't" or a "Won't" Problem:* McGrath (2007) describes a "can't" problem as one in which the student, no matter how highly motivated, is unable to do what is expected. A "won't" problem is one in which the student could do what is expected but is not motivated to do so. Each type of problem may require a different instructional adjustment. A student unable to do what is expected might need a bypass strategy; a student unwilling to do the work might need a behavior management strategy. Making this distinction can also save you time. For example, if a student fails a test because she does not feel like working on the day of the test, then a teacher's attempt to provide extra tutorial assistance will likely be wasted effort. "Can't" and "won't" problems are particularly relevant for adolescents, who are often less likely than younger students to work to please their teachers.

- *Give Students Choices:* Adding the element of choice challenges students to make decisions, encourages them to be more responsible for their own learning, and allows them to more readily demonstrate what they know by tapping into their strengths and interests (Ferlazzo, 2015; Patall, Cooper, & Robinson, 2008; Stenhoff, Davey, & Kraft, 2008). Weiser (2014) says that you can provide choice in a classroom activity just by changing the verb used in the activity. For example, Mr. Summers wanted his students to *identify* three important events in the life of Abraham Lincoln before he became president. He added choice to the assignment by suggesting his students could, instead, *interview* Abraham Lincoln, or, using a recorder, *contrast* the lives of Lincoln and Washington before they became president. To find 50 verbs to use to add choice to your classroom activities, Google weiser motivation.pdf and select "Academic Diversity: Ways to Motivate and Engage Students with Learning Disabilities." Go to page 11.

- *Select Strategies with Demonstrated Effectiveness:* Over the past three decades, an extensive body of professional literature on effective teaching practices has accumulated. Being familiar with this research can help you avoid fads and other unvalidated practices. The strategies suggested throughout this text are research-based and form a starting point for your understanding of validated practices. Such an understanding has always been important, but it is particularly important in view of the recent emphasis placed on evidence-based practices (EBPs) in IDEA and ESEA/ESSA legislation, as well as in RtI/MTSS, which requires the use of EBPs in all of its instructional tiers.

EBPs are those instructional techniques that have been shown by credible research to be most likely to improve student outcomes in a meaningful way (Cook & Cook, 2013; Torres, Farley, & Cook, 2014). Although the primary benefit of using EBPs is boosting student achievement, evidence-based teaching, when implemented with integrity, also can help schools determine when students have learning disabilities and when they fail to learn because of ineffective instruction. That is why RtI/MTSS is an accepted alternative for identifying students with learning disabilities in IDEA 2004. As indicated in Chapter 1 and throughout the text, we use the term *Research-Based Practices (RBP)* to expand the category of EBPs to include strategies for which there is some evidence but not enough to declare them EBPs (Santangelo et al., 2015).

Cook and colleagues (2008) suggest using two guidelines when deciding whether a given practice is evidence-based, one based on the quality of the research and the other on the quantity. The quality of research means that the research clearly shows that the practice leads to increased student achievement, and that no other explanations are likely. This level of quality, sometimes referred to as experimental control, can be accomplished in two ways: (1) systematically comparing the outcomes of two randomly selected groups, one that uses the practice versus a comparison or control group that does not; or (2) systematically comparing a student's performance when the practice is in place versus when it is not in place (Cook et al., 2008). It is also important to show that the technique worked again, with more and/or different students under varied classroom conditions (Torres et al., 2014). So the quantity of research, as well as the quality, are necessary for a teaching practice to be considered an EBP (Council for Exceptional Children's Interdisciplinary Research Group, 2014). Common questions about EBPs and RBPs are addressed in the Instructional Edge feature that follows.

Step 7: Evaluate Student Progress

Although teachers have more evidence-based strategies at their disposal than ever, it is still difficult to predict which will be effective for a given student. As a result, once an accommodation or adjustment is implemented, the 7 step of INCLUDE is essential: Evaluate strategy effectiveness. You can track effectiveness through grades; observations; analysis of student work; portfolios; performance assessments; and teacher, parent, and student ratings. Monitoring student progress in this way will help you decide whether to continue, change, or discontinue an intervention. In RtI/MTSS, information obtained through progress monitoring

> **RESEARCH-BASED PRACTICES**
>
> Baker and Scanlon (2016) interviewed 10 high-incidence students and found that despite having participated in their own IEP meetings, the students were unaware of what their accommodations were and even what accommodations were in general. There remains a clear need for better involving students in the process of selecting and implementing classroom accommodations.

> **FYI**
>
> To learn more about how to critically read research articles, see Tankersley, Harjusola-Webb, and Landrum (2008) and Cook, Cook, Landrum, and Tankersley (2006).

is used to assign students to instructional tiers as well as contribute to decisions regarding student eligibility for special education.

In the next section, the relationship between how you run your classroom and the diverse needs of learners is examined. As you have read, the use of effective practices allows teachers to accommodate more diversity in their classrooms while at the same time reducing the need for making more individualized adjustments. The key features that contribute to a successful classroom are shown in Figure 5.2. These features include classroom management, classroom grouping, instructional materials, and instructional methods.

INSTRUCTIONAL EDGE 5.1

Common Questions about Evidence-Based Practices

What Is the Difference Between Evidence-Based Practices and Research-Based Practices?
RBPs are supported by effective scientific research, but not to the same exacting standards as EBPs (Santangelo et al., 2015).

Are EBPs and RBPs the Same as Best Practices?
EBPs and RBPs should not be confused with what are often referred to as best practices. Although best practices can be evidence- or research-based, they often include practices that are recommended based on personal experience, opinion, and preference (Cook, Cook, Landrum, & Tankersley, 2008). In fact, so many teaching techniques have been referred to as best practices it is not at all clear which ones are based on research and which are not.

What Are Helpful Sources for Identifying EBPs and RBPs?
A recent study by Test, Kemp-Inman, Diegelmann, Hitt, & Bethune (2015) examining the trustworthiness of websites devoted to listing and describing evidence based practices found that of the 47 web sites identified, 57% met the criteria for *trust* or *trust with caution*. Fully 43% were labeled *do not trust*. The Council for Exceptional Children's Interdivisional Research Group (2014) has identified a number of credible web-based sources where you can find EBPs and RBPs. These include the following:

- National Professional Development Center on Autism Spectrum Disorders (Go to http://www.autismpdc.fpg.unc.edu. Click on Evidence-Based Practices.)
- National Secondary Transition Technical Assistance Center (Go to https://transitionta.org. Click on Effective Practices.)
- What Works Clearinghouse (http://ies.ed.gov/ncee/wwc/Publications-Reviews.aspx)
- Center on Instruction (http://centeroninstruction.org/topic.cfm?k=SE)
- Center for Parent Information and Resources (http://www.parentcenterhub.org/topics/research/#!/produced-by=1140)

If a Practice Is Evidence Based, Is It Guaranteed to Work in My Classroom?
No matter how strong the research base, a given EBP or RBP may not be equally effective in all situations (Torres et al.,

2014). We suggest asking yourself these questions before you adopt a particular practice:

- With how many learners similar to yours has the practice been used?
- What is the success rate of the practice when carried out correctly?
- How many schools/teachers in similar schools have adopted the practice?
- How often has the practice been implemented with fidelity in real-world settings?
- How many schools and teachers have carried out the practice correctly over time? (Cook & Cook, 2017; Fixsen, Blasé, Metz, & Van Dyke, 2013)

How Important Is It That I Carry Out EBPs and RBPs the Same Way They Were Done in the Research?

- Carrying out a teaching practice the same way it was done in the research is called treatment fidelity, and is important. For example, when teaching practices used in RtI are not carried out as designed, students may be unnecessarily placed in more intensive tiers or even special education.
- Making some changes to EBPs and RBPs is inevitable, though you should make adjustments only after you have first given the practice every chance to work as intended in the research. Changes should also be made without compromising the core elements that make the strategy effective (Leko, 2015).
- Even when adoption of a practice is carefully planned and executed, there are still no guarantees that it will work. That is why the progress-monitoring component of RtI that you learned about in Chapter 4 is so important.

Can I Use Practices That Are Not Evidence-Based?
Whether or not a practice is evidence- or research-based is rarely a yes-or-no decision; all teaching practices range along a continuum from ineffective to evidence-based, with plenty of gray areas in between. Still, selecting teaching practices should not be left to chance; we know enough to improve the chances of a given child considerably, and practices for which we have the most evidence should always be used before selecting practices for which we have less evidence.

FIGURE 5.2 **Overview of Classroom Environments**

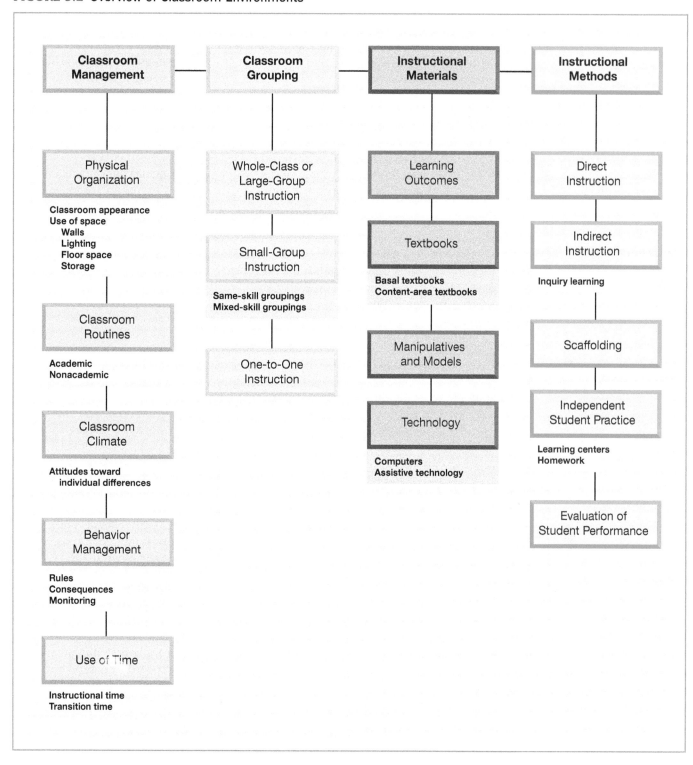

MyLab Education Self-Check 5.1

How Is an Inclusive Classroom Managed?

Classroom management comprises all of the things teachers do to organize students, space, time, and materials to maximize effective teaching and student learning (Evertson & Weinstein, 2006; Korpershoek et al., 2014). As described here, classroom management involves physical organization, routines for classroom

business, classroom climate, behavior management, and use of time. The classroom management strategies described in the following sections are part of a larger body of strategies for promoting positive student behavior called *positive behavior supports (PBS)* (Sugai & Horner, 2008). PBS is described in greater depth in Chapter 12. You also may need to use the INCLUDE strategy to make adjustments to your behavior management for students with special needs in all of these areas.

Physical Organization

The way a classroom is physically organized can affect student learning and behavior in a number of areas (Kerr & Nelson, 2009). Carefully arranged classrooms can decrease noise and disruption, improve the level and quality of student interactions, and increase the percentage of time that students spend on academic tasks (Guardino & Fullerton, 2010; Paine, Radicchi, Rosellini, Deutchman, & Darch, 1983; Sutherland, Lewis-Palmer, Stichter, & Morgan, 2008). The physical organization of a classroom influences learning conditions for all students, as well as the accessibility of instructional presentations and materials for students with sensory and physical disabilities. Physical organization includes the appearance of the classroom and the use of space, including wall areas, lighting, floor space, and storage.

Wall areas can be used for decorating, posting rules, displaying student work, and reinforcing class content, sometimes through the use of bulletin boards. For example, one teacher taught a note-taking strategy and posted the steps on a bulletin board to help her students remember them. In using wall space, keep in mind two possible problems: First, wall displays may divert students with attention problems from concentrating on instruction. These students should be placed where they are least likely to be distracted by displays. Second, students may not notice that important information appears on a display, and teachers may need to direct their attention to it. For example, Ms. Huerta posted a display showing graphic representations of the basic fractions. She reminded her students to look at these fractions while they were doing their independent math work.

Lighting, either from windows or ceiling lights, also can affect students with disabilities. Students with hearing loss might need adequate light to speech-read; they also are likely to have problems with glare in areas where the light source comes from behind the speaker. Students with visual impairments also may have difficulty working in areas that are not glare free and well lighted. Occasionally, students with learning or emotional disabilities may be sensitive to and respond negatively to certain types of light. In most cases, problems with lighting can be remedied easily by seating students away from the glare caused by sunshine coming through the classroom windows.

The organization of floor space and the kinds and placement of furniture used also need to be considered. For example, floors that do not have a nonslip surface can make wheelchair and other travel difficult for some students. Furniture that is placed in lanes can block access to the chalkboard or equipment such as computers and make mobility difficult for students in wheelchairs or students with visual impairments. Tables, pencil sharpeners, dry-erase boards, and chalkboards that are too high may prove inaccessible to students who use wheelchairs. Desks that are too low can interfere with students who have prostheses (artificial limbs). Placement and configuration of special equipment in science labs, computer centers, and vocational areas also can present difficulties in accessibility for students with special needs. For example, the lathe in the woodworking room might be positioned too high for a person in a wheelchair to operate; the spaces between work areas in the science lab might not be wide enough for a wheelchair to pass or may be difficult to navigate for a student who uses crutches or a walker. Many of these physical features of classrooms may be beyond your control. If they become a problem, seek assistance from a special education teacher.

The arrangement of your class should be predictable. This means that you should not make major changes without first considering their impact on students with disabilities and then informing these students so they have time to adapt. For example, Mr. Tate decided to move one of the bookshelves in his classroom. He noticed, however, that the new location blocked the passageway from the door to the desk of a student in his class who was blind. Mr. Tate informed the student of the move in advance, and together they worked out an alternative route to the student's desk.

The arrangement of student desks, whether in rows, circles, or small groups, can have considerable impact on students with disabilities and other special needs. For example, traditional row configurations, which provide students with an immediate, unobstructed view of the teacher, have been shown to help students with attention disorders focus better when the teacher is instructing the whole group at one time (Wannarka & Ruhl, 2008). However, the placement of desks into clusters of four works better when using mixed-ability, cooperative learning groups to help integrate a student who is socially withdrawn. Another important consideration about floor space concerns student monitoring: Teachers should be able to see all parts of the classroom at all times, whether they are teaching large or small groups or are working at their desks. Designing such visual access means that all specially designated areas in the classroom, such as learning/interest centers, computer stations, small-group instructional areas, and study carrels, need to be positioned so they can be monitored.

An additional area of physical organization is storage. For example, students with visual disabilities may need to store equipment such as audio recorders, large-print books, braille books, and magnifying devices. For other students with severe disabilities, space might also be needed to store book holders, paper holders, page turners, braces, crutches, and communication boards.

Routines for Classroom Business

Establishing clear routines in both academic and nonacademic areas is important for two reasons. First, routines that are carefully structured (that is, clear to students and used consistently) reduce nonacademic time and increase learning time. Second, you can prevent many discipline problems by having predictable classroom routines.

Most students, especially like Charlene, the student in the opening vignettes who has autism, find stability in knowing that classroom activities will be similar each day. In the absence of this stability, misbehavior often follows. Many examples of misbehavior can be related to breaks in school routines. On the day of a field trip, elementary school students are more likely to hit or push, to delay beginning assignments, and to do poor work. In middle schools and high schools, teachers often dread shortened schedules for assemblies and other school programs because of increased student behavior problems.

You can create daily classroom routines that help students learn. For example, you might expect fourth graders to enter your classroom each morning, begin their morning work, and read quietly if they finish before instruction begins. Having routines for sharing time, setting up science experiments, preparing to go to physical education, moving to the computer lab, and so on helps students meet your expectations. Routines are especially helpful to students who need a strong sense of structure in classroom life. In secondary schools, routines might include having specific lab procedures, starting each class with a five-minute review, or scheduling a particular activity on the same day every week. For example, in a geometry class, students who complete their assignments might choose to begin the day's homework, complete a math challenge activity from the electronic folder on their class instructional drive, or work on research papers or other long-term projects.

Classroom Climate

Numerous authors have noted that classroom climate contributes significantly to the number and seriousness of classroom behavior problems (Marzano & Marzano, 2003) as well as student achievement (Hattie, 2009). Classroom climate concerns the overall atmosphere in the classroom—whether it is friendly or unfriendly, pleasant or unpleasant, and so on. Climate is influenced by the attitudes of the teacher and students toward individual differences. For instance, is the classroom characterized by a cooperative or a competitive atmosphere? Is the classroom a safe place for all students to take risks? Are skills for interacting positively with students and adults actively supported in the classroom?

Teachers who communicate respect and trust to their students are more successful in creating a positive classroom environment in which fewer behavior problems occur (Arends, 2015; Marzano, 2003). For example, Mr. Elliott reprimanded a student who talked out of turn by saying, "I know you have a question about your work, and I'm glad you care enough to ask for help, but I need to have you raise your hand because I can only help students one at a time." Mr. Elliott showed respect for the student and built the student's trust by not putting her down. Yet Mr. Elliott stuck to his rule about not speaking before being called on and explained why it was important. Similarly, Ms. Belson asked Harriet to define the word *diffident*. Harriet gave an incorrect definition, saying it meant "being bored." Ms. Belson said, "Harriet, I can see how you might think the meaning is 'bored' because *diffident* looks a lot like *indifferent*. The word actually means 'lacking in confidence.'"

You can build the overall quality of your communication with your students in many small ways. For example, Mr. Rowen asking Charlene specifically about her experiences and what she was building using the 3-D blocks in her virtual game allowed him to get to know her likes and dislikes and afforded Charlene the opportunity to practice the important skill of communicating with others. Finding the time each week to speak privately with students lets them know that you care about them as individuals. Asking older students sincere questions about their friends, out-of-school activities, or part-time jobs also conveys your interest in them. Taking the time to write positive comments on papers lets students know that you appreciate their strengths and do not focus only on their special needs. When you encourage each student to achieve his or her own potential without continually comparing students to one another, you are communicating the idea that each class member has a valuable contribution to make. Teachers who fail to take these small steps toward positive communication with students or who publicly embarrass a student or punish a group because of the behavior of a few soon may create a negative classroom climate that thwarts appropriate and effective learning.

A final dimension of teacher–student communication concerns language differences. When students struggle to understand English, their behaviors may at first appear to be challenging. For example, a first grader is asked to complete several directions at one time and has a tantrum as a result of the frustration of not understanding. Similarly, a high school student apparently ignores a teacher's direction to put away project supplies and spend any remaining time beginning the homework assignment. When the teacher addresses this behavior, the student pushes everything off his desk. Is this a behavior problem or an example of misunderstanding and frustration? Teachers working with students who are not proficient English speakers should take care to distinguish problems that result from language differences from misbehavior.

Behavior Management

Behavior management, covered in greater depth in Chapter 12, refers to teacher activities that directly promote positive student behavior. It includes establishing classroom rules, providing consistent consequences, and monitoring student behavior.

Rules help create a sense of order and expectations for a classroom, and they form a significant first step in setting up a learning environment based on preventive classroom management. Teachers who are effective classroom managers have well-defined rules for their classrooms (Marzano, 2003; Olson, Platt, & Dieker, 2007). Effective classroom rules share three key characteristics: They are brief and specific, positively worded and clearly understood by students (Alberto & Troutman, 2012; Doyle, 1990), and accommodate students from different cultures (Cartledge & Kourea, 2008). Be sure to explain rules carefully to your students so that they are understood. Post rules during the first weeks of school, explain and discuss them, and model them for students. Early attention to setting your classroom expectations has a yearlong payoff. By rehearsing and focusing student attention on rules, you make them part of students' understanding of their classroom interactions. If you do not take this time to teach the rules, too often they become merely a bulletin board display, ignored by teachers and students alike.

Also, be sure that your rules accommodate students from different cultures. For example, rules about respecting other students' property may be puzzling for Latino students, for whom sharing one's belongings is a highly valued activity. Similarly, rules related to aggressive behavior may need to be enforced with care for students whose parents expect them to stand up for themselves, especially when someone says something derogatory about a student's family (Grossman, 1995). It is important to note that taking cultural differences into account does not necessarily mean that the rules need to be changed, only that the rules may need to be more carefully explained and enforced.

In addition to having clear expectations, teachers also need to tie their expectations to a set of consistent *consequences*. This means demonstrating that the same consequences apply to everyone and on a consistent basis. For example, Ms. DuBois has a rule that students are to raise their hands before speaking in class. She has also established the consequence that students receive one point for each class period they go without a single talk-out. Points earned figure into each student's grades for the class. Ms. DuBois is careful only to give points to students who meet the criterion of no talk-outs per day, regardless of who is involved or what the circumstances are, because she knows that enforcing rules arbitrarily greatly diminishes their effectiveness. Ms. DuBois also is sure to provide specific verbal praise along with the points to increase students' future chances of behaving appropriately without receiving points. Of course, Ms. DuBois realizes that sometimes rules need to be individualized, as in the case of Justin, a student with Tourette's syndrome, who is allowed one talk-out per class as specified on the behavior intervention plan (BIP) included in his IEP.

Finally, teachers need to *monitor* student classroom behaviors frequently. For example, you should scan the room to check that students are following the rules. To do this, you always need to have a clear view of the entire class, regardless of the activity in which you or the class are engaged. When student behavior is not carefully monitored, students choose not to follow the rules consistently. For example, Charmaine was a student in Ms. Patrick's fifth-grade class who had behavior problems. Ms. Patrick had a rule that students needed to complete all their independent work before they could go to the computer station to play a problem-solving game. Ms. Patrick did not have time to monitor Charmaine's behavior. One day, she saw Charmaine at the computer station and asked her whether she had completed her assignments. Not only had Charmaine not completed her assignments on that day, but she hadn't done any work for the past three days. Thereafter, Ms. Patrick was careful to monitor the work progress of all her students.

> **DIMENSIONS OF DIVERSITY**
>
> If your classroom includes students who are not native English speakers, you need to make sure that they understand classroom expectations. You may need to explain in concrete terms in a one-to-one situation what you expect, with the possible help of a translator, a student's parents, or a classmate.

Use of Time

The way teachers use time in the classroom is one of the most important aspects of classroom organization. Effectively using instructional time and managing transition time constitute two particularly important tasks.

USING INSTRUCTIONAL TIME The amount of time that students are meaningfully and successfully engaged in academic activities in school is referred to as academic learning time (Arends, 2015). Research has shown that more academic learning time in a classroom results in increased student learning (Berliner, 1990; Good & Brophy, 2003; Menzies, Lane, Oakes, & Ennis, 2017). Time usage is particularly important for students with special needs, who may need more time to learn than their peers.

Good and Brophy (2003) suggest several ways in which teachers can maximize academic learning time. One way is to minimize the time spent on organizational activities such as taking the lunch counts, completing opening activities, getting drinks, sharpening pencils, cleaning out desks, and going to the bathroom or lockers. For example, teach students how to perform organizational tasks efficiently and how to observe a firm time schedule when carrying them out. Another way is to select activities that have the greatest teaching potential and that contribute most to students' achieving the core school curriculum. Although learning activities can be fun, they should ultimately be selected for the purpose of teaching students something important. Finally, the research-based strategies described in this chapter and throughout this book for managing your classroom, grouping your students, and adapting your methods and materials also help ensure the productive use of your students' time. One specific technique to increase the academic learning time of your students is described in the Professional Edge feature.

MANAGING TRANSITION TIME Just as important as the amount of time spent in activities is the management of transition time. Transition time is the time it takes to change from one activity to another. Transition time occurs when students remain at their seats and change from one subject to another, move from their seats to an activity in another part of the classroom, move from somewhere else in the classroom back to their seats, leave the classroom to go outside or to another part of the school building, or come back into the classroom from outside or from another part of the building (Marzano, Gaddy, Foseid, Foseid, & Marzano, 2005; Paine et al., 1983). Research studies show that teachers sometimes waste academic learning time by not managing transitions carefully (McLeod, Fisher, & Hoover, 2003). Paine and colleagues (1983) suggest that you have rules devoted specifically to transitions and that you teach these rules directly to students. As with all rules, those for transitions need to be consistently monitored and reinforced.

The way you organize classroom materials also can affect the management of transitions. For example, you need to have all materials ready for each subject and activity. In addition, materials should be organized so that they are easily accessible. No matter how well organized your transitions are, you still may need to adapt them for some students with disabilities. Students with physical disabilities may need more time to take out or put away their books. Students with physical and visual disabilities may have mobility problems that cause them to take more time with such transitional activities as getting into instructional groups or moving from room to room. Furthermore, you may need an individualized system of rewards or other consequences to guide students with ADHD or behavior disorders through transition times.

Selecting the appropriate instructional grouping arrangement, the topic covered in the following section, can have a major impact on the effectiveness of your classroom practices. Other research-based practices to enhance your classroom instruction are described in the Instructional Edge feature.

MyLab Education Self-Check 5.2

PROFESSIONAL EDGE 5.1

Using "Sponges" to Increase Academic Learning Time

You almost always have times during the day when you have a minute or two before a scheduled academic activity or before the class goes to lunch, an assembly, or recess. You can fill that extra time with productive activities by using "sponges." Sponges are activities that fit into brief periods of time and give students practice or review on skills and content you have already covered in class. The following lists of sponges can help you "soak up" that extra classroom time.

EARLY ELEMENTARY SPONGES

1. Tell students to be ready to state one playground rule.
2. Tell students to be ready to list the names of classmates that begin with *J* or *M* and so on.
3. Tell students to be ready to draw something that is drawn only with circles.
4. Tell students to be ready to think of a good health habit.
5. Flash fingers—have students tell how many fingers you hold up.
6. Say numbers, days of the week, and months and have students tell what comes next.
7. Ask what number comes between two numbers: for example, 31 and 33, 45 and 47.
8. Ask students what number comes before or after 46, 52, 13, and so on.
9. Write a word on the board. Have students make a list of words that rhyme with it.
10. Ask students to count to 100 by 2s, 5s, 10s, and so on, either orally or in writing.
11. Ask students to think of animals that live on a farm, in the jungle, in water, and so forth.
12. Ask students to name fruits, vegetables, meats, and the like.
13. Ask students to list things you can touch, things you can smell, and so on.

DISMISSAL SPONGES

1. "I Spy"—ask students to find something in the room that starts with *M, P,* and so on.
2. Ask students to find something in the room that has the sound of short *a,* long *a,* and so forth.
3. Number rows or tables. Signal the number of the table with fingers, and allow students to leave accordingly.
4. Count in order or by 2s, 5s, and so on.
5. Say the days of the week, the months of the year, and so on.
6. Ask what day it is, what month it is, what date it is, or what year it is. Ask how many months are in a year, how many days are in a week, and so on.

7. Use reward activities:

   "We have had a good day! Who helped it to be a good day for all of us? Betty, you brought flowers to brighten our room. You may leave. John, you remembered to rinse your hands, good for you. You may leave. Ellen showed us that she could be quiet coming into the room today. You may leave, Ellen. Bob remembered his library book all by himself. Dawn walked all the way to the playground—she remembered our safety rules. Lori brought things to share with us. Tom surprised us with a perfect paper—he must have practiced." Students' good deeds can be grouped together to speed up dismissal. The teacher can finish with, "You're all learning to be very thoughtful. I'm very proud of all of you and you should be very proud of yourselves."

8. Use flashcards. The first correct answer earns dismissal.
9. Review the four basic shapes. Each student names an object in the room in the shape of a triangle, circle, square, or rectangle.

UPPER ELEMENTARY AND MIDDLE SCHOOL SPONGES

1. List the continents.
2. Name as many gems or precious stones as you can.
3. List as many states as you can.
4. Write an abbreviation, a roman numeral, a trademark, a proper name (biological), or a proper name (geographical).
5. Name as many countries and their capitals as you can.
6. List the names of five parts of the body above the neck that are spelled with three letters.
7. List one manufactured item for each letter of the alphabet.
8. List as many nouns in the room as you can.
9. List one proper noun for each letter of the alphabet.
10. Name as many parts of a car as you can.
11. List as many kinds of trees as you can.
12. List as many personal pronouns as you can.
13. Name as many politicians as you can.

How many sponges can you think of for your grade or subject area? Additional ideas for sponges can be found at edutopia.org. Search "academic sponge activities."

Sources: From "Effective Teaching for Higher Achievement," by D. Sparks and G. M. Sparks, 1984, *Educational Leadership*, 49(7). Reprinted with permission.

INSTRUCTIONAL EDGE 5.2

Delivering Effective Instruction in the Tier 1 Core Curriculum

You learned earlier in this chapter that the more effective your instruction is in the first place, the fewer the students who will require individualized adjustments to their instruction. RtI/MTSS's prevention-based, multi-tiered system is based on the similar idea that fewer students require instruction in more intensive tiers when evidence-based and research-based practices such as those described earlier in this chapter are effectively used in the less-intensive tiers (Vaughn et al., 2009). That is why the quality of instruction in the core curriculum, Tier 1, the place where students are first taught, is so important. A successful experience in Tier 1 bodes well for future student success (Fuchs & Vaughn, 2012). An unsuccessful experience can lead to the need for "catch-up" in more-intensive tiers, and the process of catching students up is never quick or easy (Francis, Shaywitz, Stuebing, Fletcher, & Shaywitz, 1996; Juel, 1988).

You can ensure the effectiveness of your Tier 1 core curriculum by using the following RBPs (Bursuck and Damer, 2015). Although all students benefit from these practices, students who are at risk or who have disabilities derive particular benefit from them.

- Establish a comfortable level of predictability at the beginning of lessons by telling students what they are learning, why they are learning it, and what the behavioral expectations are during the lesson.
- Actively engage students by providing them with many opportunities to respond, frequently through using unison responding.
- Present material to students in concise statements using language they understand.
- Maximize student attention and learning by employing a perky pace throughout every lesson.
- Provide support or scaffolding when students are learning new skills or content by clearly modeling new skills and providing the right amount of guided and independent practice.
- Facilitate retention by adding examples of previously learned material to examples of newly learned material.
- Correct students immediately after an error by modeling the correct answer/skill, guiding students to correct the error, and then asking the same question again so students have another opportunity to answer it.
- Continue instruction until the skill or concept presented is learned to mastery.
- Motivate students by employing a 3:1 ratio of positive to corrective teacher comments.

How Can You Group All Your Students for Instruction in Inclusive Classrooms?

Students with special needs benefit from a variety of classroom arrangements, including large- and small-group instruction, one-to-one instruction, and mixed- and same-skill groupings. The flexible use of classroom grouping arrangements is an important part of meeting individual student needs in your classroom (Broderick, Mehta-Parekh, & Reid, 2005; Huebner, 2010). Remember that the particular arrangement you choose depends on your instructional objectives as well as your students' particular needs.

Whole-Class or Large-Group Instruction

Students with special needs can benefit from both whole-class (or large-group) and small-group instruction. Tier 1 in RtI/MTSS is a combination of whole-class and small-group instruction (Gersten et al., 2009a, 2009b). One advantage of whole-class instruction is that students spend the entire time with the teacher. In small-group instruction, students spend part of the time with the teacher and also spend time working independently while the teacher works with other small groups. Research shows that the more time students spend with the teacher, the more likely they are to be engaged (Rimm-Kaufman, La Paro, Downer, & Pianta, 2005) and the more they learn (Rosenshine, 2012). This increase in learning may be because students are more likely to go off task when they are working on their own, particularly when they have learning or behavior problems. Whatever grouping arrangements you use, try to make sure that students spend as much time as possible working with you. Of course, a key advantage of co-teaching is

RESEARCH-BASED PRACTICES

Whole groups are the most common form of grouping across all grade levels, but opportunities to respond, positive feedback, and student engagement are greater during small group instruction (Hollo & Hirn, 2015).

that having two teachers in the room allows for smaller groups AND increased teacher time.

Another advantage of whole-group instruction is that it does not single out students with special needs as being different from their peers. However, you may need to modify your instruction by making adjustments within whole-group instruction for students with disabilities. For example, students in Mr. Nichols's fourth-grade class were reading *Charlotte's Web* as a large-group instructional activity. Simone read more slowly than the rest of the class. To help her keep up, Mr. Nichols provided a digital version of the book. He also gave Simone more time to answer comprehension questions about the story in class because it took her longer to look up some of the answers. In another example, before his lectures, a high school science teacher identified technical words he was going to use and then worked before school with a small group of students with vocabulary problems to help them learn the words. Tier 1 instruction in RtI is most often done in large groups. The Instructional Edge feature describes techniques that can be used to provide effective whole group Tier 1instruction in the core curriculum in RtI/MTSS.

While using RBPs in whole group Tier 1 instruction can help meet the needs of most of your students, you also need to use universal screening and progress-monitoring assessments such as those described in Chapter 4 to determine individual student needs with respect to acquiring the critical skills at your grade level and adjust your instruction based on those needs (Fuchs & Vaughn, 2012). The INCLUDE strategy described throughout this text provides a systematic approach to adjusting instruction for your students with special needs. Strategies for grouping students according to their instructional needs are described in this chapter and specific ways to adjust your instruction are described further in Chapter 9.

Small-Group Instruction

You may encounter situations in which small-group instruction is more appropriate for students with special needs. You can use same-skill groupings and mixed-skill groupings in setting up your groups.

Same-skill groupings, often referred to as *homogeneous groupings*, are helpful when some but not all students are having trouble mastering a particular skill and need more instruction and practice. For example, Ms. Rodgers was showing her students how to divide fractions that have a common denominator. She gave her class a quiz to see who had learned how to do the problems. She found that all but five students had mastered the skill. The next day, Ms. Rodgers worked with these five students while the rest of the class did an application activity. Small-group instruction is not only for students with disabilities; most students benefit from extra help in a small group at one time or another. In fact, many times students with special needs do not need extra instruction.

Small same-skill groups have also proven effective in basic skill areas when students are performing well below most of the class (Fuchs & Vaughn, 2012; Mosteller, Light, & Sachs, 1996). For example, Lori is in Ms. Hubbard's fourth-grade class and is reading at the second-grade level. Lori is learning decoding and vocabulary skills in a small group with other students who read at her level. Because the group is small and homogeneous, Ms. Hubbard is able to proceed in small steps, present many examples, and allow students to master skills before they move on. Lori is making progress and feels good about herself because she is becoming a better reader. Tier 2 and Tier 3 instruction in RtI is usually carried out in small same-skill groups.

Clearly, some students do require instruction that is more individualized and intensive than can be provided in the large group (Fuchs & Fuchs, 2015; Fuchs, Fuchs, & Compton, 2012). However, small same-skill groups should be used only when attempts to make teaching adjustments in the large group have

WWW RESOURCES

For information on how RtI/ MTSS can be implemented at the high school level, go to http:// www.rtinetwork.org. Enter "high school" into the search engine, and then click on "RtI High School Resources/RtI Action Network."

been unsuccessful. Same-skill groups tend to become permanent and take on a life of their own. Thus, the ultimate goal of any small group should be its eventual dissolution. Also, on many days students can benefit from instruction with the rest of the class. For example, Lori's group participates in large-group reading when the teacher is reading a story and the class is working on listening comprehension. Another potential problem in using same-skill groupings is the danger that students in a low-achieving group in one area will be placed in low-achieving groups in other areas even though their skill levels do not justify it. For example, just because Lori is in the lowest-level reading group does not automatically mean she needs to be in a low-achieving group in math.

Mixed skill groupings, or *heterogeneous groupings,* provide students with special needs a range of positive models for both academic and social behavior. In mixed-skill groupings students often help each other, so such groups can also be a vehicle for providing extra direct instruction to individual students, something for which classroom teachers often do not have the time. In addition, mixed-skill groups, like large groups, may be less likely to single out students with special needs.

One-to-One Instruction

Providing one-to-one instruction for students with special needs can be very effective under some circumstances. In this grouping arrangement, students work with a teacher, a paraprofessional, or a computer on well-sequenced, self-paced materials that are geared to their specific level. For example, Waldo is having trouble with addition and subtraction facts. For 15 minutes each day, he works at the classroom computer station on an individualized drill-and-practice program. Right now, he is working on addition facts through 10. When he masters these, the software will automatically provide more difficult problems. Shamika, a student with a moderate intellectual disability, works with a paraprofessional on selecting food items for a balanced lunch while the rest of the class listens to a presentation on the process of performing a nutritional analysis. One-to-one instruction is sometimes an option in the more intensive tiers in RtI/MTSS, especially when the tier involves students receiving special education (Fuchs et al., 2012).

Although one-to-one instruction may be appropriate in some circumstances, it is not necessarily the grouping arrangement of choice in either general or special education. First, it is inefficient; when it is carried out by the classroom teacher, the extensive use of one-to-one instruction results in less instructional time for everyone. Second, the logistics of one-to-one instruction sometimes require that students complete much independent work while the teacher moves from student to student. This can lead to high levels of off-task behavior, a problem many students with special needs experience (Mercer & Pullen, 2008). Third, the lack of peer models in one-to-one instruction makes it more difficult to motivate students, a problem particularly relevant at the high school level (Deshler et al., 2004). Fourth, if done as part of co-teaching, students working individually with one teacher often miss critical instruction being offered to the group by the other teacher. Habitual use of one-to-one instruction can also exclude students from critical social interactions. Fifth, there is evidence to suggest that groups as large as three are equally effective (Vaughn et al., 2003). Finally, when a student requires this type of instruction for extended periods of time, further analysis is required of her needs and instructional setting.

Although using groups effectively is an important part of an inclusive classroom, Kauffman (2011) cautions that grouping is effective because it makes effective instruction possible; grouping in and of itself is not a means of improving education (Hattie, 2009; Vaughn et al, 2010). The teaching materials you use also have a great impact on whether your students meet the standards expected of them (Coyne, Kame'enui, & Carnine, 2007). In evaluating your materials, consider the learning outcomes targeted and the quality with which the materials are designed.

MyLab Education Self-Check 5.3

How Can You Evaluate Instructional Materials for Inclusive Classrooms?

Alignment of Materials to Learning Outcomes

Instructional materials are designed to cover a range of *learning outcomes*. These outcomes reflect Bloom's revised taxonomy related to levels of thought. The six levels of thought, from lowest to highest, are remembering, understanding, applying, analyzing, evaluating, and creating (Anderson & Krathwohl, 2001, pp. 67–68):

1. *Remembering* involves retrieving, recognizing, and recalling relevant knowledge from long-term memory. For example, Ms. Lopez's American history class was studying the Revolutionary War. One of her remembering outcomes was for students to recall two major colonial leaders.

2. *Understanding* involves constructing meaning from oral, written, and graphic messages through interpreting, giving examples, classifying, summarizing, inferring, comparing, and explaining. For understanding, Ms. Lopez's students compared the family backgrounds of two colonial leaders.

3. *Applying* involves using information to solve a problem or produce some result. For this level of outcome, Ms. Lopez's students constructed a theory as to why colonial leaders refused to abolish slavery.

4. *Analyzing* is breaking up material into its parts and determining how the parts relate to one another and to an overall structure or purpose through differentiating, organizing, and attributing. For analyzing, Ms. Lopez's students differentiated how the colonists reacted to each British provocation leading up to the start of the Revolutionary War.

5. *Evaluating* involves making judgments based on criteria and standards through checking and critiquing. For this level of thought, students critiqued the colonial leaders as to their qualifications to lead the country as president.

6. *Creating,* the highest level of thought, involves putting together elements to form a coherent whole or reorganizing elements into a new pattern or structure through generating, planning, and producing. For creating, some of Ms. Lopez's students composed a song about the colonial leaders.

Keep in mind several important points when selecting the levels of thought required by your students' learning outcomes. First, in general, select outcomes reflecting a range of levels of thought, even if a range is not represented in the textbooks you are using. In the past, textbooks and teachers have tended to stress remembering at the expense of other levels of thought. Emphasizing higher-level thinking skills is more consistent with current efforts to raise learning standards such as the Common Core State Standards (National Governors Association & Council of Chief State School Officers [NGA & CCSO], 2010). Second, base your selection of outcomes on your students' strewngths and needs, not their labels. Teachers tend to choose outcomes requiring lower levels of thought for students with disabilities and other special needs, regardless of their learning profiles. Use the INCLUDE strategy to choose the appropriate level of learning for all of your students.

The nature of the instructional materials you use is another very important consideration in meeting the needs of students with special needs in your classroom. Consider the learning outcomes you desire as you select instructional materials that include textbooks and technology.

Textbooks

Basic skills textbooks, often referred to as core programs, remain the predominant vehicles for teaching foundational academic skills in today's schools (Dewitz et al., 2009; Reutzel et al., 2014). Core programs contain all the key components of the curriculum being taught for that subject. These textbooks are often comprised of an amalgam of teaching strategies. Although many of the strategies are based on research, most programs in their entirety have not been subjected to the rigorous experimentation required to call them EBPs, or even RBPs. It is important to carefully evaluate basic skill curricula yourself, prior to using them. Well-designed textbooks require fewer adjustments for students with special needs, thereby saving you much time and energy. For example, a math text that contains plenty of practice activities does not need to be adapted for students who require lots of practice to master a skill. Similarly, a science textbook that highlights critical vocabulary and includes clear context cues to help students figure out the words on their own may make it unnecessary for teachers to prepare extensive vocabulary study guides. Plus, students with special needs require more carefully designed instruction in order to be successful (Archer & Hughes, 2011; Reutzel et al., 2014). For this reason, in addition to consulting relevant websites identified earlier in this chapter in the Instructional Edge feature, we recommend further evaluating materials prior to their use. A set of questions to help you evaluate basic skills texts and materials is included in the Professional Edge feature.

While today's prescribed curriculum standards and the curricular materials to which they are aligned leave less room for changes than in the past, still, carefully evaluating basic skills texts and materials can alert you to make some

PROFESSIONAL EDGE 5.2

Guidelines for Evaluating Basic Skills Materials

To evaluate your curriculum materials, read the following evaluative questions and place an asterisk next to each that is critical for the type of material you are examining. Answer each question with yes or no. Examine all your responses in a single area, paying special attention to the questions you designated as critical. Rate each area inadequate (1), adequate (2), or excellent (3). If the area is inadequate, designate whether the features can be easily modified (M).

Rating Scale:	Inadequate 1	Adequate 2	Excellent 3	Easily modified M

1 2 3 M Effectiveness of Material

Information provided indicates successful field testing or class testing of the material.

The material has been successfully field tested with students similar to the target population.

Testimonials and publisher claims are clearly differentiated from research findings.

1 2 3 M Prerequisite Skills

Prerequisite student skills and abilities needed to work with ease in the material are specified.

Prerequisite student skills and abilities are compatible with the objectives of the material.

Prerequisite student skills and abilities are compatible with the target population.

1 2 3 M Content

Students are provided with specific strategies rather than a series of isolated skills.

The selection of subject matter, facts, and skills adequately represents standards in the content area.

The content is consistent with the stated objectives.

The information presented in the material is accurate.

The information presented in the material is current.

Various points of view—including treatment of cultural diversity, individuals with disabilities, ideologies, social values, gender roles, and socioeconomic status—are represented objectively.

The content and the topic of the material is relevant to the needs of students with disabilities.

Rating Scale:	Inadequate 1	Adequate 2	Excellent 3	Easily modified M

1 2 3 M   Sequence of Instruction

The scope and sequence of the material are clearly specified.

Facts, concepts, and skills are ordered logically.

The sequence of instruction proceeds from simple to complex.

The sequence proceeds in small, easily attainable steps.

1 2 3 M   Behavioral Objectives

Objectives or outcomes for the material are clearly stated.

Objectives or outcomes are consistent with the goals for the target population.

Objectives or outcomes are stated in behavioral terms, including the desired behavior, the conditions for measurement of the behavior, and the desired standard of performance.

1 2 3 M   Initial Assessment and Placement

The material provides a method to determine initial student placement in the curriculum.

The initial assessment for placement contains enough items to place the learner accurately.

1 2 3 M   Ongoing Assessment and Evaluation

The material provides evaluation procedures for measuring progress and mastery of objectives.

There are enough evaluative items to measure learner progress accurately.

Procedures and/or materials for ongoing progress monitoring are provided.

1 2 3 M   Instructional Input (Teaching Procedures)

Instructional procedures for each lesson are either clearly specified or self-evident.

The instruction provides for active student involvement and responses.

The lessons are adaptable to small-group and individualized instruction.

Yes   No   A variety of cueing and prompting techniques are used to gain correct student responses.

When using verbal instruction, the instruction proceeds clearly and logically.

The material uses teacher modeling and demonstration when appropriate to the skills being taught.

The material specifies correction and feedback procedures for use during instruction.

1 2 3 M   Practice and Review

The material contains appropriate practice activities that contribute to mastery of the skills and concepts.

Practice activities relate directly to the desired outcome behaviors.

The material provides enough practice for students with learning problems.

Skills are systematically and cumulatively reviewed throughout the curriculum.

Source: Adapted from *Instructional Materials for the Mildly Handicapped: Selection, Utilization, and Modification,* by A. Archer, 1977, Eugene: University of Oregon, Northwest Learning Resources System. Used by permission of the author.

adjustments. For example, a spelling program with little provision for review can be troublesome for students who have problems retaining information; you may want to develop review activities for every three lessons rather than every five, as is done in a given book. Many teachers choose to develop or collect their own materials rather than depend on published textbook series. For example, some teachers have their students read trade books instead of traditional reading books; others have their students engage in the actual writing process rather than, or in addition to, answering questions in a book. Still others involve their students in real-life problem solving in math rather than use published math texts. Even if your school does not use basic skills texts, the guidelines discussed here for teaching basic skills still apply. Of course, the selection of materials is also critical in RtI/MTSS schools where evidence-based practices are required within all of the instructional tiers. For example, having a research-based reading program as part of a core curriculum in reading in Tier 1 makes the use of proven practices more likely, provides continuity for children and adults, supplies most necessary teaching tools, and ensures a systematic progression of skills or content, not leaving instruction to chance (Bursuck & Damer, 2015).

RESEARCH-BASED PRACTICES

Reutzel and colleagues (2014) analyzed five widely-marketed core reading programs and found that the programs provided inadequate recommendations for monitoring student progress, providing students feedback, and moving students gradually towards independence. Be prepared to supplement your reading program in these areas.

Content-area textbooks, which are books used for instruction in subject areas such as science and social studies, also need to be evaluated. In secondary schools, students often are expected to read their textbooks to access curriculum content (Berkeley et al., 2014; Davilla & Talanquer, 2010). Because students are required to read and understand their texts, often without previous instruction, the texts should be written at a level at which students can easily understand them. Hiebert (2012) has experimented with a measure of difficulty called critical word factor, which defines text difficulty in terms of the number of words at a given curriculum level that students are unlikely to know. Word difficulty for her is based on frequency, decodability, the visibility of meaningful word parts, and concreteness. Certainly, text for which students are unable to independently identify and understand the meaning of at least 95 out of every 100 words read is too difficult (Bursuck & Damer, 2015). However, text may still be difficult to read independently with understanding, even if students can decipher and know the meaning of most of the words. Armbruster and Anderson (1988) and, more recently, Berkeley and colleagues (2014) refer to readable textbooks as "considerate." Considerate textbooks are easier for students to use independently and require fewer teacher adjustments. The following guidelines refer to aspects of considerate textbooks involving content, organization, and quality of writing. Research has shown that the presence of these textbook quality indicators cannot be assumed (Berkeley et al., 2014); if they are not present, you will need to adjust your instruction accordingly, guidelines for which are provided in later chapters of the text.

CHECK THE CONTENT COVERED IN THE TEXT TO SEE WHETHER IT STRESSES "BIG IDEAS" RATHER THAN FACTS IN ISOLATION "Big ideas" are important principles that enable learners to understand the connections among facts and concepts they learn (Coyne et al., 2007). For example, in a text that stressed facts in isolation, students learned that Rosa Parks was an important figure because she led the Montgomery bus boycott in 1955. In a text that stressed big ideas, students learned that the bus boycott, led by Rosa Parks in 1955, was carried out in response to the problem of segregation in the South in the early 1950s and that the boycott was the first in a series of civil rights protests eventually leading to the Civil Rights Act of 1965.

CHECK TO SEE WHETHER SUPPORT IS PROVIDED FOR STUDENT COMPREHENSION Support for student comprehension can be detected in the following three ways:

1. *Check the organization of the headings and subheadings:* Make an outline of the headings and subheadings in a few chapters. How reasonable is the structure revealed? Is it consistent with your knowledge of the subject matter?

2. *Check the consistency of organization in discussions of similar topics:* For example, in a science chapter on vertebrates, information about the different groups of vertebrates should be similarly organized; that is, if the section on amphibians discusses structure, body covering, subgroups, and reproduction, the section on reptiles should discuss the same topics, in the same order.

3. *Look for clear signaling of the structure:* A well-designed text includes information headings and subheadings. The most helpful headings are those that are the most specific about the content in the upcoming section. For example, the heading "Chemical Weathering" is a more helpful content clue than the heading "Another Kind of Weathering." A well-signaled text also includes format clues to organization. Page layouts; paragraphing; marginal notations; graphic aids; and the use of boldface, italics, and/or underlining can all serve to highlight or reinforce the structure. For example, a discussion of the four stages in the life cycle of butterflies could be signaled by using a separate, numbered paragraph for each state (that is, 1. Egg; 2. Larva; 3. Pupa; 4. Adult) and by including a picture for each stage. Finally, look for signal words and phrases that designate particular patterns of organization. For example, the

---

RESEARCH-BASED PRACTICES

Harniss, Caros, and Gersten (2007) found that students with special needs learned more when using a text that linked content information into "big ideas," helped students organize information, and provided extensive practice and review.

phrases *in contrast* and *on the other hand* signal a compare-and-contrast organization, whereas the words *first, second,* and *third* indicate an enumeration or list pattern.

CHECK TO SEE THAT IMPORTANT BACKGROUND KNOWLEDGE IS ACTIVATED

Despite the importance of background knowledge for comprehension (Beck & McKeown, 2002; Marzano, 2004), many textbooks assume unrealistic levels of students' background knowledge (Gersten, Fuchs, Williams, & Baker, 2001). A failure to activate important background knowledge may be especially problematic for students with special needs, who are more likely to lack this information (Lerner & Johns, 2014). A number of textbook features indicate adequate attention to background knowledge. For example, social studies texts often activate background knowledge by providing definitions for important vocabulary content, displaying geographical information on maps, and featuring timelines delineating when key events took place (Coyne et al., 2007). As with all of the dimensions of effective materials we have discussed, using a text that fails to adequately take background knowledge into account means that you will have to provide it.

CHECK FOR QUALITY OF WRITING The quality and clarity of writing can also affect student comprehension. Quality of writing can be evaluated in five ways:

1. *Look for explicit or obvious connectives, or conjunctions:* The absence of connectives can be particularly troublesome when the connective is a causal one (e.g., *because, since, therefore*), which is frequently the case in content-area textbooks. Therefore, look especially for causal connectives. For example, the sentence *Because the guard cells relax, the openings close* is a better explanation than the sentences *The guard cells relax. The openings close.*

2. *Check for clear references:* Another problem to watch for is confusing pronoun references when more than one noun is used. For example, consider the following: *Both the stem of the plant and the leaf produce chloroform, but in different ways. For one, the sun hits it, and then? . . .* Here, the pronouns *one* and *it* could be referring to either the stem or the leaf. Also, look out for vague quantifiers, those that do not modify the noun being quantified (e.g., *some, many, few*). For example, the sentence *Some whales have become extinct* is clearer than *Some have become extinct.* In addition, check for definite pronouns without a clear referent (e.g., *She saw him,* where the identity of *him* is not specified).

3. *Look for transition statements:* Transitions help the reader move easily from idea to idea. Given that a text covers many topics, make sure that the topic shifts are smooth. For example, in a biology chapter on the respiratory system, the text signals the transition from naming the parts of the respiratory system to describing the actual respiratory process by stating *Next, the role each of these parts of the body plays in the respiratory process will be described.*

4. *Make sure chronological sequences are easy to follow:* In a discussion of a sequence of events, the order of presentation in the text should generally proceed from first to last; any alteration of the order could cause confusion if not clearly signaled.

5. *Make sure graphic aids are clearly related to the text:* Graphic aids should contribute to understanding the material rather than simply provide decoration or fill space, should be easy to read and interpret, and should be clearly titled and labeled and referenced in the text so the reader knows when to look at them.

No matter how well designed conventional basic skill and content-area texts may be, they are still largely print-based and fixed and uniform in format. As a result, conventional materials are likely to present barriers for students with disabilities (Pisha, 2003). For example, students who are blind will need a print alternative, such as braille; students with physical challenges may be unable to

INSTRUCTIONAL EDGE 5.3

Strategies for Teaching Science to English-Learners (ELs)

ELs struggle in science (Lee & Buxton, 2013). For example, based on the 2015 National Assessment of Educational Progress (NAEP), 52 percent of ELs scored at basic or above in science compared to 79 percent of non-English learners (NCES, 2015). Although ELs share the characteristic of having limited English proficiency, it is important to realize that they are a diverse group. ELs come to your science classroom with different levels of background knowledge, literacy in their native language, family involvement in their education, intellectual ability, and motivation to do well in school, to name a few areas. All of these factors, in addition to English proficiency, should be considered when adjusting ELs' science instruction using these strategies (Lee & Buxton, 2013; Short & Echevarria, 2004/2005; Watson, 2004):

- For students in your class who speak little or no English, label parts of your classroom and lab equipment with both English names and names from the students' native language. Using Spanish, for example, the labels would be *science book/ciencialibro*. Besides helping to initiate communication with your ELs, labeling in English and another language also demonstrates to English-speaking students the difficulties students face when learning a new language. Requiring all of your students to learn both names effectively reinforces this idea.

- Place less emphasis on the traditional approach of having students read the textbook prior to engaging in a laboratory activity. Instead, start with the laboratory experience. The concreteness of laboratory experiences makes the text more comprehensible.

- Whenever possible, show objects, draw pictures, or act out the meanings of key terms. For example, when teaching the concept of *scientific classification*, one teacher demonstrated the concept by having students take off their left shoes and put them in a pile in the front of the room. The students classified the shoes in different ways, such as shoes that lace, slip on, and buckle.

- Repeat instructions, actions, and demonstrations as needed, speaking slowly and using simple sentence structure whenever possible.

- Demonstrate procedures and provide clarifying diagrams and illustrations before students begin lab work. For example, before students begin a lab exercise, provide them with a written procedural guide, go over key terms by placing them on the board, demonstrate the procedures, and actively monitor students' performance by circulating among them as they are completing the lab.

- Assign lab partners to ELs. The lab partners should be strong in science and work well with other students. Placing two ELs together in a group along with one English speaker is also effective, particularly if one of the ELs is more advanced than the other in English skills. Encouraging ELs to express their thoughts to a partner before reporting to the whole class promotes language learning and the confidence to speak out in class.

- If appropriate, enlist the support of parents in building students' background knowledge about topics before they are introduced in class. Background knowledge provided in students' native language allows them to better follow what is discussed, even if they don't know every word.

- Schedule time for review at the end of each lesson, pointing out key concepts and vocabulary while making connections to lesson objectives and state standards. This is essential, because ELs may concentrate so intently on processing language during instruction that they are unable to identify the most important information expressed.

- Give feedback to your students on their language use in class. For example, model for your students how scientists talk about their experimental findings. Have students try to use the language of scientists when orally presenting their lab reports, and give them feedback on their performance.

WWW RESOURCES

Bookshare offers free access to thousands of digital books, textbooks, teacher-recommended reading, periodicals, and assistive technology tools to all students with print-related disabilities such as visually impaired and learning disabled. For more information go to http://www.Bookshare.org.

turn the pages in a text; students with attention and organizational problems may be unable to identify main ideas; and students with reading disabilities may not be able to read material accurately and quickly enough to comprehend it. Unfortunately, teachers may lack both the time and expertise to modify these materials.

Modern digital texts can present the same content as conventional printed books but in a format that is more flexible and accessible (Anderson-Inman, 2009; Pisha & Stahl, 2005). Digital versions of texts can be easily converted to braille and virtual pages can be turned with the slight press of a switch. Electronic texts have the additional advantage of having hyperlinks to vocabulary, easily available print to text options, and other options for increased interactivity.

Manipulatives and Models

Manipulatives and models can help students like Charlene in the chapter opening vignettes who struggle with reading comprehension make connections between the abstractions often presented in school and the real-life products and situations these abstractions represent. *Manipulatives* are concrete objects used to learn mathematical concepts, properties, and procedures (Satsangi, Bouck, Taber-Doughty, Bofferding, & Roberts, 2016). Examples include blocks and counters (for example, base-10 blocks for math), fraction strips, and geoboards. *Models* provide a physical or visual representation of an abstraction (for example, a graphic organizer representing a type of word problem, a number line, or a scale model of the solar system) (Agrawal & Morin, 2016). Strategies to help students make these connections have great potential benefit for students with special needs, who may lack the background knowledge and reasoning skills to understand abstractions (Cass, Cates, Smith, & Jackson, 2003; Smith, 2004). Manipulatives are also beneficial for students such as Charlene, given her need for tactile stimulus. The use of manipulatives and models with students with disabilities has been declared an EBP (Jitendra, Nelson, Pulles, Kiss, & Houseworth, 2016). Still, as with all EBPs and RBPs, their use should be monitored carefully. To assure success, when using these tools, consider the following seven guidelines (Agrawal & Morin, 2016; Marzola, 1987; Ross & Kurtz, 1993):

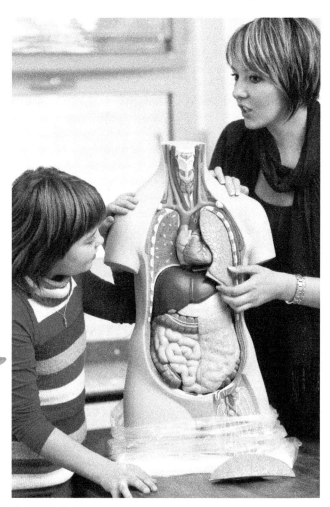

The use of manipulatives and models can make learning in science more concrete. What are ways manipulatives and models can be used to make content in other subject matter areas more concrete?

1. *Select materials that suit the concept and developmental stage of the students:* When you are first introducing a concept, materials should be easy to comprehend. Generally, the order in which you introduce materials should follow the same order as students' understanding: from the concrete to the representational to the abstract. However, not all students need to start at the same level. For example, in a biology lesson on the heart, many students benefit from viewing a three-dimensional model of a human heart, whereas other students are able to understand how a heart works just by seeing a picture of one.

2. *Use a variety of materials:* Students with disabilities may have trouble transferring their understanding of a concept from one form to another. For example, Curtis has mild intellectual disabilities. When his teacher demonstrated place value, she always used base-10 blocks. When Curtis was given a place-value problem using coffee stirrers, he was unable to do it. Curtis's teacher could have prevented this problem in the first place by demonstrating place value using a range of manipulative materials, such as coffee stirrers, paper clips, and so on.

3. *Make your manipulatives instruction more explicit by using verbal explanations whenever possible to accompany object manipulation:* Models and manipulative demonstrations should be preceded and accompanied by verbal explanations of the concept or skill being demonstrated. Verbal explanations are valuable because students may not be able to identify the important features of the model on their own. For example, Ms. Balou put a model of a two-digit-by-two-digit multiplication problem on the board. She verbally explained to her students all the steps in computing the problem and wrote each step on the Smartboard as it was completed.

4. *Encourage active interaction:* It is not enough just to have the teacher demonstrate with manipulatives or models as students observe. Students need to interact actively with models and manipulatives and receive specific corrective feedback regarding their efforts. Hands-on experience provides valuable practice and also helps them construct their own meaning from the materials.

5. *Elicit student explanations of their manipulations or use of models:* Encourage your students to verbalize what they are doing as they work with models and manipulatives. This is a good way for you to assess whether they really

MyLab Education

Video Example 5.4: Demonstrating with Manipulatives

Concrete items such as manipulatives can help students understand abstract concepts. This video shows a teacher using fruit to demonstrate fractions.

understand the concept or skill. For example, Ms. Conway had her students name the main parts of the human heart using a model. Mr. Abeles had his students explain out loud how they would subtract 43 from 52 using base-10 blocks. Although explanations can help you evaluate how your students process information, students with special needs may not be able to articulate concepts right away because of language problems or a lack of reasoning skills. These students may require frequent demonstrations of how to articulate what they are doing.

6. *Present clear guidelines for handling manipulatives to prevent management problems:* Although manipulatives can be helpful instructional tools, they also can create management problems, particularly in larger groups when your physical access to students is limited. For example, Ms. Leifheit wanted her students to manipulate blocks to show the sounds in words. Each child received three blocks. When the children heard a word such as *man*, they were to move a block as they said each sound: *m-a-n*. Ms. Leifheit had trouble getting students' attention at the beginning of the lesson because they were busy handling the blocks. She also found that students were not listening to her say the words, again because they were playing with the blocks. Ms. Leifheit decided to break the class into smaller groups so she could more carefully monitor student use of the blocks. She also established a simple rule: When the teacher is talking, students are not to touch their blocks.

7. *Move your students beyond the concrete level when they are ready:* Some students with special needs may have trouble moving from one learning stage to another. One effective way to help students make the transition from the concrete to the abstract is to pair concrete tasks with paper-and-pencil tasks, first at the representational stage and then at the abstract stage. For example, Ms. Conway had her students label a picture of a human heart (representational stage) and then draw and label their own hearts (abstract stage) after they had observed and discussed a physical model (concrete stage). Mr. Abeles had his second graders solve subtraction problems using manipulatives (concrete stage), followed by completing a worksheet of problems represented by pictures (representational stage) and then finally having the students answer problems on a traditional worksheet containing no pictures (abstract stage).

> **RESEARCH-BASED PRACTICES**
>
> There is a growing body of research attesting to the effectiveness of virtual manipulatives (Shin, Bryant, Bryant, McLenna, Hou, & Wook, 2017) as a teaching tool for students with math difficulties. See the Technology Notes in Chapter 9.

Technology

Teachers today have available to them a broad array of technologies to increase access to the general education curriculum, either by enhancing and/or supplementing their instruction or by allowing students to bypass or minimize the impact of their disabilities through assistive technology (AT). As mentioned in Chapter 1, technologies range from low- to high-tech options. One common teaching use of computers in inclusive classrooms is to employ instructional software including drill-and-practice, tutorials, simulations, games, problem solving software and Personal Learning Systems.

In general, *drill-and-practice programs* are used often with students with special needs. Such programs can supplement and/or replace worksheets and homework exercises, or help students prepare for tests. Drill-and-practice programs have been shown to be effective for these students largely because they allow students to learn in small steps, provide systematic feedback, and allow for lots of practice to mastery (Shoppek & Tullis, 2010). Still, not all drill-and-practice programs are created equal (Bursuck & Damer, 2015; Okolo, 2000). Look for programs that:

- Directly relate student responding to the instructional objective
- Have animation or graphics that support the skill being practiced
- Provide immediate feedback that helps students locate and correct their mistakes
- Store information about student performance or progress that can be accessed later by the teacher

- Have options for controlling features such as speed of problem presentation, type of feedback, problem difficulty, type of student responses, and amount of practice

Finally, drill-and practice-programs are most effective when teachers set time limits on their usage (10–15 minutes daily), use only after first teaching the concepts, and assign individually (Roblyer, 2017).

Computers also can provide initial, sequenced instruction for students, through the use of tutorials. *Tutorials* can present instruction to mastery in small, sequential steps, an instructional approach shown to be effective with students with special needs. Tutorials also can provide self-paced, one-to-one instruction at varying levels of difficulty, something teachers usually do not have time to do. Still, you need to check to be sure that students have the necessary prerequisite skills to benefit from the tutorials. In addition, tutorials may not provide sufficient review for students, and students may not be motivated enough to work through them independently (Roblyer, 2017).

Simulations are of great potential benefit in teaching students to be active learners by providing them the opportunity to confront real-life situations. Simulations can model real or imaginary systems, physical phenomena, procedures, and hypothetical situations; they can also allow students to concretely see the impact of their actions. Simulations are safe, interactive, can encourage group work, and can make the impossible possible, such as allowing students to watch muscles working by displaying the process and then visually slowing it down. Simulations work best when teachers structure students' interactions with them (Eskrootchi & Oskrochi, 2010) and when they are combined with hands-on experiences (Urban-Woldron, 2009). Less desirable features include being difficult to integrate with academic curriculum, requiring much teacher assistance, and being time consuming (Davis, 2009; Roblyer, 2017).

Games are software products that incorporate rules and/or competition into learning activities. Games can be used as rewards, provide drill in place of worksheets and exercises, encourage the development of noncognitive skills such as attention and perseverance, and teach group collaboration skills (Corbet, 2010; Hong, Cheng, Hwang, Lee, & Chang, 2009). Games should be used sparingly to sustain their ability to motivate and involve all students in a meaningful role, and should be explicitly tied to the curriculum (Rice, 2007; Roblyer, 2017).

There is also software designed specifically to teach *problem-solving* skills. Problem-solving software can be content-area specific (for example involving specific problems in math or physics) or geared to generic problem-solving skills such as gathering facts and breaking problems down into a logical series of steps. Problem-solving software can promote visualization, motivate, and make knowledge and skill instruction more relevant and practical by stressing application (Pederson, 2003). Despite its potential advantages, caution is advised as the problem-solving skills stressed do not necessarily transfer to other classroom activities and outcomes (Roblyer, 2017). As with all instructional activities, regular progress monitoring is recommended.

Personalized learning systems (PLSs) are computer-based management systems whose purposes are to provide teachers with an efficient package for assessing individual student learning needs and then prescribe an instructional experience directly tied to those needs (Cavanagh, 2014). While PLSs can potentially afford teachers with the opportunity to spend more time teaching and less time assessing and locating relevant curricular materials, as with problem solving, caution is advised, as their effectiveness has yet to be verified conclusively by research (U.S. Department of Education, 2010).

Assistive technology is an important part of an inclusive classroom. An AT device is any piece of equipment that is used to increase, maintain, or improve the functional capabilities of a child with a disability. According to the Individuals with Disabilities Act of 2004, an AT service is any item, piece of equipment, or product system, whether acquired commercially off the shelf, modified, or customized, that is used to increase, maintain, or improve the functional capabilities of a child with

TECHNOLOGY NOTES 5.1
Assistive Technology for Students with Special Needs

According to IDEA, the IEP team must consider whether a child needs assistive-technology (AT) devices and services as part of his or her plan for an appropriate education. This decision is further complicated by the fact that thousands of AT devices exist for individuals with disabilities and aging adults (Bausch & Hasselbring, 2004). That is why decisions regarding the selection of AT often include the guidance of an AT specialist. The INCLUDE strategy can also assist greatly in helping the team make this decision. What follows is a series of questions related to AT that teams may want to incorporate into the INCLUDE process. These questions were adapted from ones originally suggested by Beigel (2000); Copeland (2011); Cummings (2011); Marino, Marino, and Shaw (2006); Pedrotty-Bryant, Bryant, and Raskind (1998); and The Iris Center (2010).

EVALUATING AT USAGE

The ultimate goal of AT is to enable students to more readily meet their IEP goals. As the general education teacher, you are in the best position to evaluate the effectiveness of students' AT since you are in the position of directly observing it being used daily. Pedrotty-Bryant, Bryant, and Raskind (1998) suggest that teachers ask the following questions when determining whether the AT selected is an appropriate match for the student.

- To what extent does the AT assist the student in compensating for the disability?
- To what degree does the technology promote student independence?
- What is the student's opinion of the technology adaptation?
- What is the family's opinion of the AT?
- Is the AT efficient and easy for the student to use?
- Does the device promote meeting IEP goals and objectives in the least restrictive environment? (p. 55)

AT RESOURCES

For information about types and training in AT, go to these websites:

- ABLEDATA (http://www.abledata.com)
- Assistive Tech.net: National Public Website on Assistive Technology (assistivetech.net/contact/index.php)
- Edutopia (www.edutopia.org; click "topics"; click "all topics"; click "Assistive Technology)
- International Society for Technology in Education (http://www.ISTE.org)
- The Iris Center (https://iris.peabody.vanderbilt.edu/module/at)
- Microsoft Company (www.microsoft.com; search "assistive technology")
- National Center on Accessible Educational Materials (http://aem.cast.org)
- Tech Matrix (http://techmatrix.org)

---

a disability. As you have already learned, a range of high- to low-tech AT is available to enable students with disabilities to communicate or to access information by allowing them to bypass their disability (Bouck et al., 2012; Carpenter et al., 2015). Ways to determine the AT needs of students with disabilities are described in the Technology Notes feature. Information on using AT with students with low-incidence disabilities is covered in Chapter 6.

How Can You Analyze Instructional Methods in Relation to Student Needs?

Teachers use a number of instructional methods in class, including indirect methods of instruction, scaffolding, independent student practice, and evaluation of student performance. Each of these methods should be analyzed in relation to student needs and then used and/or adjusted as needed.

Elements of Direct Instruction

Several decades of research in teaching effectiveness have shown that many students learn skills and subject matter more readily when it is presented systematically and explicitly in what is often referred to as direct instruction (Rosenshine, 2012; Rosenshine & Stevens, 1986; Stronge, 2002). Direct instruction consists of six key elements:

1. *Review and check the previous day's work (and reteach if necessary):* This aspect of direct instruction may include establishing routines for checking homework and reviewing relevant past learning and prerequisite skills. These procedures are important for students like Manuel in the opening chapter vignettes who

might not retain past learning and/or know how to apply it to new material. For example, on Thursday Ms. Guzik taught her students how to round to the nearest whole number. On Friday she gave her class a word problem to solve that required rounding. Before the students solved the problem, she pointed to a chart in the front of the room that displayed a model of how to round numbers and suggested that they refer to this chart as they solved the problem.

2. *Present new content or skills:* When content or skills are presented, teachers begin the lesson with a short statement of the objectives and a brief overview of what they are going to present and why. Material is presented in small steps, using careful demonstrations that incorporate illustrations and concrete examples to highlight key points. Included within the demonstrations are periodic questions to check for understanding.

3. *Provide guided student practice (and check for understanding):* At first, student practice takes place under the direct guidance of the teacher, who frequently questions all students on material directly related to the new content or skill. You can involve all students in questioning by using unison oral responses or by having students answer questions by holding up answer cards, raising their hands when they think an answer is correct, or holding up a number to show which answer they think is right. For example, when asking a yes-or-no question, tell your students to hold up a 1 when they think the answer is yes and a 2 when they think the answer is no.

    This approach can be used with spelling, too. Have your students spell words on an index card and then hold up their answers. Unison responses not only give students more practice but also allow you to monitor student learning more readily. Prompts and additional explanations or demonstrations are provided during guided practice when appropriate. Effective guided practice continues until students meet the lesson objective. For example, Mr. Hayes was teaching his students how to add *es* to words that end in *y*. After modeling two examples at the board, he did several more examples with the students, guiding them as they applied the rule to change the *y* to *i* before they added *es*. Next, Mr. Hayes had students do a word on their own. Students wrote their answers on individual whiteboards and held up the boards when directed by Mr. Hayes. Mr. Hayes noticed that five students did not apply the rule correctly. He called these students up to his desk for additional instruction and had the rest of the students work independently, adding *es* to a list of words on a worksheet.

4. *Provide feedback and correction (and reteach when necessary):* When students answer quickly and confidently, the teacher asks another question or provides a short acknowledgment of correctness (for example, "That's right"). Hesitant but correct responses might be followed by process feedback (for example, "Yes, Yolanda, that's right because . . ."). When students respond incorrectly, the teacher uses corrections to draw out an improved student response. Corrections can include sustaining feedback (that is, simplifying the question, giving clues), explaining or reviewing steps, giving process feedback ("The reason we need to regroup in this subtraction problem is that the top number is smaller than the bottom number"), or reteaching last steps ("Remember, at the end of this experiment you need to tell whether the hypothesis was accepted or rejected. Let me show you what I mean"). Corrections continue until students have met the lesson objective, with praise used in moderation. Specific praise ("I'm impressed by how you drew a picture of that story problem!") is more effective than general praise ("Good job, Leon").

5. *Provide independent student practice:* Students practice independently on tasks directly related to the skills taught until they achieve a high correct rate. Practice activities are actively supervised and students are held accountable for their work.

6. *Review frequently:* Systematic review of previously learned material is provided, including the incorporation of review into homework and tests. Material missed in homework or tests is retaught.

WWW RESOURCES

For more information about a form of direct instruction with an extensive research base, consult the National Association for Direct Instruction (NIFDI) at https://www.nifdi.org/.

RESEARCH-BASED PRACTICES

Students are more engaged when they have more opportunities to respond during instruction. Research indicates positive effects on student engagement when the rate of opportunities to respond approaches three per minute (Haydon et al., 2009; Partin et al., 2010). One way to increase responding is to establish group responding signals such as thumbs up/down, stand for agree, or writing on the desk or whiteboard. Also helpful is beginning the directions for the next question (or for correction of the current question) immediately after the students respond to the first question and limiting your own talk.

MyLab Education

Video Example 5.5: Direct Instruction Spelling Lesson

Watch this video of a spelling lesson using direct instruction.

WWW RESOURCES

Use these smartphone apps to increase student engagement: Pick Me! (www.classeapps.com/), ClassCards (http://classcardsapp .com), ClassDojo (www.classdojo .com), and Kahoot (https:// getkahoot.com).

It is important to note that for older students or for those who have more subject-matter knowledge or skills, these six steps can be modified, such as by presenting more material at one time or spending less time on guided practice. For example, when a second-grade teacher presented a unit on nutrition, she spent a whole week defining and showing examples of complex carbohydrates, fats, sugar, and protein. In an eighth-grade health class, this material was covered in one day, largely because students already had much background information on this topic. Moreover, each of the direct instruction steps is not required for every lesson you teach, although they are particularly helpful to students with learning and behavior problems, who have been shown to benefit greatly from a high level of classroom structure (Archer & Hughes, 2011; Mercer & Pullen, 2008; Swanson & Deshler, 2003).

Indirect Methods of Instruction

Indirect instruction is based on the belief that children are naturally active learners and that given the appropriate instructional environment, they actively construct knowledge and solve problems in developmentally appropriate ways (Knight, 2002). This type of teaching is often referred to as *constructivistic* because of the belief that students are capable of constructing meaning on their own, in most cases without explicit instruction from the teacher (Borich, 2010; Knight, 2002). Indirect instruction is used by classroom teachers for both basic skills and content areas.

Two common indirect methods are *inquiry learning* (Jarolimek, Foster, & Kellough, 2004; Maroney, Finson, Beaver, & Jensen, 2003) and *problem-based learning* (Hung, Jonassen, & Liu, 2008). Unlike direct instruction, which is very teacher centered, in these approaches the teacher's role is that of a facilitator who guides learners' inquiry by helping them identify questions and solve problems (Hung, 2011; Jarolimek et al., 2004; Knight, 2002). The learners therefore are placed in situations that require considerable initiative and background knowledge in finding things out for themselves. In this way, students are actively involved in their own learning (Hung et al., 2008; Jarolimek et al., 2004).

You can see these elements of inquiry learning in a social studies lesson on Inuit or Native Alaskan people developed by Lindquist (1995). The goal of the lesson was for students to "realize that there are many different groups of Inuit people, each having unique customs and traditions, but whose culture has been shaped by the Far North" (Lindquist, 1995, p. 54). First, the teacher gave the students five minutes to list everything they knew about the Inuit people. The teacher then had some students share their lists with the class.

Student sharing of their background knowledge was followed by a short film on the Inuit people. After the film, the students were asked to cross out anything on their lists that the film caused them to change their minds about. When the children had revised their lists, the teacher divided the class into pairs; each pair was asked to research a different Inuit tribe. They were to gather information about food, shelter, clothing, and language. Each pair of students recorded information about their particular tribe on a data sheet and reported their information to the class. As each group reported, the teacher synthesized the information on an overhead chart, creating a graphic display for comparing and contrasting similarities and differences among the various tribes.

Scaffolding

Scaffolding is an approach that has been used successfully to support students as they develop a variety of skills, from basic academics to cognitive strategies and problem solving (Archer & Hughes, 2011; Olson et al., 2007). Scaffolds are "forms of support provided by the teacher (or another student) to help students bridge the gap between their current abilities and the intended goal" (Rosenshine & Meister, 1992, p. 26). These supports include the explicit, systematic teaching strategies that comprise direct instruction as well as the instructional enhancements for Tier 1 in RtI described earlier in the Instructional Edge feature.

With appropriate support, indirect instruction can be effective for students with special needs. What steps should this teacher take to ensure effective instruction using scaffolding?

Scaffolding is particularly helpful for students with special needs who are more likely to have problems attending to, remembering, and organizing information in a meaningful way (Archer & Hughes, 2011). As academic expectations for students continue to rise, the need to teach cognitive strategies will increase in importance. Scaffolding can help you teach these strategies more effectively.

Before using scaffolding, you first need to find out whether students have the necessary background knowledge and skills required to learn the skill or cognitive strategy you are teaching her (Rosenshine & Meister, 1992). For example, if you are teaching a student how to read her physics textbook more effectively, teaching a learning strategy is unlikely to be helpful if she lacks basic knowledge of mathematics and physical properties. Similarly, teaching a strategy for solving math word problems cannot succeed if the student does not have basic math computation skills.

Once you have checked students' background knowledge and skills, teaching higher-order cognitive strategies using scaffolding consists of six stages:

1. *Present the new cognitive strategy:* In this stage, the teacher introduces the strategy concretely, using a list of strategy steps. The teacher then models the strategy, including all "thinking" and "doing" steps. For example, Mr. Bridges is teaching his history class how geographic features and natural resources affect the growth and location of cities. First, he introduces the problem-solving strategy to his students: (a) define the problem, (b) propose hypotheses to explain the problem, (c) collect data to evaluate your hypotheses, (d) evaluate the evidence, and (e) make a conclusion. These steps are posted on the chalkboard for easy reference. Mr. Bridges then models the strategy by showing students a map of the state of Illinois and thinking out loud as he applies the steps. For example, he explains how he would sort through many pieces of information in determining which factors led to the development of Chicago (for example, being on Lake Michigan) and which did not (for example, cold climate).

2. *Regulate difficulty during guided practice:* At this stage, students begin practicing the new strategy using simplified materials so they can concentrate on learning the strategy. First, the strategy is introduced one step at a time. Students are guided carefully through the steps, with the teacher anticipating

WWW RESOURCES

Find information on how to scaffold instruction at http://iris.peabody.vanderbilt.edu. Search "scaffolding."

particularly difficult steps and completing these difficult parts of the task as necessary. Before tackling difficult problems, such as the geography of Chicago, Mr. Bridges has his students use the problem-solving steps to solve simpler problems on topics familiar to them. For example, he has them solve problems such as why the cookies someone made were dry, why a hypothetical student is late for school every day, or why the school lunches taste awful. He also helps students brainstorm ideas for how to collect data, a step that can be difficult. Mr. Bridges does this by compiling an initial list of data collection procedures for each problem. For the problem of why the cookies were dry, Mr. Bridges gives his students a list of possible data collection procedures, such as identifying the ingredients, finding out how long the cookies were baked, and figuring out how old the cookies were.

3. *Provide varying contexts for student practice:* Students practice the strategy on actual classroom tasks under the teacher's direction. The teacher starts out leading the practice, but the students eventually carry out the practice sessions in small cooperative groups. In Mr. Bridges's class, students practice the problem-solving strategy using examples from their history textbooks.

4. *Provide feedback:* The teacher provides corrective feedback to students using evaluative checklists based on models of expert problem solving carefully explained to the students. Students are encouraged to evaluate their performance using these checklists. For example, each time Mr. Bridges's students use the problem-solving strategy, they evaluate their performance by asking themselves questions such as these: Did we clearly state the problem? Did we state a complete list of hypotheses? How thorough were our data collection procedures? Were we able to evaluate all the hypotheses using the information collected? Did we interpret the results accurately? Were our conclusions consistent with our results?

5. *Increase student responsibility:* Next the teacher begins to require students to practice putting all the steps together on their own. Student independence is encouraged by removing elements of the scaffold. For example, prompts and models are diminished, the complexity and difficulty of the materials are increased, and peer support is decreased. The teacher checks for student mastery before going to the last step, independent practice.

6. *Provide independent practice:* Finally, the teacher provides the students with extensive practice and helps them apply what they have learned to new situations. For example, Mr. Bridges shows his students how problem solving can be used in other subjects, such as science.

Independent Student Practice

MyLab Education
Video Example 5.6: Scaffolding
In what ways is scaffolding demonstrated in this video?

The major purpose of practice is to help students refine or strengthen their skills in various areas. Consider the following seven guidelines for using practice activities effectively in your classroom (Good & Brophy, 2003; Harbour et al., 2015; Ornstein & Lasley, 2004; Rosenshine, 2012):

- *Students should practice only skills or content they have already learned:* This guideline is particularly important in order for students to be able to perform practice activities independently. Tasks that are too difficult can lead to high levels of off-task behavior as well as student errors that have to be untaught.

- *Practice is more effective when students have a desire to learn what they are practicing:* Whenever possible, point out to students situations in which they can use the skill in other phases of learning. For example, you may explain to your students that if they learn to read more quickly, they will be able to finish their homework in less time.

- *Practice should be individualized:* Exercises should be organized so that each student can work independently.

- *Practice should be specific and systematic:* Practice should be directly related to skills and objectives you are working on in class. This guideline is particularly important for students with special needs, who require more practice to master academic skills.

- *Students should have much practice on a few skills rather than little practice on many skills:* Focusing on one or two skills at a time is less confusing and gives students more practice on each skill.
- *Practice should be organized so that students achieve high levels of success:* Correct answers reinforce students and encourage them to do more. Most students need at least 90 percent accuracy when doing practice activities, although higher-achieving students can tolerate a 70 percent rate as long as the teacher is present to assist them.
- *Practice should be organized so that the students and teacher have immediate feedback:* You need to know how students are progressing so you can decide whether to move to the next skill. Students need to know how they are doing so they can make meaningful corrections to their work.

For students with special needs, consider these additional questions: What are the response demands of the activity? Do students have to answer orally or in writing? How extensive a response is required? Do the students have enough time to finish the activity? Response demands are important because students who are unable to meet them will not be able to do the practice activity independently. For example, Mr. Edwards is having his class practice weekly vocabulary words by orally stating their definitions. Ross stutters and is unable to answer out loud. Mr. Edwards allows Ross to submit a written list of definitions. Ms. Osborne is having her students complete short-answer questions in their chemistry books. Clarice has a physical disability and is unable to write her answers independently. She uses an adapted classroom computer to prepare her answers. Mr. Nusbaum has asked his students to write a paragraph summarizing the reasons for the stock market crash of 1929. Maurice cannot write a coherent paragraph but can answer orally into an audio recorder. Amanda writes very slowly, so Mr. Nusbaum gives her more time to complete the activity.

LEARNING CENTERS One common way of providing practice for students is through *learning centers*, classroom areas where students work alone or in groups as they engage in a variety of activities, often without the assistance of the classroom teacher (Opitz, 2007). Learning centers are called by a variety of names, including "interest centers, learning stations, activity areas, free choice areas, booths, and enrichment centers" (Patillo & Vaughn, 1992, p. 12). Well-designed learning centers can provide students with disabilities opportunities to be more actively engaged in learning, practice new skills, increase proficiency in skills acquired, and apply knowledge and skills to novel situations (King-Sears, 2007, p. 138). Learning centers can also provide teachers with ways to meet the individual needs of students with disabilities.

The key to effective use of learning centers is to design activities that are meaningful and can be accomplished independently. To do that, you must have a clear idea of what you want your students to learn ("Where are we going?"), how your students can practice information taught ("Who needs to practice what?"), and what your students' learning levels are ("What kinds of activities allow students to meaningfully practice and/or apply information learned?") (King-Sears, 2007, p. 138). Use the INCLUDE strategy to make adjustments for individual students as necessary. You can also employ a special type of teacher-led learning center by using the station-teaching option for co-teaching that you read about in Chapter 3.

> **WWW RESOURCES**
>
> Find many ideas for learning centers in literacy that are ideal for students with special needs. Go to www.fcrr.org; click "Resources" and click "Student Center Activities."

HOMEWORK Another common form of practice used by teachers is *homework*. Research shows that homework has a positive effect on student achievement when it is properly assigned and monitored (Cooper, 2006; Marzano & Pickering, 2007). Effects are greatest at upper grade levels and for lower-level tasks (Hattie, 2009).

Homework is often a challenge for students with special needs. For example, most teachers expect homework to be completed independently, and students must have the sensory, academic, and organizational skills to do so.

MyLab Education

Video Example 5.7: Parent Involvement in Student Evaluation

Watch how these educators successfully involved a parent in the evaluation process.

A student with a severe reading disability might be unable to read a chapter in a geometry book and answer the questions without some form of accommodation such as a peer reader or recorded text. Similarly, a student with fine motor difficulties might be unable to answer the questions unless allowed to do so orally or with an adapted word processor. In addition, you may need to provide this same student more time or to assign fewer questions. Therefore, it is important that you carefully examine your own particular homework requirements and modify them to ensure full participation by all your students.

Evaluation of Student Performance

The major purpose of student evaluation is to determine the extent to which students have mastered academic skills or instructional content. Chapter 4 discussed formal and informal assessments that can be used to evaluate student progress. Student evaluations are also communicated through grades, which are determined in a number of ways, including classroom tests and assignments. Because student evaluation is so important, you need to consider how classroom tests and assignments may interact with student learning needs. Most critical is that the method of evaluation measures skill or content mastery, not a student's disability. For example, Carson, a student who has ADHD, should be given tests in small segments to ensure that the tests measure his knowledge, not his attention span. Similarly, Riesa, a student with a severe learning disability in writing, needs to take an oral essay test in physics if the test is to be a valid measure of her knowledge of physics rather than her writing disability. These types of accommodations generally are enumerated on the IEP and must be implemented by the general education teacher.

The type of report-card grade used, as well as the system used to arrive at that grade, might also need to be modified for some students. For example, Hal was discouraged about always getting a C in English, no matter how hard he tried. His teacher decided to supplement his grade with an A for effort to encourage Hal to keep trying. Mr. Henning encouraged his students to come to class on time by giving them credit for punctuality.

> **MyLab Education** Self-Check 5.4

WRAPPING IT UP

Back to the Cases

Now that you have read about planning instruction by analyzing student needs, look back at the teacher stories at the beginning of the chapter. Then go to MyLab Education to apply the knowledge you've gained in this chapter to each case.

MyLab Education Application Exercise 5.1: Case Study 5.1

MR. RODRIGUEZ has provided a digital copy of the text and a daily review of previously presented content, outlines of lectures, and small-group discussions to support Manuel's learning of content. Step 7 of the INCLUDE strategy asks teachers to evaluate student progress.

MyLab Education Application Exercise 5.2: Case Study 5.2

JOSH has cerebral palsy. He is in the normal range in ability, excelling in math. However, he has a lot of trouble with muscle movements, having little use of his lower body and legs as well as problems with fine muscle coordination. As a result, Josh struggles to write quickly and correctly. Josh also has trouble with his speech; he speaks haltingly and is difficult to understand. Josh is included in Ms. Stewart's middle school English class.

MyLab Education Application Exercise 5.3: Case Study 5.3

CHARLENE is a student with autism in Mr. Rowen's fourth-grade general education class. She is considered high functioning and is on grade level in math and science but struggles with reading comprehension. Like many students with autism, she has difficulties initiating and sustaining relationships with her peers and teachers.

Summary

LO 5.1 The INCLUDE strategy is a decision-making process to help teachers make adjustments in their instruction for students with special needs. The steps in INCLUDE are: identify classroom demands; note student learning strengths and needs; check for potential paths to student success; look for possible problem areas; use information to brainstorm ways to adjust instruction; decide which adjustments to make; and evaluate student progress.

LO 5.2 An important part of the INCLUDE strategy is analyzing classroom demands. Demands covering four major areas should be analyzed: classroom management, classroom grouping, instructional materials, and instructional methods.

LO 5.3 An analysis of classroom organization involves physical organization, classroom routines, classroom climate, behavior management (including classroom rules, consequences, and monitoring), and use of time.

LO 5.4 An analysis of classroom grouping involves whole-class and small instructional groups, same-skill and mixed-skill groups, and one-to-one instruction.

LO 5.5 Classroom texts need to be analyzed with respect to how explicit and systematic they are in their presentation of skills and content. Manipulatives and models and instructional and assistive technology can provide extra instructional support for all students. Common instructional methods in need of analysis include direct and indirect instruction, independent student practice, and student evaluation. Sometimes students with disabilities or other special needs require extra support in order to be successful. These supports are called scaffolds.

APPLICATIONS IN TEACHING PRACTICE

Planning Adjustments in the Instructional Environment

Consider the following two scenarios:

- Verna is a student with a learning disability in Ms. Chang's fourth-grade class. Ms. Chang uses whole-group instruction in math. This method is sometimes hard for Verna, who is behind her peers in math. Verna is slow to remember math facts, has trouble keeping numbers straight in columns, and sometimes forgets a step or two when she is computing a problem that requires several steps.

- Mr. Howard teaches U.S. history. About half of the students in his fourth-hour class struggle in reading; four students receive special education services for learning disabilities. Mr. Howard has been assigned a special education teacher, Ms. Riley, to co-teach the class with him. Mr. Howard and Ms. Riley think the class can benefit from learning the following textbook-reading strategy (Bartelt, Marchio, & Reynolds, 1994):

  R *Review* headings and subheadings.
  E *Examine* boldface words.
  A *Ask* "What do I expect to learn?"
  D *Do* it: Read!
  S *Summarize* in your own words.

QUESTIONS

1. Identify the demands in Ms. Chang's class that are likely to be challenging for Verna.

2. Describe how Ms. Chang can use the steps in the INCLUDE strategy to help Verna succeed in the large group.

3. How can Ms. Chang use direct instruction to teach students to round numbers to the nearest 10? Design such a lesson.

4. Can Mr. Howard and Ms. Riley use the approaches for co-teaching you learned about in Chapter 3 to teach the reading strategy and still cover the history content required by the state? Explain.

5. How can they use scaffolding to teach the READS strategy?

6. Find a drill-and-practice computer program for elementary or high school students and evaluate it. Does it meet the criteria for effective instruction discussed in this chapter?

CHAPTER 6

Students with Low-Incidence Disabilities

LEARNING OUTCOMES

After you read this chapter, you will be able to:

6-1 Describe what it means to say that a student has a low-incidence disability and apply the INCLUDE strategy to effectively instruct these students in your classroom.

6-2 Outline the characteristics of students with autism spectrum disorder (ASD) and the supports they need.

6-3 Describe the characteristics of students with moderate, severe, and multiple disabilities, including intellectual disabilities and deaf-blindness, and the supports general educators can provide for them.

6-4 Explain the characteristics of students with sensory impairments (that is, vision or hearing loss) and the supports general educators can provide for them.

6-5 Explain the characteristics of students with physical, medical, and health impairments and the supports general educators can provide for them.

DAWN is a fourth-grade student at Parkview Elementary School. Although the special educator, school psychologist, and principal all indicated that they thought Dawn should spend much of the day in a separate education classroom, Ms. Burke, Dawn's mother, argued strongly that she should be educated with her peers. With some hesitation, Dawn, who has a moderate intellectual disability, is a student in Mr. Chavez's class. For the morning, she is supported by Ms. Calhoun, a paraprofessional whose responsibility is to facilitate Dawn's participation in lessons. Four times per week she leaves the classroom for 45 minutes in the afternoon for support in the special education classroom. Ms. Burke, however, is dissatisfied with Dawn's education. She has scheduled a meeting with the principal because Dawn says she usually works at a table in the back of the classroom, mostly with Ms. Calhoun, not interacting with typical peers or with Mr. Chavez.

What are the learning characteristics and needs of students like Dawn? What are appropriate expectations for Mr. Chavez to have for her this year? What are his responsibilities for ensuring that Dawn is a welcomed member of the class? What accommodations and modifications does Dawn need to succeed in fourth grade?

SEAN is a 12th-grade student identified as having autism spectrum disorder (ASD). Although he spent much of the day in a special education classroom when he was in elementary school, he now receives all his core academic instruction in general education classes. His special education teacher, Ms. Morrow, is working with him one class period each day to ensure that he understands assignments, completes the school's learning and study skills curriculum, and prepares to attend community college next year. Sean generally has done very well in high school. One of his greatest supports has been his friend Jonas, who explains when Sean does not understand a classmate's joke and inconspicuously guides Sean when he seems unsure of himself in social situations. As Sean looks forward to college, he is not worried about the academic requirements; he is a very bright young man who grasps most concepts easily. His greatest concerns are dealing with large classes, being surrounded by strangers who may not understand his special needs, and advocating for himself by going to the Office of Disability Services.

What is autism spectrum disorder? What should Sean's teachers do to help him learn? What accommodations might Sean need now, in high school, and later, in the community college?

NATALIE left sixth grade as a slightly above average student who had several close friends and who played in a community soccer league. Over the summer, though, she was struck by an automobile in a hit-and-run accident while riding her bike. Thrown more than 100 feet, she suffered a moderate traumatic brain injury and several broken bones. She spent more than two months in a hospital and rehabilitation facility and missed the beginning of seventh grade, but now she has returned to school. A medical case worker briefed Natalie's teachers about her present and likely future needs. They explained that Natalie is still experiencing headaches and dizziness, especially when tired, and that she is now reading three years below grade level. She often is anxious and is emotionally volatile, sometimes laughing inappropriately and sometimes crying. However, the case worker also explained that Natalie's skills and needs are likely to continue to change for many months and expressed optimism that she would eventually recover many of the skills she had before the accident. Natalie's mother has requested that teachers stay in close contact with her about Natalie's school performance. And Natalie says she will work hard and asks her teachers not to put her back in sixth grade again (an option not even being considered).

What are the responsibilities of general education teachers for students who have chronic or serious illnesses that may affect their school attendance and academic achievement and behavior and social skills? How could teachers help classmates understand a student's special needs and also help students be part of their class groups? How could teachers help Natalie to set goals and manage her likely frustration with her changed abilities?

Students like Dawn, Sean, and Natalie used to be considered the sole responsibility of the special education system. They might have attended a separate class for the entire school day, or they might have been educated in a separate school. Now, though, these students are likely to be members of your school's learning community because they have the same right as other students to be, as appropriate to their needs, part of a typical classroom. For Dawn, attending fourth grade with her classmates prepares her to be a valued and contributing member of her community during and after her school years, even though this educational arrangement may include an array of challenges. For Sean, being successful in college depends on receiving the strong academic background available in general education classes. For Natalie, interacting with her teachers and peers and making progress in the general curriculum can contribute to her recovery. All these students, because of their disabilities, may need specialized instruction, equipment, and other assistance.

In this chapter, you will learn about the characteristics and needs of students with low-incidence disabilities, which include autism; moderate, severe, and multiple disabilities; sensory impairments; and physical, medical, and health disabilities. The federal terms for these disabilities, the number of students with these disabilities served through the Individuals with Disabilities Education Act (IDEA), and the proportion of each group educated primarily in general education are summarized in Table 6.1. You also will explore accommodations specific to the unique needs of these students that general education teachers and other professionals can make to enable them to learn.

TABLE 6.1   School-Age Students with Low-Incidence Disabilities Receiving Special Education Services in 2015–2016[a]

Federal Disability Category	Defining Characteristics	Total Number of Students	Percentage of All Students Receiving IDEA Services	Percentage of All Students Ages 6–21	Percentage of Students in General Education 80% or More of the School Day
Intellectual disability[c]	• Significant below-average general intellectual functioning with deficits in adaptive behavior • Identified between birth and 18 years of age • Adversely affects educational performance	418,540	6.9[b]	.62	16.9
Multiple disabilities	• Two or more disabilities so interwoven that none can be identified as the primary disability • Adversely affect educational performance	125.232	2.1	.19	13.4
Deaf/Hearing impairment	• Hearing loss is permanent or fluctuating, mild to profound in nature, in one or both ears • Loss may be referred to as *hard of hearing* or *deaf* • Adversely affects educational performance	67,426	1.1	.10	60.2
Orthopedic impairment	• Physically disabling conditions that affect locomotion or motor functions • May be the result of a congenital anomaly, disease, accident, or other cause • Adversely affects educational performance	41,232	.7	.06	54.5

TABLE 6.1   (*Continued*)

Federal Disability Category	Defining Characteristics	Total Number of Students	Percentage of All Students Receiving IDEA Services	Percentage of All Students Ages 6–21	Percentage of Students in General Education 80% or More of the School Day
Other health impairment[d]	• Conditions resulting in limited strength, vitality, or alertness and caused by chronic or acute health problems • Adversely affects educational performance	907,207	15.0	1.35	65.4
Visual impairment	• Vision loss in which the student cannot successfully use vision as a primary channel for learning or has such reduced acuity or visual field that processing information visually is significantly inhibited and specialized materials or modifications are needed • Adversely affects educational performance	24,944	.4	.04	66.3
Autism	• Developmental disability characterized by impairments in communication, learning, and reciprocal social interactions • Usually identified in infancy or early childhood • Adversely affects educational performance	550,405	9.1	.82	39.9
Deaf-blindness	• Presence of both a vision loss and hearing disability that causes severe communication and related problems • Adversely affects educational performance	1,280	0.00	.00	23.2
Traumatic brain injury	• Impairment manifested by limited strength, vitality, alertness, or other impaired development resulting from a traumatic brain injury • Adversely affects educational performance	25,488	.42	.04	49.9
Developmental delay	• Significant delay in one or more of these areas: physical development, cognitive development, communication development, social or emotional development, or adaptive development • Needs special education and related services • Applicable for children ages 3–9	149,306	2.5	.22	63.7

[a]Students ages 6–21 receiving services through IDEA, Part B (U.S. Department of Education, 2017a, b). Note that the disability category developmental delay does not distinguish among children with mild versus significant disabilities; not all children in this category may have low-incidence disabilities.

[b]The most recent published educational environment data are from the 2014–2015 school year (U.S. Department of Education, 2016).

[c]Because federal categories of disability do not distinguish among students with various degrees of intellectual disability, it is difficult to provide a precise estimate of the number of students with moderate or severe intellectual disabilities. However, approximately one-third of the students in this category have moderate or severe intellectual disabilities.

[d]The category *other health impairments* includes students with ADHD who are eligible for special education (not all are, a topic presented in Chapter 8). These students have a high incidence disability. However, this category also includes students with significant health or medical conditions, and their needs are considered in this chapter.

Source: U.S. Department of Education. (2017a, b, January). "Number of students ages 6 through 21 served under IDEA, Part B, by disability and state; and Students ages 6 through 21 served under IDEA, Part B, as a percentage of the population, by disability category and state." *IDEA Section 618 data products: State tables.* Washington, DC: Author. Retrieved from https://www2.ed.gov/programs/osepidea/618-data/static-tables/index .html#partb-cc. U.S. Department of Education, Office of Special Education and Rehabilitative Services, Office of Special Education Programs. (2016, October). *38th annual report to Congress on the implementation of the Individuals with Disabilities Education Act.* Washington, DC: Author. Retrieved from https://www2.ed.gov/about/reports/annual/osep/2016/parts-b-c/38th-arc-for-idea.pdf.

What Are Low-Incidence Disabilities?

When you work with students with low-incidence disabilities, you will notice immediately the diversity of their abilities and needs, the range of educational services they access, and the variety of specialists who ensure they receive an appropriate education. The following points can help you keep in perspective the uniqueness of these students and your role in their education:

1. Students with low-incidence disabilities together make up less than 20 percent of all the students with disabilities in schools. That means that you are unlikely to teach these students every year unless your school has a program that brings together students with such disabilities from across your school district, sometimes referred to as a *cluster program* or *district class*. Otherwise and with the possible exception of students with autism, you may encounter students with low-incidence disabilities only a few times in your career.

2. Most students with low-incidence disabilities have received some type of special education service for most of their lives. They might come to kindergarten already having attended an infant program and preschool program in a daycare, inclusive preschool, or special education setting where they already have received intensive specially designed instruction. You also may find that many supports and extensive technical assistance are available for your students with low-incidence disabilities.

3. Students with low-incidence disabilities need the same type of attention from you that other students do. If you are unsure about a student's needs, it is nearly always best to rely on the same professional judgment you use in working with other students. If you encounter difficulty, you can access the technical support that special education professionals offer. Students with certain disabilities, especially significant or complex ones, often are accompanied by paraprofessionals or personal assistants, who sometimes work with them for several years. Such an individual also may be able to offer insight about responding to a given student, but the responsibility for providing the student's education in your class is yours in consultation with special education staff members.

You may have some concerns about meeting the needs of a student with a low-incidence disability in your classroom. The Working Together feature suggests questions you can ask colleagues and parents to prepare for teaching a student with a low-incidence disability. The questions address the student's strengths and potential, learning and social needs, and physical or health needs. They also cover domains in which accommodations or modifications might be needed, including the physical arrangement of the classroom. What other questions would you add?

As you anticipate teaching students with low-incidence disabilities, as well as other students with disabilities or special needs, you also should recall the notion of universal design for learning (UDL), introduced in Chapter 1 and explained in more detail in Chapter 5. By using the principles of UDL and applying them using the INCLUDE strategy, also introduced in Chapter 5, you will be able to plan and deliver instruction and evaluate student learning in a way that enables all students to access the curriculum and acquire the skills that will make it possible for them to lead productive lives.

RESEARCH-BASED PRACTICES

Sermier, Dessemontet, and Bless (2013) studied the impact of including students with intellectual disabilities on the achievement of low-, average-, and high-achieving peers. They found that inclusion had no negative effects on any of the typical students.

FYI

As a reminder of the information presented in Chapter 1, IDEA permits children ages three through nine to be identified as having a *developmental delay*, a label indicating the presence of a significant physical, intellectual, communication, or social or emotional difficulty without naming a specific disability category.

MyLab Education Self-Check 6.1

WORKING TOGETHER 6.1
Questions to Ask When Working with Students with Low-Incidence Disabilities

When you teach a student with a low-incidence disability, you probably will have concerns about the student's needs and your responsibilities for helping her succeed. What you will find is that collaboration is central to effectively educating students with these disabilities. In your conversations with special educators, related services personnel, administrators, and parents, you might ask questions such as these:

STUDENT STRENGTHS AND NEEDS

1. What are the student's greatest strengths?
2. What activities and rewards does the student most enjoy? At school? At home?
3. What are this student's interests?
4. What are the student's needs in these domains: academic? social? emotional? behavioral? physical? other?
5. Does the student have physical or health needs that require my attention? For example, does the student need to take medication? Is the student likely to have a reaction to medication? Does the student tire easily? Does the student need assistance in moving from place to place? Should I be prepared for any type of emergency related to the student's health?
6. What else should I know about this student's strengths and needs?

STUDENT GOALS

1. What are the three or four most important instructional goals for this student in my class? What are the academic, social, behavioral, emotional, and other goals?
2. What are the goals for this student in each subject (for elementary teachers)? How do the goals for this student interface with the instructional goals of this course (for secondary teachers)? Overall, how do the goals for this student represent or align with the general curriculum/standards to be met by typical students?
3. What are the goals that this student is working on throughout the day? Which goals are emphasized during different periods of the day?
4. What are goals for this student outside the IEP? Family priorities? Student priorities?

STUDENT SUPPORTS AND ACCOMMODATIONS

1. For how much time will this student participate in my class (elementary level)? Will this student be in my class every day? If not, when will the student be present?
2. If I have a question about the student, whom should I talk to? Which other professionals may be in contact with me about this student or come to my classroom?
3. Does the student have a paraprofessional or interpreter? If a paraprofessional is assigned, what responsibilities should that person carry out? For what activities should the student, not the paraprofessional, be responsible? To what extent may the paraprofessional help other students in the class?
4. What other services (for example, speech/language services, occupational therapy) will the student access? How often? Who will be in touch to let me know about these services? Will they be delivered in the classroom or in another location?
5. Do I need to adjust the physical environment for this student? If so, how?
6. Do I need to adjust my expectations for this student because of physical or health needs? If so, how? Are there restrictions on this student's participation in any class activities? If so, what?
7. How can I best adjust my teaching to foster student success?

What Are the Characteristics and Instructional Needs of Students with Autism Spectrum Disorders?

Autism was first identified as a disorder in 1943 by Dr. Leo Kanner. Since then, it has been the source of much research and ongoing professional debate about its causes and characteristics. Professionals now recognize that autism is a unique disorder that occurs in many forms, and they usually refer to this group of disabilities as autism spectrum disorders (ASDs) to convey its diverse nature. The prevalence of autism spectrum disorders has been rising steadily over the past decade, partly due to better diagnosis (Centers for Disease Control and Prevention, 2017c). ASD is believed to occur in some form in 1 in 68 children (Christensen et al., 2016) and soon may be considered a high-incidence disability. This disability affects boys more than girls in a ratio of approximately 4:1 to 5:1, and in more than half the cases it is accompanied by an intellectual or other disability (Centers for Disease Control and Prevention, 2017c). Thus, many individuals with autism spectrum disorders have average ability and some are gifted or talented (Wade & Reeve, 2014).

MyLab Education

Video Example 6.1: Olivia

Many individuals with autism spectrum disorder have average ability and some are gifted or talented (Wade & Reeve, 2014), a point clearly made in this video of Olivia describing what it is like to have this disability.

Characteristics of Students with Autism Spectrum Disorders

autism /

Although autism is like most of the other low-incidence disabilities in that it can exist in many variations, from mild to severe, and cannot be treated as a single disorder with a single set of adaptations, it does have specific characteristics.

SOCIAL RELATIONSHIPS Significant difficulty with social relationships is a defining characteristic of individuals with autism. Many students with autism resist human contact and social interactions from a very early age and have difficulty learning the subtleties of social interaction (Demopoulos, Hopkins, & Davis, 2013; Trevisan & Birmingham, 2016). These students often do not make eye contact with others, and they can seem uninterested in developing social relationships. For example, typical young children often ask the teacher to watch them do something ("Look at me!"), and they bring interesting items to share with their teacher and classmates. A young child with autism, however, may not seek out such opportunities for social interactions. In another example, Arturo, a 15-year-old with autism, was frustrated that he had no friends. However, in his conversations with peers he was observed to repeatedly list all the species of birds found in his geographic area and to never ask others about their interests. Because he could not take on the perspectives of others and did not know how to participate in the give-and-take of conversation, he was socially isolated.

COMMUNICATION A key reason students with autism spectrum disorders experience difficulty in social relationships is the challenges they face in using and responding to traditional verbal and nonverbal communication (e.g., Matson, Hess, & Mahan, 2013; Olsson, Rautio, Asztalos, Stoetzer, & Bölte, 2016). These students often have significantly delayed language development and, if they have language skills, they struggle to maintain conversation with another person. In writing about her experiences of being autistic, Temple Grandin, one of the most famous individuals with ASD and a university professor who designs livestock facilities, provides clear examples of her communication problems (Grandin, 2017). She explains that when she was young she simply did not have the words to communicate and so frequently resorted to screaming. She also comments that as she grew up, she observed others but did not understand how to fit in.

Unlike Grandin, many students with autism spectrum disorders cannot write or otherwise easily communicate about their experiences, and they may use behaviors instead of words to convey many needs. Unless they are taught alternative behaviors, they might hit a peer as a way of saying hello or run from the classroom instead of saying they do not like the assignment just given. Some students with autism have *echolalic speech*; they repeat what others have said instead of producing original communication. Strategizing to ensure productive communication is a central part of working with students with ASD.

STUDENT INTERESTS Another characteristic of students with autism is a narrow range of interests. For example, one student may be fascinated with radios to the exclusion of nearly everything else; another might focus on a single period in history and have an expert's understanding of that era. When students with autism have such interests, they can spend countless hours absorbed in a private world of exploration. They might act bored with every topic and every activity unless it relates to their special interest. This behavior sometimes has a negative impact on social relationships with peers and adults, because individuals with ASD may not discern that

Many students with autism do not have intellectual disabilities, and with appropriate supports in place they can be successful in general education classrooms learning the academic curriculum and acquiring social and other skills from peers.

others are not as interested in their preferred topic as they are, a point illustrated in the example of Arturo earlier in this section. However, researchers now are exploring how students' focused interests can be used as a tool for fostering the development of social and communication skills (Winter-Messiers & Herr, 2010).

STUDENT STRESS Students with autism have a low threshold for and difficulty in dealing with stress and may respond with anxiety (Maskey, Warnell, Parr, Le Couteur, & McConachie, 2013; Saggers, 2015). A change in classroom seating assignments could be difficult for a student with autism, as could the introduction of a new route from the classroom to the bus or the need to persist on a task with several steps. Particular noises or odors or a noisy environment such as a crowded hallway or bustling cafeteria also can be stressful. Many students with autism respond to stress with restricted and repetitive behaviors (RRB), sometimes called stereotypic behaviors. They complete the same action or motion again and again. For example, they may rock rapidly, spin an object repeatedly, or twirl their arms. In other situations, students might develop a ritual to complete a task. They might need 10 minutes to prepare to complete an assignment because they need to arrange paper and pencil on the desk in a precise pattern, check that all the books in the desk are also stored in a specific order, and make sure the desk is aligned precisely at the intersection of tiles on the classroom floor. In your classroom, you should be aware of potentially stressful situations for a student with autism. You can allow time for the student to prepare for the situation, talk about the situation well in advance, assign a peer partner to assist the student, and enlist the assistance of a special educator or paraprofessional. If a student's response to stress is demonstrated with aggressive or disruptive behavior, you should work closely with a special educator, behavior consultant, or other specialist to address the problem.

THE DIVERSITY OF STUDENTS WITH AUTISM SPECTRUM DISORDER Perhaps the most important understanding to develop about students with autism spectrum disorders is that the label given to them does not inform you of their strengths and needs. Some students with ASD have significant intellectual disabilities and may need extensive supports, a curriculum that is modified to address their needs, and support throughout their lives. Others have serious but different needs. For example, some students have extraordinary difficulty in social interactions, such as making eye contact, using facial expressions appropriately and understanding those of others, and seeking out peers and other people, even though their language and intellectual development are typical (Rodríguez-Medina, Martín-Antón, Carbonero, & Ovejero, 2016). They also may have difficulty in using language correctly, confusing whether to use first-person (*I*), second-person (*you*), or third-person (*she* or *he*) pronouns. These students may appropriately spend the school day with peers in general education classrooms and continue on to college (Ashbaugh, Koegel, & Koegel, 2017; Chown & Beavan, 2012). However, because of their difficulty with social interaction, they may struggle to make friends. Think about Sean, the student you met at the beginning of this chapter. How do his characteristics match those described in this section? What challenges might he face in college?

Instructional Supports for Students with Autism Spectrum Disorders

Although it is impossible to provide a comprehensive list of strategies for helping students with ASD to succeed in your classroom, the following suggestions illustrate how your efforts can make a significant difference in these students' lives.

RESPONDING TO BEHAVIOR Students with autism spectrum disorders often have behaviors that are unusual and can be disturbing to teachers and students who do not understand them. These behaviors also can interfere with learning. However, many of the behaviors can be changed with highly structured behavior support programs (e.g., Koegel, Vernon, Koegel, Koegel, & Paullin, 2012). Others have relatively simple solutions, and some can be ignored. For example, if a student with autism withdraws from classroom activities and begins rocking every day at about 11:00 am, it could be a signal that he is too hungry to work until the 11:45 am lunchtime. Providing a snack in a quiet corner of the classroom could reduce the problem and enable the student to remain in the general education classroom. With recognition of students' needs and appropriate interventions, many students with autism spectrum disorders can receive some or all of their education in a general education classroom (Adams, Taylor, Duncan, & Bishop, 2016; Hart, 2012).

Generally, the accommodations that help to reduce behavior problems involve creating a structured and predictable environment, which will reduce student stress and encourage appropriate social interactions (e.g., Banda, Grimmit, & Hart, 2009; de Bruin, Deppeler, Moore, & Diamond, 2013). To create a positive learning environment, establish clear procedures and routines for classroom tasks and follow them consistently. For example, in an elementary classroom, you can create procedures for students to retrieve their coats at lunchtime or begin each day with the same activities in the same order. For secondary students, you can set a clear pattern in your instruction by beginning each class with a 3-minute review followed by a 20-minute lecture followed by a 15-minute individual or small-group work session. Instead of relying on words to prompt students about these procedures, work with a special educator to create picture cards that depict the procedures. Students with ASD often respond better to pictures than words. Several specific strategies for working with students with autism spectrum disorders are summarized in the Instructional Edge feature, and the strategies presented in Chapter 12 and throughout this text likewise can be effective with these students.

INSTRUCTIONAL EDGE 6.1

Teaching Students with Autism Spectrum Disorders

Specialized techniques can be used to teach students with autism spectrum disorders (ASD). These approaches are designed to draw on students' strengths, focus their attention, and address their unique needs. Three examples of approaches demonstrated to be effective with these students are social stories, the picture exchange communication system (PECS), and visual schedules.

SOCIAL STORIES

Students with ASD often experience difficulty understanding social expectations, especially when those expectations vary across situations. Here is an example of a teacher-developed social story about talking in class:

Talking

I like to talk. It is fun to talk about many things.
It's OK to talk when I am in the cafeteria.
I can talk with my classmates when we are going from class to class.
I can talk with my friends on the bus coming to school or going home.
It is not OK to talk when my teachers have told the class to be quiet.
When the teachers are talking to us students, if I am talking I do not hear what they are saying. I make it difficult for other students to hear the teacher, too. Then they do not hear what the teachers are saying.
Talking when teachers say to be quiet is not polite. Being quiet when teachers say to be quiet is polite and helps learning.

I will try to talk only when I am in the cafeteria, going from class to class, riding the bus, or when teachers say it is OK during class.

After preparing this type of story, the teacher reads it several times with the student, preferably just before the situation in which talking is an issue. For some students, visual icons representing all the ideas would be included with the story. As the student learns to follow the advice in the story, the teacher gradually reduces repetition of the story until it is no longer needed.

How would you write a social story for situations such as these?:

- A high school student who is using profanity when speaking with adults at school
- A middle school student who does not want to transition from one activity to another during a single class period
- An elementary student who takes her shoes off when in the cafeteria

PICTURE EXCHANGE COMMUNICATION SYSTEM

The picture exchange communication system (PECS) is a strategy for teaching individuals with ASD to initiate communication with peers and others (e.g., Lerna, Esposito, Conson, & Massagli, 2014). PECS is taught to students in a highly structured series of steps. Initially, the teacher or another person working with the student exchanges a picture of a desired item (for example, a crayon, a basketball) for the actual item when the student points to it or picks it up (see Figure 6.1). No words are used.

FIGURE 6.1 **PECS Uses Pictures of Objects, Similar to Those Depicted, to Foster Communication**

As students learn the system, they begin to initiate communication by bringing a picture to another individual to obtain the pictured item or make a need known. Eventually, students use this system to form sentences and answer questions. Research has demonstrated the effectiveness of this system (e.g., Alsayedhassan, Banda, & Griffin-Shirley, 2016). If you teach students with autism, you might interact with them using PECS; a special education professional would prepare you for this communication option.

VISUAL SCHEDULES

Most students with ASD benefit when they have a clear and consistent schedule that is explained ahead of time (Knight, Sartini, & Spriggs, 2015). Working with a special educator, you can develop visual schedules that use pictures only, pictures and words, or words only (see Figure 6.2). Visual schedules can be displayed in the classroom, placed on the student's desk, or kept in an assignment notebook.

FIGURE 6.2 **A Visual Schedule Often Helps Students with Autism Manage the School Day**

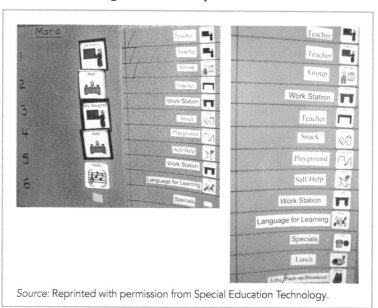

Source: Reprinted with permission from Special Education Technology.

In addition to structure, students with ASD may need opportunities during the day to work alone and be alone (Myles & Adreon, 2001). This time serves as a break from the visual and auditory stresses of the classroom and its social and communication demands. A special education teacher probably can advise you about whether this is necessary for a particular student and can assist in making arrangements for a quiet place, sometimes referred to as *home base*, in which the student can work.

FOSTERING SOCIAL INTERACTIONS To help a student with social interactions with peers and adults, you can observe the student's behavior to understand its purpose from her perspective (Banda, Hart, & Kercood, 2012; Denning, 2007). If a student has been working in a small group but suddenly leaves the group and leaves the classroom, it could be a signal that she has misunderstood a comment made by another student. Other social areas in which general education teachers can work with special educators to accommodate students with autism spectrum disorders include teaching them to wait, take turns, stop an activity before it is complete, negotiate, change topics, finish an activity, be more flexible, be quiet, and monitor their own behavior.

COMMUNICATING WITH STUDENTS Communication with students with autism is accomplished through a wide variety of strategies (Grandin, 2007; Reilly, Hughes, Harvey, Brigham, Cosgriff, Kaplan, & Bernstein, 2014). Some students with autism can communicate adequately with speech, especially when they do not feel pressured. Other students learn to communicate through sign language, just as many students who are deaf or hard of hearing do. For these students, the motor activity of signing seems to help them successfully convey their needs and preferences. For yet other students, communication boards are useful tools. By simply touching pictures, students can communicate with others even when they cannot speak the appropriate words. When communication involves following directions or mastering certain skills, video modeling, as explained in the Technology Notes feature, can be helpful. Yet other communication devices that help students who have limited speech, including those with autism, are described later in this chapter.

In general, when you learn that you will be teaching a student with autism, you should ask to meet with a special educator who can share with you the student's strengths and needs and help you plan for the school year. You also should reach out to the student's parents to establish a partnership. The diversity of students with ASD and the complexity of their needs will sometimes frustrate you and at other times make you proud to be a professional educator.

> ### RESEARCH-BASED PRACTICES
>
> In a 12-week double-blind study on the effects of a gluten-free, cassein-free diet on children with autism, a diet sometimes recommended for reducing the effects of autism, Hyman and colleagues (2016) found that the diet was well-tolerated but did not have any significant effect on the children's behavior or other symptoms associated with ASD.

MyLab Education Self-Check 6.2

TECHNOLOGY NOTES 6.1

Teaching Skills to Students with Autism Through Video Modeling

Because students with autism often respond better to pictures and other nonverbal signals than to words, one option for teaching them a wide variety of skills is *video modeling* (Burton, Anderson, Prater, & Dyches, 2013; Yakubova & Taber-Doughty, 2017). In video modeling, professionals either use a commercially available video or prepare a video that demonstrates the skill for the student. In the latter option, the individual modeling the skill could be a teacher or another professional familiar to the student, a peer, a sibling, or even the student (if the student occasionally is successful in completing the targeted skill). The video may be in a standard format, much like an instructional video you might watch. Some videos, though, are done "over the shoulder," so that it looks the way it would if the student were performing it (e.g., facing someone tying shoes versus looking down as though tying your own shoes). The student watches the video, often on a tablet, smartphone, or similar device, in order to learn the skill.

These are examples of behaviors that have been taught to students with autism through video modeling:

- Initiation of social interactions
- Conversational skills
- Reciprocal play
- Academic skills such as math
- Transition from one activity to another
- Transition from one location to another within the school
- Life skills such as making a purchase
- Functional skills such as setting the table
- Perspective taking

Would you like to learn more about video modeling? If you type the term "video modeling" into a search, you can find many additional examples of video modeling using various formats.

Video modeling is a research-based practice that assists students with autism to learn important social and functional skills.

What Are the Characteristics and Instructional Needs of Students with Moderate, Severe, or Multiple Disabilities?

multiple

Students with moderate, severe, or multiple disabilities include those whose intellectual impairments and adaptive behavior deficits are so significant and pervasive that considerable support is needed for them to learn. This group also includes students with multiple disabilities, that is, students who have two or more disabilities that significantly affect their learning. Both groups of students typically have activities and assignments that differ somewhat from those of other students in your class, but their work still should be aligned with the general curriculum for which you are responsible. These students also can benefit from social interactions with classmates who do not have disabilities.

Characteristics of Students with Moderate to Severe Intellectual Disabilities

Students with moderate to severe intellectual disabilities, like Dawn, whom you met at the beginning of the chapter, have ongoing needs for support during their school years and into adult life. Some students are able to learn academic, social,

MyLab Education

Video Example 6.2: "DON'T LIMIT ME!"—Powerful Message from Megan with Down Syndrome

This video clip holds many important messages for teachers working with students with intellectual or other disabilities, in fact, all students. https://www.youtube.com/watch?v=YOwDfnoek6E

DIMENSIONS OF DIVERSITY

Cummings and Hardin (2017) interviewed eight sets of immigrant parents of children with disabilities. They reported that parents' understanding and interaction with U.S. education professionals differed based on whether they came to this country voluntarily or as refugees. All wished to receive more communication about their children.

---

and vocational skills that enable them to live independently or semi-independently as productive adults. Others' learning will be more limited, and they may need intensive services throughout their lives. In many school districts, students with moderate or severe disabilities are integrated into general education classrooms for at least a small part of the day. This integration occurs most typically at the elementary school level but sometimes at the middle school and high school levels, often for related classes such as art, music, or physical education. Especially for older students, arts integration is less common for core academic subjects.

Most states use scores on intelligence tests and adaptive behavior scales to determine the presence of an intellectual disability. Although intelligence tests must be interpreted carefully and are not helpful in designing instruction for students, an overall IQ score of less than 70 with significant difficulty in the area of adaptive behaviors (for example, ordering a meal in a restaurant) leads to eligibility for special education in the category of intellectual disability. Students with moderate or severe intellectual disabilities generally have IQ scores of approximately 55 or below, like Dawn, introduced in the chapter opening vignettes. As you read the following sections, think about how she might learn in your classroom.

LEARNING NEEDS AND RATE Generally, students with moderate or severe intellectual disabilities have several noticeable characteristics. First, the amount of information they can learn may be limited, and second, the rate at which they learn is much slower than that of typical peers. For example, Destiny, a middle school student with a severe intellectual disability, is learning to communicate her needs to others. She has a communication device that enables her to indicate that she needs a drink of water, that she needs to use the bathroom, and that she is hungry. Her paraprofessional sometimes works with her on this skill, but her classmates also ask her questions related to these needs. Jordan, an elementary student with a moderate intellectual disability, is learning how to tell a story from a picture book and recognize his name and address. He practices these skills as opportunities arise during general instruction and when other students are completing individual assignments that are beyond his capability.

Students with moderate or severe intellectual disabilities usually also need social skills. Several goals and objectives in a student's individualized education program (IEP) may relate to participating in one-to-one or small-group interactions with peers; responding to questions asked by others; and sharing toys, games, or materials. Without direct assistance from teachers implementing inclusive practices, students with needs in these areas may have difficulty making friends throughout their school careers (Rossetti, 2015; Walton & Ingersoll, 2013).

MAINTENANCE OF LEARNED SKILLS A second characteristic of individuals with moderate or severe intellectual disabilities is that they may have difficulty maintaining their skills; without ongoing practice, they are likely to forget what they have learned (e.g., Aykut, 2012). In the classroom, you may find this means that it is not necessary to provide new activities each day. For example, Jordan, the student mentioned previously who is learning to recognize his name and address, will need computer practice on that skill for many days. In addition, once he has identified the information, he should practice printing it on cards, writing it on the chalkboard, and saying it aloud.

GENERALIZATION OF LEARNING A third characteristic of students in this group is that they may have difficulty generalizing skills learned in one setting or application to another (e.g., Goo, Therrien, & Hua, 2016; Walser, Ayres, & Foote, 2012). It is thus critical that they learn as many skills as possible in context. For example, rather than have these students practice buttoning and unbuttoning out of context, as part of a segregated classroom exercise, they can apply this skill in the morning and afternoon as they enter and leave school wearing coats or sweaters. Older students need to learn how to greet classmates and teachers appropriately; for example, with a handshake or by just saying hello instead of shouting or tightly hugging them. This skill is most easily taught as students meet and greet people throughout the school, not necessarily in a special education classroom.

Crystal's story illustrates the characteristics of students with intellectual disabilities and demonstrates the value of an inclusive education for them. Crystal is a young woman with Down syndrome, a genetic disorder that usually includes a moderate intellectual disability. Her story is typical for such a student in a school district committed to inclusive education. She attended elementary school with her peers even though she did not always learn the same things they were learning. Her teachers expected her to behave appropriately, and her peers helped her when she got confused by the teacher's directions or otherwise needed support in the classroom. As Crystal moved to middle school, she participated with peers in co-taught science and social studies classes and exploratory classes such as healthy living and technology, and she received some of her reading and math instruction in a special education classroom. In high school, she took several classes with her typical peers, including choir, U.S. history, family and consumer sciences, career exploration, and health. She also entered a vocational preparation program so she would be ready to get a job after high school. At 21, Crystal graduated from high school. She now works in a local medical office. Her job includes duplicating medical records, doing simple filing, completing errands, and helping get mail ready to send. Crystal's success as an adult is in large part a result of learning many skills while in inclusive schools.

WWW RESOURCES

http://www.nads.org
One valuable source of information about students with Down syndrome is the website of the National Association for Down Syndrome. This site includes resources, news, and information about this relatively common syndrome.

Instructional Supports for Students with Moderate to Severe Intellectual Disabilities

Are you a bit surprised at the implication in this chapter that students with significant intellectual disabilities should participate in general education? Had you assumed that they would always receive their specialized instruction in a special education classroom? Unfortunately, the latter perception is still common (Bentley, 2008), but research indicates that students with moderate or severe intellectual disabilities benefit from attending school as members of general education classrooms (e.g., Pennington, Courtade, Jones Ault, & Delano, 2016; Ryndak, Alper, Hughes, & McDonnell, 2012). The following sections highlight strategies that can help these students succeed.

MATCH EXPECTATIONS TO INSTRUCTION Students with significant disabilities are not expected to learn all the same information as other students; their curriculum is modified to match their learning needs. However, the goals and objectives on their IEPs are related to the grade-level or course competencies. In this regard, the INCLUDE strategy and collaborating with colleagues can help you effectively teach students with moderate or severe intellectual disabilities. For example, in a social studies class, the goal for most students might

Students with multiple disabilities often receive services from several professionals, including a special educator, a speech/language therapist, and a physical therapist, and you probably will collaborate with these professionals.

be to understand detailed topographical maps. At the same time, a student with a moderate intellectual disability might work to locate on a map states where relatives live, and a student with a severe intellectual disability might work to identify photos of businesses in the community. Table 6.2 provides additional examples of how the skills that might appear on a student's IEP can be mapped onto the general curriculum.

TABLE 6.2 Sample Skills from an IEP Mapped onto Fifth-Grade School Subjects

IEP Objectives	Social Studies	Math	Reading	Physical Education	Lunch
To recognize pictures for expressive communication purposes	Use daily schedule to get out book Match pictures related to social studies	Determine story problem for peers by matching same pictures	Answer questions by pointing to pictures Sequence three pictures in order to retell story	Choose equipment using photographs Choose partner using school photographs	Use pictures to request type of milk from cafeteria person Point to pictures to converse with peers
To follow directions quickly	Watch peers get out materials and follow their lead Sequence pictorial cards in order Put away materials and get ready for next subject	Watch peers get out materials and follow their lead Work on math skills as instructed Change activity when directed	Watch peers get out materials and follow their lead Find appropriate page in book Answer questions by pointing Put away materials and get ready for next subject	Line up for PE Move to area on floor by PE teacher Follow teacher and group	Line up for lunch with class Go to lunchroom Stay at table until dismissed
To interact with peers in a positive way	Sit with classmates Do not destroy peers' work Pass out materials	Sit with classmates Do not destroy peers' work Pass out materials Respond to three offers of help	Sit with classmates Choose book to read from Respond to peers' questions	Respond to peers when they initiate Share equipment Clap for peers when they do well	Respond to peers when they initiate Initiate topics using schedule and magazine Respond to peers' questions
To make decisions	Decide who will read to her Request help when needed Pick appropriate pictures from three pictures based on question	Decide which math activities to do Decide which manipulatives to use: first, second, third	Choose book to read Choose peer to read with Choose place to read	Decide which two of three exercises to do and in what order	Choose milk Choose person to sit next to Choose where to go when finished eating and with whom
To work independently	Stay on task without adult nearby for 10 minutes Raise hand to get help	Stay on task without adult nearby for 10 minutes Raise hand to get help	Stay on task without adult nearby for 10 minutes Raise hand to get help	Stay on task without adult nearby for 10 minutes Start each exercise/ activity on own Raise hand to get help	Stay on task without adult nearby for 10 minutes Obtain milk with peer support Eat meal with no prompts

Source: Downing, J. E., *Including Students with Severe and Multiple Disabilities in Typical Classrooms*, 3e, pp. 46–47, Figure 3.2. Copyright © 2008. Reprinted by permission of Paul H. Brookes Publishing Co., Baltimore, MD.

ENLIST NATURAL SUPPORT SYSTEMS Peers, older students, parent volunteers, student teachers, interns, and other individuals at school all can assist a student with a moderate or severe disability (e.g., Biggs, Carter, & Gustafson, 2017; Carter, Moss, Hoffman, Chung, & Sisco, 2011). Peers often can answer questions or respond to basic requests without adult intervention. They sometimes also can make needed adjustments in equipment, retrieve dropped articles, and get needed instructional materials for the student. Older students can serve as peer tutors or special buddies, both for instruction and for the development of appropriate social skills. Parents, student teachers, interns, and others all can assume part of the responsibility for supporting students. For example, a student teacher can work with a small instructional group that includes both typical learners and a student with an intellectual disability.

COLLABORATE WITH FAMILIES As with your other students, when you teach a student with a moderate or severe disability, you should communicate regularly with the student's parents. Families know their children better than school professionals do, and parents can provide valuable information about teaching them (Dyke, Bourke, Llewellyn, & Leonard, 2013; Jansen, van der Putten, & Vlaskamp, 2013). Parents also might have questions about how to reinforce at home the skills learned at school. Remember, too, that parents want to hear from you about their child's successes and accomplishments, not just about challenges and concerns.

Like all parents, the parents of students with moderate or severe disabilities respond to their children based on many factors, including their culture (Blacher, Begum, Marcoulides, & Baker, 2013; Sauer & Lalvani, 2017). For example, in some Puerto Rican, Mexican, and Colombian families, the mother or both parents are blamed for having a child with significant disabilities, and raising this child is seen as penance for past sins (Olivos, Gallagher, & Aguilar, 2010). These parents' degree of acceptance of a child at a low level of functioning may frustrate teachers trying to help the student to learn skills and relying on parents to practice the skills at home. For students who are bilingual, issues may arise as educators try to teach English survival words (e.g., *stop, danger*) at school when only the native language is spoken in the home.

ACCESS ASSISTIVE TECHNOLOGY Both high- and low-technology options help students learn. For example, digital cameras create infinite opportunities to take photos of signs, locations, people, and other items that can be used as tools for contextual learning. Many students who cannot use language to communicate use various types of augmentative and alternative communication (AAC), that is, various communication forms—unaided (e.g., gestures) or aided (e.g., computer software)—that enable students to convey their messages. These are addressed in the Technology Notes feature. Other students use technology to aid movement.

Students with Multiple Disabilities

Because students with multiple disabilities often have extraordinary needs, they are considered a distinct group in IDEA. Most students with multiple disabilities have an intellectual disability and a physical or sensory impairment. The needs of these students and the supports that help them succeed can be similar to those for students with moderate and severe intellectual disabilities, the differences being mostly a matter of degree and complexity. However, a few issues that particularly concern these students may arise more often. You may find that the number of special service providers who come to the classroom to work with students with multiple special needs (for example, a special educator, a paraprofessional, a speech/language therapist, an occupational therapist) is high and occasionally a distraction in the classroom. Also, care must be taken that a wheelchair, computer equipment, other therapeutic equipment, and specialized materials (for example, large books in three-ring binders made with many pictures) for a student with multiple disabilities are seamlessly integrated into classroom practices so as not to interfere with traffic patterns, safety, storage, and student attention.

Because many students with multiple disabilities have limited speech and do not easily convey their preferences and needs, communicating with them can be a challenge (Andzik, Cannella-Malone, & Sigafoos, 2016). One strategy for communication is using AAC systems, described in the previous section.

Deaf-Blindness

Although students with dual sensory impairments, or *deaf-blindness*, typically are not totally blind or deaf, they do have extraordinary needs related to navigating

TECHNOLOGY NOTES 6.2

Augmentative and Alternative Communication

Augmentative and alternative communication (AAC) is the term for an individual's use of ways other than speech to send a message to another individual, and it may substitute for speech or be an addition to speech (e.g., Alant, 2017). AAC includes:

- Nonaided communication, such as sign language, gestures, and facial expressions
- Aided communication, such as computers with specialized software or communication devices that can "speak" for the student

You might be familiar with a children's story about AAC: E. B. White's "The Trumpet of the Swan," in which Louis, a swan who cannot make the same sounds as other swans, learns to use a trumpet as his voice. Many students with low-incidence disabilities use AAC devices either as their primary means of communication or as supplements to traditional speech. These are some examples of AAC devices that your students might use:

- *Communication boards.* Some students with significant disabilities use communication boards. These boards may be as simple as a set of pictures that depict common tasks or needs. The student points to the appropriate picture using a finger, fist, elbow, eyes, or alternative means such as a head pointer. More complex communication boards are electronic.

Communication boards can be simple or sophisticated; the student's age, ability level, and communication needs all contribute to the decision about the appropriate device.

Switches can help some students to operate their computers, activate their communication boards, and participate in classroom activities.

Pointing at pictures may activate prerecorded messages, such as "I need to be excused to the restroom" and "Hello. My name is Jorge. What is your name?" For middle and high school students, communication boards can be designed to include necessary key academic vocabulary terms.

- *Switches and scanning devices.* Some students cannot push a button or point to a picture. However, they might be able to indicate a choice using a switch. Thus, when a scanning device is used, a series of options is presented (for example, "I am hungry," "I am thirsty," or "I am tired"), and the student chooses the one that communicates the intended message. The switch is the means for making the choice. The student may have the motor control to slap a large button switch to stop items being shown on a computer screen, or she may make a slight head movement that activates a switch with an electronic voice that responds.

Information about augmentative and alternative communication is available on many websites and from many organizations. One website that includes clear explanations and an array of resources is the International Society for Augmentative and Alternative Communication (ISAAC) (http://www.isaac-online.org)

---

the environment, making sense of events that most teachers and students take for granted, and learning with a limited ability to see and hear. These students sometimes have average or above-average intelligence (as did Helen Keller), but they often have intellectual or other disabilities. They typically need a wide array of special services throughout their school careers and into adulthood (Kyzar, Brady, Summers, Haines, & Turnbull, 2016).

How a student with deaf-blindness is educated in any particular school varies considerably. The student may spend most of the day in a separate class, part of the day in general education, or much of the day in that setting (refer to Table 6.1). Regardless of placement, a student who is deaf-blind needs extensive supports. Should you be informed that you will have a student with this disability, you should meet with a special educator to learn about expectations for the student, your role in the student's education, and answers to the many questions you may have. (For example, how can you assist the student to communicate with peers?) Many of the ideas in the next sections on students with either a hearing or a vision loss also may be applicable to these students.

> **MyLab Education** Self-Check 6.3

What Are the Characteristics of and Instructional Needs of Students with Sensory Impairments?

Students with *sensory impairments* have either vision loss or hearing loss so significant that their education is affected. Their specialized needs can range from minimal to complex. Because school learning relies heavily on seeing and hearing, students with these disabilities often experience academic problems and need both teacher accommodations and adaptive equipment.

In some cases, a vision or hearing problem is identified by professionals in the school setting. If you notice any of the symptoms described in the Professional Edge feature, you should alert your school nurse or health technician as well as the student's parents.

PROFESSIONAL EDGE 6.1

Warning Signs That Students May Have Vision or Hearing Loss

As a school professional, you sometimes will be in a unique position to judge whether a student may be experiencing a vision or hearing loss. If you observe any of these warning signs, you should alert your school nurse and follow district guidelines for seeking other assistance for the student.

SIGNS OF POSSIBLE VISION LOSS

- Frequent rubbing or blinking of the eyes
- Short attention span or daydreaming
- Poor reading
- Avoiding close work
- Frequent headaches
- A drop-in scholastic or sports performance
- Covering one eye
- Tilting the head when reading
- Squinting one or both eyes
- Placing head close to book or desk when reading or writing
- Difficulty remembering, identifying, and reproducing basic geometric forms
- Poor eye–hand coordination skills

SIGNS OF POSSIBLE HEARING LOSS

- Failure to pay attention to casual conversation
- Giving wrong, inappropriate, or strange responses to simple questions

- Apparently functioning below intellectual potential
- Frequent requests for information to be repeated
- Frequent and recurring ear infections
- Complaints of ringing in the ears, "head noises," and/or dizziness
- Complaints of pain in the ears or discharge
- Withdrawing from interactions with peers
- Frustration or other unexplained behavior problems
- Limited speech or vocabulary
- Frequent mispronunciation of words
- Placing head close to book or desk when reading or writing
- Watching a speaker intently to hear
- Failing to hear someone who is speaking from behind
- Turning up the volume on the television or when using the computer
- Difficulty hearing when using the phone

Sources: Warning Signs of Vision Problems, by Eye Care Council, 2017, retrieved from http://eyecarecouncil.com/about/resources-for-parents/; *Hearing loss in children* by Cleveland Clinic, 2017, retrieved from https://my.clevelandclinic.org/health/articles/hearing-loss-children; and *Hearing loss in children*, by Centers for Disease Control and Prevention, 2015, Atlanta, GA: Retrieved from https://www.cdc.gov/ncbddd/hearingloss/facts.html.

Students with Visual Impairments

Students with visual impairments cannot see well enough to use vision as a primary channel for learning without significant assistance. Generally, the term *blind* is reserved to describe the few students who have little or no useful vision. They use touch and hearing for most learning. Most students with visual impairments are *partially sighted,* meaning that they have some useful vision.

Characteristics of Students with Visual Impairments

Students with visual impairments have the same range of intellectual ability as other students, but they typically have had fewer opportunities to acquire information usually learned visually (e.g., Ivy, Lather, Hatton, & Wehby, 2016). For example, students generally learn about maps by looking at them. Although students who are blind can learn by feeling a raised map, this method is not as efficient as seeing it. The same problem can occur with academics. Students with visual impairments often experience learning difficulties simply because they cannot easily use vision to process information (Douglas et al., 2011). Think about how you read this text: You probably scan the pages, focus on words and phrases in boldface print, and visually jump between reading the type and looking at figures, features, and photos. If you could read this book only by magnifying it 15 times, by listening to it on digital recording, or by reading it in braille, you would find it much more tedious to scan, select important words and phrases, and go back and forth between components. If you multiply this dilemma across all the visual learning tasks students encounter, then you can begin to understand the challenges of learning with a visual impairment.

As is true for all individuals, students with visual impairments vary in their social and emotional development. Some students encounter little difficulty making friends, interacting appropriately with peers and adults, and developing a positive self-concept. Other students need support in these areas (Arndt, Lieberman, & James, 2014). For example, it is important to teach some students who cannot see to adhere to social norms, such as facing a person when talking, taking turns, and keeping an appropriate social distance. Conversely, teachers should keep in mind that some students might miss another student's or a teacher's puzzled expression about something they had said and continue to interact as if they were understood. Teachers also should help other students to understand that a student with a visual impairment cannot help her unusual eye movements or standing a little too close during interactions because she has difficulty judging distance.

Instructional Supports for Students with Visual Impairments

Accommodations needed by students with visual impairments depend on many factors, and the application of principles of universal design for learning (UDL), implemented by using the INCLUDE strategy, can guide your planning. First, take into account the student's overall ability level, use of learning strategies and other learning skills, and attentional and motivational levels, just as you would for any other student. Then, working with a special educator, make accommodations relative to your classroom demands, the amount of the student's residual vision, and the nature of her vision problems. Be sure to keep in mind that these students have many essential life skills to master that other students take for granted (e.g., proper eating manners, maintaining appropriate social distance during interactions, keyboarding, signature writing, and proficiency in using assistive technology). These skills sometimes are referred to as the *expanded core curriculum,*

FYI

Although a few students have guide dogs, adults are more likely to use them because of the care these animals need, the training involved in obtaining them, and the expense of maintaining them.

because they are as essential to these students as are the skills of the traditional curriculum (e.g., Lieberman, Haegele, Columna, & Conroy, 2014), and time must be made in their school careers to teach these skills. Some specific accommodations you can make and unique needs you must consider for students with visual impairments are covered in the following sections.

ORIENTATION AND MOBILITY One critical area of need for students with visual impairments is orientation and mobility, that is, the sense of where they are in relation to other objects and people in the environment and the ability to move about within a space (Cmar, 2015). For example, students with visual impairments need to understand where furniture, doorways, bookshelves, and the teacher's desk are in the classroom in relation to their own location. In addition, they need to be able to move from the classroom to the auditorium to the cafeteria and out to the bus in a timely manner. Some students will use a traditional white-tipped cane to move about; others may rely on personal global positioning system (GPS) devices.

Your first task in preparing for a student with a visual impairment might be to arrange your classroom carefully, leaving adequate space for all students to move about. Depending on the amount of sight the student has, you might need to keep furniture and supplies in consistent places and make sure the student has an opportunity to learn where everything is. If you decide to rearrange the room or move your supplies, alert the student with a visual impairment to the changes and allow opportunities to adapt to them.

TEACHING STUDENTS WITH VISUAL IMPAIRMENTS You might be asked to modify your teaching slightly to accommodate a student with a visual impairment. For example, you might need to use a whiteboard with a wide, black felt-tipped marker instead of your usual array of colors, or you might need to provide the student with paper that has heavy black lines instead of the traditional light blue ones. In addition, you should:

- Be sure to recite what is written on the board.
- Call students by name so the student with a visual impairment can learn the sounds of classmate's voices and where they are seated.
- Allow the student to move close to demonstrations and displays.
- Give specific directions instead of using general words such as *here* and *there*.
- Seat the student to optimize visual learning (e.g., away from bright light or near the front of the room).
- Possibly assign a peer buddy.

Usually, an itinerant vision specialist or another special educator will alert you to accommodations needed. They also may observe in your classroom and make suggestions on how you could improve instructional clarity for the student.

Some students with visual impairments need additional time to complete assignments, whether during class or as homework. Others may need a change-of-pace activity. A student who is fidgeting or refusing to work might be fatigued; this is a frequent problem for students who have to make extraordinary efforts to learn using residual vision. Letting the student take a break or substituting an alternative activity both helps the student and prevents discipline problems. Also keep in mind how to plan alternative learning opportunities for students. If you are talking about history and using a timeline, for example, use white glue or some other means of marking points on the timeline so a student with a visual impairment can participate meaningfully in the discussion by touching the points and feeling the distance between them. A vision specialist can help you develop such alternative learning opportunities.

LEARNING TOOLS FOR STUDENTS WITH VISUAL IMPAIRMENTS Students with visual impairments use a wide variety of devices or equipment to facilitate their learning. If they have some residual vision, they can use devices to help them

MyLab Education

Video Example 6.3: Meet Kyle

In this video you will meet Kyle, a student with a visual impairment. Pay attention to the adjustments made for him and to the many ways he is like other students his age.

WWW RESOURCES

http://afb.org
You can learn more about visual impairments by accessing the website of the American Foundation for the Blind.

acquire information visually. Some use simple devices such as magnifying lenses and bright lights to read or do other schoolwork. Others hold their books close to their eyes or at a specific angle to see the print. Many students with visual impairments use computers with speech synthesizers or text enlargers. For students who read braille, assignments can be printed on a braille printer as well as a standard printer so both teacher and student can read them. Examples of the learning tools available for students with visual impairments are included in the Technology Notes feature.

Students with Hearing Loss

Students who are deaf or hard of hearing, referred to in IDEA as being deaf or having hearing impairments, cannot hear well enough to use hearing as a primary channel for learning without significant assistance. Because a huge proportion of both formal and incidental learning occurs through understanding

TECHNOLOGY NOTES 6.3
Assistive Technology for Students with Visual Impairments

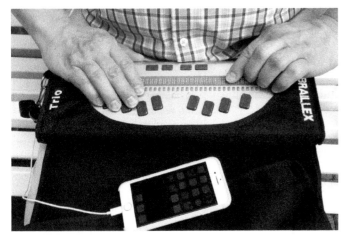

A braillewriter has six keys that the student simultaneously presses down in various combinations to produce Braille, the special system of raised dots that can be read through touch. Electronic braillewriters, some with a speech synthesizer, can be wirelessly connected to computers and other devices.

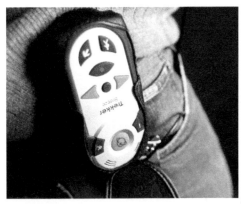

Talking personal GPS devices like the Trekker Breeze+ assist students in moving around their schools and communities; specific locations can be programmed into these devices.

Some students with low vision benefit from a video magnifier, which includes a camera, monitor, lighting, and stand. It enlarges any image placed on it and may offer varying levels of contrast and changeable colors (e.g., white print on a black background instead of the reverse).

language in casual conversations, presentations by teachers and others, and over-heard information, many professionals consider deafness and other hearing loss to be primarily language or communication impairments (Meinzen-Derr, Wiley, Grether, Phillips, Choo, Hibner, & Barnard, 2014). Small numbers of students with hearing loss are *deaf*; they cannot process linguistic information through hearing, either with or without hearing aids. Most students with hearing loss, however, are *hard of hearing*, meaning that they have some residual hearing that lets them process linguistic information, usually by using hearing aids or other assistive devices.

One key factor professionals consider in judging the seriousness of a student's hearing loss is the age when the loss occurred. Students who have been deaf or hard of hearing since birth are often at a disadvantage for language learning because they did not go through the natural process of acquiring it. These students can speak, but because they learned to talk without hearing how they sounded, their speech may be difficult to understand. They might prefer sign language and an interpreter for communicating with you and others. Students who lose their hearing after they learn language—that is, after about age five—sometimes experience fewer language and speech difficulties.

Characteristics of Students Who Are Deaf or Hard of Hearing

Students with hearing loss have the same range of intellectual ability as other students. However, if intelligence is assessed using a test based on language, students with hearing loss might have lower scores. Academically, many of these students struggle because their hearing loss affects their ability to understand language, which in turn affects their learning (Marschark, Shaver, Nagle, & Newman, 2015). For example, they might have difficulty learning vocabulary and as a result understanding the materials they read and the lessons you present (Webb, Lederberg, Branum-Martin, & McDonald Connor, 2015). They may miss subtle meanings of words, which can affect both their learning and their social interactions. One simple example can illustrate the complexity of learning language. Think of all the meanings you know for the word *can*. As a noun, it refers to a container made of metal for storing food—for example, *a can of chili*. But it also means a container with a lid, as in the type of can that tennis balls are packaged in. *Can* also has slang meanings as a synonym for both *bathroom* and *prison*. As a verb, it means "to be physically able," as in *I can lift that box*. It also refers to preserving produce from the garden, as in *I plan to can green beans this year*; to losing a job, as in *I just got canned*; and to the state of being likely, as in *Can that be true?* If you think about all the words in the English language that have multiple and sometimes contradictory meanings, it becomes easier to understand the difficulties faced by students who are deaf or hard of hearing, who may not informally learn these meanings.

Students who are deaf or hard of hearing are sometimes socially and emotionally immature (Eriks-Brophy et al., 2012). This lack of maturity occurs for two reasons. First, much of the etiquette children acquire comes from listening to others and imitating what they say and do. This learning is not available to many students who are deaf or hard of hearing. Second, these students can become confused in interactions that involve many people and multiple conversations. Because these types of situations often are uncomfortable for them, students with hearing impairments sometimes avoid them and fail to develop the social skills needed in group interactions (Antia, Jones, Luckner, Kreimeyer, & Reed, 2011; Vogel-Walcutt, Schatschneider, & Bowers, 2011). For example, Jim is a seventh-grade student with a moderate hearing loss. When students work in lab groups in Mr. George's science class, Jim tends to withdraw because he cannot follow what everyone is saying. Sometimes he tries to participate in the activity, but he often does so by making an exaggerated face or drawing a cartoon to show others. He does this even when the other students are working intently, and they become annoyed with his antics.

FYI
Hearing loss is measured by the loudness of sounds as measured in decibels (dB) and pitch or tones as measured in hertz (Hz). Normal speech is usually 55–60 dB and 500–2000 Hz; a rock band plays at about 110 dB. A hearing loss of 25–40 dB is mild; 40–60 dB is moderate; 60–80 dB is severe; and more than 80 dB is profound.

When Jim realizes his attempts to participate are not being successful, he pulls away from the group and becomes passive. Mr. George and the special education teacher are working to address this problem. Mr. George makes sure that he monitors the groups' work, and he sometimes intervenes by asking Jim a question that helps him interact appropriately with his peers.

Instructional Supports for Students Who Are Deaf or Hard of Hearing

Accommodations for students who are deaf or hard of hearing emphasize helping them use whatever residual hearing they may have and accessing language to promote formal and informal learning. Although the specific types of accommodations needed by a student you teach will be determined by the multidisciplinary team that writes the student's IEP, the following are some common ones.

TEACHING STUDENTS WHO ARE DEAF OR HARD OF HEARING Many students who are deaf or hard of hearing get some information through *speech reading*, or watching others' lips, mouths, and expressions. Given this, the teacher should always face the class when presenting information and stand where no glare or shadow makes it difficult for students to see. Using an overhead projector or Smartboard™ instead of writing on the chalkboard also is a good idea. A teacher also should stand in one location instead of moving around the room, and the student should sit near the teacher. These adjustments facilitate speech reading but also are necessary if an interpreter is present. Teachers should avoid exaggerating sounds or words; doing this makes it more difficult for the student, not easier. Teachers also should use as many visual aids as possible. Important directions can be written on the whiteboard, using either words or, for younger students, pictures. For older students, major points in a lecture can be written on a Smartboard or on the whiteboard.

As with students who have visual impairments, safety also must be kept in mind for students with hearing loss. Assigning a buddy to assist such a student during a fire, tornado, or earthquake drill is one simple strategy for addressing this issue. For other specific considerations regarding safety, a special educator with expertise in working with these students can assist you.

If a student who is deaf or hard of hearing uses sign language, you might consider enrolling in a sign class yourself and, especially in elementary and middle school, inviting a deaf education teacher to your class to teach some signs to the entire group. High school students may have an option for learning sign language as a course; in some states, it is considered a foreign language. Students generally enjoy learning some signs, and both you and they will be better able to communicate with the student who cannot hear. For example, you might use the sign for "line up" or "stay seated" instead of using words to ask students to carry out these routines. When you use the sign, everyone, including the student with hearing loss, will understand. An example of how to include students who are deaf or hard of hearing in the general education classroom is described in the Case in Practice.

LEARNING TOOLS FOR STUDENTS WHO ARE DEAF OR HARD OF HEARING Students with some residual hearing often use amplification devices such as hearing aids. If you have a student who wears hearing aids, you should be alert for signs of inattention that signal the hearing aid is not turned on or the battery needs to be replaced. Another type of amplification device is an FM system consisting of a microphone worn by the teacher and a receiver worn by the student. When the teacher talks, the sound is converted into electrical energy and carried on a specific radio frequency through the air. The receiver converts the electrical energy back to sound, amplifies it, and sends it to the student's ear.

Keep in mind that hearing aids and FM systems both amplify sounds, all sounds, so they do not separate the teacher's voice from other sounds. Thus, a

WWW RESOURCES

http://www.nad.org
The National Association of the Deaf has the goals of advocating for people who are deaf or hard of hearing, providing information on topics related to hearing loss, and serving individuals with these special needs.

CASE IN PRACTICE 6.1

Including Students Who Are Deaf or Hard of Hearing

Ms. Skinner is a fifth-grade teacher at Lunar Elementary School. This year in her class of 31, she has twin girls who both were born with profound hearing loss. Because they use sign language as their primary means of communication, they are accompanied by Ms. Mohammed, an interpreter.

Ms. Skinner discusses what it is like to teach in this class:

When I first heard I was going to get Jenna and Janice this year, I was worried. I knew they'd been in fourth grade and had done well, but there's so much more curriculum at this level. I didn't know how I was going to teach everything and also do all the work necessary for Jenna and Janice and at the same time deal with end-of-grade testing and all that pressure. As it turns out, it hasn't been much of an adjustment at all. Ms. Mohammed interprets for the girls, and she adds explanations if they need it. The hardest part for me was learning to stay in one place when I talk. For a teacher like me, who is constantly moving around the room, that has been difficult. Ms. Mohammed has taught all of us some basic signs—that puts us all in touch. I've

also incorporated more photos and other visuals into my instruction because it so helps the girls understand. Jenna and Janice have some serious academic problems, mostly related to vocabulary and understanding the subtle details of the curriculum, but the other kids just think of them as classmates—most of them have been together in school since kindergarten. I've learned a lot this year. I'm a lot more confident that I really can teach any student who comes through my door.

REFLECTION

What aspects of teaching might be particularly challenging for you if you had students like Jenna and Janice in your classroom? How would you help these students compensate for their difficulty in vocabulary? What do you imagine is the impact of having an interpreter in the classroom most of the time? What type of assistance might you ask from the twins' parents to help them master the subjects you will be teaching?

---

student wearing hearing aids can be distracted by background sounds such as the amplified noise of someone typing on the computer keyboard, a door slamming, or chairs scraping on the floor. A student using an FM device also hears the amplified sound of a teacher's jewelry hitting the microphone or the static from a teacher fingering the microphone. Any of these extraneous noises can interfere with a student's understanding of spoken information and distract from learning. Amplification clearly assists some students who have hearing loss, but it has limits.

A third type of device also is becoming common. Cochlear implants are sophisticated electronic hearing devices that are most helpful to individuals with severe or profound hearing loss. They are being used with children even under the age of two, and it is likely that you will teach a student who uses this technology. A cochlear implant has external and internal components. First, there is a receiver and stimulator system implanted under the skin in the bone behind the ear. In addition, there is an externally worn microphone, sound processor, and transmitter system that is held with a magnet, typically behind the ear. The microphone picks up sound from the environment, and the processor filters that sound and transmits it to the internal receiver; there it is turned into electric impulses, which are transmitted through the cochlea, part of the inner ear, to the brain.

Cochlear implants enable students to perceive sound, but they are not a cure for a hearing loss. Students using them usually continue to need speech/language therapy and other supports commonly used by students who are deaf and hard of hearing (Hoog, Langereis, Weerdenburg, Knoors, & Verhoeven, 2016).

Many students who have a severe or profound hearing loss use sign language. Often they use *American Sign Language (ASL)*, a distinct language that is not based on standard English grammar and structures. Learning ASL is like learning any other second language. Other students, sometimes in the elementary grades, use a manually coded English (MCE) system, such as *signed exact English (SEE)*, that is, spoken English converted to a set of signs. This option may be preferred when a goal is to have the student's reading experience and language experience be consistent. With either method, students sometimes also use *finger spelling*, in which every letter of a word is spelled out. Finger spelling may

Video Example from

MyLab Education
Video Example 6.4: How A Cochlear Implant Works by Advanced Bionics
The workings of a cochlear implant are detailed in this brief video.
https://www.youtube.com/watch?v=zeg4qTnYOpw

be needed for names or technical terms for which no signs exist. Especially in secondary schools, students who use sign language sometimes are accompanied by interpreters who translate your words and those of classmates (e.g., Berge & Thomassen, 2016).

Some high school students may use another communication option called *C-print*. Using a computer, the captionist types what is being said in class using a standard set of abbreviations. The student, usually using a second computer connected wirelessly to the computer of the captionist, reads what is being said with only a three-second delay. You can learn about other examples of technologies that support students with hearing loss in the Technology Notes feature. Keep in mind, though, that the rapid evolution of technology is making some communication approaches obsolete, and new ones are likely to be developed (Miller, 2014). If you have questions about technology for students with a hearing loss, you should seek input from a specialist in this area.

> MyLab Education Self-Check 6.4

TECHNOLOGY NOTES 6.4
Assistive Technology for Students Who Are Deaf or Hard of Hearing

Some students with hearing loss use an FM system which is sort of like a small radio station. The teacher wears a microphone, and her voice is transmitted to the receiver worn by or placed near the student.

With C-Print, generally used for older students, a typist enters the words the teacher and classmates say into a computer, and they are almost instantaneously displayed on a second computer used by the student with a hearing loss. Students may prefer this option to an interpreter because they have a transcript of the lecture or discussion.

Cochlear implants are medical devices that transmit sound directly to the brain, bypassing the ear but doing its work.

What Are the Characteristics of and Instructional Needs of Students with Physical, Medical, or Health Disabilities?

Some students receive special education and related services because they have physical disorders, chronic or acute medical problems, or health impairments that interfere with their learning. In IDEA, three categories of disabilities can be loosely grouped in this area: orthopedic impairments, other health impairments, and traumatic brain injury. Orthopedic impairments (OIs) are diseases or disorders related to the bones, joints, and muscles. Other health impairments (OHIs) include medical and health conditions such as AIDS, seizure disorders, cancer, juvenile diabetes, asthma, and combinations of disorders such as those that Cynthia, whom you met at the beginning of the chapter, is experiencing. Traumatic brain injury (TBI) is any insult to the brain caused by an external force, including injuries sustained in auto accidents and during play. Students with these kinds of disabilities, which are caused by a wide variety of physical and health problems, differ greatly in their levels of ability and academic achievement and in their needs, which can range from modest to extensive. The following sections provide just a few of the most common examples of the specific conditions that fall into these disability categories.

Orthopedic Impairments

Students with orthopedic impairments, often referred to as *physical disabilities*, are those with significant physical needs. Examples of orthopedic impairments include the following.

STUDENTS WITH CEREBRAL PALSY In public schools, the largest group of students with orthopedic impairments comprises those who have *cerebral palsy (CP)*. Some 10,000 infants and preschoolers are diagnosed each year as having this condition (Centers for Disease Control and Prevention, 2017a). Cerebral palsy occurs because of injury to the brain before, during, or after birth and results in poor motor coordination and unusual motor patterns. These problems can occur in just the arms or legs, in both the arms and legs, or in a combination of limbs, all with varying degrees of severity. CP also can affect other muscle groups, such as those controlling the head and neck. Thus, some students with cerebral palsy walk on their toes with their knees close together. Their arms may be positioned with their elbows bent and their hands positioned near shoulder height. Other students with CP need braces or a walker to move about. Yet others use wheelchairs. For some students, head supports prevent the head from lolling side to side. Intellectually and academically, students with CP can be gifted, average, or below average, or they might have intellectual disabilities.

Don is a student with cerebral palsy. His arms and hands are drawn up close to his body, and he does not control their movement. He moves around school in a motorized wheelchair, and Mike, his personal assistant, helps with personal care (e.g., going to the bathroom, eating) and tasks such as writing. Don's intellectual ability is average but his physical disabilities sometimes cause others to think he has an intellectual disability as well, especially because his speech is difficult to understand. Don's teachers have learned to engage him in class activities by asking yes-or-no questions to which he can respond fairly easily. If they ask a question requiring a longer answer, they give Don time to form the words needed and do not let other students speak for him.

STUDENTS WITH SPINAL CORD INJURIES A second orthopedic impairment is *spinal cord injury*. As the term implies, this injury occurs when the spinal cord is severely damaged or severed, usually resulting in partial or extensive paralysis (National Spinal Cord Injury Statistical Center, 2016). Spinal cord injuries most often are the result of an automobile or other vehicle accident; other common

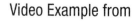

Video Example from

MyLab Education
Video Example 6.5: Runner with Cerebral Palsy Cheered by Family and Classmates
What does this video of a student with cerebral palsy supported by a teacher and his classmates tell you about your role in educating students with disabilities?
https://www.youtube.com/watch?v=MBdSSD4GWAM

WWW RESOURCES
http://www.ucp.org
Information about the causes, classification, prognosis, treatment, and psychological aspects of cerebral palsy can be found at the website for United Cerebral Palsy.

causes are falls and injuries from violence. The characteristics and needs of students with this type of injury often are similar to those of students with cerebral palsy. Judy suffered a spinal cord injury in a car accident. She was hospitalized for nearly half the school year, and at the time she returned to school, she could not walk and had the use of only one arm. She is as bright and articulate as ever and still gets in trouble when she challenges teachers' authority. What has changed is how she moves from place to place and, occasionally, her confidence that she can succeed in her life dream to be a radio broadcaster.

Cerebral palsy and spinal cord injuries are just two of many types of orthopedic impairments students can have. You also may teach students who have physical disabilities caused by amputations or birth defects that result in the absence of all or part of a limb. Likewise, you might have a student with juvenile rheumatoid arthritis, a chronic swelling of the joints usually accompanied by extreme soreness and limited mobility. Whatever orthopedic impairment a student has, your responsibility is to learn about the student's needs and work with special education professionals to ensure those needs are met through various accommodations.

Instructional Supports for Students with Orthopedic Impairments

The accommodations or modifications you make for students with physical disabilities will depend on the nature and severity of the disabilities, the students' physical status, and the students' learning capacity. For example, you need to be alert to changes you might need to make in the physical environment so that students can comfortably move into, out of, and around the classroom. Examples include rearranging classroom furniture and asking for a worktable for the student. Of course, students with orthopedic impairments also may use assistive technology, a topic you have learned about earlier in this chapter and in other chapters.

A second area of accommodation to consider for students with orthopedic impairments involves their personal needs. Many students become fatigued and might have difficulty attending to learning activities late in the school day. A few take naps or otherwise rest. Other students need to stop during the school day to take medication. Some students need assistance with personal care, such as using the bathroom and eating. Students who use wheelchairs might need to reposition themselves or be repositioned by an adult because of circulation problems. Paraprofessionals typically assume most personal-care responsibilities and those related to moving students.

It is not possible to generalize about these students' academic and social needs. Some students with orthopedic impairments enjoy school and excel in traditional academic areas. Some students with cerebral palsy are gifted. Other students with these disabilities experience problems in learning. Some are charming and gregarious students who are class leaders; others have a low self-concept and have problems interacting with peers (e.g., Pinquart & Pfeiffer, 2015). If you think about a student like Judy, the student introduced previously who has a spinal cord injury, you can imagine that her reaction to her accident and need to use a wheelchair are influenced by many factors, including her family support system, her self-concept, and her peers' reactions. The suggestions throughout this text for working with students to help them learn and succeed socially are as applicable to this group of students as to any other.

Other Health Impairments

Students with health impairments often are not immediately recognizable to a casual observer. However, when their disabilities negatively affect their education they are eligible for special education.

STUDENTS WITH SEIZURE DISORDERS   One group of health impairments is seizure disorders, or *epilepsy,* a physical condition in which the brain experiences sudden but brief changes in functioning. The result often is a lapse of attention

DIMENSIONS OF DIVERSITY

In choosing assistive technology, professionals should base decisions on a family's priorities, resources, and concerns, including stressors and cultural values, in order to avoid the possibility of assistive-technology abandonment (Etscheidt, 2016).

or consciousness and uncontrolled motor movements. A single seizure is not considered a symptom of epilepsy, but if several seizures occur, the disorder is diagnosed. About 460,000 children and adolescents have a seizure disorder, but the availability of effective medications means that most of these students rarely have a seizure (Centers for Disease Control and Prevention, 2016).

Epilepsy can produce several types of seizures. *Generalized tonic-clonic seizures* (previously called *grand mal seizures*) involve the entire body. The steps you should take when a student has a generalized tonic-clonic seizure are summarized in the Professional Edge feature. Other seizures do not involve the entire body. *Absence seizures* (previously called *petit mal seizures*) occur when students appear to blank out for just a few seconds. If they are walking or running, they might stumble because of their momentary lapse of awareness. If you observe a student with these symptoms, alert the school nurse or another professional who can further assess the student.

Although no relationship exists between seizure disorders and academic performance, you may find that a student with this disability misses more days of school than other students and is reluctant to engage in interactions with peers out of fear of their reaction to the seizures (Whiting-MacKinnon & Roberts, 2012). Students also may experience low self-esteem. If a student is likely to have recurring seizures, you may want (with student and parent support) to explain epilepsy to your class or ask a specialist to do that. What is important is that typical learners understand that, although somewhat frightening, epilepsy is not dangerous, is not controlled by the student who has the disorder, and is not contagious.

STUDENTS WITH SICKLE CELL DISEASE Another health impairment is *sickle cell disease*. This disorder is inherited and occurs most often in African American individuals, with an incidence of 1 in 365. Out of every 13 African Americans, one carries the gene for the disorder. The disease also is also found in other groups, including Greeks and Italians (Centers for Disease Control and Prevention, 2016). Sickle cell disease occurs when normally round blood cells are shaped liked sickles. This makes the blood thicker and prevents it from efficiently carrying oxygen to tissues. The effects on individuals who have this disorder are fatigue and reduced stamina, as well as mild to severe chronic pain in the chest, joints, back, or abdomen; swollen hands and feet; jaundice; repeated infections, particularly pneumonia; and sometimes kidney failure (National Institutes of Health, 2016). No reliable treatments currently are available for individuals who have

FYI

An estimated 10,270 new cases of cancer (e.g., acute lymphocytic leukemia, brain tumors, neuroblastoma) will be diagnosed among children ages birth to 14 in 2017. Approximately 1,190 children will die from this disease, a decrease of nearly 70 percent from four decades ago (National Institutes of Health, 2017).

PROFESSIONAL EDGE 6.2

What to Do When a Student Has a Seizure

As an educator in an inclusive school and as a responsible citizen, you should know how to respond when someone has a seizure. The Epilepsy Foundation recommends these steps for responding to seizures:

- Stay calm.
- Prevent injury. During the seizure, you can exercise common sense by ensuring there is nothing within reach that could harm the person if she struck it.
- Pay attention to the length of the seizure.
- Make the person as comfortable as possible.
- Keep onlookers away.
- Do not hold the person down. If the person having a seizure thrashes around, there is no need for you to restrain her. Remember to consider your safety as well.
- Do not put anything in the person's mouth. Contrary to popular belief, a person having a seizure is incapable of

swallowing her tongue, so you can relax in the knowledge that you do not have to stick your fingers into the mouth of someone in this condition.

- Do not give the person water, pills, or food until fully alert.
- If the seizure continues for longer than five minutes, call 911.
- Be sensitive and supportive, and ask others to do the same.

After the seizure, the person should be placed on her left side with the head turned. Stay with the person until she recovers, usually 5 to 20 minutes.

Further information about what to do in the case of seizures and more information about this disorder are available from the Epilepsy Foundation at (http://www.epilepsyfoundation.org/).

Source: From *Seizure First Aid*, by the Epilepsy Foundation, 2014, retrieved from (http://www.epilepsy.com/learn/treating-seizures-and-epilepsy/seizure-first-aid). Reprinted with permission.

this disease. In children, sickle cell disease can affect growth. Students with this disorder experience crises in which their symptoms are acute and include high fevers, joint swelling, and extreme fatigue; they are likely to miss school during these times. A student with this health impairment sometimes experiences cognitive impairment and often needs assistance in making up for missed instruction and encouragement for dealing with the pain and discomfort (Epping, Myrvik, Newby, Panepinto, Brandow, & Scott, 2013).

STUDENTS WITH ASTHMA OR ALLERGIES A fourth group of health impairments includes *asthma* and *allergies*. Children with asthma comprise the largest group of chronically ill children in the United States, and the number of children with these illnesses has risen sharply over the past decade (Lee, McCullough, Heider, Hanlon, & Kniffin, 2016). Approximately 6.2 million youngsters (8.4 percent) have this illness, and at any single time, most educators have two students in their classrooms who have asthma (Centers for Disease Control & Prevention, 2017b). Asthma can be triggered by allergens such as pollen, dust, and animal dander, but often it can be controlled with medication.

Allergies are the third most common chronic illness among children and adolescents. For example, approximately one in four children and adolescents has a food or digestive allergy (e.g., milk, wheat, peanuts, shellfish) (Bloom, Cohen, & Freeman, 2012). Other common causes of allergies are cat dander, insects (e.g., bee stings, ant bites), pollen and mold, and plants (e.g., poison ivy).

Only students with moderate or severe asthma or allergies may be eligible for special education services. Those with milder needs are likely to be assisted through a Section 504 plan, introduced in Chapter 2 and discussed further in Chapter 8. However, any student with these health issues may need special consideration in your classroom. For example, these students probably are absent more than other students and need assistance in mastering missed concepts. When in school, they sometimes feel tired or generally unwell, and they may need to be excused from some activities (Gibson-Scipio & Krouse, 2013). Some students use an inhaler to treat their condition; for others, emergency medication must be kept nearby, as some allergies can be life-threatening.

ADDITIONAL DISORDERS AND CONDITIONS THAT MAY AFFECT STUDENTS Students may have many other health impairments. For example, you may have a student who has been badly burned and is undergoing medical treatment and physical or occupational therapy to restore range of movement in affected limbs. You may have a student who has cancer and misses many days of school for treatments. Other health impairments your students might have include hemophilia, a genetically transmitted disease in which blood does not coagulate properly; juvenile diabetes, a condition in which the body does not produce enough insulin to process the carbohydrates eaten; AIDS; or cystic fibrosis, a genetically transmitted disease in which the body produces excessive mucus that eventually damages the lungs and causes heart failure. As noted for students with asthma or allergies, some students with these health impairments are not eligible for special education because their conditions do not negatively affect their educational performance. They are likely to receive support through Section 504 plans.

> **RESEARCH-BASED PRACTICES**
>
> Thirty adolescents with sickle cell disease reported in a survey study that their illness affected their performance in school. Although only about one-third of them received special education, as a group they were open to receiving supports that would assist them to achieve their academic goals (Crosby et al., 2015).

When a student with a disability is hospitalized for an extended period, a special educator may request the student's schoolwork. That professional will help the student keep up academically.

Instructional Supports for Students with Health Impairments

As noted throughout this discussion, the accommodations you make for students with health impairments often relate to helping them make up work missed because of absence or hospitalization and to recognizing and responding to their social and emotional needs; however, you may find that you also have questions about their academic and health needs (Wodrich & Spencer, 2007). General strategies for working with students with health impairments include these:

1. Find out the students' most difficult problems, and help them work through them. Strategies include having students write or draw about their concerns and referring students to the school counselor or social worker as you see a need.

2. Provide materials for the students about others who have a similar disease or disorder. Books, videos, websites, and other informational materials can help students with health impairments understand how others have successfully coped with their illnesses. These materials also can be useful for explaining the needs of these students to peers without disabilities.

3. Consider including death education in your curriculum if you have a student with a life-threatening condition, such as cancer. A special educator, counselor, or social worker probably can prepare a unit and help you present it. Alternatively, prepare yourself for responding to the potential death of a student and helping classmates cope with this loss.

4. Work closely with families. Parents often can be the most valuable source of information concerning their children's status and needs (Ryan & Quinlan, 2017; Trute, Benzies, & Worthington, 2012). In addition, they can alert you to upcoming changes in medications and emotional problems occurring at home, and they can help their children work on missed school assignments.

In terms of academic and curricular accommodations and modifications, you should respond to students who have health impairments as you would to students with other disabilities. Using the INCLUDE strategy, you can identify their needs. If adjustments in the environment, curriculum, or instruction are needed, you can carry them out using the suggestions made throughout the remainder of this text.

Traumatic Brain Injury

Traumatic brain injury (TBI), sometimes called *acquired brain injury*, occurs when a student experiences a trauma to the head from an external physical force that results in an injury to the brain, often including a temporary loss of consciousness. TBI is the leading cause of disability and death among children, and it has many causes, including falls, bicycle and motor vehicle accidents, sporting accidents, accidents on playground equipment, child abuse, and gunshot wounds (Brain Injury Association of America, 2015). More than 1 million children and adolescents sustain some type of TBI each year; 564,000 of those injuries result in a visit to an emergency room. Children ages 0 to 4 and 15 to 19 are the most likely to have a TBI (Centers for Disease Control and Prevention, 2017d). Although most of these injuries are mild, some 62,000 of these youngsters required hospitalization (Brain Injury Association of America, 2015). Whether TBI is the result of a severe injury or a mild one, it can have a pervasive and significant impact on a student's educational performance, and predicting the point at which she will reach her best outcomes is impossible given various lengths of recovery time and alternative patterns for treatment (Aldrich & Obrzut, 2012).

One of the most perplexing aspects of teaching students with TBI is that they can appear just as they did prior to their injuries yet have significant learning and social problems. They also can seem to be the way they were prior to the TBI one day, only to seem lethargic and incapable of learning the next. Because of the extreme variability in needs of students with TBI, the information presented in this section should be considered illustrative. If you teach a student with TBI, it is imperative to seek input from a specialist.

CHARACTERISTICS OF STUDENTS WITH TRAUMATIC BRAIN INJURY Intellectually, students with TBI might have the same abilities they had before their injury, or they might experience a loss of capacity (Fulton, Yeates, Taylor, Walz, & Wade, 2012). For example, after an automobile accident, Michael, a high school honor

---

FYI

Keep in mind that many students have more than one of the disabilities described in this chapter. For example, a student may have autism and a hearing loss, or he may have a chronic health condition and an orthopedic impairment.

RESEARCH-BASED PRACTICES

Students with disabilities are significantly more likely than other students to be bullied. Those with autism and those with orthopedic impairments are most likely to experience repeated bullying (Feather, 2016).

INSTRUCTIONAL EDGE 6.2

Teaching Students with Traumatic Brain Injury (TBI)

No single strategy is effective in working with students with TBI because their injuries and the resulting impact on learning vary widely, and because their needs change over time. You should ask special educators and other professionals how best to work with a student with TBI, and if you notice changes in the student you should alert those professionals so that appropriate adjustments can be made in the student's educational services. Here are strategies that often are helpful in meeting these students' needs:

Area of Concern	Suggested Strategies
Attention	• Use color cues (for example, highlighting in yellow key words of directions in print assignments). • Use an FM system (see further explanation in this chapter in the discussion of students with hearing loss). • Teach in small segments and allow the student to take breaks. • Provide for the student, preferably in electronic form, class notes, assignments, and other instructional information. • On any print materials, be sure that only a small amount of information appears on any single page. • Allow the student to work in a quiet area of the classroom or provide a desk carrel. • Arrange for the student to have two desks, one containing his belongings and one that is completely empty as a workspace, thus eliminating distractions. • Consistently use cue words to help the student focus (e.g., *Listen . . . , Look . . . , Write . . .*).
Memory	• Arrange for the student to use a digital recorder for recording class lectures, dictating assignments, creating reminders, and so on. • Increase your use of repetition during instruction. • Increase your use of group responding (for example, when one student gives an answer have all the students repeat it). • Request software to assist the student in written tasks (e.g., word prediction software). • Give the student checklists for activities that take place on a regular basis. • Link new information to information the student already knows.
Organization	• Establish clear, specific procedures in the classroom (e.g., where to put completed work), and be consistent using them. • Create a visual schedule for the student (as explained in this chapter related to students with autism). • Request that the student use a digital organizer and assist the student in taking advantage of the apps and software designed to aid organization. • Teach the student to set alarms and reminder functions on a smartphone or other digital organizer. • Have the student keep all materials in a single binder, divided for older students into separate sections for each class. • Color code materials (for example, math materials are printed on yellow paper and kept in a yellow folder, language arts or English materials are printed on tan paper and kept in a tan folder).
Information Processing	• Allow the student to take extra time to complete assignments or tests. • Reduce the number of items or simplify the student's way of responding so that tasks take less time (e.g., have the student write bullet points instead of sentences). • Preview for the student what is going to occur in class (e.g., what the lesson will be about, what the most critical vocabulary is, what the activity is going to be). • Ask the student to repeat directions prior to beginning a classroom task. • Simplify oral and written directions (that is, remove extraneous words, use short sentences, number the directions if possible). • Slow the pace of instruction for the student, possibly allowing the student to skip some activities to spend more time focusing on those considered most essential. • Avoid pressuring the student to work faster; focus on quality rather than quantity.

WWW RESOURCES

http://www.biausa.org
The Brain Injury Association of America website includes information about causes, cost, prevention, and treatment of TBI. It even has a kids' corner.

student who used to be a class leader, was left struggling to remaster basic math facts. His injury profoundly affected his learning. Students might experience difficulty initiating and organizing their learning tasks, remembering what they have learned, and reasoning or problem solving. They also might have difficulty processing verbal information and producing spoken and written language.

Students with TBI also may have other needs. Depending on the severity of the injury and extent of recovery, some students have limited use of their arms and legs. Others have problems in fine motor movements, such as those needed to grasp a pencil or turn the pages of a book. Yet others have limited strength and stamina. Socially and emotionally, students with TBI may have changes in their personalities; they may not be who they used to be. Many of these students remember what they were able to do prior to their injuries and sometimes become depressed as they recognize their limitations (Barlow, 2016). They also may display behavior problems when a sudden disruption in schedule occurs, as when an assembly interrupts an accustomed routine. Some of the most common challenges for students with TBI, along with potential responses teachers can make, are described in the Instructional Edge feature.

FAMILIES AND TRAUMATIC BRAIN INJURY It is especially important to mention families when discussing TBI (Durber et al., 2017). Often parents and siblings have witnessed a student in a totally unresponsive state. They might be tremendously relieved that the student survived but at the same time traumatized by the amount of physical care he needs and the drain the injury has had on the family's financial and psychological resources. Families dealing with a child with TBI may experience a range of emotions, including shock, denial, sorrow, and anger (Treble-Barna et al., 2016). Eventually, many families adapt. Regardless, you need to be sensitive to the family's stress and their changing capacity to follow up on homework as well as schoolwork to support your efforts.

MyLab Education

Video Example 6.6: Matt

This video shows Matt, a student with TBI and how he is included in the classroom environment. Pay attention to the strategies used in the classroom.

Instructional Supports for Students with Traumatic Brain Injury

If you teach a student with TBI, you might attend planning meetings to discuss the details of the student's abilities and needs and to prepare for helping the student in the classroom. This transition planning typically occurs when a student is moving from a hospital or rehabilitation center back to school and usually involves personnel from both settings.

In your classroom, accommodations relate to physical needs, instructional and organizational routines, academic content, and the social environment (Jantz, Davies, & Bigler, 2014). For example, because students with TBI need structure and routine, you should follow a consistent pattern in classroom activities, expect consistent types of student responses, and keep supplies and materials in consistent places in the classroom. If a break in routine is necessary, you can prepare the student by alerting him, assigning a buddy, and staying in close proximity.

You may need to make changes in the academic expectations for a student with TBI. Because students might know information one day but forget it the next or learn with ease sometimes but struggle to learn at other times, the need for flexibility is ongoing. Students also are likely to become frustrated with their inability to learn the way they did in the past, so your patience in reteaching information, providing additional examples and exercises, and using strategies to help them focus attention is essential.

Socially, emotionally, and behaviorally, students with TBI rely on you to set clear expectations but also to be supportive of and responsive to their changing needs. One student, Gary, had been in a coma but gradually regained enough ability to function that he returned to his middle school—at first for only an hour or two each day and eventually for the entire day. However, he continued to forget common words and grew increasingly frustrated when he could not convey messages. His teachers began providing the words he needed. Because many students with TBI seem unable to form a realistic picture of how they are functioning, you might need to confront them gently about socially inappropriate behavior. Frustrated with his language skills, Gary yelled at friends, yet his sentences remained unclear. Teachers intervened to help him learn to manage his anger and to assist friends to understand him.

In general, many of the accommodations needed by students with TBI are largely the same as those needed by students with physical or health disabilities, learning disabilities, and emotional disabilities, although some will require that you modify curriculum based on the expectations as outlined in the IEP. The uniqueness of students with TBI and the reason they are grouped as a separate category in IDEA is that their needs are difficult to predict, change either slowly

FYI

Students vary in their sensitivity to rejection. Those who are highly sensitive to rejection prior to a traumatic brain injury are at very high risk for experiencing serious social and behavioral adjustment problems after their injury (Meadows et al., 2017).

or rapidly, and vary in intensity. Teachers who are patient and willing to meet students wherever they are and work forward from there can help students with TBI achieve school success.

MyLab Education Self-Check 6.5

WRAPPING IT UP

Back to the Cases

Now that you have read about students with low-incidence disabilities, look back at the teacher stories at the beginning of the chapter. Then go to MyLab Education to apply the knowledge you've gained in this chapter to each case.

MyLab Education Application Exercise 6.1: Case Study 6.1

DAWN spends most of her day working alone with the paraprofessional. This is not at all what her mother had in mind when she insisted that Dawn be educated in a general education classroom.

MyLab Education Application Exercise 6.2: Case Study 6.2

SEAN is a twelfth-grade student identified as having autism spectrum disorder (ASD), and he has done well in high school. One of his greatest supports has been his friend Jonas, who inconspicuously guides Sean when he seems unsure of himself in social situations. As Sean looks forward to college, his greatest concerns are dealing with large classes and being surrounded by strangers.

MyLab Education Application Exercise 6.3: Case Study 6.3

NATALIE left sixth grade as a slightly above-average student who had several close friends and played in a community soccer league. Over the summer, though, she was struck by an automobile and suffered a moderate traumatic brain injury (TBI). After returning to school in seventh grade, Natalie is still experiencing physical and cognitive difficulties, but her caseworker expressed optimism that she would eventually recover many of the skills she had before the accident.

Summary

LO 6.1 Students with low-incidence disabilities comprise less than 20 percent of all students with disabilities, but they account for eight of the federal categories of disability (i.e., orthopedic impairments, other health impairments, traumatic brain injury, hearing impairments, visual impairments, deaf-blind, multiple disabilities, and autism) and part of the intellectual disabilities and developmental disabilities categories. Although you will probably teach only a few such students during your career, you will find that many of the strategies you already have learned are effective in teaching them, strategies you'll learn about for students with high-incidence disabilities also may be effective, and other professionals and parents are available to assist you in creating successful learning experiences for them.

LO 6.2 Students with autism spectrum disorders (ASDs), referred to as *autism* in federal special education law, have a wide range of intellectual and other abilities, and they have impairments in social relationships, communication, range of interests, and capacity to respond to stressful events. They need a highly-structured learning environment with clear procedures and routines. Students with autism may be high achievers or struggle to learn, but they all need specific instructional supports, and for some, some services in a separate special education setting.

LO 6.3 Students with moderate or severe intellectual disabilities or multiple disabilities learn slowly, and they usually need assistance to maintain and generalize their skills. They may not learn as much as other students or in the same ways, but their goals and objectives are aligned with the general curriculum, and they benefit from teachers who use a variety of instructional strategies and develop partnerships with parents. Students who are deaf-blind have particularly unique needs. They may or may not have additional disabilities, and they often require highly specialized instruction so that they can access learning.

LO 6.4 Students with sensory impairments (i.e., those who are blind or low vision, or deaf or hard of hearing) often have needs related to academic learning, social and emotional skills, and skills for living in their environments. They may use adaptive equipment or materials to help them learn.

LO 6.5 Some students have orthopedic impairments (i.e., physical disabilities), other health impairments (i.e., serious medical or health conditions), or traumatic brain injury (i.e., trauma to the head from an accident or other injury). Students in these groups often have medical problems that directly or indirectly affect their learning, varying intellectual levels, and social and emotional challenges, and they are likely to need a range of instructional and behavioral accommodations.

APPLICATIONS IN TEACHING PRACTICE

Planning for Students with Low-Incidence Disabilities

Mr. Walker teaches English to ninth graders. This year he will have several students with learning disabilities and emotional disabilities in his class, but his primary concern is Terrell, a young man who has cerebral palsy and limited vision. Mr. Walker has been told that Terrell has average intelligence and is quite capable of following the standard course of study for English but that he needs several specific accommodations. Mr. Walker is meeting with Ms. Bickel from the special education department to ask questions about Terrell.

Mr. Walker: I need more information about Terrell. Can he really do the work? How much can he see? How is he going to take tests? What is his assistant supposed to be doing? Am I liable if Terrell has a medical problem during class? Is it likely that will happen? I hear that Terrell has all sorts of computer equipment and a motorized wheelchair. I have 34 other students in that class period, and I'm concerned about just fitting everyone in the door, much less giving him extra attention.

Ms. Bickel: It sounds like you haven't gotten the information I thought you had. Let me try to clarify. Terrell is a very good student. He usually gets As and Bs in his core academic classes, and he is highly motivated to learn. He has every intention of going to college, and right now he hopes to be an editor. Because he can't use his voice, he talks using his communication board. I'll be working with you to be sure the board includes all the key words you want it to contain. All Terrell has to do is point his head toward the answer he wants and the laser pointer will activate the board, which says the answer out loud. One accommodation Terrell probably will need is extra time to answer; he really wants to participate but might need a moment to get the laser beam focused on the answer he wants to give. His equipment is all adapted to take into account his limited vision.

Mr. Walker: I'll have to see how that works. What does his assistant do?

Ms. Bickel: Mr. Owen is responsible for Terrell's personal care and making sure he gets from class to class. He also takes notes for Terrell and records answers Terrell gives on his communication board. He can help you out in class if there's a chance, but Terrell needs his attention much of the time.

Mr. Walker: Oh, I wasn't trying to get more help. I just need an idea of what this will be like. I need an extra place for Mr. Owen in class, don't I?

Ms. Bickel: Yes, he'll need to sit next to Terrell most of the time.

The teachers continue talking for another 45 minutes, problem solving about the space issue and trying to ensure that Terrell will experience success and that Mr. Walker understands Terrell's needs. In the first week of school, Ms. Bickel asks Mr. Walker how it is going with Terrell. Mr. Walker comments that he is surprised how smoothly things are going. Terrell spoke via the communication board in class on the first day, and the other students asked a few questions about the equipment. Most of them already knew Terrell, however, and were accustomed to interacting with him. Mr. Walker asks whether Ms. Bickel can help him deal with two other students who already seem to have behavior problems.

QUESTIONS

1. What type of disability does Terrell have? Why is he included in Mr. Walker's English class?

2. What accommodations should Mr. Walker make in his classroom and his instruction to address Terrell's special needs? If Terrell was an elementary school student or a middle school student, which accommodations would be the same? Which accommodations might be different? How? Why?

3. If you were meeting with Ms. Bickel, what additional questions would you ask about Terrell? About needed accommodations?

4. What assistance would you need from Ms. Bickel to feel comfortable teaching Terrell?

5. What would your expectation be for working with Terrell's parents? What might you learn from them that would help you be more effective in teaching Terrell? How would your expectations for working with Terrell's parents be different if he was a younger student?

6. Review the entire chapter and all the information about students with low-incidence disabilities presented in it. What are the benefits of inclusive practices related to students in this group? What concerns and questions do you have for working with students with low-incidence disabilities? Which of your personal and professional beliefs will be most challenged when you work with students with low-incidence disabilities? Why?

CHAPTER 7

Students with High-Incidence Disabilities

LEARNING OUTCOMES

After you read this chapter, you will be able to:

7-1 Explain what is meant by high-incidence disabilities, and describe their prevalence and the key elements of the federal definitions for each of the high-incidence categories.

7-2 Apply the INCLUDE strategy to adjust your classroom instruction to meet the needs of students with communication disorders.

7-3 Analyze classroom demands and the academic characteristics and needs of students with learning,

behavioral, and mild intellectual disabilities and explain how you can adjust your instruction to meet their needs using the INCLUDE strategy.

7-4 Analyze the social and emotional characteristics and needs of students with learning and behavioral disabilities, including how you can meet these needs in the classroom.

WILL is a fourth-grade student at LaForb Elementary School. Most people who know him outside school would never guess that he has a learning disability. He converses easily with children and adults, has a great sense of humor, and is renowned among his peers for his "street smarts." Unfortunately, things don't go as well for Will in school. Although he passed his third-grade end-of-grade test in math, the tests in reading and written language were another story altogether. Will reads slowly, struggling with each word, and as a result he often cannot tell his teacher what he has read. His written language is also a problem. When he does attempt a written assignment, it takes him an extremely long time to write even a few sentences. The sentences contain many misspelled words, are poorly constructed and illegible, and convey little meaning. As a fourth-grader, Will has become more disengaged from his classes. He is spending longer periods of time in the hall or the principal's office, usually for refusing to do his classwork and homework. Recently, Will's frustration has been growing as the pressure mounts to get ready for his end-of-grade tests and middle school.

What disability does Will seem to have? What factors may be contributing to his academic problems? What kinds of adjustments to her instruction should Will's teacher provide to help him progress in the general education curriculum? What other kinds of support do Will and his teacher need? Why do students like Will often become discipline problems?

RENAYE is nearly 17 and is usually in some kind of trouble in school and out. According to her grandmother, she has always been a strong-willed child, but she seems to have become more aggressive after losing her mother in a car wreck when she was in the third grade. Except in English, her favorite subject, ReNaye's grades have been going down consistently since then. She does well in English, but her math grades have been getting lower each year. For example, last year, she scored "not proficient" on the high-stakes test in math for the first time. She also frequently refuses to work in her history and science classes. In class, ReNaye gets upset easily and resorts to bullying and teasing her classmates. She has had several discipline referrals, and the principal keeps threatening to suspend her for her actions but has yet to follow through. Her attendance has been sporadic at best, and her teachers and grandmother don't know what to do to help her.

What is ReNaye's likely disability? How can her general education teachers accommodate her behavior? What kinds of support do ReNaye and her teachers need?

JEROME is included in Mr. Gonzales's third-grade class. Jerome has difficulty learning new skills and concepts in all areas, and math is no exception. Jerome's objectives on his individualized education program (IEP), based on state standards, call for learning basic addition and subtraction. Jerome processes verbal information slowly, so he struggles when learning in large groups. His problems processing language make it hard for him to pay attention for long periods of time. Jerome also has trouble remembering information from one day to the next. Just when Mr. Gonzales thinks he has learned a particular addition fact, Jerome seems baffled by it the very next day. Jerome's halting speech and slow verbal processing make interacting with his classmates awkward. Although Jerome's classmates don't pick on him, they don't seek him out as a friend either.

What is Jerome's disability? What factors are contributing to his academic and social problems? How can students such as Jerome be successfully included in general education classrooms?

Students like Will, ReNaye, and Jerome have high-incidence disabilities. These students' disabilities affect their language, learning, and behavior. You probably will teach students with high-incidence disabilities in your classroom. The expectation in the Individuals with Disabilities Education Act (IDEA) is that these students will spend most of their time in general education, while meeting the same curricular standards as their classmates without disabilities. In order to meet the goals set forth in IDEA, students with high-incidence disabilities require support from general and special education professionals. Usually this support is in the form of instructional accommodations that appear on their IEPs, or other instructional adjustments, rather than modifications, which are the responsibility of special education. For instance, Will is learning word-processing skills to help him overcome his problems with spelling and handwriting. He is also using texts on a text-to-speech handheld device in his science and social studies classes, which are sometimes co-taught. ReNaye and her teachers have developed a behavior intervention plan in which she is allowed extra access to the computer lab for attending class and complying with teachers' requests. Jerome has a mild intellectual disability. He is likely to be tested according to the state standards and his parents and teachers recognize that this is a real challenge for him. In the classroom, he is currently working on math skills at a more basic level than his classmates according to the goals set forth in his IEP. This chapter covers the characteristics and needs of students with high-incidence disabilities and the adjustments to instruction that enable them to gain better access to the general education curriculum.

What Are High-Incidence Disabilities?

Students with high-incidence disabilities have speech or language disabilities, learning disabilities, emotional disturbance, or mild intellectual disabilities. These students make up approximately 70 percent of all students who have disabilities (U.S. Department of Education, 2016). The federal terms for high-incidence disabilities and the proportion of students with these disabilities served through IDEA are summarized in Table 7.1. Students with high-incidence disabilities share three important characteristics:

1. They are often hard to distinguish from peers without disabilities, particularly in nonschool settings.
2. They often exhibit a combination of behavioral, social, and academic problems.
3. They benefit from systematic, explicit, highly structured instructional interventions such as those discussed in Chapter 5, this chapter, and throughout the remainder of this book. Having these interventions in place will help them meet the same standards as their classmates without disabilities.

In the sections that follow, we will cover the characteristics and needs of students with high-incidence disabilities, including how to adjust your instruction for them in your classroom. Students with communication disorders will be discussed first, followed by students with learning and behavioral disabilities, including those with learning disabilities, emotional disturbance, and mild intellectual disabilities.

MyLab Education Self-Check 7.1

TABLE 7.1 Proportion of Students with High-Incidence Disabilities Receiving Special Education Services in 2014–2015[a]

Federal Disability Category	Defining Characteristics	Total Number of Students	Percentage of All Students Receiving IDEA Services	Percentage of All Students Ages 6–21	Percentage of Students in General Education 80% or more of the school[b] day
Learning disabilities[a]	A heterogeneous group of disorders resulting in significant difficulties in the acquisition and use of listening, speaking, reading, writing, reasoning, and mathematical skills. Disorders are intrinsic to individuals and presumed to be due to central nervous system dysfunction. Disorders are *not* primarily due to (a) sensory or motor disorders; (b) intellectual or developmental disabilities; (c) emotional disturbance; or (d) environmental, cultural, or economic disadvantage.	2,348,891	38.8%	3.5%	69.2
Emotional disturbance[a]	Behavioral or emotional responses in school programs that are so different from appropriate age, cultural, and ethnic norms that they adversely affect academic performance. More than a temporary, expected response to stressful events in the environment. Consistently exhibited in two different settings, at least one of which is school related. Persists despite individualized interventions within the educational program.	346,488	5.7%	0.5%	46.2
Speech[a] or language[a] impairments	Speech is disordered when it deviates so far from the speech of other people that it calls attention to itself, interferes with communication, or causes the speaker or listeners distress. Three kinds of speech disorders are articulation (abnormal production of speech sounds), voice (absence of or abnormal production of voice quality, pitch, loudness, resonance, and/or duration), and fluency (impaired rate and rhythm of speech, for example, stuttering). Language is disordered when comprehension and/or use of a spoken, written, and/or other symbol system is impaired or does not develop normally. Language disorders may involve form (word order, word parts, word usage), content (word meaning), or function (words that communicate meaningfully).	1,044,286	17.2%	1.6%	86.8

[a]Students ages 6–21 receiving services through IDEA, Part B (U.S. Department of Education, 2017). Additional students receive services under Part H of the same law, and under Chapter 1.
[b]The most recent published educational environment data are from the 2014–2015 school year (U.S. Department of Education, 2016).

Source: U.S. Department of Education. (2017a, b, January). "Number of students ages 6 through 21 served under IDEA, Part B, by disability and state; and Students ages 6 through 21 served under IDEA, Part B, as a percentage of the population, by disability category and state." *IDEA Section 618 data products: State tables.* Washington, DC: Author. Retrieved from https://www2.ed.gov/programs/osepidea/618-data/static-tables/index.html#partb-cc. U.S. Department of Education, Office of Special Education and Rehabilitative Services, Office of Special Education Programs. (2016, October). *38th annual report to Congress on the implementation of the Individuals with Disabilities Education Act.* Washington, DC: Author. Retrieved from https://www2.ed.gov/about/reports/annual/osep/2016/parts-b-c/38th-arc-for-idea.pdf.

What Instructional Adjustments Can You Make for Students with Communication Disorders?

Communication is the exchange of ideas, opinions, or facts between people. Effective communication requires a sender to send a message that a receiver can decipher and understand. Students with communication disorders have problems with speech and/or language that interfere with communication. They need accommodations and adjustments to instruction that help them better receive, understand, and express oral language.

Understanding Speech Problems

Speech is the behavior of forming and sequencing the sounds of oral language (Friend, 2018; Owens, Farinella & Metz, 2015). One common speech problem is with speech articulation, resulting in the inability to pronounce sounds correctly at and after the developmentally appropriate age. For example, Stacey is in second grade but cannot pronounce the *s* sound, a sound most students master by age five. Other speech difficulties involve voice and fluency. Examples of these speech problems are shown in Figure 7.1.

Because communication is social, students with speech disorders, such as stuttering, often experience social problems. Students who can clearly communicate draw positive attention from peer relationships, but students who cannot are often avoided by their peers and sometimes ridiculed. The experience of peer rejection can be devastating, leading to a lack of confidence, a poor self-image, social withdrawal, and emotional problems later in life (Cook & Cook, 2009). For example, after years of being ridiculed by peers, Jeffrey, a high school ninth grader who stutters, speaks infrequently and has no friends. He would like to ask a girl in his math class out but is petrified he will not be able to do so without stuttering.

Understanding Language Problems

Language is a system of symbols that we use to communicate feelings, thoughts, desires, and actions. Language is the message contained in speech. Language can exist without speech, such as sign language for people who are deaf, and speech without language, such as birds that are trained to talk (Hardman, Egan, & Drew, 2016). Students who have language problems have trouble with either or both of two key parts of language: receptive language and expressive language. Receptive language involves understanding what people mean when they speak to you. Expressive language concerns speaking in such a way that others understand you. Receptive language problems occur when students are unable to understand what their teachers and peers are saying. For example,

FIGURE 7.1 Speech Problems

Articulation
1. Has difficulty pronouncing sounds correctly (at and after the developmentally appropriate age). Frequent articulation errors include *f, v, k, g, r, l, s, z, sh, ch,* and *j.* Sounds may be distorted or omitted, or one sound may be inappropriately substituted for another.
2. Speech may be slurred.

Voice
1. Speech is excessively hoarse.
2. May use excessive volume or too little volume.
3. Speech has too much nasality.
4. Speech lacks inflection.

Fluency
1. Stutters when speaking.
2. May have excessively slow rate of speech.
3. May exhibit uneven, jerky rate of speech.

Sources: "Adapting Instruction in General Education for Students with Communication Disorders," by D. Barad, 1985, unpublished manuscript, De Kalb: Northern Illinois University; and *Introduction to Communication Disorders: A Lifespan Evidence-Based Approach* (5th ed.), by R. Owens, A. Haas, and D. Metz, 2015, Boston, MA: Pearson.

FIGURE 7.2 Language Problems

Receptive Language Problems

1. Does not respond to questions appropriately
2. Cannot think abstractly or comprehend abstractions as idioms ("mind sharp as a tack"; "eyes dancing in the dark")
3. Cannot retain information presented verbally
4. Has difficulty following oral directions
5. Cannot detect breakdowns in communication
6. Misses parts of material presented verbally, particularly less concrete words such as articles (*the* book; *a* book) and auxiliary verbs and tense markers ("He *was* going"; "She *is* going")
7. Cannot recall sequences of ideas presented orally
8. May confuse the sounds of letters that are similar (*b, d; m, n*) or reverse the order of sounds and syllables in words (*was, saw*)
9. Has difficulty understanding humor or figurative language
10. Has difficulty comprehending concepts showing quantity, function, comparative size, and temporal and spatial relationships
11. Has difficulty comprehending compound and complex sentences

Expressive Language Problems

1. Uses incorrect grammar or syntax ("They walk down together the hill"; "I go not to school")
2. Lacks specificity ("It's over there by the place over there")
3. Frequently hesitates ("You know, um, I would, um, well, er, like a, er, soda")
4. Jumps from topic to topic ("What are feathers? Well, I like to go hunting with my uncle")
5. Has limited use of vocabulary
6. Has trouble finding the right word to communicate meaning (word finding)
7. Uses social language poorly (inability to change communication style to fit specific situations, to repair communication breakdowns, and to maintain the topic during a conversation)
8. Is afraid to ask questions, does not know what questions to ask, or does not know how to ask a question
9. Repeats same information again and again in a conversation
10. Has difficulty discussing abstract, temporal, or spatial concepts
11. Often does not provide enough information to the listener (saying, "*We* had a big fight with *them*," when *we* and *them* are not explained)

Sources: Based on "Instruction in General Education for Students with Communication Disorders," by D. Barad, 1985, unpublished manuscript, De Kalb: Northern Illinois University; and *Strategies for Teaching Students with Learning and Behavior Problems* (9th ed.), by S. Vaughn and C. S. Bos, 2014. Copyright © 2014 by Pearson Education, Inc.

students with receptive language difficulties may not understand questions, may have trouble following directions, and may not be able to retain information presented verbally. Students with expressive language problems are unable to communicate clearly; their spoken language may include incorrect grammar, a limited use of vocabulary, and frequent hesitations. Some common receptive and expressive language problems are listed in Figure 7.2.

Students with language problems also may have difficulty using language in social situations. For example, they may be unable to vary their conversation to match the person with whom they are talking or the context in which it is occurring. Students with language problems also may experience problems taking turns while speaking during a conversation, recognizing when a listener is not understanding the message and taking action to clarify, and in general being a considerate speaker and listener (Vaughn & Bos, 2014). As with problems in communicating clearly, challenges in using language appropriately can seriously impede students' social development and peer relationships. General education teachers can intervene in the classroom to help such students socially.

Early language development forms the underpinning for much of the academic learning that comes when students go to school. It is not surprising, then, that students with speech and language disorders are likely to have trouble with academics as well (Kamhi & Catts, 2011). Problems with sounds can result in students having difficulties acquiring word analysis and spelling skills. Receptive language problems can make comprehension very difficult and can result in trouble understanding mathematical terms such as *minus, regroup*, and *addend* and confusion in sorting out words with multiple meanings, such as *carry* and *times* (Mercer & Pullen, 2008). Further, language disabilities can seriously impede the content-area learning stressed in middle, junior high, and high school. In these settings, much information is provided orally using lecture formats, the vocabulary and concepts covered are much more abstract, and students are expected to learn with less support from the teacher. These demands are difficult for students with language disorders.

DIMENSIONS OF DIVERSITY

It is incorrect to view students as having communication disorders when they use ethnic or regional dialects, speak a form of nonstandard English learned at home, or are native speakers of languages other than English and have limited English proficiency.

RESEARCH-BASED PRACTICES

Hollo, Wehby, and Oliver (2014) studied the language development of 1,171 children with emotional and behavioral disorders (EBD) as reported in 22 research studies and found a high prevalence of language disorders. They recommended language screening for all students with EBD and language interventions for those who need it.

MyLab Education

Video Example 7.1: IEP Meeting for Student with Communication Disorders

This video shows an IEP meeting portion that deals with accommodations for a student with communication disorders. How communication disorders can be met in more natural environments is discussed.

Another part of learning independently is solving problems. Students with language disorders may have difficulty verbalizing the steps to solve a problem. For example, when Veronica, a language-proficient student, solves word problems, she talks to herself as follows: "First I need to read the whole problem. Then I need to decide what the problem is asking for and whether I need to add, subtract, multiply, or divide. Okay, the problem is asking how much Alex weighs. It says that Alex is 3 pounds heavier than Dominique and that Dominique weighs 125 pounds. So if Alex weighs 3 pounds more, his weight will be a bigger number than Dominique's, so I need to add." A student with language problems cannot talk herself through such problems.

Classroom Adjustments for Students with Communication Disorders

As discussed in Chapter 5, the <u>INCLUDE</u> strategy suggests that before you change your instruction, you should carefully consider potential student problems in view of your instructional demands. For students with speech and language problems, note especially any areas in which students are required to understand oral language (e.g., listening to a lecture or a set of verbal directions) or to communicate orally (e.g., responding to teacher questions or interacting with classmates when working in cooperative groups). The following discussion highlights specific suggestions for working with students with speech and language disorders.

CREATE AN ATMOSPHERE OF ACCEPTANCE Help students who have difficulty expressing themselves believe they can communicate without worrying about making mistakes. You can foster this nonjudgmental atmosphere in several ways. First, when a student makes an error, model the correct form instead of correcting the student's mistakes directly:

Teacher: Kareem, what did Jules do with the frog?

Kareem: Put pocket.

Teacher: Oh. He put it in his pocket?

Kareem: Yes.

Second, try to allow students who stutter or have other fluency problems more time to speak, and do not interrupt them or supply words that are difficult for them to pronounce. Offering praise or other reinforcement for successful efforts to communicate, as you would for your other students, is also helpful. Sometimes, you should praise even an attempt:

Teacher: Anthony, what did you do when you went home yesterday?

Anthony: Television.

Teacher: Great, you told me one thing you did. You watched television.

Finally, try to minimize peer pressure. One effective way to do this is to model and reinforce tolerance of individual differences in your classroom.

ENCOURAGE LISTENING AND TEACH LISTENING SKILLS Even though students spend more time listening than doing any other school activity, very little time is devoted to teaching listening skills (Lerner & Johns, 2014). Stressing listening is particularly important for students with receptive language disorders. Take the following four steps to stress listening:

1. Listen carefully yourself and praise listening among your students. For example, when Ms. Hernandez listens to a student speak, she leans forward and nods. Many of her students copy these listening behaviors.

2. Be sure to engage your students' attention before you begin speaking by increasing your proximity to the listeners, by giving direct instruction (such

DIMENSIONS OF DIVERSITY

Umansky, Valentino, and Reardon (2016) conducted a 12-year study comparing how English learners (ELs) fare in English immersion and three types of bilingual programs. They found comparable levels of English proficiency for students in all programs by the end of eighth grade. Achievement in math and English language favored English immersion programs at first, but by eighth grade children in 2 of the 3 bilingual programs had caught up and surpassed that of their English-immersion counterparts.

as, "Listen to what I'm going to say"), and by reducing competing stimuli (have only one activity going on at one time, or have only one person speak at a time). You also can use verbal, pictorial, and written advance organizers to cue students when to listen (e.g., "When we get to number 3 on this list, I want you to listen extra carefully for an error I am going to make") (Sabornie & deBettencourt, 2009).

3. Make oral material easier to understand and remember by simplifying vocabulary, simplifying sentence structure using high-frequency words, repeating important information, giving information in short segments using visual aids for emphasis, having students rehearse and summarize information, and using cues that signal when you are going to say something important (Shores, 2017).

4. Teach listening skills directly. Provide practice on skills such as predicting what might be heard, following directions, appreciating language, identifying main ideas and supporting details, drawing inferences, differentiating fact from fiction, and analyzing information critically (Bursuck & Damer, 2015).

When you speak, you also can enhance your students' listening skills by stressing words that are important to meaning. For example, say "He *hit* the *ball*" or "*He* hit the ball," depending on what you want to emphasize. Stressing inflectional patterns, such as using an upward inflection when asking a question, also helps students better understand what you are saying (Moats, 2007).

USE MODELING TO EXPAND STUDENTS' LANGUAGE   You can expand the language of students with expressive language problems by adding relevant information to student statements:

Student: John is nice.

Teacher: Yes, he is very nice, polite, and considerate of other people's feelings.

You can also expand language by broadening a minimal statement:

Student: My weekend was fun.

Teacher: You had a great time last weekend on your trip to the mountains.

Modeling to expand students' language is most effective when it is done as an ongoing part of your everyday communications. Students also can learn to model behavior for each other.

PROVIDE MANY MEANINGFUL CONTEXTS FOR PRACTICING SPEECH AND LANGUAGE SKILLS   The goal of successful language programs is to teach students to use appropriate language in a variety of social and academic situations, both in and out of school. You can help students with all types of speech and language problems meet that goal by providing as many opportunities as possible to practice language skills within meaningful contexts (Hardman et al., 2016). Practice helps students refine language skills and make them more natural and automatic. When students practice in many different contexts, they can apply what they learn more readily. For example, Ms. Crum just taught her class the meaning of the word *ironic*. During health class, the students discussed the irony of the government's warning people against fat consumption and then funding school lunches that are high in fat. During a trip to the museum, Ms. Crum pointed out the irony of the guard's telling them to be quiet when he was wearing shoes that squeaked loudly when he walked.

It is also helpful to encourage students with communication disorders to talk about events and experiences in their environment, describing them in as much detail as possible (Hardman et al., 2016). For example, Ms. Cusak, a first-grade teacher, starts every Monday by having two students tell about something they did over the weekend. Mr. Drake, a sixth-grade teacher, uses a *Saturday Night Live* format whereby students in his class act out something funny that happened to them over the weekend.

DIMENSIONS OF DIVERSITY

Carlo and colleagues (2004) improved the reading vocabulary of mixed groups of Anglo and Latino fifth graders using two strategies. They allowed native Spanish speakers access to the text's meaning in Spanish. They also presented vocabulary words in meaningful contexts and reinforced word meanings through activities that stressed spelling, pronunciation, meaningful word parts, syntax, and depth of meaning.

Finally, whenever possible, instruction should be embedded in the context of functional areas. For example, in Ms. Taylor's consumer math class, she has students go out to appliance stores, talk to salespeople about service contracts, and then describe and compare the various service contracts that are available. In Ms. Ellen's second-grade class, students invite and converse with classroom visitors.

> **MyLab Education** Self-Check 7.2

Who Are Students with Learning and Behavioral Disabilities and What Are Their Academic Needs?

INCLUDE

Students with learning and behavioral disabilities have learning disabilities, mild intellectual disabilities, and emotional disturbance. These are the students who are most likely to be included in your classroom. Students with learning disabilities achieve less than typical students academically because they have trouble with processing, organizing, and applying academic information. Students with learning disabilities are of normal intelligence, have presumably received adequate instruction, and have not been shown to be sensory impaired, emotionally disturbed, or environmentally disadvantaged. Will, one of the students described at the beginning of this chapter, has a learning disability. Students with mild intellectual disabilities are students who have some difficulty meeting the academic and social demands of general education classrooms, in large part because of below-average intellectual functioning (that is, scoring 55–70 on an IQ test). Jerome, another of the students from the opening vignettes, has a mild intellectual disability. Students with emotional disturbance are of average intelligence but have problems learning primarily because of external (acting out, poor interpersonal skills) and/or internal (anxiety, depression) behavioral adjustment problems. ReNaye from the beginning of the chapter has an emotional/behavioral disorder.

IDEA 2004 allowed school districts to use RtI to identify students with learning disabilities as an alternative to using discrepancy formulas. MTSS is a broader, general education-based means of intervening to prevent, if possible, the need for special education. The process of using the discrepancy between student ability and achievement to identify students with learning disabilities has come under attack, in large part because by the time the discrepancy is large enough to qualify for special education, students are already so far behind that catching up is difficult. Currently, the most typical way to identify students with LD is a combination of failure to respond to interventions and patterns of strengths and weaknesses according to psychological tests, the process described in the Case in Practice feature.

Students with learning disabilities, mild intellectual disabilities, and emotional disturbance differ in a number of ways (Hallahan, Kauffman, & Pullen, 2014; Sabornie, Evans, & Cullinan, 2006). The behavior problems of students with emotional disturbance are more severe (Lane, Carter, Pierson, & Glaeser, 2006), and students with mild intellectual disabilities have lower levels of measured intelligence (Polloway, Houck, Patton, & Lubin, 2017). Students with learning disabilities may have more pronounced learning strengths and weaknesses than students with mild intellectual disabilities (Spencer et al., 2014; Lerner & Johns, 2014), who are likely to show lower performance in all areas (Polloway et al., 2017). Still, the academic and social characteristics of students with these disabilities overlap considerably. All three groups may experience significant problems in academic achievement, classroom behavior, and peer relations (Gage, Lierheimer, & Goran, 2012; Stichter, Conroy, & Kauffman, 2007).

FYI

Whereas federal law uses the term *emotional disturbance*, the more accepted terminology is *children and youth with emotional or behavioral disorders* (EBD) (Kauffman & Landrum, 2017).

FYI

Because students with autism spectrum disorder comprise 8.6 percent of all students with disabilities (U.S. Department of Education, 2016), more than students with emotional disturbance and mild intellectual disabilities, they are considered by some to be a high-incidence disability (Loiacono, 2009). We include them in Chapter 6 because they generally have different educational needs than the students in this chapter.

CASE IN PRACTICE 7.1
Identifying Students with Learning Disabilities Using RtI

The RtI approach to identifying learning disabilities can be clearly seen in the accompanying progress-monitoring graph for Marni. Marni is new to the school and in fourth grade. She is able to read fourth-grade passages accurately and fluently, but struggles to understand what she is reading. Marni scored below benchmark on the fall benchmark administration of Maze, a curriculum-based measure of reading comprehension, but the RtI team decided to start her in Tier 1 because she was new to the school. The Title 1 teacher gave Marni an informal reading inventory and found that Marni had particular difficulty finding main ideas in expository text and answering inferential questions in both narrative and expository text. The core reading curriculum in Tier 1 is evidence-based. Marni's progress in reading comprehension is being monitored weekly in terms of the number of correct responses on the fourth-grade Maze. Her progress graph is divided into four parts: Tier 1, Tier 2, Tier 3, and Tier 4. In Tier 1, Marni received correctly delivered evidence-based instruction for four weeks from her general education teacher, yet she failed to make adequate progress in reading comprehension. The RtI team decided to provide her with extra small-group practice by moving her into Tier 2. Note that an aimline was drawn from her median performance in Tier 1 of 12 correct answers to the benchmark performance in May, which in grade 4 is 24 correct answers. Use of an aimline was a quick way to judge Marni's progress; if she was at or above the line, her progress would be considered adequate. If she was below the line four consecutive times, her program would need to be changed.

For Tier 2, the team suggested that Marni's teacher provide her with extra guided practice finding main ideas, constructing summaries using graphic organizers aligned with books at her instructional level, and answering inferential comprehension questions. During this time, Marni's teacher continued to monitor her progress

in reading comprehension weekly. After the paired reading was introduced, Marni's performance improved some, but wasn't sustained; she performed below her aimline for four consecutive weeks, a warning signal that she was falling farther behind her classmates. Therefore, the team proposed a Tier 3 intervention, which, in Marni's school, was not special education, but an alternative reading curriculum where she would receive small-group, intensive instruction with particular emphasis on the foundational reading skills of vocabulary and making inferences. Tier 3 was delivered by a Title 1 reading teacher five times per week for 60 minutes. Marni continued to participate in the core classroom reading program and the team continued to monitor her progress weekly.

For the first four weeks Marni was still below the aimline, but was making progress. Therefore, the team elected to keep her in Tier 3. However, after the next four weeks it was clear that her rate of progress had slowed, and rather than allowing her to fall farther behind her classmates, Marni was referred to special education. At that point, with written approval from her family, additional assessments were given to Marni by the school psychologist to see if she had processing deficits associated with a learning disability. The results showed definite problems in a number of information processing areas including working memory, oral language, and attention. After ruling out emotional, cultural, medical, and environmental factors, Marni was declared eligible for special education as a student with a learning disability. Marni remained in the same reading curriculum, but was moved to a smaller group of three taught by the special education teacher for 90 minutes per day. The small group accommodated her attention problems and allowed the teacher to provide more intensive support for Marni's skill acquisition. Increased time for reading was done in hopes of eventually catching Marni up to her classmates. The team continued to monitor Marni's reading comprehension weekly.

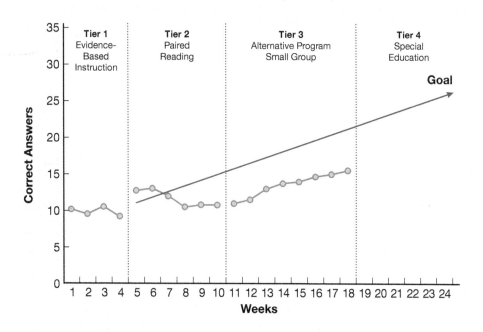

Response to Intervention (RtI), Classroom-Based Progress Graph: Marni

RESEARCH-BASED PRACTICES

Spencer and others (2014) examined the accuracy of determining the presence of a learning disability using RtI alone or in combination with standardized cognitive measures and found that using RtI with standardized cognitive measures was more accurate.

DIMENSIONS OF DIVERSITY

African American students, especially those in urban middle schools, are at greater risk of being identified as behavior disordered than white students; children from Latino or Asian families are at less risk (Greenhouse, 2015; Phippen, 2015; Waitoller, Artilers, & Cheney, 2010). What are the factors that may account for this?

DIMENSIONS OF DIVERSITY

Research has shown that reading disabilities affect boys and girls at roughly the same rate. Boys, however, are more likely to be referred for treatment, as they are more likely to get the teacher's attention by misbehaving (Lerner & Johns, 2014).

INCLUDE

FYI

McLaughlin, Speirs, and Shenassa (2014), in a 30-year longitudinal study of persons with reading disabilities, found that students experiencing severe reading problems at age seven were less likely to attain a higher level of income as an adult.

Although scientists have developed sophisticated computerized imaging techniques to detect neurological differences in children with learning and behavioral disabilities, the precise causes of these disabilities in individual children remain speculative largely because learning and behavior result from a complex interaction between students' individual characteristics, the various settings in which they learn, and the tasks or other demands they face in those settings (Hallahan et al., 2005; Shamaki, 2015; Smith & Strick, 2010). It is often difficult to identify the primary cause of a learning or behavior problem. For example, Thomas is lagging behind his classmates in acquiring a sight-word vocabulary in reading. Learning disabilities tend to run in his family, but Thomas's school district also changed reading series last year. In addition, Thomas's parents separated in the middle of the school year and divorced several months later. Why is Thomas behind in reading? Is it heredity? Is it the new reading program? Is it his parents' marital problems? All these factors may have contributed to Thomas's problem.

The most important reason students with high-incidence disabilities are grouped for discussion as students with learning and behavioral disabilities is that whatever behaviors they exhibit and whatever the possible causes of these behaviors, these students often benefit from the same instructional practices (Bateman, 2004; Coyne, Kame'enui, & Carnine, 2007). These practices are introduced in this chapter and covered in considerable depth throughout the rest of this book. For example, Raeanna has a mild intellectual disability. She has difficulty reading her classmates' social cues. As a result, she does not recognize when she is acting too aggressively with her classmates and often is rejected. Del is a student with learning disabilities. He also has trouble reading the social cues of his peers. Although Raeanna and Del may learn new social skills at different rates, both can benefit from social skills training that provides considerable guided practice and feedback on how to read social cues. The point to remember is that categorical labels are not particularly useful in describing specific students or developing instructional programs for them (Hardman et al., 2016). For example, both Damon and Aretha have learning disabilities, yet their areas of difficulty differ. Damon has a severe reading problem but excels in mathematics and various computer applications. Aretha, on the other hand, is reading at grade level but has significant problems with math. Although both students are categorized as having learning disabilities, they have very different needs. You must analyze each individual student's needs and adjust instruction, as necessary. This individualization is at the heart of the INCLUDE strategy, introduced in Chapter 5.

Students with learning and behavioral disabilities have many academic needs. They have difficulty acquiring basic skills in the areas of reading, written language, and math. They also may lack skills necessary for efficient learning, such as attending to task, memory, organizing and interpreting information, reasoning, motor coordination, independent learning skills, and academic survival skills.

Reading Skills

Students with learning and behavioral disabilities have two major types of reading problems: decoding and comprehension. Decoding problems involve the skills of identifying words accurately and fluently. Accuracy problems are most readily observed when students read orally, mispronouncing words, substituting one word for another, or omitting words (Mercer & Pullen, 2008). Students with reading fluency problems can read words accurately but do not recognize them quickly enough. They read slowly, in a word-by-word fashion, without grouping words together meaningfully (Bursuck & Damer, 2015; Hallahan et al., 2014; Lerner & Johns, 2014). Many of these reading decoding problems are exemplified in the following oral reading sample by a student with a learning disability:

> Then Ford had, uh, other i . . . a better idea. Take the worrrk to the men. He deee. . . . A long rope was hooked onto the car . . . wheels. . . . There's no rope on there. The rope pulled the car . . . auto . . . the white wheels along . . . pulled the car all along the way. Men stood still. Putting on car parts. Everybody man . . .

put on, on, a few parts. Down the assembly line went the car. The assembly line saved . . . time. Cars costed still less to buh . . . bull . . . d . . . build. Ford cuts their prices on the Model T again. (Hallahan et al., 2005, p. 370)

Here is the passage the student tried to read:

> Then Ford had another idea. Take the work to the men, he decided. A long rope was hooked onto a car axle and wheels. The rope pulled the axle and wheels along. All along the way, men stood still putting on car parts. Down the assembly line went the car. The assembly line saved more time. Cars cost still less to build. Ford cut the price on the Model T again. (Hallahan et al., 2005, p. 370)

Students who have serious difficulties decoding written words are sometimes referred to as having *dyslexia*. The Professional Edge feature discusses the meaning of this term and suggests instructional approaches for students with this disorder.

Students with learning and behavioral disabilities often have problems comprehending narrative text in the elementary grades and informational texts and advanced literature in the upper grades (Bursuck & Damer, 2015). Although these difficulties result in part from poor decoding skills, they may also occur because they lack background and vocabulary knowledge as well as strategies for identifying the key elements of stories and content-area texts. For example, after Connor's grandmother talked to him about her homeland of Vietnam, he was able to understand a well-written expository text about the Vietnam War. Todd's teacher asked him questions about a book he had just read as part of his classroom literature program. Todd was unable to tell her where the story took place (setting) or the lesson of the story (moral) because the answers to these questions were not directly stated in the story and Todd lacked the necessary inference strategies to figure them out. In another instance, Patsy was unable to answer a study question comparing the causes of World Wars I and II because she could not locate key words, such as *differences* and *similarities*. In addition, students with these disabilities may not be able to adjust their reading rate to allow for skimming a section of text for key information or for reading more slowly and intensively to answer specific questions. For example, Dennis takes a lot of time to locate key theorems in his geometry book because he thinks he needs to read every word in the chapter while he is looking for them. Students with reading problems can benefit from using a variety of Assistive Technology devices described in the Technology Notes feature.

Written Language Skills

The written language difficulties of students with learning and behavioral disabilities include handwriting, spelling, and written expression. Handwriting problems can be caused by a lack of fine motor coordination, failure to attend to task, inability to perceive and/or remember visual images accurately, and inadequate handwriting instruction in the classroom (Berninger, Nielsen, Abbot, Wijsman, & Raskind, 2008; Mercer & Pullen, 2008). Students may have problems in the areas of letter formation (is the letter recognizable?), size, alignment, slant, line quality (heaviness or lightness of lines), straightness, and spacing (too little or too much between letters, words, and lines) (Feder & Majnener, 2007).

Students with learning and behavioral disabilities also have trouble with spelling (Moats, 2007; Nag & Snowling, 2012; Wanzek et al., 2006). The English language consists largely of three types of words: those that can be spelled phonetically, those that can be spelled by following certain linguistic rules, and those that are irregular. For example, the words *cats, construction,* and *retell* can be spelled correctly by applying phonics generalizations related to consonants, consonant blends (*str*), vowels, root words (*tell*), prefixes (*re–*), and suffixes (*–ion, –s*). The word *babies* can be spelled by applying the linguistic rule of changing *y* to *i* and adding *–es*. Words such as *said, where*, and *through* are irregular and can be spelled only by remembering what they look like. Students with learning and behavioral disabilities may have trouble with all three types of words.

MyLab Education

Video Example 7.2: Reading: Direct Instruction

Becoming a fluent reader takes practice. Learn about the role of different kinds of reading practice in building fluency in this video.

RESEARCH-BASED PRACTICES

Research shows that of those children who are failing to read by the end of first grade, fewer than one in eight will ever catch up to grade level (Juel, 1988; Francis, Shaywitz, Stuebing, Fletcher, & Shaywitz, 1996; Shaywitz et al, 1999). Many at-risk readers benefit from early intervention that includes the explicit, systematic teaching of our letter–sound system, often referred to as *phonics* (Ehri, 2004).

MyLab Education

Video Example 7.3: Learning Disabilities

Watch the video and learn why students like Bridget struggle to learn and what can be done about it.

PROFESSIONAL EDGE 7.1

Understanding Dyslexia

The term *dyslexia* is used a lot. You hear that a friend's child has dyslexia, or you see a person who is dyslexic on television, or you read that Albert Einstein and Thomas Edison had dyslexia. The word *dyslexia*, which means "developmental word blindness," or, more simply, difficulty with words (Kamhi & Catts, 2011), manifests itself in both reading and spelling and is often used interchangeably with the term *reading disabilities*. Dyslexia has a medical sound to it, but until fairly recently there was little convincing evidence to show that it was medically based. Thanks to the development of computerized imaging techniques, such as functional magnetic resonance imaging (fMRI) and positron-emission tomography (PET) scanning, as well as recent studies of twins, evidence of an organic, genetic basis for reading in general (Lopez et al., 2013; Malanchini, Wang, Voronin, Schenker, Plomin, Petrill, & Kovas, 2017) and dyslexia in particular (Altarelli et al, 2014; Cui, Xia, Su, & Gong, 2016; Feng et al, 2017; Olson et al., 2013; Perrachione et al, 2016; Sela, Izzetoglu, Izzetoglu, & Onaral, 2014; Sun, Lee, & Kirby, 2010) is accumulating. For example, from an early age and often into adulthood, dyslexics show a pattern of underactivation in a region in the back of the brain that enables first accurate and then automatic reading. This pattern of underactivity appears to be present in dyslexics regardless of their age, sex, or culture (Shaywitz, 2003). That is why dyslexics have problems initially "cracking the code" and then problems later on developing reading fluency.

A common misconception about dyslexia is that it is a visual problem involving letter or word reversals (b/d, was/saw), or of "words dancing around on the page" (Hudson, High, & Al Otaiba, 2007; p. 506; Olulade, Napoliello, & Eden, 2013). In fact, such reversals are common among most beginning readers and not necessarily a sign of a reading disability. More common is their inability to identify and spell words accurately and fluently. For the latest on brain research related to learning disabilities, visit (http://www.sciencedaily.com); search *dyslexia*.

Knowing the causes of severe reading problems is one thing; knowing what to do to help students who have these problems is another altogether. Put very simply, students with dyslexia have serious problems learning to read despite normal intelligence, normal opportunities to learn to read, and an adequate home environment. Considerable evidence suggests that reading problems associated with dyslexia are phonologically based (Blachman, 1997; Bursuck & Damer, 2015; Foorman, 2003; Olulade et al., 2013; Sela et al., 2014; Stanovich & Siegel, 1994); students with dyslexia have difficulty developing *phonemic awareness*, the understanding that spoken words are made up of sounds. Phonemic awareness problems make it hard for these students to link speech sounds to letters, ultimately leading to slow, labored reading characterized by frequent starts and stops and multiple mispronunciations. Students with dyslexia also have comprehension problems largely because their struggle to identify words leaves little energy for understanding what they read. They have added trouble with the basic elements of written language, such as spelling and sentence and paragraph construction, and understanding representational systems such as telling time (Burny, Valcke, and Desoete, 2012). Dyslexia commonly is considered a type of learning disability, and in most states students with dyslexia are served under the learning disability classification of IDEA.

A large body of research (Blachman, 2000; Foorman, 2003; Haager & Vaughn, 2013; Hudson, Torgesen, Lane, & Turner, 2012; McCardle & Chhabra, 2004; Moats, 2007; National Early Literacy Panel, 2008; National Reading Panel, 2000; Shaywitz, Morris, & Shaywitz, 2008; Snow, Burns, & Griffin, 1998; Swanson, 2000) shows that students with severe reading disabilities benefit from a beginning reading program that includes the following five elements:

1. *Direct instruction in language analysis.* For example, students need to be taught skills in phonemic segmentation by orally breaking down words into their component sounds.

2. *A highly structured phonics program.* This program should teach the alphabetic code directly and systematically by using a simple-to-complex sequence of skills, teaching regularity before irregularity, and discouraging guessing.

3. *Writing and reading instruction in combination.* Students need to be writing the words they are reading.

4. *Intensive instruction.* Reading instruction should take place in groups of four or fewer and include large amounts of practice in materials that contain words they are able to decode.

5. *Teaching for automaticity.* Students must be given enough practice that they are able to read both accurately and fluently.

It is important to identify students with dyslexia and other severe reading disabilities early, before they fall far behind their peers in reading skills. You have already learned that once students fall behind in reading, they are unlikely to ever catch up. Early identification is also urgent given recent studies showing that effective language instruction appears to generate repair in underactivated sections of the brain (Odegard, Ring, Smith, Biggan, & Black, 2008; Shaywitz, 2003; Shaywitz et al, 2008; Simos et al., 2007). RtI has the potential to help educators avoid the pitfalls of the more traditional "wait to fail" discrepancy model described earlier, though it remains to be seen whether RtI can deliver timely, intensive interventions to students with reading disabilities, or whether these new systems result in delays in needed instruction, replacing "wait to fail" with a "watch them fail" approach (Reynolds & Shaywitz, 2009). See the Instructional Edge in Chapter 4 on page 110 for ways universal screening can be used to identify children at risk for reading failure early.

Additional sources of information about dyslexia include: The International Dyslexia Association (www.interdys.org), Learning Disabilities Association of America (www.ldaamerica.org), LD OnLine (www.ldonline.org), and the National Center for Learning Disabilities (www.ncld.org).

TECHNOLOGY NOTES 7.1
Using Assistive Technology (AT) in Reading

Most students with learning and behavioral disabilities have reading problems, and, unfortunately, the reading problems persist into their preteen and adolescent years. At the same time, these students are spending more time in general education classes where access to content depends on independently reading textbooks written at their frustration level. Although attempts to remediate their reading skills need to continue, AT can help students with learning and behavioral disabilities access content independently by bypassing their reading disability. A text-to-speech screen reader can be helpful for students who are unable to read their content textbooks but have good listening skills. Also, most text-to-speech applications allow the user to

adjust the speed and volume, and some applications even highlight the sentence and/or specific words being spoken (Bone & Houck, 2017; p. 49). The particular screen reading tool required depends on how it is used and the specific needs of the student. For example, some tools are better suited for students who need to touch the words as they are heard and other tools may be more beneficial because they offer a depth of content about a particular area of reading that supports a particular reading goal of the student. The various uses for screen-reader programs, along with corresponding examples of AT tools, are shown in the following table (Bisagno & Haven, 2002; Bone & Houck, 2017; Bursuck & Damer, 2015).

Use	AT Tool	Acceptable Format/Systems
Read aloud large volumes of straight text from the computer screen	ReadPlease http://www.readplease.com	Windows PC
	iPad; VoiceOver, and Siri https://www.apple.com/accessibility/iphone/vision/	Apple
Uses grammar and vocabulary-smart word prediction to help students express their ideas in writing across devices; also has speech recognition availability	Co:Writer Universal http://donjohnston.com	Google; Mac OS; Windows PC
	Kurzweil 3000 https://www.kurzweiledu.com	Firefly: Mac OS; Windows PC
Provide real-time aural feedback using natural text-to-speech voices in multiple languages and dialects	Nextup http://nextup.com/	Windows PC; PDF files, webpages, documents
Provide customized visual presentation of text as well as read aloud large volumes of straight text from handheld device that allows students to touch if needed as they read without the problem of changing screens	Kindle https://www.amazon.com	Amazon; Sony
	Audible App https://www.audible.com/howtolisten	Amazon
	Read & Write for Google https://www.texthelp.com	Google; Mac OS; Windows PC
Read aloud highlighted text on screen from various formats; converts web pages and common file types in Google Drive into spoken words	iSpeech: Chrome extensions https://www.ispeech.org/webapps/webreader	Google; Mac OS; Windows PC
	Select and Speak: Chrome extensions https://itunes.apple.com	Google; Mac OS; Windows PC
	Voice Dream Reader http://www.voicedream.com	Chrome extensions; includes text from PDFs, MS Word Docs
Read aloud text on screen from various formats even if reader leaves page; no highlighting required	Natural Reader https://www.naturalreaders.com/	Save text in Dropbox or OneDrive or is available on the web
	UDL Editions CAST http://udleditions.cast.org/	Web-based; Google, Mac, Windows PC
Provide digital text on various subjects that offer leveled supports including texthelp, which is a toolbar for individual readers	Aloud! text-to-speech app https://itunes.apple.com/us/app/aloud-text-to-speech	Apple: specifically designed for iPhone & iPad
Provide tools to organize images and geographic locations in free form maps to convey ideas for telling a story with visual representation	SpiderScribe Junior https://www.spiderscribe.net/	Google; Mac OS; Windows PC

Here are some additional suggestions when using AT for print access (Bisagno & Haven, 2002; Bursuck & Damer, 2015; Cummings, 2011):

- Using a screen writer requires having an electronic version of the text to be read. E-text can be obtained from other sources such as Bookshare.org.
- To convert course readers and text not available electronically to e-text, a scanner, optical character recognition (OCR) software, and adequate editing time are needed.
- For students who prefer a human to a computerized voice, in addition to options on the apps, you can find prerecorded audio files with human voice options.

- For more technical texts such as science and math, it is important to listen to the reading before sharing it with students because particular terms in these areas can be mispronounced by some automated voices and careful consideration of dialect is important.
- Bypass strategies using AT are not a substitute for learning how to read. Staels and Van den Broeck (2015) found that the over-use of software could have a negative impact on student word identification skills. Be sure your students are receiving systematic explicit instruction in reading decoding and comprehension as needed.

FYI

In some states such as Texas and Alabama, dyslexia is addressed outside of special education, while in others, dyslexia is not distinguished from LD.

RESEARCH-BASED PRACTICES

Meyer and Houck (2014) found that the perceptions of middle school students with disabilities towards text-to-speech software were positive. The students felt it saved time and improved their comprehension.

FYI

In manuscript writing, five letters (*q, z, u, j,* and *k*) account for 43 percent of all illegible letters written. For cursive writing, the letters *a, e, r,* and *t* account for about 50 percent of all illegible letters written (Mercer & Pullen, 2008).

Students with learning and behavior problems struggle with all areas of written expression (Graham, Collins, & Rigby-Wills, 2017; Graham & Harris, 2013). Their problems with written expression can be grouped into two major types: product problems and process problems (Isaacson, 2001; Mercer & Pullen, 2008). Their written products are often verb–object sentences; characterized by few words, incomplete sentences, overuse of simple subject–verb constructions, repetitive use of high-frequency words, a disregard for audience, and poor organization and structure; and many mechanical errors, such as misspellings, incorrect use of punctuation and capital letters, and faulty subject–verb agreements and choice of pronouns (Lerner & Johns, 2014; Mercer & Pullen, 2008).

These students also have trouble with the overall process of written communication (Harris, Graham, Brindle & Sandmel, 2009). Their approach to writing shows little systematic planning, great difficulty putting ideas on paper because of a preoccupation with mechanics, failure to monitor writing, and little useful revision (Lerner & Johns, 2014; Mercer & Pullen, 2008). A writing sample from a student who has a disability is shown in Figure 7.3. What types of product problems do you see in this sample? What process problems do you think might have led to these problems?

Math Skills

Math also can be problematic for students with learning and behavioral disabilities (Flores, Hinton, & Schweck, 2014; Powell, Fuchs, & Fuchs, 2013; Shin & Bryant, 2015; Swanson, 2011). Common problems include the following:

FIGURE 7.3 **Written Expression Sample of a 14-Year-Old Student with a Learning Disability**

1. *Problems with spatial organization.* Students may be unable to align numbers in columns, may reverse numbers (write a 9 backward, read 52 as 25), or may subtract the top number from the bottom number in a subtraction problem:

$$\begin{array}{r} 75 \\ -39 \\ \hline 44 \end{array}$$

2. *Lack of alertness to visual detail.* Students misread mathematical signs or forget to use dollar signs and decimals when necessary.

3. *Procedural errors.* Students miss a step in solving a problem. For example, they may forget to add a carried number in an addition problem or to subtract from the regrouped number in a subtraction problem:

$$\begin{array}{r} 29 \\ +53 \\ \hline 72 \end{array} \qquad \begin{array}{r} 41 \\ -28 \\ \hline 23 \end{array}$$

4. *Failure to shift mind-set from one problem type to another.* Students solve problems of one type, but when required to solve problems of another type, they solve them in the way they did those of the first type. For example, Kristy has just completed several geometry problems that required finding area. The next problem asks for the perimeter, but she continues to compute area.

5. *Difficulty forming numbers correctly.* Students' numbers are too large or are poorly formed, which makes solving computational or algebraic problems awkward, particularly when the students are unable to read their own numbers.

6. *Difficulty with memory.* Students like Jerome, the student with mild intellectual disabilities described at the beginning of the chapter, may be unable to recall basic math facts; other students may have difficulty using their working memory when solving problems involving multiple steps. For example, Adrian had difficulty solving algebra problems that required determining whether a set of five ordered pairs was a function. When he finally determined the second numbers in the pairs were mentioned only once, he had forgotten what he had found for the first numbers in the pairs.

7. *Problems with mathematical judgment and reasoning.* Students are unaware when their responses are unreasonable. For example, they do not see the obvious errors in $9 - 6 = 15$ or $4 + 3 = 43$. They may also have trouble solving word problems. For example, students may be unable to decide whether to add or subtract when solving basic word problems, focusing on cue words such as *less, more,* or *times* rather than comprehending accurately the situation described in the problem. This difficulty is shown in the following problem: "A boy has three times as many apples as a girl. The boy has 6. How many does the girl have?" Students with disabilities are likely to answer 18 instead of 2 because they think the presence of the word *times* in the problem means they need to multiply (Cawley et al., 2001, p. 325). Students with math disabilities may also have problems translating word problems into the correct algebraic equations. For example, Stacy was able to solve the problem $x + 20 = 50$. However, when given the word problem: *Serena's mom gave her 20 dollars. Serena now has a total of 50 dollars. How much money did Serena's mom give her?* she was unable to solve for the correct answer.

8. *Problems with mathematical language.* Students may have difficulty with the meanings of key mathematical terms, such as *regroup, formula, intersect,* and *minus* (Mercer & Pullen, 2008; Shin & Bryant, 2015). They also may have trouble participating in oral drills (Lerner & Johns, 2014) or verbalizing the steps in solving word, computational, or algebraic problems (Berg & Hutchinson, 2010; Shin & Bryant, 2015).

Students from culturally and linguistically diverse backgrounds may have additional problems learning math skills. Some potential trouble spots and strategies for dealing with these trouble spots are shown in the Instructional Edge feature.

FYI

Ways to increase accessibility of materials and formats for math instruction include keeping models on the board; providing graph paper to align problems; and using visual cues, such as color-coded or boldfaced signs and arrows, as reminders of direction and frames to set off problems and answers.

Learning Skills

Students with learning and behavioral disabilities have difficulty performing skills that could help them learn more readily. These include difficulties with attention, organizing and interpreting information, reasoning skills, motor skills, independent learning skills, and academic survival skills.

ATTENTION Students may have difficulty coming to attention or understanding task requirements (Cortiella & Horowitz, 2014; Hallahan et al., 2014; Swanson, 2011). For example, Janice frequently fails essay tests; she is unable to focus on key words in the questions to help her organize a response. As a result, she loses valuable writing time just staring at the question and not knowing how to begin. Benito misses important information at the beginning of science lectures because he takes five minutes to begin to attend to the teacher's presentation.

INSTRUCTIONAL EDGE 7.1

Accommodating Learners in Math Who Are Linguistically and Culturally Diverse

Math can be a challenging subject for all students, including those with learning and behavioral difficulties. While the universal nature of math can make it an area of strength for students from linguistically and culturally diverse backgrounds, English learners may still face challenges when learning math (Gay, 2010; Kersaint,

Thompson, & Petkova, 2013; Xenofontos, 2016). In the following table, Scott and Raborn (1996) present some potential trouble spots and suggested strategies for teaching math to students from linguistically and culturally diverse backgrounds.

Trouble Spot	Recommendation
Learning a new language	• Determine the student's level of proficiency in both English and the native language. • Assess math abilities in both languages. • If a student is stronger in math than in English, provide math instruction in the primary language. • Listen to the words you most frequently use in teaching math. Work together with the English as a second language (ESL) teacher to help the student learn these words or to help you learn them in the student's language. • Use a variety of ways to communicate such as gesturing, drawing sketches, writing basic vocabulary and procedures, rewording, and providing more details. • Provide time and activities that allow the student to practice the English language and the language of math.
Cultural differences	• Use word problem situations that are relevant to the student's personal cultural identity (e.g., ethnicity, gender, geographical region, age). • Share examples of the mathematical heritage of the student's culture (e.g., folk art, African and Native American probability games, measurement systems). • Involve family and community members in multicultural math.
Tricky vocabulary	• Use concrete activities to teach new vocabulary and the language of math. • Use only as many technical words as are necessary to ensure understanding. • Give more information in a variety of ways to help student understand new vocabulary. • Develop a picture file; purchase or have student make a picture dictionary of math terms and frequently-used vocabulary.
Symbolic language	• Allow student to draw pictures, diagrams, or graphic organizers to represent story problems. • Make clear the meanings and function of symbols. • Point out the interchangeable nature of operations. • In algebra, teach student to translate phrases to mathematical expressions.
Level of abstraction and memory	• Allow students to develop mathematical relationships using concrete representations accompanied by verbal descriptions. • Develop mathematical understanding from concrete to abstract form. • Use visual and kinesthetic cues to strengthen memory. • Keep distractions to a minimum.

Source: From "Realizing the Gifts of Diversity Among Students with Learning Disabilities," by P. Scott and D. Raborn, 1996, *LD Forum, 21*(2), pp. 10–18. Reprinted by permission of the Council for Learning Disabilities.

Students also may have trouble focusing on the important aspects of tasks. For example, Anita can tell you the color of her teacher's tie or the kind of belt he is wearing but nothing about the information he is presenting. When Arman tries to solve problems in math, he is unable to tell the difference between information that is needed and not needed to solve the problem.

Finally, students with learning and behavioral disabilities may have trouble sticking to a task once they have started it. This lack of task persistence is largely due to a lack of confidence resulting from a history of school failure. The emotional repercussions of school failure are covered later in this chapter in the discussion of the personal and psychological adjustment of students with learning and behavioral disabilities. Memory problems also may make learning difficult for students (Lerner & Johns, 2014; Swanson, 2011). Some problems occur when information is first learned. For example, Carla cannot remember information when it is presented just once. Sal has practiced science vocabulary many times but still cannot remember some of the terms. Students may also have trouble with working memory (Melby-Lervag & Hulme, 2013; Peijenborgh, Hurks, Aldenkamp, Vies, & Hendriksen, 2015; Swanson, 2011). For example, Denise adds a column of numbers such as 6, 8, 4, and 5. When it is time to add in the 5, she forgets that the total up to that point was 18. Rinaldo can't sustain his attention long enough to go through the problem-solving steps necessary to solve mathematical word problems. Finally, students may also fail to retain what they learn. For example, Abby correctly identified the major parts of the human digestive system in biology class on Friday, but she failed to recall them accurately when asked by the teacher to do so the following week.

ORGANIZING AND INTERPRETING INFORMATION Students with learning and behavioral disabilities may have trouble *organizing and interpreting* oral and visual information despite adequate hearing and visual skills (Learning Disabilities Association of America, n.d.); Lerner & Johns, 2014). For example, Rodney is a student with a learning disability who has trouble with visual tasks. He frequently loses his place while reading and copying; has trouble reading and copying from the chalkboard; does not notice details on pictures, maps, and photographs; is confused by worksheets containing a great deal of visual information; and often cannot remember what he has seen. LaTonya has trouble with auditory tasks. She has difficulty following oral directions, differentiating between fine differences in sounds (*e/i, bean/been*), taking notes during lectures, and remembering what she has heard.

REASONING SKILLS Students also may lack the *reasoning* skills necessary for success in school. Important reasoning skills include reading comprehension, generalization (the ability to recognize similarities across objects, events, or vocabulary), adequate background and vocabulary knowledge, induction (figuring out a rule or principle based on a series of situations), and sequencing (detecting relationships among stimuli) (Salvia et al., 2016). For example, Stu has difficulty understanding a lecture on the civil rights movement because he lacks necessary background information; he is unsure what a *civil right* is. Tamara has trouble recognizing a relationship on her own, even after repeated examples; her teacher presented five examples of how to add *s* to words that end in *y*, but Tamara still could not figure out the rule.

MOTOR SKILLS Some students with learning and behavioral disabilities may have *motor coordination and fine motor impairments* (Silver, 2006). For example, Denise is a first-grade student who has some fine motor and coordination problems. She has trouble using scissors, coloring within the lines, tying her shoes, and printing letters and numbers. Cal is in third grade. His handwriting is often illegible and messy. He is also uncoordinated at sports, which has limited his opportunities for social interaction on the playground because he is never

MyLab Education

Video Example 7.4: Adjusting Instruction for English Language Learners

This video examines the various components that teachers need to be aware of when working with students who are linguistically and culturally diverse.

selected to play on a team. Ramone is a sophomore in high school. He worries about always letting his team down because of his poor volleyball skills.

INDEPENDENT LEARNING   Students with learning and behavioral disabilities have been referred to as *passive learners,* meaning that they do not believe in their own abilities; have limited knowledge of problem-solving strategies; and even when they know a strategy, cannot tell when it is supposed to be used (Hallahan et al., 2014; Lerner & Johns, 2014). Being a passive learner is particularly problematic in the upper grades, where more student independence is expected. For example, when Laverne reads her science textbook, she does not realize when she comes across information that she does not understand. So instead of employing a strategy to solve this problem, such as rereading, checking the chapter summary, or asking for help, she never learns the information. As a result, she is doing poorly in the class. When Darrell studies for tests, he reads quickly through his text and notes but does not use strategies for remembering information, such as asking himself questions, saying the information to himself, or grouping into meaningful pieces the information he needs to learn.

ACADEMIC SURVIVAL SKILLS   Students with learning and behavioral disabilities also may have problems in the area of academic survival skills, such as attending school regularly, being organized, completing tasks in and out of school, being independent, taking an interest in school, and displaying positive interpersonal skills with peers and adults (Kerr & Nelson, 2009). For example, Duane is failing in school because he rarely shows up for class; when he does attend class, he sits in the back of the room and displays an obvious lack of interest. Nicole is always late for class and never completes her homework; her teachers think she does not care about school at all.

Learning Styles

The idea of teaching to a child's learning style has been recommended as a way to meet the individual needs of students with learning and behavioral disabilities for at least 40 years (Landrum & McDuffie, 2010). In fact, in the experience of the authors, it is difficult to have a conversation with teachers about teaching students with special needs without the topic of learning styles coming up. The assumption behind a learning styles approach is that differing students have differing preferences for how to learn and that when the mode of teaching matches that preference, achievement is enhanced (Hattie, 2009). Dunn's model of learning styles (Cassidy, 2004; Dunn, 1990), the most common, has five dimensions: biological, which includes preferences for conditions such as room temperature or lighting; emotional, such as being persistent versus needing breaks when learning; sociological, such as having a preference for working in groups or alone; physiological, including preferences for time of day or needs for mobility; and psychological, such as being impulsive versus reflective, left brained versus right brained, or a global versus analytic thinker (Hattie, 2009; Landrum & McDuffie, 2010). Examples of using a learning styles approach would include introducing content sequentially for analytic learners and using the "big picture" for global learners, teaching visual learners content using visual models rather than lecturing, and providing hands-on activities for tactile learners. Despite its broad intuitive appeal, the learning styles approach lacks a solid research base (Cuevas, 2015; Guterl, 2013; Landrum & McDuffie, 2010). Plus, the feasibility of being able to teach using one modality while excluding others is questionable at best. For example, try teaching reading visually while excluding anything auditory. For this reason, we suggest actively engaging students through all of their senses using universally designed instruction and then adjusting instruction as needed using INCLUDE.

Some parents and teachers have tried other unproven interventions in search of quick fixes for students with learning and behavioral disabilities. The issue of using unproven, controversial therapies is discussed in the Professional Edge feature.

MyLab Education

Video Example 7.5: Jennifer's Story of Self-Advocacy

One survival skill is self-advocacy. Watch as Jennifer discusses the importance of self-advocacy.

FYI

Estimates of the percentage of students with learning disabilities who are at risk for social problems range from 38 to 75 percent (Bryan, 2005).

PROFESSIONAL EDGE 7.2

Controversial Therapies in Learning and Behavioral Disabilities: What Does the Research Say?

Being the parent or teacher of a student with learning disabilities is not easy. Students with learning and behavioral disabilities often do not respond favorably to the first approach tried—or for that matter, to the first several. Failure and frustration can lead to the search for miracle cures. This problem is compounded by the fact that journals that publish research about the effectiveness of various treatments may not be read by parents and teachers. Unfortunately, this void is readily filled by a steady stream of information—much of it not substantiated by research—from popular books, lay magazines, television talk shows, and the Internet (Silver, 2006). According to Black (2016), more than 50 percent of children with chronic medical conditions, including language and learning disorders, use complementary and alternative medical techniques, and, often, parents don't tell their clinicians about it.

As a teacher, you need to be well informed about these therapies so you can give parents reliable, up-to-date information when they come to you for advice. The best way to get this information is to read professional journals. Online sites can also be helpful. Recommendations for using the Internet to evaluate controversial therapies are made at the end of this feature, including a list of reputable sites. Remember, any treatment may work for a few students, but, as you learned in Chapter 5's discussion of evidence-based practices, this is not the same as demonstrating effectiveness in a controlled research study. If you or a student's parents decide to use a controversial therapy, you must monitor its effectiveness carefully and discontinue it if necessary. Several commonly-appearing controversial therapies are summarized here, including the latest research findings for their effectiveness.

NEUROPHYSIOLOGICAL RETRAINING

In this group of approaches, learning difficulties are seen as the result of dysfunctions in the central nervous system that can be remediated by having students engage in specific sensory or motor activities. Common examples include *patterning, optometric visual training, vestibular training, applied kinesiology auditory processing training,* and the so-called *Brain Gym*[TM] (Hyatt, 2007). No research provides evidence that any of these methods improves students' cognitive functioning or reading ability (American Academy of Pediatrics, 1999, 2009; Spaulding, Mostert, & Beam, 2010).

DIET CONTROL THERAPIES

Numerous therapies involve using diet to control hyperactivity and other learning disorders. These include eliminating various artificial flavors, colors, preservatives, and refined sugar from the student's diet. Another diet therapy for learning disorders involves using megavitamins to treat emotional or cognitive disorders, while deficiencies in trace elements such as copper, zinc, magnesium, manganese, and chromium along with the more common elements of calcium, sodium, and iron are believed to cause learning disorders according to an additional theory. Combinations of herbs, spices, and other ingredients have been recommended in recent years as a treatment for ADHD, as well as for learning disabilities. A last theory claims that hypoglycemia (low blood-sugar levels) causes learning disabilities. None of the claims of these diet-related interventions has been verified by research (Barkley, 1995; Rojas & Chan, 2005; Smith & Strick, 2010).

SCOTOPIC SENSITIVITY SYNDROME

This syndrome has been defined as a difficulty in efficiently processing light, which causes a reading disorder (Irlen, 1991; Lerner & Johns, 2014). Symptoms include abnormal sensitivity to light, blinking and squinting, red and watery eyes, frequent headaches, word blurriness, print instability, slow reading, skipping and rereading lines, and difficulty reading at length because of general eye strain and fatigue (Irlen, 1991). Following a screening test, students identified as having scotopic sensitivity are treated with plastic overlays or colored lenses, which can be expensive. Although many people treated with tinted lenses claim that the lenses eliminate their symptoms and help them read better, recent research (Ritchie, Della Sala, & McIntosh, 2011) as well as a statement by the American Academy of Pediatrics (2009) shows that scientific evidence for the approach is lacking (Ritchie, Della Sala, & McIntosh, 2011). Caution is advised.

ALLERGIES

The theory is that the elimination of certain foods from the diet such as milk, chocolate, eggs, wheat, corn, peanuts, pork, and sugar can reduce the effects of learning and behavioral disabilities. Although there seems to be a relationship between allergies and brain functioning, a clear cause-and-effect relationship has yet to be established (Silver, 2006).

EMERGING THERAPIES

Health researchers have reported on a number of therapies currently being recommended to treat learning and behavior difficulties often associated with ADHD (Rojas and Chan, 2005; Searight, Robertson, Smith, Perkins, & Searight, 2012). These therapies include fatty acid supplementation, homeopathy, yoga, massage, and green outdoor settings. The researchers have concluded that the overall body of evidence does not support the use of any of these therapies either alone or in concert with treatments of established effectiveness, such as medication and behavior therapy (Rojas & Chan, 2005; Searight et al., 2012).

CONTROVERSIAL THERAPIES AND THE INTERNET

As the number of Internet sites created for specific disabilities and related health issues increases, so too does information about controversial therapies. Because information on the Internet is not reviewed for quality, Ira (2000) suggests that you do the following to determine the credibility of the various websites you visit:

1. Click on the "About Us" or "Contact Us" links or buttons at a website. These links may inform you of who is on the team of people running a particular website. Many sites, particularly those that want to prove their credibility, feature a page describing their background, history, and affiliations (the "About Us" section) and mailing and e-mail addresses and phone numbers (the "Contact Us" section).

(continued)

2. Try to establish links with other sites. Sites with reliably usable information may have endorsements from prominent special needs organizations or may have links to other websites with more information on the subject. Look for links to other associations or educational or even government-supported institutions related to the subject. The more independent sites that validate a recommendation, the more credible it is. The following are specific sites that may address doubts about the credibility of a particular controversial therapy:

http://www.interdys.org	International Dyslexia Society
http://www.ldanatl.org	Learning Disabilities Association of America
http://www.ncld.org	National Center for Learning Disabilities
www.nccam.nih.gov	National Center for Complimentary and Alternative Medicine (CAM)—National Institute of Health
www.cochrane.org	Cochrane Collaboration
www.quackwatch.org	National Council Against Health Fraud
http://www.cldinternational.org	Council for Learning Disabilities

3. Ask friends and special needs associations to recommend websites that are informative. You can also e-mail or text people you think can offer advice on the credibility of a particular site.

4. Examine the content of the site for typographical and grammatical errors. As with books, magazines, and journals, credibility is often reflected in editorial excellence.

5. Check to see how often the site is updated. A site that is updated regularly with new research findings is most likely to be run by people interested in learning the truth rather than perpetuating their own point of view.

6. Check to be sure that a given finding has been validated by a credible, refereed research publication. Many of these publications are available on the Web. Three additional sources for information on controversial therapies are (http://www.quackwatch.org), (http://understood.org), and Wikipedia. For Understood.org, search "alternative therapies." For Wikipedia, go to (http://en.wikipedia.org) and search for "alternative therapies for developmental and learning disabilities."

MyLab Education Self-Check 7.3

Students who are experiencing emotional problems might be withdrawn, anxious, or depressed. What can you do to help these students in your classroom?

What Are the Social and Emotional Needs of Students with Learning and Behavioral Disabilities?

Considering students' social needs is crucial, because students who have social adjustment problems in school are at risk for academic problems (Garwood, Vernon-Feagans, & Family Life Project Key Investigators, 2017; Lane, Wehby, & Barton-Arwood, 2005; Morgan, Farkas, Tufis, & Sperling, 2008) as well as serious adjustment problems when they leave school (Carter & Wehby, 2003; Kauffman & Landrum, 2017). Students with learning and behavioral disabilities may have needs in several social areas, including classroom conduct, interpersonal skills, and personal and psychological adjustment.

Students with learning and behavioral disabilities may engage in various aggressive or disruptive behaviors in class, including hitting, fighting, teasing, hyperactivity, yelling, refusing to comply with requests, crying, destructiveness, vandalism, and extortion (Briesch, Ferguson, Volpe, & Briesch, 2012; Friend, 2018; Hallahan et al., 2014; Marsh, 2016). Recall ReNaye, the student described in the chapter opening who exhibited a number of aggressive and disruptive behaviors. Although many of these behaviors may be exhibited by all children at one time or another, the classroom conduct of students with behavioral disorders is viewed by teachers as abnormal, and their behavior has a negative impact on the other students in class (Hallahan et al., 2014; Kauffman & Landrum, 2017). For example, Kenneth is an adolescent with learning and behavior problems. His father died last year, and his mother has been working two jobs just to make ends meet. Kenneth has begun to hang out with a rough crowd and has been getting into fights in school. He has also been talking back to his teachers frequently and refusing to comply with their requests. Kenneth's behavior has gotten so bad that other students and their parents are complaining about it to the teacher. Guidelines for disciplining students like Kenneth are described in Chapter 12.

Interpersonal Skills

Students with learning and behavioral disabilities are likely to have difficulty in social relations with their peers. Evidence for these problems comes from more than 40 years of research showing that these students have fewer friends, are more likely to be rejected or neglected by their peers (Lerner & Johns, 2014; Estell et al., 2008), and are frequently rated as socially troubled by their teachers and parents (Smith & Strick, 2010). Many of these problems can be traced to the failure of students to engage in socially appropriate behaviors or in areas such as making friends, carrying on conversations, and dealing with conflict. Recall Jerome from the beginning of the chapter; his problems processing linguistic information caused him to be socially awkward and neglected by his classmates.

There are a number of explanations for why students have social skill problems. Some students may simply not know what to do in social situations. They may lack knowledge because they do not learn from naturally occurring models of social behavior at home or in school. Students also may have trouble reading social cues and may misinterpret the feelings of others (Bauminger & Kimhi-Kind, 2008; Bryan, 2005; Lerner & Johns, 2014; Kaufman & Landrum, 2017). For example, a story was told recently about five boys sitting on the floor of the principal's office, waiting to be disciplined. Four of the boys were discussing failing or near-failing grades and the trouble they were going to be in when the fifth boy, a student with a learning disability, chimed in to say that his grandparents were coming to visit the next week.

Other students may know what to do—but not do it. For example, some students with learning and behavioral disabilities are impulsive; they act before they think. In Del's sessions with the school social worker, he is able to explain how he would act in various social situations, but in an actual social setting, he gets nervous and acts without thinking.

Some students may choose not to act on their previous knowledge because their attempts at socially appropriate behavior may have gone unrecognized, and they would rather have negative recognition than no recognition at all. For example, James was rebuffed by one group of students so often that he began to say nasty things to them just to provoke them. He also began to hang out with other students who chronically misbehaved because, according to James, "At least they appreciate me!"

Finally, some students may know what to do socially but lack the confidence to act on their knowledge in social situations, particularly if they have a history of social rejection or lack opportunities for social interactions. Consider Holly, a student who is socially withdrawn. Holly worked for a year with her school counselor to learn how to initiate a social activity with a friend but is afraid to try it out for fear of being rejected.

Personal and Psychological Adjustment

Students with little success at academics and/or social relationships may have personal and psychological problems as well (Alexander & Cooray, 2003;

Mammarella et al, 2016; Torgesen, 1991). One common personal problem is self-image. Students with learning and behavioral disabilities often have a poor self-concept; they have little confidence in their own abilities (Lerner & Johns, 2014; Silver, 2010). Poor self-image can in turn lead to learned helplessness. Students with learned helplessness see little relationship between their efforts and school or social success. When these students succeed, they attribute their success to luck; when they fail, they blame their failure on a lack of ability. When confronted with difficult situations, students who have learned helplessness are likely to say or think, "What's the use? I never do anything right anyway."

Not surprisingly, low self-esteem and learned helplessness often result in actions likely to be interpreted as a lack of motivation. For example, Denny is a 15-year-old sophomore in high school. He has been in special education since the second grade. He has never received a grade better than a C and has received quite a few Ds and Fs. Last quarter, Denny started to skip classes because he felt that even when he went to class, he did not do well. Denny is looking forward to dropping out of school on his 16th birthday and going to work for a fast-food chain, where, he reasons, at least he will be able to do the work. Of course, learning problems often coexist with motivational problems (Cambria & Guthrie, 2010; Morgan, Fuchs, Compton, Cordray, & Fuchs, 2008; Wery & Thompson, 2013), as many years of failure exact a toll on students' confidence.

Students with learning and behavioral disabilities also may have severe anxiety or depression (Alesi, Rappo, & Pepi, 2014; Maag & Reid, 2006; Mammarella et al., 2016). Depressed or anxious students may refuse to speak up when in class, may be pessimistic or uninterested in key aspects of their lives, may be visibly nervous when given an assignment, may become ill when it is time to go to school, or may show a lack of self-confidence when performing common school and social tasks. For example, Barrett is a nine-year-old boy with a consistent history of school failure. He is sick just about every morning before he goes to school. At first his mother let him stay home, but now she makes him go anyway. When at school, Barrett is very withdrawn. He has few friends and rarely speaks in class. Barrett's teachers tend not to notice him because he is quiet and does not cause problems. If you have a student in your class who you think may be depressed, consult the Diagnostic Criteria for Major Depression (American Psychiatric Association, 2013). However, caution is advised, as the research shows that although students with high-incidence disabilities tend to score higher on depression scales, few have been shown to be clinically depressed (Maag & Reid, 2006). Also keep in mind that while students with learning and behavioral disabilities are at risk for having personal and psychological adjustment problems, not all of these students have these problems. In one study, Nunez and colleagues (2005) found that just under half of the students with learning disabilities did not differ in self-concept and learned helplessness from their classmates without disabilities. Using INCLUDE to find the individual needs and strengths of your students will help ensure that you will make classroom adjustments for them based on their unique needs.

What Instructional Adjustments Can You Make for Students with Learning and Behavioral Disabilities?

INCLUDE

As you have just read, students with learning and behavioral disabilities have a range of learning and social-emotional needs. Although these needs may make learning and socializing difficult for them, students with learning and behavioral disabilities can succeed in your classroom if given support. Some initial ideas about how you can adjust your instruction for students with learning and behavioral disabilities in your classroom are discussed next. A more in-depth treatment of such instructional changes can be found in Chapters 9 through 12.

Addressing Academic Needs

As you have already learned, you can discern whether students with learning and behavioral disabilities need changes to their instruction by using the INCLUDE strategy to analyze their academic needs and the particular demands of your classroom. In most cases, students with learning and behavioral disabilities are expected to meet the same curricular expectations as their classmates without disabilities. The first thing you should do is to check students' IEPs for any listed accommodations or modifications. For students with learning and behavioral disabilities, the IEP changes will mainly be accommodations. Next, try the three types of changes described in Chapter 5: bypassing a student's need by allowing the student to employ compensatory learning strategies; making an adjustment in classroom management, grouping, materials, and methods; and providing the student with direct instruction on basic or independent learning skills. For example, Jessica, who has learning disabilities, has enrolled in Mr. Gresh's high school general science class. Mr. Gresh uses a teaching format in which the students first read the text, then hear a lecture, and finally conduct and write up a lab activity (demands). Jessica has severe reading and writing problems. She is reading at about a sixth-grade level and has difficulty writing a legible, coherent paragraph (student learning needs). However, she does have good listening skills and is an adequate note taker (student strength). In Mr. Gresh's class, Jessica will have difficulty reading the textbook and meeting the lab-writing requirements independently (problem). She will be able to get the lecture information she needs because of her good listening skills (success). Mr. Gresh, with help from Jessica's special education teacher, brainstorms a number of additional adjustments to ones already included on her IEP. He develops a study guide to help Jessica identify key points in the text (materials and methods). He also sets up small groups in class to review the study guides (grouping) and assigns Jessica a buddy to help her with the writing demands of the lab activity (bypass). Finally, Mr. Gresh and the special education teacher set up a schedule to monitor Jessica's progress in writing lab reports and reading the textbook (evaluation). Several more examples of how the INCLUDE strategy can be used to adjust instruction are provided in Table 7.2.

In what ways might students with cognitive, emotional, and behavioral disorders have difficulty learning? How can teachers address each of these areas of difficulty?

TABLE 7.2 **Adjusting Instruction for Students with Learning and Behavioral Disabilities Using Steps in the INCLUDE Strategy**

Identify Classroom Demands	Note Student Strengths and Needs	Check for Potential Successes, Look for Potential Problems	Adjust Instruction
Student desks in clusters of four	*Strengths* Good vocabulary skills *Needs* Difficulty attending to task	*Success* Student understands instruction if on task *Problem* Student off task—does not face instructor as she teaches	Change seating so student faces instructor

(continued)

TABLE 7.2 *(Continued)*

Identify Classroom Demands	Note Student Strengths and Needs	Check for Potential Successes, Look for Potential Problems	Adjust Instruction
Small-group work with peers	*Strengths* Good handwriting *Needs* Oral expressive language—problem with word finding	*Success* Student acts as secretary for cooperative group *Problem* Student has difficulty expressing self in peer-learning groups	Assign as secretary of group Place into compatible small group Develop social skills instruction for all students
Expectation for students to attend class and be on time	*Strengths* Good drawing skills *Needs* Poor time management	*Success* Student uses artistic talent in class *Problem* Student is late for class and frequently does not attend at all	Use individualized student contract for attendance and punctuality—if goals are met, give student artistic responsibility in class
Textbook difficult to read	*Strengths* Good oral communication skills *Needs* Poor reading accuracy Lacks systematic strategy for reading text	*Successes* Student participates well in class Good candidate for class dramatizations *Problem* Student is unable to read text for information	Provide digital textbook Highlight student text
Lecture on women's suffrage movement to whole class	*Strengths* Very motivated and interested in class *Needs* Lack of background knowledge	*Success* Student has near-perfect attendance and tries hard *Problem* Student lacks background knowledge to understand important information in lecture	Give student choice of video to view or leveled book to read before lecture Build points for attendance and working hard into grading system
Whole-class instruction on telling time to the quarter hour	*Strengths* Good coloring skills *Needs* Cannot identify numbers 7–12 Cannot count by 5s	*Success* Student is able to color clock faces used in instruction *Problem* Student is unable to acquire time-telling skills	Provide extra instruction on number identification and counting by 5s
Math test involving solving word problems using addition	*Strengths* Good reasoning skills *Needs* Problems mastering math facts, sums of 10–18	*Success* Student is good at solving problems *Problem* Student misses problems due to math fact errors	Allow use of calculator
Multiple-choice and fill-in-the-blanks test	*Strengths* Good memory for details *Needs* Cannot identify key words in test questions Weak comprehension skills	*Success* Student does well on fill-in-the-blank questions that require memorization *Problem* Student is doing poorly on multiple-choice parts of history tests	Use bold type for key words in multiple-choice questions Teach strategy for taking multiple-choice tests Give student choice of alternatives to show knowledge other than multiple-choice items

Addressing Social and Emotional Needs

One of the most important reasons given for inclusive education is the social benefit for students with and without disabilities (Freeman & Alkin, 2000; Friend, 2018). Unfortunately, experience shows that many students with learning and behavior problems do not acquire important social skills just from their physical presence in general education classes (Hallahan et al., 2014; Sale & Carey, 1995). Although much of the emphasis in your training as a teacher concerns academics, your responsibilities as a teacher also include helping all students develop socially, whether or not they have special needs. As with academics, the support students need depends largely on the specific social problems each student has. Students who have significant conduct problems benefit from a classroom with a clear, consistent behavior management system. In classrooms that are effectively managed, the rules are communicated clearly and the consequences for following or not following those rules are clearly stated and consistently applied. Conduct problems also can be minimized if students are engaged in meaningful academic tasks that can be completed successfully. Still, conduct problems may be so significant that they require a more intensive, individualized approach. For example, ReNaye, whom you read about at the beginning of this chapter, repeatedly talked out and loudly refused to carry out any requests her teachers made of her. Her school attendance was also spotty. ReNaye's general education teachers got together with her special education teacher to develop a behavior contract (see an example of contract in Chapter 12, pages 417–418). The contract specified that for each class ReNaye attended without incident, she would receive points that her parents would allow her to trade for coupons to buy gasoline for her car.

While today's accountability-charged school environments tend to discourage activities not directly related to academics, teaching social skills can be important for your students with disabilities. Adjustments used will depend on the types of interpersonal problems your students have. You can use social skills training for students who do not know how to interact with peers and adults (Gresham, 2015; Lane et al., 2005; McGinnis & Goldstein, 2005; Stichter et al., 2007). For example, Tammy is very withdrawn and has few friends. One day her teacher took her aside and suggested that she ask one of the other girls in class home some day after school. Tammy told her that she would never do that because she just would not know what to say. Tammy's teacher decided to spend several social studies classes working with the class on that skill and other skills such as carrying on a conversation and using the correct words and demeanor when asking another student whether he or she would like to play a game. She felt that many of the students in class besides Tammy would benefit from these lessons. First, Tammy's teacher posted the steps involved in performing these skills on a chart in front of the classroom. Then she and several students in the class demonstrated the social skills for the class. She next divided the class into small groups, and each group role-played the various skills and was given feedback by classmates and peers. To make sure that Tammy felt comfortable, the teacher put her in a group of students who had a positive attitude and liked Tammy. An example of how to carry out social skills training is presented in the Case in Practice feature. As with any type of intervention, sustained, positive results from social skills training are not guaranteed (Maag, 2006). When using social skills training, be sure to remind your students to keep using them, carefully and continually monitor their usage using the Evaluate step in INCLUDE, and reteach if needed. You will learn more about the self-management of behavior in Chapters 10 and 12.

For students who know what to do in social situations but lack the self-control to behave appropriately, self-control training can be used (Henley, 2003; Hallahan et al., 2014; Kauffman & Landrum, 2017). Self-control training teaches students to redirect their actions by talking to themselves. For example, Dominic did not handle conflict very well. When his friends teased him, he was quick to lose his temper and to verbally lash out at them. His outbursts only encouraged the students, and they continued teasing and taunting him any chance they

RESEARCH-BASED PRACTICES

Ross and Sabey (2015) reduced problem behavior and increased prosocial behavior in five elementary-aged students with serious social skills deficits. The researchers employed a Tier 2 RtI intervention that combined social skills training, with a Check-in Check-out program involving before- and after-school adult monitoring and feedback, as well as a point system to reinforce positive behavior.

INCLUDE

FYI

Motivation is an important factor in the achievement of students with learning and behavior problems (Sideridis & Scanlon, 2006). Passive learning, learned helplessness, and a low self-image all play an important part in student motivation.

RESEARCH-BASED PRACTICES

Espelage, Rose, and Polanin (2015) reduced bullying, aggression, and peer victimization among students with disabilities using a program called Second Step: Student Success Through Prevention (www.secondstep .org). The program focuses on the social emotional learning skills of empathy, bully-prevention, communication skills, and emotion regulation.

DIMENSIONS OF DIVERSITY

A small proportion of high school students with disabilities are lesbian, gay, bisexual, or transgender (LGBT). LGBT students with disabilities may need support to address socially appropriate behaviors and strategies for interpreting the messages they may receive, whether positive or negative (Duke, 2011; Harley et al., 2002).

> INCLUDE

got. Dominic's teacher taught him a self-control strategy to help him ignore his friends' teasing. Whenever he was teased, Dominic first counted to five to himself to get beyond his initial anger. He then told himself that what they were saying wasn't true and that the best way to get them to stop was to ignore them and walk away. Whenever he walked away, Dominic told himself he did a good job and later reported his efforts to his teacher.

Some students may know what to do socially but lack opportunities for using their social skills. For example, students who are newly included in your classroom and/or new to the school need opportunities to interact with class-mates to get to know them better. One way to create opportunities for social interaction is to allow students to work in small groups with a shared learning goal. For example, Thomas is a student with a mild intellectual disability who is part of Mr. Jeffreys's sixth-grade class. This is Thomas's first year in general education; until this year, he was in a self-contained special education class-room. Mr. Jeffreys has decided to use peer-learning groups in science because he thinks they will be a good way for Thomas to get to know his classmates and make some friends. Every two weeks, Thomas has the opportunity to complete various lab activities with a different group of his choice.

Students who exhibit learned helplessness can benefit from **attribution retraining** (Berkeley, Mastropieri, & Scruggs, 2011; Mercer, Mercer, & Pullen, 2010). The idea behind attribution retraining is that if you can convince students that their failures are due to lack of effort rather than ability, they will be more persistent and improve their performance in the face of difficulty (Hallahan et al., 2014). You can enhance student self-image by using the following strate-gies (Mercer & Pullen, 2008):

1. *Set reasonable goals.* When setting goals for students, make sure they are not too easy or too hard. Self-worth is improved when students reach their goals through considerable effort. Goals that are too ambitious perpetuate failure. Goals that are too easy can give students the idea that you think they are not capable of doing anything difficult.

2. *Provide specific feedback contingent on student behavior.* Feedback should be largely positive, but it should also be contingent on completion of tasks. Otherwise, students are likely to perceive your feedback as patronizing and just another indication that you think they are unable to do real academic work. Do not be afraid to correct students when they are wrong. Providing corrective feedback communicates to students that you think they can suc-ceed if they keep trying and that you care about them.

3. *Give students responsibility.* Assigning a responsibility demonstrates to stu-dents that you trust them and believe they can act maturely. Some examples for younger students include taking the class pet home over a holiday break, taking the lunch count, being a line leader, taking messages to the office, and taking attendance. For older students, try giving students input into class-room decisions such as selecting learning groups and developing their own assignments, including setting due dates.

4. *Teach students to reinforce themselves.* Students with a poor self-image say negative things about themselves. You can help students by reminding them of their strengths, encouraging them to make more positive statements about themselves, and then reinforcing them for making these statements.

5. *Give students a chance to show their strengths.* Part of the INCLUDE strat-egy is to identify student strengths and then help students achieve success by finding or creating classroom situations in which they can employ their strengths. For example, Cara cannot read very well but has an excellent speaking voice. After her group wrote a report on the 1960 presidential elec-tion, Cara was given the task of presenting the report to the whole class.

CASE IN PRACTICE 7.2

A Social Skills Training Session

Ms. Perez and her first-grade class are working on a unit on social skills in social studies. They are learning the skill of listening to someone who is talking by doing the following:

1. Look at the person who is talking.
2. Remember to sit quietly.
3. Think about what is being said.
4. Say yes or nod your head.
5. Ask a question about the topic to find out more.

Jeanine, a student in the class, has just practiced these listening skills in front of the class by role-playing the part of a student who is talking to her teacher about an assignment. In the role-play, Ms. Perez played herself. The class is now giving Jeanine feedback on her performance.

Ms. Perez: Let's start with the first step. Did Jeanine look at me when I was talking? Before you answer, can someone tell me why it's important to look at the person who is talking?

Lorna: You don't want the other person to think you're not listening. So you really have to show them you are listening.

Ms. Perez: That's right, Lorna. Well, how did Jeanine do on this one?

Charles: Well, she looked at you at first, but while you were talking she looked down at her feet. It looked like she wasn't listening.

Jeanine: I was listening, but I guess I should have looked at her all the way through.

Ms. Perez: Yes, Jeanine. To be honest, if I didn't know you better, I would have thought that you didn't care about what I was saying.

You need to work on that step. The next step is to remember to sit quietly. How did Jeanine do with this one?

Milton: I think she did well. She remembered not to laugh or play around with anything while you were talking.

Ms. Perez: I agree, Milton. Nice work, Jeanine. Now, can someone tell me what the next listening step is?

Kyrie: It's to think about what the person is saying.

Ms. Perez: Right, Kyrie. Let's let Jeanine tell us herself how she did on this one.

Jeanine: Well, I tried to think about what you were saying. Once I started to think about something else, but I did what you told us and started thinking about a question I could ask you.

Ms. Perez: Good, Jeanine. Trying to think of a question to ask can be very helpful. How do you think you did on the next step? Did you nod your head or say yes to show you were following me?

Jeanine: I think I did.

Ms. Perez: What do the rest of you think? Did Jeanine say yes?

Tara: Well, I saw her nod a little, but it was hard to tell. Maybe she needs to talk louder.

Ms. Perez: Jeanine, you need to nod more strongly or the teacher won't realize you are doing it.

REFLECTIONS

What teaching procedures is Ms. Perez using to teach her students listening skills? Do you think they are effective? What could she do to make sure that her students use this skill at school? For what settings outside school would these and other social skills be important?

Given their numbers, you will be responsible for teaching students with language, learning, and behavioral disabilities in your classroom. You have read that these students have a range of academic and social needs. This chapter has suggested ways that you can adjust your instruction to support students with high-incidence disabilities and, by so doing, ensure their success. You will be reading about additional strategies for teaching them in the chapters still to come.

MyLab Education Self-Check 7.4

MyLab Education

Video Example 7.6: Including Students with EBD in General Education

How do these teachers collaborate as they apply INCLUDE to including a student with emotional and behavior disorders in a general education classroom?

WRAPPING IT UP

Back to the Cases

Now that you have read about high-incidence disabilities, look back at the teacher stories at the beginning of the chapter. Then go to MyLab Education to apply the knowledge you've gained in this chapter to each case.

MyLab Education Application Exercise 7.1: Case Study 7.1

WILL has difficulty with two important basic skills: reading and writing. His teachers need more information about methods for supporting Will's reading and writing so that he can learn the content needed to pass his end-of-grade tests and make a smooth transition to middle school.

MyLab Education Application Exercise 7.2: Case Study 7.2

RENAYE, as you may remember, demonstrated aggressive and noncompliant behaviors. Her behavior was addressed with a behavior contract.

MyLab Education Application Exercise 7.3: Case Study 7.3

JEROME had difficulty processing verbal information. He struggled with paying attention and understanding instruction in large groups, and had difficulty remembering information from one day to the next. Jerome also was socially awkward and lacked friends in his class.

Summary

LO 7.1 Students with high-incidence disabilities are those who have speech and language disabilities, learning disabilities, emotional disturbance, or mild intellectual disabilities. These students make up approximately 80 percent of all students who have disabilities. They are often hard to distinguish, at first glance, from their peers; exhibit a combination of behavior, social, and academic problems; and benefit from systematic, highly structured interventions.

LO 7.2 Some students have communication disorders. Students with speech problems have trouble in the areas of articulation, voice, and fluency. Language problems involve receptive and/or expressive language. The academic and social performances of students with speech and language problems can be enhanced through a number of adjustments including creating an atmosphere of acceptance, actively encouraging and teaching listening skills, using modeling to expand students' language, and teaching within contexts that are meaningful for students.

LO 7.3 Students with learning and behavioral disabilities have many academic needs. They may also lack skills necessary for efficient learning, such as attending to task, memory, organizing and interpreting information, reasoning, motor coordination, independent learning skills, and academic survival skills. Classroom adjustments for students with learning and behavioral disabilities in academic areas include bypassing their disability; making an adjustment in classroom management, grouping, materials, and methods; and providing students with direct instruction on basic or independent learning skills.

LO 7.4 Students with learning and behavioral disabilities have social and emotional difficulties in classroom conduct, interpersonal skills, and personal and psychological adjustment. Classroom adjustments for students with learning and behavioral disabilities in social areas include individualized behavior management, social skills training, self-control training, and attribution retraining.

APPLICATIONS IN TEACHING PRACTICE

Using the INCLUDE Strategy with Students with High-Incidence Disabilities

Answer the following questions to show how you would apply the INCLUDE strategy to adjust instruction for the students described in the vignettes at the beginning of this chapter. To help you with this application, refer to Table 7.2, the section on the INCLUDE strategy in Chapter 5, and information gathered for Back to the Cases.

QUESTIONS

1. What communication, academic, behavioral, and social and emotional needs does each student have?

2. Keeping in mind the major aspects of the classroom environment, including classroom management, classroom grouping, instructional materials, and instructional methods, what kinds of problems are these students likely to have?

3. How would you adjust your instruction for each of these students?

4. Are the adjustments you would make reasonable in terms of teacher time and ease of implementation? What support (if any) would you need to carry them out?

5. How can you monitor the effectiveness of your instructional changes? What can you do next if your first attempt is ineffective?

CHAPTER 8

Students with Special Needs Other Than Disabilities

LEARNING OUTCOMES

After you read this chapter, you will be able to:

8-1 Describe students protected under Section 504 and general educators' responsibilities for effectively teaching them.

8-2 Explain accommodations and other instructional adjustments general education teachers can make to address the special needs of students with attention deficit–hyperactivity disorder (ADHD).

8-3 Outline how general educators provide appropriate instruction for students who are gifted and talented.

8-4 Analyze how cultural diversity influences education, critically analyzing your own response to students from cultures other than your own and your skills for addressing their needs, including those who also have disabilities.

8-5 Articulate how general educators can effectively teach students at risk for school failure, including students affected by poverty, abuse or neglect, substance abuse, and other factors, including those who have been identified as having disabilities.

ZHANG WEI is 12 years old, but after many conversations between dedicated professionals and his parents, he has been placed in fifth grade (rather than sixth) for the current school year. The reason is this: Zhang Wei has been in the United States for less than six months. He was adopted when his parents, on a church-sponsored mission trip to China, learned that he would be expelled from an orphanage on his 13th birthday, the age at which he would be considered able to function on his own. At first concerned and then alarmed when they learned that Zhang Wei also has a hearing loss, Mr. and Mrs. Davis decided to adopt him. Because of his special needs, the adoption was expedited. But Zhang Wei, who has had almost no education and no services or access to technology to address his hearing loss, now is adapting to living in a loving but vastly different home and culture, finding out about U.S. school expectations and learning English. Everyone agreed that although Zhang Wei appears to be a bright young man who is learning at a surprising rate, adjusted expectations were appropriate. He currently has a Section 504 plan because of his mild hearing loss and spends part of his day in an English as a second language (ESL) classroom with some consultation support from a deaf educator and part of his day in the general education setting. His teachers note that he is very quiet and extremely polite; they are just getting to know him. As he adjusts to his new life, school professionals and his parents plan to meet to further discuss his education.

What special needs might students from other cultures, like Zhang Wei, have? What is your responsibility for finding ways to help all your diverse students succeed in school? How are the needs of culturally and linguistically diverse (CLD) students different when they also have disabilities, whether mild or significant?

JACKSON is 17 years old and in 10th grade; he has been retained twice because of poor academic performance. He was diagnosed as having ADHD when he was in second grade, and his parents have vacillated about medication, sometimes agreeing that he should take it and other times rejecting it. Jackson has an engaging personality and many friends. His teachers try to be tolerant of his classroom behavior, but he does push limits. For example, one day in class he loudly announced that he hadn't taken his medication and so could not be responsible for his behavior. Although students were supposed to be working with partners to complete a study guide for an upcoming test, Jackson began recalling his favorite television programs from when he was "a kid." He sang the shows' theme songs, mimicked characters' voices, and asked other students to join him. Not too surprisingly, his test score was 57 percent, but Jackson claimed that he didn't understand why this happened as he had "really studied."

Does Jackson have a disability, or is he simply an example of the diversity of students in today's schools? What are his special needs? What is the responsibility of general education teachers for meeting those needs?

LYDIA is a fourth-grade student who is gifted and talented. She has been reading since age three, and she frequently borrows her sister's high school literature anthology as a source of reading material. She knew most of the math concepts introduced in fourth grade before the school year began. She has a strong interest in learning French and playing flute and piano, and she volunteers to read to residents of a local nursing home. Lydia's idea of a perfect afternoon is to have a quiet place to hide, a couple of wonderful books, and no one to bother her. Lydia's teacher, Mr. Judd, enjoys having her in class because she is so enthusiastic about learning, but he admits that Lydia's abilities are a little intimidating. He also has noticed that Lydia doesn't seem to have much in common with other students in class. She is a class leader but does not appear to have any close friends, as other students do.

To what services is Lydia entitled because of her giftedness? Is Lydia typical of students who are gifted or talented? What can Mr. Judd do to help Lydia reach her full potential? What social problems are students like Lydia likely to encounter?

TAM is a junior in high school, but he doubts that he will finish the school year. He describes school as "pointless," and he continues to come only because he would hate to hurt his mother's feelings by dropping out. He is often absent, especially from his first-block U.S. history class, and he usually does not bother to do homework or read assignments. Tam does not belong to any clubs at school or participate in any athletics. After school, Tam hangs out with his friends, often congregating in the alley behind an electronics store and not returning home until well after midnight. He is considering an offer to distribute drugs that recently was made by Michael, a 21-year-old dropout whom Tam admires. Tam has a juvenile record; he is on probation for stealing a car. Michael told him, though, that the risks of prison are minimal until he turns 18 and that his record will be expunged at that time even if he gets arrested again. Tam's rationale is that he knows many people who make money this way. Tam's teachers describe him as "unmotivated," a student who has vastly more potential than they see him using.

How many public school students are similar to Tam? What other characteristics and behaviors might Tam display in school? If Tam were your student, how would you try to reach him? What are your responsibilities to students like Tam?

Most educators agree that many students who are not eligible to receive special education have needs as great as or greater than those of students protected by the Individuals with Disabilities Education Act (IDEA). For example, Zhang Wei appears to have great potential, but he has many challenges to overcome, including adjustment to a new cultural context and learning a new language, disadvantaged by hearing loss. Even though Jackson has a significant attention problem, he does not qualify for special education. Lydia's teacher is concerned that he cannot possibly make time to provide the advanced instruction that would benefit her, but her school district does not offer any programs for students who are gifted or talented until middle school. Tam's teachers worry about his future and are frustrated that they cannot make his life better and help him reach his potential. They feel powerless to influence students like Tam, who have so many difficulties in their young lives, and they question how traditional academic standards and activities can be made relevant for those students.

This chapter is about students who are not necessarily eligible for special education whose learning is at risk and whose success often depends on the quality of the instruction they receive and the care provided by general education teachers. The students considered in this chapter fall into one or more of these groups: Those who have functional disabilities protected by Section 504, the civil rights law introduced in Chapter 1, but who are not protected by IDEA; those with attention deficit–hyperactivity disorder (ADHD), part of the group protected by Section 504 but one nearly all teachers should have detailed information about; those who are gifted and talented; those whose native language is not English and whose cultures differ significantly from those of most of their classmates; and those who are at risk because of life circumstances, including poverty, child abuse, drug abuse, transience (for example, migrant families), and other factors.

Because most of the students discussed in this chapter generally are not eligible for special education services, you might wonder why they are included in this textbook. Four reasons contribute to the rationale:

1. Students with these types of needs often benefit greatly from the same strategies that are successful for students with disabilities. Thus, one purpose is to remind you that the techniques explained throughout this text are applicable to many students, not just those who have individualized education programs (IEPs).

2. You should recognize that you will teach students with a tremendous diversity of needs resulting from many different causes, disability being just one potential factor. Creating appropriate educational opportunities for all your students is your most fundamental task as a teacher.

3. Students with a wide variety of challenges sometimes are referred for special education services because caring teachers recognize that they need help. It is essential that you realize that special education is much more than *help* and is reserved for just the specific groups of students already described in Chapters 6 and 7.

4. Although many special educators are committed to helping you meet the needs of all your students, including those at risk, they cannot take primary responsibility for teaching students like Zhang Wei, Jackson, Lydia, and Tam. These are not students who "should be" in special education. Rather, they represent the increasingly diverse range of students that all teachers now instruct. As such, they highlight the importance of creating classrooms that respect this diversity and foster learning regardless of students' unique needs, backgrounds, and experiences.

This chapter also highlights how complex student needs have become (e.g., Cooper & He, 2012; Croteau & Lewis, 2016; Endres, 2012; Ng, Hill, & Rawlinson, 2016). For example, you probably realize that students with disabilities also can have the special needs described here. That is, a student with a physical disability also might be academically gifted. A student with an intellectual disability also might live in poverty. A student with a learning disability might speak a language other than English at home. You probably recognize, too, that the student groups emphasized in this chapter are not necessarily distinct, even though it is convenient to discuss them as if they are. Students who live in poverty can also be gifted and members of a cultural minority. A physically abused student can be at risk because of drug use.

Keep in mind as you read this chapter that your responsibility as a teacher for all students—regardless of their disabilities and other special needs—is to use the principles of the INCLUDE strategy to identify strengths and needs, arrange a supportive instructional environment, provide high-quality instruction, and foster student independence. When students have multiple needs, these tasks can be especially challenging, and you should seek assistance from colleagues, parents, and other professional resources.

> **DIMENSIONS OF DIVERSITY**
>
> *Equity pedagogy* is the term that describes the use of instructional strategies that address the learning characteristics of diverse populations. If you complete an Internet search using this term, you can find research and teaching resources for effectively working with all your students.

> INCLUDE

What Are the Characteristics and Instructional Needs of Students Protected by Section 504?

In Chapter 1, you learned that some students with special needs who do not meet the eligibility criteria for receiving services through IDEA are considered functionally disabled, as defined by Section 504 of the Vocational Rehabilitation Act of 1973. The primary goal of this law is to prevent discrimination against these individuals. Students with functional disabilities are entitled to receive reasonable accommodations that help them benefit from school, as is true for both Zhan Wei and Jackson. These accommodations can include some of the same types of services and supports received by students eligible through IDEA, but there are crucial differences between the two statutes as well (Taylor, 2011; Zirkel, 2012).

Understanding Section 504

First, the definition of a disability in Section 504 is considerably broader than it is in IDEA. In Section 504, any condition that substantially limits a major life activity, such as the ability to learn in school, is defined as a *disability*. This definition means that students with a wide range of needs that do not fall within the 13 federal disability categories for education (that is, in IDEA) are eligible for assistance through Section 504, including students with significant attention problems, drug addiction, chronic health problems, communicable diseases, temporary disabilities resulting from accidents or injury, environmental illnesses, and alcoholism (Office of Civil Rights, 2015).

Second, unlike IDEA, Section 504 does not provide funds to school districts to carry out its requirements (Zirkel, 2009a). The expectation is that schools should take whatever steps are necessary, even if additional funds are required, to eliminate discrimination as defined through this statute. Third, the responsibility for making accommodations or other instructional adjustments for students who qualify as disabled through Section 504 belongs to general education personnel, not special education personnel. Special educators might provide some informal assistance, but their aid is not mandated as it is for students served through IDEA. The types of instructional support required vary based on student needs but could include alterations in the physical environment, such as providing a quiet workspace or a room with specialized lighting; modifications in instruction, such as decreasing the number of items in an assignment, allotting additional time to complete it, or providing a note-taker; organizational assistance, such as checking a student's backpack to ensure that all materials for homework are there; and making changes in a student's schedule, such as allowing a rest period. Table 8.1 summarizes these and other differences between these important laws.

The regulations governing Section 504 are in some ways similar to those for IDEA. That is, for students to receive assistance through Section 504, their needs must be assessed and a decision made concerning their eligibility (U.S. Department of Education, 2010). School districts must screen students (typically using some type of RtI or prereferral process), convene a team and obtain parent permission to evaluate student needs (although formal testing, as is typical for IDEA, is not necessarily required), determine eligibility for services, and create a plan to implement services in the general education classroom.

When students are determined eligible and have Section 504 plans, those plans cover their instructional programs as well as after-school programs, field trips, summer programs, and other extracurricular activities. The plans outline the accommodations needed, who is to implement them, and how they will be monitored (Hardcastle & Zirkel, 2012). A sample of the types of accommodations that may be incorporated into a Section 504 plan is presented in the Professional Edge feature.

Students Eligible for Services under Section 504

Approximately 1.5 percent of all K–12 students are served through Section 504 plans (Zirkel & Weathers, 2016), many of them in the three groups addressed in this chapter: students with medical or health needs, students with learning problems, and students with attention deficit–hyperactivity disorder (ADHD). The first two groups are discussed here; students with ADHD are covered in more depth in the subsequent section.

STUDENTS WITH CHRONIC HEALTH OR MEDICAL PROBLEMS Students with chronic health or medical problems—for example, those with communicable or chronic diseases or a student with a special need like Zhang Wei—who are not eligible for IDEA services according to established criteria and as determined by a multidisciplinary team comprise one of the major groups that can qualify for assistance through Section 504. For example, a student who has asthma not serious enough to be considered a disability under IDEA might have a Section 504 plan. The plan could address accommodations related to the student's need for occasional rest periods, opportunities to take medication, exemption from certain physical activities, and provisions to make up assignments and tests after absences. Similarly, a student with severe allergies might have a Section 504 plan that specifies materials in school that cannot be used (e.g., paints, chalk, peanut

TABLE 8.1   **Examples of Differences Between IDEA and Section 504**

Component	IDEA	Section 504
Purpose	To provide federal financial assistance to state and local education agencies to assist them in educating children with disabilities	To eliminate discrimination on the basis of disability in all programs and activities receiving federal financial assistance
Individuals protected	All school-age children who fall within 1 or more of 13 specific categories of disability and who, because of such disability, need special education and related services	All school-age children who have a physical or mental impairment that substantially limits or may limit a major life activity, have a record of such an impairment, or are regarded as having such an impairment (major life activities include walking, seeing, hearing, speaking, breathing, learning, reading, communicating, concentrating, thinking, working, caring for oneself, performing manual tasks, and others)
Free and appropriate public education (FAPE)	Requires that FAPE be provided only to those protected students who, because of disability, need special education or related services Defines FAPE as special education and related services; a student can receive related services under IDEA if and only if the student is provided special education and needs related services to benefit from special education Requires a written IEP and a required number of specific participants at the IEP meeting	Requires that FAPE be provided only to those protected students who, because of disability, need general education accommodations, special education, or related services Defines FAPE as general or special education and related aids and services; a student can receive related services under Section 504 even if the student is in general education full-time and is not provided any special education Does not require an IEP but does require a plan prepared by a group of persons knowledgeable about the student
Funding	Provides additional funding for protected students	Does not provide additional funds; IDEA funds may not be used to serve students protected only under Section 504
Evaluation	Requires reevaluation to be conducted at least every three years Does not require a reevaluation before a change of placement, but evaluation data, including progress toward goals and objectives, should be considered	Requires periodic reevaluation; the IDEA schedule for reevaluation can suffice Requires reevaluation before a significant change in placement
Placement procedures	An IEP meeting is required before any change in placement	A reevaluation meeting is required before any "significant change" in placement
Grievance procedures	Does not require a grievance procedure or a compliance officer	Requires districts with more than 15 employees to (1) designate an employee to be responsible for assuring district compliance with Section 504 and (2) provide a grievance procedure for parents, students, and employees
Due process	Contains detailed hearing rights and requirements	Requires notice, the right to inspect records, the right to participate in a hearing and to be represented by counsel, and a review procedure
Exhaustion	Requires the parent or guardian to pursue an administrative hearing before seeking redress in the courts	Does not require an administrative hearing prior to Office for Civil Rights involvement or court action; compensatory damages possible
Enforcement	Enforced by the U.S. Office of Special Education Programs (OSEP); compliance monitored by state department of education and OSEP	Enforced by the U.S. Office for Civil Rights

Source: From *Meeting the Needs of All Students,* by the Parent Advocacy Coalition for Educational Rights, 2004, Minneapolis, MN: Author, retrieved from (http://www.pacer.org/parent/504.html#IDEA504). Reprinted with permission from PACER Center, 952-838-9000. U.S. Department of Labor. (2017, June). *The ADA Amendments Act of 2008: Frequently asked questions.* Washington, DC: Author. Retrieved from https://www.dol.gov/ofccp/regs/compliance/faqs/ADAfaqs.htm#Q5.

PROFESSIONAL EDGE 8.1

Section 504 Accommodations

Many types of accommodations can be written into a Section 504 plan. The only guidelines are that the adjustments should be (1) individualized to meet students' needs and (2) reasonable, or designed to "level the playing field" for these students. These accommodations should go beyond those typically offered to all students (for example, allowing students to choose from among several projects or re-explaining a concept when students do not understand it). Here are some examples of classroom accommodations you might find in a Section 504 plan, depending, of course, on student needs:

RELATED TO THE PRESENTATION OF INSTRUCTION

- Make directions telegraphic—that is, concise and clear.
- Record lessons so the student can listen to them again.
- Use multisensory presentation techniques, including peer tutors, experiments, games, and cooperative groups.
- Provide practice tests that are very similar in structure and appearance to actual tests.
- Provide audio books so the student can listen to assignments instead of reading them.

RELATED TO STUDENT RESPONSES

- Establish a home–school communication system for monitoring behavior.
- Fold assignments in half so the student is not overwhelmed by the quantity of work.
- Allow the student to dictate or record responses instead of writing or typing them.
- Provide appropriate assistive technology (e.g., spell checker, word prediction software, calculator).

RELATED TO THE ENVIRONMENT/SETTING

- Seat the student nearest to where the teacher leads most instruction.
- Allow the student to work at a desk carrel or other quiet corner of the classroom.

- Permit the student to sit in the location he finds most conducive to learning (e.g., for lighting, acoustics, proximity of classmates).

RELATED TO TIME/SCHEDULING

- Allow extra time to complete assignments or take tests.
- Arrange for frequent student breaks.
- Schedule testing across more than one day.

RELATED TO ORGANIZATION

- Provide clues such as clock faces indicating beginning and ending times for instruction or assignments.
- Help the student set up a smartphone or other device with alarms to alert her to upcoming transitions.
- Help the student learn to use a smartphone or other device to record assignments, take photos of study guides, and so on.

RELATED TO STUDENT PRODUCTS

- Shorten assignments to only essential components.
- Reduce the number of examples of concepts the student is required to complete as homework.
- Allow the student to complete alternative projects or assignments.

Remember that Section 504 accommodations may vary greatly depending on a student's special needs, such as a medical condition or physical problem, drug or alcohol abuse, ADHD, or others. The INCLUDE process can help you make decisions about these students' specific needs.

Sources: Adapted from *Ideas for an IEP or Section 504 Plan,* by D. Simms, 2000, retrieved from (http://www.angelfire.com/ny/Debsimms/education.html); A. Morin (2017). *Common modifications and accommodations.* New York, NY: Understood. Retrieved from https://www.understood.org/en/learning-attention-issues/treatments-approaches/educational-strategies/common-classroom-accommodations-and-modifications; and *Sevier County (TN) School System Section 504 Examples of Program Accommodations and Adjustments,* retrieved from (http://www.slc.sevier.org/504ana.htm). Reprinted with permission from Sevier County Board of Education.

Video Example from

MyLab Education

Video Example 8.1: Section 504 of the Rehabilitation Act

Emily, a high school student, offers a succinct insight into the protections of Section 504. https://www.youtube.com/watch?v=XM3VKnGbAPE

products), guidelines for participation in physical education, and requirements for providing assignments that can be completed at home if necessary. What might a Section 504 plan for Zhang Wei include?

The increasing rate of childhood obesity has led to yet another group who might receive accommodations: students who have diabetes. The student who is diabetic might have a plan that addresses permission to use the restroom whenever requested; permission to keep a bottle of water present during class; permission to test blood glucose as necessary, including in the classroom; and postponement of high-stakes testing without penalty if blood glucose is too high or too low.

STUDENTS WITH LEARNING PROBLEMS A second group of students who may receive support under Section 504 comprises those who experience significant learning problems but who are not determined to have a learning disability (Cortiella & Kaloi, 2010; Sepiol, 2015) according to state criteria. For example,

Carson is a student who experiences extraordinary difficulty in reading. A recent evaluation led to a conclusion that he is not eligible for special education services as learning disabled because he did not meet district eligibility criteria. However, he is showing signs of anxiety related to reading tasks (e.g., crying when asked to read), and the team decided that he should have the protection of a Section 504 plan because the combination of problems is affecting his school success, a major life activity. Carson receives remedial reading instruction, but his Section 504 plan includes testing in a separate, quiet location with some tests read aloud and access to text-to-speech software for classwork.

As you can tell, some of the responsibility for implementing Section 504 plans belongs to administrators, who authorize physical modifications to classrooms and make arrangements for students, for example, to have rest periods or take medications. Your responsibility is to implement instructional accommodations outlined in the plan, such as providing assignments in advance and allowing extra time for work completion. Your interactions with students protected by Section 504 differ from your interactions with other students only in your responsibility to make the required accommodations.

MyLab Education Self-Check 8.1

How Can You Accommodate Students with Attention Deficit–Hyperactivity Disorder?

Students with attention problems have been a concern of teachers for many years. In fact, labels such as *hyperkinesis* and *minimal brain dysfunction* have been applied to these students since the 1940s (Barkley, 2015), and the first medication to help them was developed in the 1950s (Eli Lilly, 2003). The challenges that these students present for teachers, parents, and peers have raised awareness that they have a disorder, prompted research about their characteristics and needs, and fostered the development of new interventions for assisting them in school and everyday life. Some students with significant attention problems as described in this section are eligible for services through IDEA, but many receive assistance through Section 504 (Spiel, Evans, & Langberg, 2014).

The term for significant attention problems is attention deficit–hyperactivity disorder (ADHD), a condition defined in the *Diagnostic and Statistical Manual of Mental Disorders (DSM-V)* (American Psychiatric Association, 2013). ADHD is diagnosed when an individual has chronic and serious inattentiveness, hyperactivity, and/or impulsivity that is more severe and occurs more frequently than in peers.

Students with ADHD generally have multiple symptoms that are seen across two or more settings and that interfere with academic or social functioning (American Psychiatric Association, 2013). ADHD symptoms may vary somewhat by student age. The three primary categories in which ADHD is classified are these:

1. *ADHD—predominantly inattentive type.* Students in this group often appear to daydream. They may not hear teacher directions, sometimes skip parts of an assignment they do not notice, and frequently lose things. However, they do not physically move more than their peers.

2. *ADHD—predominantly hyperactive–impulsive type.* Students in this group physically move far more than their peers, and they tend to be impetuous, acting before thinking. They squirm in their seats, tap pencils or fingers, and blurt out answers during instruction.

3. *ADHD—combined type.* Students in this group display the characteristics of both other types of ADHD. They experience extraordinary difficulty both in focusing their attention and in restricting their movement.

Think about Jackson, the student you met at the beginning of the chapter. Which type of ADHD seems to best characterize him?

Estimates of the prevalence of ADHD suggest that 5 to 11 percent of all children ages 4 through 17 have at some point been diagnosed with this disorder, some 6.4 million. ADHD occurs in boys as opposed to girls at a rate of approximately 2.5 to 1 (Centers for Disease Control and Prevention, 2017a). It is one of the most commonly diagnosed childhood psychiatric disorders, and it also occurs frequently with other disabilities, including learning disabilities, autism, and emotional disabilities (e.g., Centers for Disease Control and Prevention, 2016; Hanson et al., 2013).

The causes of ADHD are not clear. Researchers have found that one important factor is heredity (Kim et al., 2017; Langner, Garbe, Banaschewski, & Mikolajczyk, 2013). Students who have ADHD are likely to have a family pattern of this disorder. Researchers also have found that the brains of individuals with ADHD are different from those of others: The amount of electrical activity is unusually low in the parts of the brain regulating attention, and the chemicals in the brain that transmit information may not function properly (Barkley, 2015). Environmental factors, including cigarette smoking and alcohol use during pregnancy, also may contribute to the development of ADHD (National Institute of Mental Health, 2013). A few authors have suggested that ADHD is caused by food additives or food allergies, inner ear problems, vitamin deficiencies, or bacterial infections, but none of these causes has been demonstrated to be valid (National Institute of Mental Health, 2016), nor have controversial treatments intended to address such causes, a topic you already explored in Chapter 7.

Usually, a diagnosis of ADHD is the result of individualized testing for intellectual ability and achievement, a medical screening completed by a doctor, and behavior ratings completed by family members and school professionals. Based on that information, a school team decides whether the student's disorder meets the criteria of other health impairment under IDEA, whether a Section 504 plan is needed, or whether no specific intervention is warranted.

Characteristics and Needs of Students with Attention Deficit–Hyperactivity Disorder

The characteristics and needs of students with attention deficit–hyperactivity disorder can vary considerably. Although all students might occasionally demonstrate some symptoms of ADHD, students diagnosed with this disorder display many of them prior to 12 years of age. Further, their symptoms are chronic and extraordinary. Consider this account from Mr. Benjamin, a high school English teacher:

> Nick challenges my skills as a teacher. Sometimes he'll be looking out the window or doodling, and yet when I call on him he knows the answer. Other times, he doesn't seem to even have processed what I'm asking. Sometimes he fidgets . . . wiggles his knee or taps with his pen. He gets frustrated easily, and if I don't pay close attention to him in class, he will give up, especially on writing assignments, and just stare until someone calls his name. I'm trying to use strategies to hold his attention—more participation opportunities for him, more changes in activities during class—and they do help. I worry about whether he's really mastering the material.

Intellectually, students with ADHD can function at any level (Neece, Baker, Crnic, & Blacher, 2013), although the disorder usually is diagnosed in students who do not have intellectual disabilities. These students' shared characteristics relate to how their brains function. That is, ADHD is not really about inattention; rather, it is the inability to *regulate* attention. The disorder develops when students fail to develop *executive functions*, that is, the ability to carry out the mental activities that help most people regulate their behavior (Barkley, 2011; Qian, Shuai, Chan, Qian, & Wang, 2013). Executive functions include these four activities:

1. *Working memory*—the ability to remember what tasks are supposed to be done and how much time there is to do them
2. *Self-directed speech*—the silent self-talk that most people use to manage complex tasks
3. *Control of emotions and motivation*—the ability to talk oneself into calming down when faced with a difficult or frustrating task
4. *Reconstitution*—the ability to combine skills learned across a variety of settings in order to carry out a new task, such as a student's knowledge that the rule for speaking in a low voice applies not only in the classroom but also in the hallways, lunchroom, and office.

Many academic problems can be related to executive functions. Students with ADHD may have difficulty in reading, especially long passages for which comprehension demands are high; in spelling, which requires careful attention to detail; in listening, especially when a large amount of highly detailed information is presented; and in math, which often requires faster computational skills than students with ADHD can handle (DuPaul, Belk, & Puzino, 2017). These students also may struggle to organize and prioritize their schoolwork, a challenge that often can be addressed with the use of apps such as those described in the Technology Notes feature.

Socially and emotionally, students with ADHD are at risk for a variety of problems (e.g., Cordier, Munro, Wilkes-Gillan, Ling, Docking, & Pearce, 2017;

MyLab Education

Video Example 8.2: Accommodations
How could you use the recommended strategies for supporting students with ADHD in your classroom?

TECHNOLOGY NOTES 8.1

Apps to Facilitate Student Organization and Learning

Many apps are available to facilitate student success. These free or inexpensive apps are examples of those that can assist students with organization and attention:

iStudiez Pro (for iOS, Android, Windows)
This app is a sophisticated electronic student planner. It lets students enter each of their courses, and for each course, they can record assignments and homework. A summary of courses and related work shows up in a "Today" section. Students also can set this app to give them reminders of assignments due, and it can help students keep track of their grades. Information can be synced across multiple devices.

Evernote (iPhone, iPad, Android, Windows)
Used by many people across work and personal contexts, this app is designed to enable users to gather and organize, in a single location, all their notes, photos, websites, lists, and related information. Students can use this app to gather information for a research paper, note assignments and due dates, save photos of the teacher's notes from the Smartboard, and so on.

Google Keep (iPhone, iPad, Android, Windows)
This note-taking app allows users to make many kinds of notes: texts, images, audio (automatically transcribed), and lists. Reminders can be set based on time or location. Other features include the option to color code notes, copy notes into a Google doc and access notes while using Docs, pin notes,

and organize notes using given labels. Keep also has an option for collaboration with others.

Google Inbox (iPhone, iPad, Android, Windows)
Inbox is designed to help organize and prioritize Gmail. It groups e-mail on the same topic, highlights details from messages, and lets the user control when some types of messages appear. This app also lets users save links they want to access later, an efficient alternative to e-mailing them.

30/30 Task Timer (iOS)
This is a simple but effective gesture-based task timer. Students list the tasks they need to complete (the number that can be in lists is unlimited), assign an amount of time to each one, and then activate the timer. Tasks can have an assigned icon and be color-coded. The timer tells students how long they have been working, notes how much time remains for the task, and alerts them when it is time to move to another task.

Studious (iOS, Android, Windows)
This app allows students to enter their class schedules, record deadlines for projects, and list test dates. Entered items can be grouped by class. This app also lets students control their phones; that is, the app can be set to silence a phone during all classes.

Source: 30/30 © 2012 Binary Hammer, LLC. App icon image with permission.

FIGURE 8.1 Behavior Characteristics of Students with Attention Deficit–Hyperactivity Disorder

Inattention
- Making careless mistakes
- Having difficulty sustaining attention/easily distracted
- Seeming not to listen
- Failing to give close attention to details in schoolwork and related activities
- Failing to finish tasks
- Having difficulty organizing
- Avoiding tasks that require sustained attention
- Losing things
- Being forgetful

Hyperactivity
- Fidgeting
- Being unable to stay seated

- Moving excessively (restlessness), including climbing on furniture and other items
- Having difficulty making and keeping friends
- Talking excessively
- Being prone to temper tantrums
- Acting in a bossy way
- Being defiant

Impulsivity
- Blurting out answers before questions have been completely asked
- Having difficulty waiting for a turn
- Interrupting conversations/intruding upon others
- Acting before thinking
- Being viewed as immature by teenage peers
- Failing to read directions

Sources: Based on "Arranging the Classroom with an Eye (and Ear) to Students with ADHD," 2001, *Teaching Exceptional Children, 34*(2), pp. 72–81; and "Psychiatric Disorders and Treatment: A Primer for Teachers," by S. R. Forness, H. M. Walker, and K. A. Kavale, 2003, *Teaching Exceptional Children, 36*(2), pp. 42–49.

Gonring, Gerdes, & Gardner, 2017). For example, they are more likely to be depressed or to have extremely low self-confidence or self-esteem. Likewise, they are likely to have conflicts with parents, teachers, and other authority figures. These students often are unpopular with peers, frequently are rejected by them, and have difficulty making friends. Students with ADHD may feel demoralized, but they also may be bossy and obstinate. Jackson, introduced at the beginning of this chapter, displays both academic and social characteristics typical of some students with ADHD.

The frequency of behavior problems of students with ADHD varies (Martel, Roberts, & Gremillion, 2013; Schultz, Evans, Langberg, & Schoemann, 2017). Students whose disorder is inattention might not act out in class, but they may be disruptive when they try to find a lost item or constantly ask classmates for assistance in finding their place in a book or carrying out directions. Students with hyperactive–impulsive disorder often come to teachers' attention immediately because they have so many behavior problems. Their constant motion, refusal to work, and other behaviors can be problematic even in the most tolerant environment. Examples of the behaviors displayed by students with ADHD are included in Figure 8.1.

Interventions for Students with Attention Deficit–Hyperactivity Disorder

As a result of a series of studies (Bloch, 2017; National Institute of Mental Health, 2009), professionals now recommend that five types of interventions be used for students with ADHD: behavior interventions, parent education, medication, academic interventions, and environmental supports.

BEHAVIOR INTERVENTIONS For responding to the behavior of students with ADHD, professionals generally recommend interventions that emphasize structure and rewards, such as specific verbal praise ("Martin, you began your work as soon as I gave the assignment") or stickers and other symbols of appropriate behavior ("Tamatha, you will earn a sticker for each five math problems you complete"). Reprimands and consequences may be needed at times, but these should be mild and used less often than rewards.

As the INCLUDE strategy outlines, you should first consider environmental demands and address these as a means of preventing behavior problems. For example, students with ADHD exhibit less acting-out behavior when they sit near

DIMENSIONS OF DIVERSITY

In a large-scale study spanning fifth, seventh, and 10th grades, Coker and his colleagues (2016) found that African American and Latino students were less likely than their Caucasian counterparts to be diagnosed with ADHD and, if diagnosed, less likely to take medication.

INCLUDE

the front of the room in an area with few visual or auditory distractions (e.g., away from posters and bulletin board displays and computers signaling with tones and music). Likewise, allowing a student to move from one desk to another in the classroom and permitting her to stand while working are examples of simple environmental support strategies that may help prevent serious behavior problems.

If a student needs to be corrected, provide a clear and direct but calm reprimand. If you say, "Tamatha, I know you are trying hard, but please try to remember to raise your hand before speaking," Tamatha might not even realize that you are correcting her. A preferred response would be to say quietly to her, "Tamatha, do not call out answers. Raise your hand." This message is much clearer.

Teachers should be proactive in designing and implementing interventions to address the needs of their students with ADHD.

PARENT EDUCATION An essential companion to behavior interventions at school is parent education that incorporates information for parents to respond to their child's behavior in home and community settings. Parent education also can effectively build the collaboration between home and school that can have a significant positive impact on the functioning of a student with ADHD (Knopf, 2016; Pfiffner, Villodas, Kaiser, Rooney, & McBurnett, 2013). Although offering parent education generally is not the sole responsibility of a new teacher, you can contribute in this area by suggesting that parents of students with ADHD be invited to sessions to learn strategies for responding to their children's behavior, ways to create a discipline system that includes both rewards and consequences, tips for helping these children to make friends, and skills for collaborating with school professionals to ensure academic success. Parents of students in middle school and high school also benefit from learning about their children's rights and responsibilities as they graduate from school and enter a college or work setting. Parents from some cultural groups may be less comfortable than other parents in seeking or participating in parent education programs (Schneider, Gerdes, Haack, & Lawton, 2013), and you may be able to assist them by explaining the offered training and encouraging them to attend. Parent education by itself usually is not sufficient to address the needs of students with ADHD, but it can help to maximize the benefits of other interventions, especially medication and behavior therapy.

MEDICATION Medication is the most common intervention for students with ADHD demonstrated by researchers to generally have significant benefit (Bachmann et al., 2017; Barkley, 2015). Prescribing medication is a decision that is made by parents with their physicians; educators may not tell parents that a child needs this intervention. Approximately 70 percent of the 6 million children ages 4 through 17 identified as having ADHD take medication (Centers for Disease Control and Prevention, 2017b), and medication is most commonly taken by students ages 9 to 12. It is considered effective in addressing ADHD symptoms for 70 percent or more of the students for whom it is prescribed, especially if combined with other interventions (e.g., behavior interventions and parent education).

The most common type of medication prescribed for students with ADHD is a group of stimulants, including Ritalin, Cylert, Adderall, and Focalin. However, students may take other medications, including antidepressants such as Norpramin, Tofranil, and Zoloft; antihypertensives such as Clonidine and Tenex; and Strattera, a medication developed specifically for this disorder. More information about the medications prescribed for ADHD is presented in Table 8.2.

TABLE 8.2   Overview of Medications Commonly Used for ADHD

Brand Name [Generic Name]	Advantages	Disadvantages	Comments
STIMULANTS			
MEDICATION TYPE: AMPHETAMINES			
Adderall [Single-entity amphetamine product]	Works quickly May last somewhat longer than other standard stimulants (3–6 hours)	High potential for abuse	May help students for whom Ritalin has not been effective
Adderall XR [Single-entity amphetamine product]	Works quickly Lasts about 12 hours	High potential for abuse	Not recommended for long-term use
Dexedrine [Dextroamphetamine]	Excellent safety record Rapid onset (20–30 minutes)	Lasts only 4 hours Must be administered frequently	Some students have fewer side effects than when on Ritalin
Dexedrine (sustained release) [Dextroamphetamine]	Excellent safety record Long lasting (6–8 hours)	Slower onset (1–2 hours)	Can be used along with standard Dexedrine, which permits once-daily dosing
Vyvanse (extended release) [Lisdexamfetamine]	Long lasting (up to 14 hours) Dosage is usually once per day	Works slowly (1–2 hours to take effect) Increased heart rate and blood pressure	Some individuals respond to this medication better than to Ritalin Less likely to be abused than other stimulant medications
MEDICATION TYPE: METHYLPHENIDATE			
Concerta [Methylphenidate]	Works quickly Lasts up to 12 hours	Not recommended for children in families with a history of tic disorders	First true once-a-day ADHD medication approved by the FDA
Ritalin [Methylphenidate]	Excellent safety record Easy to use and evaluate Works in 15–20 minutes	Lasts only 4 hours Must be administered frequently Increased heart rate and blood pressure	Most frequently prescribed medication Watch for tics or Tourette's syndrome
Ritalin SR (sustained release) [Methylphenidate]	Excellent safety record Easy to use and evaluate Long lasting (6–8 hours)	Does not work as well as regular Ritalin	Can be used along with regular Ritalin
Quillivant XR [Methylphenidate]	Long lasting (12–14 hours)	High potential for dosing problems because of liquid form	First alternative to pills; taken once daily, usually in the morning
Focalin [Dextromethylphenidate]	Works quickly Only half the dose of Ritalin is needed	Lasts only 4–5 hours Must be administered frequently	Refined form of Ritalin
Daytrana [Methylphenidate]	Patch available in varying dosages Patch may be worn for longer or shorter periods to adjust medication intake	Works slowly (1–2 hours to take effect) Patch is worn up to 9 hours Extended use may result in permanent skin discoloration at application site	Preferred when children have difficulty swallowing pills or are stigmatized by taking medication while at school

TABLE 8.2   *(Continued)*

Brand Name [Generic Name]	Advantages	Disadvantages	Comments
NON-STIMULANTS			
MEDICATION TYPE: NOREPINEPHRINE RE-UPTAKE INHIBITOR			
Strattera [Atomoxetine hydrochloride]	Lasts about 8–10 hours Noncontrolled prescription medication	Relatively new medication Long-term effects on children are not known	First nonstimulant ADHD medication approved by the FDA
MEDICATION TYPE: ALPHA ADRENERGIC AGENTS			
Intuniv (extended release) [guanfacine]	Taken once daily Can be taken by students with Tourette syndrome	Adverse effects possible if stopped suddenly May cause dizziness or light-headedness	A potential side effect is decreased appetite, a concern for some children
Kapvay (extended release) [clonidine hydrochloride]	May be taken in addition to psychostimulants Taken in the morning and at bedtime Can be taken by students with Tourette syndrome	Drowsiness is a relatively common side effect Potential for irritability	This is a medication considered an alternative for children who cannot tolerate stimulants
MEDICATION TYPE: ANTIDEPRESSANT			
Tofranil [Imipramine]	Long lasting (12–24 hours) Can be administered at night Often works when stimulants do not	Has possible side effects May take 1–3 weeks for full effects Should not be started and stopped abruptly	High doses may improve depression symptoms and mood swings

Source: From *Special Education: Contemporary Perspectives for School Professionals* (4th edition), by M. Friend, 2014, Upper Saddle River, NJ: Pearson. Reprinted with permission from Harvey C. Parker. American Academy of Child & Adolescent Psychiatry and American Psychiatric Association. (2013, July). *ADHD: Parents medication guide.* Washington, DC: Authors. Retrieved from https://www.aacap.org/App_Themes/AACAP/docs/resource_centers/resources/med_guides/adhd_parents_medication_guide_english.pdf

Despite the apparent effectiveness of medications in treating ADHD, their use remains somewhat controversial (Ahmed, McCaffery, & Aslani, 2013; Kantak & Dwoskin, 2016; Pajo & Cohen, 2013). Teachers encounter the problem of students not consistently taking their medications or sharing their medications with peers. This situation can result not only in a loss of learning, but it can potentially endanger other students. Another issue concerns the proper dosage. Some researchers contend that a dosage high enough to cause an improvement in behavior can cause lethargy, negatively affecting a student's academic learning (Rajala, Henriques, & Populin, 2012). A third area of concern pertains to side effects. Some parents and professionals note that medication may suppress weight and height gain, even though research indicates that this side effect is temporary (DuPaul et al., 2006; Faraone, Lecendreux, & Konofal, 2012). Yet other parents and professionals are concerned that taking medication may predispose children to future drug use and problems in adulthood, another perception that has not been supported by research (Golden, 2009; Winters et al., 2011).

As a teacher, your responsibilities related to medication are indirect. You should know about the medications commonly prescribed, alert your school nurse and parents if you suspect that a change in student learning or behavior might be related to medication, and be prepared to respond to parental and medical inquiries regarding the effects of medication on particular students.

ACADEMIC INTERVENTIONS Students with ADHD typically struggle with academic achievement, whether or not they take medication, although the extent

DIMENSIONS OF DIVERSITY

In a survey of 119 ethnically diverse parents of students with and without ADHD, Pham, Carlson, and Kosciulek (2010) found no differences among respondents regarding their views on the causes of ADHD. However, African American and Latino parents viewed behavioral interventions more positively than did Caucasian parents.

INCLUDE >

of their learning problems can vary considerably (Kuriyan et al., 2013; Volpe, DuPaul, Jitendra, & Tresco, 2009).

To assist students with ADHD academically, use the INCLUDE model as a strategy to design lessons and effectively teach these students. As you implement the steps of INCLUDE, keep these ideas in mind for teaching students with ADHD:

1. Try to emphasize only essential information. For example, keep oral instructions as brief as possible. Rather than giving directions by providing multiple examples and then recapping what you have said, instead list directions by number using very clear language—for example, "First, put your name on the paper. Second, write a one-sentence response for each question. Third, put your paper in the basket on the counter by the door."

2. When reading for comprehension, students with ADHD tend to perform better on short passages than on long ones. Thus, rather than have a student with ADHD read an entire story or chapter, have her read just a small part of a long story or expository passage and check comprehension at that point; then have her read another part and so on. Similarly, when older students have lengthy assignments, it is better to break them into smaller parts, assigning each component separately and checking progress.

3. In math, give students extended periods of time to complete computational work because their attentional problems interfere with their efficiency in this type of task.

4. In all large-group instruction, keep the pace perky and provide many opportunities for students to participate, such as trading answers to questions with a partner, working with manipulatives, and repeating answers as a class after one student has responded.

Additional suggestions for teaching students with ADHD are presented in the Instructional Edge feature. In addition to the types of interventions just outlined, most recommendations for helping students with ADHD academically are similar to those for students with learning and emotional disabilities and other students who need highly structured and especially clear instruction. Later chapters in this book feature many additional instructional approaches that meet the needs of students with ADHD.

ENVIRONMENTAL SUPPORTS The way you arrange your classroom can either foster learning for students with ADHD or impede it. To help students, your classroom should be free from distracting items, such as mobiles hung from the ceiling that twirl in air currents and piles of extra books or art supplies. Some students might benefit if you let them work using a *desk carrel*, a three-sided cardboard divider that blocks visual distractions. You also can provide a classroom environment conducive to learning for these students by having very clear classroom rules and routines. Further, if a change in the normal pattern of classroom activities is necessary, you can alert all students and make sure to support those with ADHD by assigning peer partners to assist them or by quietly letting them know what activity is next. Finally, you can consciously pace your instruction to mix tedious or repetitive classroom activities with those that permit students more variety and activity.

Families of Children with Attention Deficit–Hyperactivity Disorder

Just like families of other students with disabilities and special needs, families of students with ADHD cannot be described using a single set of characteristics. However, it is fair to say that for many families, having a child with ADHD affects every area of family functioning and adds significant stress for parents and siblings both at home and in interactions with school personnel (Miranda, Tárraga, Fernández, Colomer, & Pastor, 2015; Theule, Wiener, Tannock, & Jenkins, 2013).

INSTRUCTIONAL EDGE 8.1

Strategies for Teaching Students with ADHD

INTRODUCING LESSONS

Strategies such as the following provide a strong structure for your lessons, which can facilitate learning for students with ADHD:

- *Provide an advance organizer.* Prepare students for the day's lesson by quickly summarizing the order of various activities planned.
- *Review previous lessons.* Review information about previous lessons on this topic.
- *Set learning expectations.* State what students are expected to learn during the lesson.
- *Set behavioral expectations.* Describe how students are expected to behave during the lesson.
- *State needed materials.* Identify all materials that the students will need during the lesson, rather than leaving them to figure out on their own the materials required.
- *Explain additional resources.* Tell students how to obtain help in mastering the lesson.
- *Simplify instructions, choices, and scheduling.* The simpler the expectations communicated to an ADHD student, the more likely it is that he or she will comprehend and complete them in a timely and productive manner.

CONDUCTING LESSONS

Effective teachers periodically question children's understanding of the material, probe for correct answers before calling on other students, and identify which students need additional assistance. These techniques are especially important for students with ADHD.

- *Be predictable.* Structure and consistency are very important for children with ADHD. Minimal rules and minimal choices are best for these students.
- *Support student participation.* Provide students with ADHD with private, discreet cues to stay on task and advance warning that they will be called upon shortly. At all times, avoid the use of sarcasm and criticism.
- *Use audiovisual materials.* Use a variety of audiovisual materials to present academic lessons.
- *Check student performance.* Question individual students to assess their mastery of the lesson.
- *Ask probing questions.* Probe for the correct answer after allowing a child sufficient time to work out the answer to a question. Ask follow-up questions that give children an opportunity to demonstrate what they know.

- *Perform ongoing student evaluation.* Identify students who need additional assistance and provide that support, possibly through the use of peer tutoring.
- *Help students correct their own mistakes.* Describe how students can identify and correct their own mistakes.
- *Help students focus.* Remind students to keep working and to focus on their assigned task.
- *Follow-up on directions.* Check students' understanding of oral or written directions and supplement them with additional clarification as needed.
- *Lower noise level.* Monitor the noise level in the classroom, and provide corrective feedback as needed.
- *Divide work into smaller units.* Break down assignments into smaller, less complex tasks.
- *Highlight key points.* Highlight key words in the instructions on worksheets to help the student with ADHD focus on the directions.
- *Use cooperative learning strategies.* Have students work together in small groups to maximize their own and each other's learning.
- *Use assistive technology.* All students, and those with ADHD in particular, can benefit from the use of technology that makes instruction more visual and allows students to participate actively.

CONCLUDING LESSONS

Effective teachers conclude their lessons using strategies designed to alert students that instruction is ending and assist them to prepare for the next activity.

- *Provide advance warnings.* Provide advance warning—5 or 10 minutes before the conclusion—that a lesson is about to end. Use less time for younger students, more for older students who may need several minutes to complete assigned work.
- *Check assignments.* Check completed assignments for at least some students. Review student learning in order to plan the next lesson.
- *Preview the next lesson.* Instruct students on how to begin preparing for the next lesson.

Source: From Teaching Children with Attention Deficit Hyperactivity Disorder: Instructional Strategies and Practices, U.S. Department of Education, August 2013, Washington, DC: Author, retrieved from (http://www2.ed.gov/rschstat/research/pubs/adhd/adhd-teaching_pg3.html#academic).

When working with families of students with ADHD, you have to be careful not to blame parents for their children's ADHD but at the same time not to condone inappropriate student behavior that a parent might excuse by saying that the child can't help it. For example, adolescents with ADHD may have more negative moods than other teens, and they may be prone to tobacco and alcohol abuse (Owens & Bergman, 2010; Zarger & Rich, 2016). Parents and family members are faced with responding to these children's emotions and potentially harmful behaviors.

What Are the Characteristics and Instructional Needs of Students Who Are Gifted and Talented?

In addition to students who cannot meet typical curricular expectations, you also will have in your classroom students who have extraordinary abilities and skills. The term used to describe these students is gifted and talented. The federal definition for this group of students is stated in the 1988 Jacob Javits Gifted and Talented Students Education Act (Javits Act, P.L. 100–297), which identifies children and youth who possess demonstrated or potential high-performance capability in intellectual, creative, and specific academic and leadership areas, or the performing and visual arts. The federal definition further clarifies that these students need services in school that other students do not. However, unlike the services offered through IDEA, federal legislation does not require specific services for gifted and talented students, and so the extent to which programs exist is determined largely by state and local policies (National Association for Gifted Children and Council of State Directors of Programs for the Gifted, 2015). In fact, the Javits Act is not a funding mechanism for state and local programs for students who are gifted and talented; at the present time, limited funding ($12 million) is associated with this law. Its purpose is to provide a means of coordinating efforts to enhance schools' abilities to serve these students, and its emphasis is on identifying and educating students who are traditionally underrepresented in programs for students who are gifted and talented (for example, students with disabilities and those from some racial or cultural minority groups).

Because the provision of service to students who are gifted and talented varies across the United States, prevalence is difficult to determine. In today's schools, approximately 6 to 10 percent of students are considered gifted and talented (National Association for Gifted Children, 2017).

The reported prevalence of giftedness and talent is greatly affected by two factors. First, over the past several years, researchers and writers have offered alternative definitions of giftedness and questioned traditional criteria for identification that rely on intelligence measures (that is, IQ tests). For example, Gardner (1993, 2006) and his supporters argue that measured IQ is far too narrow a concept of intelligence and that a person's ability to problem solve, especially in new situations, is a more useful way of thinking about intelligence (e.g., Jessurun, Shearer, & Weggeman, 2016). They have proposed that *multiple intelligences* describe the broad array of talents that students possess and describe these nine intelligences:

1. Verbal/linguistic
2. Visual/spatial
3. Logical/mathematical
4. Bodily/kinesthetic
5. Musical
6. Intrapersonal (that is, self-understanding)
7. Interpersonal
8. Naturalist
9. Existentialist

Notice the wide range of abilities captured in this notion of intelligence. The impact of using these broader definitions is that 20 percent or more of students could be identified as being gifted or talented, according to some estimates (Callahan, 2005; Lynch & Warner, 2012). This conceptualization of giftedness is not universally accepted.

The second factor that affects the number of students identified as gifted and talented is the notion of potential. Although some students who are gifted

WWW RESOURCES

http://gifted.uconn.edu/
The University of Connecticut's Neag Center for Gifted Education and Talent Development highlights current trends in the field, programs for students who are gifted and talented, and resources to help teachers understand these students through its National Research Center on the Gifted and Talented (NRC/GT).

FYI

Giftedness traditionally has referred to students with extraordinary abilities across many academic areas and *talent* to students with extraordinary abilities in a specific area. Now, however, the terms often are used interchangeably.

and talented easily can be identified because they use their special abilities and are willing to be recognized for them, others go unnoticed (e.g., Cavilla, 2017). These students mask their skills from peers and teachers because low expectations have been set for them or their unique needs have not been nurtured. Groups at risk for being underidentified include young boys, adolescent girls, students who are so highly gifted and talented as to be considered geniuses, students from racially and culturally diverse groups, and students with disabilities (Renzulli, Baum, Hébert, & McCluskey, 2016; Stambaugh & Chandler, 2012). In many school districts, focused attention has been placed on these groups to ensure such students are identified.

MyLab Education Self-Check 8.2

Characteristics and Needs of Students Who Are Gifted and Talented

Students who are gifted and talented have a wide range of characteristics, and any one student considered gifted and talented can have just a few or many of these characteristics. The following information about student characteristics is intended to provide an overview of students who are gifted and talented and should be viewed as a sample of what is known, not a comprehensive summary.

INTELLECTUAL ABILITIES AND ACADEMIC SKILLS The area of intellectual functioning and academic skills is the most delineated aspect of gifted education. Students who are gifted and talented generally have an extraordinary amount of knowledge because of their insatiable curiosity, keen memory, unusual ability to concentrate, wide variety of interests, high levels of language development and verbal ability, and ability to generate original ideas. They also have an advanced ability to comprehend information using accelerated and flexible thought processes, a heightened ability to recognize relationships between diverse ideas, and a strong capacity to form and use conceptual frameworks. These students tend to be skilled problem solvers because of their extraordinary ability to pick out relevant information and their tendency to monitor their problem-solving efforts (Reis & Sullivan, 2009).

The intellectual abilities of students who are gifted and talented sometimes lead them to high academic achievement, but not always. Consider these three students who are gifted and talented:

- Belinda was identified as gifted and talented in second grade. She has been reading since age three, seems as comfortable interacting with adults as with peers, and invariably becomes the leader of the groups of children with whom she plays, even when they are older. She enjoys school immensely and wants to be a university professor when she grows up. Belinda is similar to Lydia, whom you read about at the beginning of this chapter.

- Tomas also is identified as gifted and talented. He has been taking violin and piano lessons since age five, and now in the seventh grade he is an accomplished pianist. He already plans to major in music theory when he goes to college, and he offers his own interpretations of both classical and contemporary music. In his academic studies, however, Tomas is slightly below average in achievement. He also is somewhat shy; he appears more comfortable with his musical instruments than with his peers.

- Charles is a sophomore in high school. He lives in a neighborhood where education is not valued and getting high grades is viewed negatively by

MyLab Education

Video Example 8.3: Nari Carter—Gifts and Talents

An expert talks about how the needs of students with gifts and talents can be somewhat similar to students with disabilities.

RESEARCH-BASED PRACTICES

Advanced Placement (AP) and International Baccalaureate (IB) programs are associated with higher student achievement and college readiness. However, Kettler and Hurst (2017) found that in suburban schools, following enrollment patterns for a decade, African American students were less likely than their Caucasian classmates to be enrolled in these programs.

Students who are gifted and talented have many profiles. They may excel in all academic areas and be highly popular with peers, or they may have specialized talents and experience feelings of isolation.

RESEARCH-BASED PRACTICES

Baudson and Preckel (2016), in a study using fictitious student descriptions, found that teachers recognized high ability of students but associated giftedness with lower social skills and higher maladjustment than those for typical learners.

neighborhood peers. As a result, the nearly straight As that used to define Charles's report cards have dropped over the past year, and now he is earning mostly Cs and Ds. Charles does not think about going to college; that does not seem like a realistic option.

How might the needs of these students differ? How could you encourage each student to reach his or her potential?

SOCIAL AND EMOTIONAL NEEDS Socially and emotionally, students who are gifted and talented can be well liked and emotionally healthy, or they can be unpopular and at risk for serious emotional problems (Gallagher, 2015; Lee, Olszewski-Kubilius, & Thomson, 2012). Affectively, they tend to have unusual sensitivity to others' feelings as well as highly developed emotional depth and intensity, a keen sense of humor that can be either supportive or hostile, and a sense of justice. They often have a sense of obligation to help others and may become involved in community service activities. Teachers sometimes assign these students to help other students, an acceptable practice unless done so often that it interferes with advanced learning opportunities. These students often set high expectations for themselves and others. That can be positive, but it also can lead to feelings of frustration, isolation, and alienation, especially when they cannot meet the expectations they have set (Christopher & Shewmaker, 2010; Worley, 2015).

Because some students who are gifted have a superior ability to recognize and respond to others' feelings, they can be extremely popular with classmates and often sought after as helpmates. However, if they tend to show off their talents or repeatedly challenge adult authority, they may be perceived negatively by peers and teachers and have problems developing appropriate social relationships (Colangelo & Davis, 2003). For example, Ms. Ogden is concerned about eighth-grader Esteban. On some days, he seems to have just a four-word vocabulary: "I already know that." He says this to his teachers, his peers, and his parents about nearly any topic under discussion. Although it is often true that Esteban does know about the subject being discussed, Ms. Ogden finds herself becoming annoyed at his style of interacting, and she knows the other students do not want to be grouped with Esteban because of it.

BEHAVIOR PATTERNS Students who are gifted and talented display the entire range of behaviors that other students do. They can be model students who participate and seldom cause problems, often serving as class leaders. In this capacity, students are sensitive to others' feelings and moderate their behavior based on others' needs. They also sometimes have behavior patterns similar to those of students diagnosed as ADHD (Rommelse et al., 2016). Occasionally, because students who are gifted and talented often have an above-average capacity to understand people and situations, their negative behavior can be magnified compared with that of other students. This behavior can be displayed through an intense interest in a topic and refusal to change topics when requested by a teacher. Other behavior problems displayed by some students who are gifted and talented include being bossy in group situations, purposely failing, and valuing and participating in counterculture activities (Francis, Hawes, & Abbott, 2016).

Interventions for Students Who Are Gifted and Talented

Although some school districts operate separate classes and programs for students who are gifted and talented, you likely will be responsible for teaching many of these students in your classroom. Four specific strategies often used to challenge students who are gifted and talented are curriculum compacting, acceleration and enrichment, specific differentiation strategies during instruction, and individualized interventions (VanTassel-Baska, 2003). As you read the following descriptions of these strategies and the examples of their implementation, think about how the INCLUDE strategy could guide you in implementing them. In the Case in Practice feature, you can see an application of instruction for a student who is gifted and has a learning disability.

⟨ **INCLUDE** ⟩

CURRICULUM COMPACTING Some students who are gifted and talented already have mastered much of the traditional curriculum content of the public schools, and they may be bored when asked to listen to a lecture or complete an assignment that does not challenge them. In *curriculum compacting*, teachers assess students' achievement of instructional goals and then eliminate instruction on goals already met. The time gained is used to pursue special interests, work with a mentor, or study the same topic at a more advanced level (Reis, Westberg, Kulikowich, & Purcell, 2016). How could you use curriculum compacting in your planned teaching?

ACCELERATION In some school districts, you may learn that *acceleration* is part of the programming available for students who are gifted and talented (Assouline et al., 2013; Dare, Dare, & Nowicki, 2017). That is, these students may skip a grade or complete the standards for two grades in a single year. In high school, acceleration may relate to a specific subject. For example, a student with extraordinary math skills might enroll in advanced coursework in that area while following the traditional curriculum for English and social studies.

CASE IN PRACTICE 8.1

Meeting the Needs of a Twice-Exceptional Student

Ms. Davis is taking a few minutes to reflect on the meeting she and her seventh-grade team had yesterday with their school psychologist, the facilitator for their school's program for students who are gifted and talented, and the special education teacher. The meeting was called because of the teachers' concerns about Isaac, a student whom the teachers characterize as a student of "contradictions." Here are examples of what they mean:

- For a multimedia project in English, Isaac produced original music and directed several classmates to produce a performance he recorded expertly using video equipment he borrowed from a teacher at the high school. The day the project was due, however, he forgot to bring it to school and told his teacher that it wasn't very good anyway.

- In social studies, Isaac can explain in detail not just the events of world history but also the societal forces that influenced them. His mother attributes this knowledge to his love of the documentaries and other programming on history available on television.

- In math, Isaac struggles. He often disrupts class by making jokes ("I know what algebra is—it's underwear for a mermaid [algae-bra]." "Did you hear what happened in the other class? Mr. Somers asked John to solve the problem 'What is $2q + 8q$?' When John said, '$10q$,' Mr. Somers said, 'You're welcome!'").

The other professionals at the meeting spent some time explaining that Isaac is *twice exceptional*; that is, he is gifted and also has a learning disability related to language

processing, mathematical reasoning, and organization. This is why he has a learning-strategies class as one of his electives and is in the co-taught English class.

In reviewing information about Isaac and discussing how to help him reach his potential (and reduce disruptions in class), the professionals talked about how to help him use his significant intellectual abilities in a constructive way. The psychologist advised the teachers that Isaac sometimes uses humor and inappropriate classroom remarks to distract his teachers so that he can avoid tasks he is afraid he may not do well. The special educator mentioned that she is concerned about Isaac's self-esteem; he told her privately that having the label *LD* (learning disability) means he's "retarded," and nothing she said seemed to change his opinion of his abilities. Suggestions for working with Isaac included giving him as many choices as possible regarding assignments; offering ways other than reading for him to acquire information; arranging peer tutoring in math, the class in which Isaac struggles the most; and guiding him to research what it means to have a learning disability.

REFLECTION

What does it mean for a student to be *twice exceptional*? Besides LD, what do you think are other disabilities that might occur with giftedness? How would such students be similar to or different from Isaac? Why might students who are twice exceptional have low self-esteem? How can you help these students succeed? Should a student like Isaac be enrolled in a program for students who are gifted? Why or why not?

ENRICHMENT *Enrichment* is an instructional approach that provides students with information, materials, and assignments that enable them to elaborate on concepts being presented as part of the standard curriculum and that usually require high levels of thinking (Brigandi, Siegle, Weiner, Gubbins, & Little, 2016; Reis, McCoach, Little, Muller, & Kaniskan, 2011). This common classroom option requires you to find related information, prepare it for the students who need it, and create curriculum-relevant alternative activities for them. For enrichment to be effective, you need to ensure that students have opportunities to complete assignments designed to encourage advanced thinking and product development, that they do such assignments in lieu of other work instead of as additional work, and that many learning resources are available to them both in and out of the classroom.

DIFFERENTIATION Perhaps one of the most practical approaches you can use for working with students in your class who are gifted and talented is to systematically plan lessons based on *differentiation*, the same approach introduced for your work with students who have disabilities (Tomlinson, 2017; Wu, 2013). Recall that differentiation is based on the understanding that students should have multiple ways to reach their potential. Just as you will analyze the strengths and needs of students with disabilities and design and evaluate effective ways to teach them, you should do the same for students who are gifted and talented. For example, Ms. Clinton's English class is reading *Romeo and Juliet*. Six students—four who have disabilities and two who are English learners—are experiencing difficulty reading the play and have been provided a version with contemporary language. The questions they are assigned once they have read the first act include these: What is the Capulet family like? The Montagues? Why don't the two families like each other? However, the pretest data of two other students indicate they are familiar with the play and know its detail. Their assignment after reading the first act is to stage that part of the play, setting it in modern times. They also are asked to explain how *Romeo and Juliet* is an example of classic tragic form, a topic they are expected to research independently.

SPECIALIZED INTERVENTIONS All of the previously described approaches may be effective for students who are gifted and talented, but students who have special circumstances—those who live in poverty, who are from nondominant cultures, or who also have disabilities—may need even further special attention (e.g., Landis & Reschly, 2013; Ritchotte, Rubenstein, & Murry, 2015). For example, some students may downplay their abilities because academic achievement is not valued in their immediate community and they fear being rejected (Cavilla, 2017; VanTassel-Baska et al., 2009). For these students, you may want to find mentors

PROFESSIONAL EDGE 8.2

Gifted Underachievers

Gifted underachievers may be students who do poorly on tests, do not turn in daily work, or achieve below grade level. At the same time, they learn quickly when interested, are highly creative, and value projects they choose themselves. The following strategies can help you better match your instruction to the needs of these students.

Provide More Flexibility to Foster Peer and Social Relationships Among Students.

- Allow students to teach classmates and others.
- Organize multiage groups across grade levels.

Assist Students with Successful Transitions.

- Develop a mentor program in which older students mentor younger students.
- Offer transition survival courses when students change grade levels/schools.
- Provide parent education programs about transitions.

Promote Empowerment and Autonomy for Students.

- Solicit student input for planning learning activities.
- Include some self-paced/mastery learning opportunities.
- Promote recognition and awards for achievement and effort.
- Provide leadership training and opportunities for students to demonstrate leadership skills.
- Involve students in evaluating school activities and providing and implementing ideas for improvement.

Improve the Learning Environment for Students.

- Expand learning beyond the classroom and into the community, including service learning.
- Create ways for students to participate in classroom and school governance.

- Use flexible instructional groups based on needs.
- Create alternative assignments that students do in lieu of traditional classwork.
- Make sure your classroom is culturally responsive; that is, respectful of students' diverse backgrounds and needs.
- Promote grading systems that encourage students to continue to try (for example, provide full credit for work, even if submitted late).
- Enlist the assistance of parents in encouraging their children and helping them manage the stresses of school.
- Encourage positive confrontation and conflict resolution.

Think about how each of these ideas applies to the grade level you plan to teach. Teachers sometimes refer to students such as gifted underachievers as "unmotivated," inferring that unless the students change, they will not learn. What is your role in motivating such students? How might your teaching strategies relate to student motivation?

Sources: Based on "Gifted and Talented Students at Risk," by K. Seeley, 2004, *Focus on Exceptional Children, 37*(4), pp. 1–9; and *Gifted and Talented Students at Risk for Underachievement* [Issue Brief], Center for Comprehensive School Reform and Improvement, 2008, Washington, DC: Author.

MyLab Education Self-Check 8.3

---

from similar backgrounds so students see that drawing on their talents can lead to positive outcomes. For some students, interacting with peers from a similar background can be helpful, especially if they are given tasks that foster critical thinking skills. In addition, students in this group may benefit when technology is integral to instruction, either as a resource for learning or a tool for accessing learning, as might be the case for students with disabilities. The Professional Edge feature provides a checklist that can be useful for recognizing students who might be gifted underachievers.

What Are the Characteristics and Instructional Needs of Students from Culturally Diverse Backgrounds?

The racial, cultural, and linguistic diversity of U.S. classrooms has been increasing for decades, and all indications are that it will continue to do so (National Center for Education Statistics, 2017b). For example, in 1972, just 22 percent of students enrolled in grades 1 through 12 were members of minority groups. In 1988 that number had grown to 32 percent, and in 2004, it had increased to 42 percent of all students. In 2014, the most recent year for which data are available, minority group students were a majority at approximately 50.5 percent, and that number is to projected to continue to increase. Approximately 9.4 percent of all U.S. public school students are English learners (National Center for Education Statistics, 2017a); approximately 77 percent of these students speak Spanish as their first language. The next most common non-English languages spoken in students' homes are Arabic, Chinese, Vietnamese, Hmong, and Somali.

WWW RESOURCES

http://ies.ed.gov/ncee/wwc/topic.aspx?sid=6
Are you wondering what the most effective interventions are for working with English learners? This website, part of the What Works Clearinghouse, answers that question and provides basic information on these interventions you might wish to use.

Approximately 14.5 percent of English learners are also identified as having disabilities and receive special education.

Although more students complete high school than ever before, evidence suggests that students from some racial/ethnic groups are less likely than other students to accomplish this critical goal. For example, in 2014–2015, dropout rates were as follows: Asian, 2.4 percent; White, 4.5 percent; Pacific Islander, 5.4; Black, 7.2 percent; American Indian/Alaska Native, 13.2 percent; and Hispanic, 9.9 percent (Digest of Education Statistics, 2017). Although some of these students may later return to complete school in a GED program, many will not. The reasons for these students' failure to complete school are complex and interrelated but involve several identifiable factors. First, students from racial and ethnic minority groups often lack role models because 80 percent of teachers (and school administrators) are from the majority Anglo-European culture (U.S. Department of Education, 2016). In addition, instructional practices can negatively affect students. In particular, traditional teaching practices that rely on whole-group instruction can disadvantage students from backgrounds whose experiences may lead them to learn best from small-group instruction that incorporates more personal attention. (e.g., Pyle, Pyle, Lignugaris-Kraft, Duran, & Akers, 2017). A blend of teaching approaches is needed. Finally, the lack of specialized school programs can penalize students. For example, few schools operate mentor programs specifically designed to connect students from diverse cultures with leaders in business, industry, and education. These contacts can be essential for helping students succeed, as is the case for Zhang Wei, whose story was part of this chapter's introduction.

Diversity and Special Education

The relationship among school failure, special education, and diverse student needs is not a comfortable one (Artiles, Kozleski, Trent, Osher, & Ortiz, 2010). Historically, students from racial and cultural minorities sometimes were inappropriately placed in special education programs based on discriminatory assessment practices. While some recent research questions the nature of the bias in the identification process (Morgan et al., 2017), bias does exist, particularly for African American students and some English learners (Ford & Russo, 2016). The reasons for such bias continue to be studied. Some researchers maintain that the issue concerns poverty more than race or ethnicity, a topic addressed later in this chapter. But bias can also be embedded within curriculum and instruction, teacher attitudes, and the special education referral process (Artiles et al., 2010; Collins, Connor, Ferri, Gallagher, & Samson, 2016).

A potentially promising way to address such bias is through a carefully designed procedure you have already learned about: response to intervention or multi-tiered system of support (Cartledge, Kea, Watson, & Oif, 2016). With these models, a team of professionals can carefully analyze several types of data and decide upon ways to increase students' rates of learning and possibly avoid consideration for special education. This form of systematic decision making is particularly important given that students' language or culture may inadvertently lead teachers to think they have a disability. When teachers collaborate with each other while systematically and consistently using a variety of increasingly intensive and research-based interventions, the hallmark of effectively implemented RtI or MTSS, it is much more likely that the student's learning problems are truly the result of a disability and not cultural or language difference (Belser, Shillingford, & Joe, 2016; Greenfield, Rinaldi, Proctor, & Cardarelli, 2010).

Students from culturally diverse backgrounds may be at risk for school failure, but your classroom culture and careful attention to their unique needs can help them achieve success.

Cultural Proficiency

Understanding the characteristics of students who are members of racially and culturally diverse groups involves recognizing that learning and behavior problems can be created and inequity result from contradictions between some students' home and community experiences and the expectations placed on them at school (Banks, 2007; Lindsey & Lindsey, 2016). This understanding also means acknowledging that teachers sometimes misunderstand students and their parents, leading to miscommunication, distrust, and negative school experiences.

If you live in an area where many different cultures are represented in a single classroom, the thought of learning about all of them can be intimidating. It is probably not possible, nor is it necessary, to learn many details about all the cultures of your students. However, it is your responsibility to learn the fundamental characteristics students might have because of their backgrounds. For example, some students might hesitate to ask questions because of concern about interacting with the teacher, who is perceived as an authority figure. If you understand this reticence, then you can make a special effort to initiate interactions with these students. Further, when a student displays troublesome behavior, you should determine whether a cultural reason may have prompted the behavior before responding to it or assuming that it represents misbehavior. Of course, you also should keep in mind that not all students from diverse backgrounds encounter these problems, nor do all families from racial or ethnic minority groups use discipline practices different from those schools use.

The INCLUDE strategy can be a valuable tool for making decisions about instruction for students from culturally and linguistically diverse groups. First, you should consider the demands of the classroom setting and identify the strengths and interests students bring to the learning environment. Next, you should look for potential problem areas throughout your entire instructional program. Use that information to brainstorm ideas for resolving the problems and select those with the most potential for success. As you go through this process, it is essential to monitor student progress and make adjustments as needed. An example of strategies related to teaching reading to students who are English learners is included in the Instructional Edge feature.

> INCLUDE

The impact of cultural and linguistic diversity in educational settings can be examined in more detail from three perspectives, each briefly considered in the following sections: how cultural factors affect student behavior, how teaching approaches can be tailored to culturally diverse groups, and how communication with nonnative English speakers can be enhanced.

CULTURAL FACTORS AND STUDENT BEHAVIOR Various cultural values can affect students' behaviors and how educators interpret these behaviors. For example, for some Native American and immigrant students, time is a fluid concept not necessarily bound by clocks (Helman, 2005). A student might come to school late by Anglo-European cultural standards that measure time precisely but on time according to events happening at the student's home. Another example of the differences between Anglo-European standards and some students' cultures concerns school participation. Hispanic students sometimes are more likely to participate when they have established close relationships with their teachers and peers (Carter Andrews & Gutwein, 2017). Contrast this fact with the common high school structure, in which one teacher sees as many as 180 students each day and often uses an instructional format that minimizes interaction. In such a setting, some Hispanic students—especially those who have only recently come to the United States—can be at a great disadvantage.

INFORMED INSTRUCTIONAL DECISION MAKING Effective decisions about teaching strategies are made by matching the needs of students from culturally diverse backgrounds to instructional approaches (Hoover, 2012; Schmeichel, 2012). For example, many African American students, as well as many Hispanic American students, respond well to cooperative rather than competitive teaching and

INSTRUCTIONAL EDGE 8.2

English Learners and Reading

Although English learners (ELs) often have trouble learning to read (Ardasheva, Tretter, & Kinny, 2012; Vaughn et al., 2008), these are ways you can make your reading instruction more meaningful for them while also building their oral language skills.

TEACH SEGMENTING AND BLENDING

When students *segment* words, they break words apart into their individual phonemes (fish = /f/-/i/-/sh/). When they *blend*, they say a spoken word when the sounds are said slowly (/f/-/i/-/sh/ = fish).

- Give ELs more opportunities to use new English vocabulary by having them blend or segment these new words before using them in complete sentences.
- Have ELs segment and blend using words from their first language. For example, have them blend a name such as *Jorgé* or clap the sounds in holidays such as *Navidad* or *Cinco de Mayo*.
- During story time, while building student vocabulary and listening comprehension skills, ask students to segment and blend words taken from a picture book about their culture.

TEACH ASSOCIATIONS BETWEEN WRITTEN LETTERS AND SOUNDS

Home, school, and community interests can be used to teach ELs the associations between written letters and sounds, or *phonics*.

- Have Spanish-speaking students sound out decodable Spanish words appearing on signs, community newspapers, and in books written in Spanish. Then have students use the English equivalents of these words in complete sentences orally, in writing, or both.
- Show students pictures of words after they have sounded them out. Doing this will ensure they are using phonics to figure out the words while also building their English vocabulary. Showing pictures also provides additional opportunities for the students and teacher to engage in dialogue about the word—and build oral language skills.
- Distinguish between errors and articulation differences. For example, José read the word *meet* as /mit/. In Spanish, a long e is often pronounced as a short *i*; therefore, *meet* could be identified correctly but pronounced as /mit/. José's teacher asked him to use the word in a sentence, which allowed her to check José's word reading skills while also reinforcing his vocabulary and syntactical knowledge by having him use the word in a sentence.

BUILD STUDENTS' READING FLUENCY

Reading fluency is the ability to read connected text accurately, quickly, and with expression and is an important bridge between word recognition and comprehension. It also requires the reader to use intonation and stress to convey meaning. Understanding the importance of reading with expression is difficult for

ELs because languages such as Spanish convey differences in meaning by changing word order.

- Read a section of text related to cultural themes, mores, values, traditions, history, or customs to students, modeling appropriate stress and intonation. Then have students read the same section back to you, provide them with feedback, and have them repeat as needed.
- For independent practice, provide digitally recorded models of orally read text. Have students try to read like the recording, and then evaluate their performance.

TEACH VOCABULARY, INCLUDING IDIOMS

As you learned in Chapter 5, ELs may learn basic vocabulary but struggle to learn the meaning of English-language idioms, such as "up the creek."

- Have students practice reading idioms with the appropriate rhythm and stress in connected speech (Celce-Murcia, 2000, p. 170)—for example, all talk and no action, talk shop, talk is cheap, talk someone's head off.
- Say each phrase and then have students repeat it, imitating your tone and inflection; discuss the meaning of each idiom (Bursuck & Damer, 2011). Also have students use each idiom in a sentence and write stories or draw pictures of idioms they choose.

ENHANCE ORAL LANGUAGE

The key to reading comprehension for ELs is knowledge of oral language (e.g., Wilson, Fang, Rollins, & Valadez, 2016). Oral language can be enhanced through student reading or by reading to students.

- Select material relevant to students' experiences and backgrounds.
- Encourage students to summarize passages using familiar words after reading or listening.
- Keep a balance between expository (informational) and narrative (storytelling) material. Schools with higher proportions of students at risk tend to stress stories despite the fact that these students have major gaps in the background knowledge required to understand these stories.
- Because ELs may be reluctant to volunteer to answer questions, call on nonvolunteers to answer in class while helping students to elaborate as they respond using modeling and guided practice.
- When you read aloud, talk slowly to give students the time needed to process what you are saying.
- When reading a long section of text, ask questions periodically rather than just at the end. This approach provides more direct support for comprehension and holds students' attention while modeling a question-asking strategy students eventually should use themselves.
- Have students write about the text they are reading or listening to in order to improve their reading comprehension skills.

learning environments. Likewise, because traditional Native American students sometimes dislike responding individually and out loud in a large-group situation, you may need to create opportunities for individual contact and quiet participation. Such instructional thinking and approaches, referred to as *equity pedagogy*, a term introduced at the beginning of this chapter, should become integral to your teaching (Valente & Danforth, 2016; Zirkel, 2008).

CROSS-CULTURAL COMMUNICATION For students who do not speak English as their native language, going to school can be a frustrating experience, resulting in some common problems. First, students who do not use English proficiently can easily be discriminated against when they are assessed, their scores reflecting their language skill more than their learning of curricular content. Second, students with limited English skills sometimes are perceived by teachers and classmates as deficient (Artiles et al., 2010; Diaz, Cochran, & Karlin, 2016). Teachers might have difficulty understanding students and assume they have limited ability, and peers may exclude them from social activities because of language differences. Third, language-related issues sometimes lead to the belief that when English is not students' primary language, these students must be segregated from other students to learn. If you understand your students' levels of language proficiency as summarized in the Professional Edge feature, you can ensure that your instruction takes language into account and avoid or reduce some of the challenges nonnative English speakers face.

For students from culturally and linguistically diverse backgrounds, home–school communication is critical. You might have difficulty even in basic communication because of language differences and the lack of availability of an interpreter. A second problem you may face concerns cultural values and parent responses to school personnel (e.g., Greenberg, 2012). For example, in a traditional Asian family, pride and shame often are emphasized and indirectness is valued. Imagine a parent conference in which an insensitive teacher describes in detail the academic and learning problems an Asian child is having and directly asks the parents whether they can assist in carrying out a home–school behavior change program. If the parents follow traditional Asian values, they might be humiliated by the public accounting of their child's failures and embarrassed at the teacher's direct and unnecessary request for their assistance.

A third problem relates to a potential discrepancy between parents' perceptions of school and how they should interact with school personnel and school staff expectations for parent involvement. For example, the parents of some students may find school foreign and intimidating and believe that their role is to listen passively to what school personnel say. Other parents may not trust educators enough to share important information with them about their children (e.g., Cherng, 2016).

MyLab Education

Video Example 8.4: Intercultural Competence
These experts offer practical advice for teachers working with diverse student groups.

Families and Diversity

Many teachers find that not only do they have to put focused effort into understanding students and family members because of language barriers and cultural differences, but also that they simply may not grasp the day-to-day realities of their students' and students' families' lives. Probably the single best strategy for improving understanding is to set aside all the books, lesson plans, and ideas about diversity and multiculturalism and simply *listen* to families (Trumbull & Pacheco, 2005). The following strategies also can contribute to building positive working relationships with the parents/families of your students from culturally and linguistically diverse groups (Colorín Colorado, 2017; Sánchez, 1999):

1. Start from a firm belief that all families are significant to their children's education and want what is best for them.

2. Critically examine your own beliefs and biases to reduce inadvertent prejudice and genuinely welcome parent/family input.

3. Analyze your interactions with students and their families as well as your written communication with them from *their* perspective, considering how you and your messages could be perceived.

PROFESSIONAL EDGE 8.3

Levels of Language Proficiency

When you teach students who are English learners, you should understand their level of language proficiency, keeping in mind that language proficiency for any single student could vary significantly depending on whether the task at hand involves speaking, listening, reading, writing, or a combination of them. This chart outlines a continuum of six levels of language proficiency, including the performance definition and some of the ways students function for each.

At the Given Level of English-Language Proficiency, English Learners will Process, Understand, Produce, or Use:

6: Reaching	• A range of grade-appropriate language for a variety of academic purposes, including precision and sophistication in relating ideas • Fluency and automaticity in response • Skillful interpersonal interactions • A variety of sentence lengths of varying linguistic complexity in extended oral or written discourse as required by the specific grade level • Oral/written communication in English comparable to that of English-speaking peers
5: Bridging	• The technical language of the content areas • A variety of sentence lengths of varying linguistic complexity in extended oral or written discourse, including stories, essays, and reports • Oral or written language approaching comparability to that of English-proficient peers when presented with grade-level material
4: Expanding	• Specific and some technical language of the content areas • A variety of sentence lengths of varying linguistic complexity in oral discourse or multiple related paragraphs • Oral or written language with minimal phonological, syntactic, or semantic errors that do not impede the overall meaning of the communication when presented with oral or written connected discourse with occasional visual and graphic support
3: Developing	• General and some specific language of the content areas • Expanded sentences in oral interaction or written paragraphs • Oral or written language with phonological, syntactic, or semantic errors that may impede the communication but retain much of its meaning when presented with oral or written narrative or expository descriptions with occasional visual and graphic support
2: Beginning	• General language related to the content area • Phrases and short sentences • Oral or written language with phonological, syntactic, or semantic errors that often impede the meaning of the communication when presented with one- to multiple-step commands, directions, or questions or a series of statements with visual and graphic support
1: Entering	• Pictorial or graphic representation of the language of the content areas • Words, phrases, or chunks of language when presented with one-step commands or directions • WH- questions (that is, questions beginning with the words who, what, where, when, why, and how) or statements with visual and graphic support

Source: WIDA. (2017, June). *WIDA performance definitions—Speaking and writing grades K–12*. Madison, WI: Author. Retrieved from https://www.wida.us/get.aspx?id=543.

4. Visit your students' neighborhoods and communities to learn about their out-of-school experiences

5. Invite parents' questions about the U.S. education system and clarify aspects of it that might be confusing (e.g., curriculum standards, scheduling quirks, grading systems, programs such as RtI/MTSS).

You can respond with respect and sensitivity to your students, as well as their families, by being careful to recognize that the most important factor about working with others is that unless you have been in their situation, you cannot completely understand it. The Working Together feature provides some

WORKING TOGETHER 8.1
Creating a School Environment for Collaborating with Parents

Collaboration between school professionals and parents and families is less about creating a set of activities than it is about forming a mindset based on "want to" rather than "ought to." This is especially important when working with families from diverse racial and cultural groups. To foster this positive approach toward working with parents and families, try these ideas:

- Survey the parents of your students to find out what information they need. Arrange to have your survey translated into the languages spoken in the homes of your students.
- Call to invite uninvolved parents to come to a school event or activity.
- Work with other professionals at your school to contact parents' places of worship for ideas on how to foster positive relationships with parents and the community.
- Let parents know a specific time and/or day of the week they can reach you by telephone or in person at school.
- Ask parents about their interests and skills and then invite them to volunteer in your classroom, possibly tutoring students or teaching mini-lessons about their hobbies or jobs.
- Provide your school e-mail address for parents who prefer this communication mode, but do not expect all parents to have technology access.

- Call parents to praise their child—and do this more than once.
- Develop home-learning activity packets that are related to your learning objectives. However, be sure they are family friendly—that is, that only basic supplies are needed to complete them.
- With parent permission, connect an uninvolved parent with a parent who is involved.
- Keep a list of community resources at your fingertips. Although your school social worker or other professionals also might have this information, you may be able to offer informal assistance in a way that is respectful and low key.
- Have your students create a newsletter to send home. In it, describe important activities. Have secondary students keep a journal for their parents, outlining what they are studying.
- Ask for parents' input regarding what works best with their child, especially regarding discipline and rewards.

Source: Adapted from *Home–School Collaboration: Building Effective Parent-School Partnerships,* by S. L. Christenson, 2002, Minneapolis: Children, Youth, and Family Consortium, University of Minnesota, retrieved December 5, 2004, from (http://www.cyfc.umn.edu/schoolage/resources/home.html). Reprinted with permission from Sandra Christenson.

suggestions for fostering collaboration with families by focusing on making them feel welcomed and valuable in their children's education.

Multicultural and Bilingual Education

Creating a classroom in which students' cultures are acknowledged and valued is a fundamental characteristic of multicultural education, that is, curriculum and instruction that reflect the diversity of society. Multicultural education begins with such basics as examining how you decorate your classroom and how you select learning materials. Do your bulletin boards display the work of students from ethnic and cultural minority groups? When you portray historical events, do you include information about members of several cultural groups? Does your classroom contain stories or literature about successful individuals from a variety of cultures? Is respect for diversity infused throughout your curriculum?

If the school in which you teach has a highly diverse student population, programs for supporting English learners (ELs) will be important and could take a number of forms (Nieto, 2013). For example, bilingual education programs are based on the assumption that students need to learn English by being immersed in an English language environment, but until a level of proficiency in English is achieved, many students do not learn concepts and skills from English language instruction. Therefore, in bilingual programs, students spend part of the school day receiving instruction in core academic areas in their native language and the remainder of the day with English-speaking students. Yet other students learn through English as a second language (ESL) programs in which instruction occurs primarily in English, although often separate from general education, and no specific attempt is made to preserve students' native language. In a few elementary schools, English learners participate in the typical classroom, with a bilingual or ESL teacher co-teaching the class for all or part of the day (Honigsfeld & Dove, 2016).

WWW RESOURCES

http://www.nabe.org
The National Association for Bilingual Education is an organization concerned with the quality of education received by students whose native language is not English. Its website includes articles, research reports, and other resources.

If you develop curiosity about your students' cultures and languages, you can be sensitive to their learning needs and responsive to them. If you consider yourself as much a learner as a teacher in interacting with these students, you will become culturally responsive and help them effectively access the curriculum and succeed in school.

MyLab Education Self-Check 8.4

What Are the Characteristics and Instructional Needs of Students Who Are at Risk?

In addition to all the other special needs you find among students, you will likely encounter one that is found in virtually every public school classroom in the country. That special need is being at risk for school failure. Students who are *at risk* are those who have been exposed to some condition or situation that negatively affects their learning, like Tam, whom you met at the beginning of this chapter. Most teachers include in this description students who were prenatally exposed to drugs, including alcohol; students who use drugs or whose family members are drug users; students who are homeless; and students who have been neglected. Others include students who are bullies and those who are victims, as well as those who have recently experienced the death of someone close to them. Students who are school phobic are at risk, as are those who are considered suicidal, physically unattractive or obese, socially underdeveloped, and slow or marginal learners. For many educators, it is difficult to understand the range of problems students face and the tremendous impact these problems have on their lives.

You might be wondering why students who are at risk are discussed in a text about students with disabilities. Three reasons are central:

1. With a well-designed education, many students who are at risk for school failure succeed in school. The strategies for adjusting to the needs of students with disabilities are usually effective for students at risk; these strategies are discussed throughout this text. By using the INCLUDE strategy, you can identify ways to help these students reach their potential.

2. Effective early school experiences for students who are at risk, increasingly based on RtI or MTSS processes, can establish a pattern of success in school learning that carries through high school (Belser et al., 2016). Without such experiences, students at risk are more likely to be identified as having learning or emotional disabilities.

3. Many students with disabilities also are students at risk. Many students with disabilities have been abused, some live in poverty, and others use illegal drugs.

Increasing your understanding of risk factors and approaches for working with students at risk benefits all students at risk for school failure, whether they have disabilities or not.

Characteristics and Needs of Students at Risk

Intellectually, socially, emotionally, behaviorally, and physically, students considered at risk are as diverse as students in the general school population. What distinguishes them from other students is the likelihood that they will struggle to obtain a high school diploma and that they will have difficulty both in school

MyLab Education

Video Example 8.5: Homeless Children in Education

This sobering video clip about the impact of homelessness on children is an important reminder for educators of their responsibilities for these students, https://www.youtube.com/watch?v=Oin2RGaJJOQ

and throughout their lives. Some students at risk also share other characteristics and needs, including a tendency to be noncompliant, problems in monitoring their own learning and behavior, language delays, difficulties with social relationships, and problems understanding the consequences of their behaviors (Deussen, Hanson, & Bisht, 2017; Severson, Walker, & Hope-Doolittle, 2007). To illustrate further the needs these students have, three representative groups of students at risk are briefly discussed in the following sections: (1) students who live in poverty, including those who are homeless; (2) students who have been abused or neglected; and (3) students who live in homes in which substance abuse occurs or who themselves are substance abusers. Keep in mind that even though this discussion treats each group as distinct for the sake of clarity, any single student could be in all three groups.

STUDENTS WHO LIVE IN POVERTY Approximately 43 percent (that is, 30.6 million) of U.S. children under 18 years of age live in low-income families, $24,036 for a family of four (Jiang, Granja, & Koball, 2017). A total of 22 percent of children live in poverty—that is, their family income is even lower, half or less of the level to be considered low income. Moreover, 30 percent of these children (that is, 16.1 million) have at least one parent who works full-time year-round; nearly half of children in low-income families live with parents who are married.

Students who live in poverty have many problems that affect their learning. These children score significantly lower on academic assessments than students who do not live in poverty, and they are more likely to have been retained at least once (e.g., Chain, Shapiro, LeBuffe, & Bryson, 2017; Claro, Paunesku, & Dweck, 2016; Herbers et al., 2012). They also might not have nutritious meals to eat, a safe and warm place to play and sleep, or needed supplies to complete homework. These students are sometimes worried about their families' circumstances, and older students might be expected to work evenings and weekends to help support the family or to miss school to babysit for younger siblings. Students living in poverty also are more likely than advantaged students to experience parental neglect, witness violence, and change schools and residences frequently, all of which may negatively affect their learning.

It is now estimated that 2.5 million children under age 18 are homeless, or one in every 30 children in the U.S. (Bassuk, DeCandia, Beach, & Berman, 2014), and they are likely to access the system of homeless shelters, on average, for up to a year (National Coalition for the Homeless, 2017). In addition to families who are homeless, many are in temporary living arrangements with relatives or friends. Homelessness results in many educational problems. Students sometimes leave their neighborhood school or transfer from school to school when they move to a shelter or stay with family or friends. This can leave gaps in their learning. Some students are placed in foster care when the family is homeless, and this arrangement affects their social and emotional adjustment. In addition to learning problems, students who live in poverty or who are homeless sometimes (although not always) display acting-out, restless, or aggressive behaviors; anxiety; depression; and regressive behaviors (Stone & Uretsky, 2016; Tyler, Hagewen, & Melander, 2011).

STUDENTS WHO ARE ABUSED OR NEGLECTED A second group of students at risk includes those who are physically abused, sexually abused, psychologically abused, or neglected. Did you know that in 2015, 1,670 children died as a result of abuse or neglect (U.S. Department of Health and Human Services, 2017)? Although the precise meaning of the term child abuse varies from state to state, it generally refers to situations in which a parent or other caregiver inflicts or allows others to inflict injury on a child or permits a substantial risk of injury to exist. Child neglect is used to describe situations in which a parent or other caregiver fails to provide the necessary supports for a child's well-being, such as basic food and shelter, education, medical care, and other items. Figure 8.2

WWW RESOURCES

http://www.nccp.org
The National Center for Children in Poverty, which is associated with Columbia University, provides a wealth of information about children living in poverty. The site includes information about immigrant children, children receiving welfare, children's health care, and many other related topics.

FYI

Homeless children have to make many educational and personal adjustments as a result of four conditions in their lives: constant moving, frequent change of schools; overcrowded living quarters; and lack of basic resources such as food, clothing, and transportation.

FIGURE 8.2 Child Abuse: A National Profile

In 2015, more than 4 million referrals were made to child protective services because of suspected abuse or neglect (a total of 7.2 million children are included in these reports). A total of 683,000 unique victims of abuse were eventually identified.

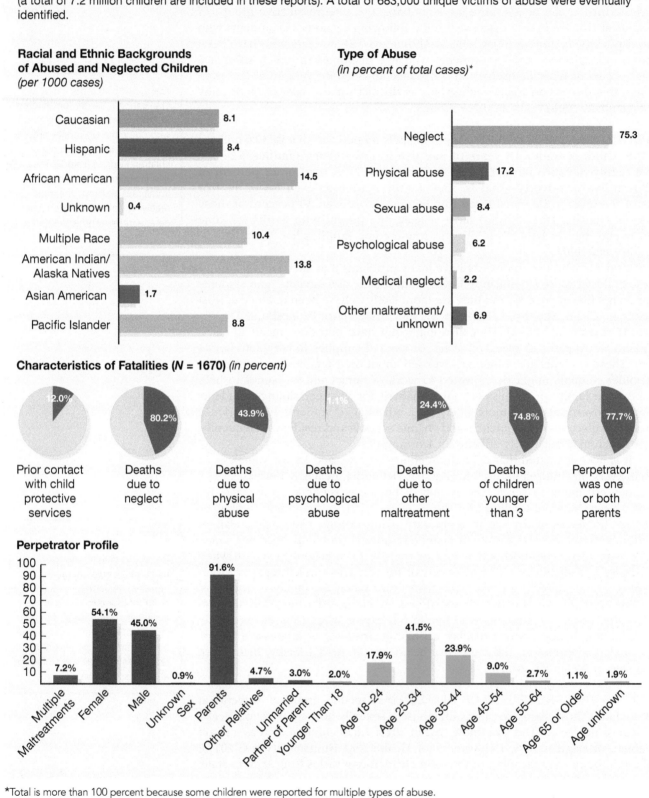

Racial and Ethnic Backgrounds of Abused and Neglected Children *(per 1000 cases)*

Caucasian	8.1
Hispanic	8.4
African American	14.5
Unknown	0.4
Multiple Race	10.4
American Indian/Alaska Natives	13.8
Asian American	1.7
Pacific Islander	8.8

Type of Abuse *(in percent of total cases)**

Neglect	75.3
Physical abuse	17.2
Sexual abuse	8.4
Psychological abuse	6.2
Medical neglect	2.2
Other maltreatment/unknown	6.9

Characteristics of Fatalities (*N* = 1670) *(in percent)*

- Prior contact with child protective services — 12.0%
- Deaths due to neglect — 80.2%
- Deaths due to physical abuse — 43.9%
- Deaths due to psychological abuse — 1.1%
- Deaths due to other maltreatment — 24.4%
- Deaths of children younger than 3 — 74.8%
- Perpetrator was one or both parents — 77.7%

Perpetrator Profile

Multiple Maltreatments	7.2%
Female	54.1%
Male	45.0%
Unknown Sex	0.9%
Parents	91.6%
Other Relatives	4.7%
Unmarried Partner of Parent	3.0%
Younger Than 18	2.0%
Age 18–24	17.9%
Age 25–34	41.5%
Age 35–44	23.9%
Age 45–54	9.0%
Age 55–64	2.7%
Age 65 or Older	1.1%
Age unknown	1.9%

*Total is more than 100 percent because some children were reported for multiple types of abuse.

Source: Children's Bureau. (2017). *Child maltreatment 2015.* Washington, DC: U.S. Department of Health & Human Services, Administration for Children and Families, Administration on Children, Youth and Families, Author. Retrieved from http://www.acfhhs.gov/programs/cb/research-data-technology/statistics-research/child-maltreatment.

summarizes the demographic characteristics of students who are abused and the individuals who abuse them.

Some students who have been abused or neglected show visible signs, such as bruises, burns, and other untreated physical problems. They also might complain of hunger. Table 8.3 provides examples of student characteristics that might signal to school professionals the presence of abuse or neglect.

You should be aware that as a teacher, you have a legal and ethical obligation to report suspected child abuse of your students (Children's Bureau, 2016). Although the specific reporting requirements for teachers vary from state to state, federal law requires that every state maintain a hotline and other systems for reporting abuse, and every state has statutes that define abuse and neglect and establish reporting procedures. If you suspect that one of your students is being abused, you should follow your school district's procedures for reporting it. If you are unsure about those procedures, you should notify your principal, school social worker, or school nurse.

STUDENTS WHO LIVE WITH SUBSTANCE ABUSE OR ARE SUBSTANCE ABUSERS A third group of students at risk for school failure comprises those involved in substance abuse. Some students' parents have abused drugs and alcohol. The impact on students can begin before they are born and often affects them throughout their lives. Babies born to mothers who drink alcohol heavily during pregnancy may have a medical condition called fetal alcohol syndrome (FAS) or a milder form known as partial fetal alcohol syndrome (PFAS). Babies with FAS or PFAS are smaller than expected, may have facial and other slight physical abnormalities, and often experience learning and behavior problems when they go to school. The prevalence estimate for these disorders varies widely, but is estimated to be as high as 2 to 5 percent of all children (Centers for Disease Control and Prevention, 2017d). Some experts estimate that as many as two-thirds of all students receiving special education services for intellectual disabilities may be affected by

MyLab Education

Video Example 8.6: Mandated Reporting—PSA for Teachers
This public service announcement, recorded in California but relevant for all teachers, is a reminder about professionals' obligation to report suspected child abuse.
https://www.youtube.com/watch?v=nlr-n-wis4g

DIMENSIONS OF DIVERSITY

Girls are slightly more likely than boys to be the victims of child maltreatment, 51.1 percent versus 48.9 percent (Children's Bureau, 2017).

TABLE 8.3   **Characteristics of Students Who Are Abused or Neglected**

• Unexplained bruises and welts	• Unexplained fractures
• Unexplained lacerations or abrasions	• Unexplained black eyes
• Unusually high compliance or passivity	• Fear of parents or going home
• Unexplained absences	• Behavioral extremes such as aggression and withdrawal
• Unattended physical problems and medical needs	• Watchfulness, as waiting for something to happen
• Hunger	• Poor hygiene
• Inappropriate dress	• Begging for or stealing food
• Constant fatigue, or falling asleep in class	• Extended stays at school
• Reported lack of adult supervision	• Mentions abusing pets or other animals
• Difficulty walking or sitting	• Wariness of adults
• Pain or itching in the genital area	• Unwillingness to change for gym
• Disclosure of maltreatment	• Bizarre, sophisticated, or unusual sexual behavior or knowledge
• Poor peer relationships	

Source: Based on Children's Bureau. (2013, July). Factsheet: What is child abuse and neglect? Recognizing the signs and symptoms. Washington, DC: Child Welfare Information Gateway, Author. Retrieved from https://www.childwelfare.gov/pubpdfs/whatiscan.pdf.

these fetal alcohol syndrome disorders (FASDs) or other alcohol-related neuro-developmental disorders (ARND). Together, FAS and PFAS are considered the leading preventable cause of childhood intellectual impairment. Students with FASDs tend to display poor judgment, for example, leaving a situation when things do not go as planned or failing to predict the consequences of their behavior.

Another type of substance abuse concerns maternal drug abuse; babies born to mothers using drugs often are low in weight at birth. They also are likely to become overstimulated, which leads to an array of behaviors associated with irritability. When these children reach school age, they are likely to experience a wide variety of learning and behavior problems (Ross, Graham, Money, & Stanwood, 2015). Some are low achievers, and others may become eligible for special education services. These children may be inattentive, hyperactive, and impulsive (National Institute on Drug Abuse, 2011).

Researchers estimate that nearly one in four children grows up in a home in which alcohol or drugs are abused. These children are at risk because of a number of factors. For example, they are at risk for being neglected or abused. In homes in which drugs are abused, children may be passive recipients of drugs that can be inhaled, or they may accidentally ingest other drugs. Students who live in homes in which alcohol or drugs are abused often display at least several of the following characteristics at school (Solis, Shadur, Burns, & Hussong, 2012):

- Lack of trust of others
- Reluctance to learn from adults
- Difficulty understanding others' emotions
- Difficulty making and keeping friends
- Problems with social skills
- Anxiety
- Widely ranging behavior problems, including hyperactivity and impulsivity
- Poor academic achievement
- Evidence of neglect (e.g., clothing, food)

DIMENSIONS OF DIVERSITY

Students who identified themselves as lesbian, gay, bisexual, or transgendered (LGBT) were 3.3 times more likely than other students to think about suicide and 2 to 3 times as likely to attempt suicide, even when compared to students who had reported equivalent levels of bullying victimization but who were not LGBT (Centers for Disease Control and Prevention, 2017c; Robinson & Espelage, 2012).

A third group of students affected by substance abuse includes those who themselves abuse drugs or alcohol. Middle and high school students' use of some substances has been declining; in 2016, 5.4 percent of eighth graders, 9.8 percent of 10th graders, and 14.3 percent of 12th graders reported using an illicit drug (including cigarettes, alcohol, and marijuana). However, adolescents' perception of the potential harmful effects of drugs likewise is decreasing, a cause for alarm (National Institute on Drug Abuse, 2016). Other drugs abused include prescription-type drugs used nonmedically, e-cigarettes, opioids, inhalants, and hallucinogens. Most youth accessing these drugs obtain them for free from family members or friends. You should be aware that students with emotional disabilities are at particularly high risk for alcohol and drug abuse (National Institute on Drug Abuse, 2010). Further, students who are substance abusers often have poor diets and sleep disturbances, feel a great deal of stress, and are at risk for depression and suicide. In school, they typically recall only information taught while they are sober, interact poorly with peers and teachers, and display excessive risk-taking behaviors.

As you can see, students who live in poverty, who are abused or neglected, and who live with substance abuse, as well as other students at risk, collectively have many characteristics and needs that affect their learning. Although some of these students are resilient and do not suffer long-term consequences from their stressful lives (Bergmann & Brough, 2012; Luthar & Eisenberg, 2017), the majority do not thrive without the support of an understanding school system and knowledgeable and committed teachers.

Interventions for Students at Risk

As a teacher, you sometimes will be faced with the frustrating situation of not being able to relieve your students of the stresses that often prevent them from learning to their potential. You can offer these students a safe environment by providing clear expectations and instructional support, making school an important place in their lives.

Generally, recommendations for intervening to teach students at risk include four goals, none of which is completely unique to these students: Set high but realistic expectations, establish peers as teaching partners, collaborate with other professionals, and support family and community involvement. Each recommendation is discussed briefly here.

SET HIGH BUT REALISTIC EXPECTATIONS When you are teaching students who are at risk, it is tempting to make assumptions about how much they are capable of learning. For example, you might think that a student who does not have books at home and whose parents are either unable or unwilling to read with her is unlikely to be a successful learner. Having low expectations—even if you think they are justified—can lead to overusing teaching strategies that emphasize lower-level academic skills. Although systematic, explicit instruction in foundational academic skills plays a key role in educating students at risk, it must be balanced with other approaches. Students need to learn sophisticated thinking processes along with basic skills, and they need to learn to construct their own knowledge along with receiving it from you, an approach consistent with implementation of the contemporary academic standards.

Care must also be taken in how students who are at-risk are grouped for instruction. In some cases, students are appropriately grouped in their classes based on their need for instruction in specific skills; they also may be grouped this way for tiered instruction that is part of an RtI or MTSS model or as part of advanced classes in some secondary schools. However, you should be aware that grouping students for instruction by perceived ability, what many professionals refer to as *tracking*, can discriminate against students at risk by creating an environment characterized by low expectations (e.g., Umansky, 2016). Other grouping arrangements are needed as well. For example, a longitudinal study of student achievement in mathematics found that when students were heterogeneously grouped in middle school math classes, they took more math classes in high school and did better in whatever classes they took than did students who had been homogeneously grouped for math in middle school (Burris, Heubert, & Levin, 2006). As a teacher, you can ensure that you do not overuse any type of grouping in your classroom, and you can work with your colleagues to create a school in which students of many different abilities learn together.

One word of caution about setting standards is necessary: Some students who are at risk live in such high-stress situations outside school that they might not have much support from their parents and other family members for completing school assignments and homework. For example, one teacher described a high school student who always slept in class. In-school suspension did not help, nor did attempts to contact the student's parents. The teacher later learned that this student left school each day, cooked dinner for her younger siblings, and

RESEARCH-BASED PRACTICES

Murillo (2017) studied the conditions under which undocumented high school students reveal their status. He found that long-standing and trusting relationships with educators were critical, but he also noted that professionals were often uncertain about how to protect students once the information was shared.

When children live in difficult circumstances, they may be at a disadvantage in their readiness for learning and ability to focus on school tasks.

then worked at a fast-food restaurant until midnight. Having high expectations is important, but they need to be tempered with understanding of the circumstances in students' lives outside school.

Ultimately, effective instruction for students at risk includes the same strategies you would use for other students, with particular attention to the physical and social-emotional challenges these students often face. Students at risk need a structured learning environment, systematic instruction in basic skill areas, and strategies for learning independence, an approach to teaching described throughout this text.

ESTABLISH PEERS AS TEACHING PARTNERS Peers learning from one another is a strategy that was recommended earlier for students from diverse cultural and linguistic backgrounds; it is also useful for at-risk students. For example, Peer-Assisted Learning Strategies (PALS) is a highly structured classwide peer-tutoring program that has been used across all grade levels to improve outcomes in reading (e.g., McMaster & Fuchs, 2016). In this program, higher-achieving students are partnered with those who are struggling, and they learn specific ways to interact with each other and reinforce each other's reading skills. Research has demonstrated that most students improve in fluency and comprehension in a PALS program.

COLLABORATE WITH OTHER PROFESSIONALS A third strategy for teaching students who are at risk involves increasing your problem-solving capability by adding the skills and resources of your colleagues. Problem solving with your colleagues about at-risk students allows you to check your own perspectives against theirs, gain access to their expertise, and coordinate your efforts. For example, if you are teaching Shaneal, a student whom you suspect has been abused, you can first ask the counselor or social worker whether there is any past documentation of abuse and you can request that one of these professionals speak with the student. For students at risk who are struggling academically, the RtI or MTSS procedures now in place in most schools can help you in identifying and implementing effective instructional strategies.

SUPPORT FAMILY AND COMMUNITY INVOLVEMENT It is essential that you maintain positive contact with parents and other caregivers of your at-risk students, just as you would with other students. However, the level of participation you can expect will vary considerably. Some parents will be anxious to ensure that their children have all the advantages an education can give them, and they will do all they can to assist you in teaching. Parents who are struggling themselves, however, probably should not be expected to participate in a traditional way in their children's education. To involve families and communities in their children's education, you might try several ideas. Sometimes it might be more appropriate to require a student to bring to school something personally important from home and to base an assignment on that, rather than to assign more traditional homework. It also can be helpful to assist parents in connecting with community resources such as health clinics and social service agencies. One school district that was struggling because of the rapidly increasing number of at-risk students worked with local religious leaders to connect families with resources and improve the communication between school personnel and families.

When you think about the diversity of students you may teach, it is easy to become overwhelmed by the challenge of meeting all students' instructional needs. Classrooms designed to celebrate diversity, rather than treat it as a deficiency or an exception, are classrooms that blend structure and flexibility and provide many options for learning.

WRAPPING IT UP

Back to the Cases

Now that you have read about students with special needs other than disabilities, look back at the teacher stories at the beginning of the chapter. Then go to MyLab Education to apply the knowledge you've gained in this chapter to each case.

MyLab Education Application Exercise 8.1: Case Study 8.1

ZHANG WEI'S story illustrates the fact that many students in today's schools have complex histories and may face multiple challenges. Think about the possibility of Zhang Wei being one of your students.

MyLab Education Application Exercise 8.2: Case Study 8.2

JACKSON, as you may recall, is having a difficult time in middle school, struggling with the large and more complex setting and concerned about the attention he draws to himself.

MyLab Education Application Exercise 8.3: Case Study 8.3

LYDIA, as you may remember, has special talents and academic ability. However, her family is very concerned that she is not getting appropriate opportunities to use her talents and academic ability.

MyLab Education Application Exercise 8.4: Case Study 8.4

TAM, a junior in high school, doubts that he will finish the school year, is often absent, does not complete assignments, and does not participate in any extracurricular activities. He has a juvenile record, is on probation for stealing a car, and is considering an offer to distribute drugs. Tam's teachers describe him as "unmotivated," but they also add that he is a student who has vastly more potential than they see him using.

Summary

LO 8.1 Some students receive specialized services through Section 504, federal legislation requiring that accommodations be provided by general educators to students who have functional disabilities (e.g., physical or medical conditions, significant learning needs) that limit their access to an education.

LO 8.2 One specific group of students who receive Section 504 assistance comprises those with attention deficit–hyperactivity disorder (ADHD), a medically diagnosed disorder characterized by chronic and severe inattention and/or hyperactivity–impulsivity. Students with ADHD may receive a variety of academic, behavior, and environmental interventions; training to assist their parents in understanding and responding to their needs; and medication.

LO 8.3 Students who are gifted and talented include those with generally high intellectual ability as well as those with talents in specific areas such as music. The interventions used most often to help them achieve school success are curriculum compacting, enrichment and acceleration, differentiation, and individualized interventions.

LO 8.4 Students from culturally and linguistically diverse backgrounds and their families sometimes have values that differ from those represented in U.S. schools. Teachers need to learn about students' cultures, teach in a manner that is responsive to those cultures, and acknowledge and value diverse cultures in the classroom in order to teach students from these backgrounds effectively.

LO 8.5 Students at risk for school failure because of environmental influences such as poverty, child abuse, and drug addiction also have special needs. Because students at risk often live in unpredictable and stressful environments, strategies for teaching them include setting appropriate expectations, establishing peers as teaching partners, collaborating with other professionals, and working closely with families and community members. Any student with a disability may also be a student at risk or have any of the other special needs outlined in this chapter.

APPLICATIONS IN TEACHING PRACTICE
Diversity in a High School Class

Ivan Robinson is a first-year teacher in a large urban school district. Although it is only the fourth week of school, he is concerned. He is confident of his knowledge of the curriculum as well as his teaching skills and he feels he has a strong commitment to teaching all the students assigned to him, but he is worried that he won't be able to meet the vast and diverse array of needs represented among his students. For example, Thuan, who just immigrated to the United States from Vietnam, speaks very little English and seems overwhelmed by nearly everything at school. Mr. Robinson can't recall ever seeing Thuan smile. Whatever topic Mr. Robinson discusses, he knows that much of the information is beyond Thuan's understanding because of language differences and that Thuan does not have the context for grasping many of the topics that are central to the curriculum. But a decision was made that Thuan should participate in Mr. Robinson's class, and so he is trying to find out how to best reach him.

Then there is Sonny. Sonny is supposed to be taking medication for ADHD, but it doesn't seem to be having the intended effect on him. At an after-school meeting, Mr. Robinson, the school psychologist, the counselor, and the assistant principal discussed the matter with Sonny, and it was noted that Sonny recently had decided he had outgrown the need for medication and sometimes was not taking it. Sonny did say, though, that a few times he decided to catch up by taking a double dose. The counselor is supposed to follow up on this unhealthy and potentially dangerous thinking about medication and keep Mr. Robinson informed. In the meantime, Sonny is in his class and, as Mr. Robinson puts it, is either "bouncing off the walls or zoned out."

Jenny is a concern as well. She and her twin sister, Jenna, are struggling academically despite receiving a lot of individual attention and having supportive parents. Neither girl's reading comprehension is strong. Both girls have been referred in the past for special education services, but neither is eligible to receive them. Mr. Robinson knows that the twins' father has been out of work for nearly a year, that the girls generally have little supervision after school, and that the family is barely getting by on donations from friends and their church. Mr. Robinson heard last week that one of the grandparents had also come to live with the family. He wonders how much of the twins' learning problems are related to their home situation.

Mr. Robinson also teaches Kimberly, who just moved into the district and is so far ahead of the other students that Mr. Robinson finds her just a bit intimidating. Two other students, Lisa and Paul, are from families that have very little; they come to school without supplies and seem reluctant to interact with the other students. And there are yet other students in his class who face challenges he knows he does not understand, from violence in their neighborhoods to homelessness to gang influence.

As he reflects on his class, Mr. Robinson realizes that more than half of the students have a special need of one kind or another, and he suspects that he knows only a fraction of their life stories. He wants to reach them all and truly make a difference in their lives, but he is not sure he can accomplish his goal.

QUESTIONS

Before you answer the following questions, place Mr. Robinson and his students in a grade level that you might teach, whether elementary, middle, or high school. After responding, discuss with your classmates what is similar across the school levels and what is different.

1. How typical is the composition of Mr. Robinson's class? What other types of diverse needs might you expect to be represented in a class you will teach?

2. What general strategies might Mr. Robinson use in his class that would benefit many students with special needs and harm none?

3. For each student with special needs Mr. Robinson has identified, consider how the INCLUDE strategy could be used. Fill in the following chart, perhaps working with a classmate to generate ideas for information not specifically outlined in the preceding student descriptions. Be sure to address academic, social-emotional, behavioral, and medical-physical needs.

	Thuan	Jenny and Jenna	Kimberly	Sonny	Lisa and Paul
Identify					
Note					
Check					
Look					
Use					
Decide					
Evaluate					

4. Mr. Settle is the special educator with whom Mr. Robinson works. What is Mr. Settle's role in assisting Mr. Robinson and other teachers in the school to meet the diverse needs of students, including those who do not have IEPs? Who else might assist Mr. Robinson as he designs instruction and plans how to help his students succeed?

5. How might Mr. Robinson work with the parents of his students to help ensure their needs are addressed?

What barriers might he encounter and how might he address them? What inadvertent biases could he have toward his students' families? How could these biases relate to your own views as a novice educator?

6. What realistic expectations can Mr. Robinson set for himself as a teacher for this school year?

CHAPTER 9

Adjusting Instruction

LEARNING OUTCOMES

After you read this chapter, you will be able to:

9-1 Analyze your basic skills instruction and describe how you can adjust it for students with disabilities and other special needs.

9-2 Analyze your content-area lessons and explain how you can make them more accessible.

9-3 Analyze and adjust independent practice activities for students.

9-4 Describe strategies for involving parents in teaching their children.

9-5 Analyze your classroom materials and activities and describe how you can modify them for students with moderate to severe intellectual disabilities.

MS. DOMANSKI is excited to teach in a fifth-grade inclusive classroom this year. Her principal told her that she would have students with high-incidence disabilities included in her class. Ms. Domanski thought they would all be about the same academically because they were all from the high-incidence group. She is finding, though, that the students are very different. Carmen, a quiet student, has a specific learning disability in reading. She reads so haltingly that she is embarrassed to read out loud in class. Her slow reading makes it hard for her to keep up with her assignments. Abdul has experienced some difficulties with math since he entered the second grade. He has trouble learning new skills unless he is given many opportunities for instruction and practice. His frequent outbursts when frustrated have affected his learning in other subjects as well. Ms. Domanski feels unsure of how to address the needs of not only these students but other students with special needs in the class, such as Albert. Albert has attention deficit–hyperactivity disorder (ADHD). He struggles with independent activities. As a result, he complains constantly about not knowing what to do, and during independent work time, he wanders around the class either getting help from other students or bothering them. Ms. Domanski is constantly on edge worrying about not embarrassing Carmen, when the next emotional outburst may erupt from Abdul, or Albert preventing other students from getting their work done. Ms. Domanski is eager to make the necessary adjustments to her instruction and create an environment in which all of her students can be successful but finds this difficult, given the different levels and problems of all the students in the room.

How can Ms. Domanski adjust her instruction for Abdul, Carmen, and Albert while still meeting the needs of the rest of her class? How might instruction for each of these students need to be different? What strategies could Ms. Domanski use that might facilitate learning for all of them?

When **MR. REEVES** found out about his incoming ninth-grade English class, he learned it was very diverse. Out of a class of 25 students, three had learning disabilities in reading and three others also struggled with reading even though they did not have disabilities. On top of that, two additional students were English learners. Although the English learners could identify words at grade level, they had trouble understanding what they read because of limited vocabulary. The principal is concerned about all of these students meeting state standards requiring that students comprehend increasingly complex text.

How can students' reading needs be addressed as they progress past the grade levels where reading instruction is a focus? What are "workaround" strategies that can assist students when text they must read is above their reading level? How will Mr. Reeves be able to meet the needs of such a broad range of students?

CHARLIE is a fifth-grade student in Ms. Fain's class who has been diagnosed with an emotional/behavioral disability and a specific learning disability. Charlie struggles mightily in math and has difficulty coping with his emotions. Charlie often exhibits disruptive behaviors in math class as he becomes frustrated when he cannot compute and solve problems like everyone else. He usually says, "I am a dummy!" and may tear up his paper and refuse to do work. Charlie has a behavior intervention plan that aims to decrease his outbursts in class.

What might be the relationship between Charlie's behavior and his academic performance? What are ways to address challenges students face in mathematics? How can Ms. Fain adjust her instruction to help Charlie become more confident and successful in her math class?

FYI

This chapter presents instructional adjustments for steps 5 and 6 of the INCLUDE strategy presented in Chapter 5:

Step 5 Use information from steps 1–4 to brainstorm ways to adjust instruction.

Step 6 Adjust instruction.

As you have already learned, the curriculum methods and materials teachers use have a strong influence on how readily students learn in the classroom. In fact, the better the materials and the teaching, the fewer the individual adjustments required for students with special needs. However, for a variety of reasons, you may not have control over the materials used in your school. Furthermore, despite your best teaching efforts, some students will still need support in order to gain access to important skills and content. For example, in the cases just described, Ms. Domanski stopped calling on Carmen to read out loud in class until she showed improvement in her reading fluency from the fluency training program being carried out by her special education teacher. Ms. Domanski paired Abdul with a study buddy who provided extra instruction for Abdul and helped him with his independent work. For Albert, Ms. Domanski made sure all directions were clearly written using words he could identify; she also gave directions for independent activities orally, guiding students through several practice examples before they were required to work independently, and she broke his assignments into several shorter activities. Most importantly, she checked to be sure that Albert had the academic skills necessary to complete the assignments independently. Ms. Domanski found that these strategies for adjusting instruction for her students with special needs helped her other students as well.

Mr. Reeves was teaching in a high school that was using response to intervention (RtI)/multiple systems of support (MTSS). He arranged for his English learners to get extra help on the meaning of upcoming vocabulary in his Tier 2 group. In class, he set up a small group that met as needed to review the pronunciations and meanings of key vocabulary prior to a section of text being assigned. This group, conducted alternately by Mr. Reeves and his co-teacher, helped both the English learners and other struggling readers in class. The students with learning disabilities were receiving instruction in reading decoding and fluency from their special education teacher. In the meantime, Mr. Reeves arranged for them to have taped texts of all of the novels to be read. Ms. Fain found extra help in math computation for Charlie in a Tier 2/RtI /MTSS group, and, to relieve the pressure on him when solving word problems in class, allowed Charlie to use a calculator until his math computation skills showed signs of improving.

The purpose of this chapter is to provide you with strategies for adjusting instruction by making changes in curriculum materials, teacher instruction, grouping, and student practice activities that are reasonable to carry out and increase the likelihood of success for students with disabilities. Remember, nearly all students with disabilities included in your classroom are expected to meet the same curricular goals as their classmates without disabilities. Therefore, most of the strategies for adjusting instruction covered in this chapter consist of supports that allow students to more readily access the general education curriculum. In addition, with RtI/MTSS being used in many schools, changes in instruction can also be carried out using more intensive instructional tiers. For example, the English learners in Mr. Reyes's class received extra vocabulary help in a Tier 2 group, while the students with learning disabilities received intensive help in word decoding and fluency in a Tier 3 reading group. Charlie, in Ms. Fain's class, received extra help with math computation in a Tier 2 math group.

INCLUDE

It is also important to note that the instructional adjustments described in this chapter can sometimes be carried out with your entire class. At other times, they might be presented for individual students or as a part of small groups. The way you choose to accommodate your students with special needs depends on classroom demands, the characteristics of individual students, and the overall level of functioning of your class. For example, in the case of Abdul, Ms. Domanski paired him with a peer to provide more direct instruction and practice because she had determined that the rest of the class did not need more guidance in the large group, and she decided that working with a classmate would be motivating for Abdul while also providing him with a good model of social behavior. If Ms. Domanski had had many other students in class struggling to learn new math concepts, she could have provided more guided practice in the large group or formed a small group to provide students who needed it with extra help. Mr. Reeves conducted a small-group vocabulary session for some of his students lacking background knowledge and provided his students with learning disabilities with assistive technology to allow them to bypass their word reading and fluency problems. Ms. Fain found extra math help for Charlie in a Tier 2 group and allowed him to bypass his difficulty with math computation when solving word problems by using a calculator. You can use the INCLUDE strategy to help you make decisions about the best way to make adjustments in your teaching for your students with special needs.

⟨ INCLUDE ⟩

As you learned in Chapter 5, and shown in Figure 9.1, adjusting your instruction involves meeting students' diverse needs by making changes to the content being taught, the process by which it is taught, and the ways students demonstrate what they have learned through products. Chapters 4 and 11 in this book describe how teachers can evaluate what students have learned by making adjustments in how students demonstrate their learning. Generally speaking, the

FIGURE 9.1 **Adjusting Instruction**

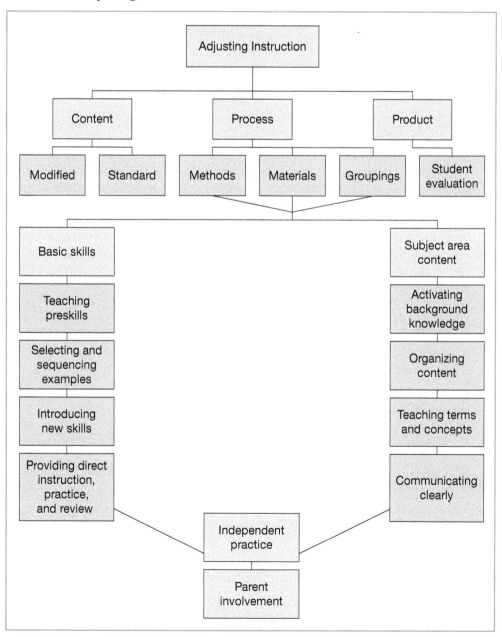

content expectations for most students with disabilities are the same as those for their peers without disabilities, although some students with learning and behavior problems may be performing well below grade level and may need to be working intensively out of level to fill in gaps in their foundational knowledge. For example, Cal is a fifth grader with learning disabilities who is reading at the second-grade level. He is in an intensive Tier 3 reading group for 60 minutes each day in an attempt to catch him up with his classmates. He participates in the vocabulary and comprehension parts of his classroom reading program by listening. His teacher has obtained audio texts for him to use in science and social studies.

The focus of this chapter is on making changes we call adjustments to the instructional process. As shown in Figure 9.1, the instructional process includes your classroom teaching methods, materials, and grouping arrangements. Strategies for adjusting instruction in basic skills are described in the first section, followed by making changes to content instruction and independent practice. Ways to involve parents in their children's education are also described. Finally, strategies for making appropriate instructional modifications are covered at the end of this chapter. As you learned in Chapters 5 and 6, instructional modifications are used for students who have more significant disabilities and who have alternative curricula (but aligned with the general curriculum) as specified on their individualized education programs (IEPs).

How Can You Make Instructional Adjustments for Students with Special Needs in Basic Skills?

Basic skills instruction means primarily instruction in the academic skills of reading, writing, and math. However, you may also apply effective principles for adjusting basic skills instruction to content areas such as science and social studies. Prior to teaching any basic skills lesson, ask yourself the questions shown in Figure 9.2. These questions reflect four essential aspects of basic skills instruction for which you may need to make adjustments for students with disabilities: preskills; the selection and sequencing of examples; the rate of introduction of new skills; and direct instruction, practice, and review. While focusing on these aspects of your teaching is relevant for all of your students, it is especially critical for students with special needs who, in the absence of careful consideration in one or more of these areas, are much less likely to acquire a foundational repertoire of basic academic skills.

Teaching Preskills

Darrell is in Ms. Rayburn's second-grade class. In language arts, he is experiencing a problem common to many students with special needs. On Tuesday, Darrell was at his desk reading a book on his favorite topic: magic. However, when Ms. Rayburn asked Darrell specific questions about the book, he was unable to

FIGURE 9.2 **Questions to Ask Yourself When Planning Basic Skills Instruction**

Do some of my students need to review lesson *preskills*? Are any students so lacking in *preskills* that they need out-of-level, intensive instruction in key foundational skills?

Do I need to adjust my *teaching examples* to clarify my instruction for some of my students?

Do I need to adjust the rate at which I introduce skills for some of my students?

Do I need to adjust the amount of *direct instruction, practice,* and *review* to assure that all of my students acquire and retain basic reading, writing, and math skills?

answer them. It turned out that Darrell was unable to identify most of the words in the book and was just pretending to read. Another student, Tamika, is in Mr. Thomas's Algebra 1 class. She is having difficulty solving basic equations with one unknown because she has yet to master basic math computational skills.

Preskills are basic skills necessary for performing more complex skills. A key aspect of effective inclusive teaching is that prior to teaching a skill, you should assess students on the relevant preskills and, if necessary, teach these skills. Darrell was unable to comprehend the book about magic because he lacked the word identification skills needed to read the words. He may need foundational instruction in basic word attack skills; he may also need to be encouraged to read trade books at his reading level. Tamika needs additional instruction and practice on her computational skills if she is going to be successful in Algebra 1. Because textbooks do not generally list preskills, you need to ask yourself continually what preskills are required, and you should be vigilant in identifying students who lack them. Some examples of preskills are shown in Figure 9.3. Looking at the instructional demands in this way is a key part of applying the INCLUDE strategy. Determining the potential impact of student preskills on instruction may mean informally assessing such skills using curriculum-based assessments like those you learned about in Chapter 4.

If you are teaching a skill and find that most of your students lack the necessary preskills, teach these preskills directly before teaching the more complex skill. If only one or two students lack preskills, you can accommodate them with extra practice and instruction through a peer or parent volunteer or with the help of a special service provider or paraprofessional. For example, Ms. Cooper was preparing a lesson on how to find the perimeter of a rectangle. Before beginning the lesson, she gave her students an addition probe and found that almost half the class was still having problems with basic addition facts. Ms. Cooper set up a peer-tutoring program in which students who knew their facts were paired with students who did not; the pairs practiced facts for 10 minutes each day for a week. Students who preferred to work alone practiced their math facts using a drill-and-practice computer-based program. Ms. Cooper still introduced finding the perimeter of rectangles as scheduled, but she allowed students to use calculators, a bypass strategy, until they had mastered their facts. As noted earlier in the chapter, you may have some students performing at a skill level so low that it precludes success in the current skill being taught. These students likely need more intensive, out-of-level instruction in a Tier 3, RtI/MTSS group or special education setting with the sole purpose of catching them up so they can meet the standards of the general education curriculum.

INCLUDE

FYI

Assessing student preskills does not always have to be done using paper-and-pencil tasks. Simply beginning each lesson with a brief oral review takes less time and can give you relevant information immediately. Preskills can also be checked through brief morning work (elementary), warm up activities (middle and high school), or by using apps such as Kahoot (https://kahoot.it/#/) and Quizlet (https://quizlet.com).

FIGURE 9.3 Examples of Preskills

SKILL TO BE TAUGHT	PRESKILLS OF CONCERN
2-digit by 1 digit division with remainder	X facts 2 digit by 2 digit subtraction
Summarize paragraph	Read paragraph accurately and fluently Identify main idea and details
Find area of rectangle	Concepts of rectangle, area, and sides 2-digit by 2-digit multiplication
Find meaning of term using Wikipedia	Use search engine Comprehend Wikipedia entry
Determine when to end sentence with an exclamation point	Use periods and question marks
X2 multiplication facts	Number concepts Count by 2s

Adapted from: Archer, A. L., & Hughes, C. A. (2011). *Explicit instruction: Effective and efficient teaching.* New York: Guilford Press.

Selecting and Sequencing Examples

INCLUDE

The way you select and sequence instructional examples also can affect how easily your students learn (Gersten et al, 2009; Koellner, Colsman & Risley, 2014). For example, Alex's practice activities for a week in Mr. Huang's third-grade math class are shown in Figure 9.4. Mr. Huang has been covering two-digit subtraction with regrouping. On Monday and Tuesday, Alex was given five of these problems and got them all right. On Wednesday, he was asked to do a mixture of problems, some requiring regrouping and some not. Alex got only three of the problems correct because he was unable to discriminate between subtraction problems that required regrouping and those that did not. He was unable to differentiate these two types of problems in part because his daily practice pages had included only one problem type and, by so doing, did not require him to attend to the most important attribute of the problems; namely, whether or not to regroup based on the numbers in the ones column. Carefully adjusting the example selection you use for instruction and student practice can help students learn to tell the difference among problem types more readily.

You can help students make key discriminations between current and previous problem types by using examples that at first require the application of only one particular skill (Carnine, Silbert, Kame'enui, & Tarver, 2010). When students can perform these problems without error, add examples of skills previously taught to help students discriminate between the different problem types. Doing this also provides students with needed review. An easy adjustment for Alex would have been to add several problems that did not require regrouping to each daily teaching and practice session once he had demonstrated that he could compute the regrouping problems accurately when they were presented alone. An additional advantage of this type of adjustment is that it will likely help other students in class as well.

Ms. Owens ran into a different example-related problem when teaching her students word problems in math. In her examples, when a word problem included the word *more*, getting the correct answer always involved subtracting, as in the following problem:

> Alicia had 22 pennies. Juanita had 13. How many more pennies does Alicia have than Juanita?

However, on her test, Ms. Owens included the following problem:

> Mark read 3 books in March. He read 4 more books in April. How many books did Mark read?

FIGURE 9.4 **Alex's Math Work**

Monday's Seatwork

2 1	3 1	2 1	3 1	6 1
3̸5	4̸2	3̸8	4̸1	7̸4
−17	−15	−19	−22	−49
18	27	19	19	25

Tuesday's Seatwork

5 1	6 1	8 1	5 1	7 1
6̸4	7̸0	9̸1	6̸8	82
−38	−32	−58	−39	−28
26	38	33	29	54

Wednesday's Seatwork

8 1	3 1	7 1	5 1	6 1
9̸6	4̸3	8̸9	6̸7	7̸5
−53	−18	−33	−28	−57
313	25	416	39	18

Several students with special needs in Ms. Owens's class subtracted 3 from 4 because they thought the presence of the word *more* signaled subtraction. Ms. Owens needed to anticipate the likelihood that some of her students would draw the wrong conclusion from her teaching and include problems of this latter type to prevent such misconceptions from occurring.

Consider this example: When Mr. Yoshida taught his students how to add –*ed* to a word ending in *y*, he demonstrated on the board as follows:

carry + ed = carried   hurry + ed = hurried

Next, Mr. Yoshida had his students add –*ed* to five words ending in *y*. Finally, he assigned students 10 practice problems in their English books that looked like this:

Write the past tense of *marry.*

A number of students were unable to answer the questions in the book, even though they knew how to add −*ed* to words ending in *y*, because the practice examples in the book required students to know the meaning of "past tense" and how to form the past tense by adding −*ed*. The book's practice activity was very different from the instructional examples Mr. Yoshida used, which only required students to add −*ed* to words ending in *y*.

Both Ms. Owens's and Mr. Yoshida's examples demonstrate an important aspect of selecting instructional examples: The range of your instructional examples should match the range of the problem types used when you assess student learning. Ms. Owens could have prevented problems in her class by expanding the range of her examples to include word problems that contained the word *more* but were not solved by subtracting. Mr. Yoshida could have better prepared his students for the practice activities in the English book by using examples that referred directly to forming the past tense by adding −*ed*. Note that some students with special needs still may struggle even when appropriate instructional examples are used. These students may require an individual adjustment that could be as simple as a reminder that the word *more* can have more than one meaning or that the past tense is formed by adding −*ed* to a verb. Or the adjustment could be as involved as providing additional instruction using multimedia to present, more dynamically, concrete representations of the different meanings of *more* or verbs ending in −*ed*. Finally, drawing upon what you have already learned, adjustments could involve teaching the preskills of understanding past tense and performing basic subtraction computations if the teachers had checked these skills prior to instruction and found the students lacking in them.

The following shows a different example selection problem. Tawana's class was learning several high-frequency sight words that appeared in their classroom reading program. On Wednesday, Tawana learned the word *man*, but on Thursday, after the word *men* was presented, she was unable to read *man* correctly. Tawana's word identification problem illustrates another example selection problem, namely, **example sequencing**. The visual and auditory similarities of *man* and *men* make learning these words difficult for many students who are at risk and students with learning disabilities, who may have trouble differentiating words that look and/or sound the same. One way to prevent this problem is to separate the introduction of *man* and *men* by introducing other dissimilar high-frequency words, such as *dog, house*, and *cat*. Students with special needs also may need adjustments to your instruction such as more practice learning the words, highlighting the differences by color coding the vowels *a* and *e*, and making the activity multisensory by having students spell the two words using letter blocks.

This same sequencing idea can be applied to teaching letter sounds. For example, when deciding on the order in which to teach the sounds, consider separating letters that look and sound the same, such as *b* and *d, m* and *n*, and *p* and *b*. The careful sequencing of instruction can also be applied to teaching higher-level content. For example, when Mr. Roosevelt, a chemistry teacher, taught the

DIMENSIONS OF DIVERSITY

Richards-Tutor, Baker, Gersten, Baker, and Smith (2016) reviewed studies examining the effectiveness of reading interventions with English learners. The researchers found that providing explicit instruction using published intervention programs was most effective. Group size and minutes of intervention were NOT significant predictors of outcomes.

INCLUDE

chemical elements, he separated those symbols that look and/or sound similar, such as bromine (Br) and rubidium (Rb), and silicon (Si) and strontium (Sr). Knowledge of how sequencing can affect learning can help you recognize the need to adjust instruction. For example, Ms. Mann, unlike Mr. Roosevelt, was unable to change the order in which she taught the chemical elements without drastically modifying her chemistry text. When she noticed that bromine and rubidium were taught closely together, she allowed more time for students to practice in their study groups before introducing another element.

Deciding the Rate of Introduction of New Skills

Students with special needs sometimes have difficulty learning skills that are introduced at too fast a rate. For example, Mr. Henry was teaching his ninth-grade English students how to proofread rough drafts of their writing for errors in using capital letters and punctuation marks. He reviewed the rules for using capital letters, periods, commas, question marks, and exclamation points. Next, he had students take out their most recent writing samples from their portfolios to look for capitalization and punctuation errors. Carmine found that he had left out capital letters at the beginnings of two sentences, but he did not find any of the punctuation errors he had made. A number of other students in the class had the same problem. The issue was that Mr. Henry had taught his students to proof-read their papers for capital letters and punctuation marks simultaneously. A better pace might have been first to work on proofreading for capitalization errors and then to add one punctuation mark at a time (first periods; then periods and *commas*; followed by periods, commas, and *question marks*; and concluding with periods, commas, question marks, and *exclamation points*). Of course, some students may still struggle with punctuation and may require adjustments such as a "cheat sheet" of punctuation rules taped to their desks and extra instruction before or after school, and/or additional small-group practice.

INCLUDE

In another example of the **rate of skill introduction**, Ms. Stevens was working on reading comprehension with her students. She introduced three new comprehension strategies at once: detecting the sequence, determining cause and effect, and making predictions. However, when applying the INCLUDE strategy using results from her universal screening measure, she recognized that Carlos, a student with a mild intellectual disability, learned best when he was taught one strategy at a time. Ms. Stevens adjusted Carlos's instruction by forming a small group with three other students who, like Carlos, would benefit from learning these comprehension strategies one by one before being asked to carry them out simultaneously. She taught the group, starting with instruction on detecting the sequence. She learned about this strategy from Mr. Wallace, her special education co-teacher. You can learn more about working with special education teachers in the Working Together feature.

These examples demonstrate an important principle about introducing new skills when you have students with special needs in your class: New skills should be introduced systematically, in small steps, and at a rate slow enough to ensure mastery before teaching more new skills. Further, you may want to prioritize skills and even postpone some, as Ms. Stevens did. In the end, failing to stress mastery of foundational skills early on by moving students through the curriculum too quickly can cause them to fall farther behind. Still, given the current atmosphere of accountability in our schools, it is often hard for teachers to slow down the rate at which they introduce new information for fear they will be unable to cover all the material that will appear on high-stakes tests. Although covering content efficiently is an important consideration, learning is usually best served when teachers carefully construct a foundation of skills and concepts based on student performance rather than on the school calendar. When you find yourself ambivalent about whether to move to the next skill, ask yourself whether it is just a small group of students not ready to move on, or a significant

WORKING TOGETHER 9.1
Asking for Help

Ms. Gabriel is starting her first year as a high school history teacher. She just found out that she will have four students with disabilities included in her fifth-period U.S. history class. The special education teacher, Mr. Colbert, left the students' "IEPs at a Glance" in her mailbox with a brief note asking her to look them over to see what kinds of accommodations she is required to make in her teaching. The IEPs state that she is supposed to adapt their homework assignments and textbook.

Ms. Gabriel is confused. In the first place, she is unsure exactly what an *accommodation* is. Second, she is concerned about the IEP accommodation that the amount of homework for the students with disabilities be reduced. She's particularly worried because this accommodation involves homework. She knows students won't like it if they know that other students are doing less homework. Ms. Gabriel feels that Mr. Colbert should have met with her to explain more clearly what she needed to do. Still, she is new

to the school and is afraid to admit she doesn't know what to do. Mr. Colbert is also the wrestling coach, and Ms. Gabriel doesn't feel very comfortable communicating with him.

- How could Ms. Gabriel request a meeting with Mr. Colbert while at the same time setting a positive tone for working together?
- What communication strategies can Ms. Gabriel employ at the meeting to both get the information she needs and establish a good working relationship with Mr. Colbert in the future?

What questions should Ms. Gabriel employ during the meeting? Make a list of these and compare them with classmates' lists, deciding on those that are most likely to lead to getting the needed information and creatively addressing the accommodations written on the students' IEPs.

- In what other ways might Mr. Colbert be helpful to Ms. Gabriel?

---

portion of the class. If it is a significant portion of your class, you are better off re-teaching for mastery before moving on. If only small numbers of students are having difficulty, provide them with extra instruction in a small group while the rest of the class is working independently. Of course, this grouping strategy can be more readily attained if you share teaching responsibilities with a co-teacher. It is also important to realize that some students, while in general education most of the time, could be receiving this kind of foundational instruction in a special education setting, and, if so, close communication relative to such issues would be extremely important.

Slowing down the rate of skills introduced is an adjustment in the way curriculum is presented, but it is not the same thing as reducing the amount of curriculum to be learned. You need to be careful not to lower the expectations for your students with special needs who are expected to meet the goals of the general education curriculum. Otherwise, they will have difficulty meeting state standards. However, for your students with moderate to severe intellectual disabilities, it may be appropriate to make an instructional modification by decreasing the amount of curriculum. For example, Ms. Evers modified Robin's curriculum by shortening her spelling lists from 15 to 3 words and selecting only high-frequency words as specified on her IEP. Strategies for making modifications for students with moderate to severe intellectual disabilities are covered in the final section of the chapter.

Providing Direct Instruction and Opportunities for Practice and Review

In Chapter 5 you read about a teaching practice called *direct instruction*, a systematic and explicit way of teaching basic skills that also includes considerable practice and review. Students who are at risk or have disabilities may require more direct instruction if they are to acquire basic academic skills. Consider the following example: Youn is in Ms. Howard's class. On Monday, Ms. Howard gave students a pretest on the 15 new spelling words for the week. On Tuesday, the students were required to use each word in a sentence. On Wednesday, the teacher scrambled up the letters in all the words and had the students put them in the correct order. On Thursday, students answered 15 fill-in-the-blank

RESEARCH-BASED PRACTICES

Joseph and colleagues (2012) reviewed the literature on a self-guided teaching practice called cover-copy-compare, a technique used most frequently in spelling and math. Cover-copy-compare requires students to view an academic stimulus such as a spelling word, cover it, copy it, and then compare it to the original. Joseph and others found considerable evidence for the effectiveness of this study strategy.

questions, each of which required one of the new spelling words. On Friday, Youn failed her spelling test even though she had successfully completed all the spelling activities for that week. Youn performed poorly because the daily spelling activities did not provide her with enough direct instruction and practice on the spelling words. Although activities such as using spelling words in sentences are valuable in the right context, they do not provide practice on the primary objective of this particular lesson, which is spelling all 15 words correctly from dictation. One way to adjust Youn's instruction would be to have a peer tutor give her a daily dictation test on all 15 words; have Youn write each missed word three times, saying each letter in the word as she writes; and then retest her on all 15 words again. Additional practice could also be provided using a drill and practice computer software program. It may also be helpful to introduce fewer words at a time, adding more words as words are mastered based on daily mini-spelling tests. Of course, it may also be beneficial to teach Youn basic strategies for spelling regular and irregular words.

This example demonstrates another problem that students with special needs have when learning basic skills: retention. Melissa had mastered addition facts with sums to 10 as measured by a probe test in October, but when she was given the same test in January, she got only half of the facts correct. Similarly, Thomas, in his civics class, could define the equal protection clause of the Constitution in November, but he could not remember what it was when asked to define it in February. A common way to adjust your instruction for such students is to schedule more review for them. This review should be more frequent following your initial presentation of the material and then can become less frequent as learning is established. For example, instead of waiting until January to review addition facts, Melissa's teacher could first provide review weekly, then every other week, and then every month. Thomas's civics teacher could periodically review key concepts and information that Thomas may need to apply later, either through homework, a learning center activity, an instructional game or contest, or a class-opening warm-up bell ringer activity. If Thomas and Melissa were the only ones in their classes in need of review, their teachers could accommodate them individually by giving them extra help before school or an alternative assignment during independent work time. The teacher or co-teacher could also operate a "flashback" or review station, sometimes with all students participating, sometimes with only the students needing review participating.

A related concern is that teaching approaches that are indirect and provide little practice may be appropriate for some students but may need to be supplemented for others. For example, Felix and Bill were learning to read in Ms. Farrell's class. Neither boy had learned the *ch* sound (as in *chin*). On Monday, Felix came across the word *chair* in a trade book he was reading. His teacher pronounced the word and said, "That sound at the beginning of *chair* is the same sound you hear at the beginning of *cherry*." The next day, Felix came to the word *chip* in his book, and he figured it out; he remembered what Ms. Farrell had told him the day before and was able to make the connection between the beginning sound in the orally presented word *cherry*, and the *ch* in *chair*, and then *chip*. For Felix, one example in his book and a brief teacher explanation were enough for learning to occur. On Monday, Bill also came across a *ch* word, and he too was told what the word was and that it began with the same sound as the word *cherry*. Unlike Felix, however, when Bill came across another *ch* word the next day, he could not remember the sound of these letters. Having the teacher tell him another word that *ch* began with was too indirect; he needed the teacher to say, "The sound of *ch* is /ch/. What's the sound of *ch*?" In addition, one practice example was not enough. Bill required more direct instruction and practice than did Felix, such as that provided in the activity shown in Table 9.1. Note also how the teacher built review into each part of the lesson to ensure student retention.

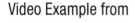

Video Example from

MyLab Education

Video Example 9.1: Classwide Peer Tutoring

Watch how you can increase direct instruction and practice through the use of peer tutors. https://www .youtube.com/watch?v=aeAjkTbyZyk

TABLE 9.1   **Direct Instruction of *ch* Sound**

Objective	After seeing a new letter combination, students will say its sound with 100 percent accuracy.
Materials Needed	Board, chart paper, Smartboard, or overhead transparency.
	Write the letter combinations that will be reviewed with the new letter combination. Use an alternating pattern to teach the new letter combination by first writing it on the board followed by one review letter combination, then by the new letter combination, followed by two review letter combinations. This pattern is continued until five letter combinations separate the last two new ones (examples: **ch** ea, **ch** th ow, **ch** ent ea re ou, **ch** ai ea ow oo le **ch**).
Time	3–5 minutes

Instructions	Teacher	Student
	1. Advance Organizer	
	2. My Turn Point to the new letter combination. **"My turn. Here's our new sound for today."** **"/ch/."** (back to starting point)	
	3. Your Turn **"Your turn. What sound?"** **"Yes, /ch/."**	/ch/
	4. Your Turn with Review Starting at the first letter combination move through the row of letters on the list. As you move through the list say, **"What sound?"** for each letter combination.	/ch/ /ea/ /ch/ /th/ etc.
	5. Individual Student Checkout Point to random letters. Starting at the first letter combination, move across the row of letters on the list just as you did in Step 4. As you point to random letter combinations on the list, say, **"Individual turns. What sound? Carmella."**	/ch/ /ea/ /ch/ /th/ etc.
Error Correction	If an error occurs, immediately return to a My Turn–Your Turn pattern. Then alternate between the missed letter combination and familiar letters until students identify the missed letter combination correctly three times.	

Source: Adapted from *Teaching Reading to Students Who Are At-Risk or Have Disabilities.* (3rd ed.), by W. Bursuck and M. Damer (2015). Boston: Pearson Education.

RESEARCH-BASED PRACTICES

Simmons and colleagues (2011) found that at-risk readers in kindergarten who received 30 minutes of extra direct instruction in early literacy skills outperformed a comparable group of kindergartners not receiving the extra instruction.

DIMENSIONS OF DIVERSITY

In Native American cultures, children learn skills by first observing them and then doing them. Native American students benefit from direct teaching that first stresses modeling or demonstrations. You can enhance demonstrations for your Native American students by showing them the final product before the demonstration (Sparks, 2000).

INCLUDE

This discussion of Felix and Bill raises an important issue: General education teachers need to know more than one approach to meet the needs of individual students, an idea at the heart of inclusive practices as well as RtI/MTSS. Felix can learn sounds with minimal instruction while reading books; Bill cannot. Bill's teacher may need to accommodate Bill and other students in the

TECHNOLOGY NOTES 9.1

Using Virtual Manipulatives to Support Instruction

Virtual manipulatives have been defined as web-based images on a computer that permit students to manipulate a visual model as if it were three-dimensional (Bouck & Flanagan, 2010; Shin et al., 2017). You learned about the use and benefits of manipulatives as physical or visual representations of abstractions in Chapter 5. Virtual manipulatives can perform the same functions as traditional manipulatives but have important advantages:

- Interactive qualities such as prompting and immediate feedback are more engaging for students.
- Screen delivery provides greater instructional control.
- Built-in visual and numeric models free students to focus on mathematical connections and relationships.
- Computer-driven representations are more age-appropriate for older students.
- Advanced subjects such as algebra can be more easily accommodated.
- Virtual manipulatives are easier to manage than physical manipulatives.
- Features such as adjustments in pace and additional practice provide greater opportunities for individualization.

Virtual manipulatives have been developed for teaching many areas of math; those areas validated by research include fractions, area and perimeter, and place value (Shin et al., 2017). Sample screen shots for teaching place value and fractions developed by the National Library of Virtual Manipulatives (NLVM) are shown in Figures 9.5 and 9.6.

Shin and colleagues (2017) recommend maximizing the effectiveness of virtual manipulatives by doing the following:

- Check students' conceptual understandings by having them verbalize their thinking and/or answer reflective questions while engaged with the virtual manipulatives.
- Try virtual manipulative teaching formats out yourself, first, to ensure clarity of presentation.
- Embed virtual manipulatives within a framework comprised of the research-based instructional practices stressed throughout this text.

Virtual manipulatives have been shown to be effective with students with disabilities, including students with autism spectrum disorders (Root, Browder, Saunders & Lo, 2017), and are available online at the National Library of Virtual Manipulatives (http://nlvm.usu.edu); Illuminations (http://www.illuminations.nctm.org/): click "Interactives"; *and* Shodor (http://www.shodor.org): click "Activities & Lessons," then click "Interactivate."

FIGURE 9.5 **Base 10 Blocks manipulative from the National Library of Virtual Manipulatives** (http://nlvm.usu.edu/en/nav/frames_asid_152_g_2_t_1.html). **Reprinted by permission of the National Library of Virtual Manipulatives.**

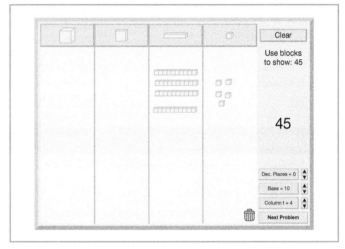

FIGURE 9.6 **Comparing fraction manipulatives from the National Library of Virtual Manipulatives** (http://nlvm.usu.edu/en/nav/frames_asid_159_g_3_t_1.html). **Reprinted by permission from the National Library of Virtual Manipulatives.**

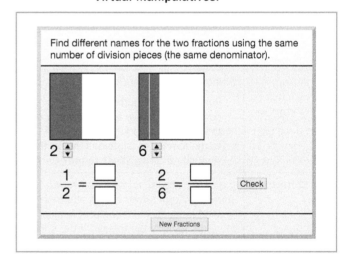

class by providing them with some direct instruction on letter–sound correspondence. This direct instruction can involve having students both say and write their sounds. Of course, as mentioned in Chapters 1 and 5, if you teach using the principles of universal design (UDL), your instruction will more likely meet the needs of all of your students in the first place.

Another example reinforces the idea that some of your students may need more direct instruction and practice. Mr. Diaz was teaching his English students

CASE IN PRACTICE 9.1

Applying INCLUDE to a Basic Skills Lesson

Ms. Dettman loves to look on the Internet for what she calls "teacher-tested" lesson plans. She found a lesson yesterday on the topic of math word problems (Bowen, n.d.), an area in which her students often struggle and where she is always looking for something different to do. The teacher who used this technique claimed that it had had a positive impact on her class's performance last year on the state's high-stakes test in math. Ms. Dettman decided to try it.

THE ONLINE LESSON

- Teacher posts a daily word problem on tagboard. The skill targeted (for example, division, fractions) varies from day to day.
- Teacher reads problem aloud first thing in the morning and students have until lunchtime to solve it.
- Students keep a special file folder containing an answer sheet for the week's problems. Students are required to show their work.
- After lunch, teacher assigns three or four students to go to the board to solve the problem. They talk aloud about how they solved the problem.
- Each child has an incentive chart posted in class. Two students collect and score papers, and points are awarded for correct answers. Students receive a prize when they reach a certain number of points, and then a new chart is posted.

STUDENTS WITH SPECIAL NEEDS

Ms. Dettman has a group of four students in class who have trouble in math; three of these students have learning disabilities in both reading and math.

LESSON DEMANDS

Ms. Dettman reviewed the demands of this activity as a beginning step in the process of determining whether any instructional adjustments would be needed. She identified the following seven demands:

1. Read the problem.
2. Identify the operation needed to solve the problem (for example, add, subtract).
3. Write a number sentence.
4. Convert the number sentence to a computation problem.
5. Solve the computation problem.
6. Label the answer.
7. Check work.

POTENTIAL PROBLEM AREAS

Next, based on the students' IEPs, as well as her previous experience teaching them, Ms. Dettman thought about parts of the lesson that might need to be adjusted. She came to these conclusions:

- Regarding the students' preskills, three of the students have reading problems, but the fact that the word problems would be read out loud eliminated the need for an accommodation such as a bypass strategy.
- The students will have trouble translating the word problems into a mathematical sentence; they all have reading compre-

hension problems and have previously struggled to pick the correct operation when they solved word problems in class.
- The four students don't know their math facts, and their computational accuracy is inconsistent, even though they understand the concepts behind the four basic operations. Computation could be a definite problem.
- None of the students struggles with handwriting, so the writing demands of solving the word problem will not be problematic.
- One student is artistically inclined, a strength on which Ms. Dettman could build.
- Different types of word problems are selected for the activity each day. This variety might confuse the four students, who seem to work best when new problem types are added gradually as others are learned.
- Student modeling of problem solving at the board by thinking out loud was a great idea, but the students with problems in math might not benefit from it without more careful structuring.

INSTRUCTIONAL ADJUSTMENTS

Ms. Dettman decided to adjust the lesson as follows in order to make it more accessible for the students in question.

- Although she would continue to work with the four students on improving the accuracy of their math computation skills, for this activity, students will be allowed to bypass their current difficulties in this area by using calculators.
- All students will be provided with a visual diagram to guide them through the problem-solving steps, along with small-group guided practice to ensure they use the strategy appropriately. Part of small-group guided practice will involve the use of teacher and student think-alouds to make the problem-solving steps more conspicuous. Students will be provided with additional small-group practice as needed.
- When students come to the board to solve problems out loud in the large group, bonus points will be awarded to those students paying careful attention, particularly to the think-aloud part.
- Only one new word problem type will be covered at a time. New types will be added as previously introduced types are mastered. Previously mastered problem types will be reviewed daily to assure retention.
- The student with artistic talent will be appointed to be the class artist. She will come to the board and draw a picture representing the problem.

REFLECTION

Why do you think Ms. Dettman made instructional *adjustments* for the four struggling students rather than instructional *modifications*? How did Ms. Dettman use the INCLUDE strategy to come up with needed changes in the lesson? How effective and feasible do you think these adjustments will be? What are the risks involved in using "teacher-tested" Internet sources? What would you do differently if you were the teacher?

Source: Based on the students' IEPs and Ms. Dettman.

INCLUDE ⟩

how to write a persuasive essay, including how to develop a thesis, add supporting details, reject counterarguments, and end with a conclusion. He described the steps in writing a persuasive essay while showing students an example of a well-written persuasive essay. He then asked the students to write a one-page persuasive essay for homework. Brenda handed in her essay the next day; although her paper showed some potential, her thesis lacked clarity, her details were sketchy, and she forgot to reject possible counterarguments. Brenda needed more instruction and guided practice on how to write a persuasive essay than Mr. Diaz had provided. Mr. Diaz could have applied the INCLUDE strategy, anticipated Brenda's problems, and provided guided practice by writing essays with the class until even lower performers such as Brenda seemed comfortable performing the task. He also could have posted an exemplar for the students having different colored markers for each of the critical components and using this as a model for the independent part of the task. Mr. Diaz used independent practice to monitor his students' performance and make adjustments for individual students using corrective feedback and more instruction, if necessary.

Finally, it is important to remember that practice is most effective when it *follows* direct instruction; practice is never an adequate substitute for direct instruction. For example, Mr. Hanesworth designed a board game in which students get to move ahead if they can answer a division fact problem. The problem is that five students in his class still do not understand the concept of division. For them, the board game practice activity is likely to result in failure. Mr. Hanesworth can adjust his instruction for these learners in a small group by providing additional instruction on division for them while allowing the rest of the class to play the board game independently. Later on, Mr. Hanesworth can reward the hard work of the small group by allowing them to practice a skill they know using a similar game-like format.

Clearly, you may need to adjust your instruction to enable students with special needs to access the curriculum. An example of using INCLUDE to do so was just presented in the Case in Practice feature. The Technology Notes feature introduced a way to use technology to enhance the math instruction of students with special needs. The Instructional Edge describes an additional option for adjusting instruction for students with special needs through Tier 2 instruction in RtI/MTSS. Students also may need adjustments when subject-area content is presented, the primary teaching focus as students move into the upper grades. Making adjustments when teaching subject matter content is the topic of the next section of the chapter.

INSTRUCTIONAL EDGE 9.1

Providing Differentiated Instruction Using Tier 2 in RtI/MTSS

When Roberto started at Stafford Middle School this year, he was flagged by the RtI team as needing help in reading comprehension due to his low score on the district-wide reading test in fourth grade. Roberto was assigned to a special Tier 2 comprehension reading class during his elective period. The class, comprised of four other students besides Roberto, meets every day for 50 minutes and is scheduled to continue at least until the end of the semester in January, unless bi-weekly progress-monitoring measures in reading comprehension as well as informal assessments by Roberto's teachers show Roberto no longer needs Tier 2 instruction or is making little or no progress and needs to be moved to Tier 3. The class is taught by Ms. Hernandez, an intervention teacher certified in special education and English and recently hired by the district to teach reading in both Tiers 2 and 3. Ms. Hernandez is teaching her group using an evidence-based program designed to help students comprehend their content-area textbooks. Ms. Hernandez is observed monthly by an instructional

coach to assure she is adhering to the prescribed program. Ms. Hernandez will share Roberto's progress-monitoring data with the RtI team. Roberto's general education teachers not on the team, as well as Roberto's parents, will be informed of Roberto's progress via e-mail.

What Is Tier 2 Instruction?

- Tier 2 consists of the instruction provided in Tier 1, plus additional small-group sessions that provide extra instruction and/or practice of targeted skills and content covered in Tier 1.

- As in Tier 1, all instruction in Tier 2 is evidence-based, includes many of the Tier 1 instructional enhancements described earlier in Chapter 5, and, like all RtI interventions, must be implemented with fidelity.

- In some schools, instruction in Tier 2 is carefully scripted using the same research-based intervention for all children having similar problems in a given area. This is called the standard protocol model. Other Rtl schools use a more individualized, problem-solving approach, whereby interventions are chosen and instructional decisions made based on graphed individual student data, much like the process used with Marni, the student in the Case in Practice in Chapter 7.

- Greater intensity is achieved in Tier 2 through additional, more systematic and focused instruction, smaller instructional groups (usually five to eight students per group), and more frequent progress monitoring (at least monthly) (Hartacher, Sanford, & Nelson, 2017).

- Tier 2 instruction is most successful when it is carefully aligned with the goals and objectives emphasized in Tier 1 (Dennis, 2015; Harn, Chard, Biancarosa, & Kam'eenui, 2011; Lane, Oakes, Ennis, & Eisner, 2014) and when it is adjusted based on student performance (Coyne et al., 2013).

Roberto, the student described earlier in the example, is receiving reading instruction using a standard protocol model that was carefully aligned with the reading demands of his general education classes. Roberto's instruction takes place in a small group (five students) and is being carried out during Roberto's elective period, as a supplement to his regular classes. Ms. Hernandez is monitoring Roberto's progress bi-weekly using Maze, a curriculum-based measure of reading comprehension.

Who Is Eligible for Tier 2 Instruction?

- Students enter Tier 2 when their performance on universal screening measures dips below benchmark scores or a set percentile, or below standard on a high-stakes or end-of-grade test.

- Although the number of students eligible for Tier 2 varies, it is estimated as being 8–15 percent (Ervin, 2017). In a class of 25 students, this would amount to as many as 3 or 4 students.

In our example, Roberto was identified as eligible for Tier 2 instruction based on his performance on the district-wide grade four reading test.

Where, When, and for How Long Does Tier 2 Instruction Take Place?

- Tier 2 instruction usually takes place in small, same-skill groupings of five to eight students, with some groups having as few as three students.

- Tier 2 groups meet three to five times per week for 20 to 40 minutes in elementary school and up to 60 minutes per session or half a block in high school (Bursuck & Damer, 2015; National High School Center, 2010).

- Tier 2 groups can take place either inside or outside the general education classroom, with some middle school groups taking place in literacy labs and even within after-school programs (Johnson, Smith, & Harris, 2009).

Roberto's Tier 2 instruction took place in an additional classroom for 50 minutes per day during his elective period.

Who Teaches Tier 2 Groups?

- Tier 2 instruction can be carried out by a variety of staff, including general education teachers, Title 1 teachers, special education teachers, and paraprofessionals, all carefully prepared to ensure instructional quality.

In the example, Roberto is being taught by an interventionist, hired specifically by the school to teach Tiers 2 and 3 in reading.

How Long Do Students Remain in Tier 2 Groups?

- The amount of time students spend in Tier 2 varies, but in many systems time in Tier 2 is of a limited duration, ranging from about 10 to 19 weeks.

- In Tier 2, student progress is monitored at least monthly.

- Students who progress to grade level exit Tier 2, although they continue to be monitored to ensure their performance is maintained. Students who fail to show progress despite receiving well-delivered Tier 2 instruction usually move to more intensive instruction in Tier 3, although students can remain in Tier 2 longer if they show significant improvement despite still performing below benchmark levels.

- Students who meet their goals early can exit Tier 2 and receive their instruction exclusively in Tier 1.

What Is the Role of the General Education Teacher in Tier 2?

- The most important role for the general education teacher is to teach Tier 1 so well that fewer students require Tier 2 instruction.

- General education teachers also play an important role in progress monitoring by regularly measuring student performance and using the results to help the Rtl team decide who exits Tier 2 and who remains.

In the example, Roberto's general education teacher communicates regularly with Ms. Hernandez regarding Roberto's grades.

- While it is a common responsibility for general elementary school teachers to teach Tier 2 groups themselves, it can be difficult to do so with quality and consistency while still completing their many other instructional responsibilities.

- General education teachers at the middle and high school levels can teach Tier 2 groups, depending on expertise as well as scheduling considerations.

- Even if you are not conducting the Tier 2 instruction, it is important to be aware of the support your students are receiving to assure that Tiers 1 and 2 are well aligned, a key ingredient of effective Tier 2 instruction (Simmons, 2015).

For more information about Rtl in middle and high schools, go to www.rti4success.org. Under "related rti topics," click "secondary schools."

FIGURE 9.7 **Questions to Ask Yourself When Planning Content-Area Instruction**

Do students have the necessary background knowledge and can they apply it to understanding the content presented?

Have I organized the content clearly so that it can be accessed by all of my students?

What essential terms and concepts do all of my students need to know and how do I make it possible for all students to learn them?

How clearly written is the textbook and other written material I am expecting my students to read for understanding? What adjustments do I need to make so that all students can learn from the text?

How clear is my oral communication? Do I give directions, ask questions, and present subject matter in a way that allows all of my students to access the content?

How Can You Make Instructional Adjustments for Students with Special Needs When Teaching Subject-Area Content?

The instruction of academic content includes areas such as social studies and science. This instruction often involves the use of textbooks and lecture–discussion formats, but it also can include other activities, such as videos, interactive online learning, hands-on activities, and cooperative learning. Although content-area instruction generally is associated with instruction in secondary schools, the information presented here is relevant for elementary teachers as well. Social studies and science have always been taught at the elementary level, and high-stakes science tests are administered as early as third grade. In this section, you learn how you can adjust your instruction to help students with special needs learn subject-area content. When planning your content-area instruction, ask the questions in Figure 9.7 related to strategies for making adjustments by activating background knowledge, organizing content, teaching terms and concepts, and using clear oral and written language. Strategies for adjusting instructional content for students in Tier 3 in RtI/MTSS are described in the Instructional Edge feature on page 297.

Activating Background Knowledge

The amount of background knowledge students have can greatly influence whether they can read subject matter with understanding. To illustrate, read this list of words:

are	making	between
only	consists	often
continuously	vary	corresponding
one	curve	points
draws	relation	variation
set	graph	table
if	values	isolated
variables	known	

Were you able to read all of them? Do you know the meanings of all these words? Now read the following passage:

If the known relation between the variables consists of a table of corresponding values, the graph consists only of the corresponding set of isolated points. If the variables are known to vary continuously, one often draws a curve to show the variation (from Michaelson, 1945, as cited in Lavoie, 1991).

Chances are, unless you are a math major, if you were asked to summarize what you just read, you would be unable to do so despite the fact that you

INSTRUCTIONAL EDGE 9.2

Providing Differentiated Instruction in Tier 3 in RtI/MTSS

A universal screening assessment given in January of kindergarten showed that while Serena was meeting benchmark standards in reading, she was below target in all four areas of number sense assessed: early numeracy, number identification, counting, and quantity discriminations. As a result, Serena received Tier 2 small-group math support consisting of 20 extra minutes of practice on math skills based on the state standards three times per week. Serena's progress-monitoring data, plus her performance on end-of-the year benchmark assessments in math, showed that she lost more ground and was well below her peers in all areas tested. In Serena's district, Tier 3 provides students with more intensive instruction without having to label them as having a disability. Serena's RtI team decided she needed and would benefit from receiving Tier 3 instruction when she enters first grade in the fall. In addition to participating in those parts of Tier 1 instruction from which the RtI team thinks she can benefit, Serena will receive 60 minutes per day of a direct instruction math program carefully scaffolded for students who are at risk. Serena's Tier 3 group will consist of three students, one of whom is disabled, and will be taught by the special education teacher, Ms. Laurel, in a small classroom off of the media center. Serena's progress will be monitored by weekly progress checks that are part of the math program as well as bi-weekly probes of number sense based on standards assessed in the universal screener.

What Is Tier 3 Instruction?

- The intent of Tier 3 in RtI/MTSS systems is to provide students with highly intensive instruction matched to their individual needs (Coolong-Chaffin & Wagner, 2015; Fuchs, Fuchs, & Compton, 2012; Zumeta, 2015). Tier 3 can be special education, but not always.

In Serena's case, the RtI team wanted to see how she responded to Tier 3 instruction before deciding to see if she had a learning disability.

- Tier 3 instruction is more concentrated than Tiers 1 and 2, focusing on a small set of foundational skills, usually in math, reading, writing, and behavior, that may or may not be at grade level (Fuchs, Fuchs, & Compton, 2012; Lemons, 2007). Intensity in Tier 3 is addressed through:
  - More frequent sessions, often of longer duration
  - Smaller groups
  - Highly individualized, systematic and explicit instruction using the instructional methods stressed in this text
  - Preparing students for making the transition from the lower to upper grades by teaching expository text comprehension, algebraic thinking, language comprehension, and self-regulatory skills
  - Ongoing progress monitoring (Gersten et al., 2009a, 2009b; Kuchle, Edmonds, Danielson, Peterson, & Riley-Tillman, 2015; Simmons, 2015).
- "Out-of-level" instruction can be used if it is determined that it is necessary to build the foundational skills needed for eventual success in grade-appropriate material (Fuchs et al., 2012).
- Prepackaged and/or commercially produced programs can also be used for Tier 3 as long as they are highly systematic, explicit, and evidence based (Bursuck & Damer, 2015; Simmons, 2015).

Serena's team decided on a commercially produced direct-instruction program that met these instructional requirements. Based on a placement test in her direct-instruction program, Serena's initial Tier 3 instruction focused on out-of-level skills that Serena had failed to acquire in kindergarten.

Who Is Eligible for Tier 3 Instruction?

- Students enter Tier 3 when the results of their progress monitoring show a clear lack of progress toward meeting specified benchmarks, or if information from cognitive assessments predicts later problems, indicating that a move directly from Tier 1 to Tier 3 is more appropriate (Chard, 2012; Fuchs et al., 2015).
- If special education is involved, then a comprehensive evaluation to determine special education needs and eligibility is required. Tier 3 typically includes approximately 2–7 percent of students (Ervin, 2017; Fuchs & Fuchs, 2015). In a class of 25 students this would amount to one or two students, although this figure may be higher in some high-poverty schools (Bursuck et al., 2004).

Serena's placement into Tier 3 was based on her progress-monitoring and benchmark assessments in kindergarten. Out of the three kindergarten classes in Serena's school, only two other students qualified for Tier 3.

Where, When, and for How Long Does Tier 3 Instruction Take Place?

- Tier 3 instruction usually takes place outside the general education classroom. In middle or high school, Tier 3 can occur during time scheduled for elective classes or study halls (Mellard & Prewett, 2010).
- On average, students participating in Tier 3 receive interventions daily, totaling from 45 to 120 extra minutes of instruction per day, in addition to time spent in their core general education program (Gersten et al., 2009a).
- In many instances Tier 3 time in high school is longer because in areas such as reading there is no core general education program. Length is dependent on multiple issues, including problem severity, subject, intervention method, and scheduling.
- With regard to group size, one-to-one instruction appears to be most effective (Gersten et al., 2009a), although groups as large as three are used in situations of limited resources and middle and high schools.

Serena's Tier 3 instruction is taking place for 45 minutes daily, in a group of three, in a setting outside of the classroom. She is also participating in Tier 1 instruction when it involves an area that is at her instructional level.

Who Teaches Tier 3 Groups?

- Tier 3 groups are most commonly taught by special education teachers, even when Tier 3 is not special education, although Tier 3 groups can be taught by general educators, speech and language pathologists, and Title 1 teachers.
- Tier 3 interventions involving behavior are likely to involve the school psychologist. *Serena's Tier 3 instruction is being provided by the special education teacher.*

(continued)

How Long Do Students Remain in Tier 3 Groups?

- Because the skill deficits of students receiving Tier 3 services are very significant, Tier 3 groups are longer term than Tier 2 groups, extending for 20+ weeks (Hartacher et al., 2017).
- While in Tier 3, students' progress is monitored as often as twice weekly (Hartacher et al., 2017); the results are used to change instruction as needed as well as determine eventual readiness to exit Tier 3 and re-enter Tiers 1 and 2.

Serena's progress will be monitored weekly. Although middle-of-the-year benchmark assessments will be given, it is likely that Serena will remain in Tier 3 at least until the end of the year, at which time her performance on benchmark assessments will be examined and her tier status re-evaluated.

What Is the Role of the General Education Teacher in Teaching Tier 3 Students?

- Even though general education teachers do not usually teach Tier 3 groups unless they have specific expertise in an area such as reading and part of their teaching assignments

includes this responsibility, they teach Tier 3 students at other times during the day.

- By applying the INCLUDE strategy, teachers can readily find out how well their Tier 3 students are meeting their classroom demands. This "window on reality" is an important part of progress monitoring for the RtI/MTSS team members as they continually evaluate the extent to which the gap between Tier 3 students and their peers is narrowing.
- Information gathered using INCLUDE also can help teachers successfully accommodate Tier 3 students in their classrooms.
- When RtI/MTSS is implemented, all teachers are responsible for all students, regardless of tier.
- The fact that students require intensive instruction in one area does not mean they cannot be successful in other areas of the general education curriculum.

Serena is at benchmark in reading and is only in Tier 3 for math. Serena's Tier 3 teacher and her general education teacher communicate regularly as to Serena's progress, particularly as it relates to her participation in the grade 1, Tier 1 math program.

probably answered yes when asked whether you could read and understand all the words individually. You may lack the background knowledge necessary to understand this very technical paragraph. The knowledge students bring to a content-area lesson is often as important for understanding as the quality of the textbook or instructional presentation (Marzano, 2004; Wood, Lapp, Flood, & Taylor, 2008; Pressley, 2000). For students to understand academic content material, they need to relate it to information they already know.

Unfortunately, teachers often fail to consider background information. Students with disabilities and students who are at risk may have two problems related to background knowledge: They may simply lack the necessary knowledge, or they may know the information but be unable to recall it or relate it to the new information being presented.

USING THE PREP STRATEGY Just as you learned about the importance of checking student preskills when teaching basic skills, it is equally important when teaching subject-matter content to see whether your students have enough background knowledge about the topic to be covered to understand it (Miller, 2016). One teaching strategy for determining how much knowledge students already have about a topic so that you can decide how much background information to present in class prior to a reading assignment is called the **PReP (PreReading Plan) strategy** (Langer, 1984; Vacca, Vacca, & Mraz, 2013). The PReP strategy has three major steps:

1. *Preview the text or lesson, and choose two to three important concepts.* For example, for a science lesson, Mr. Amin chose the concept of photosynthesis and the keywords *cycle* and *oxygen*.

2. *Conduct a brainstorming session with students.* This process involves three phases. In Phase 1, students tell you what comes to mind when they hear the concept. This gives you a first impression of how much they already know about the topic. Student responses in Phase 1 can be written or oral. The advantage of written responses is that you can assess the background knowledge of your entire class at once. The disadvantage of written responses is that for students who struggle to write, it is difficult to gauge whether an unacceptable response is due to a lack of knowledge about the topic or simply the result of a writing problem. This is a good time to adjust your instruction using INCLUDE. If students have a writing problem, modify your approach by questioning them orally or use the multiple choice option of Kahoot. If the class

is co-taught, one teacher could gather data as students respond orally, perhaps on an iPad. In Phase 2, students tell you what made them think of their responses in Phase 1. This information can help you judge the depth of and/or basis for their responses, and it also provides a springboard for students to refine their responses in Phase 3. In Mr. Amin's class, he discovered in Phases 1 and 2 that two of the students mistakenly thought that photosynthesis had to do with photography because of the presence of *photo* in the word. This error provided an opportunity to build on students' knowledge. Mr. Amin explained that *photo* means light and that in photography, a camera takes in light to make pictures. He then said that plants take in light too, and when the light combines with chemicals in the plant, carbohydrates and oxygen are made. This process is called *photosynthesis*. In this way, Mr. Amin connected what the students already knew to a concept they did not know. In Phase 3, students can add to their responses based on the discussion in Phase 2.

3. *Evaluate student responses to determine the depth of their prior knowledge of the topic.* During this step, you can decide whether students are ready to read the text and/or listen to a lecture on photosynthesis or whether they first need more information. Determining the needs of your students with respect to the demands of your instruction is an important part of INCLUDE. In Mr. Amin's class, two students continued to have trouble understanding that photosynthesis was something plants did with light to make carbohydrates and oxygen. They needed more information before they were ready to read the chapter. Mr. Amin accommodated these students by building the necessary background knowledge into his homework and daily warm-ups. The knowledge gaps for some students in his previous class had been more severe, so he showed them a video illustration of photosynthesis in the morning before school began (Miller, 2016). The video included concrete examples that weren't necessary to use with the rest of the class.

PREPARING ANTICIPATION GUIDES Anticipation guides can help you activate student knowledge about a particular topic and construct bridges to new information by encouraging students to make predictions (Readence, Moore, & Rickelman, 2000; Vacca, Vacca, & Mraz, 2013). Anticipation guides consist of a series of statements, some of which may not be true, related to the material that students are about to read (Roe, Smith, & Burns, 2011). Before teaching, students read these statements that either challenge or support ideas they may already have about the subject. This process catches their interest and gives them a reason for listening and reading. Providing questions or statements prior to reading also aids comprehension for all students, including those with disabilities.

For example, Ms. Henry constructed an anticipation guide prior to teaching a unit on the nervous system. Her anticipation guide included the following statements:

- A person cannot function without the nervous system.
- The nervous system helps us study and learn about new things.
- There are gaps between the nerve cells in our bodies.
- Nerve cells do different jobs in the body.
- The central nervous system is only one part of the nervous system.
- Our brains do not control our reflexes.
- Persons cannot hold their breath until they die.
- Some people can swim without thinking about it.

When using the anticipation guide, Ms. Henry needed to adjust her instruction for several of her students with reading problems. After distributing the guide, she met with these students in a small group and read each item out loud, clarifying terms such as *central nervous system, reflexes,* and *nerve cells.* Ms. Henry also accommodated students with reading problems by (a) highlighting important ideas from the selection, (b) dividing the text into smaller sections, (c)

MyLab Education

Video Example 9.2: Activating Background Knowledge

See how simple drills such as these, carried out using whole class or small group instruction, can be helpful in building students' background knowledge.

INCLUDE

RESEARCH-BASED PRACTICES

Vaughn and colleagues (2013) evaluated the effects of Tier 3 instruction on the reading achievement of eighth-grade students with reading difficulties who had failed the state reading test for three consecutive years. Tier 3 instruction consisted of 50 minutes of intensive instruction per day in groups of two to four students. The results showed that the students who received the Tier 3 instruction made significantly greater gains on a standardized measure of comprehension than a comparable group not receiving the Tier 3 instruction.

Video Example from

MyLab Education

Video Example 9.3: Building Background Knowledge

Watch how this teacher uses an anticipation guide to build his students' background knowledge. https://www.youtube.com/watch?v=sKlM2zCxtLM

using alternative text at students' levels, (d) simplifying the questions, (e) color coding columns to clearly differentiate *before* and *after*, (f) having these students complete the anticipation guide with peer buddies, and (g) giving students a chance to read the text at home before discussing it in school (Kozen, Murray, & Windell, 2006; Neuman, Kaefer, & Pinkham, 2017).

PROVIDING PLANNING THINK SHEETS Activating background information and building bridges to current knowledge are also of concern to teachers when asking students to write. Some researchers recommend **planning think sheets** to help writers focus on background information as well as on the audience and purpose of a paper (Englert & And, 1991). For audience, students are asked to consider who will read the paper. For purpose, students clarify why they are writing the paper (for example, to tell a story, to convey information, or to persuade someone). Finally, students activate background knowledge and organize that knowledge by asking themselves questions such as "What do I know about the topic?" and "How can I group or label my facts?" (Englert & And, 1991; Vaughn & Bos, 2014). A planning think sheet for a paper assignment might contain write-on lines for students to answer the following questions

- What is my topic?
- Why do I want to write on this topic?
- What are two things I already know that will make it easy to write this paper?
- Who will read my paper?
- Why will the reader be interested in this topic?

Students may need more teacher modeling and guided practice before being able to complete think sheets independently. You can deliver these adjustments using a small teacher-led group. You can further adjust your instruction and motivate students by providing a range of paper topics that students can choose from. Students also can be permitted to respond orally to the questions.

Organizing Content

Research shows that many students, including students with special needs, have difficulty understanding important ideas and their interrelationships in content areas (Baker, Kame'enui, Simmons, & Simonsen, 2010). These students can benefit from the use of supports or scaffolds that help them identify and understand important information. As you learned in Chapter 5, one form of support is to organize the curriculum according to big ideas rather than facts in isolation. Another form of support is to make these big ideas more evident to students through the use of advance organizers, cue words for organizational patterns, study guides, and graphic organizers. Sometimes these methods of organizing information are an integral part of your teaching plan for your whole class. Other times, these organizers function as adjustments, or scaffolds specially designed for your students with special needs using INCLUDE.

USING ADVANCE ORGANIZERS Advance organizers include information presented verbally and/or visually that makes content more understandable by putting it within a more general framework. Advance organizers are particularly effective for students with special needs who may have limited background knowledge and reading and listening comprehension skills (Swanson & Deshler, 2003). Examples of advance organizers include the following (Dean, Hubbell, Pitner, & Stone, 2012):

- Identifying major topics and activities
- Presenting an outline of content
- Providing background information
- Stating concepts and ideas to be learned in the lesson
- Motivating students to learn by showing the relevance of the activity
- Stating the objectives or outcomes of the lesson

Although a well-constructed advance organizer presented to the entire class will meet the needs of most students, those with disabilities or other special needs may benefit from a more individualized approach. For example, Mr. Serano motivated Zak by tying an advance organizer for a lesson about weather to Zak's interest in aviation. Ms. Williams explained to Rinaldo that his lesson objective was to identify and write numbers from 10 to 100. The rest of the class was learning to add two-digit numbers. Ms. Hardy used an individualized advance organizer to communicate to Carlos, who struggles with writing, that he could demonstrate what he learned in the unit on explorers by designing a map showing the countries the major explorers came from. The rest of the class wrote two-page papers about the countries involved in exploration, including the major explorers from each country.

EMPLOYING CUE WORDS FOR ORGANIZATIONAL PATTERNS Big ideas are often the central focus of an organizational pattern of information. The most common patterns of information include the descriptive list including the sequence of events in time, comparison/contrast, cause/effect, and problem/solution (Baxendell, 2003; Bursuck & Damer, 2015; Sejnost & Thiese, 2010). Each of these patterns of information can be made more conspicuous for students through the use of cue words. For example, cue words for a list, description, or sequence might include *first, second,* and *third*; cue words for comparison/contrast would be *similar, different, on the one hand,* and *on the other hand*; cue words for cause/effect might be *causes, effects, because,* and *so that*; and cue words for problem/solution would be *problem, solution,* and *resolve.* Cue words are important for students with disabilities, many of whom have difficulty telling the difference between important and unimportant information (Bursuck & Damer, 2015; Hallahan, Lloyd, Kauffman, Weiss, & Martinez, 2005).

Text that does not contain clear cue words requires students to make a number of inferences, which may be difficult for students. Rewriting the book is obviously not a reasonable way to adjust instruction. Instead, you can accommodate students by helping to make the key concepts more explicit using teaching strategies described in this text, such as study guides and graphic organizers. Or you can use alternative means of presenting the same information, such as videos or books that are more clearly written.

CONSTRUCTING STUDY GUIDES The general term study guide refers to outlines, abstracts, or questions that emphasize important information in texts. Study guides are helpful in improving comprehension for students with special needs in content-area classrooms (Conderman & Bresnahan, 2010; Mercer, Mercer, & Pullen, 2010). A common problem experienced by students at all educational levels is being able to pick out key ideas in their textbooks. That is why students can benefit from study guides, which direct them to important information by asking them questions about it. Procedures for constructing study guides are shown in the Professional Edge feature below. A sample study guide for a section of a social studies text on Truman's Fair Deal is shown in Figure 9.8.

WWW RESOURCES

To find a variety of advance organizers, Google "Advance Organizers Templates."

WWW RESOURCES

The Education Development Center's webpage for the National Center to Improve Practice in Special Education through Technology, Media, and Materials, at http://www2.edc.org/ncip, provides many ideas on how to implement research-based teaching practices with students with special needs.

FIGURE 9.8 Sample Study Guide for Truman's Fair Deal Vocabulary

Consumables are products that _____.

Some positive examples of consumables are _____, _____, and _____.

A negative example of a consumable is _____.

Big Ideas

The **problem** was that after World War II, price controls were lifted and the cost of _____, _____, and other consumer goods went _____.

The **solution** was for workers to _____.

The **effect** was that _____ and _____.

PROFESSIONAL EDGE 9.1

How to Develop Study Guides

Study guides are instructional tools that organize the presentation of information in ways that make it more accessible for all students, especially those with special needs who are included in content-area classrooms. Follow these steps to develop a study guide based on state standards, your textbook, and other information you wish to present in class.

1. Consider student qualities that could have an impact on construction of the study guide (e.g., level of background knowledge, reading level, writing skills, and level of motivation).

2. Check to see how learner friendly your text is by using guidelines covered in Chapter 5 (see pages 164–166). Where text is problematic, build supports into your study guide. For example, if text structures such as *cause and effect* and *compare and contrast* aren't explicitly signaled in the text, refer to them specifically in your study guide.

3. Read your text carefully and identify key learner outcomes. These outcomes should represent "big ideas" and key vocabulary; they should relate directly to state standards for your subject area. Add other outcomes and sources of information as needed.

4. Divide the text and corresponding classroom presentations and activities into meaningful, manageable chunks based on key outcomes identified in the entry above.

5. Write a statement for each main idea, vocabulary word, fact, or concept and then place the statements in a logical order.

6. Turn your sentences into questions. One way to do this is to delete words to create fill-in-the-blank questions. For example, the teacher who created the study guide in Figure 9.8 used the fill-in-the-blank format. She could have also used short answer questions (*What was the problem that led to the increase in worker strikes after World War II?*) or multiple choice questions (*Which of the following is a consumable product?* [a] bread [b] house [c] car [d] phone).

7. Project your questions and have students answer them as they read or listen to you teach, working in pairs or small groups. Questions can also be answered as students read independently or as review in the form of homework.

8. Develop quizzes and end-of-chapter tests based directly on content stressed in the study guide.

9. Show students how to use the study guide to prepare for quizzes and end-of-chapter tests.

10. Administer quizzes and/or tests; reteach as needed.

Study guides can be used in the following ways to adjust instruction for students (Conderman & Bresnahan, 2010; Horton, Boone, & Lovitt, 1990).

1. Allow 2 or 3 inches of margin space in the study guide in which students can take notes. Draw a vertical line to indicate the margin clearly. For example, in the study guide in Figure 9.8, the answer to the first vocabulary question is "*Consumables* are products that cannot be used over again." You may want to have students write this vocabulary word along with its complete definition in the margin. Some students find a new word easier to understand if you first use the media projector or Smartboard to discuss the definition along with a series of positive and negative examples. Specific strategies for presenting new vocabulary are presented later in the chapter.

2. Print page numbers next to the sentences in the study guide to show where to find missing words in the textbook.

3. Print the missing words at the bottom of the page to serve as cues.

4. Leave out several words for more advanced students and fewer for students with special needs. For example, in Figure 9.8, the *effect* part of the big idea could be simplified as, "The *effect* of price controls being lifted was an increase in prices leading to _____."

5. Model how to use the study guides by completing a sample study guide in front of the class while thinking out loud.

6. Arrange for reciprocal peer-teaching situations; pair students and have them take turns being the teacher and the student.

7. Use the study guide for homework assignments. Assign students a passage in the text and give them accompanying study guides (either with or without the pages marked for easy reference). Have them complete the guides and study the material for homework.

8. Ask students to keep and organize their study guides from a number of passages and to study them as they review for unit or end-of-semester tests.

9. Place reading passages, study guides, and tests on a computer. Design the study guide using a hypertext format with highlighted questions or key words containing a link to the website that will help answer the question. Be sure to take into account your students' capabilities in using computers, using INCLUDE to make adjustments as needed. Use print-to-speech software for students who have difficulty with word reading.

10. Whenever possible, write the study guide at a reading level that fits most of your students. Students with reading and writing problems may need to have the study guide read to them or respond to the questions orally.

11. To discourage students from only learning material on the study guide, supplement the study guide with other instructional methods and construct test questions that are not taken word for word from the study guide.

Study guides are not a substitute for direct instruction. The amount of direct instruction necessary varies with the difficulty of the material. In general, students need more help completing study guides for texts that assume high levels of student background knowledge and in which key information needs to be inferred as opposed to being explicitly presented. The INCLUDE strategy can help you determine whether more direct instruction is needed and whether it needs to be delivered as part of large- or small-group instruction.

> INCLUDE

CREATING GRAPHIC ORGANIZERS Another way teachers can help students organize content is to use graphic organizers. This strategy gives students a visual format to organize their thoughts while looking for main ideas (Baxendell, 2003; Dexter & Hughes, 2011). Graphic organizers can reduce cognitive demand by creating a visual representation of the most significant information in a text or lecture, a feature that is of particular benefit to students with disabilities (Singleton & Filce, 2015; p.110). Archer and Gleason (2010) suggest the following five guidelines for constructing graphic organizers:

1. Determine the critical content (for example, vocabulary, concepts, ideas, generalizations, events, details, facts) that you wish to teach your students. Helping students focus on the most critical information is important for several reasons. First, students with disabilities may have trouble identifying the most important information in an oral lesson or textbook chapter. In most cases, this will be content stressed in your state's standards. Second, it is easier for students to remember several main ideas than to remember many isolated details. Third, putting too much information on a graphic organizer can make it so visually complex that students may have trouble interpreting it.

2. Organize concepts into a concept map, a type of graphic organizer or visual representation that reflects the structure of the content, such as stories, hierarchies (top-down and bottom-up), feature analysis, diagrams, compare/contrast, and timelines. Because the purpose of a graphic organizer is to clarify interrelationships among ideas and information, you should keep it as simple as possible. Figure 9.9 shows a completed comparison/contrast concept map.

3. Design a completed concept map. Completing the map before you teach with it will ensure that the information is clear and accurate and can be presented to your students in a timely manner.

4. Create a partially completed concept map to be completed by students during instruction. Having students fill out the map as you present your lesson is an excellent way to keep them on task. Also, many students with disabilities benefit from a multisensory approach; seeing the information on the graphic, hearing it from the teacher, and writing it on the map helps them better retain the information presented.

5. Create a blank concept map for students to use as a postreading or review exercise. This structure for review is easy for students to use.

MyLab Education

Video Example 9.4: Graphic Organizer Example

Watch how the teacher in this video organized her content using graphic organizers.

FIGURE 9.9   Comparison/Contrast Concept Map

Attribute	Native Americans	Settlers
Land	Shared	Owned
	Lived close to it without changing it	Cleared it
	Respected it	Used it

Summary
Native Americans and settlers had different ideas about land. Native Americans shared the land, whereas the settlers owned individual pieces of it. Native Americans lived close to the land; they respected it and did not change it. Settlers used the land for their own gain.

Dexter and Hughes (2011) stress the importance of explicitly teaching students to use graphic organizers by providing guided practice showing how concepts are related, the differences between main and subordinate ideas, and how to put all of the pieces together to make a clear picture of the content being presented (p. 69). Steps developed by Archer and Gleason (2010) for teaching students to use graphic organizers are as follows:

1. Distribute partially completed concept maps to your students.

2. Project the map on a screen using a media projector or Smartboard displaying only those portions you wish students to attend to. Limiting the amount of information you present at one time will help students with attention problems who have trouble focusing on more than one piece of information at a time.

3. Introduce the information on the concept map proceeding in a logical order; stress the relationships among the vocabulary, concepts, events, details, facts, and so on.

4. At natural junctures, review the concepts you have introduced. You can do this by projecting the blank map and asking students questions about the content. This review is essential for students who have difficulty learning large amounts of information at one time.

5. At the end of the lesson, review the critical content again using the blank concept map. You can also have students complete the blank maps for homework. These maps will help students organize their studying and also help you find out what they have learned. Sample blank and completed maps for teaching the concept of natural resources in a science class are shown in Figures 9.10 and 9.11.

In most cases, using graphic organizers will be helpful for your entire class. Students with attention or listening problems may benefit from the additional adjustments of having a completed graphic explained to them prior to instruction for use as an advance organizer and then completing a blank organizer after instruction with the teacher or a peer for extra practice and review. Some students may find it easier to begin with partially completed graphic organizers, a practice employed by Mr. Reeves in the opening chapter vignettes. Students with gaps in background knowledge may benefit from additional work with graphic organizers that summarize background information. This can be provided as part of small-group or one-to-one instruction. For example, to prepare some of his students with special needs to complete the graphic organizer shown in Figure 9.9, Mr. Jackson read sections of two texts: one about the settlers in Ohio in the 1700s and another about the Delaware tribe, who also lived in Ohio at the time. He also adjusted his instruction by providing additional ways for students to demonstrate their knowledge of this and other differences between settlers and Native Americans by having students write short stories or produce their own picture books. Last, while students who are gifted may not need graphic organizers to conceptualize information, they may benefit from constructing their own.

FIGURE 9.10 **Partially Completed Concept Map on Natural Resources**

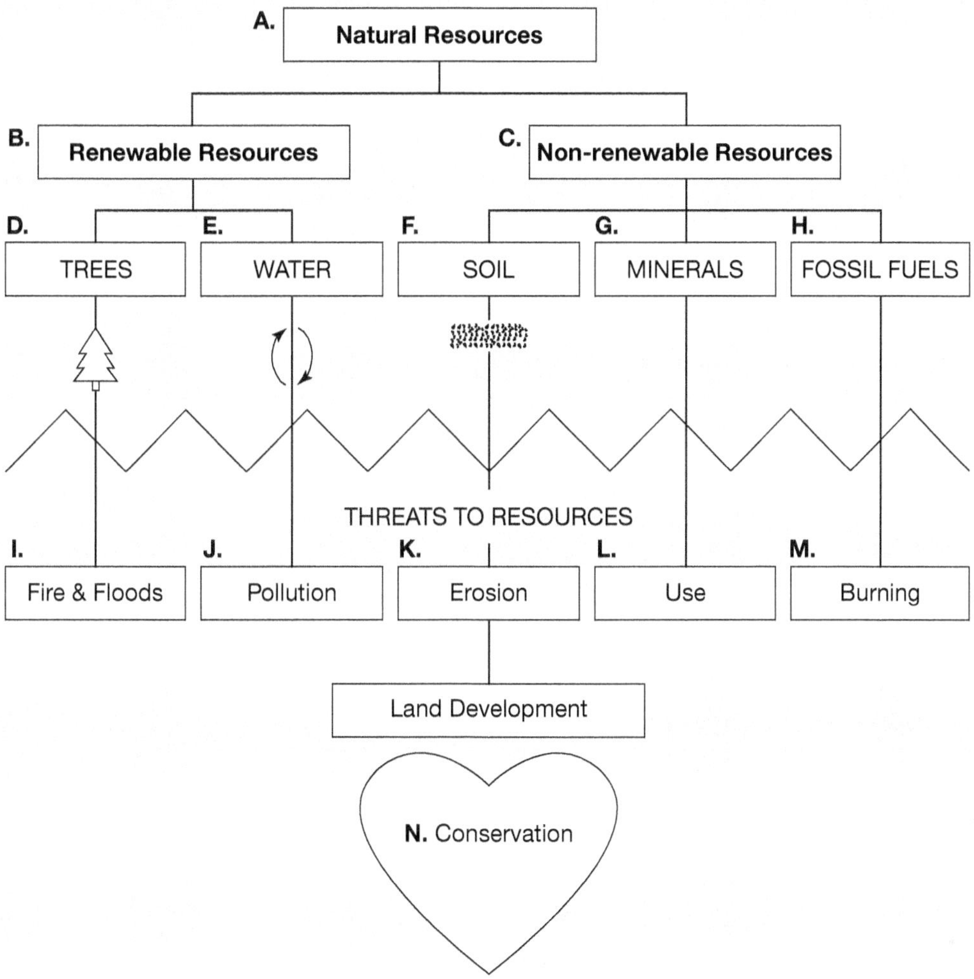

Source: From Direct instruction in content-area reading (2010) by A. Archer and M. Gleason. In *Direct Instruction Reading* by D. W. Carnine, J. Silbert, E. J. Kammenui, and S. G Tarver. Upper Saddle River, NJ: Merrill/Pearson.

Teaching Terms and Concepts

Content-area instruction is often characterized by a large number of new and/or technical vocabulary words and concepts. Students who have special needs or who are at risk are likely to have difficulty with the vocabulary and concept demands of many content-area texts and presentations. For example, consider the following passage from a general science text:

> Thousands of years ago, Scandinavia was covered by a thick ice sheet. The mass of the ice forced the crust deeper into the denser mantle. Then the ice melted. The mantle has been slowly pushing the land upward since then. This motion will continue until a state of balance between the crust and mantle is reached again. This state of balance is called *isostasy* (ie-sosstuh-see) (Ramsey, Gabriel, McGuirk, Phillips, & Watenpaugh, 1983).

Although the term *isostasy* is italicized for emphasis, other technical terms and concepts, such as *crust* and *mass*, also may pose a problem for students and require special attention. These words may be particularly difficult because students are likely to be familiar with their nonscientific meanings, which are quite different from their technical meanings (for example, *mass* as in church; *crust*

DIMENSIONS OF DIVERSITY

You can make key concepts more explicit for English learners by using teaching strategies described in this text, such as study guides and graphic organizers.

FIGURE 9.11 Completed Concept Map on Natural Resources

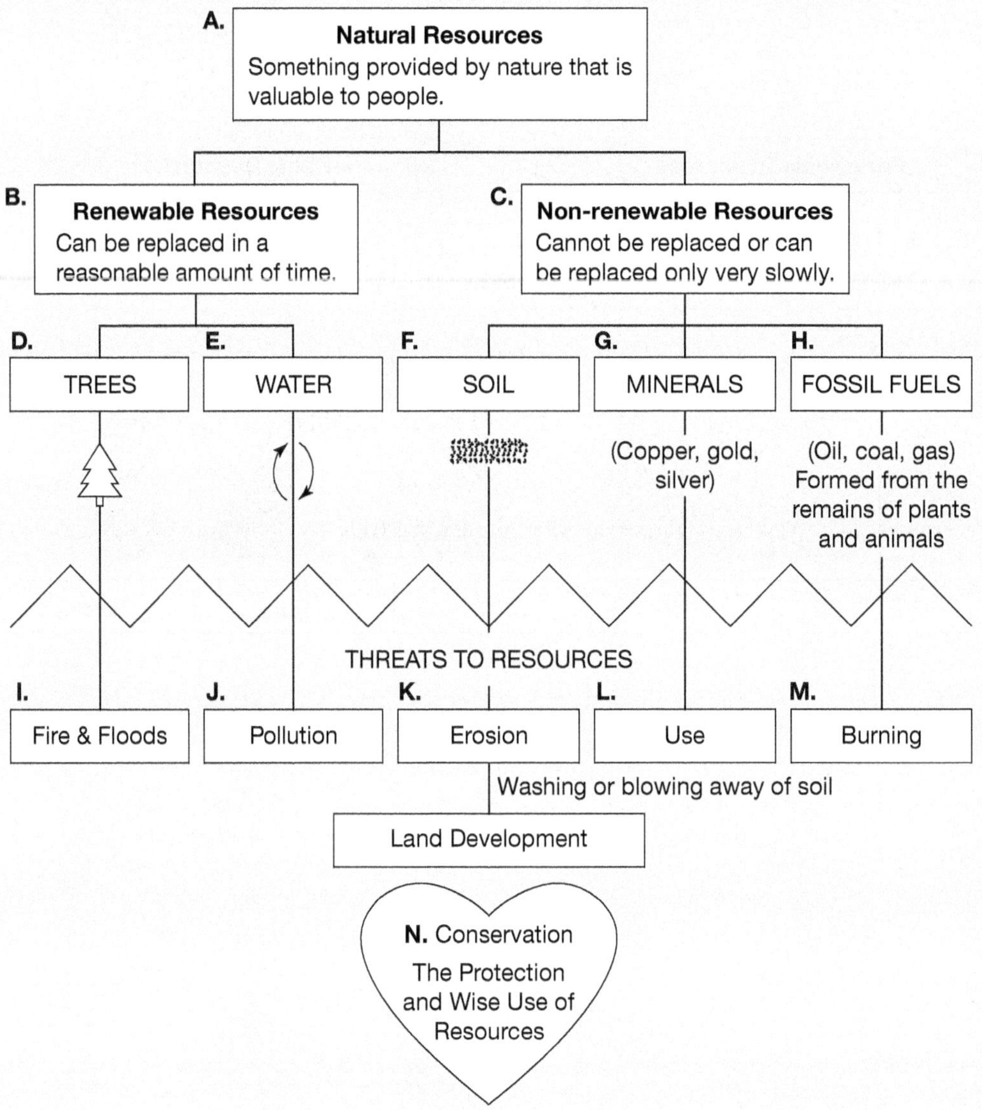

A. **Natural Resources**
Something provided by nature that is valuable to people.

B. **Renewable Resources**
Can be replaced in a reasonable amount of time.

C. **Non-renewable Resources**
Cannot be replaced or can be replaced only very slowly.

D. TREES

E. WATER

F. SOIL

G. MINERALS
(Copper, gold, silver)

H. FOSSIL FUELS
(Oil, coal, gas)
Formed from the remains of plants and animals

THREATS TO RESOURCES

I. Fire & Floods

J. Pollution

K. Erosion
Washing or blowing away of soil
Land Development

L. Use

M. Burning

N. Conservation
The Protection and Wise Use of Resources

Source: From Direct instruction in content-area reading (2010) by A. Archer and M. Gleason. In *Direct Instruction Reading* by D. W. Carnine, J. Silbert, E. J. Kammenui, and S. G Tarver. Upper Saddle River, NJ: Merrill/Pearson.

as in bread). You need to check student understanding and teach vocabulary directly, if necessary, using one of the strategies covered in this section.

USING DEFINITIONS Carnine and colleagues (2010) propose an approach to teaching terms and concepts using definitions that employ positive and negative examples following three steps:

1. State your definitions clearly and simply. Your definitions should only contain words that students already know.

   Consider the following definition of *consumables*, a word from the study guide in Figure 9.8:

   consumables: resources whose availability is permanently changed by their usage.

   This definition uses a number of words that younger or even at-risk middle or high school students might not know. Instead, consider the following more learner-friendly definition:

This teacher is modeling positive and negative examples to clarify the meaning of a new concept. How can using both examples and nonexamples help make the meaning of new terms and concepts clear?

consumables: products used by persons and businesses that must be replaced regularly because they wear out or are used up.

2. Ask students a series of questions to find out whether they can discriminate positive examples from negative examples. For example, if you were teaching *consumables* using a definition, you might say the following:

Consumables are products used by persons and businesses that must be replaced regularly because they wear out or are used up. What are consumables? ("Consumables are products used by persons and businesses that must be replaced regularly because they wear out or are used up.")

Last month we had to replace three of our light bulbs. Are light bulbs consumables? ("Yes, light bulbs are consumables.") How do you know? ("They are products that wear out and need to be replaced.")

In Ellen's neighborhood, most people have lived in the same house for more than 20 years. Are houses consumables? ("No, houses aren't consumables.") How do you know? ("Houses don't need to be replaced regularly because they don't wear out.")

Sarah was out of skin cream and hand lotion and had to go to the store to get some more. Are Sarah's skin cream and hand lotion consumables? ("Yes, Sarah's skin cream and hand lotion are consumables.") Why do you say that? ("Because she used them up and they had to be replaced.")

Randy went to the gas station to fill his tank and change his oil. Are gas and oil consumables? ("Yes, gas and oil are consumables.") How do you know? ("Because they can be used up and have to be refilled.")

The class went to the park for a picnic and went swimming in the river. Is the river a consumable? ("No, the river is not a consumable.") Why do you say that? ("Because it is not a product and can't be replaced.")

What are consumables? ("Consumables are products used by persons and businesses that must be replaced regularly because they wear out or are used up.")

3. Ask a series of open-ended questions to discover whether students can discriminate the new word from words they learned previously. For example, after teaching consumables, ask, "What are consumables?" Also ask for the definitions of words previously introduced: "What are durable goods? natural resources?"

Note the scaffolds within this lesson that are of particular benefit to students with special needs. The fact that the teacher had the students repeat the definition after it was first presented can help keep it in working memory and make it easier for them to answer the questions that follow. Also, requiring students to answer in complete sentences using the new word rather than answer with only a yes or no forces them to use the word. The more times students use a new word, the greater the likelihood they will learn it. Having the students respond in complete sentences reinforces important expressive language skills that are often problematic for students with special needs. Last, if students have been taught a word using a definition or synonym, follow your question with "How do you know?" Their reasons for answering yes or no will reveal whether they are correctly using the definition or just guessing.

TEXT TALK Text talk is a direct teaching strategy and curriculum that teaches vocabulary *in context* using definitions (Beck & McKeown, 2007; Bursuck & Damer, 2015). Students actively process the meaning of each designated vocabulary word including its connection to other words, an approach shown to be superior to traditional read-alouds in which specific words are either not called out at all or merely clarified briefly while reading (Coyne, Loftus, Zipoli, & Kapp, 2009). Use the following steps when using *Text Talk* with your students:

1. Describe the word in the context of the text (e.g., *"In this story, the ogre is opposed to everything that the people want to do: he's opposed to their wanting a holiday; he's opposed to their wanting more rest from work; and he's opposed to letting the kids play."*)

2. Explain the meaning of the word.

3. Ask the students to repeat the word so that they create a phonological representation of it.

4. Provide examples of the word in contexts other than the one used in the story.

5. Have the students make judgments about examples.

6. Ask the students to construct their own examples.

7. Reinforce the word's phonological and meaning representations by asking students to say it again. Have the students read the word if they have the skills to do that.

8. Reinforce the words on subsequent days by (a) keeping charts of the words from several stories posted on the wall; (b) placing a tally mark next to the word if children hear or use one of the words; (c) attempting to use the words in regular classroom activities that occur each day such as the morning message: *"Today is Monday. Jamal wants a **feast** for his birthday."* (Beck & McKeown, 2007; p. 256)

An example of how to use these steps to teach vocabulary directly is shown in Figure 9.12.

English learners and other learners with special needs cannot rely solely on linguistic information to learn and retain vocabulary. For these students, adjustments can include bringing in real objects and visuals, such as photographs; matching your actions with your words by conducting demonstrations; allowing students to hear and see vocabulary by using films, DVDs, and audio books; and having students engage in hands-on activities by performing pantomime and drawing pictures (Hill & Flynn, 2006). Students can also be motivated by personalizing the questions in your vocabulary instruction (Bursuck & Damer, 2015). For example, when Ms. Hendrix taught her students the meaning of *vehicle*, she included in her presentation photos of the family cars of her hard-to-motivate students. She further engaged Rohan by giving him the job of holding up the photos in front of the class during the presentation. Last, direct teaching of vocabulary can be carried out in small groups, depending on student need.

RESEARCH-BASED PRACTICES

Kuder (2017) studied recent research on effective practices for teaching vocabulary to high school students with reading disabilities. He found four practices to be most effective: mnemonic instruction, learning strategies that utilized morphemic analysis, direct instruction, and multi-media instruction.

FIGURE 9.12

Text Talk
Vocabulary Word
Feast

Explain
In the story, it said that the animals found the robbers' table full of good things to eat, and so they had a feast.
A feast is a special meal with lots of delicious food.
Say the word with me: "feast."
People usually have a feast on a holiday or to celebrate something special. We all have a feast on Thanksgiving Day.

Discuss and Summarize
- *Let's think about some examples of feasts. I will name some things and if they are examples of a feast, say, "Yum!" If they are not, don't say anything.*
  - *Eating an ice cream cone. No response*
  - *Eating at a big table full of all kinds of food. Yum!*
- *If you wanted to eat a feast, what kind of food would you want?*
- *What's the word that means a big special meal?*

Source: Based on Beck, I. L., & McKeown, M. G. (2007), "Increasing young low-income children's oral vocabulary repertoires through rich and focused instruction." *The Elementary School Journal, 107*(3), 251–271.

For example, in one of the vignettes at the beginning of the chapter, Mr. Reeves formed a small group with an English learner and two other at-risk students to teach them vocabulary for a unit he was about to introduce. For the English learner, he incorporated Spanish cognates into the lesson such as *continente* for *continent*, and *planeta* for *planet* (Miller, 2016).

MAKING CONCEPT DIAGRAMS Constructing concept diagrams is a method that combines graphic organizers with the methods just described using definitions and positive and negative examples (Boyle & Scanlon, 2010; Bulgren, Deshler, & Lenz, 2007). A sample concept diagram for the concept of nonviolent resistance is shown in Figure 9.13.

First, the teacher selects a keyword from a story or lecture. Next, she constructs a diagram that features the definition of the word; the characteristics that are always present, sometimes present, and never present; and positive and

FYI

It is estimated that teachers can realistically teach 300 words per year, which translates to about 8–10 per week (Stahl, 1999). Because there will never be enough time to teach all of the words students are unlikely to know, focus on words that are important, useful, and difficult to determine from context (Graves, 2009).

FIGURE 9.13 Concept Diagram

Concept Name: Nonviolent resistance
Definition: Protesting in a peaceful way

Always	Sometimes	Never
Peaceful	Done in a group	Violent
	Done individually	

Positive Examples	Negative Examples
Picketing	Shouting match
Boycotting	Physical attack
Sit-in	Revolutionary war
Hunger strike	Riot

MyLab Education
Video Example 9.5: Explicit Instruction
How does this teacher use positive and negative examples in teaching vocabulary to her Tier 2, RtI group?

negative examples that can be used to model the word. Finally, the teacher presents the concept diagram to students as follows (Carnine et al., 2010):

1. Present the word and its definition.

2. Discuss which characteristics are always, sometimes, and never present.

3. Discuss one of the positive examples and one of the negative examples in relation to the characteristics.

4. Check other positive and negative examples to discover whether they match the characteristics.

Communicating Clearly

In effective instruction, ideas are clearly tied together, which enables students to understand them more easily. The need for instructional clarity applies to both your written communication and oral communication. Written communication, in many school situations, involves the use of textbooks and other teacher-generated items such as handouts, homework, and written tests. Oral communication can include instructional behaviors such as giving directions, asking questions, and delivering lectures.

When a textbook is not written clearly or a lecture is not presented clearly, students have to make critical connections between ideas on their own, a skill that many students who are at risk may not have. Students may not be able to recognize that they do not understand the material, or they may not be aware of strategies to try when instruction is difficult to understand. For example, when reading a text, they may not know how to use keywords and headings or how to look at the end-of-chapter questions to get main ideas. During oral presentations, students may not feel comfortable asking questions to clarify the information presented because often they are not sure what to ask and are afraid of looking stupid. Finally, students may lack the background knowledge necessary to construct meaning on their own. If you communicate clearly and use materials that do so as well, students with special needs can be more successful and the need for adjusting your instruction, while still necessary, will be reduced.

COMMUNICATING CLEARLY IN WRITING The importance of clear written communication is illustrated by these two textbook passages about western migration in the United States:

> Many of the farmers who moved in from New England were independent farmers. Land cost about a dollar an acre. Most men could afford to set up their own farms. Livestock farming was quite common on the frontier. Hogs could be fed in the forests. The cost of raising hogs was low (Senesh, 1973, as cited in Armbruster, 1984).

> Most of the farmers who moved in from New England were independent farmers. Being an independent farmer means that the farmer can afford to own his own farm. Around 1815, most men could afford their own farms because lands were cheap—it cost only about a dollar an acre. Many of these independent farms were livestock farms. For example, many frontier farmers raised hogs. Hog farming was common because hogs were inexpensive to keep. The cost of raising hogs was low because the farmer did not have to buy special feed for the hogs. The hogs did not need special feed because they could eat plants that grew in the surrounding forests. (Armbruster, 1984)

The second passage is much easier to understand; it requires fewer inferences by the reader and fewer adjustments by the teacher. It also defines *independent farmer* for the reader. If students were reading the first passage, you might have to provide this definition—which you could do orally or in a study guide, in large or small groups depending on your students' needs. The reason farmers turned to raising livestock can be inferred from the first paragraph, but it is stated directly in the second. For students reading the first paragraph, teachers may need to pose questions prior to reading to establish an understanding of this relationship: For example, "Why did the farmers turn to raising livestock?" Vocabulary not explained clearly in context may need to be covered more directly in large or small groups using strategies for teaching vocabulary covered in this and the next chapters.

Another aspect of written language that can make comprehension more difficult is the use of pronouns. A general rule of thumb is that the closer a pronoun is to its referent, the easier it is to translate. Consider the following section of text:

> Now life began to change. The Eskimo hunters could see that these tools were useful. So they became traders, too. They trapped more furs than their families needed. Then they brought the furs to the trading posts. There they could trade the furs for supplies they had never had before. Because the new tools helped Eskimo hunters get along better, they became part of the Eskimo environment (Brandwein & Bauer, 1980).

Many readers may have trouble figuring out whom *they* refers to in this passage. Although the placement of most pronouns is not this problematic, understanding pronouns can be difficult for students with special needs. However, students can be taught to make sense of pronouns (Carnine et al., 2010). Before students read, identify unclear pronouns. Have students underline the pronouns in a passage. Then show them how to find the pronouns' referents by asking questions. Consider the following example:

Passage
Curtis and Dorva skipped school. They were grounded for a week. He was sorry. She got mad.

Student Questioning
Teacher: "Curtis and Dorva skipped school." Who skipped school?
Students: Curtis and Dorva.
Teacher: "They were grounded for a week." Was Curtis grounded?
Students: Yes.
Teacher: Was Dorva grounded?
Students: Yes.
Teacher: "He was sorry." Was Curtis sorry?
Students: Yes.
Teacher: Was Dorva sorry?
Students: No.
Teacher: "She got mad." Did Dorva get mad?
Students: Yes.

Depending on the level of sophistication of your class, this instruction could be done with the entire class or performed as an instructional adjustment for individual students who struggle to understand sentences containing pronouns. The adjustment could also be made as part of a Tier 2 group.

COMMUNICATING CLEARLY ORALLY Just as the quality of textbook writing affects student learning, so too does the quality of teachers' oral communication. Three particularly important areas of oral language are giving directions, asking questions, and presenting subject matter (such as in a lecture).

Giving oral directions is the most common way that teachers tell their students what they want them to do. When directions are not clear and have to be repeated, valuable instructional time is wasted. Consider this set of directions given by a middle school teacher at the beginning of a social studies lesson:

Unclear Instruction

> All right, everyone, let's settle down and get quiet. I want you all to get ready for social studies. Shh. . . . Let's get ready. Alice and Tim, I want you to put those worksheets away. We need our books and notebooks (Evertson et al., 1983, p. 143).

How clear is the teacher about what she wants her students to do? Now read this alternative set of directions:

Clearer Instruction

All right, everyone, I want all of you in your seats facing me for social studies. [Teacher pauses.] Now, I want you to get out three things: your social studies book, your spiral notebook, and a pencil. Put everything else away so that you have just those three things—the social studies book, the spiral notebook, and the pencil—out on your desk. [As students get out their materials, the teacher writes "Social Studies, page 55, Chapter 7 on Italy" on the whiteboard. She waits until students have their supplies ready and are listening before she begins talking.] (Evertson et al., 1983, p. 143)

In the first example, the teacher does not get the students' attention before giving them directions. She is also unclear in communicating what she wants her students to do. For example, the words *settle down* and *get ready* are not defined for the students. In the second example, the teacher first gets her students' attention and then very specifically states all the things they need to do.

Lavoie (2007) has suggested four guidelines for giving directions that are helpful either for your entire class or as instructional adjustments for individual students with special needs:

1. State commands specifically, using concrete terms. In the Clearer Instruction example, the teacher was very specific about what the students needed to do to get ready for social studies. They had to get out three things: their books, notebooks, and pencils. The first teacher told them only to "get ready."

2. Give "bite-size" directions; avoid a long series of directions. The second teacher first had her students sit down and face her; then she had them take out their materials; finally, she had them turn to the chapter they were going to read that day.

3. Whenever possible, accompany explanations with a demonstration. For example, Mr. Gaswami asked his students to take out their science books, turn to the beginning of the chapter, identify five keywords, and define them using the glossary. Mr. Gaswami showed his students what he wanted them to do by opening his book to the chapter, pointing out that the keywords were italicized, and then defining several keywords to demonstrate how to find and paraphrase the meanings using the glossary in the back of the book. He also displayed pictorial images of these directions on the board to help students read and remember all the steps.

4. Use cuing words such as "Look up here" and "Listen, please" before giving directions. Gestures such as a raised hand are also effective in getting students' attention.

Asking students questions is a vital part of instructional clarity. The way you question your students is important for several reasons. Questioning is a quick way of assessing what your students have learned. In addition, questioning through the use of follow-up probes can help you analyze your students' errors. Finally, you can adjust your instruction by varying the types of questions asked depending on the needs of your students.

Wilen, Ishler, Hutchinson, and Kindsvatter (1999) suggest the following guidelines for using questions in your classroom:

1. *Phrase questions clearly to ensure that students know how to respond.* For example, a vague question such as "Why were bank failures and the stock market crash of 1929 important?" forces students to guess rather than to consider carefully a direct response to the question. Better wording would be "What were the two primary causes of the Great Depression?"

2. *Provide a balance between higher- and lower-level questions.* The important point to keep in mind is that both kinds of questions are important.

FYI

Another use of cueing is to let a student know that he or she can expect to be called on to respond orally when you present a particular signal that only the student knows. This way the student can attend to a lesson with less anxiety about speaking in class.

Lower-level, or convergent, questions help you find out whether students have the basic understanding necessary for higher-level thought. Further, critical and creative thinking can be developed by using convergent and evaluative questions. Although incorporating more higher-level skills into the curriculum is positive, it is important to realize that lower-level knowledge is still important, particularly for students with special needs, who may not readily acquire lower-level knowledge. Failing to help these students acquire this understanding can prevent them from ever developing higher-level understanding. Also, lower-level questions can give students an opportunity to succeed in class. You can adjust your instruction by varying the proportion of lower- and higher-level questions for your students with special needs. For example, Jerome was reluctant to volunteer in class for fear of answering incorrectly. When his teacher Ms. Gonzales asked him a question, he would just frown and not say anything. Ms. Gonzales devised a plan whereby she would give Jerome the questions she was to ask him in advance; she also focused on lower-level questions to further build his confidence. When Jerome began to respond to her questions consistently, Ms. Gonzales gradually introduced unplanned and higher-level questions.

3. *Adapt questions to the language and skill level of the class, including adjusting your questions for individual students in the class.* Your questions should accommodate a range of needs, from lower-performing students to gifted students. For example, a question for a lower-performing student might be, "From what you have just read, how does the demand for a product affect its supply?" For students with more skills, the question might become, "Going beyond the article a little, how does price affect supply and demand and at what point is market equilibrium reached?"

4. *Vary the wait time depending on the nature of the question asked.* If the question covers review material or material of little difficulty, the wait time—or time you allow your students to think about the answer—is brief. However, if a question covers material that is new and/or difficult for your students, give them more time to think before responding. In general, teachers tend to give their students too little think time (Stahl, 1994). Extending thinking time to just three seconds between the end of a question and the start of an answer benefits students in a number of ways:

- Students give longer, more accurate answers.
- The number of times students don't respond decreases.
- Many more students volunteer answers.
- More students with special needs volunteer answers.
- More capable students are less likely to dominate class discussions. (Bursuck & Damer, 2015).

   Some of your students with disabilities may require an even longer thinking time. For example, Ted has a mild intellectual disability and processes oral language more slowly than his peers. In addition to controlling the level of questions she asks him, his teacher allows Ted at least five seconds to respond.

5. *Involve all students in classroom questioning by calling on nonvolunteers as well as volunteers.* Calling on all students also allows you to monitor student learning efficiently. In addition, calling on nonvolunteers (who frequently are students with disabilities or other special needs) demonstrates that you hold them accountable for listening and leads to higher levels of on-task behavior. However, as mentioned before, you should adjust your questions based on student ability to maximize the likelihood of student success. Finally, for lower-level questions, consider using choral responding or having all students respond at once together. Unison responding allows more student opportunities for practice and recitation and can lead to higher levels of correct responses and on-task behavior (Bursuck & Blanks, 2010).

FYI

There is an app called Stick Pick (https://itunes.apple.com/us/app/stick-pick/id436682059?mt=8) that is for randomly calling on students, but it also lets teachers designate which students are higher/lower in terms of academics and gives them questions designed on that basis.

RESEARCH-BASED PRACTICES

Middle school students with special needs taught to self-question outperformed comparable students in their comprehension of social studies content (Berkley, Marshak, Mastropieri, & Scruggs, 2011).

RESEARCH-BASED PRACTICES

Okolo, Ferretti, and MacArthur (2007) analyzed discussions in four middle school history classes. They found that the teacher who had the most student participation and highest state test scores responded to students on an individual basis, used repetition, and personalized history by linking it to students' thoughts and experiences.

6. *Scaffold incorrect answers and "no responses."* Often students with disabilities will not attempt to answer questions because they are worried about making errors in front of their classmates or are unsure of their speech. Even when you increase thinking time, some of these students will not volunteer answers and, when you call on them, will say, *"I don't know,"* or silently shrug their shoulders. Increase your support for these students using this four-step "cue-clueing procedure" suggested by Bursuck and Damer (2015). For example, Ms. Baroody asked the class, *"What is one detail in this section that led me to decide the main idea is 'Mae was fascinated by science?'"* She scaffolded her instruction for Lovelle, a student with a learning disability whose hand wasn't raised, as follows:

1. First Ms. Baroody provided a cue, *"Lovelle, what are some of the things that Mae was doing in this section that showed she was fascinated with learning science?"*

2. Next, Ms. Baroody gave Lovelle a three-second thinking pause to formulate an answer. He still didn't respond, so she moved to step 3.

3. Ms. Baroody increased her support and provided a cue so obvious she was certain it would lead Lovelle to the right answer. *"Lovelle, look at sentence 4 and read it."* (Lovelle read: "Mae spent many hours at the library reading books about science and space.") Then Ms. Baroody asked, *"So where did she go to learn more about science?"* (Lovelle answered, "The library.")

4. Ms. Baroody then reinforced and expanded Lovelle's answer to bolster his confidence: *"Yes, that's absolutely right, Lovelle. The information in the book describing how Mae went to the library and spent all that time reading about science and space was a clue that she must really like science"* (Bursuck & Damer, 2015, p. 294).

INCLUDE ⟩

Use the INCLUDE strategy to ensure that the questions you ask in class match the instructional levels of your students. For example, as part of a curriculum modification stated on her IEP, Melissa was learning to identify numbers from 100 to 999; the rest of the class was learning long division. During a class presentation on how to solve three-digit division problems, Mr. Henry called on Melissa to identify the hundreds-place number that was being divided. Sam, another student in the class, was expected to learn the same long division problems as everyone else, but he was clearly having trouble doing so, as judged by his homework and in-class performance. Mr. Henry questioned him in a different way by asking him to explain the first step in solving the problem after it had already been solved at the board.

Communicating clearly to your students when you are presenting subject-area content orally, such as in a lecture, also is important. The following section of a lecture was delivered during a geography lesson on Italy:

Teacher 1

Italy is in southern Europe, down by France and the Mediterranean Sea. It's a peninsula in the Mediterranean. There are a lot of beautiful islands in the Mediterranean off of Italy and Greece as well. Sardinia and Sicily are islands that are part of Italy. Corsica, Capri, and some other islands like Crete and Cyprus are in the same part of the world, but they don't belong to, although they may be close to, Italy. You could turn to the map of Europe that's in your text to see where Italy is (Evertson et al., 1983, pp. 143–144).

The language used by this teacher lacks clarity. For example, he presents information about a number of islands but is unclear in explaining how these islands relate to the main topic, which seems to be the location of Italy. The teacher is also vague when he says, "[The islands] don't belong to, although they may be close to, Italy." In addition, the teacher uses the word *peninsula* but does not define it. Finally, this explanation needs the visual display of a map to bring clarity to it, but the teacher refers to a map only at the end of the explanation, almost as an afterthought. Then, rather than require students to refer to it, he leaves them with the impression that its use is voluntary. The only students who will know where Italy is after this lecture are those who already knew before the lecture. Many students with special needs will likely be left behind. An example of another lecture on the same topic is much clearer:

Teacher 2

Now, I want all eyes on me. [The teacher then gestures to the world map next to her. The continent of Europe is highlighted.] The continent we have been studying the past month is highlighted here on this map of the world. What continent is it? [The teacher calls on a nonvolunteer who is also a struggling student to identify the continent. The teacher then shows a map of Europe with the countries they have already studied highlighted: France, Switzerland, and Austria.] What are the names of these countries that we have already studied? [The teacher has the class respond in unison and then shows the map of Europe with Italy highlighted.] This is the new country we are studying today. It is called *Italy*. [The teacher writes the word *Italy* on the board as she says it.] What is this country called? [The teacher has the class respond in unison.] Italy is a large peninsula shaped like a boot that extends into the Mediterranean Sea. [The teacher writes *peninsula* on the board, sounding out the syllables as she writes.] What's the word everyone? [Because students have studied the word once before, the teacher calls on a nonvolunteer to define it.] Corrine, what is a *peninsula*?

Although this teacher's presentation is much clearer, she may still need to adjust instruction for her students. For example, Juan, a student with attention problems, may respond better to a video than to a teacher lecture. Carmen, who has a learning disability, has trouble organizing information presented orally and may benefit from using a graphic organizer of the key geographical features of Italy. Damon, a struggling student who has difficulty retaining information, may be assisted by completing a blank copy of the graphic organizer as part of a student study team. Of course, other students in the class may benefit from these adjustments as well.

MyLab Education 9.2 Self-Check

What Adjustments Can You Make for Students to Help Them Succeed in Independent Practice?

As discussed in Chapter 5, the main purpose of practice activities is to provide students with opportunities to refine skills or solidify content that they have already learned and to allow you to monitor their performance. To achieve these purposes, students should be able to independently complete practice activities such as seatwork, practice that is included as part of independent learning centers, and homework assignments.

Even under ideal circumstances and with the best intentions, it is difficult to design practice activities that meet the needs of all students in your class. Problems arise because of individual characteristics, and individual adjustments need to be made using INCLUDE. For example, students with severe reading problems may have difficulty reading directions that are clear to everyone else. Students with attention problems may have trouble answering questions that have multiple

INCLUDE

steps. Students with physical disabilities may be unable to perform the writing requirements of their assignments. In the case of students with severe intellectual disabilities, practice activities may need to be modified so they are consistent with the students' skill levels and the goals and objectives on their IEPs.

Adjusting Seatwork Assignments

Here are five adjustments you can make to directions to ensure that students with special needs know what to do before working independently. Use INCLUDE to figure out whether these adjustments need to be done with your entire class or with only one or a small group of students:

1. Verbally present the tasks. This strategy can be applied to the whole class, particularly when many students are having problems with the directions. You can adjust directions further to meet the needs of individual students by employing physical or pictorial prompts following the directions or pairing a worksheet with a digital recording that explains the directions.

2. Add practice examples that you can do with the whole class or a small group of students who are having particular difficulty.

3. Write alternative sets of directions. You can project these, or you can distribute individual copies to students.

4. Highlight the important words in the directions.

5. Have students help each other when the directions are difficult.

Adjusting Homework Assignments

As they do with in-class practice activities, students with special needs may have difficulty completing traditional homework assignments. A major reason for student failure to complete homework assignments independently, successfully, and without undue stress is that the assignments are too difficult to begin with. Before you give your students an assignment, ask yourself the following questions:

1. What skill (for example, reading, written expression, or math) demands does the assignment make on the students? Are the students capable of meeting these skill demands?

2. What background knowledge (for example, vocabulary or concepts) does the assignment demand of the students? Are the students capable of meeting the demand for background knowledge?

3. Is the purpose of the assignment clear to students?

4. If the assignment involves skill practice, does it include a lot of practice on a few skills rather than a little practice on a lot of skills?

5. Are clear, written directions provided for how to complete the assignment?

6. Is enough time allotted to complete the assignment?
   Even if you answered yes to all these questions, students with special needs may require some of these additional adjustments:

   - Students with reading problems may need extra assistance with homework directions from you, a classmate, or a study group.
   - Students with physical disabilities may need assignments shortened, or they may need to respond orally rather than in writing.
   - Students who read, write, and/or compute more slowly may need fewer or shorter assignments or extra time to complete assignments.

   Remember to use the INCLUDE strategy to make adjustments that fit your assignments and the individual characteristics of your students with special needs.

FYI

As you learned in Chapter 5, another way to provide extra practice for students is in independent learning centers. Use INCLUDE as needed to modify the learning outcomes, materials, and ways students respond in your learning centers.

INCLUDE

WWW RESOURCES

QR codes can be a useful tool for making directions understandable for any kind of practice activity. First, audio record directions on a free site. Then, create a QR code to link to this URL, and paste the QR code onto the master worksheet or web page for the assignment. Students who need oral directions can use their own smartphones or any other device with a QR code reader to access the directions. Providing this support takes only a minute or two and enables students to independently access the support. Using QR codes works across grade levels.

WWW RESOURCES

For homework help, students can go to www.infoplease.com, search "homework," and then be linked instantly to information on the academic subject of their choice, including math, English, literature, social studies, and science. Students can also be linked to tutorials in a wide range of subject areas.

Finally, the success of homework also depends on the involvement of parents. Parent involvement is particularly important for students with disabilities because they are more likely to struggle with homework. Parents play two key roles: overseeing the homework process while their children are at home and communicating with the school regularly about homework. Parents can oversee the homework process by having daily discussions about homework with their children, creating an environment at home that is conducive to getting homework done, supervising homework activities periodically during the time set for homework, and providing support and encouragement for homework completion (Bursuck et al., 1999).

Despite the importance of homework, home–school communication about it sometimes is a problem (Harniss, Epstein, Bursuck, Nelson, & Jayanthi, 2001; Munk et al., 2001; Warger, 2017). Parents of students with special needs may want much more communication with teachers about homework and feel that teachers should make more of an effort to initiate such communication (Munk et al., 2001). Likewise, teachers may feel that parents do not initiate communication about homework often enough, take homework seriously enough, and follow through with commitments they make about helping their children with homework (Epstein et al., 1997).

Contacts with parents about homework can be increased by conducting parent–teacher meetings in the evenings for working parents and by taking advantage of e-mail, a great potential time-saver (Harniss et al., 2001). Another strategy for increasing communication is to establish a homework hotline that can be accessed by phone or a website that provides certain types of homework assistance. You can also involve parents in the homework process at the beginning of the school year and on an ongoing basis thereafter using checklists, newsletters, informed notes, phone calls, and parent discussion groups (Margolis, 2005). For example, at the open house at the beginning of the school year, Ms. Ordonez gives parents information about course assignments for the semester, homework support available in the classroom, and policies on missed homework and extra-credit assignments. She then sends home school progress updates every four weeks; the progress reports include a section on homework completion.

Teachers also can ask parents whether they want to have homework information sent home daily, to sign that they reviewed their children's homework, and to note their children's efforts and describe their difficulties. By signing assignments and indicating their children's effort or difficulty in completing them, parents communicate to their children that they and the teacher are working together and care about homework being completed (Margolis, 2005). It is also important to understand that homework may be a lower priority for families when compared to other home issues. For example, Mr. Gentry knew that Dominique's family had recently been evicted from their apartment and were living in their car. Until Dominique's family was able to find another place to live, Mr. Gentry arranged for him to complete his homework before or after school. Ultimately, the most effective way of warming parents to the homework process is to only send homework that students can complete successfully and independently.

These students are practicing their reading in a learning center. What adjustments might teachers need to make when planning learning centers for their students with disabilities?

MyLab Education 9.3 Self-Check

RESEARCH-BASED PRACTICES

Langberg and others (2015) studied a sample of 104 middle school students diagnosed with ADHD and followed them for 18 months. They found that: (1) students with ADHD turned in on average 12 percent fewer homework assignments; (2) the lower completion rates were largely due to deficient homework materials management abilities; and (3) problems with homework had an adverse effect on their grades.

How Can You Involve Parents in Teaching Their Children?

Teachers are always looking for ways to find extra help for students who take more time to learn new content or skills. That is why we often hear teachers say, "If only his parents would work with him more at home." Although we know parents can promote learning by showing affection for their children, by displaying interest in their children's schoolwork, and by expecting academic success, the effectiveness of parents tutoring their children at home is less clear. The results of research on the effectiveness of parent teaching are mixed; some experts say it is effective whereas others question it (Erion, 2006; Mercer & Pullen, 2008). When determining whether to involve parents in tutoring their children, Mercer and Pullen (2008) suggest taking the following factors into account:

1. Are there reasons for deciding against tutoring (for example, parent lacks technical background to effectively assist in tutoring, mother–father disagreement over the necessity of tutoring, health problems, financial problems, marital problems, or a large family with extensive demands on parental time)?

2. Do parents have the resources of a professional (for example, a teacher) to answer their questions about the tutoring? The success of home tutoring may depend on cooperative efforts.

3. Can the sessions be arranged at a time when there is no interruption from siblings, callers, or other demands? Children need sustained attention in order to learn.

4. Will the child become overwhelmed with academic instruction and resent the home sessions or feel overly pressured?

5. Do the parents become frustrated, tense, disappointed, or impatient during the tutorial sessions? These parents may spend their time better with the child in activities that are mutually enjoyable.

6. Do the tutorial sessions create tensions among family members? For instance, do the siblings view the sessions as preferential treatment?

7. Does the parent resent tutoring the child or feel guilty every time a session is shortened or missed? Are the sessions usually enjoyable and rewarding?

Of course, if you decide to have parents tutor their child, the same strategies for teaching skills and content to students with special needs covered earlier in this chapter still apply. For example, only skills or content at a student's level should be presented, and the progression of skills or content should be gradual and based on student mastery. In addition, parents should be carefully prepared to present new information or skills clearly and enthusiastically and to provide appropriate corrections and encouragement as needed. Parents should also limit the length of the tutoring sessions to 15 minutes for children up to grade six and 30 minutes for older students and should begin and end each session with an activity that the child enjoys and is successful at (Mercer & Pullen, 2008). Also, care must be taken to select the most appropriate time to tutor and to select a place that does not restrict the activities of other family members and is not too distracting. Finally, tutoring should be held at the same time and place to establish a clear routine (Mercer & Pullen, 2008).

FYI

The number of students enrolled in online classes has skyrocketed (Watson, Murin, Vashaw, Gemin, & Rapp, 2014). For information on promising practices in online learning for students with disabilities, go to The Center on Online Learning and Students with Disabilities (COLSD) http://centerononlinelearning.org/.

MyLab Education 9.4 Self-Check

How Can You Make Instructional Modifications for Students with Moderate to Severe Intellectual Disabilities?

Students with moderate to severe intellectual disabilities often cannot perform some or all of the steps in tasks carried out every day by students without disabilities. In the past, this inability to perform tasks in the same way as other students was interpreted to mean that these students could not benefit from these activities. Today, the emphasis is on making modifications for students with moderate to severe disabilities so that they can meet the same curricular standards but in a more functional way, as guided by their IEPs (Cushing, Clark, Carter, & Kennedy, 2005; Hollingshead, Carnahan, Lowrey, & Snyder, 2017; Nolet & McLaughlin, 2005).

One way to allow students with moderate to severe intellectual disabilities to meet state standards and participate more fully in your classroom is by modifying their materials and activities by conducting an environmental inventory (Vandercook, York, & Forest, 1989) as part of the MAPS person-centered planning process (New Jersey Coalition for Inclusive Education, 2013). The planning process involves asking yourself these questions:

1. What is the standard involved?
2. What does a person who does not have a disability have to do in this environment to meet the standard?
3. Can the person who has a disability participate just like everyone else? If not, what is the discrepancy?
4. What types of supports and/or modifications can be put in place to increase the participation level or independence of the student with special needs?
5. What IEP goals (functional outcomes) can the student meet as a result of this participation?

An example of how this process is used in a classroom environment is shown in Figure 9.14. This example involves Roberto, a student with moderate to severe intellectual disabilities whom you read about at the beginning of Chapter 4. Roberto is in Ms. Benis's sixth-grade science class. The class is working in small groups on depicting the steps in the recycling process for paper, metal, and plastic, part of the state science standards. Each group is studying a different recycled material. Roberto lacks the motor and intellectual skills necessary to participate like everyone else.

Ms. Benis decides to modify instruction for Roberto. She assigns him to the group that his friend Seth is in. She also decides to use different materials with Roberto. Ms. Benis has a paraprofessional help Roberto find pictures of recycled products; Seth helps Roberto paste these pictures onto the group's diagram. Mr. Howard, Roberto's special education teacher, helps Roberto identify recycled products in grocery stores and restaurants. Roberto's parents help him sort the recycling at home. All of these activities help Roberto meet the state standard related to the recycling process as well as his IEP goals, which follow:

- Use appropriate communication skills when engaged in a conversation.
- Communicate his wants and needs to peers and staff by using picture symbols or verbally.
- Answer simple questions from peers and staff using a minimum of three-word sentences.
- Count and say the number of items.
- Follow one or two-step directions with minimum prompts.

Examples of making instructional modifications using INCLUDE are described in the Case in Practice feature.

RESEARCH-BASED PRACTICES

Matzen, Ryndak, and Nakao (2010) found that students with significant disabilities received more instruction, experienced less downtime, and engaged in fewer problem behaviors in general education settings. Lee, Wehmeyer, Soukup, and Palmer (2010) discovered further that when modifications were provided, students were more academically engaged and teachers spent less time managing behavior.

WWW RESOURCES

Find information on research-based practices for helping students with severe intellectual disabilities access the general education curriculum at www.ccsso.org. Search "research-based practices." Go to www.georgiastandards.org, click "Georgia Performance Standard (GPS)," and then click "standards for students with significant cognitive disabilities."

FIGURE 9.14 **Environmental Inventory Process**

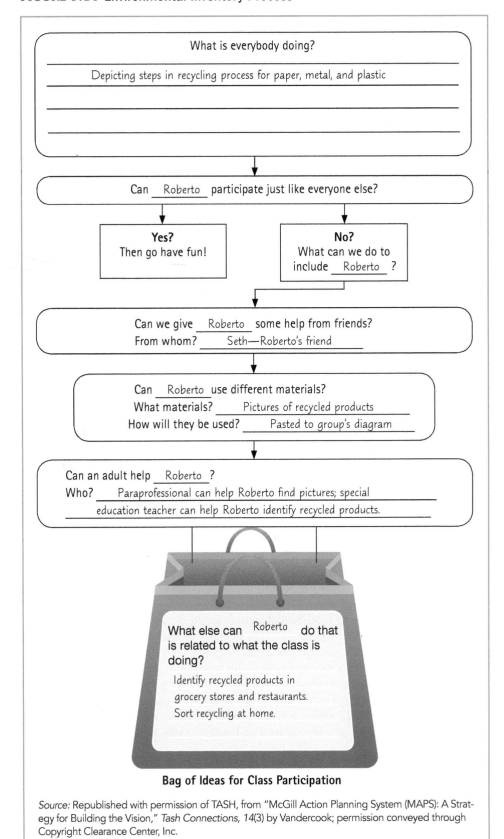

What is everybody doing?

Depicting steps in recycling process for paper, metal, and plastic

Can   Roberto   participate just like everyone else?

Yes?
Then go have fun!

No?
What can we do to
include   Roberto ?

Can we give   Roberto   some help from friends?
From whom?   Seth—Roberto's friend

Can   Roberto   use different materials?
What materials?   Pictures of recycled products
How will they be used?   Pasted to group's diagram

Can an adult help   Roberto ?
Who?   Paraprofessional can help Roberto find pictures; special
education teacher can help Roberto identify recycled products.

What else can   Roberto   do that
is related to what the class is
doing?

Identify recycled products in
grocery stores and restaurants.
Sort recycling at home.

Bag of Ideas for Class Participation

Source: Republished with permission of TASH, from "McGill Action Planning System (MAPS): A Strategy for Building the Vision," *Tash Connections, 14*(3) by Vandercook; permission conveyed through Copyright Clearance Center, Inc.

CASE IN PRACTICE 9.2

Making Instructional Modifications in a Middle School Consumer and Food Science Class

In this case, based on one reported in Kleinert, Green, Hurte, Clayton, and Oetinger (2002), Mr. Gagliano is teaching a middle school consumer and food science class. He recently taught a unit on cooking and nutrition, including how to shop for food. The targeted state standards for the unit were as follows:

1. Students demonstrate the knowledge and skills needed to remain physically healthy.
2. Students evaluate consumer products and services and make effective consumer decisions.

One part of the unit covered vegetarianism. The goal was for the students to plan, shop for, and cook a vegetarian meal. After defining *vegetarianism* and providing a brief history of vegetarianism in the United States, Mr. Gagliano planned to show a video on the Food and Drug Administration (FDA) nutritional guidelines, including how to decipher nutritional information on a food product label. Mr. Gagliano then planned to break the class into four groups and assign each group the task of designing a vegetarian meal meeting FDA nutritional guidelines.

Ramone is a student with moderate intellectual disabilities who is included in Mr. Gagliano's class. Ramone can do basic math at about the second-grade level and reads below the first-grade level. Although his oral language skills are adequate to carry on a conversation, his ability to interact with others in a small group is limited. Ramone's IEP objectives include the following:

1. Prepare one basic meal independently.
2. Use a calculator to budget money while shopping.
3. Make purchases with the "next-dollar" strategy (for example, paying $6.00 and "one more dollar for cents" for an item that costs $6.62).
4. Increase functional sight-word vocabulary to 200 words.
5. Work appropriately in small groups for up to 30 minutes.

Mr. Gagliano and Ms. Henning, Ramone's special education teacher, met to decide how Ramone's instruction during this unit could be modified. They agreed that the curricular demands for the rest of the class were not appropriate for Ramone, and they planned the following instructional modifications based on Ramone's IEP:

1. Ramone will record the possible choices for the menu (for example, main dishes, dessert, drink). He will actively participate in the making of the final choices and will record them via dictation using computers/Chromebooks/iPads.
2. Ramone will record the choices for the grocery list. He will also be assigned the job of checking the kitchen to make sure that items on the list are not already there.
3. Ramone will practice reading the words from the grocery list with the help of his group.
4. Ramone will assist with the shopping, using his calculator to budget the group's money, making purchases using the "next-dollar" strategy, and reading his grocery words to find his items. Ramone will be assisted by his group as needed.
5. Ramone will assist the group in cooking the meal.

Following the activity, Ramone, with assistance from Mr. Gagliano and Ms. Henning, evaluated his performance using checklists based on his related IEP objectives. The evaluations were placed in Ramone's alternate assessment portfolio.

REFLECTION

Do you think it was appropriate for the teachers to plan instructional modifications for Ramone rather than instructional adjustments? How were the expectations for Ramone different from those for his classmates? How were they similar? Should students such as Ramone get credit for meeting state standards when their instruction is modified? How useful is the INCLUDE strategy in planning instructional modifications for students with moderate to severe disabilities?

Source: Based on "Creating and Using Meaningful Alternate Assessments," *Teaching Exceptional Children,* 34(4).

MyLab Education 9.5 Self-Check

WRAPPING IT UP

Back to the Cases

Now that you have read about adjusting instruction for students with special needs, look back at the teacher stories at the beginning of the chapter. Then go to MyLab Education to apply the knowledge you've gained in this chapter to each case.

MyLab Education Application Exercise 9.1: **Case Study 9.1**

MS. DOMANSKI notes that Carmen is willing to read in front of the class when she has had time to practice the passage first within a small Tier 2 group. Abdul had been showing signs of losing the motivation to try new math skills. Ms. Domanski has increased the number of examples and practice opportunities each time she introduces a new skill and provides oral and written directions for all seatwork activities. Another teacher has suggested that she use an advance organizer whenever she introduces a new skill. Albert, as you may remember, struggles to independently complete practice activities in learning centers. Ms. Domanski has taken several steps to help him.

MyLab Education Application Exercise 9.2: **Case Study 9.2**

MR. REEVES'S incoming ninth-grade English class is very diverse, including three students with a variety of learning disabilities, two English learners, and three students who struggle in reading even though they do not have disabilities. Although the English learners can identify words at grade level, they have problems understanding what they are reading because of limited vocabulary. The principal is concerned about all of these students meeting state standards.

MyLab Education Application Exercise 9.3: **Case Study 9.3**

In addition to his behavior intervention plan, Mr. Fain decides on a number of adjustments he can make to his instructions to prevent CHARLIE from becoming frustrated in math.

Summary

LO 9.1 Teachers may need to adjust basic skill instruction in the areas of preskills; selecting and sequencing examples; the rate of introduction of new skills; and the amount of direct instruction, practice, and review.

LO 9.2 In teaching subject-area content to students with special needs, teachers may need to adjust instruction when activating background knowledge, organizing content, and teaching terms and concepts.

LO 9.3 Teachers can improve clarity in written communication by selecting printed materials that clearly tie ideas together, having clear pronoun referents, and requiring fewer student inferences. Teachers can improve oral communication by giving clear directions, asking questions appropriately, and presenting subject matter using direct, unambiguous language.

LO 9.4 Teachers may need to adjust independent practice activities such as seatwork, those found in independent learning centers, and homework.

LO 9.5 Students with moderate to severe intellectual disabilities often cannot perform some or all of the steps in everyday learning tasks. These students require instructional modifications based on an alternative standards-based curriculum as set forth on their IEPs. Teachers can use an environmental inventory as part of the MAPS person-centered planning process as well as the INCLUDE strategy to modify classroom activities for these students.

APPLICATIONS IN TEACHING PRACTICE
Developing a Repertoire of Instructional Adjustments

You want to teach your class to spell the following contractions: *can't, aren't, couldn't, shouldn't, wouldn't, don't, won't,* and *isn't.* Your class includes students with special needs.

QUESTIONS

1. What preskills should you be concerned with, how can you assess them, and what can you do with students who do not know them?

2. How can you sequence instruction? Why did you choose this particular sequence?

3. How can you provide direct instruction, practice, and review for your students?

4. At what rate should you introduce the contractions?

5. How can you evaluate whether your students have learned the contractions?

6. After evaluating your students, you found that two or three of them still hadn't learned the contractions. What should you do next?

Develop a graphic organizer for a major concept in Chapter 1 of this text.

QUESTIONS

1. How did you select the concept? Is it a big idea?

2. How would you use the graphic organizer to teach students the concept?

3. How might you adjust your use of the graphic organizer for students who are at-risk or have other special needs?

Design a lesson to teach the concept of *adjusting instruction* using a definition.

QUESTIONS

1. Is your definition stated clearly, simply, and concisely?
2. What positive and negative examples did you use?
3. How can you find out whether your students know the meaning of the concept?
4. How can you find out whether your students can differentiate this concept from other concepts presented in the text?
5. How would you teach the concept using a concept diagram format?
6. Why would this approach to teaching definitions be beneficial for students with special needs? Under what circumstances might the approach need to be adjusted and how would you do it?

You are teaching a lesson on the respiratory system. First you describe the respiratory process (for example, diaphragm contracts; air rushes into nose and/or mouth; air travels down trachea; air enters lungs through bronchial tubes; and so forth) using a chart showing the key parts of the respiratory system (for example, nose, throat and trachea, bronchial tubes, lungs). Next, you plan to have students work in small, heterogeneous groups on labeling a model of the respiratory system and describing all the key steps in the respiratory process.

QUESTIONS

1. How can you use an environmental inventory to modify this lesson for a student with a moderate to severe intellectual disability?
2. Using INCLUDE, what other modifications might you make for this student?

CHAPTER 10

Strategies for Independent Learning

LEARNING OUTCOMES

After you read this chapter, you will be able to:

10-1 State ways that teachers can encourage student self-awareness, self-advocacy, and self-determination.

10-2 Explain how teachers can create their own learning strategies.

10-3 Describe the steps involved in teaching learning strategies, analyzing each step and discussing why it is important for building independent strategy usage.

10-4 List, describe, and justify the teaching of research-based learning strategies in the areas of reading and reading comprehension; listening and note taking; written expression; math problem solving; and time and resource management, and explain how they can be applied to the students you will be teaching.

10-5 Explain how methods of teaching learning strategies can be applied to helping students perform strategies independently.

GERALD is a student with learning disabilities in Mr. McCrae's ninth-grade English class. Gerald has had problems in the area of written expression throughout his school years, consistently failing to meet standards on the state high-stakes assessment. It is not that he does not have good ideas. When Gerald talks about what he is going to write, it sounds great. However, when he tries to capture his ideas on paper, he becomes very frustrated. Writing is difficult for Gerald. He writes a lot down but his papers lack organization. They rarely have good introductions and conclusions, and the bodies of the papers are usually out of sequence. Gerald also makes a lot of mechanical errors; his papers are full of misspellings, and he frequently leaves out punctuation marks and capital letters. When asked by Mr. McCrae why he does not proofread his papers, Gerald responded that he does.

What can Mr. McCrae do to help Gerald learn to organize his papers better? How can Mr. McCrae help Gerald with writing mechanics without discouraging him from writing? What strategies would help Gerald proofread his papers better for spelling, mechanical, and organizational errors?

TRACI is a student with learning disabilities in Ms. Cord's fourth-grade class. Last year, Traci didn't meet standards on the state high-stakes assessment in math, but her scores were not low enough to make her eligible for special education services. Traci has trouble solving word problems in math because she does not have a systematic way of working on them. When she starts a problem, she looks for the numbers right away rather than first reading the problem carefully. For example, one day she saw the numbers 23 and 46 in a problem and automatically added them to get a sum of 69. The problem called for subtraction, but Traci did not know that because she had not read the problem.

What learning problems might Traci have that are interfering with her ability to solve math word problems? What strategies might help Traci solve math word problems more successfully? How can Ms. Cord teach Traci to learn these strategies and apply them independently?

RON is a 12th-grade student with a moderate intellectual disability who spends part of his day in content specific classes, such as co-taught English IV and American History II, with general education peers. The remainder of Ron's time is spent in classes related to his occupational course of study stressing vocational skills. Ron has problems with organization. He is often late for school, because, according to his parents, he rarely plans ahead and is always getting his materials ready for school at the last minute. Ron is usually late for class as well. He says that he cannot keep track of what he needs to bring to each class, so he is constantly going back to his locker, which makes him late. His locker is a complete mess. Ron has received negative feedback from his school-based vocational training experiences as he works to develop his career portfolio as part of his graduation requirement. In the afternoons, Ron has a part-time job helping to clean copying and fax machines in a work-study program. His supervisor has expressed concern that Ron has been late for work several times and frequently misses his bus after work, causing his coworkers to have to drive him home. Growth in organizational skills would help Ron be more successful in his academic work and in his vocational experiences.

How likely is it for general education teachers to have students like Ron in their classes? What can Ron's general education teachers do to help him become better organized?

Gerald, Traci, and Ron share a common problem: They are unable to meet independently the academic and organizational demands of school. Being able to work and solve problems independently has become increasingly important as more and more students are expected to meet state and federal standards and as the demands of the twenty-first-century job market have become increasingly complex. Gerald needs to be able to organize his papers better, not just in English but in all areas, because teachers often judge quality on the basis of organization, neatness, and the number of spelling or punctuation errors. Traci needs to solve problems more systematically, not just in math but in other classes and outside school as well. Ron needs a strategy for managing his time: Being punctual and having the necessary supplies or materials are essential for success on his alternate assessments as well as eventually in the world of work. The fact is, as students move through the grades and on to careers or post-secondary education, more independence is expected and necessary for success.

Students need to perform independently in five key areas: gaining information, storing and retrieving information, expressing information, self-advocating, and managing time (Deshler et al., 2001; Lenz, 2006). Gaining information involves skills in listening to directions during lessons and on the job and in reading and interpreting textbooks, source books, and Internet and other media. Storing information consists of strategies for taking notes and preparing for tests or other evaluations. Students also need to retrieve information when needed. For example, they need to remember how to carry out a task such as cleaning and clearing a table or how to follow safety procedures during science lab. Expressing information includes taking tests and writing papers. It also involves employment tasks such as developing a printed menu for a fast-food restaurant. Self-advocacy skills build student self-determination, helping students set realistic school or life goals and develop and carry out a plan to meet those goals. Finally, students need to have the time management skills to organize their time and efforts toward meeting their goals.

Although all these skills become more important as students progress through school, independence should be stressed at all levels of instruction. Unfortunately, many students—including those who have disabilities, are at risk, or have other special needs—lack basic independent learning skills. Traditionally, when students needed learning-strategy instruction, they were referred to special education classes, remedial reading or math programs, or special study-skills courses. But in inclusive classrooms, learning strategies can be taught to students with disabilities or other special needs in several ways. Moreover, learning strategies often can be covered in class so that all students can benefit. For example, when Mr. Cooper discovered that many of his students in U.S. history were having trouble taking notes, he presented a note-taking strategy to his whole class. Similarly, Ms. Carpenter taught her biology class a strategy for taking multiple-choice tests because her students were scoring low as a group on these kinds of questions.

When students have more intensive skill needs, more individualized strategy instruction might take place outside the classroom, sometimes in a Tier 2 response-to-intervention (RtI) or Multi-Tier System of Supports (MTSS) group. For example, some students with special needs may need to have a strategy broken down into small steps, view multiple demonstrations of a strategy, and practice it many times before they learn it. If the collaborative support of other education professionals is lacking, as might occur in co-teaching when a general educator does not want to devote time to such instruction, this level of teaching may be difficult to deliver within the time and curricular constraints of the general education classroom. Ron, from the chapter-opening case, has just such extraordinary needs. He needs a strategy designed specifically for his organizational problems; a plan for getting to his afternoon job on time would not be relevant for the rest of his classmates. In cases such as these—in which a special educator teaches a strategy to individual students whether in your classroom or in another setting—your job is to encourage and monitor student use of the strategy in your class and to provide students with feedback on their performance. However, in most cases, you can teach many of these skills in your class while still covering the required academic content. In fact, teaching learning strategies to students allows you to cover more material because your students become able to learn on their own.

You should do all you can to encourage the use of independent learning strategies and teach them to your students. This chapter focuses on ways you can build student independence in learning by encouraging student self-awareness and self-advocacy skills, developing and teaching independent learning strategies directly in class, and teaching students to use specific strategies on their own.

How Can You Encourage Student Self-Awareness, Self-Advocacy, and Self-Determination?

As students move through elementary, middle, and high school and on to post-secondary education or the world of work, the level of independence expected of them increases. Teachers expect students to come to class on time, master content through reading and lectures, keep track of assignments, organize study and homework time, set realistic career goals, and participate in curricular and extracurricular activities to meet these career goals. Students also must recognize when they have a problem and know where to go for help. Clearly, students need to look out for themselves, to become self-advocates. Self-advocacy is an important part of self-determination, or the ability to make decisions and direct behavior so that the desired goals are achieved (Wehmeyer, Shogren, Toste, & Mahal, 2017). Although the goal of becoming self-determined is important for all students, it is particularly important for students with special needs, who, as you learned in Chapter 7, are at risk for learned helplessness and low self-esteem.

Adjusting to changing expectations can be difficult for all students, but especially for those with disabilities. In Chapter 2, you learned about a process to help students take control of their lives called person-centered planning. However, for person-centered planning to be successful, students need to be self aware and must not be afraid to stand up for themselves. Unfortunately, many students with special needs are not aware of their strengths and weaknesses (Walker & Test, 2011; Scanlon & Mellard, 2002) and lack self-advocacy skills (Durlak, Rose, & Bursuck, 1994; Prater, Redman, Anderson, & Gibb, 2014). Fortunately, self-advocacy skills can be taught to students of all ages and disabilities (Durlak et al., 1994; Prater et al., 2014; Test, Fowler, Brewer, & Wood, 2005).

In effective student self-advocacy training, students learn their strengths and weaknesses, the potential impact of these strengths and weaknesses on their performance, the support they need to succeed, and the skills required to communicate their needs positively and assertively. Generally speaking, special educators have much of the responsibility for teaching self-advocacy directly. However, general education teachers are in a good position to teach all students about the opportunities and expectations of the adult world related to self-awareness and self-advocacy.

For example, in applying the steps in INCLUDE, when Ms. Gay observed that Meredith was getting Fs on her independent work in class, Ms. Gay surmised that Meredith's problem was at least in part due to her being afraid to ask for help. Ms. Gay decided to spend five minutes with the whole class talking about knowing when and how to ask for help. She felt this discussion would help Meredith and other students in the class be more assertive when they encountered difficulty in their work. In another situation, Cecil, a student with a vision impairment who was in Mr. Jordan's algebra class, sat in the front row but was still unable to see the problems on the Smartbboard because Mr. Jordan wrote the numbers too small. However, Cecil did not feel comfortable asking Mr. Jordan to write larger when he could and also accompany his visual presentations with clear verbal explanations. With his special education teacher, Cecil practiced asking Mr. Jordan for help. Cecil then asked Mr. Jordan directly, who responded that it would be no problem to write bigger. Mr. Jordan also gave Cecil some additional pointers on how to describe his disability and how to ask his teachers for accommodations. Read more about the importance of student self-advocacy in Working Together 10.1.

RESEARCH-BASED PRACTICES

Shogren, Villarreal, Lang, and Seo (2017) found that students who were more self-determined (i.e., autonomous, psychologically empowered, and self-realized) were more likely to benefit from school supports designed to enhance their transition to adulthood. A high level of self-determination also promotes more positive reading and writing outcomes (Wehmeyer et al., 2017).

FYI

Papay, Unger, Williams-Diehm, and Mitchell (2015) recommend teaching self-determination at the elementary school level. One way is through the Self-Determination Game, a series of questions aligned with elements of self-determination. Questions focus on hypothetical "what ifs," with each participant answering from his/her own perspective.

INCLUDE

RESEARCH-BASED PRACTICES

Neale and Test (2010) successfully taught third- and fourth-grade students with high-incidence disabilities to express their learning preferences in an individualized education program (IEP) meeting using a learning strategy called "I Can Use Effort."

WORKING TOGETHER 10.1

Fostering Team Communication and Self-Advocacy

Avery was a student with a disability in reading and writing in Mr. Katz's biology class. At Avery's IEP meeting at the end of the previous school year, his team decided that Avery needed extended time taking classroom and standardized tests because of his slow reading rate. The team also agreed that if Avery found he needed adjustments to his instruction in other areas, he was to let Mr. Katz know. Avery told the team that he didn't always feel comfortable asking for accommodations, so his special education teacher agreed to coach him on how to ask for support, as needed, when Avery came to his class for resource. Avery began the year with no problems, but when Mr. Katz's

homework assignments became longer and more difficult, Avery struggled to complete them. As Mr. Katz was a stickler for homework being handed in on time, Avery's grades in biology began to suffer. Avery knew he needed to talk with his teachers about this but was too embarrassed. As a result, he received a grade of D in Biology for the first grading period.

Why is it important for students with disabilities to be able to advocate for themselves?

Why do you think a problem has occurred in this case?

What steps should the IEP team take to support Avery?

How Can You Effectively Teach Independent Learning Strategies in Class?

MyLab Education

Video Example 10.1: Self-Advocacy

Watch this student with disabilities talk about her experiences with self-advocacy. https://www.youtube.com/watch?v=CqtO3cvdom8

INCLUDE

In addition to teaching students to advocate for their own educational needs, another way you can help your students become more independent is to teach them strategies for learning how to learn (Lenz, 2006). These methods are collectively referred to as learning strategies. Learning strategies are techniques, principles, and rules that enable a student to learn to solve problems and complete tasks independently (Gildroy & Deshler, 2008; Lenz, Ellis, & Scanlon, 1996). Learning strategies, which are similar to study skills, not only emphasize the steps needed to perform a strategy (for example, steps to follow in reading a textbook) but also stress why and when to use that strategy as well as how to monitor its usage. For example, when Ms. Blankenship taught her students a strategy for reading their textbook, she pointed out that the strategy would save them time yet improve their test scores. She also taught them to judge how well they were using the strategy by filling out a simple checklist as they read. As shown in Figure 10.1, this section of the chapter covers the process of teaching independent learning strategies in the areas of reading, math problem solving, written expression, listening/note taking, and time and resource management. This process includes selecting well-designed strategies based on student needs. The Case in Practice feature shows how the INCLUDE strategy can be used to select the appropriate learning strategies for your students.

An important component of teaching learning strategies effectively is that they be well designed. As you recall from the discussions of effective materials and Universal Design for Learning (UDL) in Chapters 5 and 9, the better your materials and instruction are designed, the greater the chance that they will work for your students with disabilities or other special needs without requiring you to make major adjustments. Some effective guidelines for designing learning strategies are presented in the Professional Edge feature; the specific strategies described later in the chapter all follow these design principles. It is also important to select strategies based on student needs.

For students to use learning strategies independently, they must first learn to perform them accurately and fluently. Research shows that most students benefit when the teacher directly explains how learning strategies can help them complete academic tasks (Lenz, 2006). However, students vary in the amount of structure they need to acquire learning strategies (Lenz, 2006). Some students can construct successful strategies on their own from repeatedly completing tasks in their classes (Pressley & Hilden, 2006). Other students may need simple prompts and models to develop strategies. This level of structure usually

FIGURE 10.1 **Process of Teaching Independent Learning Strategies**

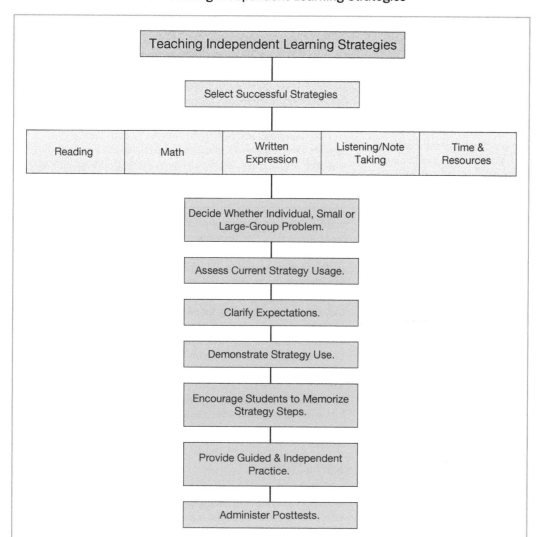

can be delivered by the general education teacher in a large-group setting. Still other students may require more intensive instruction, often in a small group, that includes explicit describing and modeling of a specific strategy as well as extensive practice and feedback about how to apply the strategy to their course demands (Archer & Hughes, 2011; Swanson, 2001). This more intensive instruction can be delivered through co-teaching (Conderman & Hedin, 2013) or in Tier 2 or 3 of an RtI or MTSS system, depending on the degree of student need. The following research-based steps for teaching independent learning strategies are recommended (Schumaker & Deshler, 2006), provided you have already selected successful strategies and decided whether the situation represents an individual, small, or large-group problem:

1. Assess current strategy use.
2. Clarify expectations.
3. Demonstrate strategy use.
4. Encourage students to memorize strategy steps.
5. Provide guided and independent practice.
6. Administer posttests.

These steps incorporate many of the effective teaching practices described in Chapters 5 and 9, and they would also qualify as evidence-based practices for

⟨ INCLUDE

CASE IN PRACTICE 10.1

Using INCLUDE and Co-Teaching to Guide Instruction in Learning Strategies

Mr. Devereau taught social studies at Martin Luther King Jr. Middle School. He had a reputation for expecting a lot from his students; throughout the year, he expected them to be able to learn an increasing amount of subject matter independently.

Prior to the first day of school, Mr. Devereau was informed that his first-period class included eight students with learning disabilities and two with behavior disorders. He was also told that a special education teacher, Ms. Finch, was assigned to the class as a co-teacher. Mr. Devereau had never before had this many students with disabilities in one class; he also had never worked with a co-teacher. Still, he was hopeful that Ms. Finch would be able to help him, so he set up an appointment to meet with her. Here is part of their conversation:

Ms. Finch: What demands do students have to meet to be successful in your class?

Mr. Devereau: I expect students to begin to learn on their own. That is what is expected when they get to high school. Some of my class material is flipped. Students watch narrated Power-points of my lectures on their own, outside of class, taking notes as they watch. We then discuss the lectures in class, where I respond to any questions they may have.

Ms. Finch: How does your grading system work?

Mr. Devereau: Grades are based on student performance on two multiple-choice tests and a five-page report on a famous person in pre–Civil War America.

Ms. Finch: Based on how your class is structured, my concern is that the students' IEPs show that they all are likely to have problems finding main ideas in both the textbook and the class lectures. But I know of some learning strategies that would help them be more successful in these areas.

Mr. Devereau: That sounds good. It's likely that other students in the class would benefit from these strategies as well.

Mr. Devereau and Ms. Finch decided to each take a strategy. Mr. Devereau would teach the note-taking strategy while he was lecturing in class. Ms. Finch would assist by modeling note taking at the board and/or monitoring student note-taking performance and providing corrective feedback as necessary. Ms. Finch was to teach the students two textbook-reading strategies: one for scanning a text and another for summarizing the big ideas in the text. She was to work on these strategies daily during the last 15 minutes of class until the students were able to perform them independently. While Ms. Finch and Mr. Devereau thought that the students with special needs also would have trouble with the multiple-choice tests and the five-page report, they decided that covering these strategies at the same time would be too much. However, they agreed to show the students how the strategies they were learning for note taking and text-book reading could also help them with their tests and research paper. Last, both teachers felt that the students with disabilities would need more practice than other students to master the strategies. Therefore, they agreed to integrate strategy practice into a learning station once per week for three weeks, with some students getting extra practice while others received helpful review.

REFLECTION

How did Mr. Devereau and Ms. Finch use INCLUDE to help their students? Do you think taking the time to teach strategies to the whole class undermines the coverage of content needed to pass state tests? Why or why not? In what areas might the students benefit from acquiring learning strategies?

WWW RESOURCES

The Wrightslaw website (http://www.wrightslaw.com) can be a valuable resource for all involved in student development of self-advocacy skills. Under "Topics," which appears on the left side of your screen, scroll down and click "Self-Advocacy."

INCLUDE >

RtI or MTSS. Use the INCLUDE strategy to help you determine the level of structure you need to provide to students as you deliver each step.

Assess Current Strategy Use

Students often are receptive to instruction when they can clearly see what problems they are having and how the strategy you are teaching can help them overcome these problems. Therefore, learning-strategy instruction begins with an assessment of how well your students can currently perform a skill, a part of the N and C steps of INCLUDE. As you learned in Chapter 4, specific learning strategies can be assessed using direct-observation checklists, analyses of student products, and student self-evaluations.

You also need to assess whether your students have the preskills necessary to perform the strategy. For example, students who can discriminate between main ideas and details in a lecture are ideal candidates for learning a note-taking strategy; students who can read all the words on a test and understand the class content will benefit most from a test-taking strategy. In contrast, students who cannot identify most of the words in their texts are not logical candidates for learning a textbook-reading strategy; students whose assignments are too

PROFESSIONAL EDGE 10.1

Developing Your Own Learning Strategies

You can use the guidelines here either to create your own learning strategies or to evaluate ones that are commercially produced. By following these suggestions (Conderman, Hedin, & Bresnahan, 2013; Sabornie & DeBettencourt, 2009), based on ones originally proposed by Ellis, Lenz, and Sabornie (1987), you can develop learning strategies tailored for the students in your class.

1. Identify skill areas that are problematic for most of your students, such as taking multiple-choice tests or writing lecture notes.

2. For each skill area, specify student outcomes, such as scoring at least 10 percent higher on multiple-choice tests or writing down key main ideas and details from a lecture.

3. List a set of specific steps students need to follow to reach the identified outcomes. You may want to ask other students who have good test-taking and note-taking skills what they do. Presented here is a sample reading comprehension strategy called *TRAP* (Hagaman, Casey, & Reid, 2016):

   T   *Think* before you read.

   R   *Read* a paragraph.

   A   *Ask* yourself, "What was this paragraph mostly about?"

   P   *Put* it into your own words.

4. Your strategy should contain no more than eight steps. More steps make the strategy difficult to remember.

5. Your steps should be brief; each should begin with a verb that directly relates to what students are to do.

6. To help students remember the steps, encase the strategy in a mnemonic device (for example, the acronym *TRAP* for the reading strategy just presented).

7. The strategy should cue students to perform behaviors for thinking (remembering), for doing (reading), and for self-evaluation (surveying or checking their work).

8. A textbook-reading strategy developed by teachers (Conderman et al., 2013) that meets the guidelines for developing an effective learning strategy follows:

   B   *Break* reading into smaller parts.

   I   *Identify* confusing words or phrases.

   R   *Reword* or *rephrase* to clarify.

   D   *Decide* if it makes sense.

   S   *Summarize* in your own words.

difficult for them will not benefit from a strategy to help them organize their independent practice activities.

As you have learned, students with special needs often lack critical preskills. Before you decide to teach a particular strategy, you should identify its preskills and assess them separately. If most students lack the preskills, they can be taught

Demonstrating the use of a learning strategy involves explaining both the thinking and the doing parts of a process, showing examples and nonexamples of effective strategy use, and checking learners' understanding. How do these steps help students with special needs acquire learning strategies?

as part of your everyday instruction. If only a few have problems with preskills, these students need to receive additional instruction in class, with a peer or adult tutor; through co-taught lessons; or in a learning center, Tier 2 or Tier 3 in RtI or MTSS, or special education setting.

Clarify Expectations

Learning strategies have the potential to empower your students because they enable them to learn and succeed in and out of school on their own, without getting too much help from others. When you introduce learning strategies to students, you need to point out their potential benefits clearly and specifically. Carefully explained expected outcomes can be motivating, particularly as students get older and teacher encouragement alone may no longer be enough to keep them interested.

> INCLUDE

The first step in getting and keeping students motivated to learn is to provide a strong rationale for why learning the strategy is important. This rationale should be directly tied to current student performance as well as to the demands of your class, two essential pieces of information derived from the INCLUDE process. For example, when introducing a new note-taking strategy, Mr. Washington pointed out that the class was able to identify on average only half of the main ideas presented on a note-taking pretest. He also told his class that half of the material on his tests would come from information presented during his lectures. Finally, Mr. Washington explained that taking good notes can help students outside school as well; in many job situations, employers give directions that need to be written down.

The next step in clarifying expectations is to explain specifically what students should be able to accomplish when they have learned the skill. For example, Ms. Thompson told her class that after learning a textbook-reading strategy, they would be able to do their homework faster. Also, give students an idea of how long it will take them to learn the strategy. You could make a chart showing the instructional activities to be covered each day and the approximate number of days it will take to learn the strategy. The advantage of presenting the information on a chart is that steps can be checked off as completed. The act of checking off completed activities can be very motivating for students, and it is also a way of demonstrating self-monitoring, an effective independent learning skill discussed later in this chapter.

RESEARCH-BASED PRACTICES

Research shows that students are more motivated to learn when instruction (a) leads to success, (b) is thematic in orientation, (c) allows for student choice, (d) is relevant, and (e) builds collaborative relationships (Cambria & Guthrie, 2010).

Demonstrate Strategy Use

In demonstrating strategies, keep in mind three important points. First, remember that the process one goes through in performing a task or solving a problem should be carefully explained. For example, demonstrate both thinking and doing behaviors. Talking aloud to yourself while performing the skill is particularly important for many students with disabilities, who often do not develop spontaneously organized thinking patterns. Co-teachers sometimes accomplish this by having one teacher describe the strategy or deliver content while the other models how to talk to oneself to learn the strategy or apply it during instruction, in essence, being the "student brain." Learning strategy instruction can also be delivered through an RtI or MTSS system. A model RtI program at the high school level is described in Instructional Edge 10.1.

Second, present both positive and negative examples of appropriate strategy use, carefully explaining why they are positive or negative. This explanation can help students tell the difference between doing a strategy the right way and doing it incorrectly, a distinction that can be difficult for students with special needs to make without direct instruction. For example, Mr. Washington demonstrated effective and ineffective note-taking strategies using a Smartboard. As students listened to a short videotaped lecture, he took notes systematically, writing down key ideas and details. Next, using the same lecture, he demonstrated ineffective note taking by trying to write down every word. While negative examples are indeed helpful, you should use positive examples at least three

INSTRUCTIONAL EDGE 10.1

A Model High School RtI Program

A common refrain about RtI or MTSS is that there are few models to guide practice at the secondary level. Fisher and Frey (2011) have presented a two-year case study of a successful RtI implementation at an ethnically diverse urban high school in the American Southwest. The RTI program resulted in improved student achievement, attendance, and grade-point averages, and a decrease in special education referrals. Fisher and Frey made these suggestions for designing and implementing RtI in high schools based on their successful experience.

FOCUS ON QUALITY CORE INSTRUCTION

Evidence-based Tier 1 instruction is at the heart of RtI and was the main focus of this project. The teachers agreed to:

- Establish a specific purpose or content focus for each lesson.
- Continually demonstrate expert thinking for students by using think-alouds.
- Carefully scaffold student practice in both small and large groups.
- Provide direct explanation as needed, but eventually withdraw supports to encourage independent student thinking.
- Encourage student engagement by having students work collaboratively with their classmates to ensure a firm understanding of the content.
- Require students to apply what they have learned by engaging in tasks aligned with lesson purposes and focus of instruction.

Over the two years of the project, 50 percent or more of the Tier 1 instruction was devoted to students interacting with each other over the content, and the average lecture, which included teacher modeling, was 12.4 minutes.

USE CORE COMPETENCIES TO MONITOR STUDENT PROGRESS

In traditional high schools, progress is often monitored through grades, which represent performance on elements such as classroom assignments, homework, tests, and projects that may or may not be related to teacher performance objectives. In the RtI model described here, project teachers:

- Developed their own curriculum-based assessments based on key learnings or competencies in their classrooms.
- Carefully aligned the competencies with state standards.
- Planned instruction based on student performance on the competency assessments.
- Used student performance data to identify students in need of additional instructional support, either as a part of differentiated instruction in Tier 1 or more intensive interventions in Tiers 2 and 3.
- Expected all students to meet the competencies; students who struggled were provided with supplemental or intensive instruction until they passed.
- Used only the results of the teacher-made competency tests to guide decision making related to RtI.

SCHEDULE INTERVENTIONS TO SUPPLEMENT, NOT SUPPLANT, CORE INSTRUCTION

- Because all students were expected to attain the core curricular objectives or competencies, they all remained in the core curricular program.
- The teachers took charge of the support process using the results of progress monitoring data from the competency tests. As a result, most support took place as a part of small-group instruction in the general education classroom and the general education teachers directed the process.

DEDICATE RESOURCES TO SUPPORT INTERVENTION EFFORTS

Although the general educators were the driving force behind the project, after a year it became evident that someone needed to be available to coordinate all of the supplemental and intensive intervention efforts. The school hired a coordinator with a background in reading who, in addition to coordinating the interventions, introduced screening measures in reading, math, and writing to help identify students with more significant academic needs.

To learn more about RtI at the high school level, go to http://www.rti4success.org; under "Related RTI Topics," click "Secondary Schools."

---

times more often to guard against the possibility of unwittingly modeling and supporting an ineffective practice.

Third, after you demonstrate, ask frequent questions to monitor student understanding and determine whether more demonstration is needed. Keep in mind that for many students, including those with disabilities, one demonstration may not be enough.

Encourage Students to Memorize Strategy Steps

The purpose of having students memorize the steps in the strategy is to make it easier for them to recall the strategy when they need to use it. To help students learn the steps, you can post them prominently in your classroom at first so that you and your students can refer to them throughout the class or day. Students also should practice saying the strategy steps. To practice, students could pair off and quiz each other, or you could ask students the strategy steps before and after class. For example, each day during the last several minutes of class, Ms. Henry quizzed four of her social studies students on the steps of a strategy for paraphrasing text.

Even though memorizing a strategy can help students recall it, you may not want to spend too much time on this step, particularly for some of your students with learning disabilities, who may have memory problems. For these students, you might include the steps to all the strategies they are learning in a special section of their assignment or class notebooks. For strategies used most often, cue cards listing strategy steps can be taped to the inside covers of textbooks or notebooks, or stored, sometimes in picture form, on students' smartphones or tablets.

Provide Guided and Independent Practice

Because students must learn how to perform strategies accurately and fluently before they can attempt them independently, they need considerable practice. Five ways of providing practice on learning strategies are suggested. One way is to have students use controlled materials when they are first learning a strategy. Controlled materials generally are materials at the student's reading level, of high interest, and relatively free of complex vocabulary and concepts. Because controlled materials remove many content demands on the learner, they allow students to focus all their energy on learning the strategy. Controlled materials also foster initial success, which is important for motivation. For example, Mr. Bernard was teaching his students a strategy for taking essay tests in current events. At first, he had his students practice this strategy on simply worded, one-part essay questions about material familiar to the students, such as people and events in the areas of rock music, movies, television, and sports. As students became better at using the strategy, Mr. Bernard gradually introduced more complex questions on less familiar topics, such as the malaria eradication in Africa and opioid addiction in the United States. Finally, he used sample test questions.

A second way to provide students with practice is first to guide them and then to allow them to perform independently. *Guided practice* means giving students verbal cues when they are first attempting a skill. For example, before and while her students were practicing a strategy, Ms. Waters asked them questions such as "What will you do first?" "Why did you do that?" "What should you do after you are done with the strategy steps?" "Which key words are you going to look for in the questions?" "How will you know which are the main ideas?" and "Was the sentence I just read a main idea? Why?" Of course, guided practice of this nature could also be accomplished using parallel teaching, a model of co-teaching described in Chapter 3. Once most students seem able to answer your reminder questions, you can gradually stop asking them so that students are eventually performing independently. Some students may need little guided practice or none at all and can be allowed to work independently right away.

A third practice technique is to give feedback that is specific and encourages students to evaluate themselves (Lenz, 2006; Lenz et al., 1996). For example, Dominique has just performed the steps of a proofreading strategy in front of the class. Her teacher says, "Good job, Dominique! I knew you could do it." Denise performed the same strategy in front of her class and her teacher asked, "How do you think you did? What do you need to focus on most the next time?" The feedback Dominique received does not clearly tell her what she did right, nor does it encourage self-evaluation. The feedback given to Denise encourages self-evaluation, a critical part of independent learning. Of course, if Denise cannot evaluate her own performance at first, the key parts of good performance have to be pointed out to her and practice on self-evaluation provided. More ideas for helping students monitor their performance are described later in the chapter.

A fourth aspect of practicing learning strategies is to praise students only when they have produced work that is praiseworthy. Praise that is not tied to student performance or is exaggerated, often for the purpose of enhancing student self-image, may only reinforce the student's sense of inadequacy. For example, because of a history of failure in learning situations, students with special needs often see little relationship between their efforts and classroom success. When you give nonspecific praise to these students, it is easier for them to attribute your praise to something other than competence, such as sympathy ("I'm so bad at this, she has to pretend I did well").

Fifth, encourage students to reinforce themselves and to take responsibility for both their successes and their failures. For example, after doing well on a note-taking strategy, Alicia was encouraged by her teacher to say, "I did a good job. This time I paid attention and wrote down all the main ideas. I need to do the same the next time." Alicia's teacher was showing her how to attribute her success to factors under her control. This approach can help her become a more active, independent learner.

MyLab Education

Video Example 10.2: Taking Notes in Content Area Reading

Watch this video of the teaching of a note-taking strategy. How did the teacher manage to teach the strategy and still cover class content?

Administer Posttests

When it appears from your practice sessions that most students have acquired the strategy, give them the pretest again, this time as a posttest, to test their mastery. If, according to your posttest, students have not acquired the strategy, identify where the breakdown occurred and then provide additional instruction and/or practice. If more than 20 percent of the students need extra practice or instruction, they can receive additional help in a large or small group. Using small groups is easier when you have a co-teacher in your classroom. If fewer than 20 percent of the students require more assistance, they can be provided with more individualized practice by the classroom teacher before or after school by a co-teacher in an alternative teaching group, special education teacher, or other support staff, or in a Tier 2 or Tier 3 intervention group.

MyLab Education 10.1 Self-Check

FYI

Classrooms employing inquiry-, problem-, or project-based learning provide excellent opportunities for students to practice independent learning strategies.

FYI

Knowing which strategies to teach your students is an important outcome of using the INCLUDE strategy.

What Are Some Examples of Successful Learning Strategies?

There is a growing number of research-based learning strategies that work for students who are at risk or who have special needs. As shown in Figure 10.1, these strategies cover many areas, including reading and reading comprehension, listening and note taking, written expression, math problem solving, and time and resource management. An array of strategies that incorporate many of these effective practices is summarized in the following sections. Many of these strategies can be used with students at all levels—elementary, middle, and high school. While most of the strategies are framed with acronyms to help students remember the steps, this mnemonic device is a supplement, and not a substitute, for the systematic, explicit method of teaching learning strategies described in the previous section.

Word Identification and Reading Fluency Strategies

Students cannot always depend on the teacher to help them figure out difficult words. They also need to read fluently enough so that they can understand what they are reading and finish assignments in a timely manner. The next two strategies are designed to help students help themselves in the important areas of word identification and reading fluency.

IDENTIFYING WORDS IN TEXTBOOK READING Middle and high school students are likely to encounter technical words in their content-area textbooks that have multiple syllables, making them difficult for some students to identify. One strategy designed to help students with special needs identify difficult words in their textbook reading (Archer, Gleason, & Vachon, 2003, p. 95) helps students break apart words and then put them back together. First, teach your students to break words apart on paper by having them do the following:

1. Circle the word parts at the beginning of the word (prefixes).
2. Circle the word parts at the end of the word (suffixes).
3. Underline the letters representing vowel sounds in the rest of the word.
4. Say the parts of the word.
5. Say the parts fast.
6. Make it a real word.

Once your students can perform all of these steps by writing them, they are gradually encouraged to perform the steps in their heads, as follows (Archer et al., 2003, p. 95):

1. Look for word parts at the beginning and end of the word, and vowel sounds in the rest of the word.
2. Say the parts of the word.
3. Say the parts fast.
4. Make it a real word.

To be successful with this strategy, students need to be able to perform two critical preskills. They need to know sounds the vowels make, and they need to be able to pronounce prefixes and suffixes. Students lacking these preskills need to be taught the skills prior to strategy instruction. For words that have parts difficult to decode, encourage students to say the parts they know and then use the strategy described next for using the context to figure out the word. Of course, it is fair to get help from a classmate or the teacher if all these strategies have been tried and students are still unable to figure out the word.

WARF To be successful in understanding content-area textbooks, students need to read quickly enough so that they can think about word meaning rather than focus their energy on word identification. Students also may have to adjust their rate of reading, depending on their purpose for reading (Mercer & Pullen, 2009). Minskoff and Allsopp (2003) suggest a strategy to help students who can read accurately at least at the third-grade level but need to increase and/or adjust their reading speed. It is called *WARF:*

W *Widen* your eye span.
A *Avoid* skip-backs.
R *Read* silently.
F *Flex* your reading rate.

When teaching *WARF:*

- For the **W** step, students first are taught to widen their eye span and not read word by word. They are taught to group words, not reading the articles (for example, *the* or *a*) or auxiliary words (for example, *is* or *are*), so they can focus on words that give meaning. They also are taught to try to group words meaningfully (for example, for the words *a sunny day,* focus on *sunny* and *day*).
- In the **A** step, students are taught to avoid skip-backs by keeping reading if they do not understand something; using context clues to gain understanding; and only going back if these efforts are unsuccessful.

WWW RESOURCES

The Strategic Instructional Model (SIM) provides a wealth of research-based learning strategies for students. SIM is found on the Internet at sim.kucrl.org. To get to specific strategies, click "View All SIM Curricula."

WWW RESOURCES

For more detailed information about WARF and other practical learning strategies, Google "The Learning Toolbox," and click on "Strategies."

- In the **R** step, students are taught to read silently, avoiding reading aloud in a whisper by pressing their lips together.
- In the final step, **F**, students learn to change their reading rate depending on the difficulty and/or familiarity of the material. For example, when students are looking for information, they need to know to read quickly as they search for key words on the page. When students read important information they must understand or memorize, they need to be aware to read more slowly. Conversely, if students are reading information they know well, they can adjust their rate and read faster.

Vocabulary Strategies

In addition to being able to identify technical vocabulary, students also must know what words mean if they are to understand what they read. Strategies for using direct instruction to teach new vocabulary were covered in Chapter 9. However, as you learned in Chapter 9, teachers realistically only have the time to teach about 300 new vocabulary words per year (Stahl, 1999). You can teach your students to figure out the meaning of a word independently by teaching them to:

- Know the meaning of common word parts or morphemes (e.g., *ex* = out; *il* = not; *est* = the most) along with the meaning of the term's *root word* (a single word that cannot be broken into parts), *prefix* (a word part added to the beginning of a word that changes its meaning), and *suffix* (a word part added to the ending of a word that changes its meaning). For a list of common morphemes to teach your students, go to **www.leonsplanet.com**. Scroll to the Complete Index. Then, scroll down to ***M.*** Click "Morphemes."
- Break words into prefixes, suffixes, and root words.
- Look for context clues by examining the words and sentences around a given word.
- Come to a conclusion about the meaning of a word based on its meaningful parts and context (Baumann, Edwards, Boland, Olejnik, & Kameenui, 2003).

Reading Comprehension Strategies

Reading comprehension strategies are intended to help students meet the independent reading demands of content-area classes, particularly in the middle and upper grades. Although reading primarily involves textbooks, there is an increasing emphasis on having students read and understand a variety of primary source books and media as well. The following are examples of proven reading comprehension strategies designed to help students of all grade levels.

SCROL One example of a reading comprehension strategy is *SCROL* (Grant, 1993). The *SCROL* strategy enables students to take notes while they are reading, an important study strategy, and to use text headings to aid their comprehension and help them find and remember important information. The *SCROL* strategy has five steps:

S *Survey* the headings. In the assigned text selection, read each heading and subheading. For each heading and subheading, try to answer the following questions: What do I already know about this topic? What information might the writer present?

C *Connect.* Ask yourself, "How do the headings relate to one another?" Write down key words from the headings that might provide connections between them.

R *Read* the text. As you read, look for words and phrases that express important information about the headings. Mark the text to point out important ideas and details. Stop to make sure that you understand the major ideas and supporting details. If you do not understand, reread.

O *Outline.* Using indentations to reflect structure, outline the major ideas and supporting details in the heading segment. Write the heading and then try to outline each heading segment without looking back at the text.

RESEARCH-BASED PRACTICES

Schmitt, Hale, McCallum, and Mauck (2011) found that struggling readers provided with an audio version of text did not comprehend any better than students at comparable levels who just read the same passages silently. Although audio text can be a helpful bypass strategy for students, it is often not an appropriate substitute for instruction in language comprehension.

RESEARCH-BASED PRACTICES

Helman, Calhoon, and Kern (2015) used a clue word strategy like the one just described to successfully increase student proficiency in reading science vocabulary.

FIGURE 10.2

Highlight It!

1. Read section.

2. Pause and Think.

3. Highlight.

4. Re-read Highlighting.

5. Self-Check:
   Does it make sense?
   Do I have the main idea(s)?
   Do I have several key details?

6. Pair/Share/Compare
   "I highlighted . . ."
   "I highlighted this because . . ."
   (Justify and Explain Thinking)

7. Discussion: How is our highlighting similar and different?

8. Community Share: Report Out

Source: Based on Englert, C. S., Mariage, T. V., & Okolo, C. M. (2009). Informational Writing Across the Curriculum. In G. Troia (Ed.), *Writing Instruction and Assessment for Struggling Writers: From Theory to Evidence-Based Practices* (pp. 132–164). New York: Guilford Press.

FIGURE 10.3

Mark It!

1. Read and **highlight.**
2. **Mark** the text with symbols. Make notes in the margins to record your thoughts and strategies.
3. Pause and Think.
4. Self-Check:
   Do my marks and notes make sense?

5. Pair/Share/Compare
   "Here's what I marked. . . ."
   "I made these marks because . . ."
   "The *strategy* I used was . . ."
   "I was thinking. . . ."
   (Justify and Explain Thinking)
   "Questions or comments?"

6. Discussion: How are we similar or different?

7. Community Share: Report Out

Mark-It Symbols

PK: Prior knowledge
Q: Question
CL: Clarify (idea or word)
P: Predict
S: Summarize
I: Imagery
C: Connect (self, text, world)
MI: Main Idea
D: Detail
** Key point
?   Confusing part

Source: Based on Englert, C. S., Mariage, T. V., & Okolo, C. M. (2009). Informational Writing Across the Curriculum. In G. Troia (Ed.), *Writing Instruction and Assessment for Struggling Writers: From Theory to Evidence-Based Practices* (pp. 132–164). New York: Guilford Press.

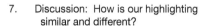

L *Look* back. Now look back at the text and check the accuracy of the major ideas and details you wrote. Correct any inaccurate information in your outline. If you marked the text as you read, use this information to help you verify the accuracy of your outline.

Advise students to follow steps 3–5 (**R–L**) every time they encounter a section with headings in the text they are reading. Taking notes using *SCROL* improves student comprehension while also providing students with a product that can help them study more effectively for tests.

Students often struggle with the R step of *SCROL* that involves marking the important ideas and details. Englert, Mariage, and Okolo (2009) developed the *Highlight It!* and *Mark It!* strategies to help students identify and then elaborate on main ideas and details. Cue cards used to guide students through the *Highlight-It!* and *Mark-It!* steps are shown in Figures 10.2 and 10.3. *Highlight It!* focuses on the meaning in the text, whereas in *Mark-It!* students elaborate on the meaning by questioning the author's ideas and themselves, making personal connections, predicting ideas, using imagery, and clarifying text. To teach both strategies, first model the strategies. Then perform the strategies with your students, focusing on a section of text. Last, have your students collaborate with partners on performing the strategies and share the results with the class.

RESEARCH-BASED PRACTICES

Reading strategies are more effective when combined with instruction in written expression. Teachers taught both a deep reading strategy, *TWA* (Think before reading; think While reading; think After reading) and a writing strategy, *PLANS* (Pick goals; List ways to meet goals; And make Notes and Sequence notes). The combined use of *TWA* and *PLANS* led to student gains in both reading comprehension and writing (Mason, Snyder, Sukhram, & Kedem, 2006).

PARS *PARS* is a simplified textbook-reading strategy that is good for younger students and students without much experience using textbook-reading strategies (Cheek & Cheek, 1983; Reid, Lienemann & Hagaman, 2013). The four steps of *PARS* follow:

P *Preview* the material by scanning the chapter and surveying the introductory statement, headings, graphic aids, and chapter summary to identify main ideas.

A *Ask* questions that relate to the main ideas discovered when surveying the chapter.

R *Read* the chapter to answer the questions developed.

S *Summarize* the main ideas in the chapter.

Remember that just telling students the steps of a learning strategy is not enough. Letting students watch you perform the strategy and then carefully guiding students as they learn to perform it are essential if students are to learn to use PARS to gain access to the content of their textbooks more independently.

CAPS You have learned that students who can comprehend narrative text are able to identify key parts of stories called story grammars (see the Case in Practice in Chapter 4). *CAPS* is a self-questioning strategy that guides students as they look for these important story elements (Leinhardt & Zigmond, 1988). The strategy is composed of the following steps:

C Who are the *characters*?

A What is the *aim* of the story?

P What *problem* happens?

S How is the problem *solved*?

CAPS is particularly effective for reading narrative text in elementary school.

POSSE Another reading comprehension strategy is *POSSE* (Englert, 2009; Englert & Mariage, 1991). This strategy includes many research-based reading comprehension practices such as graphic organizers, text structures, stimulation of student background knowledge, and self-monitoring. The steps in this strategy are as follows:

P *Predict* ideas.

O *Organize* the ideas.

S *Search* for the structure.

S *Summarize* the main ideas.

E *Evaluate* your understanding.

When students are predicting in the *P* step, they can be given a sentence starter such as "I predict that . . ." For this step, students are taught to activate background knowledge by brainstorming what the text will be about using text clues or signals from a variety of sources, including the title, headings in bold, pictures, keywords, and so on. In the *O* step, students organize their background knowledge and/or predictions into a semantic or concept map. The *S* step has students search the text to confirm their predictions and find the main ideas. In the next *S* step, students state what each paragraph is mainly about. In the *E* step, evaluate, students question themselves by turning each paragraph main idea into a question; compare their predictions and findings; clarify any misunderstandings by asking questions about unfamiliar vocabulary terms or other text information; predict what the next paragraph will be about; and, finally, summarize the entire reading section. Graphic organizers for each *POSSE* step can be found at **www.nbss.ie**. Search "posse"; click "Posse—Reading and Learning Strategy."

A technique used for teaching the POSSE strategy steps is a process called reciprocal teaching. **Reciprocal teaching** is a way to teach students to comprehend reading material by providing them with teacher and peer models of thinking behavior and then allowing them to practice these thinking behaviors with their peers (Palincsar & Brown, 1988). At first, the teacher leads the dialogue, demonstrating how the strategies can be used during reading. As instruction goes

These students are engaged in a structured dialogue about the text they are reading, a peer-mediated comprehension strategy called reciprocal teaching. What strategies must students be taught before they can practice reciprocal teaching?

on, the teacher gives the students more and more responsibility for maintaining the dialogue. Eventually, students are largely responsible for the dialogue, although the teacher still provides help as necessary. The most important part of the technique is the teacher's releasing control and turning the dialogue over to the students (Englert & Mariage, 1991).

MAIN-I A key preskill for POSSE and most other textbook comprehension strategies is the ability to identify the main ideas of a paragraph or series of paragraphs in expository text (Gajiria, Jitendra, Sood, & Sacks, 2007; Wexler, Reed, Mitchell, Doyle, & Clancy, 2015), the purpose behind the *MAIN-I* strategy (Boudah, 2013), with the following steps:

> **M**ake the topic known.
> **A**ccent at least two essential details.
> **I**nk out the clarifying details.
> **N**otice how the essential details are related.
> **I**nfer the main idea.

In the *Topic* step, students are taught to identify the subject of the paragraph or section or who or what it is mainly about. There are two types of *Details. Essential* details are directly related to the topic and say something specific about it. *Clarifying* details say more about one of the other essential details but not something specific and new about the topic. Essential details hold the key to the final step of identifying the *Main Idea*. In this step, students look carefully at the essential details and classify them by asking themselves these questions:

- How do these sentences go together?
- What is the author saying about the topic between the lines?
- Do these sentences give us examples or characteristics of an important point about the topic?
- What is the "big idea" or point made in these sentences?
- What's the main idea (Boudah, 2013; p. 151)?

In the last step, students are prompted to *infer* the main idea by putting it in their own words, making a main idea statement. To demonstrate how *MAIN-I* might work, consider this example from Bursuck and Damer (2015). To determine the main idea, "Suzanne is freezing in the cold," Mrs. Whitlaw's students first must know *who or what was talked about the most* in the paragraph (**M** step). Although Suzanne's name might be mentioned once or twice in the paragraph, students need to recognize the "the red-faced girl" and "the shivering huddled form" as essential details (**A** step) and cross out "cobblestone streets" and Suzanne's "brother Rob" as clarifying details (**I** step). Next, the students need to see how the *essential details are related*. If text in the paragraph mentions that Suzanne's lips were blue, she was outside on a freezing day, her face was red from the cold, and she couldn't wait for the warm bus to arrive, students classify these ideas and notice that Suzanne is very cold (**N** step). Last, students infer the main idea statement: "Suzanne is freezing in the cold" (second *I* step).

While the strategies described here are helpful for struggling readers, students can also benefit from technology such as the Reading Pen, an assistive technology device featured in Technology Notes 10.1, that allows students at a reading level well below grade level to access text content independently.

SLICK A common accommodation for students with reading disabilities is the bypass strategy of providing them with an oral text such as when using the Reading Pen just described. However, some students still struggle to understand a text, even when they no longer have to read it. *SLiCK* (Boyle et al., 2002) is a strategy designed to help students comprehend digitally recorded textbooks. It involves the following steps:

S   *Set* it up.
L   *Look* ahead through the chapter.
C   *Comprehend.*
K   *Keep* it together.

In the **S** step, the student sets it up by opening the textbook to the start of the assigned section; readying a worksheet containing the *SLiCK* strategy steps at

TECHNOLOGY NOTES 10.1
The Reading Pen

As students progress into the upper grades, the demand for being able to read accurately and fluently increases. At the same time, school reforms have led to the adoption of increasingly higher standards requiring students to read texts of ever-increasing complexity. These increased reading demands can be particularly problematic for students with special needs, many of whom continue to struggle to read accurately and fluently when they enter middle and high school. While struggling readers continue to need intensive skill instruction to help them eventually read grade-level text independently, they may need additional support in the short run to keep up with their assignments in subject matter classes. Assistive technology can enable struggling readers to independently read textbooks above their reading level. Digital texts are most commonly used for this purpose, but another promising device is the *Wizcom Reading-pen©*. The pen, powered by two AA batteries, is a portable assistive device that the student runs over words just like a highlighter to scan either a word or line of text. The pen then reads the text aloud or converts it to text in Windows. In addition, the pen can display the syllables of a scanned word and display the dictionary definitions of the word on its small screen. Headphones can be used so that only the student using the device can hear the speech. Like all technology, the pen has positive and negative aspects:

Positive Aspects of the Reading Pen
1. Available for K–12 and more advanced editions.
2. Comfortable earbuds provide privacy.
3. Can be programmed for either left- or right-handed users.
4. Reads words and sentences in an electronically generated voice.
5. Construction of both the pen and earbuds is sturdy.

Negative Aspects of the Reading Pen
1. Careful scanning across text is necessary for accuracy.
2. Additional practice is needed for students who have weak coordination.
3. Reading different fonts can pose problems.
4. Occasionally the pen misreads text and rescanning is necessary.
5. The pen can prove frustrating by slowing reading down and impeding comprehension if students aren't adequately trained on how to use it.
6. Students may have other reasons besides word identification for their reading difficulties, such as deficits in background knowledge and language comprehension.
7. Research validating the effectiveness of the pen is limited.

the top, with spaces to record key information such as headings, subheadings, and key vocabulary words. In the **L** step, the student looks ahead through the chapter using the recorded book, player, and print textbook. The student notes keywords, headings, and subheadings and records them on the worksheet. In the comprehend, or **C**, step, the student reads along with the recording, pausing to record important details under the headings and subheadings previously identified. The student is encouraged to think of big ideas by writing mini-summaries as he or she reads. In the final step, **K**, the student combines all of the mini-summaries to get the big picture about what the section of text means. Boyle and colleagues (2002) report that students acquire the **S** and **L** steps quickly, while the **C** and **K** steps require considerable teacher modeling and practice before they are learned.

Listening and Note-Taking Strategies

Students in all grades need to be able to understand information presented orally by their teachers. In elementary school, students are required to follow many oral directions and listen when the teacher is reading aloud or presenting information. In middle school, junior high, and high school, where lecturing is a common way for teachers to present subject-area content, students are required to discern and record key information in lectures so they can study it later. As you have already learned, students with special needs may have problems understanding information presented orally (Boyle, Forchelli & Cariss, 2015). These problems can make access to the general education curriculum more difficult for them. The listening and note-taking strategies described in the next section were designed to help all students learn more successfully from their teachers' presentations.

SLANT Students who are engaged in class are more likely to be successful (Elliott, 2015; Jung-Sook, 2013). The *SLANT* strategy (Ellis, 1991; Gildroy & Deshler, 2008) is designed to increase student involvement in class lectures or discussions. Greater student involvement increases the likelihood that students will listen more carefully and take better notes. *SLANT* includes the following steps:

> **S** *Sit* up.
> **L** *Lean* forward.
> **A** *Activate* your thinking.
> **N** *Name* key information.
> **T** *Track* the talker.

> **S** Sit up, remind students that slouching or putting their heads down in class makes their bodies want to fall asleep and causes them to miss a lot of information.
> **L** Tell students that leaning forward shows they are interested in the information, even when they are not, and that often they can train their minds to follow their bodies.
> **A** Activating your thinking involves having your students ask themselves questions such as, "What is this about?" or "What is important to remember?" This step also involves asking the teacher a question when they don't understand.
> **N** Students answer teacher questions, share their ideas, and respond to others' comments.
> **T** Track the talker; encourage students to keep their eyes on the teacher or whoever else is talking because this prevents them from daydreaming or being distracted by other things.

TASSEL As students move into the upper grades, they are required to take notes for longer periods of time. Longer lectures require sustained attention, a skill that is often problematic for students with disabilities (Smith & Strick, 2010). The *TASSEL* strategy is recommended for students who have trouble maintaining their level of attention (Minskoff & Allsopp, 2003). It includes the following steps:

MyLab Education

Video Example 10.3: SLANT Strategy

Watch a teacher introduce the SLANT strategy to a seventh grade class.

T *Try* not to doodle.

A *Arrive* at class prepared.

S *Sit* near the front.

S *Sit* away from friends.

E *End* daydreaming.

L *Look* at the teacher.

For the **E** step, encourage students to monitor their attention. When they find they are daydreaming, they should immediately change their position, sit forward, and make eye contact with the teacher. Then they should write down whatever the teacher is saying, regardless of its importance. For the **L** step, encourage students to keep their eyes on the teacher when they are not taking notes or looking at the whiteboard, overhead, PowerPoint presentation, or computer screen (Minskoff & Allsopp, 2003).

CUES *CUES* is a strategy for taking lecture notes that has been validated for use in middle school inclusive science classes (Boyle, 2011), although it is general enough to work in other subject-matter classes as well.

C *Cluster* together 3–6 main points of the lecture.

U *Use* teacher cues to record ideas: number cues (e.g., there were three elements involved) and importance cues (e.g., this is very important to remember).

E *Enter* important vocabulary.

S *Summarize* quickly and whenever possible.

If you plan to give a brief lecture, make your own set of notes prior to the instruction. Doing so helps keep you on message, and the notes can also provide a helpful model for your students. When first teaching students to use *CUES*, it helps to break the lecture into shorter, meaningful segments of 10–15 minutes each. Students can then compare their notes to a model or share notes with a partner after each section. It also helps to slow the pace of the lecture and liberally use pauses, gestures, and emphasis cues to signal the need to record what was just said.

In addition, try posting the CUES steps prominently in your classroom. When you lead whole-group instruction, employ think-alouds to explicitly tell your students which steps you are performing and why. Finally, evaluate your students' notes regularly using peer, self, and teacher assessment.

Smartpens (Gittlin, 2013) are an extension of the reading pen technology, described in the Technology Notes feature, that can be used in conjunction with note-taking strategies such as *CUES*. Smartpens use Livescribe© software that makes oral, digital recordings of lectures as students are taking written notes, storing them in Wi-Fi for easy later retrieval and study. This device may be a particularly helpful note-taking accommodation for students with special needs who may have difficulty keeping up with the instructor and/or identifying key ideas on the spot. With more traditional lecture recordings, it is difficult and time-consuming to locate places in the lecture that need clarification. With the smartpen, students can access what the teacher said at any point in the written notes. For example, Denise noted in writing during class that some businesses were able to thrive during the great depression, but she failed to write down which businesses. With her Smartpen using Livescribe, she simply tapped on the word businesses at the place in her notes where this idea was presented, and she was able to retrieve a recording of her teacher identifying the businesses in question.

To learn *CUES* or any other note-taking strategy, students need the preskill of being able to tell the difference between main ideas and details. Some students choose key words that represent main ideas, but others attempt to write down everything and should be taught directly how to differentiate main ideas and details. For example, Mr. Abeles discovered that many students in his world history class were unable to identify the main ideas in his lectures. First, he explained the difference between main ideas and details: A *main idea* is what a whole section or passage is about; a *detail* is what just one part of a section

FYI

Today's schools increasingly try to limit lecturing and engage students in more inquiry-based teaching such as problem and project-based learning (Wiek, Xiong, Brundires, & van der Leeuw, 2014). Inquiry-based approaches require more student independence, the goal of strategies recommended in this chapter. Scaffolding, a method of student support described in Chapter 5, may also be needed when students are faced with tasks that require more independence.

RESEARCH-BASED PRACTICES

Peverly and colleagues (2007) found that the speed at which students were able to produce written letters accounted more for quality note taking than either student memory or the ability to listen for main ideas. What implications does this have for instruction?

or passage is about. For several weeks he stopped after presenting a section of material and put three pieces of information on the board—one main idea and two details. He asked the students which was the main idea and why. When his students were doing well at these tasks, Mr. Abeles had them write their own main ideas for a section of a lecture, which were shared with the class, and then he provided corrective feedback as necessary.

Writing Strategies

Another area that requires student independence is writing and proofreading papers. Self-regulated strategy development (*SRSD*) is a process of teaching writing that has an extensive research base (Gillespie & Graham, 2014; Harris et al., 2017). The steps or teaching stages in this process are similar to those described early in the chapter for teaching learning strategies and are *Develop it, Discuss it, Model it, Memorize it, Support it,* and *Practice it* (Harris et al., 2017).

POW AND TREE   *SRSD* can be used to teach students *POW* and *TREE*, two research-based practices designed to increase student writing competence (Harris et al., 2017). A description of the steps in both of these strategies is shown in Figure 10.4.

POW and TREE can be used for any writing assignment, be it persuasive, informative, or narrative. *TREE* is used for persuasive essays. *POW* prompts students to select a topic, think about what they are going to say about the topic,

FIGURE 10.4 **Strategies for Persuasive Writing**

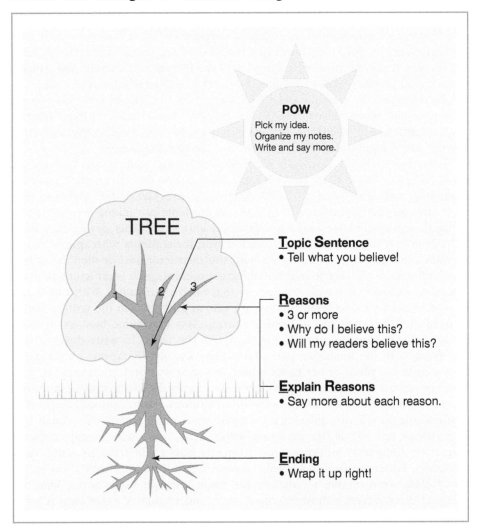

POW
Pick my idea.
Organize my notes.
Write and say more.

TREE

Topic Sentence
• Tell what you believe!

Reasons
• 3 or more
• Why do I believe this?
• Will my readers believe this?

Explain Reasons
• Say more about each reason.

Ending
• Wrap it up right!

FIGURE 10.5 **Pattern Guide for Comparison/Contrast *POW* Paper**

Compare/Contrast

What is being compared and contrasted?
Deep dish pizza and regular pizza

On what characteristics?
Crust

Both same | Alike? White flour | Different? Deep dish is thicker | In contrast to

On what characteristics?

Similarly | Alike? | Different? | However

Source: From "A Case for Writing Intervention: Strategies for Writing Informational Text," by C. S. Englert, T. E. Raphael, L. M. Anderson, H. M. Anthony, K. L. Fear, and S. L. Gregg, 1988, *Learning Disability Quarterly, 3*(2), p. 108. Reprinted with permission from Council for Learning Disabilities.

and consider their purpose for writing and audience. Students are also encouraged to make notes as they plan while recognizing that they will generate new ideas as they continue to write. For example, Alex selected the topic of pizza to write about for the class newsletter. He decided to focus on pizza, and to do a compare-contrast piece focusing on Chicago style and New York style pizza. To facilitate his use of *POW,* his teacher encouraged him to use a **pattern guide**, which is a graphic organizer designed to help students organize their papers. A sample pattern guide for Alex's comparison/contrast article is shown in Figure 10.5. Notice that the words not in boxes—*Both same, In contrast to, Similarly,* and *However*—are key words frequently used when making comparisons. These words help students make the transition to writing sentences. In Figure 10.5, two kinds of pizza are being compared and contrasted. The student might write, "The crusts of Chicago style and New York style pizza are the same in that they both are made mainly of white flour. This is in contrast to their thickness; Chicago style pizza has a thicker crust."

When the time comes to write, the teacher demonstrates and thinks aloud to show students how to take the information gathered in the planning and organizing steps and produce a first draft. Using the pizza comparison as an example, you can compose an essay comparing two kinds of pizza using a Smartboard or overhead projector, thinking out loud as you write. You can involve students by asking questions such as, "What would a good topic sentence be? Is this a good example? How do you think I should end this? Why?" You could also have students write the paper along with you.

TREE reminds students that persuasive essays have important components. These components were shown in Figure 10.4 and include a clear statement of

WWW RESOURCES

The Write Site (http://www.writesite.org) allows students to take on the roles of journalists and editors to research, write, and publish their own newspapers. The site provides unit outlines, handouts, exercises, downloadable teaching materials, information about how to write, and more.

FIGURE 10.6 Sample *TREE* Outline

Alex		
T		Chicago style pizza is better than New York style pizza.
R		Chicago style pizza is cheesier.
E		The deep dish makes room for more cheese.
R		Chicago style pizza is saucier.
E		The thick crust can hold more sauce.
R		Chicago style pizza has a tastier crust.
E		The crust has some cornmeal in it to make it flakier.
E		Chicago style pizza is superior to New York style pizza. It is so good I could eat it every day.

Source: Based on "Teaching Spelling, Writing and Reading for Writing" by K. R. Harris et al., 2017, from *Teaching Exceptional Children, 49*(4).

FYI

One hundred words account for 50 percent of the words children use in their writing; 1,000 words account for 89 percent; and 3,000 account for 97 percent (Graham, 1999). High-frequency words should be an important part of your spelling instruction. So should instruction in common spelling patterns.

WWW RESOURCES

Two software programs designed to help students plan and organize research projects through outlines and concept maps are *Inspiration* and *Mindmeister*. For more information about these programs, go to http://www.inspiration.com and https://www.mindmeister.com/education-software.

belief, reasons for a belief that are carefully explained, and an effective ending. It is also important to stress that writing should be fun to read and write, and that writing that makes sense, has an engaging opening, and a strong ending is more likely to convince the reader (Harris et al., 2017). An example of how Alex used TREE to plan a persuasive essay on why Chicago style pizza is better than New York style pizza is shown in Figure 10.6.

Editing Editing teaches students to critique their own writing and to identify areas in which they need clarification or assistance, an important self-evaluation skill. Effective editing is a two-step process involving student self-evaluation and peer editing. For self-evaluation, students reread and evaluate their drafts, starring sections of the paper they like best and putting question marks in the margins beside passages they think may be unclear. Finally, students think of two questions to ask their peer editors. For example, Jorge asked his peer editor whether he had used capital letters and punctuation correctly. He was also concerned about whether his paper was long enough and asked for suggestions on how to add information.

For **peer editing**, several steps are followed. First, the writer reads the paper to a peer editor while the editor listens. The peer editor then summarizes the paper. Next, the editor evaluates the paper, sharing with the writer an analysis of salient features of the writing that might guide a revision or lead to improvements. For example, the peer editor might suggest that the writer add key words or reorganize the paper for clarity. Then the peer editor and the writer brainstorm ways to improve the paper.

A research-based strategy called *TAG* can help students with the peer-editing process (Carlson & Henning, 1993; MacArthur & Stoddard, 1990). The *TAG* strategy involves three simple steps:

T *Tell* what you like.
A *Ask* questions.
G *Give* suggestions.

As with all strategies, students need to be provided with models and guided practice for doing these steps prior to doing them independently.

In the *revising* step, students decide on changes to be made using their self-evaluation marks and peer feedback. Englert and colleagues (1988) suggest that the teacher model how to insert or change the order of information, providing a rationale for any changes. All modifications are made directly on the first draft.

Last, the teacher and student have a conference, and changes in writing mechanics are suggested. Following this conference, a final draft is composed on clean sheets of paper or electronically.

When students have to proofread their papers independently, they might use a strategy called *COPS* (Alley, 1988; Reid, Lienemann, & Hagaman, 2013). In the *COPS* strategy, students question themselves as follows:

C Have I *capitalized* the first word and proper nouns?

O How is the *overall appearance* of my paper? Have I made any handwriting, margin, or messy errors? Is my formatting correct? Are my fonts consistent?

P Have I used end *punctuation*, commas, and semicolons carefully?

S Do words look like they are *spelled* right? Can I sound them out or use the dictionary?

Although *COPS* has been shown to be effective, students need preskills to perform this strategy adequately. Before teaching *COPS*, consider the following questions: Can the students recognize misspelled words? Do the students know rules for using capital letters and punctuation? Can they apply these rules? Can the students use a dictionary? If the answer to any of these questions is no, teach these skills directly before teaching students the *COPS* strategy.

REPORT WRITING Report writing is something many students prefer to avoid, largely because they lack a systematic way of writing successfully. Graham, Harris, and MacArthur (2006) report success teaching students a six-step report-writing strategy originally developed by MacArthur, Schwartz, Graham, Malloy, and Harris (1996). The steps in the strategy are as follows:

1. Choose a topic.

2. Brainstorm all you know and would like to know about the topic.

3. Organize your ideas by main points and details on a web-type graphic organizer, where main ideas and subordinate ideas are linked together through the use of lines and arrows.

4. Read to find new information and verify the accuracy of information already generated. (Add, delete, and modify items on the web as necessary.)

5. Write your report using the information you organized on the web, but continue planning as you write.

6. Check to be sure you used everything you wanted from the web. (p. 291)

In Graham and others (2006), the report-writing strategy was co-taught by general and special educators using many of the suggestions for teaching a learning strategy described earlier in the chapter. First, they clarified expectations by carefully describing the qualities of a good report and showing the students actual examples of well-written reports. Next the teachers encouraged students to memorize the strategy, and then the special education teacher demonstrated how to use the strategy while holding a running dialogue with herself. For example, to show the students how to keep themselves focused, she asked herself, "What do I need to do?" To show the students how to keep themselves on task, the teacher said to herself, "Keep going." To demonstrate how to self-monitor, the teacher said, "Does this part make sense?" To show students how to cope with frustration, she said, "I can do this."

For guided practice, the teachers adjusted their instruction. The special education teacher co-wrote reports with some of the students with special needs in an alternative group, while the general education teacher worked with the remainder of the class in a large group, providing reduced support. Once students were writing independently, the teachers required them to reflect on what they were doing in a daily journal. Students were also reminded to continue to manage the writing process by talking to themselves. In all, it took the students six weeks to master the report-writing

INCLUDE

DIMENSIONS OF DIVERSITY

SRSD has been used to improve the persuasive writing skills of both students with Autism Spectrum Disorder (Assaro-Saddler & Bak, 2014) and students with emotional and behavioral disabilities (Mastropierir et al., 2015).

WWW RESOURCES

Find strategies for writing lab and class reports in science inspired by Universal Design for Learning (UDL) at http://www.cast.org; search for "free learning tools," and then click "cast science writer."

TECHNOLOGY NOTES 10.2

Using Web-Based Programs to Improve Student Writing Performance

A number of software programs are available to help students with disabilities overcome writing problems (Beam & Williams, 2015; Gillette, 2006; Sessions, Kang, & Womack, 2016; Vue et al., 2016).

Software Programs that Can Read Digitized Text

- Write OutLoud (Don Johnston Incorporated) (http://www.donjohnston.com)
- Read OutLoud (Don Johnston Incorporated) (http://www.donjohnston.com)
- Kurzweil 3000 (Kurzweil Educational Systems) (http://www.kurzweiledu.com)
- Read & Write Gold (http://www.texthelp.com)

Software Programs that Assist Students with Planning Compositions

- Draft Builder (Don Johnston Incorporated) (http://www.donjohnston.com)
- Inspiration (Inspiration) (http://www.inspiration.com)
- Popplet (http://www.popplet.com)
- SimpleMind+ (http://www.simpleapps.eu)
- Story Wheel (http://my.kindertown.com/apps/story-wheel)
- The Brainstormer (http://www.tapnik.com/brainstormer/)

Talking Word Processors

- IntelliTalk III (IntelliTools) (www.specialneedscomputers.ca/index.php?1=product_list&m=212)
- Word 2010 (Microsoft) (http://www.microsoft.com)

Voice Recognition Software

- Scansoft Dragon Naturally Speaking (http://www.texthelp.com)
- Word 2010 Microsoft (http://www.microsoft.com)

What types of assistive technology might help this student with her journal entries?

Word Prediction Software

- Co:Writer: Don Johnston Incorporated (http://www.donjohnston.com)
- Read & Write Gold (http://www.texthelp.com)

Other Sites That Provide Information about Apps and Internet Sources:

- Association of American Educators (https://www.aaeteachers.org). Search "16 writing apps."
- Reading Rockets (http://www.readingrockets.org). Search "writing apps."
- Commonsense media (https://www.commonsensemedia.org). Search "lists of storytelling apps."

---

strategy—time that the teachers felt was well spent, given the improvement in student reports that resulted.

Technology can be of great help to all writing, including those who struggle with writing. Various web-based resources and Google extensions are listed and described in Technology Notes 10.2 and 10.3.

Strategies for Problem Solving in Math

Increasingly, teachers are focusing on problem solving as a major component of the math curriculum. This concentration is consistent with the math standards developed by the National Council of Teachers of Mathematics (2000), recommendations of the National Mathematics Advisory Panel (2008), and rigorous standards developed by many states that all stress the importance of teaching problem solving. However, research indicates that if students with special needs are to become effective and efficient problem solvers, they must be directly taught how to problem solve. A common (but by no means the only) way to introduce problem solving to students in a classroom context is through word problems. An effective technique for teaching word problems for students with special needs is presented in the Professional Edge feature.

MyLab Education

Video Example 10.4: Strategies for Learning About Operations

Note how learning strategies help these students solve number operations while reducing the need for memorization.

TECHNOLOGY NOTES 10.3
Google Extensions for Assisting Writers

Extensions are tools that can be added to the browser. They are designed to work in combination with websites and the documents in Google Drive. Extensions are found and downloaded from the Chrome Web Store, and are collected and managed in a dedicated tab of the browser. The Chrome Web Store is similar to the app store, but it is dedicated to only extensions. Icons of active extensions are placed in the toolbar for easy access. Whereas apps are standalone applications that run in their own windows or tabs within the browser, extensions work within the browser in an unobtrusive way.

Extension	Use
for Google Chrome https://chrome.google.com/webstore/detail/readwrite-for-google-chro/inoeonmfapjbbkmdafoankkfajkcphgd?hl=en-US	• For websites, a pop-up toolbar is available with supports, like text-to-speech with synchronized highlighting, a talking dictionary, a picture dictionary, and annotation tools. • For Google Docs, the toolbar adds functions for dictation and word prediction. • For PDF documents within Google Drive, the Read&Write extension opens those documents in new tabs that contain text-to-speech tools, as well as various note-taking and annotation tools. • There is an available add-on tool called Snapverter, which performs optical character recognition (OCR) on inaccessible text. By using the Snapverter add-on, students can convert smartphone photographs of hard-copy handouts into text that can be read aloud by Read&Write for Google.
Ginger https://chrome.google.com/webstore/detail/spell-checker-and-grammar/kdfieneakcjfaiglcfcgkidlkmlijjnh?hl=en	• This is a contextual spelling and grammar checker. Students can copy and paste a piece of writing into the Ginger pop-up window to get advanced editing assistance. It goes further than Google Docs spell checker in that it considers words in the context of entire sentences and identifies more errors, such as homonym confusion. • The extension also has a rephrasing tool, which makes suggestions for better sentence organization and word choice.
Mercury Reader https://chrome.google.com/webstore/detail/mercury-reader/oknpjjbmpnndlpmnhmekjpocelpnlfdi?hl=en	• Eliminates advertisements, etc. that can be distracting on website text for students with attention issues. The extension extracts website text from images and advertisements. • The text can be adjusted by font and size to meet the needs of individual students. • The text can be saved to an account or sent to a Kindle e-reader.
Note Anywhere https://chrome.google.com/webstore/detail/note-anywhere/bohahkiiknkelflnjjlipnaeape-fmjbh	• Notes can be made by students on any website and in any position. • Notes get saved in real time and can be moved by the mouse in a drag-and-drop method. When you revisit the page again, the notes get loaded automatically. • Options to change the style of notes and a notes summary feature are also available.

STAR The *STAR* strategy has been used successfully to teach older students with disabilities to solve math problems, including algebra (Gagnon & Maccini, 2001, p. 10). It consists of the following steps:

S   *Search* the word problem, reading the problem carefully and writing down knowns or facts.

T   *Translate* the word problem into an equation in picture form by choosing a variable, identifying the operation, and representing the problem through manipulatives or picture form.

A   *Answer* the problem.

R   *Review* the solution by rereading the problem and checking the reasonableness of the answer.

Examples of how STAR can be used to solve division problems with integers are shown in Figure 10.7. Note how the teacher moves students beyond the concrete application phase and into semi-concrete and abstract phases. For

FIGURE 10.7 **Using the STAR Strategy to Solve Division Problems with Integers**

Sample problem: Suppose the temperature changed by an average of –2°F per hour. The total temperature change was –16°F. How many hours did it take for the temperature to change?

Phase of Instruction	⭐ **Star Strategy**
1. Concrete Application	Prompts students to:
Students use blocks to represent the problem. General guidelines: inverse operation of multiplication.	Search problem (read carefully, ask questions, write down facts); translate the problem using blocks; answer the problem using the tiles; and review the solution (reread the problem, check reasonableness and calculations).

Algebra tiles: ▨ = 1 unit

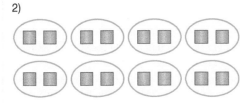

1)
Students begin with no tiles on the workmat.

2)

3)

a. Count the number of sets of –2 needed to obtain –16.

b. Students add 8 sets.

c. Students count the number of sets needed (8).

2. Semiconcrete Application	Prompts students to:
Students draw pictures of the representations.	Search problem (read carefully, ask questions, write down facts); translate (represent) the problem via drawings and write down the equation; answer the problem using drawings and write the answer; and review the solution (reread the problem, check reasonableness and calculations).
3. Abstract Application	Prompts students to:
Students first write numerical representations: –16 ÷ 2 = *x*, apply the rule for dividing integers to obtain *x* = 8, and reread and check the answer.	Search problem (read carefully, ask questions, write down facts); translate the problem into an equation; answer the problem (apply the rule for division of integers); and review the solution (reread the problem, check reasonableness and calculations).

Source: Republished with permission of Council for Exception Children, from "Preparing Students with Disabilities for Algebra." *Teaching Exceptional Children, 34*(1) by J. Gagnon and P. Maccini (2001); permission conveyed through Copyright Clearance Center, Inc.

example, she starts with blocks (concrete) and moves to pictures (semi-concrete) and then to numerals (abstract). Moving students beyond concrete representations is important for students with special needs, because if they are to become independent learners, they must be able to work at an abstract level. Although these students benefit from working with manipulatives and other concrete representations, teachers must make sure to move them to more abstract levels as soon as they are able. Another approach to helping students solve math word problems is described in Professional Edge 10.2.

LAMPS The *LAMPS* strategy (Reetz & Rasmussen, 1988) can be used as an aid to help remember the steps in regrouping or carrying in addition:

L *Line up* the numbers according to their decimal points.
A *Add* the right column of numbers and ask . . .
M *"More* than 9?"* If so, continue to the next step.
P *Put* the 1s below the column.
S *Send* the 10s to the top of the next column.

PROFESSIONAL EDGE 10.2

The Key-Word Strategy for Solving Math Word Problems: Is There a Better Way?

The key-word strategy is an example of an ineffective strategy that many students with special needs use or are taught to use in solving math word problems (Kelly & Carnine, 1996). In this approach, students associate key words such as *more, in all, gave away,* and *left over* with certain mathematical operations. The key-word strategy is attractive to teachers and students because sometimes it works. For example, the word *more* is commonly associated with subtraction, as in the following problem:

Jose has 15 cents. Carmen has 10 cents. How much *more* money does Jose have?

Unfortunately, many times the word *more* appears in word problems that call for addition, as in the following problem:

Charmaine had 15 cents. Her mother gave her 10 *more* cents. How many cents does she have now?

Kelly and Carnine (1996) suggest teaching students with special needs a more effective strategy for solving math word problems using problem maps and math fact families. Their strategy for teaching single-operation addition and subtraction problems follows.

For any addition/subtraction situation, there are two "small" numbers and a "big" number (the sum).

An addition/subtraction number family is mapped this way:

$$\xrightarrow{\quad 7 \quad 9 \quad} 16$$

The preceding family represents the following addition/subtraction facts:

$$7 + 9 = 16 \qquad 16 - 9 = 7$$
$$9 + 7 = 16 \qquad 16 - 7 = 9$$

A missing *big* number implies addition:

$$\xrightarrow{\quad 8 \quad 22 \quad} \square \qquad 8 + 22 = \square$$

A missing *small* number implies subtraction:

$$\xrightarrow{\quad \square \quad 22 \quad} 30 \qquad 30 - 22 = \square$$

or

$$\xrightarrow{\quad 8 \quad \square \quad} 30 \qquad 30 - 8 = \square$$

These maps can then be applied to a variety of addition and subtraction word problems. Kelly and Carnine (1996, p. 6) give the following example involving comparison problems:

In comparison problems, the difference between two values being compared may be information given in a problem (for example, Marco sold 57 fewer subscriptions than Lui) or

the unknown in a problem. (For example, How much heavier was Mary?) Because of the words *sold fewer* in the following problem, many students with LD will subtract.

Marco sold 57 fewer magazine subscriptions than Lui. Marco sold 112 subscriptions. How many subscriptions did Lui sell? (*Excerpt reprinted with permission from Council for Learning Disabilities.*)

Students can use number families to avoid this confusion. The first step is to represent the problem using a number family; students must determine whether each of the two numbers given in the problem is a small number or the big number. The students are shown a simple way to do this:

They find the sentence that tells about the comparison and read it without the difference number. For example, students are taught to read the first sentence without the 57: "Marco sold fewer subscriptions than Lui." Because Marco sold fewer subscriptions, Marco is represented by a small number. By default, Lui is the big number. The students write M for Marco and L for Lui:

$$\xrightarrow{\quad M \quad} L$$

The word problem also gives a number for the difference between Marco and Lui. That number always has to be a small number. Marco sold 57 fewer, so 57 is the other small number:

$$\xrightarrow{\quad 57 \quad M \quad} L$$

Next, the students read the rest of the problem. The problem asks about Lui and gives a number for Marco, so the students draw a box around L and replace the M with 112:

$$\xrightarrow{\quad 57 \quad \cancel{M} \, 112 \quad} \boxed{L}$$

Because the problem gives both small numbers, the students write an addition problem:

$$\begin{array}{r} 57 \\ +112 \\ \hline \end{array}$$

The answer tells how many magazine subscriptions Lui sold.

Stein, Kinder, Silbert, and Carnine (2005) and Seethaler, Powell, and Fuchs (2010) offer similar word problem strategies as applied to multiplication, division, and multistep word problems. Flores, Hinton, & Burton (2016) and Pfannenstiel, Pedrotty-Bryant, Bryant, & Porterfield (2015) successfully taught students with difficulties in math to solve word problems using a strategy similar to that used by Kelly and Carnine, only they referred to the small and big numbers as "parts" and "whole."

Source: Data from B. Kelly & D. Carnine (1996). "Teaching Problem-Solving Strategies for Word Problems to Students with Learning Disabilities." *LD Forum,* 21(3) 5–9.

SLOBS To help with borrowing in subtraction, teach students to follow the steps in the *SLOBS* strategy (Reetz & Rasmussen, 1988):

S *Smaller:* Follow steps.
L *Larger:* Leap to subtract.
O *Cross off* the number in the next column.
B *Borrow* by taking one 10 and adding to the next column.
S *Subtract.*

For the problem:

$$\begin{array}{r} 72 \\ -46 \\ \hline \end{array}$$

Students look at the top number on the right to see whether it is smaller or larger than the bottom right number. If it is smaller, the students follow the rest of the steps. They cross off the number in the next column to the left to borrow one unit from that column (reducing that number by one) and add it to the other column. In the problem shown, they borrow 10 from the left column and then subtract. If the number is larger, students proceed directly to the subtract step. They repeat the steps if more digits are to be subtracted.

FOIL The *FOIL* strategy (Crawford, 1980) helps prevent algebra students from missing one of the four products needed to calculate multiplication of a binomial by another binomial. Students follow these four steps:

F   Multiply *first* terms.
O   Multiply *outermost* terms.
I   Multiply *innermost* terms.
L   Multiply *last* terms.

For example, the *FOIL* strategy can be applied to the following problem:

$$(x + 4)\,(x + 3)$$
$$A \quad\ B \quad\ C \quad\ D$$

In the **F** step, the student multiplies the first two factors in each binomial, $x \times x = x^2$, or using the letters, *AC*. Next, in the **O** step, the student multiplies the first factor in the first binomial and the second factor in the second binomial, $x \times 3 = 3x$, or *AD*. Then, in the **I** step, the student multiplies the second factor of the first binomial and the first factor of the second binomial, $4 \times x = 4x$, or *BC*. Finally, in the **L** step, the second factors of both binomials are multiplied: $4 \times 3 = 12$, or *BD*. This strategy applies only to the special case of multiplying two binomials.

Strategies for Managing Time and Resources

A lack of organization is a common characteristic of students with disabilities (Langberg et al., 2011; Lerner & Johns, 2014; Silver, 2010), as is true for Ron, one of the students introduced at the beginning of the chapter. Students need to be able to organize their school materials as well as their homework and time. Demands for organization become particularly problematic once students reach middle school, where increases in class size and the number of teachers, greater workloads, and a reduction in adult supervision all create the need for greater student independence (Langberg et al., 2011). Being organized requires the skills of executive functioning previously described in Chapter 7, skills that help students regulate their actions by getting themselves started, focusing on what needs to be done, maintaining focus on the task at hand, keeping counterproductive emotions at bay, and employing short-term memory skills to keep relevant problem solving information readily accessible (Langberg, Dvorsky, & Evans, 2013). Langberg and others (2011) developed and validated the Homework, Organization, and Planning Program (HOPS), a program that can increase organization skills, decrease homework problems, and, as shown in one study, reduce academic problems and increase GPAs (Langberg, Epstein, Urbanowicz, Simon, & Graham, 2008). HOPS consists of three parts: organizing school materials, homework management, and time management and planning. For school materials organization, through the use of a detailed checklist, students are taught a systematic strategy for organizing their school binder, book bag, and locker. Students are also taught a system for assuring that the transfer of homework materials to and from school goes smoothly. In the homework management component, students are taught how to use a planner to accurately and consistently record homework projects and tests. Part 3, time management and planning, teaches students to break study and project tasks into manageable segments and plan for their timely completion. HOPS also

Strategies for managing time and organizing materials help provide the structured routines that many students need to succeed in school. What are the three steps in teaching students how to use weekly assignment calendars?

employs a reward system to maintain student motivation to succeed, and it includes a parent component with the eventual goal of turning operation of the program over to parents if feasible. Whether or not you use HOPS, efforts to improve your students' organization skills should be comprehensive and cover the same basic areas.

A number of smartphone or tablet apps are also available to help students better manage their lives. A list of these developed by Yu (2016) is shown in Table 10.1. As with all technology, be sure students are able to use the apps as they are intended, and monitor usage continually to determine whether students are using the apps as intended.

WWW RESOURCES

For a wealth of strategies, checklists, and other materials for keeping students organized, Google "organization checklists for students" and choose from many sites of interest.

TABLE 10.1   Sample Smartphone or Tablet Apps to Self-Manage

Category	Apps	Descriptions
Student Planner	iHomework[a] myHomework Student[a,b] Planner[b] HomeWork[b] Homework Planner[b]	Track classes, tests, and assignments Develop to-do lists and set up reminders Enter time-, block-, and period-based schedules
Generic Planner	Awesome Calendar Lite[a] Opus Domini Mobile[a] Schedule Planner[a,b]	Plan daily or weekly activities by priority Create task lists Enter daily notes
Simple To-Do List[c]	Conqu[a,b] gTasks[a,b] Priorities[a] SmallTask[a] Todoist[b]	Create tasks and subtasks based on time and locations Develop repeating tasks (e.g., weekly reading) Set up reminders

[a]iOS app, [b]Android app, [c]Students with disabilities are recommended to use simple and explicit apps.

Source: "Just Do It! Reducing Academic Procrastination of Secondary students," by Z. Yu, 2016. Reprinted with permission from Council for Learning Disabilities.

How Can Students Learn to Use Strategies Independently?

Some students may have trouble using a learning strategy independently, even after they have learned how to do it. Their problem could be that they do not know when to use a strategy or how to keep track of how well they are using it, and how to change their behavior, if necessary.

Three strategies that can help students perform tasks more independently are self-instruction, self-monitoring, and self-questioning. Like all learning strategies, these "self" strategies may need to be carefully taught using the teaching practices described in this chapter.

Self-Instruction

In **self-instruction**, learners are taught to use language to guide their performances. In essence, students are taught to talk themselves through a task. The idea is that if they can talk themselves through a task, they will not need help from anyone else. Self-instruction has been successfully used to teach students with disabilities strategies for math, test taking, reading comprehension, and writing (Korinek & DeFur, 2016; Reid et al., 2013; Uberti, Mastropieri, & Scruggs, 2004).

Before teaching self-instruction, be sure students have engaged in some form of self-assessment and are aware of their own particular strengths and weaknesses, an essential preskill for self-instruction. Then, begin teaching self-instruction techniques by explaining that self-instruction involves giving oneself directions on how to do a task. For example, self-instruction can be used to help get seatwork done or to remember to use a strategy for a multiple-choice test. Next, ask students to identify a situation that requires the use of a specific skill, such as getting their seatwork done in reading or taking a 10-minute science quiz on Friday. Demonstrate how to write down the steps needed to perform that task. For example, to get independent classwork done, the student first decides how much effort to put into this task. Next, he or she decides what is supposed to be done. Finally, the student decides what the first step in completing the task should be, what the next step should be, and so forth, until the assignment is done. When students are finished, they praise themselves for a job well done. Ask students to rehearse the steps through self-talk or peer review, going over all the steps involved in completing a written classwork task from beginning to end.

After you have demonstrated how to apply self-instruction, have the students practice in a role-play situation and give them feedback. In the independent classwork task, for example, you could project a sample reading task and demonstrate the steps by thinking out loud. The students could then practice in pairs and give each other feedback, with you monitoring and also giving feedback. Even after all of this careful instruction, students still can forget the purpose of certain strategies, forget to use the strategies, or not understand when and where to use the strategies. Wery and Niefield (2010) developed the form shown in Figure 10.8 to guide students as they try to independently select and use learning strategies they have been taught to use in class.

Self-Monitoring

In **self-monitoring**, students watch and check themselves to make sure they have performed targeted behaviors. Self-monitoring has been shown to be effective in

FIGURE 10.8 **Sample Reading Strategies Notebook**

Alonzo's Reading Strategies Notebook Table of Contents	
Identifying hard words	**Page**
Using word parts	3
Reading fluency	
WARF	4
Reading comprehension	
SCROL	5
Highlight it!	6
Mark it!	7
MAIN-I	8

Source: Republished with permission of Council for Exceptional Children, from "Supporting Self-Regulated Learning with Exceptional Children." *Teaching Exceptional Children, 42*(4) by J. Wery & J. Nietfeld (2010); permission conveyed through Copyright Clearance Center, Inc.

making positive changes in the academic and social behavior of students with disabilities (Daly & Ranalli, 2003; Wills & Mason, 2014). It is a critical aspect of independent learning, which often requires students to check their performance to see whether it is effective and make a change when a particular strategy is not working (Hallahan, Llyod, Kauffman, Weiss, & Martinez, 2005; Reid et al., 2013). Self-monitoring also can be a strong motivator for students by providing them concrete evidence of their progress.

In teaching self-monitoring to your students, first explain to them that it is a way they can check their own behavior to make sure they are doing the right thing. Ask the students to identify a learning strategy they need to use in class. For example, students may select a strategy such as the *COPS* proofreading strategy described earlier in the chapter.

The next step is to select a practical and expedient way for students to measure the behavior. One possibility is to have them use a checklist of strategy steps and then record the number of steps completed. For example, Yashika recorded the steps of the *SCROL* strategy he completed when reading a section in his science text.

Brimijoin, Marquisse, and Tomlinson (2003) report a teacher using a car windshield metaphor to teach students to monitor their understanding. The teacher asked, "How many [of you] are clear as glass about how greatest common factor works? How many have bugs on your windshields? How many have windshields covered with mud?" (p. 70).

Self-Questioning

Self-questioning is a form of self-instruction in which students guide their performance by asking themselves questions. The idea behind self-questioning is that if students can guide their own behavior by asking themselves questions, then they will not always need a teacher or other adult present to perform.

In teaching students self-questioning, have them first identify the duties or tasks that are required in class. For example, students can identify steps needed to proofread a written paper, such as checking the correct use of capital letters, punctuation, spelling, and appearance. Have students write these tasks in question form, asking, for example, "Have I capitalized all words correctly? Have I used the right punctuation marks in the right places? Have I spelled all the words correctly? Is my paper neat?"

As in self-monitoring, the next step is to select a practical and expedient way for students to measure the behavior, such as recording behaviors as they occur using a checklist. Students might practice self-questioning in pairs

WWW RESOURCES

For more information on self-monitoring strategies, go to http://www.pbisworld.com; click on "Tier 2," and then click on "Self Monitoring."

MyLab Education

Video Example 10.5 Self: Management: Brandon's MotivAider and Picture Schedule

This video shows several ways a student is learning to self-monitor his independent work completion in class

RESEARCH-BASED PRACTICES

Joseph, Alber-Morgan, Cullen, and Rouse (2016) reviewed 35 studies that involved the use of self-questioning as an aid to reading comprehension. The researchers found that self-questioning is effective for improving reading comprehension across a range of diverse learners and educational settings.

for feedback. Other practical measures include keeping task questions on index cards and putting them in a convenient place or creating a list and/or taking a picture and storing it in an organizational app. For example, students might put the proofreading questions on an index card and tape it to the inside cover of their notebooks, or consult a video of themselves proofreading on a file stored in their smartphones.

> **MyLab Education** 10.3 Self-Check

WRAPPING IT UP

Back to the Cases

Now that you have read about strategies for independent learning, look back at the teacher stories at the beginning of the chapter. Then go to MyLab Education to apply the knowledge you've gained in this chapter to each case.

MyLab Education Application Exercise 10.1: Case Study 10.1

GERALD has problems in written expression, including organization and mechanical errors. Mr. McCrae has determined that organization is most important, because the mechanical errors can be corrected after Gerald has produced an organized written product.

MyLab Education Application Exercise 10.2: Case Study 10.2

TRACI, as you may recall, struggled with solving word problems. After helping her with a strategy for solving such problems, Ms. Cord reflects on Traci's skills in other academic areas.

MyLab Education Application Exercise 10.3: Case Study 10.3

RON often came unprepared to class. However, after several weeks of his teachers working with him, he now is coming to class with all of the books and materials he needs. In fact, he completed his homework assignments every day this week.

Summary

LO 10.1 General education teachers can help all their students, including students with disabilities and other special needs, become independent learners. One way teachers can build student independence is to encourage student self-awareness, self-advocacy, and self-determination.

LO 10.2 When designing your own learning strategies, identify skill areas problematic for most of your students, specify learning outcomes for each area, and list a set of steps students need to follow to reach the identified outcomes. Steps should number no more than eight, be brief and encased in a mnemonic, and cue students to think, do, and self-evaluate.

LO 10.3 Another way to help students become more independent is to design and teach effective learning strategies in class. Methods of teaching learning strategies to students include assessing current strategy use, clarifying expectations, demonstrating strategy use, encouraging students to memorize strategy steps, providing guided and independent practice, and administering posttests.

LO 10.4 Many successful strategies that can help students become independent learners are available in the areas of reading and reading comprehension, listening and note taking, writing, problem solving in math, and managing time and resources.

LO 10.5 Three strategies that can help students learn to use learning strategies independently are self-instruction, self-monitoring, and self-questioning.

APPLICATIONS IN TEACHING PRACTICE
Designing Strategies for Independence

Latasha is a student who has moderate hearing loss. Although her hearing aid helps, she still has to depend on speech reading to communicate. She also speaks slowly and has trouble saying high-frequency sounds such as *sh* and *t*. Latasha has a poor self-image and is reluctant to interact with her peers and teachers. Design a self-advocacy program for Latasha.

QUESTIONS

1. What skills would you teach Latasha to use for self-advocacy?
2. How would you get Latasha to use these skills in your class and in other in-school and out-of-school situations?

Cal is a student with organizational problems; he is chronically late for class and rarely finishes his homework. Design an organizational strategy for Cal using the guidelines for developing strategies covered in this chapter.

QUESTIONS

1. How would you teach the organizational strategy you have designed using the guidelines covered in this chapter for effectively teaching a learning strategy?
2. How would you teach Cal to apply the strategy independently using self-instruction? Self-monitoring? Self-questioning?

Evaluate the design of any one of the learning strategies in the chapter using the guidelines in Professional Edge 10.1.

QUESTIONS

1. Is there anything you would change about the strategy? How would you teach the strategy using the six steps described in this chapter?
2. How would you help students apply the strategy independently using the three "self" strategies discussed in this chapter?

CHAPTER 11

Evaluating Student Learning

LEARNING OUTCOMES

After you read this chapter, you will be able to:

11-1 Analyze demands that occur before, during, and after classroom testing and describe adjustments that can be made for students with special needs.

11-2 Describe and provide a rationale for grading practices that can benefit all of your students.

11-3 Explain when and how report card grades can be individualized for students with special needs.

11-4 Explain the potential benefits of using performance-based and portfolio assessments with students with disabilities. Identify features of each that may cause problems for students with disabilities, and describe adjustments that could be made to ameliorate these difficulties.

STACI is a student in Ms. Stevens's earth science class. Staci has a learning disability in reading; she reads slowly and often has difficulty understanding what she is reading. As a result, Staci's IEP indicates that she is to receive extended time when taking classroom tests. During the past grading period, Ms. Stevens gave four multiple-choice tests, each worth 20 percent of the final grade. Scores on homework assignments counted for the remaining 20 percent. Staci earned a grade of B on her homework, but, despite receiving extended time taking the tests, she had two Ds, one C, and one F. Ms. Stevens assigned her an overall grade of D. Ms. Stevens felt this was a fair grade because Staci had extra time to take the tests; plus, most of Staci's peers scored much higher on the tests. Ms. Stevens is also committed to keeping her reputation as a teacher with high standards. When Staci received her grade, she asked her parents why she should work so hard when she couldn't seem to get good grades anyway. Staci's parents felt that she had improved during the last grading period but that her grade did not show it. They were afraid that Staci would stop trying and eventually drop out of school.

What adjustments to classroom testing can Ms. Stevens make to improve Staci's test performance? What types of classroom evaluation besides classroom tests might she use to better reflect Staci's classroom progress? How can Ms. Stevens adjust her grading procedures to keep Staci motivated without sacrificing grading accuracy and lowering her standards?

AMELIA is in Ms. Robinson's third-grade class. She is an English learner and has some trouble in reading but always tries hard and completes her classroom work. Ms. Robinson is pleased with her progress and believes that students need to be rewarded for their effort or they will cease to be motivated. Amelia's EL teacher agrees, reasoning that her English is just beginning to show improvement and she doesn't want to do anything to risk that. As a result, Ms. Robinson has given Amelia A's in reading for the first two grading periods. Recently, Amelia's parents became very upset when they learned that Amelia was reading only at the first-grade level according to district standardized tests. They wondered how she could have done so poorly on the standardized tests when she has been bringing home A's on her report card.

What would you tell Amelia's parents if she were in your class? How could you change your grading procedures to prevent communication problems like this from occurring?

RONALD is a student with a moderate intellectual disability who is in Mr. Henry's fourth-grade math class. On the basis of his current performance in math, which is at the first-grade level, Ronald's individualized education program (IEP) team set math goals for him in the areas of basic addition and subtraction. The rest of the class is working on more difficult material—for example, the introduction of factors and multiples—based on the fourth-grade math standards. Ronald has an IEP objective for the second grading period of computing in writing, within 20 minutes, 10 two-digit by two-digit addition problems without regrouping with 80 percent accuracy. While he takes an alternate assessment in math rather than a grade level standardized test, this objective is aligned with state standards. Ronald received direct instruction on these problems from Mr. Brook, his special education teacher, who co-teaches with Mr. Henry. As a result, he met his goal for the grading period.

School policy mandates letter grades. Are students like Ronald expected to meet the same standards as his classmates without disabilities? How should Mr. Henry grade Ronald? What other approaches can he use to evaluate Ronald's performance in his class?

Although high-stakes tests have become the predominant method of evaluating student learning, teachers continue to play an important role in determining student progress. The information teachers collect during classroom evaluation activities can indicate whether their teaching has been effective and can help them alter instruction as needed. Classroom evaluations also are helpful in giving students (and their parents) an idea of how well they are performing in school.

Even though evaluation activities are very important, the ways in which students are evaluated most frequently—testing and grading—can be problematic for students with disabilities, their teachers, and their parents. For example, Staci and her earth science teacher have a problem because Staci's test scores more often reflect her learning disability than her knowledge of earth science. Amelia's teacher has a problem in communicating the meaning of Amelia's grades to her parents. She graded Amelia based on Amelia's progress and effort in class. Amelia's parents, however, thought she was being graded in comparison with her peers and therefore expected their daughter to be performing at or above grade level, not below. Ronald's teacher needs to give Ronald a grade even though he has different curricular goals than the other students in the class. Further complicating these problems is the current climate of accountability and the related expectation that most students with disabilities will meet the same standards as their peers without disabilities. This expectation makes it imperative that adjustments in evaluation be made without compromising students' ability to meet standards on high-stakes tests. As you work with students with disabilities or other special needs, you will experience these and other challenges in evaluating their learning. In this chapter, you learn a number of ways to address these dilemmas.

How Can Adjustments Be Made for Students with Special Needs When Giving Classroom Tests?

Although testing has always been a major part of U.S. education, the current emphasis on rigorous standards and students leaving school truly ready for work or postsecondary education promises to make educators rely even more on tests in the future (National Center on Educational Outcomes, 2016). This increasing emphasis on test performance includes focus on the test performance of students with disabilities. As described in the vignette about Staci at the beginning of this chapter, testing can be a very trying experience for many of these students and their families.

Most important in testing students with disabilities is ensuring that test results reflect their knowledge and skills, not their disabilities. Fortunately, classroom tests can be designed or adjusted in ways that help you test students with disabilities fairly and with a reasonable amount of accuracy. As shown in Table 11.1, adjustments for students with special needs can be made in three contexts: before the test, during the test administration, and after the test as part of the grading procedures. Many of these adjustments also can benefit students who do not have disabilities.

Students can help each other prepare effectively for tests using directly taught study strategies. What strategies might these students be using to prepare for an upcoming test?

Adjustments Before the Test

STUDY GUIDES You can prepare a *study guide* that tells students what to study for the test. A study guide can help students avoid wasting valuable time studying

TABLE 11.1 **Examples of Testing Adjustments**

Before the Test	During the Test	After the Test
Study guide	Alternative forms of questions	Changed letter or number grades
Practice test	Alternative test sites	Changed grading criteria
Individual tutoring	Alternative response modes	Alternatives to letter and number grades
Teaching test-taking skills		
Modified test construction		

everything indiscriminately and instead help them concentrate on the most important information. For example, Acrey, Johnstone, and Milligan (2005) suggest using a "countdown study guide." A week prior to the test, give students a blank one-week organizer with enough blank space for each day. At the beginning of each class have the students write down what they will do that day to prepare for the test. Roditi and colleagues (2005) recommend providing students with a list of the major topics to be covered on the exam along with four columns: (a) "I am missing this information; I need to get it," (b) "I don't know this," (c) "I remember this topic but need to read it over one more time," and (d) "I know this well enough to answer questions on a test." The columns help students decide how much time to spend on each topic included on the test (Lagares & Connor, 2010, p. 64).

PRACTICE TESTS Practice tests can clarify your test expectations and also benefit the class by familiarizing students with the test format. Practice tests are also helpful to students who have trouble following directions and to those who are anxious about taking tests and often fail to cope immediately with an unfamiliar test format. The effect of practice tests can be enhanced by making the testing conditions as similar as possible to those students will encounter during the actual test (Conderman & Pederson, 2010). Many students with disabilities also benefit from *tutoring* before tests. Tutoring can be offered before or after school and may be carried out by peer tutors or paraprofessionals. Tutors can provide guidelines for what to study or can help directly with particularly difficult content.

TEST-TAKING SKILLS Another option is to teach students *test-taking skills*. This option can help students take your classroom tests and state high-stakes tests as well. Students may need a number of test-taking skills, including ones for studying for tests, taking objective tests, and writing essay tests. With respect to *studying for tests*, students often are required to remember a lot of material. This can be difficult for students with learning or intellectual disabilities, who may have memory problems. Students can benefit from strategies that help them remember important content for tests. For example, Georgia uses a memorization technique called chunking. After she studies a chapter in her text, she tries to recall five to seven key ideas. These key thoughts help trigger her recall of more significant details. After reading a chapter about the life of Harriet Tubman, for example, she remembers information in chunks—Tubman's early years, her experiences with the underground railroad, and so on. These general ideas help her remember details such as when Harriet Tubman was born and how many slaves she helped to free.

Mnemonic devices also can help students remember information for tests. Mnemonics impose an order on information to be remembered using words, poems, rhymes, jingles, or images to aid memory. For example, Mr. Charles wants his class to remember the six methods of scientific investigation. He tells the students to think of the word *chrome* (Cermak, 1976). The following six steps make up the *CHROME* strategy:

C Categorization
H Hypothesis
R Reasoning

FYI

Planning tests and testing adjustments at the beginning of instruction helps you clarify what is essential to teach and achieve a good match between your tests and instruction.

WWW RESOURCES

The Study Guides and Strategies website (http://www.studygs.net) provides study guides as well as strategies for preparing for and taking tests. The site provides study skills resources, including several links to study skills guides and interactive tutorials. Information is available in multiple foreign languages.

O   Observation
M   Measurement
E   Experimentation

Another mnemonic device that can help students remember definitions and factual information is called the keyword method, not to be confused with the key-word method used to teach math word problems that was referred to in Chapter 10 (Mastropieri, 1988; Uberti, Scruggs, & Mastropieri, 2003). The **keyword method** uses visual imagery to make material more meaningful to students and hence easier to remember. First, a vocabulary word or fact is changed into a word that sounds similar and is easy to picture. For example, to help remember that the explorer Hernando de Soto came from Spain, students might be shown the picture in Figure 11.1, a bull (to symbolize Spain) at a counter sipping a soda (the keyword for *de Soto*) (Carney, Levin, & Levin, 1993). When students are asked to name an explorer who came from Spain, they are told to think of the keyword for de Soto. Next, they are told to think back to the picture the keyword was in and remember what was happening in the picture. Finally, they are told to answer the question (Who was an explorer from Spain?).

Mercer, Mercer, and Pullen (2010) suggest a strategy for teaching students to create their own mnemonics called *FIRST*. The steps are:

Form a word that shows an important part of the skill or fact (for example, HOMES for each of the Great Lakes).

Insert extra letters to form a mnemonic word if needed (for example BrACE for remembering the unseen scientific objects of black holes, antimatter, cosmic rays, and earth's core.

Rearrange letters to form a mnemonic word when order isn't important.

Shape a sentence to form a mnemonic (for example, **S**ally **L**ikes **A**ll **N**ice **T**eachers for the *SLANT* strategy described in Chapter 10 for paying attention in class.

Try combinations of the first four steps to form a mnemonic.

FIGURE 11.1 Keyword for de Soto

Source: Carney, R. N., Levin, M. E., & Levin, J. R. (1993). "Mnemonic strategies: Instructional techniques worth remembering." *Teaching Exceptional Children, 25*(4), 24-30. Council for Exceptional Children (CEC).

Many students do poorly on tests because they do not *study for tests systematically*. Teach students to organize their materials so that they avoid wasting time searching for such items as notes for a particular class or the answers to textbook exercises. Making random checks of students' notebooks is one way to find out how well organized they are. For example, Ms. Barber stresses note taking in her fifth-grade social studies class. Every Friday afternoon, she checks the notebooks of five students. She gives students bonus points if they have notes for each day and if their notes are legible and include key information. Also teach students strategies for how to process material when they are studying. For example, Ms. Treacher shows her third graders a verbal rehearsal strategy for learning spelling words. She says the word, spells it out loud three times, covers the word, writes the word, and then compares her spelling to the correct spelling. Another effective rehearsal strategy is for students to ask themselves questions about the most important information to be learned.

Students, including those with special needs, may not test well because they lack strategies for actually *taking tests*. For example, Sal rarely finishes tests in science because he spends too much time on questions that he finds difficult. Laura has trouble with true–false questions because she does not pay attention to key words such as *always, never, usually,* and *sometimes.* Lewis's answers to essay questions contain much irrelevant information and do not focus on what the questions are asking. The Professional Edge feature offers suggestions for teaching students strategies for taking objective tests. These strategies also work for taking high-stakes tests.

Students also need strategies for taking essay tests. Performing well on essay tests requires that students know the content covered; can follow directions, including identifying and understanding key words; and can organize their ideas. All these areas can be problematic for students with disabilities. Thierren, Hughes, Kapelski, and Mokhtari (2009) successfully taught seventh- and eighth-grade students with learning and writing disabilities to answer essay questions using the *ANSWER* strategy, described as follows:

Analyze the action words in the question by reading the question carefully and underlining the key words.

Notice the requirements of the question. Mark each and change the question into your own words.

Set up an outline listing your main ideas for the essay question.

Work in detail by adding important details to the outline that you plan to include in your essay.

Engineer your answer by including an introductory sentence and detailed sentences about each of the main ideas in your outline.

Review your answer by checking that all parts of the question have been answered and edit your essay. (p. 17)

All students benefit from tests that are written clearly and assess pertinent knowledge or skills. Thus, everything that you have learned about writing good tests in your teacher-education program applies here. Still, test items can be reasonably well written but constructed in a way that results in problems for students with special needs. When this situation occurs, *modified test construction* is necessary. For example, Carmen has difficulty reading tests that are visually cluttered. She might benefit from triple spacing between test items and extra space between lines. Juan scores poorly on tests because the items contain complex sentences with many words that are above his reading level and that his teacher did not use while teaching.

Practical ways of constructing objective tests that allow you to measure student knowledge more accurately are shown in the Professional Edge feature. Strategies for constructing test items for English learners are shown in the Instructional Edge feature.

WWW RESOURCES

Create all kinds of game-like tools for studying at Quizlet (www.quizlet.com) and Kahoot (www.kahoot.com).

RESEARCH-BASED PRACTICES

Feldman, Kim, and Elliott (2011) found that testing accommodations based on student IEPs improve the test performance, test-taking self-efficacy, and motivation of adolescents with learning disabilities.

FYI

While many of the Before Testing adjustments relate directly to the middle and high school levels, most apply to elementary-school children as well.

PROFESSIONAL EDGE 11.1

Adjustments in Test Construction for Students with Disabilities

All of your students will do better on clearly written tests that ask questions pertaining specifically to the material covered in class and in the textbook. But your students with disabilities especially require well-phrased and visually accessible tests if they are to succeed at test taking. Consider the following guidelines, most of which apply to both paper and pencil and electronic tests:

1. Paper and pencil tests should be typewritten and photo-copied. For electronic tests, make sure the font is large enough and formatting clear.

2. Make tests visually uncluttered by leaving sufficient space between items (3 spaces) and between lines within items (1½ spaces). Do not crowd pages with items; keep wide margins.

3. Use symmetrical spacing. For multiple-choice tests, align possible responses vertically rather than horizontally, and type the question and possible responses on the same page. Permit students to circle the letter of the correct answer rather than write it in front of the item.

4. Provide additional spacing between different types of test questions and separate directions and a sample item for each type of test question.

5. Provide symbols, icons, and/or pictorials to prompt students to pay attention to directions (Elliott et al., 2010) and depict important content (Roach, Beddow, Kurz, Kettler, & Elliott, 2010).

6. For completion, short-answer, and essay questions, leave sufficient space to write the answer. Students do not do as well when they must continue their answers on the back of the page or on the next page. For completion, keep each blank close to the end of the sentence or stem to prevent reading comprehension issues.

7. Leave space for students to answer on the test rather than using machine scoring or answer sheets. Some students have difficulty transferring answers from one page to another.

8. For students who read slowly and students who have organizational problems, avoid the following constructions in matching items: long matching lists—keep lists to five or six items and group by concepts; lengthy items; and drawing lines to the correct answer, which can be confusing. Lists with 10 to 15 entries in the first column can be simplified by preselecting three to four choices from the second column for each item in the first column. Record these choices beside the item in the first column and have the student select the correct answer from the smaller pool.

Consider the following example:
Match the definition on the left with the word on the right by writing the letter for the word in the blank next to the definition.

1.	in a sudden way _____	a.	brightness
2.	not able _____	b.	visitor
3.	to make bright _____	c.	suddenly
4.	one who visits _____	d.	happiness
5.	in a happy way _____	e.	rearrange
6.	to tell again _____	f.	brighten
7.	to arrange beforehand ___	g.	retell
8.	state of being happy ___	h.	prearrange
9.	to arrange again _____	i.	unable
10.	state of being bright ___	j.	happily

These questions will be less confusing if you change them using the guidelines just described:

1.	*in a sudden way* ___	a.	brightness
		b.	visitor
		c.	suddenly
		d.	retell

9. Change fill-in-the-blank items to a multiple-choice format for the blank. Students select the correct answer only from the choices given. This adjustment can benefit students with memory issues by changing the task from one of recall (memory) to one of recognition.

10. Consider color-coding, underlining, enlarging, or highlighting key words and mathematical symbols.

11. Avoid confusing negatives such as "All of the above except D and E.," or "Which of the following is NOT an example of . . . ?"

12. To reduce stress and put some fun into testing, devise items that relate to students' lives such as referring to the local food market when questioning students about food groups for a nutrition test (Savage, Savage, & Armstrong, 2006) and involve students in the testing process by allowing them to develop test questions (Edyburn, 2009).

13. Keep tests short; if two or three questions will do, avoid asking 10.

Source: Based on Assessing universal design for classroom testing, by B. B. Frey and J. P. Allen, 2010, Annual Meeting of the American Educational Research Association, Denver, CO; Test better, teach better, by J. Popham, 2003, Alexandria, Va.: ASCD; Fair isn't always equal: Assessing and grading in the differentiated classroom, by R. Wormeli, 2006, Portland, Maine: Stenhouse Publishers; and Classroom assessment: Supporting teaching and learning in real classrooms, 2005, Upper Saddle River, NJ: Pearson-Merrill-Prentice Hall.

Adjustments During the Test

In the Chapter 4 Professional Edge 4.1 you learned that providing accommodations on standardized/high stakes tests improves the accuracy of the results for students with special needs. These adjustments involved making changes

INSTRUCTIONAL EDGE 11.1

Testing English Learners in Math Problem Solving

Recent research reveals two important findings about English learners (ELLs) and tests. The bad news is that the test scores of ELs in all subject areas, including math, are much lower than those of native English speakers (National Center for Educational Statistics, 2012). The poorer test performance of ELs in math occurs not because they know less about the math content but because they have a hard time understanding the language used in test items. In effect, the language demands of the test render the test invalid and unfair. However, the good news is that test scores for ELs can be improved by decreasing the complexity of the language (Abedi, Hofstetter, & Lord, 2004). In fact, simplifying the language of test items is more helpful to ELs than translating the items into their native language (Educational Testing Service, 2009). Here are some examples of how you can simplify language when writing math problems for your students (Abedi et al., 2004):

- Change unfamiliar or infrequently used nonmath vocabulary. For example, the phrase "a certain business concern" is unfamiliar and difficult to understand; the substituted phrase "Acme Company" is more common and easier to understand.
- Change the voice of verbs from passive to active. For example, change "If a marble is taken from the bag" to "If you take a marble from the bag."
- Shorten the length of noun phrases. For example, the phrase "the pattern of the puppy's weight gain" can be changed to "the pattern above."
- Replace conditional clauses with separate sentences or change the order of the conditional and main clauses. For example, consider the sentence, "If two batteries in the sample were found to be dead, then the workers had to

inspect all of the batteries." This sentence can be simplified by changing it into two sentences: "The workers found two dead batteries in the sample. Because of this, they had to inspect all of the batteries." You could also change the order of the clauses: "The workers had to inspect all of the batteries when they found that two batteries in the sample were dead."

- Remove or change relative clauses. For example, change "What is the total number of newspapers that Lee delivers in five days?" to "How many papers does Lee deliver in five days?"
- Change complex question phrases to simple question words. For example, change "which is the best approximation of the number . . . ?" to "approximately how many . . . ?"
- Make abstract wordings more concrete. For example, change "2,675 radios sold" to "2,675 radios that Mr. Jones sold."

Examine the following word problem:

Students in Mr. Jacob's English class were giving speeches. Each student's speech was 7–10 minutes long. Which of the following is the best estimate for the total number of student speeches that could be given in a two-hour class?

a. 4 speeches
b. 8 speeches
c. 13 speeches
d. 19 speeches

What problems do you think an English learner might have with this question? How would you change the item to make it more understandable?

---

to test scheduling, timing, method of presentation, and method of response. All these ways of adjusting how standardized tests are given are just as important to use in your classroom testing program. If changes in test construction are intended for the whole class, they can be incorporated into the original test file before printing. However, when changes are intended only for one or two students, you can make them as students take the test. Test adjustments of particular concern for classroom tests include using alternative forms of questions, allowing alternative response modes, and using alternative testing sites.

ALTERNATIVE FORMS OF QUESTIONS Ms. Minter's co-teacher, Ms. James, was working with Barry on his test-taking skills. She was helping Barry consider each answer choice in multiple-choice questions carefully, rather than always picking the first choice. Ms. James began by using an alternative form of question for Barry. When using *alternative forms of questions*, the teacher changes the type of question asked (for example, multiple-choice instead of essay questions) or the construction of the question (for example, adding a word bank for fill-in-the-blank questions). Ms. James used an alternative form of question by decreasing the number of choices on Barry's test items from four to two to make it easier to apply the strategy; on Barry's tests, she blackened two of the four choices. Eventually, however, she added choices to be sure that Barry was able to take the same tests as his classmates. Ms. James used this type of adjustment for another

FYI

When testing students with reading disabilities in areas other than reading, use a Google extension and give students the option of wearing earbuds so that the test can be read to them. Other software such as Read and Write Gold can do the same.

DIMENSIONS OF DIVERSITY

Some African American, Brazilian American, Filipino American, and Hawaiian students are accustomed to working at a measured pace. These students may benefit from extended time when taking tests (Grossman, 1995). Teachers should observe students to document their work pattern before considering this adjustment.

PROFESSIONAL EDGE 11.2

Teaching Test-Taking Strategies for Objective Tests

You can help your students approach their objective tests more systematically by teaching them the following six rules for responding to multiple-choice and true–false items (Scruggs & Mastropieri, 1988):

1. *Respond to the test maker's intention:* Answers to test questions should take into account the way material is treated in class. For example, Rob had this item on his social studies test:

   During the occupation of Boston, the British received their most severe losses at Bunker Hill.

   True
   False

   Even though Rob had learned at a recent trip to the museum that the Battle of Bunker Hill was actually fought on Breed's Hill, his teacher had not brought up this point in class. Therefore, Rob responded by circling *True*.

2. *Anticipate the answer:* Before students attempt to answer the question, they should fully understand its meaning. Therefore, they should try to figure out the answer before they read the possible answers. For example, Armand was answering the following multiple-choice item:
   What does an astronomer study?
   a. plants
   b. music
   c. history
   d. stars
   After he read the question, Armand thought about the word *astronomy* and what his teacher had talked about in class, such as the fact that astronomers use telescopes and that they look at stars and planets. He then read all the possible choices and circled *d. stars* as the correct answer.

3. *Consider all alternatives:* Many students with special needs, such as students with learning or intellectual disabilities or attention deficit–hyperactivity disorder (ADHD), tend to answer too quickly, choosing the first available choice. Students should be encouraged to read all the choices before responding. Students can monitor their behavior by putting a checkmark next to each choice after they have read it.

4. *Use logical reasoning strategies to eliminate unlikely answers:* Even if students do not know the answer to a question, they can improve their chances of getting it right by using what knowledge they do have to eliminate unlikely choices. For example, Dolores read the following item:
   In which country would it be impossible to use a sled in the winter?
   a. Guatemala
   b. Canada
   c. Zimbabwe
   d. Norway

Dolores did not know the geographical locations of Guatemala or Zimbabwe, but she did know that Canada and Norway are countries where it snows often. She then took a guess between *a* and *c* and chose *a*, the correct answer. By eliminating two of the items, she improved her chance of getting the question right by 25 percent.

5. *Use time wisely:* As already mentioned, a frequent test-taking problem is failing to budget time. While taking tests, students should check the time periodically to make sure they have enough time left to answer the remaining questions. You can assist students by communicating the time remaining on the chalkboard several times during the testing period or by displaying a digital countdown timer. Students also can be taught to estimate the amount of time they should spend on each question. For example, if students are taking a 50-item test in a 50-minute period, they should figure on spending no more than one minute per question. After 25 minutes, they can then check to see that they have completed at least 25 items. Finally, teach students to spend more time on items on which they have at least partial knowledge and less time on questions for which they have no knowledge.

6. *Guess, if all else fails:* Most tests do not have a penalty for guessing. On standardized tests especially, tell your students that if they do not answer a question, they have no chance of getting it right, but if they guess, they have a 50 percent chance of getting true–false questions right and a 25 percent chance of getting most multiple-choice questions right.

STRATEGIES USING THINK-ALOUDS

Teaching test-taking strategies explicitly and systematically can help ensure students will be able to apply the strategies in completing actual classroom tests. Once you have selected a strategy aligned with your tests, show your students how to use it. Be sure your demonstration includes thinking aloud about what the strategy is, why it is important, and when and where to use it. Provide students with both guided and independent practice using the strategy and offer systematic corrections, as needed. Notice how the teacher in this example uses a think-aloud to teach the strategy of *anticipating the answer* that you just read about:

OK. The question is asking me what an astronomer studies. I'm going to try to figure out the answer before I even look at the choices, because that will make picking the right answer easier. This is helpful for Ms. Busey's tests because she always tests us on things she's talked about in class. So, let's see. What has Ms. Busey said in class about astronomy? Well, she's been telling us about how astronomers use these powerful telescopes to look at stars and planets. So, the answer probably will have something to do with stars and planets. In looking at the possible answers, the choices of plants, music, and history don't make sense, but choice d is stars. That must be the right answer.

student with reading comprehension difficulties by underlining key words in each question. She gradually eliminated the underlining as the student showed he was able to identify the key words in questions without them. Both of these adjustments could be easily accomplished before printing the test by making the changes electronically.

ALTERNATIVE TEST SITES Using alternative test sites is an adjustment that involves changing the location where a student with a disability is tested. For example, testing in the resource room might help students with attention problems (by allowing them to take their tests in a setting with fewer distractions) and students with written language problems (by permitting them to answer test questions orally). Changing the test site also can protect students who are taking the test in a different way from being embarrassed. However, testing in a separate setting has potential drawbacks. For example, students may be reluctant to leave a familiar location and there is time lost moving between locations. Also, using change of site as an accommodation can lead to other potentially helpful accommodations being overlooked such as teaching test-taking skills. Therefore, before sending a student out of class to take a test, we recommend trying other options first. For example, Ms. Edwards allows her students to choose whether or not to have a test read aloud to them. Those who do not want the test read aloud can work independently while she reads the test to the rest of the students. She also gives the students to whom she reads the test more help with directions and the meanings of key vocabulary or difficult questions without, of course, giving the answers away. Mr. Collins and Ms. Klein are co-teaching. Mr. Collins supervises students taking the test silently while Ms. Klein reads the test to another group of students. If a student's IEP specifies that testing must occur in a separate setting, be sure to coordinate your plans in advance with the special education teacher to avoid scheduling problems.

ALTERNATIVE RESPONSE MODES As with standardized tests, sometimes it is appropriate to allow students to respond to a classroom test using an alternative response mode. For example, Ms. Lemon allowed several of her students who struggled with written expression to write bullet points instead of paragraphs on her essay tests. Mr. Oliver accommodated Julian, a student with physical disabilities, by allowing him to respond orally on a science test using speech to text software.

Adjustments After the Test

You also may need to use alternative test-grading procedures for students, including changing letter or number grades, changing the grading criteria, and using alternatives to traditional letters and numbers.

Changing letter or number grades by adding written comments or symbols or by giving multiple grades can help clarify what a test grade means. For example, Seth, a student with a moderate intellectual disability, was tested only on questions covering standards stressed on his IEP. His teacher, Mr. Grassley, placed an asterisk next to his grade of B, indicating that his test covered less content than that given to the rest of the class. Giving multiple grades can also be helpful on tests that require written responses. For example, on an English test, Jacinto is required to write an essay on the character Boo Radley in the novel *To Kill a Mockingbird*. When his teacher grades his essay, she assigns him one grade based on the quality of his analysis of the character and another grade for writing mechanics.

A second option is to change the grading criteria, or the basis on which the grade is based. For example, Seth's teacher could give him a grade of B by basing his grade on fewer questions. In some cases, you may also want to base a student's test grade on the percentage correct of the items tried instead of on the total number of questions. This adjustment may help students who work accurately but slowly. Giving partial credit is another possible option. For example, when Ms. Jordan grades student answers to math word problems, she

MyLab Education

Video Example 11.1: Testing Adjustments

How do the teachers in this video adjust testing for their students with special needs?

FYI

Allowing retakes is a practice that facilitates student mastery. Recording students' highest retake grade rather than an average of their retakes encourages task persistence (Wormelli, 2006).

gives students points for underlining key words in the question and setting up the equation correctly even if they still get the final answer wrong. These points can motivate students who are improving but do not increase their test scores significantly. While in some cases changing the grading criteria can be an effective motivator, changing the criteria can send a message that standards have been reached, when in fact they have not. Be sure to accompany any change in criteria with a clear message for the student and parents indicating what you have done.

A third grading option is using alternatives to letter and number grades, such as pass/fail grades and checklists of skill competencies. For example, Matt could be given a grade of P (pass) because he mastered 7 of 10 key concepts in the chapter, or he could be rated on a competency checklist showing which key concepts in the chapter he learned. Although all of these test-grading adjustments allow students to be more successful, remember that grades or percentages do not constitute feedback; learners need specific feedback if they are to improve on future work (Munk, 2009). In addition, care must be taken to assure that students are prepared to meet state standards. For example, Matt's teacher needs to be certain that the content for which Matt is held responsible reflects state standards and that reducing the content for which he is held responsible will not interfere with his attainment of state standards.

Having *grading rubrics* with clear descriptors results in a more accurate representation of students' learning at the end of a grading period. In addition, basing a grade primarily on mathematical averages often distorts the accuracy of grades (Marzano, 2010). A strategy designed to help students use grading rubrics to improve their performance is described in the Professional Edge feature. A sample rubric designed for English-learners to use to evaluate their effort is shown in Figure 11.2.

FIGURE 11.2 Effort Rubric Adapted for English-Learners

4		I worked until I finished. I tried even when it was difficult. This lesson helped me learn more English.
3		I worked until I finished. I tried even when it was difficult.
2		I tried, but I stopped when it was too difficult.
1		I didn't try.

Source: From *Classroom Instruction That Works with English Language Learners* (2006), by J. D. Hill and K. M. Flynn, Alexandria, VA: ASCD. Reprinted with permission from Association for Supervision and Curriculum Development (ASCD).

PROFESSIONAL EDGE 11.3

Using Grading Rubrics with Students

The use of grading guidelines called *rubrics* helps students do the following:

- Better understand their teachers' expectations
- Monitor their progress
- Judge the quality of their work (Wormeli, 2006)

Jackson and Larkin (2002) created the *RUBRIC* strategy to help students with special needs use rubrics to assess the quality of their work. To teach students to carry out the strategy, explain what rubrics are by showing students some examples. Internet resources for finding rubrics include RubiStar (http://rubistar.4teachers.org) and Teachnology (http://www.bestteachersites.com/). Search "rubrics."

Once students know what rubrics are, they are ready to apply the *RUBRIC* strategy. In general, follow the same steps described in Chapter 10 for teaching learning strategies, including clarifying expectations, demonstrating strategy use, and providing guided and independent practice.

R *Read the rubric and material to be graded.* Encourage students to familiarize themselves with the criteria to be applied to each component of the task. Getting the "big picture" prevents students from diving into the task without thinking, a common problem for students with disabilities.

U *Use the rubric to get an initial score.* Students work individually and apply the rubric to one of their products, giving it a score. They should ask questions about the clarity of the scoring guidelines as well as verbalize their thought processes to someone else, receiving feedback as needed.

B *Bring a buddy to help you rate again.* Students select a buddy to help them rate the product again.

R *Review material together.* The student and the buddy then review the material, forming a team to compare scores and ideas. They then present their scores to the larger group of students, explaining how they used the rubric and why they agreed or disagreed. Next, the group gives the team feedback on how they applied the rubric.

I *Identify and award scores together.* The team uses the feedback to identify and award a new set of scores.

C *Check the scores again.* Students check their work.

Source: Adapted from Goodrich, as cited in "Rubric: Teaching Students to Use Grading Rubrics," by C. W. Jackson and M. J. Larkin, 2002, *Teaching Exceptional Children, 35*(1), 40–45.

MyLab Education Self-Check 11.1

How Can Adjustments in Report-Card Grading Be Made for Students with Special Needs?

Report-card grading is perhaps the most prevalent and controversial evaluation option used in schools. The practice of grading by letters and percentages began in the early twentieth century, a time of great faith in the ability of educational measures to assess students' current levels of learning accurately and also predict future levels of learning. High grades were seen as a sign of accomplishment, intended to spur students on to even greater achievements. Those who received low grades were either placed in basic-level or special classes or were encouraged to join the workforce (Cohen, 1983).

Times certainly have changed. Laws have been passed guaranteeing that our evaluations do not discriminate on the basis of disability, race, or ethnicity. These laws also guarantee an appropriate education for all students, not just those who can succeed with minimal intervention. Further, our ability to compete in the global economy depends on better educational outcomes for all citizens, not just a privileged few. These changes have led to new challenges for our grading systems. For example, how can evaluations be modified to ensure that they do not discriminate against students with disabilities? How can they be used to motivate students to stay in school, to communicate educational competence and progress to parents and students, and to guide our teaching as we strive to meet the needs of an increasingly diverse student body?

Report card grades for students with disabilities and other students with special needs must be carefully explained to prevent misunderstandings. What should this teacher be sure to communicate to this parent about her child's grades?

Although answers to these and other questions about grading are beginning to emerge, in large part professionals continue to use a grading system that was intended to fulfill a purpose much more narrow in scope. The use of traditional letter and number grades has caused problems for teachers, who must communicate with many audiences, including parents, students, administrators, and legislators. These audiences often are looking for information that is not readily communicated using a single number or letter (Jung & Guskey, 2012; Marzano, 2010). For example, students may be interested in how much progress they have made, whereas their parents want to know how their children compare to their classmates as well as to children nationwide. Principals, on the other hand, may need to provide college admissions offices with indicators of student potential to do college work. Teachers also are increasingly left with many conflicting concerns about grading, including upholding the school's standards, maintaining consistency with other teachers' evaluations, being honest with students, justifying grades with other students, motivating students for better future performance, communicating accurately to the students' next teachers, and avoiding the reputation of being an "easy" teacher (Munk & Bursuck, 2003).

Increased inclusion in schools has put even more burdens on grading systems. As illustrated in the vignettes at the beginning of the chapter, grading can present serious challenges for students with disabilities and their teachers. Staci was not a good test taker, yet 80 percent of her report-card grade in earth science was based on her test performance. She was concerned that her grade did not recognize her effort or progress in class. Amelia's parents were surprised to find that their daughter had received A's in reading all year but was reading below grade level on a recent standardized achievement test. Ronald was working on math skills that were more basic than those the rest of the class covered, and his teacher was unsure how to grade his performance. Add to these problems the concern that grades need to relate to student performance on state high-stakes assessments or universal screening and progress-monitoring measures used in RtI, despite the fact that the purposes and formats for these indicators of student achievement are often very different and the accuracy of test scores can be adversely affected by poor test-taking skills.

Despite these challenges, a number of reasons support the continued use of grades. First, many parents want to see how their children compare to other students, and they demand grades. In addition, grades are efficient and can make decision making easier, particularly for schools making decisions about promotion to the next grade level and for colleges and universities making admissions decisions (Munk & Bursuck, 2001). Despite their many limitations, grades are likely to be used by teachers and schools for many years to come. Teachers need to recognize the limitations, however, and, when necessary, adjust grading systems to ensure they are fair to all students. Perhaps most important, teachers must never lose sight of the fact that the primary purpose of grades is to support students in their pursuit of learning (Brookhart, 2017).

The next section is divided into two topics. First, grading practices will be described that benefit all students, including students with disabilities. Second, strategies for individualized grading will be covered. Individualized grading is carried out almost exclusively with students with significant intellectual disabilities, as specified in their IEPs.

Grading Practices That Benefit All Students

A common practice among teachers is to factor in both learning and learning-related behaviors such as attendance, homework, and effort when calculating student grades. The idea behind this approach is that because grades are earned, effort should be rewarded. Giving credit for learning-related behaviors is also used to sustain students' motivation in the face of what are often less than optimal achievement outcomes. However, there is an emerging consensus among educators that learning is best served when grades are solely achievement based (Brookhart, 2017; Marzano, 2010; Wormeli, 2006). The rationale behind achievement-based grading is that when grades stress learning, learning becomes more valued and more likely to become the focus of students' attention. Of course, a key assumption behind achievement-based grading is that an effective system of standards-based instructional practices is in place that maximizes the likelihood of student success. That said, it is important to note that giving credit for behavior can be appropriate if it is a carefully considered accommodation written into the IEP of a student with a disability.

One way to ensure that report card grades communicate accurately and clearly while also recognizing the importance of learning-related behaviors is to provide additional information for parents that clarifies the meaning of students' grades. The form this information takes depends on school policy, which largely determines how all aspects of grading are handled. Some school districts may allow clarifying information to appear directly on the report card, but in most cases, that information needs to be communicated separately. Providing clarifying information can be used with most students in your class, but it is most appropriate for students with disabilities (1) who are working toward the same learning standards as the rest of the class, (2) whose progress is being appropriately monitored, and (3) who are receiving accommodations and adjustments that result in reasonable access to the general education curriculum (Munk, 2007).

Adding information to clarify letter and number grades can be accomplished by supplementing them with written or verbal comments, logs of student activities, and portfolios. Written or verbal comments can be used to clarify areas such as student performance levels as compared with peers and the extent of student effort. For example, Robert scored below standard for the grading period; his teacher commented that he had read more trade books but that these books were below grade level.

Comments about student performance levels can prevent misunderstandings, particularly when parents find their children are performing below standard on state tests or on RtI or MTSS universal screening assessments. For instance, in the chapter-opening vignette, Amelia's mother thought her daughter's high grade

DIMENSIONS OF DIVERSITY

Cultural expectations and standards strongly influence how families interpret and react to their children's grades. As a teacher, you cannot take for granted that all parents will respond in the same way to their children's grades. Communication is the key.

RESEARCH-BASED PRACTICES

Welsh and D'Agastino (2009) studied the relationship between teachers' grading practices and student proficiency levels on high-stakes standards-based achievement tests. They found that the more teachers graded students based on performance on state standards, and the less they counted effort, the higher were their students' proficiency levels on high-stakes tests.

The adoption of achievement-based report cards does not mean that important learning-related behaviors such as attendance, tardiness, work habits, and homework should be ignored. The key point is that such behaviors should be nurtured "by coaching, not reporting" (Brookhart, 2017; p. 21).

in reading meant that she was reading at grade level. Providing Amelia's parents with an explanation would have put her grade in context.

Finally, the basis for arriving at number or letter grades on report cards is often not clear. For example, does the grade represent a student's performance in comparison with his or her classmates, student progress, effort, or other factors? Failure to clarify the basis for grades can lead to issues of fairness raised by students, as shown in the Case in Practice feature, as well as communication problems with parents, as shown in the Working Together feature.

CASE IN PRACTICE 11.1

Fairness

Ms. Rodriguez had never questioned her decision to become a middle school science teacher—that is, not until last week. She has always had students with disabilities as class members and felt comfortable being able to meet their individual needs while maintaining high standards. This year, she has three such students: one with learning disabilities, another who has an emotional disability, and a third with a mild intellectual disability. All three students have testing or grading accommodations written into their IEPs. To complicate matters, for the first time this year, her students without disabilities are complaining. Tricia wants to know why Tyrell is allowed extra time to take his tests. She feels she would do better, too, if given extra time. Monikee questions why Maya receives extra points for coming to class but she does not. Even Dayrone, who never complains about anything, wants to know why Garrett has to learn fewer vocabulary words than the rest of the class.

Ms. Rodriguez has always believed that fairness means everyone should receive what he or she needs, which is not necessarily the same thing. Still, she has to think carefully about how best to respond to her students' concerns about fairness. She believes she can likely appeal to Tricia's independence and sense of right and wrong if she can get her to think more clearly about the situation. So, Ms. Rodriguez tells Tricia, "You

don't think it's fair. Please write me a note about your point of view, and we'll talk about it later." Monikee will require a different approach. Because she thrives on Ms. Rodriguez's attention, Ms. Rodriguez concludes that she is complaining because she needs something special, too. Ms. Rodriguez tells her, "Is there something you would like to work on and receive points?" Ms. Rodriguez is concerned that students like Dayrone complain when they feel the teacher is unsure about a classroom policy. Ms. Rodriguez believes that, in general, it is important to respond to complaints of unfairness consistently and without explanation. Therefore, she says to Dayrone, "I can't make comments about anyone else's work. May I help you with your own?" (Welch, 2000, p. 37).

REFLECTION

What are the different ways Ms. Rodriguez responds to her students' complaints about the fairness of Tyrell, Monikee, and Garrett's grading adjustments? What do you think the impact of each adjustment will be on their learning? Can you think of other ways she could have responded to her students' complaints? What could Ms. Rodriguez do in the future to prevent complaints about fairness?

WORKING TOGETHER 11.1

Communicating with Parents About Grades

Mr. and Mrs. Washington's son Delarnes is in Mr. Campbell's junior English class. Delarnes received an F in English for the last marking period, and Mr. and Mrs. Washington are upset. They know Delarnes is working hard in the class because they are spending a lot of time helping him with his English homework at night. They schedule a meeting with Mr. Campbell to learn more about the problem.

When Mr. and Mrs. Washington arrive at the meeting, Mr. Campbell is seated at a table with the chairperson of the English department, Dr. West. The Washingtons hadn't expected someone else to be at the meeting, and it makes them fear that Delarnes has done something terrible. After asking the Washingtons to sit down, Mr. Campbell introduces Dr. West, who talks for what seems like forever about the state English standards and how the state "seems to be setting the bar higher every year."

The Washingtons aren't sure how the state standards affect Delarnes's English grade but are afraid to ask. Mr. Washington is beginning to grow impatient. He had expected the meeting to be

about helping Delarnes. Next Mr. Campbell says that although Delarnes seems to be working hard, he has failed both of the grammar tests during the quarter, and his essay on Frederick Douglass has received a score of D–. Mrs. Washington helped Delarnes outline that paper but hasn't heard anything about it since. Delarnes hasn't told his parents about the grammar tests. When Mr. Campbell asks the Washingtons if they will help Delarnes more at home, Mr. Washington explodes, saying that they *have* been helping him at home, asking why they haven't been told about Delarnes's problem in English before, and demanding that the school do something to help him.

Why is it sometimes difficult to communicate with parents about the meaning of their children's grades?

What problems with Mr. Campbell's grading system are in evidence here? What grading adjustments can Mr. Campbell employ to prevent this problem from happening again? Do you think the way Mr. Campbell conducted the meeting may have contributed to the problem? What could he have done differently?

FIGURE 11.3 **Daily Scorecard**

Student	Homework		Instruction	Practice	Physical Demeanor	Exit Ticket		Other
Dolores	4/10	40%	needs more instruction	guided practice	looking more confident	2/4	50%	more support
Darren	10/10	100%	engaged skill learned	independent practice	focused confident	4/4	100%	next skill

Source: Based on *Differentiation from planning to practice, grades 6–12,* by R. Wormeli, 2007, and "Formative assessment made easy: Templates for collecting daily data in inclusive classrooms," by K. F. Cornelius, 2014, *Teaching Exceptional Children, 47(2),* 112–118.

Report-card grades are primarily summative in nature, occurring after instruction to communicate student learning at a given point in time (Cornelius, 2014). As such, report card grades provide few specifics about student growth or progress. Formative data reflects what is happening during instruction and can thus provide a useful supplement to summative grades. The use of one type of formative assessment in grading, portfolios, is described later in the chapter. Another useful way to supplement report card grades with formative data is to use a strategy like the daily scorecard of student activities and achievement (Cornelius, 2014; Wormeli, 2007) shown in Figure 11.3. The figure shows information for two students in Ms. Henry's Algebra 1 class: Dolores, a student who has math disabilities, and Darren, who has ADHD. Ms. Henry is working on the skill of simplifying terms such as $5 + x(x - 7) = $ ____. According to the figure, on yesterday's 10 homework problems requiring simplification, Dolores only answered four problems correctly; Darren, on the other hand, scored 100 percent. On that day's instruction, Ms. Henry provided more guided practice for Dolores (and others who were having difficulty with simplification), but allowed students like Darren to solve problems independently to build their fluency. After more guided practice, Ms. Henry recorded that Dolores was feeling more confident, though on an exit quiz she still only scored 50 percent. She will need more support, and a decision will need to be made regarding how to provide it. Darren is ready to move on to a different skill. Ms. Henry uses her daily scorecard to construct weekly progress reports for Dolores, Darren, and any other students who may be struggling, and clarifies their report card grades based on information collected on the scorecards completed during the grading period. Of course, you can also supplement your report card grades by collecting data on an Excel spreadsheet, a digital calendar, or using self-sticking notes.

Whatever type of daily records are used, entries should at least include the date, the student's name, the classroom activity, and a brief description of the observation. For example, Ms. Parks was concerned about the progress of one of her students, Carrie, in the area of word-identification skills. Each day during an hour-long literature class, Ms. Parks observed how Carrie approached the trade books she was reading. One day she recorded that Carrie spontaneously used the parts of a multisyllable word to figure out its pronunciation and meaning. Mr. Edwards was interested in how Ricardo was progressing in biology lab. He recorded the steps Ricardo completed successfully while conducting various dissections over time in biology class. Information taken from observations can be summarized periodically. These summaries can then be shared with parents as often as necessary to clarify student report card grades.

As we have said, teachers become frustrated when they have to communicate multiple messages using a single grade. Prototypes have emerged in the literature that can help solve this problem (Brookhart, 2017; Guskey et al., 2010; Marzano, 2010; Wormeli, 2006). For example, Ms. Lsu wanted to tell her students' parents which standards her students had met by reporting on the quality of the products they had produced, such as tests, reports, and projects. However, she also wanted to tell parents about the processes involved in developing the products, such as the effort that went into creating them and the work habits

FYI

While computerized grade books are increasingly popular and available, Guskey and Jung (2016) remind us that teacher judgment is often more accurate and reliable than computer-generated algorithms for assigning grades. Why do you think that is so?

FIGURE 11.4 Individualized Grading Report for Taylor

Subject	Standards	Grade	Previous Grade	Effort	Absences	Tardiness
Geometry	Applying and using standards of indirect punishment	D	C	Excellent __ Satisfactory __ Needs improvement √	5	3
	Representing problem situations with geometric models	C	C			
English	Writing personal narratives	A	A	Excellent √ Satisfactory __ Needs improvement __	0	0
	Responding reflectively to a variety of texts	B	B			
			Grading Key			
		Grade	Student Rating	Rating		
		A	3.00 – 4.00	Advanced		
		B	2.50 – 2.99	Proficient		
		C	2.00 – 2.49	Basic		
		D	1.00 – 1.99	Below Basic		
		F	Below 1.00	No Success		

Source: Based on *Developing standards-based report cards*, by T. R. Guskey and J. M. Bailey, 2010, Thousand Oaks, CA: Corwin; and *Communicating student learning and formative assessment & standards-based grading*, by R. S. Marzano, 2010, Bloomington, IN: Marzano Research Laboratory.

Video Example from

You Tube

MyLab Education

Video Example 11.2: Standards-Based Report Cards

Watch this video about the differences between traditional report cards and those that are standards-based. Which type of report card would work better for students with special needs? http://www.youtube.com/watch?v=0RoSs-bQeBc.

her students had displayed. In addition, Ms. Lsu wanted to communicate how much her students had progressed. Fortunately, Ms. Lsu's school had just adopted a grading report format such as the one shown in Figure 11.4. Note that Ms. Lsu used letter grades to evaluate her student Taylor's products for the marking period. As shown in the figure, the letter grades were based on a four-point scale keyed to levels of competence in the state standards. Four-point scales have been shown to be more accurate than the more prevalent 100 point scales (Marzano, 2010). Ms. Lsu was also able to communicate Taylor's level of effort using the three-point scale of *Outstanding, Satisfactory*, and *Needs Improvement*. Finally, Taylor's progress was communicated by reporting his grades for the previous grading period.

Teachers who grade effectively also avoid giving zeroes for work not submitted or tests missed due to unexcused absences. Some teachers give zeroes for missing assignments on the grounds that it teaches students personal responsibility (Munk, 2007). The truth is that the practice of giving zeroes for work not submitted is full of problems (Brookhart, 2017). First, a grade of zero distorts the final grade and diminishes its value as an indicator of what was learned (Wormeli, 2006). For example, Cherise had the following scores on five classroom quizzes: 70, 68, 63, 73, and 0. She received a zero on quiz five because of an unexcused absence. Cherise's average score for the quizzes with a score of zero figured in was 55 percent. She received a grade of F despite the fact that she passed every quiz she took. Giving Cherise a zero for the quiz distorted the evidence of what she learned and was very likely to undermine her motivation. Missing work and missed tests also may result from organizational problems related to a learner's disability or life circumstances beyond her control. For example, Cherise was involved in family child care. On the day of the quiz, she had to take her younger brother to the doctor because her mother was working.

Wormeli (2006) suggests giving a grade of 60 rather than zero as a way of lessening the impact of a missed assignment or test. The grade of 60 percent could be made contingent upon making up the work. This strategy of giving a minimum grade instead of a zero can also be applied to quarterly report card grades (Wormeli, 2006). This approach is called minimum quarter grading. Although minimum grading can lessen the numerical impact of a zero (Cherise would have averaged 67 percent, rather than 55 percent, the difference between passing and failing), in our view, there are more proactive ways to solve the problem of giving zeroes. First, make sure all students understand your grading policies for late or missed work. Second, allow students to turn in late work for full or partial credit. Third, increase the level of communication regarding assignments, tests, and due dates. Fourth, have students complete projects in segments with separate scores for each segment. Finally, for students with disabilities, consider setting an IEP goal for improving time management, including the self-monitoring of work completion (Munk, 2007).

Another grading practice that can benefit all your students is to report student progress more frequently. Report-card grades come out infrequently. Students as well as parents need more frequent feedback than that. Of course, the frequency with which you provide student progress reports will vary depending on the student as well as the time demands made on you as a teacher. Last, the ultimate purpose of grades is to communicate accurately student mastery of agreed upon learning standards. Because some commonly-used grading practices undermine this purpose, they are to be avoided. These practices include allowing extra credit and bonus points, giving group grades, and grading on a curve (Wormeli, 2006).

Using Individualized Grading with Students with Disabilities

Individualized grading is called for when a learner has a disability that requires modified curricular expectations. Merely having an IEP, trying hard, failing because of missed work, or receiving poorly administered accommodations or adjustments is not enough to qualify a student for individualized grading (Munk, 2007).

Individualized grading involves making judgments in a systematic way. It is done in conjunction with the student's IEP, which makes individualized grading legally binding. Individualized grading includes standards-based grading and basing all or part of the grade on progress on IEP objectives. Both approaches are summarized and described in the following subsections.

USING STANDARDS-BASED GRADES Jung and Guskey (2007) recommend a variation of standards-based grading model as a way of individualizing report-card grades for students with disabilities. While most if not all grading is currently standards-based, in Jung and Guskey's model, the IEP team first reviews grade-level standards to determine whether an accommodation or modification is needed. Because accommodations merely involve access to the general education curriculum, if a standard only requires an accommodation, there is no need to modify the grade-level standard or the grading process. As long as the appropriate accommodations are in place for both instruction and assessment, students with disabilities can be graded on the grade-level standard the same as everyone else. For example, Juan, a student with learning disabilities, is enrolled in a biology class. Juan has a reading disability, but with a digital text, recorder, and oral tests as accommodations, he can meet the same biology standards as his classmates without disabilities. Therefore, in grading whether he met the standard for comparing and contrasting the structure and function of the organic molecules of carbohydrates, proteins, and lipids, there is no need for a grading accommodation. The expectations are the same for Juan as for everyone else. If modifications

Video Example from YouTube

MyLab Education
Video Example 11.3: Zero Grades
How would you respond to the person in this video who is critical of the practice of not giving zeros? https://www.youtube.com/watch?v=phb8fsyoAXw

FYI

Individualized grading needs to be closely coordinated with the IEP-required collection of progress monitoring data by the special education teacher.

are required, then the IEP team needs to align IEP goals to grade level standards, taking into account the student's functional level and the resulting need to modify them. The general and special education teachers then work together to grade the student based on the modified standards. Germaine is a student with an intellectual disability who requires a modification in standards. His IEP team decided that he could meet the standard related to comparing organic molecules just described for Juan by identifying foods in the grocery store that consisted primarily of proteins, carbohydrates, and lipids, and comparing their respective nutritional benefits.

Although Jung and Guskey's standards-based grading model is most commonly used with students with intellectual disabilities, it may also be used for students with learning and behavior disabilities who are performing significantly below grade level. For example, Patrice is a fifth grader with learning disabilities. One of the fifth-grade reading standards is to be able to read grade-level text with purpose and understanding. Patrice is receiving intensive reading instruction to help her meet her long-term goal of grade-level reading, but at the present time, she is reading at the third-grade level. Her IEP team decided to have her reading grades be based on reading fourth-grade material with understanding.

Research results for standards-based grading are encouraging (Brookhart, 2017). In one study, parents liked its clarity, general education teachers thought it improved communication even though it required extra work, and both general and special educators felt it improved their communication (Guskey, Swan, & Jung, 2010). Still, standards-based grading may need to be combined with the other ways to differentiate report-card grades described in the previous section. For example, Jung and Guskey (2007) recommend marking grades based on modified standards with an asterisk to make it clear that the student is not performing at grade level. This grading strategy would be helpful in the case of Patrice just described. In addition, because standards-based grading does not take effort or progress into account, a separate grade for these dimensions of student performance may need to be provided.

BASING ALL OR PART OF THE GRADE ON PROGRESS ON IEP OBJECTIVES For this type of individualized grading, progress on IEP objectives is used as the basis for part or all of a student's report-card grade (Munk, 2003). Grading on the basis of progress on IEP objectives would have been appropriate for Ronald, the student in the opening vignette whose math curriculum was modified on his IEP. Whereas the rest of the class was working on decimals, he was working on two-digit by two-digit addition problems without regrouping. Because his IEP objective was to score 80 percent or better when given 10 of these problems, his fourth-grade teacher and special education teacher agreed to give him an A if he met his objective, a B if he scored between 70 and 80 percent, a C if he scored between 60 and 70 percent, and so forth. To ensure that Ronald's mother had an accurate picture of Ronald's standing in relation to his peers, Ronald's teacher included a written comment on Ronald's report card indicating that his grade was based on modified curricular objectives based on his individual needs.

Basing grades on progress on IEP objectives also can be helpful for students who are in special education but do not have modified curricular expectations. For example, Manny is a student with a learning disability who is included in Mr. Ottens's middle school science class. Manny receives pullout services in writing but is still expected to meet the same curriculum standards in science as his classmates. During Manny's IEP conference, it was decided that 10 percent of his science grade would be determined by progress on an IEP objective stating that "Manny will write complete sentences using correct spelling, grammar, and sentence structure." Mr. Ottens agreed to evaluate Manny's written work in science using these criteria. Mr. Ottens would give a writing grade along with a regular grade for each assignment Manny submitted. Manny's average writing grade would count 10 percent toward his report-card grade in science.

WWW RESOURCES

Find out about testing and grading policies being used around the country by visiting the website of the Council of Chief State School Officers (CCSSO) (http://www.ccsso.org). Search "testing policies" and "grading policies."

Basing all or part of a student's daily work grade or report-card grade on IEP objectives, as was done for Ronald and Manny, is advantageous because it:

1. Allows the team to consider how and when IEP objectives can be addressed in the general education classroom.

2. Informs students, parents, and teachers which objectives are important and how supports can be provided.

3. Ensures that a student's grade reflects progress on skills that have been identified as most important for him by the team.

4. Eliminates the redundancy of reporting grades separately from progress on IEP objectives.

5. Improves communication among parents, students, and teachers about grading in the general education classroom.

Of course, basing grades or progress on IEP objectives carries the risk that students with disabilities will be evaluated using criteria unrelated to expectations in general education. When curricular objectives in general and special education are out of sync, student access to the general education curriculum is compromised. That is why, to the maximum extent possible, IEP objectives should be based on standards articulated in the general education curriculum. It is also why Manny's IEP team only counted writing as 10 percent of his science grade.

Legalities of Individualized Grading

Individualizing grading is legal for students with disabilities as long as the modifications that comprise them appear on students' IEPs. Individualized grading should not be used with students without IEPs unless it is available to all students in the class or school (Salend & Duhaney, 2002). All school districts have some grading policies, and you should check to see whether individualized grading is covered by them. The Professional Edge feature presents a more in-depth discussion of the legalities of grading students with disabilities.

> **DIMENSIONS OF DIVERSITY**
>
> Many metropolitan school districts provide teachers the service of having testing information translated into languages as diverse as Chinese, Korean, Tagalog, and Arabic.

As an alternative to pencil-and-paper tests, performance-based tests allow students to demonstrate their knowledge and skills through application in real-world contexts. What are some of the ways to support students with special needs as they participate in performance-based assessment?

PROFESSIONAL EDGE 11.4

The Legalities of Grading Students with Disabilities

Report-card grades often are used to make important educational decisions about students such as eligibility for honors awards, graduation, and admission to post-secondary education. Because of the importance of grades, teachers need to exert great care when modifying grading systems for students with disabilities. Although most schools have a written grading policy containing guidelines for giving and interpreting grades, many such policies focus on the grading scale and the schedule for reporting grades to parents, not on judgments required for grading students with disabilities (Munk, 2003).

The following are some commonly asked questions and answers about grading students with disabilities (Salend & Duhaney, 2002; U.S. Department of Education, 2008). As legal guidelines for grading are constantly being refined, you should consult your school policies and your building administrator prior to changing your grading system. It is also important to document all grading accommodations and modifications for students with disabilities on their IEPs.

1. *May I give modified grades to a student with a disability who is in my classroom and receiving accommodations?* Accommodations do not alter the standards or course expectations, but ensure success with the course content or requirements. Modified grades imply altering the course standards. You can modify the grades of a student with a disability, but only if it is done through the IEP process.

2. *If a student enrolled in my class has alternative curricular objectives specified on her IEP, can I exclude her from my regular grading system and evaluate her based on her IEP objectives?* Yes, you may grade her solely on the basis of her IEP objectives. Otherwise, you should consult with a special educator about the required grading practices.

3. *May I collaborate with a student's special education teacher to decide how to assign the student a grade?* Collaborating with a student's special education teacher is entirely appropriate (and desirable).

4. *If I want to communicate to parents and employers that a student in my class has a modified curriculum, may the student's transcript reflect that the class was a special education class?* No. It is illegal to specify that a class is *special education*. However, there is general agreement that alternative terms can be used to communicate curricular differences. None of these terms, which are set by school districts and not individual teachers, has been officially sanctioned by the courts. Terms such as *basic, level 1,* or *modified curriculum* can be used as long as they are also used in courses besides those for students with disabilities, such as classes within gifted and talented programs. Asterisks or other symbols can also be used to communicate a modified curriculum as long as courses for all students are handled in a similar way. Transcripts sent to postsecondary schools can contain courses designated as modified when families and students are informed and give their written consent (Salend, 2005).

5. *May we exclude grades earned in separate special education classes or general education classes taken with support when we calculate districtwide GPAs and rank students for purposes of creating an honor roll or assigning scholarships?* Grades earned by students in special education classes or general education classes taken with support cannot be dismissed arbitrarily or categorically by the district. However, districts can implement a system of weighted grades that assigns points to grades depending on the difficulty of the subject matter. Weighted systems are permissible as long as they are fair and simple to understand. Districts also can establish a list of core courses that must be completed to be eligible for honors, class rankings, or participation in certain activities. Again, the important consideration is that all students are similarly affected, not just students with disabilities.

MyLab Education Self-Check 11.2

How Can Performance-Based Assessment Benefit Students with Special Needs?

Ms. Johnson is just completing a unit on persuasive writing and has her students write letters to the editor of a local newspaper, trying to persuade readers to support the building of a new county facility for elderly people. Mr. Repp is teaching drawing to scale as part of a map-reading unit and has his students make maps of the neighborhood that could be used by visitors from another country. Ms. Overton's class is working on basic bookkeeping skills and has her students plan a budget for a fundraiser to earn money to build a new swing set for the playground.

All of these teachers are checking their students' progress with a method of evaluation called performance-based assessment. **Performance-based assessment** "provides students with opportunities to demonstrate their mastery of a skill or concept through performance of a task" (Haager & Klingner, 2004, p. 66). Performance-based assessment measures learning processes rather than focusing only on learning products. It frequently involves using authentic learning tasks, or tasks that are presented within real-world contexts and lead to real-world outcomes (Hilliard, 2015). Performance-based assessments are likely to play an increasing role in evaluating students as problem-based learning and an emphasis on student-led instruction evolves in order to tap student college and career readiness in a global economy (Council of Chief State School Officers, 2015; Darling-Hammond, Wilhoit, & Pittenger, 2014).

Mr. Repp could have asked his students to compute the mileage between several cities using a mileage key, a more traditional map-reading assignment. Instead, he has them create their own maps within a real context because he wants to see how well they can apply what they have learned to an actual problem. Not only does Mr. Repp evaluate students' maps, but he also evaluates parts of the learning process, such as how well his students select and implement learning strategies and collaborate with their classmates during problem solving.

Using performance assessments can be very helpful for students with disabilities and other special needs who may be members of your classroom. Performance-based assessments offer students options for demonstrating their knowledge that do not rely exclusively on reading and writing, areas that often impede the successful testing performance of students with disabilities. For example, Calvin, a struggling reader in Mr. Repp's class, completed the map activity successfully but would have had trouble with a traditional paper-and-pencil test of the same material.

Performance-based tests also are not subject to the same time constraints as traditional tests. This flexibility can benefit students who need more time, such as those with reading fluency problems, or students who need to work for shorter time periods, such as those with attention deficit–hyperactivity disorder. Again, using the example of Mr. Repp's map-drawing activity, students had some time limits (they had to finish in one week), but they did not have to do the entire project in one sitting.

Students with disabilities also may have particular difficulty making the connection between school tasks and tasks in the real world. Performance assessments can help them understand this connection, particularly if an assessment is followed up with instruction directly geared to skill applications. For example, Ms. Johnson, whose students were required to write letters to the editor, discovered that many of her students were unable to support their arguments directly with specific examples. She therefore spent some class time demonstrating to students how they could support their arguments and guiding them through several practice activities.

As you can see, using performance assessment has many potential benefits for students with special needs. Nonetheless, you may still need to make adjustments for students with disabilities when they participate in performance assessments (Haager & Vaughn, 2013). For example, Gregory is a student with cerebral palsy in Mr. Repp's social studies class. Gregory has very little control over fine motor movements in his hands. As a result, he is unable to write or draw. Gregory obviously needs to have the drawing-to-scale map task adapted. One possible adjustment would be to have Gregory make an audiotape to accompany the map that would provide visitors from another country with a self-guided tour. Or consider Rhonda, a student with a learning disability who has difficulty expressing herself in writing. Rhonda is included in Ms. Johnson's class. The class is writing letters to the editor as a way of practicing persuasive writing skills. As an adjustment, Ms. Johnson has Rhonda develop an oral editorial that is sent to the local public radio channel. In some cases, then, adjustments for performance-based tests can be made just as readily as those made for traditional tests.

Some students with special needs may have problems with performance tests that are more difficult to adapt. For instance, students might have difficulty

DIMENSIONS OF DIVERSITY

Research shows that performance assessments can lead to a better understanding of the content knowledge of English learners and improve their academic performance (Abedi, 2010).

RESEARCH-BASED PRACTICES

Evans and Lyons (2017) found that the New Hampshire Performance Assessment of Competency Education (NH PACE), a statewide performance-based test of competency in English, language arts, math, and science, was comparable to a standard high-stakes test in determining student proficiency.

making the connection between school tasks and real-world tasks. You need to teach these students directly how to make those connections. For example, Ms. Riley's class is learning to compute subtraction problems. As a performance-based test, Ms. Riley has her class compare prices of various brands of the same products in the grocery store and compute price differences using subtraction. Cleo, a student in the class who has a mild intellectual disability, is unable to perform the task because he has never used subtraction as it applies to money or products in the grocery store. The next day in class, Ms. Riley includes examples of subtracting amounts of money in her daily instruction. She also includes word problems dealing with the subtraction of money, some of which involve grocery store products. This accommodation helps Cleo make the connection between money, subtraction, and the supermarket.

Students with special needs also may lack important preskills necessary for problem solving. You need either to teach these preskills or allow such students to bypass the preskills altogether to carry out performance-based tasks. For example, Sam has a learning disability in math; he does not know basic math facts and as a result cannot get Ms. Riley's product comparisons correct. Ms. Riley allows him to perform the task with a calculator. She also requires that he spend five minutes per day using a computer-based math fact program until he learns basic math facts. Anna has visual disabilities; another student reads to her the prices of the brands and she writes them down.

For students with moderate to severe intellectual disabilities, you may need to modify or scale down performance-based tasks by using the guidelines for developing alternate assessments described in Chapter 4 and the environmental inventory process described in Chapter 9. For example, Derek has a severe intellectual disability and lacks basic math skills other than simple number identification. Ms. Riley has Derek participate in the same task as the other students but has him perform an easier step. She has Derek pick groups of products that students are to compare. This task is more consistent with Derek's IEP goal of being able to classify similar objects, such as three kinds of cola or two types of bread.

Finally, students with disabilities or other special needs may have trouble meeting the problem-solving demands of performance-based tests. For example, Peter has attention deficits and approaches problems impulsively; he rushes to find an answer and fails to consider all the options. For Peter, performance-based tests are important because they give him the opportunity to learn critical self-control and problem-solving skills. Nonetheless, for students like Peter to succeed, performance-based tasks need to be modified and problem-solving skills need to be taught directly. For example, Mr. Kelsey's students are applying work they have done in computing areas and perimeters to the task of planning a garden. Before having students design their own gardens, Mr. Kelsey carefully demonstrates how he would design his. This demonstration is very helpful for students in the class, such as Peter, who are not natural problem solvers and need a model to guide them. Mr. Kelsey also scales down Peter's assignment, asking him to design only one section of a smaller garden. Finally, before allowing Peter to construct his design, Mr. Kelsey has Peter verbally explain it to him to ensure that Peter has carefully thought through his idea.

As you can see, the use of performance-based tests with students with disabilities can be helpful, but it can also be problematic. For this reason, we recommend a balanced approach that uses performance-based tests in conjunction with other classroom-based and standardized tests.

MyLab Education

Video Example 11.4: Performance-Based Tests and Learning Standards

Why are performance-based assessments useful in evaluating the performance of students with disabilities on state standards?

MyLab Education Self-Check 11.3

How Can Portfolio Assessment Benefit Students with Special Needs?

Portfolio assessment is a method of evaluation in which a purposeful collection of student work is used to determine student effort, progress, and achievement in one or more areas (Barrett, 2007; Gronlund, 2006). A portfolio collection differs from testing in that it is able to address improvement, effort, and achievement within the realm of more functional projects that include authentic tasks (Clancy & Gardner, 2017; p. 95). Portfolios include evidence from many different sources such as checklists, scrapbooks, observations, drawings, reading lists, photographs, self-evaluations, reflections, letters, video or audio recordings, progress reports, test reports, homework, rating scales, scored samples such as curriculum-based assessment probes, and rubrics. They are most often used to evaluate progress on classroom instruction and not as a substitute for high stakes tests.

Portfolios can be very helpful for teachers working with students with disabilities. Portfolios can assist teachers in evaluating student progress toward IEP objectives and in guiding instruction. For example, Ms. Pohl is interested in finding out whether the extra math practice sheets she is sending home with Robert are improving his scores on weekly math computation tests. She consults Robert's portfolio and finds that his performance has improved quite a bit over the last two months. Ms. Pohl tells Robert's parents of his progress. They agree to continue the extra practice for at least another month. Portfolios also emphasize student products rather than tests and test scores. This emphasis benefits students with special needs, many of whom are poor test takers. Portfolios also may highlight student strengths better than traditional tests, which tend to have a narrow academic focus. For example, Leshonn's teacher uses portfolios to evaluate her history students. Leshonn has problems in reading and writing but has good artistic ability and excellent oral language skills. During the last marking period, his class studied the growth of suburban areas after World War II, subject matter based on the state standards. Leshonn designed a scale model of Levittown, one of the first planned communities. He also developed a recorded explanation to go with the model that explained the key features of the community. His performance on these projects was excellent and enabled him to raise his overall grade for the class because his scores on the two tests given during the marking period were low.

Finally, a key component of portfolio assessments is student self-evaluation. As you have already learned, students with special needs often are described as not being involved in their own learning; they can benefit greatly from self-evaluation. For example, students might complete a self-assessment after they have finished a unit of instruction. This evaluation can then become a part of the students' portfolios.

You may have to make adjustments when using portfolios with students with disabilities, particularly in selecting and evaluating portfolio pieces. For example, Jerome was asked to select an example of his best work in written expression for his portfolio. However, he was uncertain what "best work" meant: Was it the paper that he tried his hardest on? Was it the paper that was the hardest to write? Or was it the one that he or his teacher liked best? Because he did not know, Jerome simply selected one paper at random. Similarly, when Thanh was asked to evaluate his efforts to solve a word problem in geometry for his portfolio, all he could come up with was whether he had the correct answer. You should teach students such as Jerome and Thanh how to select and evaluate portfolio pieces.

A key part of being an effective teacher is to be able to accurately evaluate student learning. As a teacher, you are in the best position to gauge student learning because you are privy to what students are accomplishing on a daily basis; high-stakes tests, on the other hand, measure student learning only once

DIMENSIONS OF DIVERSITY

Barootchi and Keshavarz (2002) found that portfolio assessments increased Iranian English learners' achievement and feelings of responsibility toward monitoring their own academic progress.

MyLab Education

Video Example 11.5: Portfolio Assessment: Writing Folder

Watch how one teacher uses portfolio assessment. Why might this approach benefit students with disabilities? How might the portfolio process need to be adjusted?

FYI

Although portfolios are potentially valuable evaluation tools, they should supplement, not supplant, standardized achievement, psychological-, and curriculum-based measures.

WWW RESOURCES

For more information on digital portfolio software, go to http://www.superschoolsoftware.com (click on "Portfolios").

per year. Traditional classroom testing and grading are the most frequently used methods of classroom evaluation, though performance-based tests and portfolios are used as well. All forms of classroom evaluation can be problematic for students with disabilities included in your class, but if carried out carefully, employing strategies covered in this chapter, they can facilitate their learning, communicate that learning clearly to the appropriate audiences, and help ensure a successful inclusive experience.

ePortfolios (EPs) are digitized collections of artifacts used to provide important information about students' performances over a period of time (Clancy & Gardner, 2017). EPs have a number of advantages over more traditional portfolios, advantages that may be particularly helpful for students with disabilities. EPs:

- Showcase student performance in a number of ways including video, digital photos, sound clips, animation, diagrams, text, and podcasting which provide multimedia displays and assessment possibilities that demonstrate and develop understanding through authentic tasks (Abrami, Venkatesh, Meyer, & Wade, 2013; Barrett, 2007).
- Incorporate many different formats that they have the potential to communicate student strengths and weaknesses more accurately and in greater depth (Clancy & Gardner, 2017); they are also easier to reproduce, distribute, and access (Black, 2010; Trexler, 2015).
- Have been shown to support skills associated with executive functioning such as reflection and goal setting (Abrami et al, 2013; Clancy & Gardner, 2017), skills that are challenging for students with disabilities.
- Foster self-advocacy and related skills needed for students to make a successful transition to adult life (Black, 2010). Students assume more ownership for their learning and better understand their strengths and limitations, knowledge helpful for setting individual goals (Abrami et al., 2013; Black, 2010).
- Scaffold attempts at knowledge construction, helping to develop skills for lifelong learning and problem-based learning concepts (Abrami et al., 2013; Chang & Tseng, 2011).
- Organize learning materials in a way that illustrates the process of learner development and provides remote access and easier input from peers, parents, and teachers (Abrami et al., 2013).

With only an Internet connection, and the assistive technology that may be needed to bypass physical and learning disabilities, students can build their portfolios using platforms such as Epearl, Think.com, Web 2.0, open source, blogging, and various Google applications including Google Groups, iGoogle, eBlogger, Google Docs, Google Notebook, Google Page Creator, and Google Reader.

The Technology Notes feature describes an ePortfolio system that was used successfully with elementary-aged students.

TECHNOLOGY NOTES 11.1

Using ePortfolios (EPs)

Abrami and colleagues (2013) used ePEARL to help students construct a process portfolio: a purposeful collection of work that tells the story of a student's effort, progress, and/or achievement in one or more curricular areas. The process portfolio scaffolds student knowledge attainment by supporting reflection, conferencing, and other processes of self regulation. ePEARL takes students through three phases of portfolio construction: planning, performance, and reflection. It has a number of features designed to support students with portfolio construction including a text editor, audio recorder, and the ability to attach work completed using other software including videos, slideshows, podcasts, scanned images, and photos of paper-based work.

In the planning phase, students are guided to describe the specific task comprising the artifact, setting outcome and process goals, identifying strategies to meet goals, and providing a place for teachers to scaffold and give feedback. A sample plan used in Abrami and others' study for a student participating in Readers Theater, a program designed to build reading fluency, is shown in Figure 11.5.

Phase 2 involves performance, or doing. In this phase students create a new piece of work, link it to existing work, attach digital files to document work completed, and, as in phase 1, leave space for teacher feedback. An example of phase 2 products is shown in the artifact index in Figure 11.6. The index includes the title of each artifact, date modified, number of file attachments (A),

FIGURE 11.5

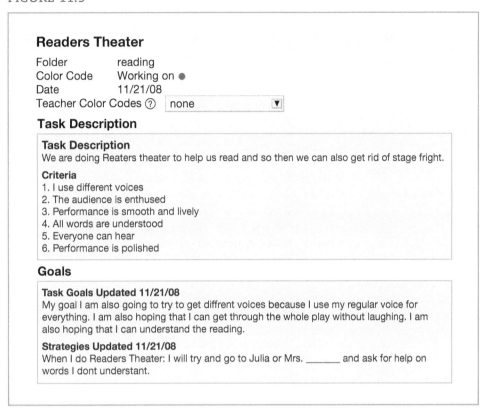

Readers Theater

Folder   reading
Color Code   Working on ●
Date   11/21/08
Teacher Color Codes ⑦ [none   ▼]

Task Description

Task Description
We are doing Reaters theater to help us read and so then we can also get rid of stage fright.

Criteria
1. I use different voices
2. The audience is enthused
3. Performance is smooth and lively
4. All words are understood
5. Everyone can hear
6. Performance is polished

Goals

Task Goals Updated 11/21/08
My goal I am also going to try to get diffrent voices because I use my regular voice for everything. I am also hoping that I can get through the whole play without laughing. I am also hoping that I can understand the reading.

Strategies Updated 11/21/08
When I do Readers Theater: I will try and go to Julia or Mrs. _____ and ask for help on words I dont understant.

FIGURE 11.6

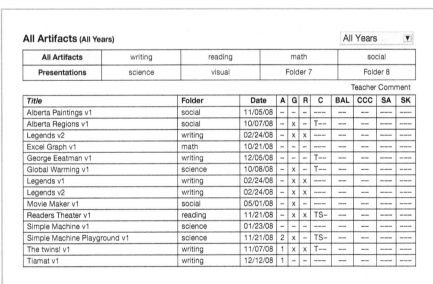

All Artifacts (All Years)   [All Years   ▼]

All Artifacts	writing	reading	math	social
Presentations	science	visual	Folder 7	Folder 8

Teacher Comment

Title	Folder	Date	A	G	R	C	BAL	CCC	SA	SK
Alberta Paintings v1	social	11/05/08	–	–	–	–––	––	––	–––	–––
Alberta Regions v1	social	10/07/08	–	x	–	T––	––	––	–––	–––
Legends v2	writing	02/24/08	–	x	x	–––	––	––	–––	–––
Excel Graph v1	math	10/21/08	–	–	–	–––	––	––	–––	–––
George Eeatman v1	writing	12/05/08	–	–	–	T––	––	––	–––	–––
Global Warming v1	science	10/08/08	–	x	–	T––	––	––	–––	–––
Legends v1	writing	02/24/08	–	x	x	–––	––	––	–––	–––
Legends v2	writing	02/24/08	–	x	x	–––	––	––	–––	–––
Movie Maker v1	social	05/01/08	–	x	–	–––	––	––	–––	–––
Readers Theater v1	reading	11/21/08	–	x	x	TS–	––	––	–––	–––
Simple Machine v1	science	01/23/08	–	–	–	–––	––	––	–––	–––
Simple Machine Playground v1	science	11/21/08	2	x	–	TS–	––	––	–––	–––
The twins! v1	writing	11/07/08	1	x	x	T––	––	––	–––	–––
Tiamat v1	writing	12/12/08	1	–	–	–––	––	––	–––	–––

if goals met (G), if reflection completed (R), and if comments provided by the teacher (T) or student (S). The remaining columns relate to other outcomes required by government education policy.

In Phase 3, the reflection phase, students reflect on their work, share it, get feedback from teachers, peers, and parents, edit the work, and send it to a folder for final presentation. Examples of student reflections and teacher feedback for the Readers Theater artifacts are shown in Figure 11.7.

As a result of participating in the study, the reading, writing and self-regulatory skills of students motivated to use the software improved significantly (Abrami et al., 2013). Also of note is that ePearl comes with wikis and tutorials to help teachers with implementation. Still, while ePEARL in specific, and EPs in general may be of potential benefit to students with disabilities, caution is advised. You have already read about the potential limitations of portfolio use in general with students with disabilities. Those same limitations apply to EPs.

(continued)

FIGURE 11.7

Feedback

Teacher Feedback	Peer Feedback
Teacher Updated 11/23/08 You have a lot of goals and strategies. They are all good so let's see if we can work together to reach them. They would make a difference to all your reading skills and your presentation skills.	**Updated 01/14/08** I really liked your play because it was really funny. I think it could be a little louder. Try reading it to your brother. Can he hear you?

Edit Feedback

Reflections

Reflections Updated 01/12/09

I think I did pretty well I've met all of my goals, I think I could have done better because I dont really look at the crowd because I get nervice, but the bad thing is that not many people could hear what I was saying, most of the people were going haa, what is she saying? When I look at the crowd I do a really wierd smile, kind of like I'm wierd too. Any idea's?

A couple of people said to try it out on crowd before we share with the classes. I think that my friends are really great with giving me advice. I will share everything with my friends because they can help me with everything. I'm glad I know them The teacher said that i should meet my goals and try and have fun with your Readers Theater and see what happends, JUST HAVE FUN!

Of particular relevance with respect to this study is that the students selected for the research were motivated to use the software; students not motivated were excluded from the study. Given a history of failure, struggling learners, including students with disabilities, may not be as motivated because they don't value the intended outcomes or may not think those outcomes are even possible.

MyLab Education Self-Check 11.4

WRAPPING IT UP

Back to the Cases

Now that you have read about evaluating student learning for all students, look back at the stories at the beginning of the chapter. Then go to MyLab Education to apply the knowledge you've gained in this chapter to each case.

MyLab Education Application Exercise 11.1: Case Study 11.1

STACI, as you may recall, struggled during tests because of her reading problem, a common challenge for students with learning disabilities. Many teachers face the same dilemma as Ms. Stevens: How can she provide Staci with an opportunity to demonstrate her learned knowledge and skills that will not be affected by her reading disability?

MyLab Education Application Exercise 11.2: Case Study 11.2

AMELIA reads at a lower level than her classmates but receives A's. Her parents have questions about her grade in reading, and so do some of her classmates.

MyLab Education Application Exercise 11.3: Case Study 11.3

RONALD will be in your classroom this year. You have thought carefully about the issue of modifying your grading procedures to reflect Ronald's learning and progress in your class.

Summary

LO 11.1 Adjustments can be made before testing, during testing, and after testing. Adjustments before the test include study guides, practice tests, tutoring, teaching test-taking skills and strategies, and modifying test construction. During the test, you can make alternative forms of questions and allow alternative ways of administering tests. Adjustment after the test involve grading tests and include changing letter or number grades, changing the criteria on which grades are based, and using alternatives to letter and number grades.

LO 11.2 Practices in report-card grading that can benefit all students include using differentiated report cards, avoiding the use of zeroes, and reporting progress more frequently than the minimum required.

LO 11.3 Individualized grading is for students who have a modified curriculum and involves standards-based grading and grading on the basis of IEP objectives.

LO 11.4 Performance-based assessment measures learning processes rather than focusing exclusively on learning products and frequently involves authentic, or real-world tasks. This type of assessment can be helpful in evaluating the performance of students with special needs because it does not rely exclusively on formats that create problems for students with disabilities. However, adjustments may need to be made for them. Portfolio assessment also can benefit students with special needs. Portfolios typically contain the observable evidence or products of performance assessment, such as anecdotal records, interviews, work samples, and scored samples. Students with disabilities may need to be taught how to select and evaluate their portfolio pieces.

APPLICATIONS IN TEACHING PRACTICE
Making Adjustments When Evaluating Students with Special Needs

Eugene is a high school student who is included in Ms. Howard's American history class. Eugene has a specific learning disability that affects his written expression, spelling, reading fluency, and organization. He is receiving a number of adjustments in Ms. Howard's class, including a digital text with accompanying study guide, help with organizing an assignment notebook from his special education teacher, and use of an electronic speller in class. The grading elements in Ms. Howard's class are multiple-choice/essay tests (60 percent), two-page research reports (25 percent), and end-of-chapter questions for homework (15 percent). Eugene is trying very hard but is barely passing Ms. Howard's class, having received a D– for the last grading period.

QUESTIONS
1. What factors might be responsible for Eugene getting such a low grade?
2. What grading adjustments might be helpful for him?

Tara and Jamie are students in your fourth-grade class. Tara has a learning disability and receives intensive reading instruction in the resource room. Her short-term objectives for this grading period include reading a first-grade literature book at a rate of 20 words correct per minute with four or fewer errors per minute and discerning who the main character of the story is, what the main problem in the story is, and how the problem is solved.

Jamie is a student with moderate intellectual disabilities. You are about to start a unit on adding and subtracting fractions. The IEP objective for Jamie is to identify and demonstrate the meaning of the fractions ¼, ⅓, and ½.

QUESTIONS
1. At the end of the grading period, should you give Tara a grade in reading? Why or why not?
2. Assuming that Tara has met her short-term objectives in reading, what do you think her grade for the marking period should be? Should her grade be modified in any way?
3. Describe a performance-based test that you could use to measure Jamie's knowledge of her target fractions.
4. What problems might Jamie have with your performance-based tests? What accommodations and modifications might you need to make to accommodate her?

CHAPTER 12

Responding to Student Behavior

LEARNING OUTCOMES

After you read this chapter, you will be able to:

12-1 Outline classroom strategies that promote students' positive behavior and prevent misbehavior.

12-2 Explain simple techniques for responding to individual student misbehavior.

12-3 Describe the purpose of a functional behavior assessment (FBA) and steps for deciding how to respond to chronic, inappropriate individual student behavior.

12-4 Outline systematic approaches for increasing positive behaviors and decreasing negative behaviors.

12-5 Identify how to help students manage their own behavior.

PAUL is a ninth-grade student struggling in many ways. He currently is eligible for special education as other health impaired (OHI) because of significant attention deficit–hyperactivity disorder (ADHD). However, in a school district in another state, he previously had been labeled at various times emotionally disabled (ED) and mildly intellectually disabled (ID-mild). He takes medication for ADHD, but he still has extraordinary difficulty focusing on learning tasks, a problem that is already affecting his academic performance in high school and causing his teachers to express concern. Paul takes another medication to address anxiety, and at a local clinic he also sees a private counselor as well as attending counseling with his family. Paul's parents have stated repeatedly that they will not allow professionals to again label their son as "crazy." They attribute most of his current problems at school and his need for medication to issues during his elementary and middle school years, including an incident involving assault against a teacher that was settled without formal charges being filed. Paul's teachers know that the situation is complicated by the fact that his mother also takes medication and has a history of mental health issues and that the family recently has been investigated for child neglect. Paul's school attendance is inconsistent, and in class he often puts his head on his desk, violating a school rule by covering his head with his hoodie. When asked about his plans for the future, Paul generally shrugs and does not offer any answers. Outside of school, Paul seems more engaged. He has several friends and helps a neighbor who works on cars (and receives a small amount of pay for this). In his family, he is required to complete many chores, including babysitting for his younger brother, who has autism, during his parents' frequent absences from home.

What factors might be affecting Paul's academic performance and behavior at school? What responsibilities do Paul's teachers have for understanding his situation and intervening to help him increase his engagement and learning rate? What strategies might his teachers use to accomplish these goals? How should teachers respond when parents may not be able or willing to partner in contributing to their child's education?

J.R. is a seventh-grade student with an emotional disability who is transitioning from a self-contained special education class to a blend of services in general education and a resource class setting. Mr. George, his social studies teacher, is concerned about two problems that are having a negative impact on J.R.'s learning. First, J.R. tends to display behaviors the school psychologist termed *oppositional*: He directly and loudly refuses to complete some assignments, he challenges Mr. George's directions, and he criticizes the way Mr. George teaches. The second issue concerns other students' interactions with J.R. Mr. George overheard a group of students discussing J.R., and they mentioned several incidents that happened in the past, one in elementary school. The students were agreeing that they did not want to work with J.R. or socialize with him away from school. Mr. George has asked Ms. Rogers, the special educator, to schedule at least one observation in his class so that she sees J.R.'s behaviors in the general education classroom firsthand in preparation for revising J.R.'s behavior intervention plan (BIP).

What are your responsibilities for addressing the social interaction and behavior problems of students such as J.R.? What is a behavior intervention plan, and what is your role in implementing it? How can general education teachers help to ensure that students with disabilities have positive interactions with their classmates and other peers?

ARTHUR is a fourth-grade student with autism who spends most of his day in general education with his classmates and teacher Ms. Collins. At the beginning of the school year, Arthur seemed to succeed both academically and behaviorally, but that has changed. Even with an hour of daily co-teaching with Mr. Sanders, a special education teacher, challenges have emerged. For example, Arthur is very rigid concerning where he sits in the classroom. When the teachers explained that seats were being re-arranged for a class activity, Arthur got upset, putting his head down and, in another instance, he ran from the classroom. When stressed, he tends to rock in his seat. But at other times he chews on his T-shirt and sometimes bites his arm; the latter is most likely to occur when the classroom is very noisy as students participate in a range of highly engaging instructional tasks. Recently, Arthur has twice hit other students when they told him it was their turn, not his, and his teachers are searching for strategies to address this and the growing list of other inappropriate classroom behaviors. Ms. Collins and Mr. Sanders are frustrated because they view Arthur as a very capable student, but his behavior is having a negative impact on his achievement. The simple ideas they have tried (e.g., giving Arthur a break from the classroom stressors, rewarding appropriate behavior) have not been effective, and so they have scheduled a meeting with the school psychologist and district autism specialist to discuss additional options.

What purpose might Arthur's behavior be serving for him? How could Ms. Collins and Mr. Sanders constructively respond to Arthur's behavior? How could they help him to manage his own behavior? What is a teacher's responsibility for supporting a student like Arthur?

B ehavior is a concern for all teachers. Whether you teach five-year-olds in a kindergarten class or 17-year-olds in 11th-grade English, the environment you create in your classroom affects whether students' inappropriate behaviors escalate or improve, and your response to such behaviors significantly influences students' learning (Allen et al., 2013; Garwood & Vernon-Feagans, 2017). The public is concerned about student behavior, too. Despite the fact that total incidents of school violence have decreased significantly over the past 20 years (Musu-Gillette, Zhang, Wang, Zhang, & Oudekerk, 2017), Americans still list lack of discipline and related behavior issues among the top three problems facing public schools (Musu-Gillette et al., 2017). The Professional Edge feature takes a brief look at the topic of school violence and related student warning signs.

To begin a discussion of preventing student behavior problems and responding to inappropriate behavior, we present three key concepts that provide a context for the rest of the chapter. First, remember that the root word of *discipline* is *disciple*, meaning "a follower of a teacher." Even though discipline often is associated with obedience, discipline mostly is about learning. It is a means of ensuring that students have the maximum opportunity to learn from their teachers. Discipline is never an end in and of itself, nor is it about control or power. In this chapter, you will be finding ways to enhance your students' learning and help them to reach their potential by preventing and responding to behavior problems by fostering appropriate classroom discipline and teaching appropriate behaviors.

Second, teacher beliefs about discipline have a strong cultural basis, and some evidence suggests that a teacher is far more likely to refer students for discipline problems when they are from a culture other than the teacher's (Allen, 2013; Mason, Gunersel, & Ney, 2014). In addition, teachers may unintentionally vary their use of discipline techniques (for example, talking to the student versus taking away a privilege) depending on the student's culture or ethnicity (Jensen, 2004; Rausch & Skiba, 2006). All teachers have an obligation to monitor their own behavior to ensure that their responses are not biased. Third, over the past decade, researchers have worked to identify interventions for preventing

DIMENSIONS OF DIVERSITY

Teacher bias in responding to student behavior has been repeatedly documented. For example, Silva, Langhout, Kohfeldt, and Gurrola (2015), in a large-scale study, found that girls and Caucasian students were significantly more likely than boys and African American students to receive positive reports for "good" behavior while the latter students were more likely to receive conduct reports for "bad" behavior.

PROFESSIONAL EDGE 12.1

Preventing School Violence

As a school professional, you have a responsibility to be alert for students who are at high risk for committing acts of violence against themselves or others. Most of these students display early warning signs that should signal to you a need for help, but there is no single profile of such students. As you review the warning signs listed here, keep in mind that if you have serious concerns about a student, you should ask for assistance from your colleagues, including school counselors, social workers, psychologists, and administrators, and, with their support, work with parents and the student to address the issues at hand. Think about which of these signs could apply to Paul, the student you met at the beginning of the chapter.

EARLY WARNING SIGNS OF POTENTIAL FOR VIOLENCE

- *Social withdrawal:* Some students gradually withdraw from social contact because of depression, rejection, or a lack of confidence; they may have attempted suicide.
- *Excessive feelings of isolation:* Although most students feel isolated occasionally, a sense of isolation sometimes is associated with aggression and violence.
- *Excessive feelings of rejection:* Some aggressive students who are rejected by peers seek out other aggressive students who in turn reinforce their aggressive tendencies.
- *Victimization by others:* Students who have been physically or sexually abused are at risk of becoming violent.
- *Feelings of being picked on and persecuted:* Students who believe they are teased, bullied, or humiliated at home or at school may vent their feelings through aggression or violence.
- *Low school interest and poor academic performance:* A drastic change in school performance or poor school achievement accompanied by frustration can be a warning sign for acting out.
- *Interest in violence:* Students at risk may show violence in their writing and drawings and may be attracted to music and social media sites emphasizing violence.

- *Uncontrolled anger:* Getting angry is natural, but if a student is frequently and intensely angry in response to minor incidents, it may signal a potential for violence.
- *Patterns of impulsive and chronic hitting, intimidating, and bullying behavior:* If behaviors such as these are not addressed, they can escalate to violence.
- *Display of behavior of concern to others:* In many cases, students who commit violence displayed behavior prior to the attack that raised concern for a teacher, parent, or other adult.
- *History of violent and aggressive behavior:* Unless a student with a history of aggressive and violent acts receives counseling, the behaviors are likely to continue and even escalate.
- *Intolerance for differences and prejudicial attitudes:* Intense prejudice (regarding, for example, race, ethnicity, religion, gender, or sexual orientation) may lead to violence against individuals perceived to belong to the targeted group.
- *Drug and alcohol use:* The use of drugs and alcohol tends to reduce self-control, thus increasing the chance of being either a perpetrator or victim of violence.
- *Affiliation with gangs:* Students who are members of gangs that support antisocial values may act on group beliefs.
- *Inappropriate access to, possession of, and use of firearms:* Students who have a history of aggression, impulsiveness, or other serious emotional problems should not have access to firearms and other weapons.
- *Serious threats of violence:* One of the most reliable indicators that a student is likely to commit a violent act is a specific and detailed threat, sometimes but not always directed at an individual or shared with a friend or on social media.

Source: Adapted from *Early Warning, Time Response: A Guide to Safe Schools,* by U.S. Department of Education, Special Education and Rehabilitative Services, 1998, Washington, DC: Author. Retrieved from (http://cecp.air.org/guide/guide.pdf); and Vossekuil, B., Fein, R. A., Reddy, M., Borum, R., & Modzeleski, W. (2004, July). *The final report and findings of the safe school initiative: Implications for the prevention of school attacks in the United States.* Washington, DC: U. S. Department of Education and U.S. Secret Service. Retrieved from http://www2.ed.gov/admins/lead/safety/preventingattacksreport.pdf.

behavior challenges as well as techniques for addressing common and intense behavior problems. Their work has been collected at the U.S. Office of Special Education Programs (OSEP) National Technical Assistance Center on Positive Behavioral Interventions and Supports (PBIS) (U.S. Department of Education, 2017). **Positive behavioral interventions and supports (PBIS)**, and variations of this specific work sometimes called the more general term **positive behavior supports (PBS)**, are research-based, systemic approaches designed to enhance the learning environment and improve outcomes for students.

PBIS interventions are grouped by their intensity (e.g., Horner, Sugai, & Fixsen, 2017). The first level is called *primary prevention* and is considered a universal level of intervention. That is, it is designed to create schoolwide and classroom environments that address the needs of approximately 80 percent of students (Lane, Oakes, Menzies, Oyer, & Jenkins, 2013). The second level, *secondary prevention* or group level, is designed to quickly and efficiently address student behavior problems in order to prevent them from becoming more serious,

WWW RESOURCES

http://www.pbis.org/
To learn more about PBIS, including explanations of primary, secondary, and tertiary interventions, visit the National Technical Assistance Center on Positive Behavioral Interventions and Supports.

MyLab Education

Video Example 12.1: Basic Principles of Classroom Management

This brief overview of classroom management is a preview of many topics that will be addressed in this chapter.

and it addresses an additional 15 percent or so of students (Lane, Capizzi, Fisher, & Ennis, 2012), usually through small-group interventions. The final level, *tertiary prevention* or individual level, includes intensive interventions for the 5 percent or so of students whose behavior problems are chronic or exceptionally serious.

The PBIS structure is similar in important ways to that used for response to intervention (RtI) for student problems related to reading and other academic areas. You also may recall that in many locales, RtI and PBIS systems now are blended into a single integrated structure referred to as a multi-tiered system of supports (MTSS). In the Professional Edge feature you can learn how some school professionals are incorporating interventions related to behavior into their intervention procedures.

Many issues are beyond a teacher's control—you do not have the power to increase the financial support available to schools, nor can you remove the public pressures that surround many school reform initiatives. However, teachers ultimately are accountable for student outcomes, and those who actively, carefully, and creatively apply approaches to create a positive learning environment, build students' skills as members of their classroom community, teach appropriate behaviors, and effectively address student behavior challenges will have a positive influence on student learning (e.g., Floress, Rock, & Hailemariam, 2017; Gut, Reimann, & Grob, 2013). The sections that follow present a wide array of procedures grounded in the three key concepts just outlined to assist you to reach that goal.

PROFESSIONAL EDGE 12.2

Response to Intervention, Multi-Tiered Systems of Support, and Positive Behavior Supports

Response to intervention (RtI) was developed primarily to address students' academic challenges through increasingly intensive interventions carefully monitored by frequent data collection. PBIS was developed to accomplish similar goals by focusing on students' behavior challenges. MTSS blends these efforts. In previous chapters, you have reviewed examples of interventions for academic concerns. The following applies the practice of using three-tiered interventions to the social/behavior domain.

Tier 1: Universal interventions (effective for 80–85 percent of students)

- Clear schoolwide rules and expectations, including procedures for the lunchroom, procedures for entering and leaving the building or campus as school begins and ends, and so on
- Character-building programs for all students
- Social skills instruction for all students
- Procedures for deescalating disruptive behavior by establishing cooling off times and locations for student reflection
- Monitoring of student behavior using naturally occurring measures, such as discipline referrals

Tier 2: Selected interventions (effective for an additional 10–15 percent of students)

- Structured social skills training designed for small groups
- Group counseling
- Mentoring programs

- Daily behavior report cards
- Use of structured reward programs for appropriate behavior
- Progress monitoring frequently (at least every 2–4 weeks)

Tier 3: Targeted interventions (effective for the remaining 1–5 percent of students)

- Implementation of functional behavior assessments (described later in this chapter)
- Specific student instruction on appropriate behaviors to replace inappropriate behavior while serving the same function
- Involvement of agencies outside the school, possibly including juvenile justice, mental, and social services
- Individual counseling, possibly including the family and possibly delivered at the student's home
- Individually designed behavior intervention plan (described later in this chapter)
- Frequent progress monitoring, as often as daily or weekly

Research on the use of positive approaches to respond to student behavior concerns indicates that it has many benefits. These include an emphasis on student strengths rather than problems, consideration of effective instructional practices, clear communication among colleagues and with parents, and attention to data collection (e.g., Flannery, Fenning, Kato, & McIntosh, 2014; Garbacz, McIntosh, Eagle, Dowd-Eagle, Hirano, & Ruppert, 2016; Pavri, 2010).

How Can You Use Positive Behavior Supports to Prevent Discipline Problems?

The beginning point for addressing student behavior problems is to focus on how to *prevent* them (Bradshaw, Waasdorp, & Leaf, 2015; Landrum, Scott, & Lingo, 2011); these are the primary prevention strategies addressed in PBIS as Tier 1. In nearly all situations, you can create a caring and positive instructional environment conducive to learning (Belt & Belt, 2017; Knoff, 2012) and avoid teaching in a classroom in which the stress level is high and "keeping control" is a constant struggle.

Instructional Environments Conducive to Learning

In Chapter 5, you learned that many factors contribute to creating an instructional environment that fosters student learning. Many of these same factors also promote appropriate classroom behavior. For example, you learned that teachers need to set clear expectations in their classrooms through rules that students understand and follow (Reinke, Herman, & Stormont, 2013).

Another key factor related to the instructional environment and discipline is establishing clear classroom routines. Routines should be established for beginning the school day or class period, transitioning from one activity to another, moving about in the classroom, and ending the school day or class period. Students who have routines are less likely to misbehave because they can meet classroom expectations for behavior. In classes such as art, music, drama, and physical education, in which students may be very active participants, routines are especially important.

EFFECTIVE CLASSROOM COMMUNICATION Teachers who treat their students with respect and trust are more successful than other teachers in creating a positive classroom environment in which fewer behavior problems occur (e.g., Winkler, Walsh, de Blois, Maré, & Carvajal, 2017).

Communication between teacher and students is integral to fostering this trust and respect. However, teacher–student communication is a complex matter, and problems often arise. For example, sometimes teachers provide students with too much information or information that is not clear, and students become confused. And sometimes teachers give one message with words but convey another message with their tone of voice or nonverbal behaviors.

Another dimension of teacher–student communication concerns language differences. When students struggle to understand English, their behaviors may at first appear to be challenging. For example, a first-grader is asked to complete several directions at one time and has a tantrum as a result of the frustration of not understanding. Similarly, a high school student apparently ignores a teacher's direction to put away project supplies and spend any remaining time beginning the homework assignment. When the teacher addresses this behavior, the student pushes everything off his desk. Is this a behavior problem or an example of misunderstanding and frustration? Teachers working with students who are not proficient English speakers should take care to distinguish problems that result from language differences from misbehavior.

The overall quality of your communication with your students is built in numerous small ways. For example, finding time each week to speak privately

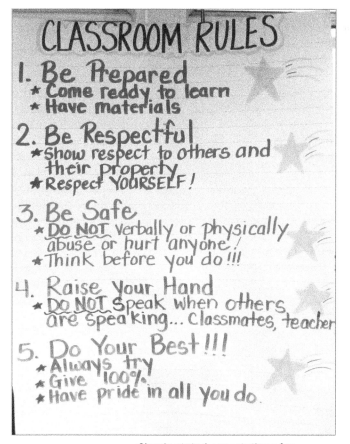

Clearly stated expectations for behavior, generated with student input and directly discussed with them, can foster a positive classroom climate conducive to learning and acceptance of diversity.

with students lets them know that you value them as individuals. Asking older students sincere questions about their friends, out-of-school activities, and part-time jobs also conveys that you care. Taking the time to write positive comments on papers shows students that you appreciate their strengths and are not focusing only on their needs. Using nonverbal signals (e.g., thumbs up or thumbs down) instead of, or in addition to, verbal communication also can facilitate understanding (Jamie & Knowlton, 2007).

EFFECTIVE TEACHING METHODS Another critical strategy for preventing behavior problems is to provide instruction that is relevant, interesting, individualized, and active in addition to being at students' instructional level (McComas, Downwind, Klingbeil, Petersen-Brown, Davidson, & Parker, 2017; Nurmi, 2012). Recall from Chapters 9 and 10 that learning is enhanced through the use of clear and systematic instructional approaches that actively engage students in learning. We remind you of this information because effective instruction plays a critical role in classroom behavior management. Students who are given boring, outdated, or impossibly difficult-to-read materials and no choice in assignments, who are asked to complete seemingly endless worksheets with little instructional value, who have few opportunities to create their own learning through projects or activities, or who seldom see their own culture reflected in their learning tasks are likely to misbehave.

FOSTERING POSITIVE STUDENT INTERACTIONS Another key to preventing behavior problems is to foster positive student interactions; simply mixing students with and without disabilities in single classrooms may not result in an integrated social system for them. To develop respect for one another, an appreciation for diversity, and sensitivity to others who are not exactly like themselves could be among the most important lessons you teach your students (Aasebø, Midtsundstad, & Willbergh, 2017).

One way to promote positive interactions among students with and without disabilities is to provide opportunities for them to interact in meaningful ways. In both elementary and secondary classrooms and regardless of the academic content being addressed, this means structuring activities and assigning students to groups so that interacting becomes part of classroom instruction. Formal strategies for doing this are introduced in the next section of this chapter. Arranging service-learning activities in which students with and without disabilities all participate is another way to encourage interactions (Anderson & Gurnee, 2016). For instance, students might work together to pick up debris from a local park, visit a senior citizen center, or contact local government officials to support a new health and fitness initiative.

Creating special programs is yet another way to accomplish the goal of meaningful interactions. For example, in one high school, peer buddies were assigned to provide students with significant intellectual disabilities with more and better opportunities to participate in general education classes (Copeland et al., 2004). In this program, students without disabilities were paired with students with disabilities to provide academic and social support. Group interviews of participating nondisabled students revealed that these students discovered many ways that their classmates with disabilities were socially isolated in schools. They also learned that they could foster social interaction by advocating for their buddies, facilitating interactions with other students, and modeling appropriate social interactions.

You may be able to identify many other strategies for fostering interactions between students with and without disabilities, interactions that build positive social relationships. How could you do this in an elementary classroom? A middle school class? A high school class? Even a small amount of attention on your part to arranging such interactions can benefit all your students (e.g., Lo, Correa, & Anderson, 2015). The Case in Practice feature illustrates the importance of fostering positive student interactions.

CASE IN PRACTICE 12.1

Intervening to Promote Positive Social Interactions

Ms. Giano, a middle school teacher, is in a quandary. This afternoon she received a phone call from Mr. Perez concerning Jesse, his son. Mr. Perez related that Jesse had come home from school looking disheveled, carrying torn books and papers. At first he wouldn't tell his father what had happened, but eventually he related the story. Jesse has albinism. He has very little pigment in his skin, hair, and eyes. His skin is very pale, and his hair appears almost white. In addition, Jesse has a serious vision problem related to his albinism, and he also has been identified as having a learning disability. He told his father that several of his classmates had begun making fun of him on the walk to the bus and then continued on the bus. They had been doing this almost since the beginning of the school year, but things had been getting worse lately. Today, Jesse explained, he couldn't stand it anymore and he lunged at the boys. The bus driver intervened, but all the boys now were to be brought back to school by their parents for fighting.

Mr. Perez was upset. He also mentioned to Ms. Giano that Jesse had asked him not to call the school, saying that he would deal with the situation and accept the discipline for fighting on the bus. He was afraid that his classmates' bullying would become even worse if it was made an issue. Mr. Perez is not satisfied; he wants something done to stop the teasing and protect his son. He is concerned that Jesse is becoming discouraged and has read about the association between such bullying and depression, especially among middle and high school students.

REFLECTION

If you were Ms. Giano, what would you say to Mr. Perez? What is the role of general education teachers in ensuring that students are treated respectfully? How would you address this issue with Jesse? With the other boys? If you think they should have an additional consequence, what should it be? What might you try as an all-homeroom activity to foster better understanding among your diverse students?

Schoolwide Strategies

One additional prevention strategy goes beyond your classroom. PBIS supports the use of schoolwide prevention strategies that are developed in a systematic way (for example, Coffey & Horner, 2012; McIntosh, Kelm, & Canizal Delabra, 2016), often by a committee of several teachers and administrators. These schoolwide strategies require a commitment to implementation from every teacher, specialist, and other staff member in the school (Feuerborn & Tyre, 2016). For example, a common schoolwide expectation is that students will be respectful of themselves, of others, and of property. In the cafeteria, the specific expectations might include these:

- Use a soft voice at all times.
- Ask for assistance if something is spilled or dropped.
- Remove all trays and dispose of all trash when you are finished eating.

What might the specific applications be for a locker room? A student commons area? On the bus?

RESEARCH-BASED PRACTICES

Video modeling, introduced in Chapter 6, has been demonstrated to be an effective strategy for teaching communication and social skills to students with autism (Puckett, Mathur, & Zamora, 2017).

How Can You Promote Positive Group Behavior?

In effective classrooms, teachers and students respect each other, and students are busily engaged in learning (Johnson & Gooliaff, 2013); a clear sense of classroom community exists. Students attend to their work, interact with each other politely and without verbal or physical fighting, and ignore the occasional misbehavior of classmates instead of encouraging it. You can promote positive behaviors such as these by using behavior management strategies designed specifically for the whole class (e.g., Chafouleas, Hagermoser Sanetti, Jaffery, & Fallon, 2012; State, Harrison, Kern, & Lewis, 2017). For example, all students might participate in discussing classroom discipline issues, helping each other monitor their behavior, and earning privileges or rewards as individuals or as members of learning groups. The following sections describe additional effective whole-group strategies: peer-mediated instruction and group contingency systems.

Implement Peer-Mediated Instruction

Peer-mediated instruction is the term for structured and interactive systems in which students teach each other. It enables teachers to change from traditional whole-group teaching approaches, and a strong research base demonstrates that peer-mediated instruction improves students' social relationships, decreases student behavior problems, and improves students' academic outcomes (e.g., Scruggs, Mastropieri, & Marshak, 2012; Wexler, Reed, Pyle, Mitchell, & Barton, 2015). J.R., who you met at the beginning of the chapter, might benefit from peer-mediated instruction.

PEER TUTORING In **peer tutoring**, pairs of students are given formal roles for promoting each other's achievement (Bowman-Perrott et al., 2013; Jones, Ostojic, Menard, Picard, & Miller, 2017). The tutor role most often is held by a peer in the same class, but the tutor could also be from another class or school. *Tutees* are the students who receive the instruction from peer tutors.

One example of a highly structured peer-tutoring program is **Peer-Assisted Learning Strategies (PALS)** (McMaster & Fuchs, 2016). It has been implemented with positive results for students with learning and behavioral disabilities (Santangelo, Ruhaak, Kama, & Cook, 2013; Sporer & Brunstein, 2009) and English learners (Wayman, McMaster, Sáenz, & Watson, 2010). For example, a group of first-grade teachers implemented PALS for their students with and without disabilities (Baker, Gersten, Dimino, & Griffiths, 2004). Several years after the initial successful research study, the teachers were still using the peer-tutoring program effectively at least twice each week in math. Because the program includes a built-in data collection system, they were able to report that the effect on student academic achievement was highly positive. The teachers also noted that PALS had a positive impact on student social development. They found that the program taught students to work effectively with many different peers, instead of just their friends, by helping them to learn how to say positive things to one another. This result carried far beyond the math instructional period and is a specific example of how peer-mediated instructional approaches facilitate positive behaviors.

Developing Peer-Tutoring Programs   Developing a peer-tutoring program can be as simple or complex as you want it to be. You can create your own system within your classroom, partner some or all your students with another group of students, or help coordinate a schoolwide tutoring program. Alternatively, you may decide to use a research-based approach, such as PALS, mentioned earlier, or **Classwide Peer Tutoring (CWPT)** (e.g., Lundblom & Woods, 2012; Scruggs, Mastropieri, & Marshak, 2012), in which all the students in a class take on the roles of tutor and tutee in turn and follow a set of clear steps for helping each other learn. CWPT is described in Figure 12.1.

Generally, the steps for setting up a peer-tutoring program of your own are these:

1. *Selecting tutors:* To create a same-age tutoring program in your classroom, consider pairing students who are both high achievers rather than pairing a high achiever with a low achiever. Then pair other students whose understanding of the topic at hand is similar. This arrangement reduces the problem of high achievers becoming impatient with low achievers and the concern about high-achieving students missing their own opportunities for learning. Another approach is to pair students randomly and use a reciprocal tutoring approach, in which both students alternate between the tutor and tutee roles. To create a cross-age tutoring approach, older students tutor younger ones, either within a school or across school levels (e.g., older elementary students tutor younger ones, middle school students tutor elementary students, or

MyLab Education

Video Example 12.3: Peer Tutoring

This video illustrates Classwide Peer Tutoring, a specific peer tutoring approach that can be implemented across grade levels and that has a strong research base.

FIGURE 12.1 **Steps in Classwide Peer Tutoring**

1. Assign all students to tutoring pairs that change periodically, perhaps weekly or biweekly.
2. Assign each tutoring pair to one of two classroom teams.
3. Teach all students a specific series of steps for presenting and practicing content.
4. Teach all students specific strategies for correcting tutees and rewarding correct responses.
5. Provide tutoring pairs with daily assignments.
6. Instruct tutors to keep score: When a tutee answers a question correctly, a point is scored for the team.
7. Announce the winning team and post point totals.
8. Reward the winning team with a privilege or class applause.
9. Reverse the tutor/tutee arrangement each session, or have both students take the tutor role within each session.

high school students tutor middle school students). Twelfth-graders might be paired with ninth- or tenth-grade students. Remember, sometimes students with disabilities can serve as tutors to their classmates. An older student without a disability can be an ideal tutor for a younger student with a disability. Also, an older student who has a learning or intellectual disability or who is at risk for school failure can be an effective tutor for a younger student with or without a disability. In other words, you can structure a tutoring program in many ways. What is important is making deliberate decisions about structure based on the strengths and needs of the students.

2. *Deciding how much tutoring should occur:* The specific time allocated to peer tutoring depends on the needs of the students and the structure of the program. In many cases tutoring in elementary schools occurs two to four times each week for 20 or 30 minutes, and as often as daily for a class period in high schools, particularly when it is structured as an elective course for tutors (Baker et al., 2004; Calhoon & Fuchs, 2003). Tutoring, of course, should not detract from the rest of tutors' or tutees' core educational programs.

3. *Providing time for peer tutoring:* Peer tutoring can occur as part of independent work time or as a periodic activity in which an entire class participates. Cross-age tutoring needs to occur on a schedule that accommodates both the tutor and the tutee. In some middle schools and high schools, peer tutoring is a service-learning activity that is an elective course or a course for students hoping one day to be teachers. In such cases, tutoring occurs during the class period available for the tutor, and it might occur in the tutee's classroom, the library or media center, or a study hall or advisory classroom.

4. *Selecting content and format for tutoring:* Effective peer-tutoring programs provide practice on skills already taught by the teacher and use standard formats that help tutors know how to do their job (Galbraith & Winterbottom, 2011). For example, many elementary peer-tutoring programs have tutors and tutees working on basic math facts, spelling or vocabulary words, and comprehension questions from social studies and science concepts already taught. In middle and high schools, peer tutoring may occur to review vocabulary, concepts, and skills or to provide assistance to a student in a core academic class (for example, algebra or biology) that the tutor has successfully completed. Further, tutors should be given explicit directions to follow so that the tutoring format is highly structured. For example, tutors might be instructed to begin a vocabulary session by reviewing all eight words from last time and then showing each new word, waiting for a response, and marking the response as correct or incorrect. The tutor praises correct responses, corrects errors, and asks the tutee to repeat the corrected responses. Having well-defined procedures helps keep participants in tutoring sessions on task.

5. *Training tutors:* Professionals generally agree that effective peer-tutoring programs carefully prepare tutors for their teaching roles (e.g., Topping,

WWW RESOURCES

The What Works Clearinghouse offers summaries on the effectiveness of a variety of programs for improving student behaviors. You can access it at this website (http://ies.ed.gov/ncee/wwc/), and then click on the icon for behavior.

Buchs, Duran, & van Keer, 2017). Tutor training should provide procedures for tutoring, give tutors a way to track tutee learning, teach positive interaction skills, and include problem solving so that tutors know what to do if the tutoring is not working.

Supporting Peer-Tutoring Programs   A training program for peer tutors should include follow-up and assessment. For example, in a cross-age tutoring program, it is important to bring tutors together periodically to discuss how they are doing and how they have resolved problems and to thank them for their work. When tutoring extends beyond your own class group, it is a nice touch to provide tutor appreciation certificates or other recognition. Sometimes paraprofessionals or parent volunteers can assist with the management and supervision of peer-tutoring programs, taking that burden off of you and other teachers.

Keep in mind that support for peer-tutoring programs often depends on communication with your principal or other administrators as well as parents and other community members. If you implement a peer-tutoring program, you should invite your principal or the appropriate administrator to observe the program in action. You also should alert parents and explain your instructional approach. Periodic notes or updates provided on your website or in your electronic newsletter can keep parents informed of the accomplishments of the program. In middle schools and high schools, where peer tutoring might be an elective or service learning course, information on the program can be added to the school website, possibly with a list of frequently-asked questions and information for signing up as a tutor or tutee.

COOPERATIVE LEARNING   Another peer-mediated instructional approach is **cooperative learning**. It has been employed as a strategy for achieving racial and cultural integration, assisting socially isolated learners, fostering inclusive education for students with disabilities and other special needs, and accommodating culture-based learning styles (Jacobs, Power, & Loh, 2016).

Cooperative learning generally has four essential characteristics:

MyLab Education

Video Example 12.4: Cooperative Learning

Watch an example of students engaging in a cooperative learning activity.

1. Students in the groups have *positive interdependence.* Either they reach their goal together, or no one can achieve it. For example, in Mr. Reilly's classroom, the students earn points when all the members in their cooperative groups get at least 70 percent on their weekly review quiz. Group members work very hard to help all members learn the material so their shared goal can be reached.

2. Cooperative learning requires face-to-face interactions. In Mr. Sutter's class, students have opportunities to work directly with their group members to accomplish learning goals related to reviewing the use of advertising approaches in magazines. Alternatively, students may interact in real-time electronically using social media or an electronic learning platform such as Schoology or Google Hangouts.

3. Members of cooperative groups have individual accountability. On the weekly vocabulary test in Ms. Mather's chemistry class, students who have difficulty learning are not excused from taking the test, nor are high achievers permitted to answer for all group members. Each member is required to make a contribution.

4. Cooperative learning stresses student interpersonal skills, such as how to ask questions, praise classmates, and help another student learn. When Ms. Bolter notices positive interpersonal interactions among her seventh-grade English students, she gives them "Bolter Bucks" to spend on a variety of privileges and rewards.

These social and interactive components of cooperative learning make it unique. They are not possible when teachers engage in traditional classroom procedures in which students compete against one another (for example, a classroom game that can have only one winner) nor in individualistic approaches in which students are compared only to themselves, as is common in special education settings. That means that this approach is especially important in inclusive schools. It helps students learn to work together, which, in turn, prevents behavior problems.

Developing Cooperative Learning Programs To achieve the best results with cooperative learning, several ideas should be kept in mind. First, the makeup of the groups should be based on the age, abilities, maturity, and needs of your students, and they generally should reflect the heterogeneity of your students. The number of students in each group may range from three to six, depending on student characteristics. Second, students should be taught cooperative skills that include how to speak positively to each other and how to provide feedback to peers (Lehraus, 2015). Third, students should be assigned to specific roles in their groups. Common roles include *leader, recorder, encourager,* and *timekeeper.*

The next step in cooperative learning is to select a specific program to guide student interactions. Many options exist. Some programs can be used for any subject matter. Some give students specific roles for learning part of the material being covered and teaching it to other group members. Yet other programs have clear reward structures so that all group members succeed in their learning. Two examples of specific cooperative learning programs are described in the Instructional Edge feature.

Supporting Cooperative Learning Programs Once students are established in cooperative groups, your role becomes one of monitoring and managing your class (Gillies, 2016). For example, if you notice that a student is having difficulty

INSTRUCTIONAL EDGE 12.1

Cooperative Learning in Action

Many cooperative learning programs have been developed that provide effective ways to foster student interactions, prevent behavior problems, and increase student learning. Here are two examples.

NUMBERED HEADS TOGETHER

Numbered Heads Together (Hunter, Dieker, & Whitney, 2016; Kagan, 1990) has these steps:

1. Students are assigned to cooperative groups (usually four or five in a group) and count off by number.
2. The teacher then poses a question to the group and students are asked to "put their heads together" to be sure all group members know the answer.
3. After a brief time, the teacher reconvenes the whole class and calls out a number.
4. All the students with that number stand, and one student responds to the question, or they all write down the answer and hold it up for the teacher to see.
5. Students responding correctly score points for their teams.

This simple cooperative learning approach can be used for questions with single correct answers as well as for those with many responses.

JIGSAW CLASSROOM

Jigsaw Classroom (Aronson, 2005; Berger & Hänze, 2015; Darnon, Buchs, & Desbar, 2012) uses these steps:

1. Students are assigned to heterogeneous work groups.
2. Each member of the work group also is assigned to a separate expert group.
3. Work groups meet and decide which member to assign to which expert group. For example, in a unit on the Midwest, experts might be assigned for four topics: geography, economy, culture, and cities.
4. All team members then read the material, with each member focusing on his expert topic.
5. After reading, team members join their respective expert groups, which are composed of all students in the room who share the same expert topic.
6. The expert groups review their portion of the instructional material and then return to teach it to their work-group members.
7. Group members ask each expert questions to help clarify the information being presented.
8. After all the group members have taught their segments of the information and the groups have had an opportunity to review their learning, a quiz or other evaluation procedure is used, and each group member is graded individually on this assessment.

Several variations of this popular cooperative learning approach have been developed (for example, Holliday, 2002; Sahin, 2011), with changes such as giving the expert groups a quiz prior to their teaching information to their peers.

in a group, you might decide to join that group briefly to judge whether students can resolve the problem themselves or need your assistance. If a student seems to be struggling because of the complexity of the lesson content, you can make an on-the-spot adaptation to help the student and the group. If a student is being disruptive, your proximity might be sufficient to settle that student. As you monitor, you also can observe students' use of cooperative skills and check the progress of their learning.

INCLUDE

By applying the INCLUDE strategy, you quickly can see that many of the teaching strategies presented in this text can be incorporated into cooperative learning experiences, for example, learning strategies introduced in Chapter 10 (e.g., *TASSEL, POWER, READS*). Cooperative groups provide a constructive classroom structure, one that builds self-esteem, engages students in order to build group spirit and prevent behavior problems, and provides opportunities for adapting instruction for individual needs.

Use Group Contingencies

Another straightforward way to prevent behavior problems in your classroom is to use group contingency systems (Maggin, Johnson, Chafouleas, Ruberto, & Berggren, 2012; Pennington & McComas, 2017). In these systems, the goal is to promote positive behavior by allowing students to earn a group reward based on the performance of particular students. Many group contingency options exist. Here are two examples:

- *Small-group contingency:* In small-group contingency, the class is rewarded based on the performance of a selected group of students. For example, if four selected students complete the assigned work, the entire class will earn five minutes of instructional computer time at the end of the class. This approach is helpful if one or two students tend to have behavior problems. It avoids placing too much pressure on one student, as would happen if the reward was based on just that student's performance, but at the same time it fosters desired student behavior.
- *Whole-group contingency:* In whole-group contingency, reward is based on the performance of all class members. For example, if 80 percent of all the students in an algebra class complete their assigned in-class work during the week, on Friday no homework will be assigned.

Group contingencies can be powerful classroom tools for teachers, but care must be taken in developing them. For example, one or two students may sabotage the group by deliberately misbehaving. Or one student may not be capable of performing at the level required for the group to be rewarded. In such cases, this may not be the most effective strategy to implement, and other approaches—those already discussed and those in the sections that follow—should be considered.

MyLab Education 12.1 Self-Check

What Are Positive Behavior Strategies for Responding to Minor Individual Behaviors?

For some students, including students with special needs, the steps you take to create a positive and productive learning environment may not be sufficient to eliminate behavior problems. These students may need much more specialized

INCLUDE

approaches—secondary prevention or Tier 2 strategies—and you will find it helpful to follow the steps of the INCLUDE model outlined in Chapter 5 when planning and implementing these strategies. However, before you decide to use that approach, try several simpler strategies. Teachers have long relied on the principle of least intervention in addressing student behavior needs. The strategies described in the following sections include minimal interventions, such as "catch 'em being good," and techniques for managing students' surface behaviors.

Use Minimum Interventions

Teachers sometimes contribute unintentionally but significantly to student misbehavior. They do this by inadvertently bringing out negative student behaviors and responding too strongly to minor misbehaviors, actions that sometimes cause students to misbehave more. For example, when asked directly to begin work, a student might refuse. However, when given a choice regarding which assignment to do first, the student might comply. Similarly, when reprimanded for using profanity in the classroom, some students will use the reprimand as a signal to continue the language to get further attention. Ignoring occasional inappropriate language might lessen the problem.

When working with students with special needs, it is essential to stay alert to how you might be contributing to a student's behaviors, either through your own responses to the behavior or through your classroom structure and lesson format. Two examples of minimum interventions teachers use to address minor student misbehavior follow.

"CATCH 'EM BEING GOOD" A versatile and long-recognized strategy for reducing inappropriate student behavior and increasing appropriate behavior is called "catch 'em being good." In short, when a student is behaving according to expectations, you acknowledge and reward the behavior (e.g., Collins & Cook, 2016; Lum, Tingstrom, Dufrene, Radley, & Lynne, 2017). For example, if third-grader Connor enters the room and immediately begins his work, you might say to him, "I like the way you went right to your desk, Connor. That's exactly what you're supposed to do!" This comment has the effect of rewarding Connor's behavior. At the same time, it clearly lets other students know that going directly to one's seat is a behavior they should do, too. In a middle school or

When teachers use minimum interventions, perhaps standing in close proximity to a misbehaving student, they often can avoid escalating the situation and may thus prevent more serious behavior problems from occurring.

high school social studies class, a teacher might privately say to a student who is chronically late, "I noticed you were at your seat with materials ready when the bell rang. Nice going." Although the privacy of the comment eliminates its potential positive impact on other students, it has the benefit of preventing student embarrassment.

MAKE HIGH-PROBABILITY REQUESTS FIRST Another minimal strategy for encouraging appropriate behavior involves thinking carefully about the sequence of tasks requested of students. For example, Banda and Kubina (2006) describe a successful strategy for helping students with autism who have difficulty transitioning between activities in the classrooms, such as halting work on a language arts assignment to get ready to leave the classroom to go to physical education. With this approach, make several simple requests the student is likely to complete prior to making the targeted request. For example, if it is time for first-grader Angel to put away his crayons and join a group reading a story, first get Angel's attention by saying something like, "Angel, give me five." Follow this with asking Angel to tell you his address (or another appropriate piece of personal information that he is learning and likely to share). Next, ask him to shake hands, another behavior he knows and usually readily does. Finally, request that Angel leave his coloring and join the reading group. Each request should be followed by verbal praise (for example, "Right" or "Good job"). Other learners with disabilities also may respond well to this easily implemented intervention (Clinton & Clees, 2015). How do you think it would work with a student with an intellectual disability? Emotional disability?

DIMENSIONS OF DIVERSITY

McComas, Downwind, Klingbeil, Petersen-Brown, Davidson, and Parker (2017) studied the behavior of American Indian youth, finding that when teachers gave these students more opportunities to respond during instruction and praised them, they were more likely to be on task; when these practices were not used, the opposite was truly, that is, off-task behavior increased.

Manage Students' Surface Behaviors

Another relatively simple strategy for responding to student behaviors is managing their surface behaviors (Dhaem, 2012; Redl, 2007). Long and Newman (1971) proposed long ago that a teacher's initial response to student behavior often determines whether a problem situation develops and how intense it is. If a teacher treats a minor misbehavior as a major infraction, the result might be a strong negative student response followed by a stronger teacher response and, ultimately, a serious behavior incident. For example, if a student mutters under her breath something negative about an assignment and the teacher responds by asking in a stern voice, "What did you say?" the situation will likely escalate. The student might reply, "Nothing," the teacher may repeat the request, and the student may eventually say something that requires a negative consequence.

Such interactions can be avoided if teachers are prepared to shift the focus of the interaction. Suggestions for heading off such problems include purposefully ignoring minor incidents and using humor to defuse tense classroom situations. Examples of additional initial response techniques are outlined in the following Professional Edge feature.

These low-intrusion techniques are most suited to minor misbehaviors and unlikely to resolve serious discipline issues. Also, responding to students' surface behaviors sometimes can have the effect of increasing them. For example, if you use humor with a student and she responds by talking back, then your humor may be increasing rather than decreasing the inappropriate behavior. If this happens, switch to another approach or work with colleagues to examine the behavior more carefully and devise a more individualized response to it, as described in the remainder of this chapter.

MyLab Education 12.2 Self-Check

PROFESSIONAL EDGE 12.3

Strategies for Managing Students' Surface Behaviors

You sometimes will be faced with the dilemma of how to respond to students' *surface behaviors*—minor inappropriate behaviors that students display, such as refusing to work, sitting with their head down, and calling out answers (Newcomer, 2009). In some cases, these behaviors may be symptoms of serious problems that need the careful attention of a functional behavior assessment (described later in this chapter). However, a first approach can be to use simple techniques, such as the following, to deal with problem behaviors as soon as they occur:

1. *Planned ignoring:* If a student's behavior is not likely to harm others or spread to others, you might decide to ignore it. For example, a student who repeatedly sighs loudly could be signaling a loss of interest; instead of responding to the sighing, recognize that the student needs to change activities soon. If you ignore inappropriate behavior, you should be sure to give the student attention for appropriate behavior.

2. *Signal interference:* Use nonverbal signals, such as eye contact and gestures (for example, putting your finger to your lips to request silence) to communicate with students.

3. *Proximity control:* Sometimes simply moving closer to a misbehaving student will resolve the problem. However, if the behavior continues, it may mean that your nearness is rewarding the student and a different technique should be used.

4. *Interest boosting:* If a student appears to be losing interest in a task or activity, refocus attention immediately by asking a specific question about her progress or otherwise paying specific attention to her work.

5. *Tension reduction through humor:* For some minor misbehavior, try humor. For example, suppose a student who was frustrated with an assignment tossed a textbook into the trash can. Instead of scolding or lecturing, the teacher exclaimed "Two points!" and then went on to assist the student with the assignment. Care must be taken, though, that the humor neither rewards the behavior nor is perceived as embarrassing or criticizing the student.

6. *Hurdle help:* Beginning an assignment can be overwhelming for some students. You can help them begin and avoid

a behavior issue by assisting with the first example, asking questions to facilitate their thinking, prompting them to follow steps, or literally cutting an assignment into parts and giving them one small part at a time.

7. *Support from routine:* Creating more structure in the classroom can avert discipline problems. For example, expecting all students to enter class, sit down, and begin the warm-up work by the time the bell rings may help some students avoid being disruptive. Displaying the schedule or agenda for the day or class (possibly with small pictures or icons to support students who cannot easily read the information) and using clear patterns for classroom activities also can help eliminate disruptions.

8. *Direct appeal to valued areas:* Students sometimes see their schoolwork as irrelevant. If you can identify a meaningful context for assigned work, students may be more likely to complete it. For example, work with decimals can be related to sports statistics.

9. *Removing seductive objects:* When students bring distracting items to school (for example, the latest electronic gadget), teachers usually should hold them for safekeeping. Other objects in the classroom environment also can become a focus for misbehavior. For example, if you set up an intriguing science lab, cover the materials until it is time to use them.

10. *Antiseptic bouncing:* When behavior is starting to become an issue or you see signals that a behavior problem is likely to occur (for example, a student seems to be angry as she comes into the classroom), consider giving the student the opportunity to move to a quiet corner of the classroom or to step outside the room to reduce tension. Doing so will help some students calm down and avoid trouble. Similarly, some students will benefit from being sent on a simple errand that takes them out of the classroom and provides them with a purposeful activity.

Source: Adapted from "Management of Surface Behavior: A New Look at an Old Approach," by J. W. Maag, 2001, *Counseling and Human Development*, 33(9), pp. 1–10.

How Can Functional Behavior Assessment and Behavior Intervention Plans Help You Respond to Serious Individual Behaviors?

When students with disabilities have chronic and significant behavior problems, you are not expected to design and use Tier 3 or tertiary prevention—that is, individual—strategies by yourself. You will find that the Individuals with Disabilities Education Act (IDEA) contains many provisions that guide how teachers and other school personnel should respond to serious student behaviors (von Ravensberg & Blakely, 2014; Yell & Gatti, 2012). These procedures, addressing everything from contacting parents to guidelines related to suspension and expulsion, are summarized in Figure 12.2.

FIGURE 12.2 IDEA Provisions Related to Discipline

IDEA includes several provisions for addressing issues that relate to students with disabilities and their behavior. The following list is a sample of those provisions:

- Parents must be given an opportunity to participate in all meetings with respect to the identification, evaluation, and educational placement of the student and the provision of a free, appropriate public education. This provision applies to behavior problems as well as academic problems.
- School personnel can consider on a case-by-case basis unique circumstances that may affect decisions about a change in placement for a student who violates a school's student conduct code.
- When a student's placement is changed because of her behavior, her education must continue so that progress can continue toward the accomplishment of IEP goals and, for some students, objectives. Access to the general curriculum must be assured, and any behavior intervention plan must continue.
- Within 10 school days of a decision to change the placement of a student because of a behavior code infraction, school officials must hold a special meeting to complete *manifestation determination*; that is, a decision about whether the behavior is related to the student's disability or poor implementation of the IEP. If the behavior is related to the disability, a functional behavior assessment (FBA) must be completed and a behavior intervention

plan (BIP) must be created and implemented. (Details on these topics are included later in this chapter.)

- School officials can remove a student to an appropriate interim alternative educational setting or suspend him for not more than 10 days in the same year (to the extent that such alternatives are applied to students without disabilities) if he violates the school's student conduct code.
- Parents must be notified of all procedural rights under IDEA, including expanded disciplinary rights, not later than the day on which the decision to take disciplinary action is made.
- School personnel may remove a student with a disability to an interim alternative educational setting for up to 45 school days if the student has brought a weapon to school or a school function, knowingly possesses or uses illegal drugs or sells or solicits the sale of a controlled substance while at school or a school function, or causes serious bodily injury to another person. This action may be taken whether or not the behavior is found to be related to the student's disability, and it may extend beyond 45 days if that policy is in effect for other students and the student's behavior is not related to the disability.
- In the case of a student whose behavior impedes her learning or that of others, the IEP team must consider, when appropriate, strategies to address that behavior. The FBA must look across contexts to include school, home, and community.

Sources: Based on *Highlights of New Legislation to Reauthorize the Individuals with Disabilities Education Act (IDEA), PL 108–466: The Individuals with Disabilities Education Improvement Act of 2004*, by J. West, L. Pinkus, and A. Singer, January 2005, Washington, DC: Washington Partners; and *What Every Teacher Should Know about IDEA 2004*, by M. Madlawitz, 2006, Boston: Allyn & Bacon.

In addition, you will work with a team of colleagues to complete a more detailed analysis of the behaviors of concern and to plan, carry out, and evaluate systematically the effectiveness of a range of interventions (Dufrene, Kazmerski, & Labrot, 2017). This legislatively mandated approach, referred to as **functional behavior assessment (FBA)**, is an evidence-based, problem-solving process implemented for any student with a disability who has chronic, serious behavior problems (e.g., Heffernan & Lyons, 2016).

FBA is a detailed and documented set of procedures designed to improve educators' understanding of exactly what a problem behavior looks like: where it occurs, when it occurs, and what function it serves for the student. FBA leads to ideas about how to change the behavior and a specific plan for doing so (Stoiber & Gettinger, 2011). An FBA and *behavior intervention plan (BIP)* must be included as part of a student's individualized education program (IEP) whenever it is needed; these procedures are not only for students whose disability is emotional or based in behavior (Oram, Owens, & Maras, 2016). For example, a student with autism might need these procedures to address her difficulty in transitioning from one school activity to another. It is possible that the professionals meeting about Arthur, the fourth-grade student described in the chapter opening, will undertake writing an FBA for him. For J.R., also introduced at the beginning of the chapter, a team will work to revise the behavior intervention plan because it has not resulted in improved outcomes.

Understanding the Rationale for Functional Behavior Assessment

When a student displays behaviors that are especially aggravating or seem directed at purposely causing a classroom disruption, it is tempting to respond

RESEARCH-BASED PRACTICES

In a study of schools across 37 states, Freeman, Simonsen, McCoach, Sugai, Lombardi, and Horner (2016) found that, despite various challenges, high schools implementing PBIS with fidelity report positive outcomes related to student behavior and attendance.

simply by trying to stop the behavior and get back to the business of educating the student. However, if you do not understand why the behavior is occurring and how to address that underlying cause, the behavior will likely recur.

In FBA, inappropriate behaviors are viewed as serving a function or purpose for the student. Understanding this function will help you identify the actual problem the student is experiencing and decide how to respond to it instead of to the symptomatic behavior (Gongola & Daddario, 2010; Lloyd, Weaver, & Staubitz, 2016). Functions of behavior include avoiding something (for example, assignments, people) or obtaining something (for example, attention, help). Put simply, this conceptualization of student behaviors suggests that before you respond, you should ask, "Why is the student doing this?" Table 12.1 describes in more detail some common student behaviors and their possible functions.

An example can help clarify the idea of identifying the function of behaviors. Daniel is in the sixth grade. When the sixth-grade teaching team meets to discuss student problems, Mr. Adams expresses concern that Daniel often uses profanity in class. Ms. Jefferson adds that Daniel picks fights with other students several times each week. Dr. Hogue agrees that Daniel is having problems and recounts a recent incident in which he was sent to the office. As the teachers talk, they begin to look past Daniel's specific behaviors and focus instead on the function the behaviors are serving. They realize that in one class, Daniel was disruptive when a difficult assignment was being given; in another, the problem was occurring as quizzes were being returned; and in the third, the incident happened immediately before Daniel's turn to give an oral book report. The teachers agree that Daniel's intent has been to escape situations in which he fears he might fail.

Once you identify the function of a problem behavior, you can assist the student in changing the behavior. In Daniel's case, it would be easy for the

TABLE 12.1   **Possible Functions of Student Behaviors**

Function	Goal	Example of Behavior
Power/control	Control an event or a situation	Acts to stay in the situation and keep control: "You can't make me!"
Communication	Convey information to another	Hits head against the desk when tired of the assignment or activity
Protection/escape	Avoid a task or activity; escape a consequence; stop or leave a situation	Has a tantrum at the start of every math lesson; skips social studies class
Attention	Become the center of attention; focus attention on self	Puts self in the forefront of a situation or distinguishes self from others—for example, burps loudly during class instruction
Acceptance/affiliation	Become wanted or chosen by others for mutual benefit	Hangs out with troublemakers; joins a clique or gang
Self-expression	Express feelings, needs, or preoccupations; demonstrate knowledge or skill	Produces inappropriate drawings—for example, of aerial bombings, body parts, occult symbols
Gratification	Feel good; have a pleasurable experience; reward oneself	Acts to get or maintain a self-determined reward—for example, hoards an object, indulges in self-gratifying behavior at others' expense
Justice/revenge	Settle a score; get or give restitution, apology, or punishment	Destroys others' work; meets after school to fight; commits acts of vandalism

Source: Based on "Our Five Basic Needs: Application for Understanding the Function of Behavior," by L. M. Frey and K. Wilhite, 2005, *Intervention in School and Clinic, 40*, pp. 156–160.

teachers to decide on a reward system to get Daniel to swear less in Mr. Adams's class. However, that solution would have more to do with the teachers' need to have well-mannered students than with Daniel's need to avoid the possibility of failing. An alternative approach would be to teach Daniel replacement behaviors (McKenna, Flower, & Adamson, 2016). For example, they could teach him to request his quizzes before the start of class or perhaps to participate in the after-school homework club that includes a group that studies for quizzes. He also could be taught to use words to explain that he is feeling anxious about failure, even by simply asking his teachers for a brief break. He also could be taught simple relaxation techniques. Thus, the question of intervening to address Daniel's behavior has shifted from "How can we get Daniel to be less disruptive in the classroom?" to "How can we teach Daniel and help him use more appropriate strategies in situations in which he fears he will fail?"

This approach to understanding student behavior requires looking for patterns in a student's behavior and describing them clearly in concrete terms. It takes more time and effort, but it greatly increases the likelihood that you and your colleagues will be able to design an effective intervention to assist the student. In addition, you should keep in mind that although many of the students involved in functional assessment and the development of a behavior plan have high-incidence disabilities, this method of addressing behavior was first used with individuals with significant intellectual disabilities, primarily to develop appropriate social and communication behavior. Certainly, this method also can be used appropriately to help students with those disabilities succeed in your classroom. The Case in Practice feature explores using functional assessment for such students.

The following sections present in more detail the process of completing FBAs. The procedure includes these specific steps (Cipani, 2018):

1. Verifying the seriousness of the problem
2. Defining the problem behavior in concrete terms
3. Collecting data to better understand the behavior
4. Analyzing the data and forming hypotheses about function
5. Developing a behavior intervention plan (BIP)
6. Implementing the plan and gathering data on its impact on the behavior
7. Monitoring intervention effectiveness and proceeding to appropriate next actions

Verifying the Seriousness of the Problem

The first step in functional assessment is to determine whether supportive strategies such as those already introduced in this chapter have been implemented in the student's classroom(s). For example, if you have a student who is bullying others, a topic addressed in the Professional Edge feature, your team might ask you to complete a questionnaire about the tactics you have used to address the student's behavior, and a psychologist, special education teacher, or other educator may observe and interview the student. In cases of acting-out behavior, other students also may be observed. The latter approach is used to determine whether the student's behavior is typical or significantly different from that of classmates.

Defining the Problem Behavior

The second step of FBA is to ensure that the behaviors of concern are defined and described in a specific way. Teachers working with students with serious behavior problems often use a type of verbal shorthand to describe their concerns. They may refer to a student as "disruptive," "always off task," or "unmotivated." Although these general statements may have specific meaning to the teachers making them, they are too vague and tend to be too subjective to be useful in addressing the student's behaviors. The alternative is to describe behaviors

CASE IN PRACTICE 12.2

Supporting a Student with Autism Using Functional Behavior Assessment

Mary Elizabeth, a student with autism, just moved to the area. At her previous school, she spent most of her day in the general education classroom with the support of an instructional assistant and a special educator. She was nearly at grade level in math and just a year or so behind in reading.

In her first week at John Glenn Elementary School, however, Mary Elizabeth repeatedly tried to bite and hit staff and students, had several noisy tantrums, and refused to attempt any academic tasks. On two different days, it took two adults to remove her from the general education classroom. Ms. Lieberman, the third-grade teacher, was astonished at this disastrous beginning, especially because she had carefully prepared her other students for their new classmate and had done some quick reading about what to expect of a student with autism.

Within the week, Ms. Lieberman was distraught and became more so when the instructional assistant quit. Mr. Poulos, the school psychologist, quickly called together the team, including Ms. Lieberman and himself as well as special education teacher Ms. Daugherty, principal Dr. Cook, and Mary Elizabeth's parents, Mr. and Mrs. O'Toole. Mary Elizabeth refused to be part of the meeting, but Ms. Daugherty spoke with her individually about the problems and ideas to address them.

The team's task was to complete the FBA checklist included here. Although occasional incidents still occurred, the team was successful in addressing Mary Elizabeth's behavior problems and helping her adjust to her new school.

REFLECTION

Working with your classmates, complete as many items on the checklist as possible (for example, write a definition of the behavior, identify replacement behaviors, and so on). What aspects of the FBA and BIP process seem straightforward? Which seem challenging? If you were Ms. Lieberman, what types of assistance would you request during the transition time as the behavior plan was being implemented? What expectations would you have for all the other people at this meeting to participate in implementing an intervention?

Source: Based on *Functional Behavior Assessment/Behavior Intervention Plan Checklist*, Center for Effective Collaboration and Practice, 2000. Originally retrieved August 12, 2007, from http://cecp.air.org/fba/problembehavior3/appendixa.htm. Now available from https://dpi.wi.gov/sites/default/files/imce/sped/doc/fba-bip-toolkit.docx.

Functional Behavior Assessment/Behavior Intervention Plan Checklist

Student _____ Date _____

Team leader _____ Grade _____

Behavior(s) of concern _____

_____

Yes   No

1. Is the student behavior of concern clearly defined?
2. Have replacement behaviors that serve the same function (or result in the same outcome) for the student been identified, along with the circumstances under which they should occur?
3. Are multiple sources of information available that have been collected from various individuals (for example, teachers, parents, classmates, student)? At least two separate indirect measures and multiple direct measures (for example, ABC charts, scatterplots) that capture multiple occurrences/nonoccurrences of the behavior (and its context) should be in agreement.
4. Does the information gathered by the team indicate a consistent behavior pattern?
5. Is the hypothesis statement written according to the three-term contingency (that is, under x conditions, the student does y in order to achieve z) so that an intervention plan can be easily produced?

Yes   No

6. Is the plan aligned with student needs and assessment results?
7. Does the plan address all aspects of the social/environmental contexts in which the behavior of concern has occurred?
8. Is there a strategy to verify the accuracy of the hypothesis statement?
9. Does the plan address both short-term and long-term aspects of student behavior (and its social/environmental context), including procedures to eliminate reliance on unacceptable behavior?
10. Does the plan include practical ways to monitor both its implementation (for example, checklist) and effectiveness as a behavior intervention plan?
11. Does the plan include ways to promote the maintenance and generalization of positive behavior changes in student behavior?
12. Is the plan consistent with systems of student behavior change and support available in the school?

in specific and concrete terms: "Yesterday during the first 30 minutes of language arts, Michael left his desk six times"; "When I ask Chenille a direct question, she looks away and does not answer"; "Juan talks out three to five times each class period—he does not raise his hand." If several behaviors are identified, it often is most helpful to prioritize the one that should be addressed first instead of trying to design interventions for several behaviors at one time.

PROFESSIONAL EDGE 12.4

Bullying: The Problem and Some Interventions

As noted at several points in this textbook, bullying is a serious problem. Some 21 percent of students ages 12 to 18 report having been bullied at some point at school (National Center for Education Statistics, 2017), whether through being made fun of; being pushed, shoved, or tripped; threatened with harm; purposely excluded; pressed to do things they didn't want to do; or victimized through destruction of their property.

WHAT IS BULLYING?

Bullies generally consider themselves bigger, stronger, more popular, or in some other way more powerful than their victims. Bullying can take several forms and may occur in face-to-face or electronic interactions:

- Physical violence
- Verbal taunts, name-calling, put-downs
- Threats and intimidation
- Extortion or stealing money or possessions

Students who are bullied often are perceived as different for various reasons:

- Appearance (for example, overweight, clothing different than that of peers, presence of a disability)
- Intellect (too smart or not smart enough)
- Racial or ethnic heritage
- Socioeconomic background
- Cultural or religious background
- Sexual orientation

WHAT CAN EDUCATORS AND SCHOOLS DO?

Teachers and other school professionals can help all students feel safe using strategies such as these:

A. Intervene when an incident occurs:

- Intervene calmly but immediately if bullying is observed, possibly enlisting assistance for a colleague or administrator.
- Separate the children involved and make sure everyone is safe; reassure students.
- Meet any immediate medical or mental health needs.
- Model respectful behavior when you intervene.
- Avoid these common mistakes:
  - Ignoring the bullying or thinking students can work it out without adult help.
  - Trying to sort out the facts without time to investigate and analyze what occurred.
  - Forcing other students to say publicly what they saw.

- Questioning the students involved in front of other students.
- Talking to the students involved together—talk to them only separately.
- Making the students involved apologize or patch up relations on the spot.

- Get police help or medical attention immediately if warranted (e.g., weapon involved, hate-motivated violence, illegal acts, sexual abuse)

B. Find out what happened:

- Get the story from several sources, both adults and students.
- Listen without blaming.
- Do not call the act "bullying" while you are trying to understand what happened, but determine if it is bullying.
- Determine if there a power imbalance (e.g., physical, social, verbal).
- Ask if the student bullied is worried that it will happen again.
- If the students have dated, access resources for that particular type of bullying.
- Similarly, gang violence requires different interventions.

C. Support the students involved:

- Support the students who are bullied.
- Listen to and focus on the student, assuring him/her that bullying is not his/her fault.
- Give advice about what to do; try to resolve the situation while protecting the bullied student.
- Be persistent and follow-up.
- Avoid these common mistakes:
  - Telling the student to ignore the bullying.
  - Blaming the student for being bullied. Even if he or she provoked the bullying, no one deserves to be bullied.
  - Encouraging physically fighting back against the student who is bullying.
  - Encouraging parents to contact the other parents involved. It may make matters worse.
- Address bullying behavior:
  - Make sure the student knows what the problem behavior is.
  - Show students that bullying is taken seriously.
  - Work with the student to understand some of the reasons why he or she is bullied.

Source: Adapted from National Center on Safe Supportive Learning Environments. (2017). *Module 1: Understanding and intervening in bullying behavior* [handout]. Washington, DC: American Institutes for Research. Retrieved from https://safesupportivelearning.ed.gov/sites/default/files/sssta/20121108_20120928ClsrmMod1HandoutsFINAL1.pdf.

Collecting Data to Better Understand the Behavior

The third step in FBA requires systematically gathering information about a behavior's occurrence and the situation in which it occurs (Lee, Vostal, Lylo, & Hua, Y., 2011). By doing this, team members are able to judge more accurately whether the behavior follows a particular pattern, for example, occurring during certain types of activities or at certain times of the day. Identifying a pattern can assist team members in understanding the function and seriousness of the behavior in relation to teachers' classroom expectations. At the same time, by measuring the behavior when it becomes a concern and continuing to do so after a plan for addressing it has been implemented, team members can decide whether their efforts to change the behavior have been successful. Sometimes you may be able to observe and record student behavior yourself. However, if this is not feasible, a school psychologist, special education teacher, administrator, paraprofessional, or another professional may help to complete this task. Especially in middle and high school, a specialist such as those just mentioned may be able to contribute valuable insights on student behavior across classes and teachers. Examples of commonly used behavioral data collection strategies include these:

ANECDOTAL RECORDING When you keep written notes of a student's actions or words, gathered while they happen or shortly thereafter, you are completing *anecdotal recording*. One valuable use of this strategy involves recording specific incidents, including what happened immediately before the behavior (antecedents) and what happened as a result of the behavior (consequences). This approach is called an *antecedents–behaviors–consequences (ABC) analysis*. For example, whenever Ms. Carlisle directs the class to form cooperative groups (antecedent), Carlos loudly announces he's not working in groups, gets up from his seat, and heads for the classroom door (behavior). Ms. Carlisle get to the door before him, blocks his exit, and tells Carlos to join his group (consequence). By observing Carlos and keeping an ongoing ABC log of Carlos's behaviors in the classroom (e.g., Carlos complies with Ms. Carlisle's direction, or Carlos changes direction and sits down at a table in the corner of the classroom, putting his head down), Ms. Carlisle has found that whenever the class is transitioning from one activity to another, especially one that is challenging for Carlos, he is likely to state he will not participate and defy Ms. Carlisle. A sample ABC analysis is shown in Figure 12.3.

EVENT RECORDING One straightforward way to measure a behavior is to count how many times it occurs in a given period of time. This approach, called *event*

> **WWW RESOURCES**
>
> At Free Printable Behavior Charts.com (http://www.freeprintablebehaviorcharts.com/), you will find many easy-to-use templates for gathering data on student behavior, grouped by type of behavior to be recorded and age of the student. Also available on the site are charts for behavior contracts as well as charts you could share with parents.

FIGURE 12.3 **Sample ABC Analysis**

Student Name: Denton R. **Date:** 11/12/18
Location: Math—Mr. B **Observer:** Mr. D
Start Time: 1:02 **Stop Time:** 1:15

Antecedents	Behaviors	Consequences
1:03 Students get out books and open to begin class.	D. pulls out his cap and puts it on.	Students around D. start laughing and saying, "Hey."
1:05 Teacher notices D. and tells him to remove cap.	D. stands, slowly removes cap, and bows.	Students applaud.
1:14 Teacher asks D. a question.	D. says, "Man, I don't know."	Another student says, "Yeah, you're stupid." Others laugh.

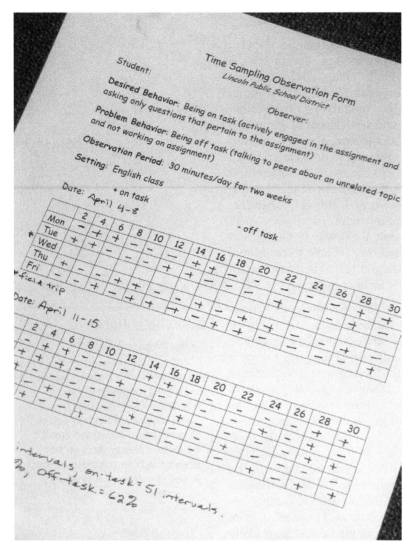

Gathering data about student behavior, often in collaboration with special educators and other colleagues, is essential for understanding it, designing a strategy to address it, and later for determining the effectiveness of that strategy.

recording, is appropriate when the behavior is discrete—that is, when it has a clear starting and stopping point. For example, it might be appropriate to count the number of times John is late to class during a week or the number of times David blurts out an answer during a 30-minute large-group social studies lesson. Conversely, event recording probably will not be helpful in measuring Jane's tantrum or Jesse's delay in starting his assignment, because these behaviors have more to do with how long they last than with the number of times they occur.

PERMANENT PRODUCT RECORDING If your concern about student behavior relates to academics, it may be simplest to keep samples of work as a means of measuring behavior, a strategy called *permanent product recording.* For example, if students in a U.S. history class regularly have to respond to 10 discussion questions during a single class session, you might keep Sam's completed work to document the percentage of questions he is attempting or the percentage of his responses that are correct.

DURATION RECORDING For some behaviors, the concern is the length of time the behavior lasts. The strategy of *duration recording* might be used with a young student who cries each morning at the start of the school day, a middle school student who takes an extraordinary amount of time to locate all her learning materials, or a high school student who delays beginning assignments.

TIME SAMPLING *Time sampling* involves periodic observation of a student. For example, if you wanted to observe whether Patricia interacted with classmates during a 20-minute group assignment, you could divide the time into ten two-minute observations. At the end of each two-minute interval, you would glance to see whether Patricia was interacting at that moment and record your observation accordingly. This system also can help you to observe several students at one time: By glancing at three different students and immediately recording the behavior of each one, you can look at the behavior patterns of each student during a single observational period. The risk in time sampling is that the behaviors you observe at each sampling are not typical of what has occurred until that moment. Usually this is not a problem if the length of the interval is kept brief enough. A teacher who uses time sampling often needs a signal to alert her to observe and record the behavior. For example, she might install a repeating timer app on her smartphone and keep the phone in her pocket. Each time the phone vibrates the teacher gathers data. Time sampling sometimes is most easily accomplished through collaboration with a colleague in co-teaching or teaching assistant.

OTHER DATA SOURCES Functional behavior assessment rarely consists of just classroom observations. Most likely, team members will ask questions about your perceptions of how the student's behavior has developed or changed and your attempts to contact the parents and otherwise address the behavior. Family members may be interviewed, and an analysis of the structure, length, and characteristics of the student's entire school day may be considered, as may the physical classroom environment and classroom climate. The student also is likely to be interviewed; her perspective can add important information to other data gathered (Storey & Post, 2012). Any factor that might contribute to the behavior needs to be explored.

Professionals sometimes say that such precise behavior measurement and exhaustive consideration of the causes of the behavior are not realistic. It is true that you would not routinely have the time to use these strategies. However, when you are faced with a student whose behavior is particularly persistent and puzzling, or the one or two students in a class identified as needing Tier 3 interventions, the time you and the team take to analyze it systematically can give you a clearer picture of how to address the problem and effectively alleviate it.

Analyzing the Data and Forming Hypotheses

At the fourth step in FBA, all the pieces come together. Consider, for example, Kyle, whose middle school teachers had expressed concern about his frequent loud and profane outbursts during class. Conducting five 20-minute observation sessions revealed that Kyle spoke loudly using profanity an average of 2.2 times per session (event recording) during large-group instruction (classroom environment). An ABC analysis illustrated that the talking out occurred when the teacher asked the whole class to read a paragraph in the book, review a chart or graph, or complete some other reading-related task (anecdotal recording). The other students looked at and laughed at Kyle after the talk-outs. The teacher nearly always corrected Kyle, and in just over half the instances, he challenged the teacher's reprimand, saying for example, "I did not," or pounding his fists on his desk and then putting his head down. In an interview, Kyle said that he got called on in class only when he did not know the answer, and he said he knew more than teachers gave him credit for.

In analyzing these data, Kyle's teachers and other team members hypothesized that his talking out served two functions: First, it was a means of avoiding being called on when the question required a reading task, an area of significant academic difficulty for Kyle. Second, it was a means of getting attention from both peers and the teachers. This step in the process is something like detective work. With the data collected, team members try to identify patterns in the behavior, purposes it might serve for the student, and factors that might make the behavior better or worse. In Kyle's case, the teachers recognized that instead of responding to the profanity and outbursts, they needed to address his fear and need for positive attention.

Developing a Behavior Intervention Plan

Once hypotheses have been generated, team members can develop a behavior intervention plan (BIP) based on them (Crone, Hawken, & Horner, 2015; Oram, Owens, & Maras, 2016). This fifth step in functional behavior assessment may include any number of interventions. For example, the BIP might include modifying the physical or instructional arrangement of the classroom (seating Kyle nearer to where the teacher usually stands or using more cooperative groups), changing antecedents (permitting students to ask each other for help while reading the material being discussed), altering consequences (the teacher ignoring at least some occurrences of the talking out), or teaching alternative behaviors to the student (having Kyle record his own behaviors and reward himself for raising his hand). It also might incorporate teaching replacement behaviors, as noted earlier and as explained in this brief video (http://www.youtube.com/watch?v=8uaEXTwCOis), or it could include modifying curricular materials (using fewer questions for which reading is required) or implementing a bypass strategy such as digital text (Gongola & Daddario, 2010). Different types of rewards and consequences that you might specify in a BIP are presented later in this chapter.

MyLab Education

Video Example 12.5: Functional Behavior Assessment

This video summarizes the compents of and steps for completing a functional behavior assessment and behavior intervention plan. https://www.youtube.com/watch?v=Qaz5kcS2oD4

Implementing the Plan

Once the BIP has been developed, you and the team, often including the student, reach the sixth step in functional behavior assessment: implementing your plan. Teachers and other professionals implementing the BIP should monitor the consistency with which they implement the plan; if the plan is not carried out as designed it is far less likely to be successful. In addition, if peers or family members have implementation responsibilities, every effort should be made to ensure that their roles are reasonable, that they understand and can carry out their parts of the plan, and that any concerns they have are addressed (Simpson, Peterson, & Smith, 2011). Throughout implementation, data on the BIP's impact should be gathered so that monitoring, described next, will be facilitated.

Monitoring the Plan's Effectiveness

You began the process of FBA by gathering information about the student's behavior prior to thinking about how to respond to it. The behavior records you keep as you implement the BIP enable you to determine whether the plan is working (Storey & Post, 2012). To proceed with the seventh step, monitoring the plan, you and the team use the same recording strategies presented in the third step of FBA. Remember that behavior does not change rapidly; the team should be committed to following the plan for a specified period of time—perhaps two or three weeks or even more—before deciding whether it is effective.

As you monitor the plan, you may observe any of a number of effects. First, the inappropriate behavior may stop completely or the desired behavior may be displayed consistently. If this happens, you may decide to gradually withdraw the plan. For example, if you are intervening to eliminate a student's profane language use in class and no profane language is occurring, then you can gradually increase the length of time without profanity required to earn a reward and then move to using just verbal praise. This is called *fading out* a reward system.

Second, the plan you are implementing may have value but needs modification. Perhaps it requires too much time to implement or the rewards need adjustment. Such alterations are not unusual; simply modify the plan and continue to monitor its effectiveness. For example, if you created a point system for your tenth-grade keyboarding student that includes earning points for being seated when the bell rings, turning homework in at the beginning of class, and having an assignment notebook and pen in class, you might discover that the system is too difficult to monitor. You might then eliminate the points for everything except homework for a student who chronically fails to come to class on time with assignments in hand.

Third, the plan may not be working. As you track the number and duration of tantrums for one of your students, you might learn that they are occurring more often and lasting longer. When a situation like this occurs, the team responsible for the IEP needs to analyze what is happening and create an alternative plan, again following the steps that have been outlined. If other options do not seem appropriate, a more significant change, such as a change in the student's placement, may need to be considered.

Finally, it is imperative that you work closely with parents as well as your colleagues to resolve student behavior problems. Parents sometimes can clarify reasons a student suddenly is behaving in a particular way (for example, a death in the family, a divorce, an unusually exciting weekend trip, a cultural response to a school activity). In addition, they can reinforce school messages at home and help provide rewards at home earned by appropriate behavior during the school day. Parents are likely to be members of the team completing the functional behavior assessment and behavior intervention plan, and their contributions cannot be emphasized enough. You increase options for responding to student behavior by creating partnerships with parents, even when you may disagree with their perceptions, a topic addressed in the Working Together feature.

FYI

Community involvement can be very successful at reducing student behavior problems. Mentors, volunteers, and safety patrols are among the options that have demonstrated positive results (Green, Xuan, Kwong, Anderson, & Leaf, 2016; Sheldon, Epstein, Hutchins, & Thomas, 2012).

WORKING TOGETHER 12.1
When Differences of Opinion Occur

Few people would disagree that collaboration is essential for working with students with disabilities, and most professionals enjoy their interactions with colleagues and parents. However, collaboration can be challenging when differences of opinion occur. Think about conflicts such as the one described here. Consider role-playing this interaction with your classmates to practice using the suggestions offered.

Ms. Bonnet requests a meeting with you. She is quite upset, accusing you of treating her daughter Taylor unfairly. She says Taylor has told her that other students are misbehaving more than she is but that you discipline only her. Ms. Bonnet wants you to stop and apologize to Taylor.

- It is tempting in this type of interaction to become defensive, explaining that you have been fair and that Taylor is not telling the whole story. Instead, first be sure that Ms. Bonnet has relayed her story. When she finishes speaking, paraphrase what she has said, succinctly summarizing the information without making any judgments—for example, "Taylor has told you that other students misbehave but that I discipline only her." Notice that you are not necessarily agreeing with this perspective, only restating it.
- Try asking Ms. Bonnet for a specific example of what Taylor has described. That may help you to understand more about the situation.

- If Taylor is not present, it probably would be best to leave this matter unresolved and to arrange a meeting that includes her. That way, the situation can be more fully explored.
- As you discuss the situation with Taylor and her mother, ask Taylor what she thinks would make things more fair. You do not necessarily have to agree with her perspective, but it is important to know what she thinks should occur.
- Develop a strategy to address Taylor's concerns, and try it for a week. This might include touching base momentarily with Taylor each day or keeping a record of your interactions with her. Even if you believe that Taylor's accusations are wildly inaccurate, trying to verbally reinforce her appropriate behavior can help to ease the tension.
- Consider the possibility that Taylor may be accurate in her perception. Are you inadvertently noticing her because her voice tends to be louder than the voices of other students? Could you be responding to a cultural difference? Are you especially watchful of her because you know that she has a behavior intervention plan?

Situations that involve conflict can be stressful, but with careful communication and a willingness to consider others' opinions, you can successfully address them.

MyLab Education 12.3 Self-Check

How Do Behavior Intervention Plans (BIPS) Address Serious Individual Behaviors?

The FBA procedure provides educators with clear guidelines for assisting students with significant behavior problems. The strategies that are part of that process usually are carried out across time in a consistent and well-documented manner and include many of the interventions described in this section. They also may involve the use of contracts, in which the expectations for behavior are specified and rewards and consequences are clearly spelled out. The interventions covered in the following sections include increasing desirable behaviors, decreasing undesirable behaviors, and using behavior contracts. Some of these interventions, especially those for increasing desirable behaviors, might be used with many different students. Others are most likely implemented only with students with extraordinary behavior challenges.

> **WWW RESOURCES**
>
> Dignity in Schools (http://www.dignityinschools.org/) is an organization with the goal of ending bias in school responses to students, including suspensions and expulsions, and fostering the treatment of all students with dignity and respect.

Increasing Desirable Behaviors

All students, even those who display challenging behaviors, have some appropriate behaviors you should increase. The primary strategy for increasing appropriate behavior is called *reinforcement*. Reinforcement is any response or consequence that increases a behavior (e.g., Cipani, 2018; Markelz & Taylor, 2016).

It is important for you to keep in mind that reinforcement can increase negative as well as positive behaviors. For example, when a teacher puts a sticker on a student's chart because the student completed his assignment without calling out for unneeded help, the student has been rewarded and is more likely in the future to continue to work independently; a positive behavior has been increased or reinforced. However, when a teacher says, "Take your hoodie off!" to a student who is violating that school rule, the student also has been rewarded, this time by gaining the teacher's attention. The student is more likely in the future to keep his hood on his head, and so an undesirable behavior has been increased or reinforced.

POSITIVE AND NEGATIVE REINFORCEMENT Any time you respond to a behavior with a consequence that makes it more likely for the behavior to occur again, you are using positive reinforcement (Storey & Post, 2017). When you reward a student for appropriate behavior and that behavior increases, positive reinforcement has occurred. For instance, if you tell a student that she may use the classroom computer after she completes five math problems and she completes all the problems, you are positively reinforcing math problem completion through computer rewards. Think about Arthur, introduced at the beginning of the chapter. How might his teacher, Ms. Wright, use positive reinforcement to help him increase appropriate classroom behavior?

Negative reinforcement operates somewhat differently. Suppose you set up a system with your ninth-grade English students whereby they must have their homework signed each night by their parents until they have brought it back to school on time at least 9 out of 10 times. Because students see having their homework signed by their parents as an undesirable consequence, they will increase their promptness in turning in homework to avoid the consequence. Any increase in behavior to avoid a consequence is the result of negative reinforcement (Schieltz, Wacker, & Romani, 2017). Although negative reinforcement can be effective, positive reinforcement usually should be tried first because having students work toward a positive outcome is preferable to having them work under the threat or perceived threat of a negative consequence.

Some professionals object to frequently using positive reinforcement with students. They maintain that general, overly positive praise can negatively affect students' motivation (e.g., "you did an amazing job" when the work was adequate), and they also fear it teaches students they are entitled to a payoff for appropriate behavior (e.g., May, 2017). These professionals contend that students should complete their schoolwork and behave appropriately simply because these are the right things to do, referred to as having internal motivation. Although learning and behaving appropriately because of internal motivation, rather than the expectation of external rewards, or external motivation, certainly is preferable, some students who struggle to learn and behave as expected are simply not able or likely to do so. These students may behave and respond appropriately in school because of internal motivation only when they are extremely interested in a subject or topic or experience repeated success over an extended period of time. Additional strategies, including reinforcement, provide the support they need to succeed in their learning.

TYPES OF REINFORCERS To ensure that positive reinforcement is successful for students with special needs, keep in mind that many different types of rewards can be used. Four of these types are as follows:

1. *Social reinforcers* are various types of positive consequences that a teacher, parent, or peer can give a student to reward appropriate behavior and increase it (Kang et al., 2013). These reinforcers might include a positive phone call home to parents, a pat on the back or hug, verbal praise, or selection as Classroom Citizen of the Month. Social reinforcers, especially clear and specific verbal praise, always should be tried before other positive reinforcers because they are the most natural type of reward in a school environment. If you find

---

DIMENSIONS OF DIVERSITY

Latino students screened and found at risk of developing emotional or behavioral disabilities reported that they believed they were more likely to succeed in school when their teachers were flexible (e.g., with assignment deadlines), provided extra help, and communicated to students a sense of warmth and caring (Balagna, Young, & Smith, 2013).

it necessary to employ other types of rewards, you should use them only in conjunction with social reinforcers. Your long-term goal should always be to have students respond to rewards that occur naturally in their classroom. Note, too, that social reinforcers often should be given privately to avoid embarrassing students, especially those with serious behavior problems.

2. *Activity reinforcers* involve activities such as playing computer games, being allowed to listen to music on a cellphone, having extra recess, helping a teacher in another class, and participating in other coveted individual or group pastimes. Generally, activities that directly relate to a student's educational goals (for example, practicing math skills on the computer) are preferable to those that are solely recreational (for example, playing a noneducational computer game).

3. *Tangible reinforcers* are prizes and other objects that students can earn as symbols of achievement and that students want to obtain. A student who is earning a coupon for a fast-food meal for completing assignments in class is receiving a tangible reinforcer. Putting stickers on papers is another example of this type of reinforcer. When tangible reinforcers are used, the amount must be appropriate for the amount of positive behavior required (that is, small rewards for short periods of relatively simple behaviors; larger rewards for longer periods of more difficult appropriate behavior).

4. *Primary reinforcers* are foods and other items related to human needs that a student finds rewarding. They are much more basic than secondary reinforcers, which comprise the three types just described. Primary reinforcers used in schools often are edible and might include a piece of candy or a piece of fruit. Although you might occasionally employ primary reinforcers, generally you should use them only if a student is incapable of understanding more natural rewards or other types of rewards are not effective. This is important for two reasons. First, the potential negative impact of food reinforcers on student health is a concern, and second, food reinforcers are not a natural part of the school learning process. If you plan to use primary reinforcers, such as food, check with a school administrator to find out about local policies governing their use. Also check with parents, both for permission and about possible student food allergies. Keep in mind nutritional issues as well.

EFFECTIVE USE OF POSITIVE REINFORCERS In addition to understanding the different types of positive reinforcers, you need to know some guidelines for using them effectively. Three principles are key:

1. *Make sure that the positive reinforcers are clear and specific and that students understand the relationship between their behavior and rewards:* The rewards students earn need to be specific. For example, rewarding a student with time on the computer is not precise enough. If it is a reward, the amount of computer time for the specific behavior displayed should be clarified. Clarity and specificity are especially important when you use verbal praise. Saying to a student, "Good job!" is far less effective than saying, "Good job! You asked three other students for help before you asked me."

2. *Vary how much and how often you reward students:* If a student displays very little positive behavior, you may reward it heavily at first just to increase it. As the student learns to use the appropriate behavior more readily, you should decrease the amount and intensity of the reward. For example, if at first you were reinforcing a student with points toward a reward to be selected by the student from a menu of options for every five minutes the student worked without speaking to other students, you might gradually change the reward so the student must work appropriately for seven minutes and then 10 minutes to earn the points.

3. *Make sure a student desires the reward selected:* If you propose to make a positive phone call home when a student participates in group work but the

student does not care what his parents think, then your reward is unlikely to work. Instead the student may be far more motivated to choose three homework problems *not* to do. You can determine your students' preferences for rewards by asking them what types of incentives they like or having them rank their preferences from a list of rewards you provide.

Related to the concept of reward desirability is that of *satiation*. That is, a student who receives the same reward over a period of time eventually may no longer find it rewarding (Contrucci-Kuhn, Lerman, & Vondran, 2006). If five minutes of free time is given repeatedly, after a while the student may come to expect the free time and not work to receive it. When this happens, it is important to change the reward. You often can avoid the problem of satiation by using a *reinforcement menu*, which is a list of rewards from which students may choose. The menu can be posted in the classroom, or students can keep individual lists. Some rewards might be reserved for extraordinary performance. Many websites provide ideas for rewards and other ways to increase student behavior. Some of these are outlined in the Technology Notes feature.

Decreasing Undesirable Behaviors

Many teachers find that some students with special needs have inappropriate classroom behaviors that need to be decreased. These might include aggressive behaviors such as calling classmates names and poking, pinching, and hitting others; verbal outbursts such as using profanity and making nonsense statements during large-group instruction; and other behaviors such as copying others' work and refusing to work. Just as some strategies increase desirable behaviors, other strategies are designed to decrease undesirable behaviors, both based, as noted earlier, on a functional behavior assessment and development of a behavior intervention plan.

TECHNOLOGY NOTES 12.1

Help on the Web for Responding to Student Behavior

The Internet is a valuable resource for information about fostering positive behavior and responding to misbehavior. Here is a sampling of particularly valuable websites:

DR. MAC'S (MCINTYRE'S) AMAZING BEHAVIOR MANAGEMENT ADVICE SITE

http://www.behavioradvisor.com
This website lives up to its name. It offers basic information for new teachers related to setting up positive classroom behavior management systems, strategies for addressing common student behavior problems, examples and explanations of interventions such as contracts and token economies, and links to hundreds of additional websites. This site also provides a teacher bulletin board for posting problems and receiving assistance.

CLASSROOM MANAGEMENT: RESOURCE ROUNDUP

https://www.edutopia.org/classroom-management-resources
The website Edutopia has gathered a lengthy list of resources related to behavior management. To access the list and the hyperlinked sites, search using the term "classroom management resources."

CENTER FOR PARENT INFORMATION AND RESOURCES

http://www.parentcenterhub.org/behavior-atschool/#
This federally funded center includes an extensive set of resources related to behaviors. It explains strategies such as the Good Behavior

Game, a classwide positive behavior strategy, addresses topics such as avoiding power struggles, and provides links and information about functional behavior assessment and behavior intervention plans.

PROJECT IDEAL (INFORMING AND DESIGNING EDUCATION FOR ALL LEARNERS)

http://www.projectidealonline.org/index.php
Project IDEAL was developed to educate teachers regarding working effectively with students with disabilities. Among the modules of information available is one on overall classroom management strategies and their impact on student learning. Another module provides detailed information on responding to student behavior. All the modules, which are complete with activities, presentations, and case studies, can be accessed from the tab at the top of the page labeled "Modules."

YOUTH VIOLENCE PREVENTION

https://www.cdc.gov/violenceprevention/youthviolence/index.html
The violence prevention webpage of the Centers for Disease Control and Prevention contains a special section related to youth violence. It includes a wealth of information on preventing school violence. It includes statistics, strategies teachers and administrators should use, insights on face-to-face bullying and cyberbullying, and links to many additional resources.

Decreasing behavior generally is accomplished through one of these four strategies:

1. Differential reinforcement of behaviors that are incompatible with the undesirable behavior
2. Extinction, or ignoring the behavior until the student stops it
3. Removing something desirable from the student
4. Presenting a negative or aversive consequence

The latter two strategies—removing something desirable and presenting a negative or aversive consequence—are considered *punishment*. Punishment occurs when a consequence applied has the effect of decreasing a behavior. Punishment violates the principles of PBS and should be employed only when accompanied by strategies that increase desired behaviors. Each of the four strategies for decreasing undesirable behaviors is explained in the following sections.

DIFFERENTIAL REINFORCEMENT OF INCOMPATIBLE AND OTHER BEHAVIORS Inappropriate behaviors can be decreased by increasing related appropriate behaviors through reinforcement (LeGray, Dufrene, Mercer, Olmi, & Sterling, 2013). Perhaps you have a student like Patrick in your classroom. Patrick has a severe learning disability. He tends to be very dependent on you for affirmation that he is doing his work correctly; he seems to be constantly at your elbow asking, "Is this right?" To change this behavior, you might want to teach Patrick to set a timer to stay in his seat and then praise Patrick when he works independently at his desk. This technique is called differential reinforcement of incompatible behaviors. You are teaching and reinforcing a positive behavior that is preferred—working independently at the student's own desk—that is incompatible with the negative behavior—being at your desk asking for affirmation (Wheatley, West, Charlton, Sanders, Smith, & Taylor, 2009). You also could decide to reward Patrick for asking a classmate for assistance—that is, by reinforcing other behaviors incompatible with dependence on the teacher.

EXTINCTION Another approach to decreasing negative behavior is extinction. To extinguish a behavior, you stop reinforcing it; eventually, the behavior decreases (e.g., Liddon, Kelley, & Podlesnik, 2017). This strategy often is appropriate when a student has a minor but annoying undesirable behavior, such as tapping a pencil or rocking a chair, which you inadvertently have been reinforcing by calling attention to it or otherwise responding to it. However, extinction is appropriate only when the behavior is minor and does not threaten student well-being. Also, before an ignored behavior will decrease, it will likely increase; that is, at first the student might tap the pencil more loudly or rock more rapidly before stopping. If you respond to the behavior at this higher level (by telling the student to stop the noise or to keep still), you can inadvertently reward the student for the exaggerated behavior through your response. If you think you cannot ignore a behavior while it increases, then extinction is not the strategy to use.

REMOVING REINFORCERS In some instances, you can decrease inappropriate behavior by taking away from the student something desired, a strategy called removal punishment. One example of removal punishment is response cost, which involves taking away a privilege, points, or some other reward (Lee, Penrod, & Price, 2017; Nolan & Filter, 2012). An informal use of response cost occurs when a teacher takes away recess, a field trip, or attendance at an assembly because of misbehavior. More systematically, a student may lose the privilege of helping in the classroom because she refuses to begin assigned tasks. If you are considering using response cost, keep in mind that it is effective only if the student currently has reinforcers you can remove. For example, denying a student access to a special school program will decrease his negative behavior only if he wants to attend the program. Also, response cost sometimes fails because the negative behavior is being reinforced so strongly that the response cost is not effective. For example, every time Laquan uses profanity or makes a rude remark during class, he loses a point toward the reward available to every student: a homework-free weekend. However, Laquan's classmates usually give him considerable attention for his colorful language by laughing, calling out to him, or giving him a thumbs-up. Laquan's use of profanity is so strongly reinforced by his peers' reactions to it that the loss of points is not a powerful enough response cost to cause him to change his behavior. Keep in mind, too, that response cost may be effective with a limited implementation, that is, taking away five minutes of recess rather than all of it. Finally, because response cost teaches a student only what *not* to do, it is essential that you simultaneously teach the student desired behaviors—what she *should* do.

Another removal punishment strategy you may have heard of is time-out, which involves removing a student from opportunities for reward (Bon & Zirkel, 2014; Donaldson & Vollmer, 2011). Many elementary school teachers use a simple form of time-out when they require students who are misbehaving on the playground to spend a few minutes in a "penalty box." The reward from which students are removed is playtime with classmates. Time-out can be used in a number of ways depending on the age of the student, the nature of the inappropriate behaviors, and the student's response to isolation. For example, it may be sufficient in a kindergarten or first-grade classroom to have a time-out chair in a quiet corner of the classroom. When Heather pushes another child, she is told to sit in time-out, where she can observe other students in the reading circle but cannot interact with them. If this is not effective, then placing a carrel on the student's desk or using a screen (possibly made from a large box) around a chair might be the next step. For older students and for those with more challenging behaviors, the time-out may need to be in a location totally removed from the student's class. For example, when Louis swears at his teacher, he is sent to the time-out room, a small, undecorated room with just a desk and chair that adjoins the counselor's office. However, for Cherri, time-out means going to Ms. Eich's room across the hall, where she doesn't know the students.

Several factors must be kept in mind if time-out is being considered as a behavior intervention. First, you should think about an appropriate length of time for the time-out. Generally, it should be brief, just a few minutes for young students and never for an extended period of time, even for older students. Second, time-out is effective only if the student was being reinforced by the activities in your classroom. If the student was not engaged, time-out is unlikely to have the desired effect. Finally, neither the act of taking a student to time-out nor the location of the time-out should be reinforcing. For example, if Jadyn is accompanied by a paraprofessional to a time-out setting located in an empty classroom, but the paraprofessional talks with Jadyn and helps him create geometric patterns on the whiteboard, the attention and activity are likely to be strong reinforcers. Instead of decreasing Jadyn's inappropriate classroom behavior, this poorly designed time-out may increase the behavior.

Time-out, especially time-out that removes students from their learning environment, has become controversial (Bon & Zirkel. 2014; Walsh, 2013). Many professionals note that the negative effects of this punishment strategy on students can be significant and that it sometimes is used excessively and inappropriately (Council for Children with Behavior Disorders, 2009). For example, some students who prefer to be alone may find time-out rewarding. Other strategies that teach appropriate behavior are strongly preferred as an alternative, and some school districts now prohibit the use of time-out.

NEGATIVE CONSEQUENCES The final strategy for decreasing undesirable student behavior, presentation punishment, is the least preferable, because it involves presenting negative consequences to students (Lee, 2013; Mallett, 2016). For example, when a teacher verbally reprimands a student, the *reprimand* is a negative consequence intended to decrease student misbehavior. It is a mild punisher, one of the most common used in schools.

Another type of presentation punishment is *overcorrection*, in which a student is directed to restore a situation to its original condition or a better condition.

DIMENSIONS OF DIVERSITY

Punishments vary from culture to culture. Your students may come from families that use punishments such as shame, ostracism, and physical punishment. Your knowledge of how students are punished at home should help you understand how they may respond to punishment in school.

This strategy is useful when a student has damaged classroom property or otherwise created a mess. For example, a student who scribbles on a whiteboard might be assigned to erase and wash all the boards in the room. A student who writes on a desktop might be required to stay after school to clean all the desktops in the classroom. This strategy can make clear the undesirable consequences of negative behaviors, but it is not without problems. First, the student must be willing to complete the overcorrection activity. In fact, it might be extremely difficult to get the student to comply. If a student refuses to complete the task, a confrontation might occur. In addition, the overcorrection requires close teacher supervision. A student should not be left alone to complete the assigned task, which could translate into a significant time commitment from the teacher.

Physical punishment is another traditional presentation punishment. Although corporal punishment, carried out within specific guidelines, still is permitted in schools in 19 states, most educators strongly oppose its use because of its negative effects (Raskin, 2013; Sparks & Harwin, 2016). For example, punishment often suppresses a student's undesirable behavior but does not change it, and the behavior may recur when the student perceives a chance to "get away with it" or another negative behavior may occur in place of the original, punished behavior. Some students may learn to associate school with punishment, causing them to dislike school or even to avoid attending. Further, when students crave attention, no matter the cost, punishment can increase inappropriate student behavior. Finally, when teachers punish students, they are modeling negative behavior themselves.

In general, then, the message for you as a teacher responding to student behaviors in class is this: Increasing positive behaviors through the use of reinforcers, especially when these desirable behaviors can substitute for undesirable behaviors, is the preferred approach to behavior management. If you find it necessary to decrease undesirable behaviors, the preferred strategies are teaching and reinforcing positive replacement behaviors and extinction. Removal or presentation punishment should be a last resort, used only as part of an ongoing behavior intervention plan and involving a team decision.

> **FYI**
>
> Although not considered an appropriate practice by professional educators, when school districts allow corporal punishment they usually have clear guidelines, including obtaining advance parent permission, specifying how punishment is administered, and requiring the presence of a witness.

Using Behavior Contracts

Using behavior contracts is one straightforward way to apply the strategies for increasing and decreasing behavior. A behavior contract is an agreement between the teacher and student that clearly specifies the expectations for the student, the rewards for meeting those expectations, the consequences of not meeting them, and the timeframe for which the agreement is valid (Bowman-Perrott, Burke, de Marin, Zhang, & Davis, 2015).

Contracts are best used with students like Joseph and perhaps Paul from the chapter-opening vignettes, who are old enough to understand the purpose of a contract and its specific requirements and whose disabilities either do not affect their cognitive functioning or affect it only marginally. However, simple contracts can be used with almost any student. As you review the sample contract in Figure 12.4, notice that it has more detail than some student contracts you may have seen. For students with special needs who have behavior challenges, contracts with less detail often are ineffective in changing behavior.

The original and still most comprehensive information on how to write student behavior contracts comes from Homme (1970). He stressed the following points:

1. The reward that goes with the contract should be immediate; that is, as close in time as possible to the performance of the desired behavior.

2. An initial contract should call for and reward small amounts of the desired behavior. For example, requiring a student to read an entire book to earn a reward probably would be too frustrating a task for a student with a reading problem. Instead, the student could be rewarded for each chapter (or even each chapter section or page) completed.

FIGURE 12.4 **Sample Student Contract**

Student Name: Mia
Class: U.S. History
Teacher: Mr. Lee

I agree to do these things (what, how much, how well, how often, how measured):

Every day when the bell rings, I will be in my seat with my book, iPad, notebook, and a pen ready. During class, I will answer questions only when called on (2 warnings per class for calling out).

For doing them I will receive (what, how much, how often, when):

1 point/day for being prepared, 1 point/day for appropriate class participation. Every time I accumulate 8 points, I may earn 5 extra-credit points toward my course grade.

Outstanding performance will be if I

Keep my contract 5 days in a row (10 points in a 5-day week)

My bonus for outstanding performance is

The option of skipping 1 homework assignment during the week after the bonus is earned with full credit given for the skipped assignment.

If I don't meet the terms of my contract, this is the consequence:

If fewer than 5 points are earned in a week, I forfeit participating in the History Jeopardy! competition the following Monday.

This contract will be renegotiated on

October 19, 2018

Mia   *Mr. Lee*
Student signature   **Teacher signature**

September 15, 2018   *September 15, 2018*
Date   **Date**

3. Rewards should be distributed frequently in small amounts. This approach has been proven more effective than using fewer but larger rewards.

4. A contract should call for and reward accomplishments rather than obedience. That is, it should reward the completion of assigned work or appropriate behavior rather than teacher-pleasing behaviors such as staying in one's seat.

5. The performance should be awarded only after it has occurred. This rule seems obvious but is often overlooked. Students who are allowed privileges or rewards before or during assigned work are far less likely to complete it successfully than those who are rewarded after it.

6. The contract must be fair. The amount of work required of the student and the payoff for completing the work must be balanced.

7. The terms of the contract should be clear to the student. The contract should be put in writing in language the student understands and discussed with the student. If the student is not able to understand a contract, this strategy is probably not appropriate. Both the student and the teacher should sign the contract.

8. The contract must be honest. The teacher should be willing to carry out the terms of the contract as written and do so immediately. In practice, this means that you should be sure you can deliver on the promises you make.

WWW RESOURCES

Would you like to learn more about specific behavior management strategies and access resources to help you implement them? The website of the National Center on Intensive Interventions has collected this information in a readily accessible table (http://www.intensiveintervention.org/behavior-strategies-and-sample-resources).

9. The contract should be positive. It should specify student accomplishments and rewards rather than restrictions and punishments.

10. The contract should be used systematically. If the contract is enforced only occasionally, the result may be worse (or at least very confusing) for the student than not using one at all.

MyLab Education Self-Check 12.4

How Can You Help Students Manage Their Own Behavior?

The strategies just outlined for increasing positive and decreasing negative student behavior rely on the teacher providing rewards or consequences to the student. Another set of strategies, far less teacher directed, involves having students take an active role in regulating their own behavior (Joyce-Beaulieu & Sulkowski, 2015; Sebag, 2010). These strategies are preferred because they promote student independence by giving students skills they can use in many school settings and outside school as well. They have been used with young children and middle and high school students; with students who have learning disabilities, emotional disabilities, autism, and intellectual disabilities, as well as other special needs; and with a wide range of academic and social behaviors.

Cognitive Behavior Management Strategies

In **cognitive behavior management (CBM)**, students are taught to monitor their own behavior, make judgments about its appropriateness, and change it as needed (for example, Knoff, 2012; Meichenbaum, 1977; Zirpoli, 2016). Many elements of CBM were introduced in Chapter 10 as a means of increasing student independence in academic learning and organization. In this chapter, they are applied to helping students manage their own classroom conduct and social behavior in a variety of situations. For example, Paul, the student identified as having ADHD introduced at the beginning of this chapter, might be able to use CBM to manage his own classroom behavior. Two specific CBM strategies are commonly used to teach students how to manage their own behavior. These are self-monitoring and self-reinforcement.

SELF-MONITORING Students learn to monitor and record their own behavior in *self-monitoring*. For example, a student might keep a daily tally of the number of assignments completed or the number of times he waited until the teacher was between instructional groups to ask a question. A student might also use self-monitoring to track the rate at which she completes and turns in homework assignments, level of anxiety and constructive responses to reduce that anxiety, or any other behavior (Farmer & Chapman, 2016; Minahan & Rappaport, 2012). Students with more advanced skills could even wear earbuds to listen to timed signals and record whether they are on task at each sound of the tone. Students also can self-record their nonacademic behaviors. For instance, they can tally the number of times they leave their seat without permission or ask permission before leaving the classroom. Think about how Paul, introduced at the beginning of the chapter, could benefit from such a strategy.

SELF-REINFORCEMENT Another CBM strategy, *self-reinforcement*, often is used in conjunction with self-monitoring. In this approach, students self-evaluate and then judge whether they have earned a reward. For example, Eric might award himself three points for a high self-monitoring score, two points for an average score, and no points for a low score. When he accumulates 20 points, he chooses a reward from his personal reinforcement menu. His favorite reward might be working on a timeline for critical events of the twentieth century. The teacher periodically checks the accuracy of Eric's self-evaluation and self-reinforcement. He earns a bonus point for being accurate in his assessment of himself, even if that assessment is occasionally negative. If Eric has to give himself no points for a low score and his teacher checks his accuracy that day, he receives a bonus point because he accurately assessed his work.

Teaching Cognitive Behavior Management Strategies

Generally, teaching a CBM strategy to a student with special needs involves three main steps, consistent with steps for strategy instruction you learned in Chapter 10:

1. *Discuss the strategy with the student and present a rationale for its use:* If you cannot clarify for the student what the strategy is or how it works, he might not be a good candidate for CBM. To check understanding, ask the student to explain the approach back to you. You can even summarize the goal of the strategy and the rewards and consequences in a contract.

2. *Model for the student what you expect:* For example, you might use an old sample of the student's work and walk through the strategy you plan to use, such as showing the amount of completed work that represents a high score or a low score. Alternatively, you might use a brief role-play to demonstrate to the student how to self-monitor behavior and record it.

3. *Provide practice and feedback:* For this step, the teacher rewards the student for correctly using the strategy until the student is confident enough to use it without such support. If you are teaching a student to use CBM, use reinforcers with the student until she has mastered the strategy. Even after mastery, it is helpful to reward the student periodically for successfully self-managing behavior. This step can be enhanced by helping the student develop a personal reinforcement menu so rewards are meaningful. Parents and colleagues sometimes can assist in implementing this step.

Although CBM is not appropriate for every student behavior problem, it has the advantage of teaching a student to monitor and take responsibility for his own behavior (Niesyn, 2009; Weisz et al., 2017). Because of increased student responsibility, cognitive behavior management is a far more effective long-term

FYI

Think about the INCLUDE strategy. How could you use its steps to guide your problem solving about students whose behavior is disruptive in your class?

WWW RESOURCES

On the website of the Association of American Educators (http://www.aaeteachers.org/), if you click on the "about us" button you will find a valuable resource to guide you in your career as an educator, that is, a set of ethical principles. Reflect on how they should guide all your work with students, including those with disabilities and other special needs.

You could be the teacher that makes all the difference in the lives of your students, helping them to reach their academic potential, helping them to develop appropriate behaviors, and giving them the foundation to lead successful adult lives.

strategy for some students than are more traditional classroom rewards. Students can transfer self-management strategies to other classrooms and teachers and even into adult life. By collaborating with special education teachers and other school professionals, you can design a CBM program that could have a long-lasting positive student impact.

Final Thoughts About Including Students with Special Needs and the INCLUDE Strategy

With your understanding of strategies and approaches for responding to student behavior, you now have the final ingredient for making your classroom a place where students with special needs want to come and want to learn. You know about the foundations of special education and the procedures followed for identifying students with disabilities. You have a strategy—INCLUDE—for guiding your decisions about student needs and interventions that can be embedded within your curriculum and lesson plans. You know about the importance of having the support and assistance of colleagues and parents, whether for planning an instructional program for a student, teaching with you in the classroom, or problem solving when concerns arise. You also understand some of the most important characteristics and needs of students with disabilities and other special needs. You have learned many strategies for helping students succeed in your classroom, including creating a positive instructional environment, assessing student needs, implementing instructional interventions, helping students be independent, and evaluating their learning. And you have learned several approaches for responding to students' discipline, behavior, and social needs.

If you keep that in mind and use the knowledge you have gained, you will positively touch the lives and learning of all the students who call you *teacher*. You will help all your students reach their potential so that they can become productive individuals who contribute to their communities, living happy, constructive, and fulfilled lives. And those former students will remember that you were that special teacher who made all the difference.

Video Example from YouTube

MyLab Education

Video Example 12.6: People with Disabilities Can Succeed

What is most important is the statement that appeared in the first chapter of this text: Students with disabilities and other special needs are children and youth first, and you can be the teacher that makes all the difference in their lives. https://www.youtube.com/watch?v=v4Nq-bLkvP8

MyLab Education Self-Check 12.5

WRAPPING IT UP

Back to the Cases

Now that you have read about responding to student behavior, look back at the teacher stories at the beginning of the chapter. Then go to MyLab Education to apply the knowledge you've gained in this chapter to each case.

MyLab Education Application Exercise 12.1: Case Study 12.1

PAUL is a ninth-grade student struggling in many ways. He currently is eligible for special education as other health impaired (OHI) because of significant attention deficit–hyperactivity disorder (ADHD).

MyLab Education Application Exercise 12.2: Case Study 12.2

J.R. is a seventh-grade student with an emotional disability who is transitioning from a self-contained special education class to a blend of services in general education and a resource class setting. Mr. George, his social studies teacher, is concerned about two problems that are having a negative impact on J.R.'s learning.

ARTHUR is a fourth-grade student with autism who spends most of his day in general education with his classmates and teacher Ms. Collins. At the beginning of the school year, Arthur seemed to succeed both academically and behaviorally, but that has changed.

Summary

LO 12.1 *Positive behavioral interventions and supports (PBIS)* is a systematic approach for addressing prevention as well as the more intensive interventions needed by some students with disabilities or other special needs. By setting clear expectations, fostering respect and communication, and establishing effective teaching methods, teachers can create a positive classroom learning environment that encourages appropriate behavior and discourages inappropriate behavior.

LO 12.2 Group techniques, such as peer-mediated instruction, also can promote positive student behavior. Peer tutoring and cooperative learning help students learn social skills, prevent behavior problems, build classroom community, and enhance student learning. Some students need additional supports and may respond to low-intrusion strategies such as "catch 'em being good," managing surface behaviors, and direct instruction in social skills.

LO 12.3 When behavior problems are serious and persistent, you may participate in functional behavior assessment (FBA) with your team to prepare and follow a behavior intervention plan (BIP) tailored to the student's needs. Such a plan may be part of the IEP if the need arises for any student with a disability.

LO 12.4 A behavior intervention plan may include one or more strategies for increasing desirable student behavior (for example, teaching replacement behaviors, reinforcement of preferred behaviors) or decreasing undesirable student behavior (for example, extinction, removal punishment); it also may be presented to the student in the form of a behavior contract.

LO 12.5 For some students, cognitive behavior management strategies such as self-monitoring and self-reinforcement also can be employed. Such techniques help students learn to manage their own behavior.

APPLICATIONS IN TEACHING PRACTICE

Developing Strategies for Responding to Individual Student Behavior

Ms. Caldwell is a second-year teacher who is very concerned about the behavior of Russell, a student identified as having a learning disability and behavior problems. Russell tends to be the class clown. He makes flippant remarks that border on being disrespectful of other students and Ms. Caldwell. He often is reprimanded for chatting with other students instead of listening and then complaining that he doesn't know how to do the assignment that was just explained. The other students generally like Russell, and they sometimes directly or indirectly, through their laughter, urge him to engage in more classroom antics.

Ms. Caldwell is not alone in her concern about Russell's behavior. Other teachers report a similar pattern. All are concerned that, unless his behavior improves, his troubling behaviors may develop into more serious ones that could jeopardize his learning and his relationships with peers, teachers, and others. Ms. Caldwell's tally of classroom incidents from the last week suggests that Russell was reprimanded at least six times in a single 45-minute period. The reprimands tend to occur when the class is transitioning from one activity to another—for example, from a large-group lecture to an individual assignment.

Ms. Caldwell, special education teacher Mr. Clark, counselor Ms. Lassaux, and parent Ms. Pinelli have been meeting about Russell. The first step in their functional behavior assessment was to think about whether any simple strategies have been effective and about the intent of Russell's behavior. They decide that the behaviors he has been displaying probably have to do with seeking attention from both peers and teachers, but they conclude that current interventions are inadequate. Using observational data from the classroom and interview information from other teachers, the lunchroom supervisor, and Russell himself, they spend considerable time discussing what sources of appropriate attention are available to Russell, and they weigh the pros and cons of various alternatives for responding to Russell's behavior. They also engage in a conversation about the impact other students are having on maintaining Russell's behavior when they encourage him. Ms. Caldwell is convinced that if Russell's peers were not providing him with an audience, many of his problems might take care of themselves.

QUESTIONS

Before you answer the questions that follow, decide the grade level you wish to attribute to Russell—elementary, middle, or high school.

1. What strategies could Ms. Caldwell and other teachers use to address the group response to Russell's behavior? What cautions would you have for them in trying these strategies?

2. What simple strategies outlined early in this chapter could Ms. Caldwell use to help Russell behave more appropriately in class? For each strategy, identify potential positive outcomes that could occur, as well as potential problems.

3. What information about Russell do you think the team gathered? How can this information be used

to help them create a behavior intervention plan? What additional information might be needed?

4. What is an example of a behavior that Ms. Caldwell could teach Russell as a replacement for one of his behaviors of concern? What ideas do you have for the best way to teach it?

5. What types of reinforcement might work for Russell? How can Ms. Caldwell decide which reinforcers to use if reinforcement is the strategy selected? Which types of reinforcers would you avoid in this case?

6. Is Russell a good candidate for cognitive behavior management? Why or why not? If you decided to try a CBM strategy, how would you go about it?

7. How should Russell and his mother be involved in the discussion about his behavior? What contributions could each make?

academic learning time The time students are meaningfully and successfully engaged in school.

academic survival skills Skills needed to succeed in school, including regular and punctual attendance, organization, task completion, independence, motivation, and appropriate social skills.

accommodations A component of special education services comprising supports provided to help students gain full access to class content and instruction, and to demonstrate accurately what they know; for example, digital text and extended time on assignments and tests.

ADA *See* Americans with Disabilities Act.

ADD *See* attention deficit disorder.

adequate yearly progress (AYP) The minimum level of improvement, set by each state, that schools and districts must achieve toward reaching the goals of the No Child Left Behind Act of 2001.

ADHD *See* attention deficit–hyperactivity disorder.

advance organizer Information, often presented as organizational signals, that makes content more understandable by putting it within a more general framework.

alternate assessment A form of functional assessment for students with severe disabilities who are unable to participate in the standard state- and district-wide assessment programs.

alternative forms of questions Testing adaptations that involve changing the construction of a test item or substituting one kind of test item for another. Examples of alternative forms of questions include reducing the choices on a multiple-choice item from four to two or adding a word bank to fill-in-the-blank items.

alternative test site A type of testing accommodation that involves changing the location where a student with a disability is tested to make sure the results of the test are accurate. An example is testing a student with attention problems in a room having fewer distractions.

alternative ways of administering tests Testing adaptations that involve changing the ways students respond on tests and/or the ways teachers give tests. An example of changing the way students respond on tests is responding orally to written test items. An example of changing the way teachers give tests is giving a test orally.

alternatives to letter and number grades Ways to evaluate student test performance using pass–fail grades and/or checklists of student skills.

Americans with Disabilities Act (ADA) Civil rights law passed in 1990 that protects individuals with disabilities from discrimination and requires building and transportation accessibility and reasonable accommodations in the workplace.

Americans with Disabilities Act Amendments (ADAA) Federal law passed in 2008 extending the rights of individuals with disabilities, birth to death, and based on the 1990 Americans with Disabilities Act.

annual goal Broad statement describing estimated yearly outcomes for a student with a disability. Annual goals address areas of identified needs.

annual review Yearly process of convening a team that includes a parent, teacher, administrator, and others as needed to review and update a student's IEP.

anticipation guide Series of statements, some of which may not be true, related to material that is about to be presented during instruction, given to students as a way of activating their knowledge by making predictions about the topic.

assessment Process of gathering information to monitor progress and make educational decisions.

assistive technology (AT) Any of a wide variety of technology applications designed to help students with disabilities learn, communicate, and otherwise function more independently by bypassing their disabilities.

attention deficit disorder (ADD) Term sometimes used as a synonym for attention deficit–hyperactivity disorder.

attention deficit–hyperactivity disorder (ADHD) Medical condition in which students have significant inability to attend, excessive motor activity, and/or impulsivity.

attribution retraining Teaching program that increases student task persistence and performance by convincing them that their failures are due to effort and can therefore be overcome.

augmentative and alternative communication (AAC) Ways other than speech to send a message to another individual, including nonaided communication such as using sign language or gestures and facial expressions and aided communication such as using computers or other simple or complex devices as communication tools.

authentic learning tasks Tasks used in performance-based assessment that are based on real-world contexts and lead to real-world outcomes.

autism Condition in which an individual lacks social responsiveness from a very early age, has a high need for structure and routines, and demonstrates significant language impairments. These characteristics interfere with learning.

autism spectrum disorder (ASD) Contemporary term used to convey the diversity of autism and related disorders, from classic autism that usually includes intellectual disabilities, to Asperger syndrome in which individuals may be intellectually gifted.

avoid giving zeroes Practice of not giving a student a grade of zero for work not submitted in order to lessen the impact of a missed assignment or test.

behavior contract Agreement between a teacher (or other adult) and student that clearly specifies student performance expectations, rewards for meeting expectations, consequences of not meeting expectations, and the timeframe for which the agreement is valid.

behavior intervention plan (BIP) A detailed strategy, developed on the basis of a functional behavior assessment, to address significant behavior problems being experienced by a student with a disability. The plan typically includes detailed descriptions of interventions, persons responsible, a timeline, and methods for data collection. This plan is required by federal law when a student with a disability has significant behavior problems.

bilingual education program Education approach in which students with limited English skills learn core subjects in a separate setting in their native language and spend the remainder of their school day with English-speaking peers.

Brown v. Board of Education Supreme Court decision in 1954 that established that it is unlawful and discriminatory to create separate schools for African American students. This concept of "separate cannot be equal" was later applied to students with disabilities.

bypass strategies Ways of receiving or expressing information that allow students to gain access to or demonstrate mastery of the curriculum in alternate ways. For example, a bypass strategy for a student with a reading disability would be a digitized book.

CBA See curriculum-based assessment.

CBM See cognitive behavior management or curriculum-based measurement.

changing letter or number grades A way of clarifying letter and number grades by supplementing them with other ways of evaluating and reporting learner progress, such as written or verbal comments, logs of student activities, and portfolios.

child abuse Situation in which a parent or other caregiver inflicts or allows others to inflict injury on a child, or permits a substantial risk of injury to exist.

child neglect Situation in which a parent or other caregiver fails to provide the necessary supports for a child's well-being.

chunking Memorization strategy in which students are taught to remember five to seven key ideas at one time.

classwide peer tutoring (CWPT) Peer-mediated instruction in which all students in a class are partnered. Both students serve as the tutor and tutee following a clear procedure, and they are rewarded for demonstrating appropriate social behaviors.

clear written communication Written products used during instruction such as textbooks, handouts, and tests that clearly tie ideas together, enabling students to understand them more readily.

cognitive behavior management (CBM) Behavior management strategy in which students learn to monitor and change their own behavior.

collaboration A style of interaction professionals use in order to accomplish a goal they share, often stressed in inclusive schools.

competency checklist Evaluation technique in which student learning is checked against a listing of key concepts, ideas, or skills being taught.

concept diagram Specific type of graphic organizer used to present vocabulary words that includes definitions and characteristics.

concept map Graphic organizer showing relationships among concepts of instruction as well as essential characteristics of the concepts.

consultation Specialized problem-solving process in which one professional with particular expertise assists another professional or parent who needs the benefit of that expertise; used as an instructional approach for some students with disabilities.

controlled materials Instructional materials at the student's reading level, of high interest and free of complex vocabulary and concepts; often used while teaching students a learning strategy.

cooperative learning Student-centered instructional approach in which students work in small, mixed-ability groups with a shared learning goal.

co-teaching Instructional approach in which two or more teachers or other certified staff share instruction for a single group of students within a single classroom setting.

critical word factor A method of defining text difficulty in terms of the number of words in a given text that students are unlikely to know. Word difficulty is based on word frequency, decodability, morphology, and concreteness.

cross-age tutoring Peer-tutoring approach in which older students tutor younger ones.

cross-categorical approach Instructional approach in which the cognitive, learning, affective, and social and emotional needs of students, not their disability labels, form the basis for planning and delivering instruction.

curriculum-based assessment (CBA) Method of measuring the level of achievement of students in terms of what they are taught in the classroom.

curriculum-based measurement (CBM) A particular kind of curriculum-based assessment characterized by a research base establishing its technical adequacy as well as standardized measurement tasks that are fluency based.

curriculum placement Type of assessment decision concerning where to begin instruction for students.

daily activity log Strategy for providing ongoing information for students and their parents about learning by noting daily observations of student work, effort, and outcomes.

deaf Hearing impairment in which the individual cannot process linguistic information through hearing with or without the use of hearing aids and relies on visual and other input for learning.

deaf-blind Condition in which an individual has both significant visual and hearing impairments that interfere with learning.

developmental delay Significant delay in one or more of the following areas leading to the need for special education and related services: physical development, cognitive development, communication development, social or emotional development, or adaptive development. Applicable only for children ages 3–9.

developmental disability A significant, chronic condition, typically physical, cognitive, or a combination of both, that results in the need for special education and related services. IDEA permits the use of this term in lieu of a more specific disability label for children until age 9.

diagnosis Type of assessment decision concerning whether or not a student meets established federal guidelines for being classified as having a disability and, if so, the nature and extent of the disability.

differential reinforcement of incompatible behaviors Reinforcing an appropriate behavior that is incompatible with another undesirable behavior in order to increase the positive behavior.

differentiated instruction A form of instruction that meets students' diverse needs by providing materials and tasks of varied levels of difficulty, with varying degrees of support, through multiple instructional groups and time variations.

differentiated report cards Report cards that have individualized provisions for students, including additional information to clarify grades and separate grades for different grading elements such as progress and effort.

direct instruction Research-based instructional approach in which the teacher presents subject matter using a review of previously taught information, presentation of new concepts or skills, guided practice, feedback and correction, independent student practice, and frequent review.

disability Condition characterized by a physical, cognitive, psychological, or social difficulty so severe that it negatively affects student learning. In the Americans with Disabilities Act, a disability is defined as a condition that limits some major life activity.

discipline Term to describe the set of classroom expectations, including rules for behavior, that serves as a means for facilitating student learning.

Down syndrome Most prevalent type of biologically caused cognitive disability, caused by the failure of one pair of chromosomes to separate at conception.

due process Procedures outlined in IDEA for ensuring that parents' and children's rights are protected and for resolving disputes between parents and school district personnel concerning any aspect of special education.

ED See emotional disturbance.

Education for All Handicapped Children Act (EHCA) See Public Law 94-142.

Elementary and Secondary Education Act (ESEA) Federal law passed in 2002, also know as the *No Child Left Behind Act*, that has a primary goal of ensuring that all students, including those who live in poverty and who have disabilities, have equal access to a high-quality education.

emotional disturbance (ED) Condition in which an individual has significant difficulty in the social and emotional domain, so much so that it interferes with learning.

English-language learners (ELLs) Students whose native language is not English and who are developing their English skills while in school.

environmental inventory Assessment procedure, often used for students with moderate or severe disabilities, designed to find out what adaptations or supports are needed to increase student participation in classroom and community environments.

evidence-based practice Instructional techniques that have been shown by research to be most likely to improve student outcomes in a meaningful way.

example selection Teacher choice of examples during instruction. Example selection directly affects student understanding of instruction.

example sequencing Order of presentation of examples during instruction. Example sequence directly affects student understanding of instruction.

expressive language An individual's ability to communicate meaning clearly through speech.

extinction Strategy for decreasing negative behavior by no longer reinforcing it; most effective when the undesirable behavior has been inadvertently reinforced by the teacher.

family-centered practices Approach for working with families based on the notion that outcomes are best for students when their families' perspectives are respected, family input is sincerely sought, and families gain information that can assist them to make the best decisions for their children.

FAS *See* fetal alcohol syndrome.

FBA *See* functional behavior assessment.

fetal alcohol syndrome (FAS) Medical condition caused by prenatal maternal abuse of alcohol, often resulting in slight physical abnormalities and learning, cognitive, or emotional disabilities.

fetal alcohol syndrome disorder (FASD) Disorder associated with maternal alcohol consumption during pregnancy that typically results in the baby being small in size, having physical anomalies, and having an intellectual disability.

frame of reference An individual's predisposition to respond to a situation in a certain way based on his background, education, experiences, and work history.

functional behavior assessment (FBA) The process of gathering detailed data on a student's behavior and the context in which it occurs for the purpose of determining the reasons for it and creating a behavior intervention plan. This process is required by federal law when a student with a disability has significant behavior problems.

functional curriculum Instructional approach in which goals and objectives are based on real-life skills needed for adulthood. Examples of skills addressed in a functional curriculum include shopping and making purchases; reading common signs such as exit, stop, and sale; riding public transportation; and interacting with peers and adults.

gifted and talented Demonstrated ability far above average in one or several areas, including overall intellectual ability, leadership, specific academic subjects, creativity, athletics, or the visual or performing arts.

grading criteria The standard on which a student's academic performance is evaluated and graded.

graphic organizer Visual format that helps students to organize their understanding of information being presented or read and the relationships between various parts of the information.

handicap Term, generally no longer preferred, to describe disabilities.

hard of hearing Hearing impairment in which an individual has some hearing through which to process linguistic information, possibly with the assistance of hearing aids or other assistive devices.

hearing impairment Condition in which an individual has the inability or a limited ability to receive information auditorily such that it interferes with learning.

high-incidence disability Any of the most common disabilities outlined in IDEA, including learning disabilities, speech or language impairments, mild mental retardation, and serious emotional disturbance.

high-stakes tests Assessments designed to measure whether students have obtained state learning standards.

IEP *See* individualized education program.

IFSP *See* Individualized Family Service Plan.

INCLUDE strategy A strategy for accommodating students with special needs in the general education classroom.

inclusive practices Term to describe a professional belief that students with disabilities should be integrated into general education classrooms whether or not they can meet traditional curricular standards and should be full members of those classrooms.

indirect instruction A type of teaching based on the belief that children are naturally active learners and that given the appropriate instructional environment, they actively construct knowledge and solve problems in developmentally appropriate ways.

individualized education program (IEP) Document prepared by the multidisciplinary team or annual review team that specifies a student's level of functioning and needs, the instructional goals and objectives for the student and how they will be evaluated, the nature and extent of special education and related services to be received, and the initiation date and duration of the services. Each student's IEP is updated annually.

individualized family service plan (IFSP) Education plan for children receiving services through P.L. 99-457. Similar to an IEP.

individually administered diagnostic test Diagnostic achievement test given to one student at a time, often administered by a special education teacher or school psychologist, useful as a diagnostic measure. These tests provide more specific information than group-administered achievement tests do.

Individuals with Disabilities Education Act (IDEA) Federal education law that updates the 1975 Education for All Handicapped Children Act and ensures that students with disabilities receive special education and related services through prescribed policies and procedures.

Individuals with Disabilities Education Improvement Act (IDEA) Public Law 101-476. Current federal special education law.

inquiry learning The most common method of nondirect instruction.

instructional accommodations Services or supports provided to help students gain full access to class content and instruction, and to help them demonstrate accurately what they know.

instructional evaluation Type of assessment decision concerning whether to continue or change instructional procedures that have been initiated with students.

instructional modifications Changes in classroom instruction that involve altering student content expectations and performance outcomes.

intellectual disability Term sometimes used as a synonym for *mental retardation*.

intervention assistance team Group of professionals, including general education teachers, that analyzes the strengths and problems of referred students to identify strategies to address the problems. If not successful, this team may recommend that a student be assessed to determine special education eligibility.

keyword method Mnemonic for remembering definitions and factual information in which visual imagery is used to enhance recall.

LD *See learning disability.*

learned helplessness Characteristic of some students with disabilities in which they see little relationship between their own efforts and school or social success, often resulting in a belief that they cannot perform challenging tasks.

learning disability (LD) Condition in which a student has dysfunction in processing information typically found in language-based activities, resulting in interference with learning. Students with learning disabilities have average or above-average intelligence but experience significant problems in learning how to read, write, and/or do math.

learning strategies Techniques, principles, or rules that enable a student to solve problems and complete tasks independently.

least restrictive environment (LRE) The setting as similar as possible to that for students without disabilities in which a student with a disability can be educated, with appropriate supports provided. For most students, the LRE is a general education classroom.

low-incidence disability Any of the less common disabilities outlined in IDEA, including multiple disabilities, hearing impairments, orthopedic impairments, other health impairments, visual impairments, deaf-blindness, autism, and traumatic brain injury.

LRE *See least restrictive environment.*

mainstreaming Term for placing students with disabilities in general education settings when they can meet traditional academic expectations with minimal assistance, or when those expectations are not relevant.

MDT *See multidisciplinary team.*

mediation Process in which a neutral professional assists parents and school district personnel in resolving disputes concerning any aspect of a student's special education.

mixed-skill grouping Classroom grouping arrangement in which students are clustered for instruction without focusing on specific skill needs. Also referred to as *heterogeneous grouping.*

mnemonic A device or code used to assist memory by imposing an order on the information to be remembered.

modifications Special education service for students with significant disabilities that comprises changes to *what* the student learns, usually implying that some of the standard curriculum is removed or significantly altered.

multicultural education Approaches to education that reflect the diversity of society.

multidisciplinary team (MDT) Team including teachers, specialists, administrators, and parents who assess a student's individual needs, determine eligibility for special education, and develop the IEP.

multiple disabilities Condition in which individuals have two or more of the disabilities outlined in IDEA, although no one can be determined to be predominant.

multi-tiered system of support (MTSS) A comprehensive, evidence-based approach to responding quickly to students' academic and behavioral challenges; it is based on principles of response to intervention and positive behavior supports.

negative reinforcement A potential negative consequence to a behavior that causes the behavior to increase.

No Child Left Behind Act of 2001 (NCLB) Reauthorization of the Elementary and Secondary Education Act of 1965; this law set high standards for student achievement and increased accountability for student learning and criteria by which teachers are considered highly qualified.

one-to-one instruction Classroom grouping arrangement in which individual students work with either a teacher or computer in materials geared to their level and at their own pace.

oral communication Providing information orally to students such as giving directions, asking questions and presenting subject matter.

oral directions Teachers orally telling students what they want them to do.

organizational patterns Ways in which content area texts are written to reflect main ideas, such as compare-contrast, cause-effect, and problem solution.

orthopedic impairments (OI) Physical conditions that seriously impair the ability to move about or to complete motor activities and interfere with learning.

other health impairments (OHI) Medical or health conditions such as AIDS, seizure disorders, cancer, juvenile diabetes, and asthma that are serious enough that they negatively affect a student's educational performance.

paraprofessional Noncertified staff member employed to assist certified staff in carrying out education programs and otherwise help in the instruction of students with disabilities.

partially sighted Condition in which an individual has a significant visual impairment but is able to capitalize on residual sight using magnification devices and other adaptive materials.

pattern guide A graphic organizer designed to help students organize their written papers.

peer-assisted learning strategies (PALS) Research-based form of reciprocal classwide peer tutoring designed to assist struggling students across all grade levels to learn key math and reading skills.

peer editing Component of student writing in which students review, evaluate, and provide feedback to each other about their written work.

peer-mediated instruction Structured and interactive systems in which students teach each other, including peer tutoring and cooperative learning.

peer tutoring Student-centered instructional approach in which pairs of students help one another and learn by teaching.

performance-based assessment Method of evaluation that measures what students can do with knowledge rather than measuring specific bits of knowledge the student possesses.

planning think sheet Set of questions to which students respond as a strategy for assisting them to help writers focus on background knowledge as well as on the audience and purpose of a paper, in preparation for writing.

portfolio assessment Method of evaluation in which a purposeful collection of student work is used to determine student effort, progress, and achievement in one or more areas.

positive behavior supports Research-based, systemic approaches related to student behavior and designed to enhance the learning environment and improve outcomes for students.

positive behavioral interventions and supports (PBIS) Strategies for preventing behavior challenges as well as techniques for addressing common and intensive behavior problems; PBIS is based on clearly defined outcomes, behavioral and biomedical science, research-validated practices, and systematic approaches.

positive reinforcement A consequence to a behavior that causes it to increase. Also called a *reward.*

PReP (PreReading Plan) strategy Strategy for determining how much background information students have about a topic.

presentation punishment Presenting negative consequences as a strategy for decreasing behavior.

preskill Basic skill necessary for performing a more complex skill.

program evaluation   Type of assessment decision concerning whether a special education program should be terminated, continued as is, or modified.

program placement   Type of assessment decision concerning where a student's special education services will take place.

progress on IEP objectives   A type of individualized grading accommodation in which a student's grade is based on the measurable goals and objectives and progress-monitoring components of the IEP.

psychological test   Test designed to measure how efficiently students learn in an instructional situation; often used to assess intelligence and to determine whether learning disabilities exist.

Public Law 94-142   Education for All Handicapped Children Act; first federal special education law that incorporated many of the rights captured today in the Individuals with Disabilities Education Improvement Act (IDEA).

questioning   Process whereby teachers stimulate student thought and assess student learning.

rate of skill introduction   The pace at which new skills are introduced during instruction.

receptive language   An individual's ability to understand what people mean when they speak.

reciprocal teaching   Teaching students to comprehend reading material by providing them with teacher and peer models of thinking behavior and then allowing them to practice these thinking behaviors with their peers.

reciprocal tutoring   Same-age tutoring approach in which students in the same class are randomly assigned and take turns teaching each other. See also reciprocal teaching.

rehearsal strategy   Test-taking strategy that involves saying information out loud, repeating it, checking it for accuracy, and repeating it again as part of studying.

related services   Services students with disabilities need to benefit from their educational experience. Examples of related services include transportation, speech therapy, physical therapy, and counseling.

removal punishment   Taking away from a student something that is desired as a strategy for decreasing inappropriate behavior.

report student progress more frequently   Strategy for improving parent-teacher communication by reporting their child's progress more frequently than standard report card grading.

resource room   Special education setting in which a special education teacher works with groups of students with disabilities for parts of the school day.

response cost   Type of removal punishment in which a student loses privileges or other rewards as a consequence of inappropriate behavior.

response to intervention (RtI)   An approach for the identification of learning disabilities based on whether student learning progress improves or fails to improve after the student receives increasingly intense, research-based interventions; the latter may be an indication of a learning disability.

same-age tutoring   Peer-tutoring approach in which students in the same class or grade level tutor one another, typically with higher-achieving students assisting lower-achieving students.

same-skill grouping   Classroom grouping arrangement in which all students needing instruction on a particular skill are clustered for that instruction. Also referred to as homogeneous grouping.

scaffolding   Instructional approach for teaching higher-order thinking skills in which the teacher supports student learning by reviewing the cognitive strategy to be addressed, regulating difficulty during practice, providing varying contexts for student practice, providing feedback, increasing student responsibility for learning, and creating opportunities for independent student practice.

screening   Type of assessment decision concerning whether or not a student's academic or behavior performance is different enough from that of his or her peers to merit further, more in-depth assessment. See also universal screening.

Section 504   The section of the Vocational Rehabilitation Act of 1973 that prohibits discrimination against all individuals with disabilities in programs that receive federal funds.

self-advocacy   Extent to which a student can identify supports needed to succeed and communicate that information effectively to others, including teachers and employers.

self-control training   A strategy in which students who lack self-control are taught to redirect their actions by talking to themselves.

self-determination   Providing meaningful opportunities for students with disabilities to express their needs and goals so that their wishes guide decision making.

self-instruction   Strategy in which students are taught to talk themselves through tasks.

self-monitoring   Strategy in which students are taught to check whether they have performed targeted behaviors.

self-questioning   Strategy in which students are taught to guide their performance by asking themselves relevant questions.

separate grades   Differentiating report cards by assigning grades for different grading elements, such as effort and progress.

shared problem solving   Process used by groups of professionals, sometimes including parents, for identifying problems, generating potential solutions, selecting and implementing solutions, and evaluating the effectiveness of solutions.

short-term objective   Description of a step followed in order to achieve an annual goal.

social skills training   Strategies for improving students' social interaction skills through modeling and guided and independent practice with feedback.

special education   Specially designed instruction provided by the school district or other local education agency that meets the unique needs of students identified as disabled.

specially designed instruction (SDI)   Required service for all students with IEPs that is instruction tailored to meet assessed individual student needs; it usually addresses academic skills, but also includes communication, behavior, social, vocational, and functional domains as needed.

speech articulation   The ability to produce sounds correctly at the age where they would normally be expected to develop.

standardized achievement test   Norm-referenced test designed to measure academic progress, or what students have retained in the curriculum.

standards-based grading model   Individualized form of report card grading whereby students are graded based on standards modified according to the dictates of their IEPs.

study guide   General term for outlines, abstracts, or questions that emphasize important information in texts.

stuttering   Speech impairment in which an individual involuntarily repeats a sound or word, resulting in a loss of speech fluency.

supplementary aids and services   Term in IDEA for a range of supports provided in general education classes and other education-related settings that enable students with disabilities to be educated with students who are not disabled to the maximum extent appropriate.

surface behaviors   Initial student behaviors that teachers could interpret as misbehavior. Responding appropriately to surface behaviors can prevent them from escalating into more serious discipline problems.

TBI   See traumatic brain injury.

team   Formal work group that has clear goals, active and committed members, leaders, clear procedures followed in order to accomplish goals, and strategies for monitoring effectiveness.

3-year reevaluation   Triannual process of reassessing the needs of a student with a disability, carried out by a multidisciplinary team.

tier 1 instruction   Instruction in RtI that is evidence-based and provided to all students in a class.

tier 2 instruction   Tier 2 in RtI consists of instruction provided in Tier 1 plus additional small-group sessions that provide extra practice of targeted skills and content covered in Tier 1.

tier 3 instruction   Tier 3 in RtI consists of highly intensive instruction matched to the individual needs of students who continue to struggle, despite well delivered, evidence-based instruction in Tier 2.

time-out   Type of removal punishment in which a student is removed from opportunities for reward. An example of time-out is a "penalty box" for misbehavior on the playground.

transition plan   Document for students with disabilities who are at least 14 years old that describes strategies for assisting them to prepare to leave school for adult life.

transition time   The time it takes a group of students to change from one classroom activity to another.

traumatic brain injury (TBI)   Condition in which an individual experiences a significant trauma to the head from an accident, illness, or injury and that affects learning.

treatment fidelity   Carrying out the teaching practice the same way it was done in the research.

universal design   The design of instructional materials, methods, and assessments that are compatible with a diverse range of student needs and minimize the need for labor-intensive adaptations.

universal screening   The process used in RtI to assess all students in order to identify those who are having difficulty learning despite evidence-based Tier 1 instruction.

visual impairment   Condition in which an individual has an inability or a limited ability to receive information visually, so much so that it interferes with learning.

(NCEE2009-4067). Washington, DC: National Center for Education Evaluation and Regional Assistance, Institute for Education Sciences, U.S. Department of Education. Retrieved from http://ies.ed.gov/ncee/wwc/publications/practiceguides/.

Aasebø, T. S., Midtsundstad, J. H., & Willbergh, I. (2017). Teaching in the age of accountability: Restrained by school culture? *Journal of Curriculum Studies, 49,* 273–290.

Abedi, J. (2010). *Performance assessments for English language learners.* Stanford, CA: Stanford University, Stanford Center for Opportunity Policy in Education.

Abedi, J., Hofstetter, C. H., & Lord, C. (2004). Assessment accommodations for English language learners: Implications for policy-based empirical research. *Review of Educational Research, 74*(1), 1–28.

Able, H., Sreckovic, M. A., Schultz, T. R., Garwood, J. D., & Sherman, J. (2015). Views from the trenches: Teacher and student supports needed for full inclusion of students with ASD. *Teacher Education and Special Education, 38,* 44–57.

Abrami, P. C., Venkatesh, V., Meyer, E. J., & Wade, C. A. (2013). Using electronic portfolios to foster literacy and self-regulated learning skills in elementary students. *Journal of Educational Psychology, 105*(4), 1188.doi:10.1037/a0032448

Aceves, T. C. (2014). Supporting Latino families in special education through community agency-school partnerships. *Multicultural Education, 21*(3-4), 45–50.

Acrey, C., Johnstone, C., & Milligan, C. (2005). Using universal design to unlock the potential for academic achievement of at-risk learners. *Teaching Exceptional Children, 35,* 22–31.

Adams, C., Gaile, J., Lockton, E., & Freed, J. (2015). Integrating language, pragmatics, and social intervention in a single-subject case study of a child with a developmental social communication disorder. *Language, Speech, and Hearing Services in Schools,* 294–311.

Adams, R., Taylor, J., Duncan, A., & Bishop, S. (2016). Peer victimization and educational outcomes in mainstreamed adolescents with autism spectrum disorder (ASD). *Journal of Autism and Developmental Disorders, 46*(11), 3557–3566.

Adcock, J., & Cuvo, A. (2009). Enhancing learning for children with autism spectrum disorders in regular education by instructional modifications. *Research in Autism Spectrum Disorders, 3,* 319–328.

Addy, S., Engelhardt, W., & Skinner, C. (2013). *Basic facts about low-income children* (children under 18 years, 2011). New York, NY: National Center for Children in Poverty, Columbia University. Retrieved from http://www.nccp.org/publications/pub_1074.html

Adlof, S. M., Catts, H. W., & Lee, J. (2012). Kindergarten predictors of second versus eighth grade reading comprehension impairments. *Journal of Learning Disabilities, 43*(4), 332–345.

Agran, M., Wehmeyer, M., Cavin, M., & Palmer, S. (2010). Promoting active engagement in the general education classroom and access to the general education curriculum for students with cognitive disabilities. *Education and Training in Autism and Developmental Disabilities, 45*(2), 163–174.

Agrawal, J., & Morin, L. L. (2016). Evidence-based practices: Applications of concrete representational abstract framework across math concepts for students with mathematics disabilities. *Learning Disabilities Research & Practice, 31*(1), 34–44.

Ahmed, R., McCaffery, K. J., & Aslani, P. (2013). Factors influencing parental decision making about stimulant treatment for attention-deficit/hyperactivity disorder. *Journal of Child and Adolescent Psychopharmacology, 23,* 163–178.

Al Otaiba, S., Connor, C. M., Folsom, J. S., Wanzek, J., Greulich, L., Schatschneider, C., & Wagner, R. K. (2014). *Exceptional Children, 81*(1), 11–27.

Alant, E. (2017). *Augmentative and alternative communication: Engagement and participation.* San Diego, CA: Plural Publishing.

Al-Azawei, A., Serenelli, F., & Lundqvist, K. (2016). Universal design for learning (UDL): A content analysis of peer-reviewed journal papers from 2012 to 2015. *Journal of the Scholarship of Teaching and Learning, 16*(3), 39–56.

Alberto, P., & Troutman, A. C. (2012). *Applied behavior analysis for teachers* (9th ed.). Upper Saddle River, NJ: Prentice Hall.

Aldrich, E. M., & Obrzut, J. E. (2012). Assisting students with a traumatic brain injury in school interventions. *Canadian Journal of School Psychology, 27,* 291–301.

Alesi M., Rappo, G., & Pepi, A. (2014). Depression, Anxiety at School and Self-Esteem in Children with Learning Disabilities. *Journal of The Psychologically Abnormal Child* 3:125. doi:10.4172/2329-9525.1000125

Alexander, R., & Cooray, S. (2003). Diagnosis of personality disorder in learning disability. *The British Journal of Psychiatry, 182,* 28–31.

Allen, J., Gregory, A., Mikami, A., Lun, J., Hamre, B., & Pianta, R. (2013). Observations of effective teacher-student interactions in secondary school classrooms: Predicting student achievement with the Classroom Assessment Scoring System—Secondary. *School Psychology Review, 42,* 76–98.

Allen, Q. (2013). "They think minority means lesser than": Black middle-class sons and fathers resisting microaggressions in the school. *Urban Education, 48,* 171–197.

Alley, G. R. (1988). Effects of generalization instruction on the written language performance of adolescents with learning disabilities in the mainstream classroom. *Reading, Writing, and Learning Disabilities, 4,* 291–309.

Allinder, R. M., Bolling, R. M., Oats, R. G., & Gagnon, W. A. (2000). Effects of teacher self-monitoring on implementation of curriculum-based measurement and mathematics computation achievement of students with disabilities. *Remedial and Special Education, 21,* 219–226.

Alquraini, T. A. (2013). An analysis of legal issues relating to the least restrictive environment standards. *Journal of Research in Special Educational Needs, 13,* 152–158.

Alsayedhassan, B., Banda, D. R., & Griffin-Shirley, N. (2016). A review of picture exchange communication interventions implemented by parents and practitioners. *Child & Family Behavior Therapy, 38*(3), 191–208.

Altarelli, L., Leroy, F., Monzalvo, K., Fluss, J., Billard, C., Dehaene-Lambertz, G., Galaburda, A. M., & Ramus, F. Planum temporale asymmetry in developmental dyslexia: Revisiting an old question. *Human Brain Mapp, 35*(12), 5717–5735. Epub, 2014, July 10.

American Academy of Child & Adolescent Psychiatry and American Psychiatric Association. (2013, July). *ADHD: Parents medication guide.* Washington, DC: Authors. Retrieved from https://www.aacap.org/App_Themes/AACAP/Docs/resource_centers/adhd/adhd_parents_medication_guide_201305.pdf

American Academy of Pediatrics. (1999). *The treatment of neurologically impaired children using patterning.* Retrieved from http://aappolicy.aappublications.org/cgi/reprint/pediatrics;104/5/1149.pdf

431

American Academy of Pediatrics. (2009). Joint statement—learning disabilities, dyslexia, and vision. *Pediatrics, 124*(2), 837–844.

American Psychiatric Association. (2013). *Attention deficit/hyperactivity disorder fact sheet.* Arlington, VA: Author. Retrieved from http://www .dsm5.org/Documents/ADHD%20Fact%20Sheet.pdf

American Psychiatric Association. (2013). *Diagnostic and statistical manual of mental disorders* (5th ed., text rev.). Washington, DC: Author.

Anastasiou, D., & Kauffman, J. M. (2012). Disability as cultural difference: Implications for special education. *Remedial and Special Education, 33*, 139–149.

Anderson, D. H., Munk, J. H., Young, K. R., Conley, L., & Caldarella, P. (2008). Teaching organizational skills to promote academic achievement in behaviorally challenged students. *Teaching Exceptional Children, 40*(4), 6–13.

Anderson, L. B. (2007). A special kind of tutor. *Teaching PreK–8, 37*(5). Retrieved from http://www.teachingk-8.com/archives/articles/a_special_kind_of_tutor_by_linda_brown_anderson.html

Anderson, L. W., & Krathwohl, D. R. (Eds.). (2001). *A taxonomy for learning, teaching and assessing: A revision of Bloom's taxonomy of educational objectives: Complete edition.* New York: Longman.

Anderson, S., & Gurnee, A. (2016). Home-Grown Citizens. *Educational Leadership, 73*(6), 72–75.

Anderson-Inman, L. (2009). Supported etext: Literary scaffolding for students with disabilities. *Journal of Special Education Technology, 24*(3), 1–7.

Andzik, N. R., Cannella-Malone, H. I., & Sigafoos, J. (2016). Practitioner-implemented functional communication training: A review of the literature. *Research and Practice for Persons with Severe Disabilities, 41*, 79–89.

Angelov, A. S., & Anderson, S. L. (2012). On the outside looking in: An African American family's experience in an individualized education plan meeting. *Mid-Western Educational Researcher, 25*(3), 1–20.

Antia, S. D., Jones, P., Luckner, J., Kreimeyer, K. H., & Reed, S. (2011). Social outcomes of students who are deaf and hard of hearing in general education classrooms. *Exceptional Children, 77*, 489–504.

Archer, A. L., Gleason, M. M., & Vachon, V. L. (2003). Decoding and fluency: Foundation skills for struggling older readers. *Learning Disability Quarterly, 26*, 89–101.

Archer, A., & Gleason, M. (2010). Direct instruction in content-area reading. In D. W. Carnine, J. Silbert, E. J. Kame'enui, & S. G. Tarver (Eds.), *Direct instruction reading* (5th ed., pp. 273–318). Upper Saddle River, NJ: Merrill/Pearson.

Archer, A., & Hughes, C. A. (2011). *Explicit instruction: Effective and efficient teaching.* New York: Guilford Press.

Ardasheva, Y., Tretter, T. R., & Kinny, M. (2012). English language learners and academic achievement: Revisiting the threshold hypothesis. *Language Learning, 62*, 769–812.

Arends, R. (2015). *Learning to teach.* New York, New York: McGraw-Hill.

Armbruster, B. B. (1984). The problem of "inconsiderate text." In G. G. Duffy, L. R. Roehler, & J. Mason (Eds.), *Comprehensive instruction: Perspectives and suggestions* (pp. 202–217). New York: Longman.

Armbruster, B. B., & Anderson, T. H. (1988). On selecting "considerate" content. *Remedial and Special Education, 9*(1), 47–52.

Arndt, K., Lieberman, L., & James, A. (2014). Supporting the social lives of adolescents who are blind: Research to practice. *Clearing House: A Journal of Educational Strategies, Issues and Ideas, 87*, 69–74.

Aron, L., & Loprest, P. (2012). Disability and the education system. *Future of Children, 22*(1), 97–122.

Aronson, E. (2005). *Jigsaw in 10 easy steps.* Middletown, CT: Social Psychology Network. Retrieved from http://www.jigsaw.org/index.html

Artiles, A. J., & Kozleski, E. B. (2016). Inclusive education's promises and trajectories: Critical notes about future research on a venerable idea. *Education Policy Analysis Archives, 24*(43). http://dx.doi .org/10.14507/epaa.24.1919

Artiles, A. J., Harris-Murri, N., & Rostenberg, D. (2006). Inclusion as social justice: Critical notes on discourses, assumptions, and the road ahead. *Theory into Practice, 45*, 260–268.

Artiles, A., Kozleski, E., Trent, S., Osher, D., & Ortiz, A. (2010). Justifying and explaining disproportionality, 1968–2008: A critique of underlying views of culture. *Exceptional Children, 76*, 279–299.

Asaro-Saddler, K., & Bak, N. (2014). Persuasive writing and self-regulation training for writers with autism spectrum disorders. *Journal of Special Education, 48*(2), 92–105.

Ashbaker, B. Y., & Morgan, J. (2013). *Paraprofessionals in the classroom: A survival guide* (2nd edition). Boston, MA: Pearson.

Ashbaugh, K., Koegel, R. L., & Koegel, L. K. (2017). Increasing social integration for college students with autism spectrum disorder. *Behavioral Development Bulletin, 22*, 183–196.

Asher, A., & Nichols, J. D. (2016). Collaboration around facilitating emergent literacy: Role of occupational therapy. *Journal of Occupational Therapy, Schools & Early Intervention, 9*(1), 51–73.

Ashton, T. M. (1999). Spell checking: Making writing meaningful in the inclusive classroom. *Teaching Exceptional Children, 32*(2), 24–27.

Assouline, S. G., Colangelo, N., Heo, N., & Dockery, L. (2013). High-ability students' participation in specialized instructional delivery models: Variations by aptitude, grade, gender, and content area. *Gifted Child Quarterly, 57*, 135–147.

Aykut, C. (2012). Effectiveness and efficiency of constant-time delay and most-to-least prompt procedures in teaching daily living skills to children with intellectual disabilities. *Educational Sciences: Theory and Practice, 12*(1), 366–373.

Azad, G. F., Kim, M., Marcus, S. C., Sheridan, S. M., & Mandell, D. S. (2016). Parent-teacher communication about children with autism spectrum disorder: An examination of collaborative problem-solving. *Psychology in the Schools, 53*(10), 1071–1084.

Azad, G. F., Locke, J., Downey, M. M., Xie, M., & Mandell, D. S. (2015). One-to-one assistant engagement in autism support classrooms. *Teacher Education and Special Education, 38*, 337–346.

Bachmann, C. J., Wijlaars, L. P., Kalverdijk, L. J., Burcu, M., Glaeske, G., Schuiling-Veninga, C. C., & . . . Zito, J. M. (2017). Trends in ADHD medication use in children and adolescents in five western countries, 2005–2012. *European Neuropsychopharmacology, 27*, 484–493.

Bahr, K. M. (2015). Special needs: Financial costs and financial planning challenges. *Journal of Accounting & Finance (2158-3625), 15*(7), 41–52.

Bailey, J., & McTighe, J. (1996). Reporting achievement at the secondary level: What and how. In T. R. Guskey (Ed.), *Communicating student learning: 1996 Yearbook of the Association for Supervision and Curriculum Development* (pp. 119–140). Alexandria, VA: ASCD.

Bailey, M. P., & Bauer-Jones, K. (2015). Florida Senate Bill 1108: A case study and analysis of implications and impact. *Journal of Cases in Educational Leadership, 18*(1), 53–65.

Baio, J. (2012, March). Prevalence of autism spectrum disorders—Autism and Developmental Disabilities Monitoring Network, 14 Sites, United States, 2008 [National Center on Birth Defects and Developmental Disabilities]. *Surveillance Summaries, 61* (SS03), 1–19.

Baker, D., & Scanlon, D. (2016). Student perspectives on academic accommodations. *Exceptionality, 24*(2), 93–108. DOI:10.1080/0936 2835.2015.1064411

Baker, J. M., & Zigmond, N. (1995). The meaning and practices of inclusion for students with learning disabilities: Implications from the five cases. *The Journal of Special Education, 29*, 163–180.

Baker, S. K., Kame'enui, E. J., Simmons, D. C., & Simonsen, B. (2007). Characteristics of students with diverse learning and curricular needs. In M. D. Coyne, E. J. Kame'enui, & D. W. Carnine (Eds.),

Effective teaching strategies that accommodate diverse learners (4th ed.) (pp. 23–44). Upper Saddle River, NJ: Merrill/Pearson.

Baker, S., Gersten, R., Dimino, J. A., & Griffiths, R. (2004). The sustained use of research-based instructional practice: A case study of peer-assisted learning strategies in mathematics. *Remedial and Special Education, 25,* 5–24.

Balagna, R. M., Young, E. L., & Smith, T. B. (2013). School experiences of early adolescent Latinos/as at risk for emotional and behavioral disorders. *School Psychology Quarterly, 28,* 101–121.

Balcazar, F. E., Taylor-Ritzler, T., Dimpfl, S., Portillo-Pena, N., Guzman, A., Schiff, R., & Murvay, M. (2012). Improving the transition outcomes of low-income minority youth with disabilities. *Exceptionality, 20,* 114–132.

Balu, R., Zhu, P, Doolittle, F., Schiller, E., Jenkins, J., & Gersten, R. (2015). *Evaluation of Response to Intervention Practices for Elementary School Reading.* (NCEE 2016-4000). Washington, DC: U.S. Department of Education, Institute of Education Sciences. Retrieved from http://ies.ed.gov/ncee/pubs/20164000/pdf/20164000.pdf

Banda, D. R., & Kubina, R. M. (2006). The effects of a high-probability request sequencing technique in enhancing transition behaviors. *Education and Treatment of Children, 29,* 507–515.

Banda, D. R., Hart, S. L., & Kercood, S. (2012). Decreasing disruptive vocalizations of a student with high-functioning autism across three general education classrooms. *Preventing School Failure, 56,* 104–109.

Banda, D., Grimmit, E., & Hart, S. (2009). Activity schedules: Helping students with autism spectrum disorders in general education classrooms manage transition issues. *Teaching Exceptional Children, 41*(4), 16–21.

Banks, J. (2007). *Educating citizens in a multicultural society* (2nd ed.). New York: Teachers College Press.

Banks, T., & Zionts, P. (2009). Teaching a cognitive behavioral strategy to manage emotions: Rational emotive behavior therapy in an educational setting. *Intervention in School and Clinic, 44*(5), 307–313.

Barkley, R. (1995). *Taking charge of ADHD: The complete authoritative guide for parents.* New York: Guilford Press.

Barkley, R. A. (2006). *Attention-deficit hyperactivity disorder: A handbook for diagnosis and treatment* (3rd ed.). New York: Guilford Press.

Barkley, R. A. (2011). Attention-deficit/hyperactivity disorder, self-regulation, and executive functioning. In K. D. Vohs & R. F. Baumeister (Eds.), *Handbook of self-regulation: Research, theory, and applications* (2nd ed., pp. 551–563). New York, NY: Guilford Press.

Barkley, R. A. (2015). *Attention-deficit hyperactivity disorder: A handbook for diagnosis and treatment* (4th ed.). New York, NY: Guilford Press.

Barlow, K. M. (2016). Postconcussion syndrome: A review. *Journal of Child Neurology, 31,* 57–67.

Barnett, W. S., & Nores, M. M. (2012). *Investing in early childhood education: A global perspective.* New Brunswick, NJ: National Institute for Early Education Research, Rutgers University. Retrieved from http://nieer.org/sites/nieer/files/Investing%20in%20Early%20Childhood%20Eduation%20A%20Global%20Perspectivei.pdf

Barootchi, N., & Keshavarz, M. H. (2002). Assessment of achievement through portfolios and teacher-made tests. *Educational Research, 44,* 279–288.

Barrella, K., Besden, C., Crow, N., Greenberg, M., Shrieves, G., Smith, K. A., & Vickroy, M. (2011). Striving to provide innovative orientation and mobility services in times of diminishing resources. *Journal of Visual Impairment & Blindness, 105,* 587–590.

Barrett, H. C. (2007). Researching electronic portfolios and learner engagement. THE REFLECT Initiative. *Journal of Adolescent and Adult Literacy, 50*(6), 436–449. doi:10.1598/JAAL.50.6.2

Barringer, M. S., & Dixon, S. R. (2017). School psychologists. In R. J. Sternberg, R. J. Sternberg (Eds.), *Career paths in psychology: Where your degree can take you* (pp. 469-485). Washington, DC: American Psychological Association.

Bartelt, L., Marchio, T., & Reynolds, D. (1994). The READS strategy. Unpublished manuscript, Northern Illinois University.

Bassuk, E. L., DeCandia, C. J., Beach, C. A., & Berman, F. (2014, November). *America's youngest outcasts: A report card on child homelessness.* Washington, DC: National Center on Family Homelessness, American Institutes for Research. Retrieved from http://www.air.org/sites/default/files/downloads/report/Americas-Youngest-Outcasts-Child-Homelessness-Nov2014.pdf

Bateman, B. D., & Linden, M. A. (2006). *Better IEPs: How to develop legally correct and educationally useful programs* (4th ed.). Verona, WI: IEP Resources.

Bateman, B. E. (2004). Achieving affective and behavioral outcomes in culture learning: The case for ethnographic interviews. *Foreign Language Annals, 37*(2), 240–253.

Bateman, B., Warner, J., Hutchinson, E., Dean, T., Rowlandson, P, Gant, C., Grundy, J., Fitzgerald, C., & Stevenson, J. (2004). The effects of a double blind, placebo controlled, artificial food colourings and benzoate preservative challenge on hyperactivity in a general population sample of preschool children. *Archives of Disease in Childhood, 89,* 506–511.

Baudson, T. G., & Preckel, F. (2016). Teachers' conceptions of gifted and average-ability students on achievement-relevant dimensions. *Gifted Child Quarterly, 60,* 212–225.

Baumann, J. F., Edwards, E. C., Boland, E. M., Olejnik, S., & Kame'enui, E. J. (2003). Vocabulary tricks: Effects of instruction in morphology and context on fifth-grade students' ability to derive and infer word meanings. *American Educational Research Journal, 401*(2), 447–494.

Bauminger, N., & Kimhi-Kind, I. (2008). Social information processing, security of attachment, and emotion regulation in children with learning disabilities. *Journal of Learning Disabilities, 41*(4), 315–332.

Bauml, M. (2016). The promise of collaboration. *Educational Leadership, 74*(2), 58–62.

Bausch, M., & Hasselbring, T. (2004). Assistive technology: Are the necessary skills and knowledge being developed at the preservice and inservice levels? *Education and Special Education, 27*(2), 97–104.

Baxendell, B. W. (2003). Consistent, coherent, creative: The 3 C's of graphic organizers. *Teaching Exceptional Children, 35*(3), 46–53.

Beam, S., & Williams, C. (2015). Technology-mediated writing instruction in the early literacy program: Perils, procedures, and possibilities. *Computers in the Schools, 32*(3/4), 260–277. doi:10.1080/07380569.2015.1094320

Beck, I. L., & McKeown, M. G. (2002). *Bringing words to life.* New York: Guilford.

Beck, I. L., & McKeown, M. G. (2007). Increasing young, low-income children's oral vocabulary repertoires through rich and focused instruction. *Elementary School Journal, 107*(3), 251–271.

Beebe, S. A., & Masterson, J. T. (2012). *Communication in small groups: Principles and practices.* Boston, MA: Allyn & Bacon.

Beebe, S. A., Beebe, S. J., & Redmond, M. V. (2014). *Interpersonal communication: Relating to others* (7th edition). Upper Saddle River, NJ: Pearson.

Begay, R. C., Brown, B. G., & Bounds, R. G. (2015). Disability as a human perception: Personal and professional reactions to American Indian families' narratives about their children's disabilities [corrected]. In C. A. Marshall, E. Kendall, M. E. Banks, R. S. Gover, C. A. Marshall, E. Kendall, . . . R. S. Gover (Eds.), *Disabilities: Insights from across fields around the world, Vol 1: The experience: definitions, causes, and consequences* (pp. 87–106). Santa Barbara, CA: Praeger/ABC-CLIO.

Beigel, A. R. (2000). Assistive technology assessment: More than the device. *Intervention in School and Clinic, 35,* 237–245.

Belser, C. T., Shillingford, M. A., & Joe, J. R. (2016). The ASCA model and a multi-tiered system of supports: A framework to support students of color with problem behavior. *Professional Counselor, 6,* 251–262.

Belt, A., & Belt, P. (2017). Teachers' differing perceptions of classroom disturbances. *Educational Research, 59,* 54–72.

Benner, G. J., Nelson, J., Sanders, E. A., & Ralston, N. C. (2012). Behavior intervention for students with externalizing behavior problems: Primary-level standard protocol. *Exceptional Children, 78,* 181–198.

Bennett, A. (1932). *Subnormal children in elementary grades.* New York: Columbia University, Teacher's College, Bureau of Publications.

Bennett, C. I. (2003). *Comprehensive multicultural education: Theory and practice* (5th ed.). Boston: Allyn & Bacon.

Bennett, M. S., Erchul, W. P., Young, H. L., & Bartel, C. M. (2012). Exploring relational communication patterns in prereferral intervention teams. *Journal of Educational & Psychological Consultation, 22,* 187–207.

Bennett, S. M., & Gallagher, T. L. (2013). High school students with intellectual disabilities in the school and workplace: Multiple perspectives on inclusion. *Canadian Journal of Education, 36*(1), 96–124.

Bentley, J. (2008). Lessons from the 1%: Children with labels of severe disabilities and their peers as architects of inclusive education. *International Journal of Inclusive Education, 12,* 543–561.

Berg, D., & Hutchinson, N. (2010). Cognitive processes that account for mental addition fluency differences between children typically achieving in arithmetic and children at-risk for failure in arithmetic. *Learning Disabilities: A Contemporary Journal 8*(1), 1–20.

Berge, S. S., & Thomassen, G. (2016). Visual access in interpreter-mediated learning situations for deaf and hard-of-hearing high school students where an artifact is in use. *Journal of Deaf Studies and Deaf Education, 21,* 187–199.

Berger, R., & Hänze, M. (2015). Impact of expert teaching quality on novice academic performance in the Jigsaw cooperative learning method. *International Journal of Science Education, 37,* 294–320.

Bergmann, S., & Brough, J. (2012). *Reducing the risk, increasing the promise: Strategies for student success.* New York, NY: Routledge/Eye on Education.

Berkeley, S., King-Sears, M. E., Hott, B. L., & Bradley-Black, K. (2014). Are history textbooks more "considerate" after 20 years? *The Journal of Special Education, 47*(4), 217–230.

Berkeley, S., Mastropieri, M. A., & Scruggs, T. E. (2011). Reading comprehension strategy instruction and attribution retraining for secondary students with learning and other mild disabilities. *Journal of Learning Disabilities, 44*(1), 18–32.

Berkley, S., Marshak, L., Mastropieri, M. A., & Scruggs, T. (2011). Improving student comprehension of social studies text: A self-questioning strategy for inclusive middle school classes. *Remedial and Special Education, 32,* 105–113.

Berliner, D. (1990). What's all the fuss about instructional time? In M. Ben-Peretz, & R. Bromme (Eds.), *The nature of time in schools: Theoretical concepts, practitioner perceptions.* New York: Teachers College Press. Retrieved from http://courses.ed.asu.edu/berliner/readings/fuss/fuss.htm

Berlowitz, M. J., Frye, R., & Jette, K. M. (2017). Bullying and zero-tolerance policies: The school to prison pipeline. *Multicultural Learning and Teaching, 12*(1), 7–25.

Berninger, V. W., Nielsen, K. H., Abbott, R. D., Wijsman, E., & Raskind, W. (2008). Writing problems in developmental dyslexia: Under-recognized and under-treated. *Journal of School Psychology, 46*(1), 1–21.

Bettini, E. A., Crockett, J. B., Brownell, M. T., & Merrill, K. L. (2016). Relationships between working conditions and special educators' instruction. *Journal of Special Education, 50,* 178–190.

Biggs, E. E., Carter, E. W., & Gustafson, J. (2017). Efficacy of peer support arrangements to increase peer interaction and AAC use. *American Journal on Intellectual and Developmental Disabilities, 122,* 25–48.

Biggs, E. E., Gilson, C. B., & Carter, E. W. (2016). Accomplishing more together: Influences to the quality of professional relationships between special educators and paraprofessionals. *Research & Practice for Persons with Severe Disabilities, 41,* 256–272.

Birdsall, P., & Correa, L. (2007, March/April). Gifted underachievers. *Leadership, 21*–23.

Bisagno, J. M., & Haven, R. M. (2002, Spring). Customizing technology solutions for college students with learning disabilities. International Dyslexia Association quarterly newsletter, *Perspectives, 21* 26. Retrieved from LDONLINE, http://www.ldonline.org/ld_indepth/technology/customizing_technology.html

Blacher, J., Begum, G. F., Marcoulides, G. A., & Baker, B. L. (2013). Longitudinal perspectives of child positive impact on families: Relationship to disability and culture. *American Journal on Intellectual and Developmental Disabilities, 118,* 141–155.

Blachman, B. A. (2000). Phonological awareness. In M. L. Kamil, P. B. Mosenthal, P. D. Pearson, & R. Barr (Eds.), *Handbook of reading research: Volume III* (pp. 483–502). Mahwah, NJ: Lawrence Erlbaum Associates.

Blachman, B. A. (Ed.). (1997). *Foundations of reading acquisition and dyslexia: Implications for early intervention.* Mahwah, NJ: Lawrence Erlbaum Associates.

Black, J. (2010). Digital transition portfolios for secondary students with disabilities. *Intervention in School and Clinic, 46*(2), 118–124.

Black, J. B. (2016). *Looking for a quick fix? Controversial therapies in the treatment of language and learning disorders.* Cullowhee Conference—2016. http://www.wcu.edu/WebFiles/Looking foraQuickFix_HANDOUT.pdf

Blain-Moraes, S., & Chau, T. (2012). Challenges of developing communicative interaction in individuals with congenital profound intellectual and multiple disabilities. *Journal of Intellectual & Developmental Disability, 37,* 348–359.

Blake, J. J., Lund, E. M., Zhou, Q., Kwok, O., & Benz, M. R. (2012). National prevalence rates of bully victimization among students with disabilities in the United States. *School Psychology Quarterly, 27,* 210–222.

Blanchett, W. J., Brantlinger, E., & Shealey, M. W. (2005). *Brown 50 years later—Exclusion, segregation, and inclusion. Remedial and Special Education, 26,* 66–69.

Blankenship, C., & Lilly, M. (1981). *Mainstreaming students with learning and behavior problems.* New York: Holt, Rinehart & Winston.

Blatt, B. (1958). The physical, personality, and academic status of children who are mentally retarded attending special classes as compared with children who are mentally retarded attending regular class. *American Journal of Mental Deficiency, 62,* 810–818.

Bloch, M. H. (2017). Editorial: The continuing contributions of multi-modal treatment of attention over nearly two decades to initial attention-deficit hyperactivity disorder pharmacotherapy and long-term clinical course. *Journal of Child Psychology and Psychiatry, 58,* 637–639.

Bloom, B., Cohen, R. A., & Freeman, G. (2012, December). Summary health statistics for U.S. children: National Health Interview Survey, 2011. *Vital Health Statistics, 10*(254). Hyattsville, MD: National Center for Health Statistics, Centers for Disease Control and Prevention. Retrieved from http://www.cdc.gov/nchs/data/series/sr_10/sr10_254.pdf

Bohanon, H., Gilman, C., Parker, B., Amell, C., & Sortino, G. (2016). Using school improvement and implementation science to integrate multi-tiered systems of support in secondary schools. *Australasian Journal of Special Education, 40,* 99–116.

Bon, S. C., & Zirkel, P. A. (2014). The time-out and seclusion continuum: A systematic analysis of the case law. *Journal of Special Education Leadership, 27*(1), 35–45.

Bondy, A. (2012). The unusual suspects: Myths and misconceptions associated with PECS. *Psychological Record, 62*, 789–816.

Bone, E. K., & Bouck, E. C. (2017). Accessible text-to-speech options for students who struggle with reading. *Preventing School Failure, 61*(1), 48–55. DOI: 10.1080/1045988X.2016.1188366

Booster, G. D., DuPaul, G. J., Eiraldi, R., & Power, T. J. (2012). Functional impairments in children with ADHD: Unique effects of age and comorbid status. *Journal of Attention Disorders, 16*, 179–189.

Borich, G. D. (2010). *Effective Teaching Methods: Research Based Practices* (7th ed). Boston: Pearson.

Bouck, E. C., & Flanagan, S. M. (2010). Virtual manipulatives: What they are and how teachers can use them. *Intervention in School and Clinic, 45*(3), 186–191.

Bouck, E. C., Shurr, J. C., Kinsey, T., Jasper, A. D., Bassette, L., Miller, B., & Flanagan, S. M. (2012). Fix it with TAPE: Repurposing technology to be assistive technology for students with high-incidence disabilities. *Preventing School Failure: Alternative Education for Children and Youth. 56(2)*, 121–128.

Boudah, D. J. (2013). The main idea strategy: A strategy to improve reading comprehension through inferential thinking. *Intervention in School and Clinic, 49(3)*, 148–155.

Bowen, S. (n.d.). Daily story problem. Retrieved from http://www.pacificnet.net/~mandel/math.html

Bowman, L. (2011). Americans with Disabilities Act as amended: Principles and practice. *New Directions for Adult And Continuing Education, 132*, 85–95.

Bowman-Perrott, L. (2009). Classwide peer tutoring: An effective strategy for students with emotional and behavioral disorders. *Intervention in School and Clinic, 44*, 259–267.

Bowman-Perrott, L., Burke, M. D., de Marin, S., Zhang, N., & Davis, H. (2015). A meta-analysis of single-case research on behavior contracts: Effects on behavioral and academic outcomes among children and youth. *Behavior Modification, 39*, 247–269.

Bowman-Perrott, L., Davis, H., Vannest, K., Williams, L., Greenwood, C., & Parker, R. (2013). Academic benefits of peer tutoring: A meta-analytic review of single-case research. *School Psychology Review, 42*, 39–55.

Boyle, E. A., Washburn, S. G., Rosenberg, M. S., Connelly, V. J., Brinckerhoff, L. C., & Banerjee, M. (2002). Reading's SLiCK with new audio texts and strategies. *Teaching Exceptional Children, 35*(2), 50–55.

Boyle, J. R. (2011). Strategic note-taking for inclusive middle school science classrooms . *Remedial and Special Education, 34*(2), 78–90.

Boyle, J. R., Forchelli, G. A., & Cariss, K. (2015). Note-taking interventions to assist students with disabilities in content area classes. *Preventing School Failure, 59(3)*, 186–195.

Boyle, J., & Scanlon, D. (2010). *Methods and strategies for teaching students with mild disabilities: A case-based approach.* Belmont, CA: Wadsworth, Cengage Learning.

Boyle, J., & Weishaar, M. (2001). The effects of a strategic notetaking technique on the comprehension and long-term recall of lecture information for high school students with LD. *Learning Disabilities Research and Practice, 16*, 125–133.

Bradshaw, C. P., Waasdorp, T. E., & Leaf, P. J. (2015). Examining variation in the impact of school-wide positive behavioral interventions and supports: Findings from a randomized controlled effectiveness trial. *Journal of Educational Psychology, 107*, 546–557.

Brain Injury Association of America. (2004). *Causes of brain injury.* McLean, VA: Author. Retrieved from http://www.biausa.org/Pages/causes_of_brain_injury.html

Brain Injury Association of America. (2015). *Brain injury in children.* Vienna VA: Author. Retrieved from http://www.biausa.org/Default.aspx?PageID=3597011& A=SearchResult&SearchID=10306192&ObjectID=3597011&ObjectType=1

Brandon, R., Higgins, K., Pierce, T., Tandy, R., & Sileo, N. (2010). An exploration of the alienation experienced by African American Parents from their children's educational environment. *Remedial and Special Education, 31*, 208–222.

Brandwein, P. F., & Bauer, N. W. (1980). *The United States, living in our world: Research, evaluation, and writing.* Barton R. Clark et al., consulting social scientists. San Francisco and New York: Center for the Study of Instruction/Harcourt Brace Jovanovich.

Briesch, A. M., Ferguson, T. D., Volpe, R. J., & Briesch, J. M. (2012). Examining teachers' perceptions of social-emotional and behavioral referral concerns. *Remedial and Special Education, 34*(4), 249–256.

Brigandi, C. B., Siegle, D., Weiner, J. M., Gubbins, E. J., & Little, C. A. (2016). Gifted secondary school students: The perceived relationship between enrichment and goal valuation. *Journal for the Education of the Gifted, 39*, 263–287.

Brimijoin, K., Marquisse, E., & Tomlinson, C. A. (2003). Using data to differentiate instruction. *Educational Leadership, 60*(5), 70–73.

Brock, M. E., Biggs, E. E., Carter, E. W., Cattey, G. N., & Raley, K. S. (2016). Implementation and generalization of peer support arrangements for students with severe disabilities in inclusive classrooms. *Journal of Special Education, 49*, 221–232.

Broderick, A., Mehta-Parekh, H., & Reid, D. K. (2005). Differentiating instruction for disabled students in inclusive classrooms. *Theory into Practice, 44*(3), 194–202.

Brooke, V., Revell, G., & Wehman, P. (2009). Quality indicators for competitive employment outcomes: What special education teachers need to know in transition planning. *Teaching Exceptional Children, 41*(4), 58–66.

Brookhart, S. M. (2017). *How to use grading to improve learning.* Alexandria, Va.: ASCD.

Browder, D. M., Wakeman, S. Y., & Flowers, C. (2006). Assessment of progress in the general curriculum for students with disabilities. *Theory into Practice, 45*(3), 249–259.

Browder, D. M., Wakeman, S. Y., Spooner, F., Ahlgrin-Delzell, L., & Algozzine, B. (2006). Research on reading instruction for individuals with significant cognitive disabilities. *Exceptional Children, 72*, 392–408.

Brown, D., Pryzwansky, W. B., & Schulte, A. C. (2013). *Psychological consultation and collaboration: Introduction to theory and practice* (7th ed.). Upper Saddle River, NJ: Pearson/Merrill.

Brownell, M. T., Smith, S. J., Crockett, J. B., & Griffin, C. C. (2012). *Inclusive instruction: Evidence-based practices for teaching students with disabilities* [What Works for Special-Needs Learners Series]. New York, NY: Guilford.

Brownstein, R. (2010). Pushed out. Education Digest: Essential Readings Condensed for Quick Review, 75(7), 23–27.

Bryan, R. R., McCubbin, J. A., & van der Mars, H. (2013). The ambiguous role of the paraeducator in the general physical education environment. *Adapted Physical Activity Quarterly, 30*, 164–183.

Bryan, T. (2005). Science-based advances in the social domain of learning disabilities. *Learning Disability Quarterly, 28*(2), 119–121.

Bryan, T. H., & Bryan, J. H. (1986). *Understanding learning disabilities* (3rd ed.). Palo Alto, CA: Mayfield.

Bryan, T., Burstein, K., & Bryan, J. (2001). Students with learning disabilities: Homework problems and promising practices. *Educational Psychologist, 36*(3), 167–180.

Buchanan, R., Nese, R. T., & Clark, M. (2016). Stakeholders' voices: Defining needs of students with emotional and behavioral disorders transitioning between school settings. *Behavioral Disorders, 41*, 135–147.

Bulgren, J., Deshler, D. D., & Lenz, K. (2007). Engaging adolescents with LD in higher order thinking about history concepts using integrated content enhancement routines. *Journal of Learning Disabilities, 40*(2), 121–133.

Bullara, D. T. (1993). Classroom management strategies to reduce racially biased treatment of students. *Journal of Educational and Psychological Consultation, 4*(4), 357–368.

Burdette, P. (2012). *Principal preparedness to support students with disabilities and other diverse learners: A Policy Forum proceedings document.* Alexandria, VA: National Association of State Directors of Special Education, Project Forum.

Burny, E., Valcke, M., & Desoete, A. (2012). Clock reading: An under-estimated topic in children with mathematics difficulties. *Journal of Learning Disabilities, 45*(4), 351–360.

Burris, C. C., Heubert, J. P., & Levin, H. M. (2006). Accelerating mathematics achievement using heterogeneous grouping. *American Educational Research Journal, 43*, 105–136.

Bursuck, W. D., & Blanks, B (2010). Evidence-based early reading practices within a response to intervention system. *Psychology in the Schools, 47*(5), 421–431.

Bursuck, W. D., & Damer, M. (2015). *Teaching reading to students who are at-risk or have disabilities: A multi-tier approach* (3rd ed.). Upper Saddle River, NJ: Pearson Education.

Bursuck, W. D., & Lessen, E. (1987). A classroom-based model for assessing students with learning disabilities. *Learning Disabilities Focus, 3*(1), 17–29.

Bursuck, W. D., Harniss, M. K., Epstein, M. H., Polloway, E. A., Jayanthi, M., & Wissinger, L. M. (1999). Solving communication problems about homework: Recommendations of special education teachers. *Learning Disabilities Research and Practice, 14*, 149–158.

Bursuck, W. D., Smith, T., Munk, D., Damer, M., Mehlig, L., & Perry, J. (2004). Evaluating the impact of a prevention-based model of reading on children who are at risk. *Remedial and Special Education, 25*, 303–313.

Burton, C. E., Anderson, D. H., Prater, M., & Dyches, T. T. (2013). Video self-modeling on an iPad to teach functional math skills to adolescents with autism and intellectual disability. *Focus on Autism and Other Developmental Disabilities, 28*, 67–77.

Bushaw, W. J., & Lopez, S. J. (2012). Public education in the United States: A nation divided. *Phi Delta Kappan, 94*, 8–25.

Butler, D. L., & Schnellert, L. (2012). Collaborative inquiry in teacher professional development. *Teaching and Teacher Education: An International Journal of Research and Studies, 28*, 1206–1220.

Byrd, E. (2011). Educating and involving parents in the response to intervention process: The school's important role. *Teaching Exceptional Children, 43*(3), 32–39.

Byrnes, M. (2008a). Educators' interpretations of ambiguous accommodations. *Remedial and Special Education, 29*(5), 306–315.

Byrnes, M. (2008b). Writing explicit, unambiguous accommodations. *Intervention in School and Clinic, 44*(1), 18–24.

Calhoon, M. B., & Fuchs, L. S. (2003). The effects of peer-assisted learning strategies and curriculum-based measurement on the mathematics performance of secondary students with disabilities. *Remedial and Special Education, 24*, 235–245.

Callahan, C. M., (2005). Identifying gifted students from underrepresented populations. *Theory into Practice, 44*, 98–104.

Cambria, J., & Guthrie, J. T. (2010). Motivating and engaging students in reading. *The NERA Journal, 46*(1), 16–29.

Cameron, D. L., & Cook, B. G. (2013). General education teachers' goals and expectations for their included students with mild and severe disabilities. *Education and Training in Autism and Developmental Disabilities, 48*, 18–30.

Capio, M., Swanlund, L., & Kelly, M. S. (2016). School social workers and the prereferral process: Problem-solving teams and data-driven decision making. In C. Rippey Massat, M. S. Kelly, R. Constable, C. Rippey Massat, M. S. Kelly, R. Constable (Eds.), *School social work: Practice, policy, and research* (pp. 239–268). Chicago, IL: Lyceum Books.

Carey, T., & Carifio, J. (2012). The minimum grading controversy: Results of a quantitative study of seven years of grading data from an urban high school. *Educational Researcher, 41*(6), 201–208.

Carlo, M. S., August, D., Mclaughlin, B., Snow, C. E., Dressler, C., Lippman, D. N., Lively, T. J., & White, C. E. (2004). Closing the gap: Addressing the vocabulary needs of English-language learners in bilingual and main-stream classrooms. *Reading Research Quarterly, 39*, 188–215.

Carlson, C., & Henning, M. (1993). The TAG peer editing procedure. Unpublished manuscript, Northern Illinois University.

Carlson, J. S., Maupin, A., & Brinkman, T. (2010). Recent advances in the medical management of children with attention deficit/hyperactivity disorder. In P. C. McCabe & S. R. Shaw (Eds.), *Psychiatric disorders: Current topics and interventions for educators* (pp. 71–80). Thousand Oaks, CA: Corwin.

Carnahan, C. R., Williamson, P., Clarke, L., & Sorensen, R. (2009). A systematic approach for supporting paraeducators in educational settings: A guide for teachers. *Teaching Exceptional Children, 41*(5), 34–43.

Carnes, S. L., & Quinn, W. H. (2005). Family adaptation for brain injury: Coping and psychological distress. *Families, Systems, and Health, 23*, 186–203.

Carney, R. N., Levin, M. E., & Levin, J. R. (1993). Mnemonic strategies: Instructional techniques worth remembering. *Teaching Exceptional Children, 25*(4), 24–30.

Carnine, D. W. (1981). High and low implementation of direct instruction teaching techniques. *Education and Treatment of Children, 4*, 42–51.

Carnine, D. W., Silbert, J., Kame'enui, E. J., & Tarver, S. G. (2010). *Direct instruction reading* (5th ed.). Upper Saddle River, NJ: Merrill/Pearson.

Carpenter, L. B., Johnston, L. B., & Beard, L. A. (2015). *Assistive technology: Access for all students* (3rd ed.). Boston: Pearson.

Carter Andrews, D. J., & Gutwein, M. (2017). "Maybe that concept is still with us": Adolescents' racialized and classed perceptions of teachers' expectations. *Multicultural Perspectives, 19*(1), 5–15.

Carter, E. W., & Wehby, J. H. (2003). Job performance of transition-age youth with emotional and behavioral disorders. *Exceptional Children, 69*, 449–465.

Carter, E. W., Asmus, J., Moss, C. K., Biggs, E. E., Bolt, D. M., Born, T. L., & . . . Weir, K. (2016). Randomized evaluation of peer support arrangements to support the inclusion of high school students with severe disabilities. *Exceptional Children, 82*, 209–233.

Carter, E. W., Lane, K., Cooney, M., Weir, K., Moss, C. K., & Machalicek, W. (2013). Parent assessments of self-determination importance and performance for students with autism or intellectual disability. *American Journal on Intellectual and Developmental Disabilities, 118*, 16–31.

Carter, E. W., Moss, C. K., Asmus, J., Fesperman, E., Cooney, M., Brock, M. E., & ... Vincent, L. B. (2015). Promoting inclusion, social connections, and learning through peer support arrangements. *Teaching Exceptional Children, 48*(1), 9–18.

Carter, E. W., Moss, C. K., Hoffman, A., Chung, Y., & Sisco, L. (2011). Efficacy and social validity of peer support arrangements for adolescents with disabilities. *Exceptional Children, 78*, 107–125.

Carter, E. W., Swedeen, B., & Moss, C. K. (2012). Engaging youth with and without significant disabilities in inclusive service learning. *Teaching Exceptional Children, 44*(5), 46–54.

Carter, E., O'Rourke, L., Sisco, L., & Pelsue, D. (2009). Knowledge, responsibilities, and training needs of paraprofessionals in elementary and secondary schools. *Remedial and Special Education, 30,* 344–359.

Cartledge, G., & Kourea, L. (2008). Culturally responsive classrooms for culturally diverse students with and at risk for disabilities. *Exceptional Children, 74,* 351–371.

Cartledge, G., Kea, C. D., Watson, M., & Oif, A. (2016). Special education disproportionality: A review of response to intervention and culturally relevant pedagogy. *Multiple Voices for Ethnically Diverse Exceptional Learners, 16,* 29–49.

Casanova, U., & Berliner, D. (1986). Should students be made test-wise? *Instructor 95*(6), 22–23.

Cass, M., Cates, D., Smith, M., & Jackson, C. (2003). Effects of manipulative instruction on solving area and perimeter problems by students with learning disabilities. *Learning Disabilities Research & Practice, 18*(2), 112–120.

Cassidy, S. (2004) Learning Styles: An overview of theories, models, and measures. *Educational Psychology, 24*(4), 419–444, DOI: 10.1080/0144341042000228834

Castillo, J. M., March, A. L., Tan, S. Y., Stockslager, K. M., Brundage, A., Mccullough, M., & Sabnis, S. (2016). Relationships between ongoing professional development and educators' perceived skills relative to Rtl. *Psychology in the Schools, 53,* 893–910.

Castro-Villarreal, F., Villarreal, V., & Sullivan, J. R. (2016). Special education policy and response to intervention: Identifying promises and pitfalls to advance social justice for diverse students. *Contemporary School Psychology, 20,* 10–20.

Catts, H. W., & Kamhi, A. G. (2011). *Language and reading disabilities.* (3rd ed.). Boston: Allyn and Bacon (Pearson).

Causton, J., & Theoharis, G. (2013). Inclusive schooling: Are we there yet? *School Administrator, 70*(2), 19–25.

Causton-Theoharis, J. (2014). *The paraprofessional's handbook for effective support in inclusive classrooms.* Baltimore, MD: Paul H. Brookes.

Causton-Theoharis, J. N. (2009). The golden rule of providing support in inclusive classrooms: Support others as you would wish to be supported. *Teaching Exceptional Children, 42*(2), 36–43.

Causton-Theoharis, J., Theoharis, G., Bull, T., Cosier, M., & Dempf-Aldrich, K. (2011). Schools of promise: A school district-university partnership centered on inclusive school reform. *Remedial and Special Education, 32,* 192–205.

Causton-Theoharis, J., Theoharis, G., Orsati, F., & Cosier, M. (2011). Does self-contained special education deliver on its promises? A critical inquiry into research and practice. *Journal of Special Education Leadership, 24*(2), 61–78.

Cavanagh, S. (2014). What is personalized learning? Educators seeking clarity. *Education Week.* Retrieved from www.edweek.org/ew/articles/2014/10/22/09p1-overview.h34.html

Cavilla, D. (2017). Observation and analysis of three gifted underachievers in an underserved, urban high school setting. *Gifted Education International, 33*(1), 62–75.

Cawley, J., Hayden, S., Cade, E., & Baker-Kroczynski, S. (2002). Including students with disabilities into the general education science classroom. *Exceptional Children, 68,* 423–436.

Cawley, J. F., Parmar, R., Foley, T. E., Salmon, S., & Roy, S. (2001). Arithmetic performance of students: Implications for curriculum. *Learning Disabilities Research & Practice, 13*(2), 311–328.

Celce-Murcia, M. (2000). *Discourse and context in language teaching: A guide for language teachers.* New York: Cambridge University Press.

Center for Appropriate Dispute Resolution in Special Education (CADRE). (2014, January). *IDEA special education due process complaints/hearing requests: Including expedited hearing requests. A guide for parents of children & youth (ages 3–21).* Center for Appropriate Dispute Resolution in Special Education (CADRE). Eugene, OR: Author. Retrieved from http://files.eric.ed.gov/fulltext/ED555851.pdf

Center for Appropriate Dispute Resolution in Special Education (CADRE). (2013 April). Fundamental attributes of exemplary state special education dispute resolution systems. Eugene, OR: Author. Retrieved from http://files.eric.ed.gov/fulltext/ED558062.pdf

Center on Education Policy [CEP]. (2011). *State high school tests: Changes in state policies and the impact of the college and career readiness movement.* Washington, DC: Center on Education Policy.

Centers for Disease Control and Prevention. (2011, December). *Attention-deficit/hyperactivity disorder: Treatment.* Atlanta, GA: Author. Retrieved from http://www.cdc.gov/ncbddd/adhd/treatment.html

Centers for Disease Control and Prevention. (2011, September). *Sickle cell disease (SCD): Data and statistics.* Atlanta, GA: Author. Retrieved from http://www.cdc.gov/ncbddd/sicklecell/data.html

Centers for Disease Control and Prevention. (2012, August). *Fetal alcohol spectrum disorders (FASDs).* Atlanta: Author. Retrieved from http://www.cdc.gov/ncbddd/fasd/data.html

Centers for Disease Control and Prevention. (2013, May). *Attention-deficit/hyperactivity disorder (ADHD): Data and statistics.* Atlanta, GA: Author. Retrieved from http://www.cdc.gov/ncbddd/adhd/data.html

Centers for Disease Control and Prevention. (2013a, June). *Autism spectrum disorders (ASDs): Prevalence and statistics.* Atlanta, GA: Centers for Disease Control and Prevention. Retrieved from http://www.cdc.gov/ncbddd/autism/data.html

Centers for Disease Control and Prevention. (2013b, March). *Injury prevention and control: Traumatic brain injury.* Atlanta, GA: Author. Retrieved from http://www.cdc.gov/traumaticbraininjury/statistics.html#A

Centers for Disease control and Prevention. (2013c, May). *Epilepsy: Frequently asked questions.* Atlanta, GA: Author. Retrieved from http://www.cdc.gov/epilepsy/basics/faqs.htm

Centers for Disease Control and Prevention. (2015). *Hearing loss in children.* Atlanta, GA: Author. Retrieved from https://www.cdc.gov/ncbddd/hearingloss/facts.html

Centers for Disease Control and Prevention. (2016, August). *Sickle cell disease: Data and statistics.* Atlanta, GA: Author. Retrieved from https://www.cdc.gov/ncbddd/sicklecell/data.html

Centers for Disease Control and Prevention. (2016, November). *Attention-deficit/hyperactivity disorder (ADHD): Facts about ADHD.* Atlanta, GA: National Center on Birth Defects and Developmental Disabilities, Author. Retrieved from https://www.cdc.gov/ncbddd/adhd/facts.html

Centers for Disease Control and Prevention. (2016, September). *Epilepsy in children.* Atlanta, GA: National Center for Chronic Disease Prevention and Health Promotion, Division of Population Health, Author. Retrieved from https://www.cdc.gov/features/epilepsy-in-children/

Centers for Disease Control and Prevention. (2017a, March). *Autism spectrum disorder (ASD): Data and statistics.* Atlanta, GA: Division of Birth Defects, National Center on Birth Defects and Developmental Disabilities, Author. Retrieved from https://www.cdc.gov/ncbddd/autism/data.html

Centers for Disease Control and Prevention. (2017b, February). *Data and statistics for cerebral palsy.* Atlanta, GA: Division of Birth Defects and Developmental Disabilities, National Center on Birth Defects and Developmental Disabilities, Author. Retrieved from https://www.cdc.gov/ncbddd/cp/data.html

Centers for Disease Control and Prevention. (2017c, February). Most recent asthma data. Atlanta, GA: National Center for Environmental Health, Author. Retrieved from https://www.cdc.gov/asthma/most_recent_data.htm

Centers for Disease Control and Prevention. (2017d, April). *TBI: Get the facts*. Atlanta, GA: National Center for Injury Prevention and Control, Division of Unintentional Injury Prevention, Author. Retrieved from https://www.cdc.gov/traumaticbraininjury/get_the_facts.html

Centers for Disease Control and Prevention. (2017e, February). *Attention-deficit/hyperactivity disorder (ADHD): Data and statistics*. Atlanta, GA: National Center on Birth Defects and Developmental Disabilities, Author. Retrieved from https://www.cdc.gov/ncbddd/adhd/data.html

Centers for Disease Control and Prevention. (2017f, February). *Attention-deficit/hyperactivity disorder: State-based prevalence data of parent reported ADHD medication treatment*. Atlanta, GA: National Center on Birth Defects and Developmental Disabilities, Author. Retrieved from https://www.cdc.gov/ncbddd/adhd/medicated.html

Centers for Disease Control and Prevention. (2017g, March 9). *Lesbian, gay, bisexual, and transgender health: LGBT youth*. Atlanta, GA: Author. Retrieved from https://www.cdc.gov/lgbthealth/youth.htm

Centers for Disease Control and Prevention. (2017h, June). *Fetal alcohol spectrum disorders (FASDs): Data and statistics*. Atlanta, GA: National Center on Birth Defects and Developmental Disabilities, Author. Retrieved from https://www.cdc.gov/ncbddd/fasd/data.html

Cermak, L. S. (1976). *Improving your memory*. New York: Norton.

Chaffin, J. (1975). Will the real "mainstreaming" program please stand up! (Or . . . should Dunn have done it?). In E. L. Meyen, G. A. Vergason, & R. J. Whelan (Eds.), *Alternatives for teaching exceptional children*. Denver, CO: Love.

Chafouleas, S. M., Hagermoser Sanetti, L. M., Jaffery, R., & Fallon, L. M. (2012). An evaluation of a classwide intervention package involving self-management and a group contingency on classroom behavior of middle school students. *Journal of Behavioral Education, 21*(1), 34–57.

Chain, J., Shapiro, V. B., LeBuffe, P. A., & Bryson, A. M. (2017). Academic achievement of American Indian and Alaska native students: Does social emotional competence reduce the impact of poverty? *American Indian and Alaska Native Mental Health Research, 24*(1), 1–29.

Chang, C., & Tseng, K. (2011). Using web-based portfolio assessment system to elevate project-based learning performances. *Interactive Learning Environments, 19*(3), 201–230. Doi:10.1080/10494820902809063

Chapman, C., & Hyatt, C. H. (2011). *Critical conversations in co-teaching: A problem-solving approach*. Bloomington, IN: Solution Tree Press.

Chard, D. J. (2012). A glass half full: A commentary on the special issue. *Journal of Learning Disabilities, 45(3)*, 270–273.

Chard, D. J. (2013). Systems impact: Issues and trends in improving school outcomes for all learners through multi-tier instructional models. *Intervention in School and Clinic, 48*(4), 198–202.

Cheatham, G. A., & Jimenez-Silva, M. (2012). Partnering with Latino families during kindergarten transition: Lessons learned from a parent-teacher conference. *Childhood Education, 88*, 177–184.

Cheatham, G. A., Hart, J. E., Malian, I., & McDonald, J. (2012). Six things to never say or hear during an IEP meeting: Educators as advocates for families. *Teaching Exceptional Children, 44*(3), 50–57.

Cheek, E. H., Jr., & Cheek, M. C. (1983). *Reading instruction through content teaching*. Columbus, OH: Merrill.

Chen, F., Planche, P., & Lemonnier, E. (2010). Superior nonverbal intelligence in children with high-functioning autism or Asperger's syndrome. *Research in Autism Spectrum Disorders, 4*, 457–460.

Chenoweth, K. (2016). ESSA offers changes that can continue learning gains. *Phi Delta Kappan, 97*(8), 38–42.

Cherng, H. S. (2016). Is all classroom conduct equal?: Teacher contact with parents of racial/ethnic minority and immigrant adolescents. *Teachers College Record, 118*(11), 1–32. Retrieved from http://www.tcrecord.org/Content.asp?ContentId=21625

Children's Bureau. (2013, July). *Factsheet: What is child abuse and neglect? Recognizing the signs and symptoms*. Washington, DC: Child Welfare Information Gateway, Author, Department of Health and Human Services. Retrieved from https://www.childwelfare.gov/pubpdfs/whatiscan.pdf

Children's Bureau. (2016). *Mandatory reporters of child abuse and neglect*. Washington, DC: Child Welfare Information Gateway, Author, Department of Health and Human Services. Retrieved from https://www.childwelfare.gov/topics/systemwide/laws-policies/statutes/manda/

Children's Bureau. (2017). *Child maltreatment 2015*. Washington, DC: U.S. Department of Health & Human Services, Administration for Children and Families, Administration on Children, Youth and Families, Author. Retrieved from http://www.acfhhs.gov/programs/cb/research-data-technology/statistics-research/child-maltreatment.

Childs, K. E., Kincaid, D., George, H. P., & Gage, N. A. (2016). The relationship between school-wide implementation of positive behavior intervention and supports and student discipline outcomes. *Journal of Positive Behavior Interventions, 18*, 89–99.

Chin, S. B., Bergeson, T. R., & Phan, J. (2012). Speech intelligibility and prosody production in children with cochlear implants. *Journal of Communication Disorders, 45*, 355–366.

Chopra, R. V., Sandoval-Lucero, E., Aragon, L., Bernal, C., De Balderas, H. B., & Carroll, D. (2004). The paraprofessional role of connector. *Remedial and Special Education, 25*, 219–232.

Chown, N., & Beavan, N. (2012). Intellectually capable but socially excluded? A review of the literature and research on students with autism in further education. *Journal of Further and Higher Education, 36*, 477–493.

Christensen, D. L., Baio, J., Braun, K. V. N., Bilder, D., Charles, J., Constantino, J. N . . . Yeargin-Allsopp, M. Prevalence and characteristics of autism spectrum disorder among children aged 8 years—Autism and Developmental Disabilities Monitoring Network, 11 Sites, United States, 2012. (2016, April). *Morbidity and Mortality Weekly Report (MMWR), 65*(3), 1–23. Retrieved from https://www.cdc.gov/mmwr/volumes/65/ss/ss6503a1.htm

Christopher, M. M., & Shewmaker, J. (2010). The relationship of perfectionism to affective variables in gifted and highly able children. *Gifted Child Today, 33*(3), 20–30.

Christopolos, F., & Renz, P. (1969). A critical examination of special education programs. *Journal of Special Education, 3*, 371–379.

Cianca, M., & Wischnowski, M. (2012). Collaborating with parents of students with disabilities. *Educational Horizons, 91*(1), 26–29.

Cipani, E. (2018). *Functional behavioral assessment, diagnosis, and treatment: A complete system for education and mental health settings* (3rd edition). New York, NY: Springer.

Clancy, M., & Gardner, J. (2017). Using digital portfolios to develop non-traditional domains in special education settings. *International Journal of ePortfolio, 7*(1), 93–100.

Clark, S. K., & Byrnes, D. (2012). Through the eyes of the novice teacher: Perceptions of mentoring support. *Teacher Development, 16*(1), 43–54.

Clarke, B., Baker, S., Smolkowski, K., & Chard, D. J. (2008). An analysis of early numeracy curriculum-based measurement: Examining the role of growth in student outcomes. *Remedial and Special Education, 29*, 46–57.

Clarke, L. S., Haydon, T., Bauer, A., & Epperly, A. C. (2016). Inclusion of students with an intellectual disability in the general education classroom with the use of response cards. *Preventing School Failure, 60*, 35–42.

Claro, S., Paunesku, D., & Dweck, C. S. (2016). Growth mindset tempers the effects of poverty on academic achievement. *PNAS Proceedings of the National Academy of Sciences of the United States of America*, *113*(31), 8664–8668.

Clayton, J. K., & Goodwin, M. (2015). Culturally competent leadership through empowering relationships: A case study of two assistant principals. *Education Leadership Review*, *16*, 131–144.

Clayton, J., Burdge, M., Denham, A., Kleinert, H. L., & Kearns, J. (2006). A four-step process for accessing the general curriculum for students with significant cognitive disabilities. *Teaching Exceptional Children*, *38*(5), 20–27.

Cleveland Clinic. (2017). *Hearing loss in children*. Retrieved from https://my.clevelandclinic.org/health/articles/hearing-loss-children

Clinton, E., & Clees, T. J. (2015). High-preference strategies and other interspersal procedures for learners with disabilities: A review of the literature. *Journal of Special Education Apprenticeship*, *4*(2), Article 4. Retrieved from http://scholarworks.lib.csusb.edu/josea/vol4/iss2/4

Cmar, J. L. (2015). Orientation and mobility skills and outcome expectations as predictors of employment for young adults with visual impairments. *Journal of Visual Impairment & Blindness*, *109*, 95–106.

Coffey, J. H., & Horner, R. H. (2012). The sustainability of schoolwide positive behavior interventions and supports. *Exceptional Children*, *78*, 407–422.

Cohen, S. B. (1983). Assigning report card grades to the mainstreamed child. *Teaching Exceptional Children*, *15*, 186–189.

Coker, D. L., & Ritchey, K. D. (2010). Curriculum-based measurement of writing in kindergarten and first grade: An investigation of production and qualitative scores. *Exceptional Children*, *76*, 175–193.

Coker, T. R., Elliott, M. N., Toomey, S. L., Schwebel, D. C., Cuccaro, P., Emery, S. T., & . . . Schuster, M. A. (2016). Racial and ethnic disparities in ADHD diagnosis and treatment. *Pediatrics*, *138*(3).

Colangelo, N. (2002, Fall). Counseling gifted and talented students. *National Research Center on the Gifted and Talented Newsletter*. Storrs, CT: National Research Center on the Gifted and Talented. (ERIC Document Reproduction Service No. ED447662)

Colangelo, N., & Davis, G. A. (Eds.). (2003). *Handbook on gifted education* (3rd ed.). Boston: Allyn and Bacon.

Collins, K. M., Connor, D., Ferri, B., Gallagher, D., & Samson, J. F. (2016). Dangerous assumptions and unspoken limitations: A disability studies in education response to Morgan, Farkas, Hillemeier, Mattison, Maczuga, Li, and Cook (2015). *Multiple Voices for Ethnically Diverse Exceptional Learners*, *16*, 4–16.

Collins, L. W., & Cook, L. (2016). Never say never: The appropriate and inappropriate use of praise and feedback for students with learning and behavioral disabilities. In B. G. Cook, M. Tankersley, T. J. Landrum, B. G. Cook, M. Tankersley, T. J. Landrum (Eds.), *Instructional practices with and without empirical validity* (pp. 153–173). Bingley, United Kingdom: Emerald Group Publishing.

Colorín Colorado. (2017, June). How to reach out to parents of ELLs. Arlington, VA: WETA. Retrieved from http://www.colorincolorado.org/article/how-reach-out-parents-ells

Compton, M. V., Appenzeller, M., Kemmery, M., & Gardiner-Walsh, S. (2015). Itinerant teachers' perspectives of using collaborative practices in serving students who are deaf or hard of hearing. *American Annals of the Deaf*, *160*, 255–272.

Conderman, G. (2011). Methods for addressing conflict in cotaught classrooms. *Intervention in School and Clinic*, *46*, 221–229.

Conderman, G., & Bresnahan, V. (2010). Study guides to the rescue. *Intervention in School and Clinic*, *45*(3), 169–176.

Conderman, G., & Hedin, L. R. (2013). Co-teaching with strategy instruction. *Intervention in School and Clinic*, *49*(3), 156–163.

Conderman, G., & Johnston-Rodriguez, S. (2009). Beginning teachers' views of their collaborative roles. *Preventing School Failure*, *53*, 235–244.

Conderman, G., & Pedersen, P. (2010). Preparing students with mild disabilities for taking state and district tests. *Intervention in School and Clinic*, *45*(4), 232–241.

Conderman, G., Bresnahan, V., & Hedin, L. (2011). Promoting active involvement in today's classrooms. *Kappa Delta Pi Record*, *47*, 174–180.

Conderman, G., Hedin, L., & Bresnahan, V. (2013). *Strategy Instruction for Middle and Secondary Students with Mild Disabilities: Creating Independent Learners*. Thousand Oaks, CA: Corwin Press.

Conderman, G., Koman, K., Schibelka, M., Higgin, K. L., Cooper, C., & Butler, J. (2013). *Learning strategies for adolescents with mild disabilities*. Lisle: Illinois: Paper presented at the Illinois Council for Exceptional Children Conference, November 8.

Connor, D. J., & Ferri, B. A. (2007). The conflict within: Resistance to inclusion and other paradoxes in special education. *Disability & Society*, *22*, 63–77.

Conoley, J. C., & Conoley, C. W. (2010). Why does collaboration work? Linking positive psychology and collaboration. *Journal of Educational and Psychological Consultation*, *20*, 75–82.

Contrucci-Kuhn, S. A., Lerman, D. C., & Vondran, C. M. (2006). Analysis of factors that affect responding in a two-response chain in children with developmental disabilities. *Journal of Applied Behavior Analysis*, *39*, 263–280.

Cook, B. G., & Cook, L. (2017). Do research findings apply to my students? Examining study samples and sampling. *Learning Disabilities Research & Practice*, *32*(2), 78–84.

Cook, B. G., & Cook, S. C. (2011, July). *Thinking and communicating clearly about evidence-based practices in special education*. Arlington, VA: Division for Research, Council for Exceptional Children. Retrieved from http://www.cecdr.org/pdf/Thinking_and_Communicating_Clearly_About_Evidence-based_Practices_in_Special_Education.pdf

Cook, B. G., & Cook, S. C. (2013). Unraveling evidence-based practices in special education. *Journal of Special Education*, *47*, 71–82. doi:10.1177/0022466911420877

Cook, C. R., Mayer, G., Wright, D., Kraemer, B., Wallace, M. D., Dart, E., & . . . Restori, A. (2012). Exploring the link among behavior intervention plans, treatment integrity, and student outcomes under natural educational conditions. *Journal of Special Education*, *46*, 3–16.

Cook, J. L., & Cook, G. (2009). *Child development: Principles and perspectives*. Boston: Pearson.

Cook, L., & Friend, M. (2010). The state of the art of collaboration on behalf of children with disabilities. *Journal of Educational and Psychological Consultation*, *20*, 1–8.

Coolong-Chaffin, M., & Wagner, D. Using brief experimental analysis to intensify Tier 3 reading interventions. *Learning Disabilities Research & Practice*, *30*(4), 193–200.

Cooper, H. (1989). Synthesis of research on homework. *Educational Leadership*, *47*(3), 85–91.

Cooper, H., Robinson, J. C., Patall, E.A. (2006). Does homework improve academic achievement? A synthesis of research, 1987–2003. *Review of Educational Research*, *76*(1), 1–62.

Cooper, J. E., & He, Y. (2012). Journey of "becoming": Secondary teacher candidates' concerns and struggles. *Issues in Teacher Education*, *21*, 89–108.

Cooper, S. M. A. (2002). Classroom choices for enabling peer learning. [Electronic version]. *Theory into Practice*, *41*(1), 53–57.

Copeland, C. A. (2011). School librarians of the 21st century: Using resources and assistive technologies to support students' differences and abilities. *Knowledge Quest*, *39*(3), 64–70.

Copeland, S. R., Hughes, C., Carter, E. W., Guth, C., Presley, J. A., Williams, C. R., et al. (2004). Increasing access to general education: Perspectives of participants in a high school peer support program. *Remedial and Special Education, 25*, 342–352.

Corbet, S. (2010, September 15). Learning by playing: Video games in the classroom. *The New York Times.* Retrieved from http://www .nytimes.com/2010/09/19/magazine/19video-t.html

Cordier, R., Munro, N., Wilkes-Gillan, S., Ling, L., Docking, K., & Pearce, W. (2017). Evaluating the pragmatic language skills of children with ADHD and typically developing playmates following a pilot parent-delivered play-based intervention. *Australian Occupational Therapy Journal, 64*(1), 11–23.

Cornelius, K. E. (2014). Formative assessment made easy: Templates for collecting daily data in inclusive classrooms. *Teaching Exceptional Children, 47*(2), 112–118.

Cortiella, C. & Horowitz, S. H. (2014). *The state of learning disabilities: Facts, trends and emerging issues.* New York: National Center for Learning Disabilities.

Cortiella, C., & Kaloi, L. (2010). Meet the new and improved Section 504. *Exceptional Parent, 40*(2), 14–15.

Cott, A. (1977). *The orthomolecular approach to learning disabilities.* New York: Huxley Institute.

Cott, A. (1985). *Help for your learning disabled child: The orthomolecular treatment.* New York: Time Books.

Council for Children with Behavioral Disorders. (2009, May). *CCBD position summary: The use of seclusion in school settings.* Arlington, VA: Council for Exceptional Children.

Council for Exceptional Children's Interdivisional Research Group (2014). Evidence-based special education in the context of scarce evidence-based practices. *Teaching Exceptional Children, 47*(2), 81–84.

Council of Chief State School Officers. (2015). *Comprehensive statewide assessment systems: A framework for the role of state education agency in improving quality and reducing burden.* Washington, DC: Author.

Council of Chief State School Officers. (2016). *ESSA: Key provisions and implications for students with disabilities.* Washington, DC: Author. Retrieved from http://www.ccsso.org/Documents/2016/ESSA/ESSA_Key_Provisions_Implications_for_SWD.pdf

Courtade, G., & Browder, D. M. (2011). *Aligning IEPs to common core standards.* Verona, WI: Attainment Company.

Coutinho, M. J., & Oswald, D. P. (2000). Disproportionate representation in special education: A synthesis and recommendations. *Journal of Child and Family Studies, 9*(2), 135–156.

Coyne, M. D., Kame'enui, E. J., & Carnine, D. W. (2007). *Effective teaching strategies that accommodate diverse learners.* Upper Saddle River, NJ: Merrill/Pearson.

Coyne, M. D., Loftus, F., Zipoli, R., & Kapp, S. (2009). Direct vocabulary instruction in kindergarten: Teaching for breadth versus depth. *The Elementary School Journal, 110*(1), 1–18.

Coyne, M. D., Simmons, D. C., Hagan-Burke, S., Simmons, L. E., Kwok, O., Kim, M., . . . Rawlinson, D. M. (2013). Adjusting beginning reading intervention based on student performance: An experimental evaluation. *Exceptional Children, 80*(1), 25-44.

Crawford, C. G. (1980). *Math without fear.* New York: New Viewpoints/Vision Books.

Crawford, L. (2014). The role of assessment in a response to intervention model. *Preventing School Failure. 58*(4), 230–236.

Crone, D. A., Hawken, L. S., & Horner, R. H. (2015). *Building positive behavior support systems in schools: Functional behavioral assessment* (2nd edition). New York, NY: Guilford.

Crosby, L. E., Joffe, N. E., Irwin, M. K., Strong, H., Peugh, J., Shook, L., & . . . Mitchell, M. J. (2015). School performance and disease interference in adolescents with sickle cell disease. *Physical Disabilities: Education and Related Services, 34*, 14–30.

Croteau, S. M., & Lewis, K. (2016). "Just like the other boys": Meeting the needs of gender diverse students. *Journal of Cases in Educational Leadership, 19*, 102–113.

Crouch, R., Keys, C. B., & McMahon, S. D. (2014). Student–teacher relationships matter for school inclusion: School belonging, disability, and school transitions. *Journal of Prevention & Intervention in the Community, 42*(1), 20–30.

Cuevas, J. (2015). Is learning-styles based instruction effective? A comprehensive analysis of recent research on learning styles. *Theory and Research in Education, 13(3),* 308-333.

Cui, Z., Xia, Z., Su, M., Shu, H., & Gong, G. Disrupted white matter connectivity underlying developmental dyslexia. *Human Brain Mapp, 37*(4), 1443–1458. Epub, 2016, Jan 20.

Cullinan, D. (2007). *Students with emotional and behavioral disorders: An introduction for teachers and other helping professionals* (2nd ed.). Upper Saddle River NJ: Pearson Merrill/Prentice Hall.

Cummings, E. O. (2011). Assistive and adaptive technology resources. *Knowledge Quest, 39*(3), 70–73.

Cummings, K. P., & Hardin, B. J. (2017). Navigating disability and related services: Stories of immigrant families. *Early Child Development and Care, 187*, 115–127.

Cummings, K. P., & Hardin, B. J. (2017). Navigating disability and related services: Stories of immigrant families. *Early Child Development and Care, 187*, 115–127.

Currie-Rubin, R., & Smith, S.J. (2014). Understanding the roles of families in virtual learning. *Teaching Exceptional Children, 46(5),* 117–126.

Cushing, L. S., Clark, N. M., Carter, E. W., & Kennedy, C. H. (2005). Access to the general education curriculum for students with significant cognitive disabilities. *Teaching Exceptional Children, 38*(2), 6–13.

Daly, B., Kral, M., & Brown, R. (2008). Cognitive and academic problems associated with childhood cancers and sickle cell disease. *School Psychology Quarterly, 23*, 230–242.

Daly, P. M., & Ranalli, P. (2003). Using countoons to teach self-monitoring skills. *Teaching Exceptional Children, 35*(5), 30–35.

Danneker, J., & Bottge, B. (2009). Benefits of and barriers to elementary student-led individualized education programs. *Remedial and Special Education, 30*, 225–233.

Darden, E. C. (2013). What's so special about an IEP? *Phi Delta Kappan, 94*(6), 66–67.

Dare, A., Dare, L., & Nowicki, E. (2017). Concurrent enrollment: Comparing how educators and students categorize students' motivations. *Social Psychology of Education, 20*, 195–213.

Darling-Hammond, L., Wilhoit, G., & Pittenger, L. (2014). Accountability for college and career readiness: Developing a new paradigm. *Education Policy Analysis Archives, 22*(86). Retrieved from https://doi .org/10.14507/epaa.v22n86.2014

Darnon, C., Buchs, C., & Desbar, D. (2012). The Jigsaw technique and self-efficacy of vocational training students: A practice report. *European Journal of Psychology of Education, 27*, 439–449.

Data Accountability Center. (2012). *Part B child count: 2011.* Retrieved from https://www.ideadata.org/arc_toc13.asp#partbCC

Data Accountability Center. (2013, July). *Teachers employed (FTE) to work with children, ages 6 through 21, who are receiving special education under IDEA, Part B, by qualification status and state: Fall 2010* [Table B2-2]. Retrieved from https://www.ideadata.org/TABLES35TH/B2-2_unsuppressed.pdf

Davila, K., & Talanquer, V. (2010). Classifying end-of-chapter questions and problems for selected general chemistry textbooks used in the United States. *Journal of Chemical Education, 87*, 97–101. doi:10.1021/ed8000232

Davis, L. E. (1986, March). *A recipe for the development of an effective teaching clinic*. Washington, D.C: ERIC Clearinghouse. Retrieved from http://eric.ed.gov/?id=ED275028

Davis, M. (2009). Simulated vs. hands-on lab experiments: New model is likely to require more actual lab work for those taking Advanced Placement online. *Digital Directions, 2*(4), 32–33.

Davis, S. (2012). Preventing gifted/talented children from being harmed by bullying. *Understanding Our Gifted, 24*(3), 4–10.

Daviss, W., Diler, R., & Birmaher, B. (2009). Associations of lifetime depression with trauma exposure, other environmental adversities, and impairment in adolescents with ADHD. *Journal of Abnormal Child Psychology, 37*, 857–871.

de Bruin, C. L., Deppeler, J. M., Moore, D. W., & Diamond, N. T. (2013). Public school–based interventions for adolescents and young adults with an autism spectrum disorder: A meta-analysis. *Review of Educational Research, 83*(4), 521–550.

De Neve, D., & Devos, G. (2017). How do professional learning communities aid and hamper professional learning of beginning teachers related to differentiated instruction? *Teachers and Teaching: Theory and Practice, 23*, 262–283.

Dean, C. B., Hubbell, E. R., Pitler, H., & Stone, B. (2012). *Classroom instruction that works*. (2nd ed.). Denver: ASCD.

Delaney, L., & Smith, J. P. (2012). Childhood health: Trends and consequences over the life course. *Future of Children, 22*, 43–63.

Delgado, R. (2010). "Poco a poquito se van apagando": Teachers' experiences educating Latino English language learners with disabilities. *Journal of Latinos and Education, 9*, 150–157.

Demopoulos, C., Hopkins, J., & Davis, A. (2013). A comparison of social cognitive profiles in children with autism spectrum disorders and attention-deficit/hyperactivity disorder: A matter of quantitative but not qualitative difference? *Journal of Autism and Developmental Disorders, 43*, 1157–1170.

Denham, A., & Lahm, E. A. (2001). Using technology to construct alternate portfolios of students with moderate and severe disabilities. *Teaching Exceptional Children, 33*(5), 10–17.

Denning, C. B. (2007). Social skills interventions for students with Asperger syndrome and high-functioning autism: Research findings and implications for teachers. *Beyond Behavior, 16*(3), 16–23.

Dennis, S. M. (2015). Effects of Tier 2 and Tier 3 interventions for second graders with mathematics difficulties. *Learning Disabilities Research & Practice, 30*(1), 29–42.

Dennison, P. E., & Dennison, G. E. (1994). *Brain Gym™ teacher's edition: Revised*. Ventura, CA: Edu-Kinesthetics.

Deno, S. L. (2003). Developments in curriculum-based measurement. *Journal of Special Education, 37*, 184–192.

Deno, S. L., Reschly, A. L., Lembke, E. S., Magnusson, D., Callender, S. A., & Windram, H., et al. (2009). Developing a school-wide progress-monitoring system. *Psychology in the Schools, 46*, 44–55. http://dx.doi.org/10.1002/pits.20353

Deno, S. L., Reschly-Anderson, A., Lembke, E., Zorka, H., & Callender, S. (2002). A model for school wide implementation: A case example. Paper presented at the annual meeting of the National Association of School Psychology, Chicago, IL.

Deshler, D. D., Lenz, B., Bulgren, J., Schumaker, J. B., Davis, B., Grossen, B., & Marquis, J. (2004). Adolescents with disabilities in a high school setting: Student characteristics and setting dynamics. *Learning Disabilities—A Contemporary Journal, 2*(2), 30–48.

Deshler, D. D., Schumaker, J. S., Lenz, B. K., Bulgren, J. A., Hock, M. F., Knight, J., & Ehren, B. J. (2001). Ensuring content-area learning by secondary students with learning disabilities. *Learning Disabilities Research & Practice, 16*(2), 96–108.

DeSimone, J. R., & Parmar, R. S. (2006). Middle school mathematics teachers' beliefs about inclusion of students with learning disabilities. *Learning Disabilities Research and Practice, 21*, 98–110.

Dessemontet, R., Bless, G. G., & Morin, D. D. (2012). Effects of inclusion on the academic achievement and adaptive behaviour of children with intellectual disabilities. *Journal of Intellectual Disability Research, 56*, 579–587.

Dettmer, P., Knackendoffel, A. P., & Thurston, L. P. (2013). *Collaboration, consultation, and teamwork for students with special needs* (7th ed.). Upper Saddle River, NJ: Pearson/Allyn & Bacon.

Deussen, T., Hanson, H., & Bisht, B. (2017). *Are two commonly used early warning indicators accurate predictors of dropout for English learner students? Evidence from six districts in Washington state* (REL 2017-261). Retrieved from http://www.eric.ed.gov/contentdelivery/servlet/ERICServlet?accno=ED573197

Dewitz, P., Jones, J., & Leahy, S. (2009). Comprehension strategy instruction in core reading programs. *Reading Research Quarterly, 44*(2), 102–126.

Dexter, D. D., & Hughes, C. A. (2011). Graphic organizers and students with learning disabilities: A meta-analysis. *Learning Disability Quarterly, 34*(1), 51–72.

Dhaem, J. (2012). Responding to minor misbehavior through verbal and nonverbal responses. *Beyond Behavior, 21*(3), 29–34.

Diaz, A., Cochran, K., & Karlin, N. (2016). The influence of teacher power on English language learners' self-perceptions of learner empowerment. *College Teaching, 64*, 158–167.

Dieker, L. (2013). *Demystifying secondary inclusion*. Naples, FL: Dude Publishing.

Digest of Education Statistics. (2017, February). *Percentage of high school dropouts among persons 16 to 24 years old (status dropout rate) and number of status dropouts, by noninstitutionalized or institutionalized status, birth in or outside of the United States, and selected characteristics: Selected years, 2006 through 2015 (Table 219.80)*. Washington, DC: U.S. Department of Commerce, Census Bureau, American Community Survey, Author. Retrieved from https://nces.ed.gov/programs/digest/d16/tables/dt16_219.80.asp

Diliberto, J. A., & Breaver, D. (2012). Six tips for successful IEP meetings. Teaching *Exceptional Children, 44*(4), 30–37.

Doman, G. (2005). What to do about your brain injured child (30th anniversary ed.). Garden City Park, NY: Square One Publishers.

Doman, G., & Delacato, D. (1968). Doman–Delacato philosophy. *Human Potential, 1*, 113–116.

Dombeck, J. L., & Al Otaiba, S. (2016). Curriculum-based measurement for beginning writers (K–2). *Intervention in School and Clinic, 51*(5), 276–283.

Donaldson, J. M., & Vollmer, T. R. (2011). An evaluation and comparison of time-out procedures with and without release contingencies. *Journal of Applied Behavior Analysis, 44*, 693–705.

Douglas, G., McLinden, M., McCall, S., Pavey, S., Ware, J., & Farrell, A. (2011). Access to print literacy for children and young people with visual impairment: Findings from a review of literature. *European Journal of Special Needs Education, 26*, 25–38.

Douglas, H. A. (2014). Promoting meaning-making to help our patients grieve: An exemplar for genetic counselors and other health care professionals. *Journal of Genetic Counseling, 23*, 695–700.

Douglas, S. N., Chapin, S. E., & Nolan, J. F. (2016). Special education teachers' experiences supporting and supervising paraeducators: Implications for special and general education settings. *Teacher Education and Special Education, 39*, 60–74.

Doyle, W. (1990). Classroom management techniques. In O. C. Moles (Ed.), *Student discipline strategies* (pp. 83–105). Albany, NY: State University of New York Press.

Doyle, W. (2006). Ecological approaches to classroom management. In C. Evertson, & C. Weinstein (Eds.), *Handbook of classroom management: Research, practice, and contemporary issues* (pp. 97–125). New York: Erlbaum.

Dray, B. J., & Wisneski, D. B. (2011). Mindful reflection as a process for developing culturally responsive practices. *Teaching Exceptional Children, 44*(1), 28–36.

Dufrene, B. A., Kazmerski, J. S., & Labrot, Z. (2017). The current status of indirect functional assessment instruments. *Psychology in the Schools, 54,* 331–350.

Duke, N. K. (2000). 36 minutes per day: The scarcity of informational texts in first grade. *Reading Research Quarterly, 35,* 202–224.

Duke, T. S. (2011). Lesbian, gay, bisexual, and transgender youth with disabilities: A meta-synthesis. *Journal of LGBT Youth, 8*(1), 1–52. Retrieved from: http://dx.doi.org/10.1080/19361653.2011.519181

Dukes, C., & Lamar-Dukes, P. (2009). Inclusion by design: Engineering inclusive practices in secondary schools. *Teaching Exceptional Children, 41*(3), 16–23.

Dulaney, S. K. (2013). A middle school's response-to-intervention journey: Building systematic processes of facilitation, collaboration, and implementation. *NASSP Bulletin, 97,* 53–77.

Dunn, L. M. (1968). Special education for the mildly handicapped—Is much of it justifiable? *Exceptional Children, 35,* 5–22.

Dunn, R. (1990). Understanding the Dunn and Dunn learning styles model and the need for individual diagnosis and prescription. *Journal of Reading, Writing and Learning Disabilities International, 6*(3), 223–247.

DuPaul, G. J., Belk, G. D., & Puzino, K. (2017). Evidence-based interventions for attention deficit hyperactivity disorder in children and adolescents. In L. A. Theodore (Ed.), *Handbook of evidence-based interventions for children and adolescents* (pp. 167–179). New York, NY: Springer.

DuPaul, G. J., Jitendra, A. K., Volpe, R. J., Tresco, K. E., Lutz, J. G., & Vile Junod, R. E. (2006). Consultation-based academic interventions for children with ADHD: Effects on reading and mathematics achievement. *Journal of Abnormal Child Psychology, 34*(5), 633–646.

Dupper, D., & Montgomery Dingus, A. (2008). Corporal punishment in U.S. public schools: A continuing challenge for school social workers. *Children & Schools, 30,* 243–250.

Durber, C. M., Yeates, K. O., Taylor, H. G., Walz, N. C., Stancin, T., & Wade, S. L. (2017). The family environment predicts long-term academic achievement and classroom behavior following traumatic brain injury in early childhood. *Neuropsychology,* doi:10.1037/neu0000351

Durlak, C. M., Rose, E., & Bursuck, W. (1994). Preparing high school students with learning disabilities for the transition to postsecondary education: Teaching the skills of self-determination. *Journal of Learning Disabilities, 27,* 51–59.

Dussault, M., Deaudelin, C., Royer, N., & Loiselle, F. (1999). Professional isolation and occupational stress in teachers. *Psychological Reports, 84,* 943–946.

Dwyer, K., Rozewski, D., & Simonsen, B. (2012). A comparison of function-based replacement behaviors for escape-motivated students. *Journal of Emotional and Behavioral Disorders, 20,* 115–125.

Dyke, P., Bourke, J., Llewellyn, G., & Leonard, H. (2013). The experiences of mothers of young adults with an intellectual disability transitioning from secondary school to adult life. *Journal of Intellectual & Developmental Disability, 38,* 149–162.

Dykeman, B. F. (2009). Response to intervention: The functional assessment of children returning to school with traumatic brain injury. *Education, 130,* 295–300.

Dyson, L. (2010). Unanticipated effects of children with learning disabilities on their families. *Learning Disability Quarterly, 33,* 43–55.

Educational Testing Service (2009). *Guidelines for the Assessment of English Language learners.* Retrieved from https://www.ets.org/s/about/pdf/ell_guidelines.pdf

Edwards, C. C., & DaFonte, A. (2012). The 5-point plan: Fostering successful partnerships with families of students with disabilities. *Teaching Exceptional Children, 44*(3), 6–13.

Edyburn, D. (2009). RTI and UDL interventions. *Journal of Special Education Technology, 24*(2), 46–47.

Ehri, L. C. (2004). Teaching phonemic awareness and phonics: An explanation of the National Reading Panel meta-analyses. In P. McCardle, & V. Chhabra (Eds.), *The voice of evidence in reading research* (pp. 153–186). Baltimore, MD: Brookes.

Elbaum, B., Blatz, E. T., & Rodriguez, R. J. (2016). Parents' experiences as predictors of state accountability measures of schools' facilitation of parent involvement. *Remedial and Special Education, 37,* 15–27.

Elbaum, B., Moody, S. W., & Schumm, J. S. (1999). Mixed-ability grouping for reading: What students think. *Learning Disabilities Research and Practice, 14,* 61–66.

Eli Lilly. (2003). *The history of ADHD.* Retrieved from http://www.strattera.com/1_3_childhood_adhd/1_3_1_1_2_history.jsp

Elliott, S. M., Kettler, R. J., Beddow, P. A., Kurz, A., Compton, E., McGrath, D., & Roach, A.T. (2010). Effects of using modified items to test students with persistent academic difficulties. *Exceptional Children, 76,* 475–495.

Elliott, S. N. (2015). Measuring opportunity to learn and achievement growth: Key research issues with implications for the effective education of all students. *Remedial and Special Education, 36*(1), 58–64.

Ellis, E. (1991). *SLANT: A starter strategy for participation.* Lawrence, KS: Edge Enterprises.

Ellis, E. (1996). Reading strategy instruction. In D. Deshler, E. Ellis, & K. Lenz (Eds.), *Teaching adolescents with learning disabilities: Strategies and methods* (2nd ed., pp. 61–125). Denver, CO: Love.

Ellis, E., Lenz, B. K., & Sabornie, E. (1987a). Generalization and adaptation of learning strategies to natural environments: Part 1: Critical agents. *Remedial and Special Education, 8*(2), 6–24.

Ellis, E., Lenz, B. K., & Sabornie, E. (1987). Generalization and adaptation of learning strategies to natural environments: Part 2: Research into practice. *Remedial and Special Education, 8*(2), 6–23.

emerging issues. New York: National Center for Learning Disabilities.

Emmer, E. T., Evertson, C. M., Sanford, J. P., Clements, B. S., & Worsham, M. E. (1983). *Organizing and managing the junior high classroom.* Austin: Research and Development Center for Teacher Education, University of Texas.

Endres, C. (2012). Removing barriers, building futures: Educating homeless students. *School Business Affairs, 78*(4), 8–9.

Englert, C. S. (2009). Connecting the dots in a research program to develop, implement, and evaluate strategic literacy interventions for struggling readers and writers. *Learning Disabilities Research & Practice, 24*(2), pp. 104–120.

Englert, C. S., Mariage, T. V., & Okolo, C. M. (2009). Informational Writing Across the Curriculum. In G. Troia (Ed.), *Writing Instruction and Assessment for Struggling Writers: From Theory to Evidence-Based Practices* (pp. 132–164). NY: Guilford Press.

Englert, C. S., Zhao, Y., Dunsmore, K., Collings, N. Y., & Wolbers, K. (2007). Scaffolding the writing of students with disabilities through procedural facilitation: Using an internet-based technology to improve performance. *Learning Disability Quarterly, 30,* 9–29.

Englert, C., & And, O. (1991). Making strategies and self-talk visible: Writing instruction in regular and special education classrooms. *American Educational Research Journal, 28*(2), 337–372.

Englert, C., & Mariage, T. (1991). Making students partners in the comprehension process: Organizing the reading "POSSE." *Learning Disability Quarterly, 14*, 123–138.

Enriquez, L. E. (2011). "Because we feel the pressure and we also feel the support": Examining the educational success of undocumented immigrant Latina/o students. *Harvard Educational Review, 81*, 476–500.

Epilepsy Foundation. (2014). Seizure first aid. Retrieved from http://www.epilepsy.com/learn/treating-seizures-and-epilepsy/seizure-first-aid

Epping, A. S., Myrvik, M. P., Newby, R. F., Panepinto, J. A., Brandow, A. M., & Scott, J. P. (2013). Academic attainment findings in children with sickle cell disease. *Journal of School Health, 83*, 548-553.

Epstein, M. H., Polloway, E. A., Buck, G. H., Bursuck, W. D., Wissinger, L., Whitehouse, F., & Jayanthi, M. (1997). Homework-related communication problems: Perspectives of general education teachers. *Learning Disabilities Research and Practices, 12*, 221–227.

Erchul, W. (2011). School consultation and response to intervention: A tale of two literatures. *Journal of Educational & Psychological Consultation, 21*, 191–208.

Eriks-Brophy, A., Durieux-Smith, A., Olds, J., Fitzpatrick, E. M., Duquette, C., & Whittingham, J. (2012). Communication, academic, and social skills of young adults with hearing loss. *Volta Review, 112*, 5–35.

Erion, J. (2006). Parent tutoring: A meta-analysis. *Education and Treatment of Children, 29*(1), 79–106.

Ervin, R.A. (2017). *Considering Tier 3 Within a Response-to-Intervention Model.* http://www.rtinetwork.org/essential/tieredinstruction/tier3/consideringtier3

Eskrootchi, R., & Oskrochi, G. R. (2010). A study of the efficacy of project-based learning integrated with computer-based simulation-STELLA, *Educational Technology & Society, 13*(1), 236–245.

Espelage, D. L., Rose, C. A., & Polanin, J. R. (2015). Social-emotional learning program to reduce bullying, fighting, and victimization among middle school students with disabilities. *Remedial and Special Education, 36*(5), 299–311.

Espin, C., Wallace, T., Campbell, H., Lembke, E. S., Long, J. D., & Ticha, R. (2008). Curriculum-based measurement in writing: Predicting the success of high-school students on state standards tests. *Exceptional Children, 74*, 174–193.

Estell, D. B., Jones, M. H., Pearl, R., Van Acker, R., Farmer, T. W., & Rodkin, P. C. (2008). Peer groups, popularity, and social preference. *Journal of Learning Disabilities, 41*(1), 5–14.

Etscheidt, S. (2006). Behavioral intervention plans: Pedagogical and legal analysis of issues. *Behavioral Disorders, 31*, 223–243.

Etscheidt, S. K. (2006). Progress monitoring: Legal issues and recommendations for IEP teams. *Teaching Exceptional Children, 38*(3), 56–60.

Etscheidt, S. L. (2016). Assistive technology for students with disabilities: A legal analysis of issues. *Journal of Special Education Technology, 31*, 183–194.

Evans, C. M., & Lyons, S., (2017). Comparability in balanced assessment systems for state accountability. *Educational Measurement: Issues and Practice, 36*(3), 24–34.

Evans, R. (2012). Getting to no: Building true collegiality in schools. *Independent School, 71*, 99–107.

Evertson, C. M., & Weinstein, C. S. (2006). Classroom management as a field of inquiry. In C. M. Evertson, & C. S. Weinstein (Eds.), *Handbook of classroom management: Research, practice, and contemporary issues* (pp. 3–16). Mahwah, NJ: Lawrence Erlbaum Associates.

Evertson, C. M., Emmer, E. T., Clements, B. S., Sanford, J. P., Worsham, M. E., & Williams, E. L. (1983). *Organizing and managing the elementary school classroom.* Austin: Research and Development Center for Teacher Education, University of Texas.

Eye Care Council. (2017). *Warning signs of vision problems.* Retrieved from http://eyecarecouncil.com/about/resources-for-parents/

Fairbanks, S., Sugai, G., Guardino, D., & Lathrop, M. (2007). Response to intervention: Examining classroom behavior support in second grade. *Exceptional Children, 73*, 288–310.

Falkmer, M., Anderson, K., Joosten, A., & Falkmer, T. (2015). Parents' perspectives on inclusive schools for children with autism spectrum conditions. *International Journal of Disability, Development and Education, 62*(1), 1–23.

Faraone, S. V., Lecendreux, M., & Konofal, E. (2012). Growth dysregulation and ADHD: An epidemiologic study of children in France. *Journal of Attention Disorders, 16*, 572–578.

Farmer, R. F., & Chapman, A. L. (2016). *Behavioral interventions in cognitive behavior therapy: Practical guidance for putting theory into action* (2nd edition). Washington, DC: American Psychological Association.

Farmer, T. W., Farmer, E. M. Z., & Brooks, D. S. (2010). Recasting the ecological and developmental roots of intervention for students with emotional and behavior problems: The promise of strength-based perspectives. *Exceptionality, 18*, 53–57.

Feather, K. A. (2016). Antibullying interventions to enhance self-efficacy in children with disabilities. *Journal of Creativity in Mental Health, 11*, 409–422.

Feder, K. P., & Majnemer, A. (2007). Handwriting development, competency, and intervention. *Developmental Medicine & Child Neurology, 49*(4), 312–317.

Feingold, B. F. (1975). *Why your child is hyperactive.* New York: Random House.

Feistritzer, C. E. (2011). *Profile of teachers in the U.S. 2011.* Washington, DC: National Center for Education Information.

Feldman, E., Kim, J., & Elliott, S. N. (2011). The effects of accommodations on adolescents' self-efficacy and test performance. *The Journal of Special Education, 45*(2), 77–88.

Feng X., Li L., Zhang M., Yang X., Tian M., Xie W., Lu Y., Liu L., Bélanger, N. N., Meng, X., & Ding, G. (2017). Dyslexic children show atypical cerebellar activation and cerebro-cerebellar functional connectivity in orthographic and phonological processing. *Cerebellum, 16*(2), 496–507.

Ferguson, P. M. (2002). A place in the family: An historical interpretation of research on parental reactions to having a child with a disability. *Journal of Special Education, 36*, 124–130.

Ferlazzo, L. (2015). *Building a community of self-motivated learners: Strategies to help students thrive in school and beyond.* New York: New York: Routledge.

Fernandez, N., & Hynes, J. W. (2016). The efficacy of pullout programs in elementary schools: Making it work. *The Journal of Multidisciplinary Graduate Research, 2*(3), 32–47.

Feuerborn, L. L., & Tyre, A. D. (2016). How do staff perceive schoolwide positive behavior supports? Implications for teams in planning and implementing schools. *Preventing School Failure, 60*(1), 53–59.

Feuerborn, L. L., Sarin, K., & Tyre, A. D. (2011). Response to intervention in secondary schools. *Principal Leadership, 11*(8), 50–54.

Fiedorowicz, C. (2005). *Neurobiological basis of learning disabilities: An overview.* Retrieved from http://www.ldac-taac.ca/Research/neurobiological-e.asp

Finkbeiner, C., & Lazar, A. M. (Eds.). (2015). *Getting to know ourselves and others through the ABCs: A journey toward intercultural understanding* (pp. 71–83). Charlotte, NC: IAP Information Age Publishing.

Fisher, D., & Frey, N. (2011). Implementing RTI in a high school: A case study. *Journal of Learning Disabilities, 46*(2), 99–114.

Fisher, M., & Pleasants, S. L. (2012). Roles, responsibilities, and concerns of paraeducators: Findings from a statewide survey. *Remedial and Special Education, 33*, 287–297.

Fishman, C. E., & Nickerson, A. B. (2015). Motivations for involvement: A preliminary investigation of parents of students with disabilities. *Journal of Child and Family Studies, 24*, 523–535.

Fitzell, S. (2013). *Co-teaching and collaboration in the classroom* (2nd edition). Manchester, NH: Cogent Catalyst Publications.

Fitzell, S. G. (2013). *Paraprofessionals and teachers working together: Highly effective strategies for the inclusive classroom* (3rd edition). Manchester, NH: Cogent Catalyst Publications.

Fitzgerald, J. L., & Watkins, M. W. (2006). Parents' rights in special education: The readability of procedural safeguards. *Exceptional Children, 72*, 497–510.

Fixsen, D., Blasé, K., Metz, A., & Van Dyke, M. (2013). Statewide implementation of evidence-based programs. *Exceptional Children, 79*(2), 213–230.

Flannery, K. B., Fenning, P., Kato, M. M., & McIntosh, K. (2014). Effects of school-wide positive behavioral interventions and supports and fidelity of implementation on problem behavior in high schools. *School Psychology Quarterly, 29*, 111–124.

Fleischer, D. Z., & Zames, F. (2001). *The disability rights movement: From charity to confrontation*. Philadelphia: Temple University Press.

Fleischman, S. (2012, Winter). Before choosing, ask three questions. *Better: Evidence-Based Magazine*. Retrieved from http://education.jhu.edu/PD/newhorizons/Better/articles/winter2012.html

Flores, M. M., Hinton, V. M., & Burton, M. E. (2016). Teaching problem solving to students receiving tiered interventions using the concrete-representational-abstract sequence and schema-based instruction. *Preventing School Failure, 60*(4), 345–355.

Flores, M. M., Hinton, V. M., & Schweck, K. B. (2014). Teaching multiplication with regrouping to students with learning disabilities. *Learning Disabilities Research & Practice, 29*(4), 171–183.

Floress, M. T., Rock, A. L., & Hailemariam, A. (2017). The Caterpillar Game: A classroom management system. *Psychology in the Schools, 54*, 385–403.

Foegen, A. (2008). Algebra progress monitoring and interventions for students with learning disabilities. *Learning Disability Quarterly, 31*, 65–78.

Foegen, A., & Morrison, C. (2010). Putting algebra progress monitoring into practice: Insights from the field. *Intervention in School and Clinic, 46*(2), 95–103.

Foegen, A., Stecker, P. M., Genareo, V. R., Lyons, R., Olson, J. R., Simpson, A., Romig, J. E., & Jones, R. (2016). Using an online tool for learning about and implementing algebra progress monitoring. *Teaching Exceptional Children, 49*(2), 106–114.

Foorman, B. R. (Ed.). (2003). *Preventing and remediating reading difficulties: Bringing science to scale*. Baltimore, MD: York.

Foorman, B. R., Goldenberg, C., Carlson, C. D., Saunders, W. M., & Pollard-Durodola, S. D. (2004). How teachers allocate time during literacy instruction in primary-grade English language learner classrooms. In P. McCardle, & V. Chhabra (Eds.), *The voice of evidence in reading research* (pp. 289–322). Baltimore, MD: Paul H. Brookes.

Ford, D. Y. (2012). Culturally different students in special education: Looking backward to move forward. *Exceptional Children, 78*, 391–405.

Ford, D. Y., & Russo, C. J. (2016). Historical and legal overview of special education overrepresentation: Access and equity denied. *Multiple Voices for Ethnically Diverse Exceptional Learners, 16*, 50–57.

Forness, S., & Knitzer, J. (1992). *A new proposed definition and terminology to replace "serious emotional disturbance" in individuals with disabilities education act*. Alexandria, VA: The National Mental Health and Special Education Coalition.

Foster, M. (1995) African American teachers and culturally-relevant pedagogy. In J. A. Banks, & C. A. M. Banks (Eds.), *Handbook of research on multicultural education* (pp. 570–581). New York: Macmillan.

Foster, M. (1997). *Black teachers on teaching*. New York: New Press.

Fox, G. L., Nordquist, V. M., Billen, R. M., & Savoca, E. F. (2015). Father involvement and early intervention: Effects of empowerment and father role identity. *Family Relations: An Interdisciplinary Journal of Applied Family Studies, 64*, 461–475.

Francis, D. J., Shaywitz, S. E., Stuebing, K. K., Shaywitz, B. A., & Fletcher, J. M. (1996). Developmental lag versus deficit models of reading disability: A longitudinal, individual growth curves analysis. *Journal of Educational Psychology, 88*(1), 3–17.

Francis, G. L., Blue-Banning, M., Turnbull, A. P., Hill, C., Haines, S. J., & Gross, J. S. (2016). Culture in inclusive schools: Parental perspectives on trusting family-professional partnerships. *Education and Training in Autism and Developmental Disabilities, 51*, 281–293.

Francis, R., Hawes, D. J., & Abbott, M. (2016). Intellectual giftedness and psychopathology in children and adolescents: A systematic literature review. *Exceptional Children, 82*, 279–302.

Frea, W. (2010). Preparing adolescents with autism for successful futures. *Exceptional Parent, 40*(4), 26–29.

Freeman, J., Simonsen, B., McCoach, D. B., Sugai, G., Lombardi, A., & Horner, R. (2016). Relationship between school-wide positive behavior interventions and supports and academic, attendance, and behavior outcomes in high schools. *Journal of Positive Behavior Interventions, 18*, 41–51.

Freeman, S. F. N., & Alkin, M. C. (2000). Academic and social attainments of children with mental retardation in general education and special education settings. *Remedial and Special Education, 21*(1), 3–18.

Freeman-Green, S. M., O'Brien, C., Wood, C. L., & Hitt, S. B. (2015). Effects of the SOLVE strategy on the mathematical problem solving skills of secondary students with learning disabilities. *Learning Disabilities Research & Practice, 30*(2), 76–90.

Frey, L. M., & Wilhite, K. (2005). Our five basic needs: Application for understanding the function of behavior. *Intervention in School and Clinic, 40*, 156–160.

Friend, M. (2000). Perspective: Myths and misunderstandings about professional collaboration. *Remedial and Special Education, 21*, 130–132, 160.

Friend, M. (2013). Inclusive practices. In J. A. Banks (Ed.), *Encyclopedia of diversity in education* (pp. 1144–1147). Thousand Oaks, CA: Sage.

Friend, M. (2018). *Special education: Contemporary perspectives for school professionals* (5th edition). Upper Saddle River, NJ: Merrill/Pearson.

Friend, M. (2014a). *Co-Teach!: Building and sustaining classroom partnerships in inclusive schools* (2nd ed.). Greensboro, NC: Marilyn Friend, Inc.

Friend, M. (2014b). *Special education: Contemporary perspectives for school professionals* (4th edition). Upper Saddle River, NJ: Merrill/Pearson.

Friend, M. (2016). Welcome to co-teaching 2.0. *Educational Leadership, 73*(4), 16–22.

Friend, M., & Barron, T. (2015). School to school collaboration. In J. D. Wright (Ed.), *International encyclopedia of the social & behavioral sciences* (2nd edition) (Vol. 21, pp. 112–118). Oxford: Elsevier.

Friend, M., & Barron, T. (in press). Collaborating with colleagues to increase student success. In B. Billingsley & J. McCleskey (Eds.), *High leverage practices in special education.* New York: Routledge.

Friend, M., & Cook, L. (2013). *Interactions: Collaboration skills for school professionals* (7th ed.). Upper Saddle River, NJ: Pearson/Merrill.

Friend, M., & Cook, L. (2017). *Interactions: Collaboration skills for school professionals* (8th ed.). Upper Saddle River, NJ: Pearson.

Friend, M., Cook, L., Hurley-Chamberlain, D., & Shamberger, C. (2010). Co-teaching: An illustration of the complexity of collaboration in special education. *Journal of Educational & Psychological Consultation, 20,* 9–27.

Fuchs, D., & Fuchs, L. (2017). Critique of the national evaluation of response to intervention: A case for simpler frameworks. *Exceptional Children, 83(3),* 255–268.

Fuchs, D., & Fuchs, L. S. (2015). Rethinking service delivery for students with significant learning problems: Developing and implementing effective instruction. *Remedial and Special Education, 36(2),* 105–111.

Fuchs, D., Compton, D. L., Fuchs, L. S., Bryant, V. J., Hamlett, C. L., & Lambert, W. (2012). First-grade cognitive abilities as long-term predictors of reading comprehension and disability status. *Journal of Learning Disabilities, 45(3),* 217–231.

Fuchs, D., Fuchs, L. S., & Stecker, P. M. (2010). The "blurring" of special education in a new continuum of general education placements and services. *Exceptional Children, 76,* 301–323.

Fuchs, D., Fuchs, L.S., & Compton, D.L. (2012). Smart RTI: A next-generation approach to multi-level prevention. *Exceptional Children, 78(3),* 263–279.

Fuchs, L (2017). Curriculum-based measurement as the emerging alternative: Three decades later. *Learning Disabilities Research & Practice, 32(1),* 5–7.

Fuchs, L. S., Fuchs, D., Hamlett, C. L., & Stecker, P. M. (1991). Effects of curriculum-based measurement and consultation on teacher planning and student achievement in mathematics operations. *American Educational Research Journal, 28,* 617–641.

Fuchs, L. S., Fuchs, D., Hintze, J., & Lembke, E. (2007). Progress monitoring in the context of response to intervention. Presentation at the National Center on Student Progress Monitoring Summer Institute: Nashville.

Fuchs, L. S., Fuchs, D., Kazdan, S., Karns, K., Calhoon, M. B., Hamlett, C. L., & Hewlett, S. (2000). Effects of workgroup structure and size on student productivity during collaborative work on complex tasks. *Elementary School Journal, 100,* 201–210.

Fuchs, L. S., Fuchs, D., Powell, S. R., Seethaler, P. M., Cirino, P. T., & Fletcher, J. M. (2008). Intensive intervention for students with mathematics disabilities: Seven principles of effective practice. *Learning Disability Quarterly, 31(2),* 79–92.

Fuchs, L. S., Hamlett, C. L., & Fuchs, D. (1997). *Monitoring basic skills progress: Basic reading* (2nd ed.) [Computer software, manual, and blackline masters]. Austin TX: PRO-ED.

Fuchs, L. S., Hamlett, C. L., & Fuchs, D. (1998). *Monitoring basic skills progress: Basic math computation* (2nd ed.) [Computer software, manual, and blackline masters]. Austin TX: PRO-ED.

Fuchs, L. S., Hamlett, C. L., & Fuchs, D. (1999). *Monitoring basic skills progress: Basic math concepts and applications* [Computer software, manual, and blackline masters]. Austin TX: PRO-ED.

Fuchs, L.S., & Vaughn, S. (2012). Responsiveness-to-intervention: A decade later. *Journal of Learning Disabilities, 45(3),* 195–203.

Fulk, B. M. (2011). Effective communication in collaboration and consultation. In C. G. Simpson, J. P. Bakken, C. G. Simpson, & J. P. Bakken (Eds.), *Collaboration: A multidisciplinary approach to educating students with disabilities* (pp. 19–30). Waco, TX: Prufrock Press.

Fulton, J. B., Yeates, K. O., Taylor, H. G., Walz, N. C., & Wade, S. L. (2012). Cognitive predictors of academic achievement in young children 1 year after traumatic brain injury. *Neuropsychology, 26,* 314–322.

Furtak, E. M., Seidel, T., Iverson, H., & Briggs, D. C. (2012). Experimental and quasi-experimental studies of inquiry-based science teaching: A meta-analysis. *Review of Educational research, 82(3),* 300–329.

Gable, R., Hester, P., Rock, M., & Hughes, K. (2009). Back to basics: Rules, praise, ignoring, and reprimands revisited. *Intervention in School and Clinic, 44,* 195–205.

Gage, N. A., Lewis, T. J., & Stichter, J. P. (2012). Functional behavioral assessment-based interventions for students with or at risk for emotional and/or behavioral disorders in school: A hierarchical linear modeling meta-analysis. *Behavioral Disorders, 37,* 55–77.

Gage, N. A., Lierheimer, K. S., & Goran, L. G. (2012). Characteristics of students with high-incidence disabilities broadly defined. *Journal of Disability Policy Studies, 23,* 168–178.

Gagnon, J. C., & Maccini, P. (2001). Preparing students with disabilities for algebra. *Teaching Exceptional Children, 34(1),* 8–15.

Gajiria, M., Jitendra, A.K., Sood, S., & Sacks, G. (2007). Improving comprehension of expository text in students with LD: A research synthesis. *Journal of Learning Disabilities, 40(3),* 210–225.

Galbraith, J., & Winterbottom, M. (2011). Peer-tutoring: What's in it for the tutor? *Educational Studies, 37,* 321–332.

Gallagher, J. J. (2015). Peer acceptance of highly gifted children in elementary school. *Journal for the Education of the Gifted, 38(1),* 51–57.

Gannotti, M., Oshio, T., & Handwerker, W. P. (2012). Caregiver practices of families of children with and without physical disability. *Journal of Developmental and Physical Disabilities,* doi:10.1007/s10882-012-9318-9

Garbacz, S. A., & McIntyre, L. L. (2016). Conjoint behavioral consultation for children with autism spectrum disorder. *School Psychology Quarterly, 31,* 450–466.

Garbacz, S. A., McIntosh, K., Eagle, J. W., Dowd-Eagle, S. E., Hirano, K. A., & Ruppert, T. (2016). Family engagement within schoolwide positive behavioral interventions and supports. *Preventing School Failure, 60,* 60–69.

Gardner, H. (1993). *Multiple intelligences: The theory in practice.* New York: Basic Books.

Gardner, H. E. (2006). *Multiple intelligences: New horizons in theory and practice.* New York: Basic Books.

Garwood, J. D., & Vernon-Feagans, L. (2017). Classroom management affects literacy development of students with emotional and behavioral disorders. *Exceptional Children, 83,* 123–142.

Garwood, J. D., Vernon-Feagans, L., & the Family Life Project Key Investigators. (2017). Classroom management effects literacy development of students with emotional and behavioral disorders. *Exceptional Children, 52(1),* 123–142.

Gay, G. (2002). Culturally responsive teaching in special education for ethnically diverse students: Setting the stage. *Qualitative Studies in Education, 15(6),* 613–629.

Gay, G. (2010). *Culturally responsive teaching: Theory, research, and practice* (2nd ed.). New York: Teachers College Press.

Gelbar, N. W., Anderson, C., McCarthy, S., & Buggey, T. (2012). Video self-modeling as an intervention strategy for individuals with autism spectrum disorders. *Psychology in the Schools, 49,* 15–22.

Gelbart, W.R. (2016). Students with learning disabilities and computer-based high stakes testing. *Intervention in School and Clinic, online First,* Retrieved from: http://journals.sagepub.com/doi/abs/10.1177/1053451216676796

Gersten, R., Baker, S. K., & Marks, S. U. (1998). *Teaching English language learners with learning difficulties.* Eugene, OR: Eugene Research Institute.

Gersten, R., Beckmann, S., Clarke, B., Foegen, A., Marsh, L., Star, J. R., & Witzel, B. (2009a). *Assisting students struggling with mathematics: Response to intervention (RtI) for elementary and middle school. A practice guide* (NCEE 2009–4060) [Electronic version]. Washington, DC: National Center for Education Evaluation and Regional Assistance, Institute of Education Sciences. Retrieved from http://ies.ed.gov/ncee/wwc/publications/practiceguides/

Gersten, R., Chard, D. J., Jayanthi, M., Baker, S. K., Morphy, P., & Flojo, J. (2009). Mathematics instruction for students with learning disabilities: A meta-analysis of instructional components. *Review of Educational Research, 79*, 1202–1242. doi:10.3102/0034654309334431

Gersten, R., Compton, D., Connor, C. M., Dimino, J., Santoro, L., Linan-Thompson, S., & Tilly, W. D. (2009b). *Assisting students struggling with reading:Response to intervention and multi-tier intervention for reading in the primary grades, A practice guide* (NCEE 2009–4045) [Electronic version]. Washington, DC: National Center for Education Evaluation and Regional Assistance, Institute of Education Sciences, U.S. Department of Education. Retrieved from http://ies.ed.gov/ncee/wwc/publications/practiceguides/

Gersten, R., Fuchs, L. S., Williams, J. P., & Baker, S. (2001). Teaching reading comprehension strategies to students with learning disabilities: A review of research. *Review of Educational Research, 71*, 279–320.

Gersten, R., Jayanthi, M., & Dimino, J. (2017). Too much, too soon?: Unanswered questions from national response to intervention evaluation. *Exceptional Children, 83(3)*, 244–254.

Giangreco, M. F. (2007). Extending inclusive opportunities. *Educational Leadership, 64*(5), 34–37.

Giangreco, M. F. (2013). Teacher assistant supports in inclusive schools: Research, practices and alternatives. *Australasian Journal of Special Education, 37*, 93–106.

Giangreco, M. F., Doyle, M., & Suter, J. C. (2012). Constructively responding to requests for paraprofessionals: We keep asking the wrong questions. *Remedial and Special Education, 33*, 362–373.

Giangreco, M. F., Suter, J. C., & Doyle, M. (2010). Paraprofessionals in inclusive schools: A review of recent research. *Journal of Educational & Psychological Consultation, 20*, 41–57.

Gibson-Scipio, W., & Krouse, H. J. (2013). Goals, beliefs, and concerns of urban caregivers of middle and older adolescents with asthma. *Journal of Asthma, 50*(3), 242–249.

Gilbertson, D., Duhon, G., Wi, J. C., & Dufrene, B. (2008). Effects of academic response rates on time-on-task in the classroom for students at academic and behavioral risk. *Education and Treatment of Children, 31*, 153–165.

Gildroy, P., & Deshler, D. (2008). Effective learning strategy instruction. In R. J. Morris & N. Mather (Eds.) *Effective Learning Strategy Interventions for Students with Learning and Behavioral Challenges* (pp. 288–301). New York, NY: Routledge.

Gillanders, C., McKinney, M., & Ritchie, S. (2012). What kind of school would you like for your children? Exploring minority mothers' beliefs to promote home-school partnerships. *Early Childhood Education Journal, 40*, 285–294.

Gillespie, A., & Graham, S. (2014). A meta analysis of writing interventions for students with learning disabilities. *Exceptional Children, 80(4)*, 454–473.

Gillette, Y. (2006). Assistive technology and literacy partnerships. *Top Lang Disorders, 26*(1), 70–81.

Gillies, R. M. (2016). Cooperative learning: Review of research and practice. *Australian Journal of Teacher Education, 41*(3), 39–54.

Gitlin, S. (2013). Will smartpen innovations change how teachers and students write and draw? EdTECH:FOCUS ON K-12. Retrieved from

http://www.edtechmagazine.com/k12/article/2013/06/will-new-smartpen-innovations-change-how-teachers-and-students-write-and-draw

Goh, A. E., & Bambara, L. M. (2012). Individualized positive behavior support in school settings: A meta-analysis. *Remedial and Special Education, 33*, 271–286.

Golden, S. M. (2009). Does childhood use of stimulant medication as a treatment for ADHD affect the likelihood of future drug abuse and dependence? A literature review. *Journal of Child & Adolescent Substance Abuse, 18*, 343–358.

Goldman, S. R., Braasch, J. L. G., Wiley, J., Graesser, A. C., & Brodowinska, K. (2012). Comprehending and learning from internet sources: Processing patterns of better and poorer learners. *Reading Research Quarterly, 47*(4), 356–381. DOI:10.1002/rrq.027

Goldstein, H., Moss, J. W., & Jordan, L. J. (1965). *The efficacy of special class training on the development of mentally retarded children* (U.S. Office of Education Cooperative Research Program Project No. 619). Urbana: University of Illinois Institute for Research on Exceptional Children. (ERIC Document Reproduction Service No. ED002907)

Goldstein, J., & Behuniak, P. (2012). Assessing students with significant cognitive disabilities on academic content. *The Journal of Special Education, 46*(2), 117–127.

Gongola, L. C., & Daddario, R. (2010). A practitioner's guide to implementing a differential reinforcement of other behaviors procedure. *Teaching Exceptional Children, 42*(6), 14–20.

Gonring, K., Gerdes, A., & Gardner, D. (2017). Program for the education and enrichment of relational skills: Parental outcomes with an ADHD sample. *Child & Family Behavior Therapy, 39*(1), 19–42.

Gonzalez, L., & Cramer, E. (2013). Class placement and academic and behavioral variables as predictors of graduation for students with disabilities. *Journal of Urban Learning, Teaching, and Research, 9*, 112–123.

Goo, M., Therrien, W. J., & Hua, Y. (2016). Effects of computer-based video instruction on the acquisition and generalization of grocery purchasing skills for students with intellectual disability. *Education and Training in Autism and Developmental Disabilities, 51*, 150–161.

Good, T. L., & Brophy, J. E. (1986). School effects. In M. C. Wittrock (Ed.), *Handbook of research on teaching* (3rd ed., pp. 570–602). Upper Saddle River, NJ: Prentice Hall.

Good, T. L., & Brophy, J. E. (2003). *Looking in Classrooms* (9th ed.). Boston, Ma.: Allyn & Bacon.

Graham, S. (1999). Handwriting and spelling instruction for students with learning disabilities: A review. *Learning Disability Quarterly, 22*(2), 78–98.

Graham, S., & Harris, K. (2013). Common core state standards, writing, and students with LD: Recommendations. *Learning Disabilities Research and Practice, 28*(1), 28–37.

Graham, S., & Harris, K. R. (1987). Improving composition skills of inefficient learners with self-instructional strategy training. *Topics in Language Disorders, 7*(4), 66–77.

Graham, S., & Harris, K.R. (2013). Common core standards, writing, and students with LD: Recommendations. *Learning Disabilities Research & Practice, 28*(1), 28–37.

Graham, S., Collins, A. A., & Rigby-Wills, H. (2017). Writing characteristics of students with learning disabilities and typically achieving peers: A meta-analysis. *Exceptional Children, 83*(2), 199–218.

Graham, S., Harris, K. R., & MacArthur, C. (2006). Explicitly teaching struggling writers: Strategies for mastering the writing process. *Intervention in School and Clinic, 41*(5), 290–294.

Graham, S., Hebert, M., & Harris, K.R. (2015). Formative assessment and writing. *The Elementary School Journal, 115*(4), 498–522.

Grandin, T. (2002). *Teaching tips for children and adults with autism.* Salem, OR: Center for the Study of Autism. Retrieved from http://www.autism.org/temple/tips.html

Grandin, T. (2007). Autism from the inside. *Education Leadership, 64*(5), 29–32.

Grandin, T. (2017). *Temple Grandin: An inside view of autism.* San Diego, CA: Autism Research Institute. Retrieved from https://www.autism.com/advocacy_grandin

Grant, R. (1993). Strategic training for using text headings to improve students' processing of content. *Journal of Reading, 36,* 482–488.

Grantham, T. C. (2012). Eminence-focused gifted education: Concerns about forward movement void of an equity vision. *Gifted Child Quarterly, 56,* 215–220.

Graves, M. F. (2009). *Teaching individual words: One size does not fit all.* New York, NY: Teachers' College Press and International Reading Association.

Green, J. G., Xuan, Z., Kwong, L., Anderson, J. A., & Leaf, P. J. (2016). School referral of children with serious emotional disturbance to systems of care: Six-month clinical and educational outcomes. *Journal of Child and Family Studies, 25,* 3728–3738.

Greenberg, J. (2012). Educational engagement practices of urban immigrant Latina mothers. *Journal of Ethnic & Cultural Diversity in Social Work, 21,* 231–248.

Greenfield, R., Rinaldi, C., Proctor, C. P., & Cardarelli, A. (2010). Teachers' perceptions of a response to intervention (RTI) reform effort in an urban elementary school: A consensual qualitative analysis. *Journal of Disability Policy Studies, 21,* 47–63.

Greenhouse, J. (2015, July 15). The complicated problem of race and special education. *The Huffington Post.* Retrieved from http://www.huffingtonpost.com/entry/racism-inherent-in-special-education-leads-to-marginalization_us_55b63c0ae4b0224d8832b8d3

Gregory, A., Skiba, R. J., & Noguera, P. A. (2010). The achievement gap and the discipline gap: Two sides of the same coin? *Educational Researcher, 39,* 59–68.

Grenier, M., & Yeaton, P. (2011). Previewing: A successful strategy for students with autism. *Journal of Physical Education, Recreation & Dance (JOPERD), 82,* 28–32.

Gresham, F. (2015). Evidence-based social skills interventions for students at risk for EBD. *Remedial and Special Education, 36*(2), 100–104.

Gresham, F. M., Van, M. B., & Cook, C. R. (2006). Social skills training for teaching replacement behaviors: Remediating acquisition deficits in at-risk students. *Behavior Disorders, 31*(4), 363–377.

Griffin, M. M. (2011). Promoting IEP participation: Effects of interventions, considerations for CLD students. *Career Development for Exceptional Individuals, 34,* 153–164.

Gronlund, G. (2006). *Make early learning standards come alive: Connecting your practice to state guidelines.* St. Paul, MN: Red Leaf Press.

Grossman, H. (1995). *Special education in a diverse society.* Boston: Allyn & Bacon.

Guardino, C. A. and Fullerton, E. (July/Aug, 2010). Changing behaviors by changing the classroom environment. *Teaching Exceptional Children, 42*(6), pp. 8–13. Accessed November 6, 2013.

Gul, S., & Vuran, S. (2010). An analysis of studies conducted video modeling in teaching social skills. *Educational Sciences: Theory and Practice, 10,* 249–274.

Guskey, T. R. (2006). Making high school grades meaningful. *Phi Delta Kappan, 87*(9), 670–675.

Guskey, T. R., & Jung, L. A. (2016). Grading: Why you should trust your judgement. *Educational Leadership, 73*(7), 50–54.

Guskey, T. R., Swan, G., & Jung, L. A. (2010, May). *Developing a statewide, standards-based report card: A review of the Kentucky initiative.*

Paper presented at the annual meeting of the American Educational Research Association, St. Louis, Mo.

Gut, J., Reimann, G., & Grob, A. (2013). A contextualized view on long-term predictors of academic performance. *Journal of Educational Psychology, 105,* 436–443.

Guterl, S. (2013, September 20). Is teaching to a student's "learning style" a bogus idea? *Scientific American.* Retrieved from https://www.scientificamerican.com/article/is-teaching-to-a-students-learning-style-a-bogus-idea/

Gyamfi, P., Walrath, C., Burns, B., Stephens, R., Geng, Y., & Stambaugh, L. (2010). Family education and support services in systems of care. *Journal of Emotional and Behavioral Disorders, 18,* 14–26.

Haager, D., & Klinger, J. K. (2004). *Differentiating instruction in inclusive classrooms: The special educator's guide.* Boston: Allyn & Bacon.

Haager, D., & Vaughn, S. (2013). Common core state standards and students with learning disabilities: Introduction to the special issue. *Learning Disabilities Research and Practice, 28*(1), 1–4.

Haager, D., & Vaughn, S. (2013). The common core state standards and reading: Interpretations and implications for elementary students with learning disabilities. *Learning Disabilities Research, 28*(1), 5–16.

Hagaman, J. L., Casey, K. J., & Reid, R. T. (2016). Paraphrasing strategy instruction for struggling readers. *Preventing School Failure, 60*(1), 43–52.

Hale, J. E. (2016). Thirty-year retrospective on the learning styles of African American children. *Education and Urban Society, 48,* 444–459.

Hallahan, D. P., Kauffman, J. M., & Pullen, P. C. (2014). *Exceptional learners: An introduction to special education* (14th ed.). Upper Saddle River, NJ: Pearson.

Hallberg, U. (2014). Differences in health and well-being of parents of children with disabilities. *International Journal of Qualitative Studies on Health and Well-Being, 9* doi:10.3402/qhw.v9.24343

Hamilton, L., Halverson, R., Jackson, S., Mandinach, E., Supovitz, J., & Wayman, J. (2009). *Using student achievement data to support instructional decision making* (NCEE 2009-4067). Washington, DC: National Center for Education Evaluation and Regional Assistance, Institute of Education Sciences, U.S. Department of Education. Retrieved from http://ies.ed.gov/ncee/wwc/publications/practiceguides/.

Hammill, D. (1990). On defining learning disabilities: An emerging consensus. *Journal of Learning Disabilities, 23*(2), 74–84.

Hang, Q., & Rabren, K. (2009). An examination of co-teaching: Perspectives and efficacy indicators. *Remedial and Special Education, 30,* 259–268.

Hanson, E., Cerban, B. M., Slater, C. M., Caccamo, L. M., Bacic, J., & Chan, E. (2013). Brief report: Prevalence of attention deficit/hyperactivity disorder among individuals with an autism spectrum disorder. *Journal of Autism and Developmental Disorders, 43,* 1459–1464.

Harbour, K. E., Evonovich, L. L., Sweigart, C. A., & Hughes, L. E. (2015). A brief review of effective teaching practices that maximize student engagement. *Preventing School Failure, 59*(1), 5–13.

Hardcastle, L. A., & Zirkel, P. A. (2012). The "new" Section 504: Student issues in the wake of the ADAAA. *Journal of Cases in Educational Leadership, 15*(4), 32–39.

Hardman, M. L., Egan, M. W., & Drew, C. J. (2016). *Human exceptionality: School, community, and family, IDEA 2004 update edition* (12th ed.). Boston: Allyn and Bacon.

Harlaar, N., Cutting, L., Deater-Deckard, K., DeThorne, L.S., Justice, L. M., Schatschneider, C., Thompson, L. A., & Petrill, S. A. (2010). Predicting individual differences in reading comprehension: A twin study. *Annals of Dyslexia, 60,* 265–288.

Harley, D. A., Nowak, T. M., Gassway, L. J., & Savage, T. A. (2002). Lesbian, gay, bisexual, and transgender college students with disabilities: A look at multiple cultural minorities. *Psychology in the Schools, 39*, 525–538.

Harn, B. A., Chard, D. J., Biancarosa, G., & Kam'eenui, E. J. (2011). Coordinating instructional supports to accelerate at-risk first-grade readers' performance: An essential mechanism for effective RtI. *Elementary School Journal, 112*, 332–355.

Harniss, M. K., Caros, J., & Gersten, R. (2007). Impact of the design of U.S. history textbooks on content acquisition and academic engagement of special education students: An experimental investigation. *Journal of Learning Disabilities, 40*(2), 100–110.

Harniss, M. K., Epstein, M. H., Bursuck, W. D., Nelson, J., & Jayanthi, M. (2001). Resolving homework-related communication problems: Recommendations of parents of children with and without disabilities. *Reading and Writing Quarterly, 17*, 205–225.

Harris, K. R., Graham, S., Aitken, A. A., Barkel, A., Houston, J., & Ray, A. (2017). Teaching spelling, writing, and reading for writing. *Teaching Exceptional Children, 49*(4), 262–272.

Harris, K. R., Graham, S., Brindle, M., & Sandmel, K. (2009). Metacognition and Children's Writing. *Handbook of metacognition in education*, 131.

Harris, K. R., Graham, S., Mason, L. H. (2003). Self-regulated strategy development in the classroom: Part of a balanced approach to writing instruction for students with disabilities. *Focus on Exceptional Children, 35*(7), 1–16.

Harris, S. F., Prater, M. A., Dyches, T. T., & Heath, M. A. (2009). Job stress of school-based speech-language pathologists. *Communication Disorders Quarterly, 30*, 103–111.

Harrison, J. R., Vannest, K., Davis, J., & Reynolds, C. (2012). Common problem behaviors of children and adolescents in general education classrooms in the United States. *Journal of Emotional and Behavioral Disorders, 20*, 55–64.

Harry, B. (2008). Collaboration with culturally and linguistically diverse families: Ideal versus reality. *Exceptional Children, 74*, 372–388.

Hart, J. E. (2012). Navigating autism's swirling waters. *Phi Delta Kappan, 94*(4), 24–27.

Hart, J. E., & Brehm, J. (2013). Promoting self-determination: A model for training elementary students to self-advocate for IEP accommodations. *Teaching Exceptional Children, 45*(5), 40–48.

Hartacher, J. E., Sanford, A., & Walker, N. N. (2017). *Distinguishing Between Tier 2 and Tier 3 Instruction in Order to Support Implementation of RtI.* http://www.rtinetwork.org/essentasil/tieredinstruction/tier3/distinguish...tier-2-and-tier-3-instruction-in-order-to-support-implementation-of-rti

Hartman, M. (2009). Step by step: Creating a community-based transition program for students with intellectual disabilities. *Teaching Exceptional Children, 41*(6), 6–11.

Hartmann, E. (2011). *Universal design for learning. Practice perspectives—highlighting information on deaf-blindness* [Number 8]. Monmouth, OR: National Consortium on Deaf-Blindness. Retrieved from http://www.eric.ed.gov/contentdelivery/servlet/ERICServlet?accno=ED531767

Hartmann, E. S. (2016). Understanding the everyday practice of individualized education program team members. *Journal of Educational & Psychological Consultation, 26*, 1–24.

Hartzell, R., Liaupsin, C., Gann, C., & Clem, S. (2015). Increasing social engagement in an inclusive environment. Education and Training in Autism and Developmental Disabilities, 50, 264–277.

Harvard Family Research, P. (2010). *Parent-teacher conference tip sheets for principals, teachers, and parents.* Cambridge, MA: Author. Retrieved from http://hfrp.org/var/hfrp/storage/fckeditor/File/FI-ConferenceTipSheet-111810.pdf

Hasbrouck, J. E., & Tindal, G. (2006). Oral reading fluency norms: A valuable assessment tool for reading teachers. *The Reading Teacher, 59*(7), 636–644.

Hattie, J. (2009). *Visible learning: A synthesis of over 800 meta-analyses relating to achievement.* London: Routledge.

Hawkins, R., Musti-Rao, S., Hughes, C., Berry, L., & McGuire, S. (2009). Applying a randomized interdependent group contingency component to classwide peer tutoring for multiplication fact fluency. *Journal of Behavioral Education, 18*, 300–318.

Haydon, T., Mancil, G. R., & VanLoan, C. (2009). Using opportunities to respond in a general education classroom: A case study. *Education and Treatment of Children, 32*, 267–278.

Hazelkorn, M., Bucholz, J. L., Goodman, J. I., Duffy, M., & Brady, M. P. (2011). Response to intervention: General or special education? Who is responsible? *Educational Forum, 75*(1), 17–25.

Heath, D. (1993). Using portfolio assessment with secondary LED students yields a cross-cultural advantage for all. *BeOutreach, 4*(1), 27.

Heffernan, L., & Lyons, D. (2016). Differential reinforcement of other behaviour for the reduction of severe nail biting. *Behavior Analysis in Practice, 9*, 253–256.

Heitin, R. (2017). *Writing IEP goals.* Retrieved from http://www.wrightslaw.com/info/goals.lesson.heitin.htm.

Helman, A. L., Calhoon, M. B., & Kern, L. (2015). Improving science vocabulary of high school English language learners with reading disabilities. *Learning Disability Quarterly, 38*(1), 40–52.

Helman, C. (2005, July). Cultural aspects of time and ageing. *Science and Society* [National Center for Biotechnology Information, EMBO Report, Suppl. 1], 54–58. Retrieved from http://www.nature.com/embor/journal/v6/n1s/full/7400402.html

Henfield, M. S., & Washington, A. R. (2012). "I want to do the right thing but what is it?": White teachers' experiences with African American students. *Journal of Negro Education, 81*, 148–161.

Henley, M. (2003). *Teaching self-control: A curriculum for responsible behavior* (2nd ed.). Bloomington, IN: National Education Service.

Herbers, J. E., Cutuli, J. J., Supkoff, L. M., Heistad, D., Chan, C., Hinz, E., & Masten, A. S. (2012). Early reading skills and academic achievement trajectories of students facing poverty, homelessness, and high residential mobility. *Educational Researcher, 41*, 366–374.

Hertberg-Davis, H. (2009). Myth 7: Differentiation in the regular classroom is equivalent to gifted programs and is sufficient—classroom teachers have the time, the skill, and the will to differentiate adequately. *Gifted Child Quarterly, 53*, 251–253.

Hessler, T., Konrad, M., & Alber-Morgan, S. (2009). 20 ways to assess student writing. *Intervention in School and Clinic, 45*, 68–71.

Hetzroni, O. E., & Shrieber, B. (2004). Word processing as an assistive technology tool for enhancing academic outcomes of students with writing disabilities in the general classroom. *Journal of Learning Disabilities, 37*, 143–154.

Hiebert, E.H. (2012). Curious George and Rosetta Stone: The role of texts in supporting automaticity for beginning reading. In T. Raskinski, C. Blachowicz, & K. Lems (Eds.), *Fluency instruction: Research-based practices* (2nd ed., pp. 289–309). New York: Guilford Press.

Hill, J., & Flynn, K. (2006). *Classroom instruction that works with English language learners.* Alexandria, VA: Association for Supervision and Curriculum Development.

Hilliard, P. (2015). *Performance-Based Assessment: Reviewing the Basics.* George Lucas Educational Foundation. Retrieved from https://www.edutopia.org/blog/performance-based-assessment-reviewing-basics-patricia-hilliard

Hinkelman, L., & Bruno, M. (2008). Identification and reporting of child sexual abuse: The role of elementary school professionals. *Elementary School Journal, 108*, 376–391.

Hintze, J. M. (2007). Conceptual and empirical issues related to developing a response-to-intervention framework. Paper presented at the National Center on Student Progress Monitoring, Washington, DC. Retrieved from http://studentprogress.org/doc/Hintze2008 ConceptualandEmpiricalIssuesofRTI.doc

Hintze, J. M., Christ, T. J., & Methe, S. A. (2006). Curriculum-based assessment. *Psychology in the Schools, 43*(1), 45–56.

Hmelo-Silver, C. E., Duncan, R. G., & Chinn, C. A. (2007). Scaffolding and achievement in problem-based and inquiry learning: A response to Kirschner, Sweller & Clark (2006). *Educational Psychologist, 42*(2), 99–107.

Hobbs, N. (1975). *The futures of children.* San Francisco: Jossey-Bass.

Holbrook, M. D. (2007). *Standards-based individualized education program examples.* Alexandria, VA: National Association of State Directors of Special Education. Retrieved October 8, 2017 from http://www.nasdse.org/portals/0/standards-basediepexamples.pdf.

Holliday, D. C. (2002). *Jigsaw IV: Using student/teacher concerns to improve Jigsaw III.* (ERIC Document Reproduction Service No. ED465687)

Hollingshead, A., Carnahan, C. R., Lowrey, K. A., & Snyder, K. (2017). Engagement for students with severe intellectual disability: The need for a common definition in inclusive education. *Inclusion, 5*(1), 1–15.

Hollo, A., & Hirn, R. G. (2015). Teacher and student behaviors in the contexts of grade-level and instructional grouping. *Preventing School Failure, 59*(1), 30–39.

Hollo, A., Wehby, J. H., & Oliver, R. M. (2014). Unidentified language deficits in children with emotional and behavioral disorders: A meta-analysis. *Exceptional Children, 80*(2), 169–186.

Homme, L. (1970). *How to use contingency contracting in the classroom.* Champaign, IL: Research Press.

Hong, J., Cheng, C., Hwang, M., Lee, C., & Chang, H. (2009). Assessing the educational value of digital games. *Journal of Computer-Assisted Learning, 25*(5), 423–437.

Honigsfeld, A., & Dove, M. G. (2010). *Collaboration and co-teaching: Strategies for English learners.* Thousand Oaks, CA: Corwin.

Honigsfeld, A., & Dove, M. G. (2016). Co-teaching ELLs: Riding a tandem bike. *Educational Leadership, 73*(4), 56–60.

Hoog, B. E., Langereis, M. C., Weerdenburg, M., Knoors, H. T., & Verhoeven, L. (2016). Linguistic profiles of children with CI as compared with children with hearing or specific language impairment. *International Journal of Language & Communication Disorders, 51*, 518–530.

Hoover, J. J. (2012). Reducing unnecessary referrals: Guidelines for teachers of diverse learners. *Teaching Exceptional Children, 44*(4), 38–47.

Hoppey, D., & McLeskey, J. (2013). A case study of principal leadership in an effective inclusive school. *Journal of Special Education, 46*, 245–256.

Horner, R. H., Sugai, G., & Fixsen, D. L. (2017). Implementing effective educational practices at scales of social importance. *Clinical Child and Family Psychology Review, 20*, 25–35.

Horton S. V., Boone R., Lovitt T. (1990). Teaching social studies to learning disabled high school students: Effects of a hypertext study guide. *British Journal of Educational Technology, 21*, 118–131. Google Scholar CrossRef

Hosp, J. L. (2008). Best practices in aligning academic assessment with instruction. In A. Thomas, & J. Grimes (Eds.), *Best practices in school psychology* (5th ed., pp. 363–376). Bethesda, MD: National Association of School Psychologists.

Hosp, J. L., & Reschly, D. J. (2004). Disproportionate representation of minority students in special education: Academic, demographic, and economic predictors. *Exceptional Children, 70*, 185–199.

Hosp, M. K., & Hosp, J. (2003). Curriculum-based measurement for reading, spelling, and math: How to do it and why. *Preventing School Failure, 48*(1), 10–17.

Howell, K. M., & Morehead, M. K. (1993). *Curriculum-based evaluation for special and remedial education* (2nd ed.). Columbus, OH: Merrill.

Huberman, M., Navo, M., & Parrish, T. (2012). Effective practices in high performing districts serving students in special education. *Journal of Special Education Leadership, 25*(2), 59–71.

Hudson, R. F., Torgesen, J. K., Lane, H. B., & Turner, S. J. (2012). Relations among reading skills and sub-skills and text-level reading proficiency in developing readers. *Reading and Writing: An Interdisciplinary Journal, 25*(2), 483–507.

Hudson, R.F., High, L., & Al Otaiba, S. (2007). Dyslexia and the brain: What does current research tell us? *The Reading Teacher, 60*(6), 506-515.

Huebner, T. A. (2010). Meeting students where they are. *Educational Leadership, 67*(5), 79–81.

Hughes, C., & Dexter, D. D. (2010). *Universal screening within a response to intervention model.* http://www.rtinetwork.org/learn/research/universalscreening-within-a-rti-model

Hughes, E. M., Powell, S. R., Lembke, E. S., & Riley-Tillman, T. C. (2016). Taking the guesswork out of locating evidence-based mathematics practices for diverse learners. *Learning Disabilities Research & Practice, 31*, 130–141.

Hulac, D., & Benson, N. (2010). The use of group contingencies for preventing and managing disruptive behaviors. *Intervention in School and Clinic, 45*, 257–262.

Hung, W. (2011). Theory to reality: A few issues in implementing problem-based learning. *Educational Technology Research and Development, 59*(4), 529–552.

Hung, W., Jonassen, D. H., & Liu, R. (2008). Problem-based learning. *Handbook of Research on Educational Communications and Technology, 3*, 485–506.

Hunter, W. C., Dieker, L. A., & Whitney, T. (2016). Consultants and coteachers affecting student outcomes with numbered heads together: Keeping all engaged. *Journal of Educational & Psychological Consultation, 26*, 186–199.

Hurley, K. D., Lambert, M. C., Epstein, M. H., & Stevens, A. (2015). Convergent validity of the strength-based behavioral and emotional rating scale with youth in a residential setting. *Journal of Behavioral Health Services Research, 42*(3), 346–354.

Hyatt, K. J. (2007). Brain Gym™ building stronger brains or wishful thinking? *Remedial and Special Education, 28*(2), 117–124.

Hyman, S. L., Stewart, P. A., Foley, J., Cain, U., Peck, R., Morris, D. D., & . . . Smith, T. (2016). The gluten-free/casein-free diet: A double-blind challenge trial in children with autism. *Journal of Autism and Developmental Disorders, 46*, 205–220.

Ira, V. B. (2000). Safe and secure on the web: Pointers on determining a web site's credibility. *Exceptional Parent, 30*(1), 148.

Irlen, H. (1991). *Reading by the colors: Overcoming dyslexia and other reading disabilities through the Irlen method.* Garden City Park, NY: Avery.

Isaacson, S. (2001). Written language. In P. J. Schloss, M. A. Smith, & C. N. Schloss (Eds.), *Instructional methods for secondary students with learning and behavior problems* (3rd ed., pp. 222–245). Boston: Allyn and Bacon.

Ivy, S. E., Lather, A. B., Hatton, D. D., & Wehby, J. H. (2016). Toward the development of a self-management intervention to promote pro-social behaviors for students with visual impairment. *Journal of Special Education, 50*, 141–150.

Jackson, C. W., & Larkin, M. J. (2002). RUBRIC: Teaching students to use grading rubrics. *Teaching Exceptional Children, 35*(1), 40–45.

Jacob Javits Gifted and Talented Students Education Act of 1988, 20 USC §3065.

Jacobs, G. M., Power, M. A., & Loh, W. I. (2016). *The teacher's sourcebook for cooperative learning: Practical techniques, basic principles, and frequently asked questions.* New York, NY: Skyhorse Publishing.

Jamie, K., & Knowlton, E. (2007). Visual supports for students with behavior and cognitive challenges. *Intervention in School and Clinic, 42*(5), 259–270.

Jang, H., Reeve, J., & Deci, E. L. (2010). Engaging students in learning activities: It is not autonomy support or structure but autonomy support and structure. *Journal of Educational Psychology, 102*(3), 588–600.

Jansen, S. G., van der Putten, A. J., & Vlaskamp, C. (2013). What parents find important in the support of a child with profound intellectual and multiple disabilities. *Child: Care, Health and Development, 39*(3), 432–441.

Jantz, P. B., Davies, S. C., & Bigler, E. D. (2014). *Working with traumatic brain injury in schools: Transition, assessment, and intervention.* New York, NY: Routledge.

Jarolimek, J., Foster, C. D., & Kellough, R. D. (2004). *Teaching and learning in the elementary school* (8th ed.). Upper Saddle River, NJ: Prentice Hall.

Jenkins, J. (2009). Measuring reading growth: New findings on progress monitoring. *New Times for DLD, 27*, 1–2.

Jenkins, J. R., Schiller, E., Blackorby, J., Thayer, S., & Tilly, W. (2013). Responsiveness to intervention in reading: Architecture and practices. *Learning Disability Quarterly, 36*, 36–46.

Jensen, R. J. (2004). Discipline preferences and styles among Latino families: Implications for special educators. *Multiple Voices, 7*(1), 60–73.

Jenson, W. R., Sheridan, S. M., Olympia, D., & Andrews, D. (1994). Homework and students with learning disabilities and behavior disorders: A practical, parent-based approach. *Journal of Learning Disabilities, 27*, 538–549.

Jessurun, J. H., Shearer, C. B., & Weggeman, M. P. (2016). A universal model of giftedness—An adaptation of the Munich model. *High Ability Studies, 27*, 113–128.

Jiang, Y., Granja, M. R., & Koball, H. (2017, January). *Basic facts about low-income children under 18 years, 2015.* New York, NY: National Center for Children in Poverty (NCCP), Columbia University. Retrieved from http://www.nccp.org/publications/pub_1170.html

Jimerson, S. R., Burns, M. K., & VanDerHeyden, A. M. (2016). From response to intervention to multi-tiered systems of support: Advances in the science and practice of assessment and intervention. In S. R. Jimerson, M. K. Burns, A. M. VanDerHeyden, S. R. Jimerson, M. K. Burns, & A. M. VanDerHeyden (Eds.), *Handbook of response to intervention: The science and practice of multi-tiered systems of support* (2nd edition) (pp. 1–6). New York, NY: Springer Science + Business Media.

Jimerson, S. R., Burns, M. K., & VanDerHeyden, A. M. (2016). *Handbook of response to intervention: The science and practice of multi-tiered systems of support* (2nd edition). New York, NY: Springer.

Jitendra, A. K., Nelson, G., Pulles, S. M., Kiss, A. J., & Houseworth, J. (2016). Is mathematical representation of problems an evidence-based strategy for students with math difficulties? *Exceptional Children, 83*(1), 8–25.

Johns, B. H. (2016). *Your classroom guide to special education law.* Baltimore, MD: Paul H. Brookes.

Johnson, C., & Gooliaff, S. (2013). Teaching to strengths: Engaging young boys in learning. *Reclaiming Children and Youth, 21*(4), 28–31.

Johnson, E. S., Pool, J., & Carter, D. R. (2013, March) *Screening for Reading Problems in Grades 4–12.* Retrieved from http://rtinetwork.org/

Johnson, E., & Arnold, N. (2004). Validating an alternate assessment. *Remedial and Special Education, 25*, 266–275.

Johnson, E. S., Smith, L., & Harris, M. L. (2009). *How RTI Works in Secondary Schools.* Thousand Oaks, CA: Corwin.

Jolliffe, W. (2007). *Cooperative learning in the classroom: Putting it into practice.* Thousand Oaks, CA: Sage.

Jones, G., Ostojic, D., Menard, J., Picard, E., & Miller, C. J. (2017). Primary prevention of reading failure: Effect of universal peer tutoring in the early grades. *Journal of Educational Research, 110*, 171–176.

Jones, N. D., Buzick, H. M., & Turkan, S. (2013). Including students with disabilities and English learners in measures of educator effectiveness. *Educational Researcher, 42*, 234–241.

Jones, S. K. (2015). Teaching students with disabilities: A review of music education research as it relates to the Individuals with Disabilities Education Act. *Update: Applications of Research in Music Education, 34*(1), 13–23.

Jones, V. F., & Jones, L. S. (2004). *Comprehensive classroom management: Creating communities of support and solving problems* (7th ed.). Boston: Allyn and Bacon.

Joseph, L. H., Konrad, M., Cates, G., Jajcner, T., Eveleigh, E., & Fishley, K. M. (2012). A meta-analytic review of cover-copy-compare and variations of the self-management procedure. *Psychology in the Schools, 49*(2), 122–136.

Joseph, L. M., Alber-Morgan, S., Cullen, J., & Rouse, C. (2016). The effects of self-questioning on reading comprehension: A literature review. *Reading & Writing Quarterly, 32*(2), 152–173.

Joy, S., & Kolb, D. A. (2009). Are there cultural differences in learning style? *International Journal of Intercultural Relations, 33*, 69–85.

Joyce-Beaulieu, D., & Sulkowski, M. L. (2015). *Cognitive behavioral therapy in K–12 school settings: A practitioner's toolkit.* New York, NY: Springer.

Juel, C. (1988). Learning to read and write: A longitudinal study of 54 children from first through fourth grades. *Journal of Educational Psychology, 80*(4), 437–447.

Jung, L. A., & Guskey, T. R. (2011). Fair and accurate grading for exceptional learners. *Principal Leadership, 12*(3), 32–37.

Jung, L. A., & Guskey, T. R. (2012). *Grading Exceptional and Struggling Learners.* Thousand Oaks, CA: Corwin.

Jung, L., & Guskey, T. R. (2007). Standards-based grading and reporting: A model for special education. *Teaching Exceptional Children, 40*(2), 48–53.

Jung-Sook, J. (2013). The relationship between student engagement and academic performance: Is it a myth or reality? *The Journal of Educational Research, 107*(3), 177–185.

Juul, H., Poulsen, M., & Elbro, C. (2014). Separating speed from accuracy in beginning reading development. *Journal of Educational Psychology, 106*(4), 1096–1106.

Kagan, S. (1990). A structural approach to cooperative learning. *Educational Leadership, 47*(4), 12–15.

Kahn, L. G., Lindstrom, L., & Murray, C. (2014). Factors contributing to preservice teachers' beliefs about diversity. *Teacher Education Quarterly, 41*(4), 53–70.

Kaldenberg, E. R., Watt, S. J., & Therrien, W. J. (2015). Reading instruction in science for students with learning disabilities: A meta-analysis. *Learning Disability Quarterly, 38*(3), 160–173.

Kamhi, A. G., & Catts, H. W. (2011). *Language and reading disabilities*. (3rd ed.). Boston: Allyn and Bacon (Pearson).

Kampwirth, T. J., & Powers, K. M. (2012). *Collaborative consultation in the schools: Effective practices for students with learning and behavior problems* (4th ed.). Upper Saddle River, NJ: Pearson.

Kampwirth, T. J., & Powers, K. M. (2016). *Collaborative consultation in the schools: Effective practices for students with learning and behavior problems* (5th edition). Boston, MA: Pearson.

Kang, S., O'Reilly, M., Rojeski, L., Blenden, K., Xu, Z., Davis, T., & . . . Lancioni, G. (2013). Effects of tangible and social reinforcers on skill acquisition, stereotyped behavior, and task engagement in three children with autism spectrum disorders. *Research in Developmental Disabilities: A Multidisciplinary Journal, 34*, 739–744.

Kantak, K. M., & Dwoskin, L. P. (2016). Necessity for research directed at stimulant type and treatment-onset age to access the impact of medication on drug abuse vulnerability in teenagers with ADHD. Pha*rmacology, Biochemistry and Behavior, 14*(5), 24–26.

Katz, J. (2013). The three block model of universal design for learning (UDL): Engaging students in inclusive education. *Canadian Journal of Education, 36*(1), 153–194.

Kauffman, J. M. (2011). Toward a science *of education: The battle between rogue and real science*. Verona, WI: Attainment.

Kauffman, J. M. (2015a). Opinion on recent developments and the future of special education. *Remedial and Special Education, 36*, 9–13.

Kauffman, J. M. (2015b). Why exceptionality is more important for special education than exceptional children. *Exceptionality, 23*, 225–236.

Kauffman, J. M., & Badar, J. (2014). Instruction, not inclusion, should be the central issue in special education: An alternative view from the USA. *Journal of International Special Needs Education, 17*(1), 13–20.

Kauffman, J. M., &, Landrum, T. J. (2017). *Characteristics of emotional and behavioral disorders of children and youth* (11th ed.). Upper Saddle River, NJ: Merrill/Pearson.

Kavale, K. A., & Forness, S. R. (2000). History, rhetoric, and reality: Analysis of inclusion debate. *Remedial and Special Education, 21*, 279–296.

Kellems, R. O., Springer, B., Wilkins, M. K., & Anderson, C. (2016). Collaboration in transition assessment: School psychologists and special educators working together to improve outcomes for students with disabilities. *Preventing School Failure, 60*, 215–221.

Kelly, B., & Carnine, D. (1996). Teaching problem-solving strategies for word problems to students with learning disabilities. *LD Forum, 21(3)*, 5–9.

Kelly, M. S., Constable, R., Capio, M., Swanlund, L., Thomas, G., & Leyba, E. G. (2016). School social workers and the special education process: From assessment to individualized education programs to school social work services. In C. Rippey Massat, M. S. Kelly, & R. Constable (Eds.), *School social work: Practice, policy, and research* (pp. 269–298). Chicago, IL: Lyceum Books.

Kern, L., & Clemens, N. H. (2007). Antecedent strategies to promote appropriate classroom behavior. *Psychology in the Schools, 44*(1), 65–75.

Kerr, M. M., & Nelson, C. M. (2009). *Strategies for managing behavior problems in the classroom* (6th ed.). Upper Saddle River, NJ: Merrill/Pearson.

Kersaint, G., Thompson, D. R., Petkova, M. (2013). *Teaching mathematics to English-language learners* (2nd ed.). New York, NY: Routledge.

Ketterlin-Geller, L. R., Baumer, P., & Lichon, K. (2015). Administrators as advocates for teacher collaboration. *Intervention in School and Clinic, 51*(1), 51–57.

Kettler, T., & Hurst, L. T. (2017). Advanced academic participation: A longitudinal analysis of ethnicity gaps in suburban schools. *Journal for the Education of the Gifted, 40*(1), 3–19.

Killu, K. (2008). Developing effective behavior intervention plans: Suggestions for school personnel. *Intervention in School and Clinic, 43*, 140–149.

Kim, A., Vaughn, S., Klinger, J. K., Woodruff, A. L., Reutebuch, C. K., & Kouzekanani, K. (2006). Improving the reading comprehension of middle school students with disabilities through computer-assisted collaborative strategic reading. *Remedial and Special Education, 27*(4), 235–249.

Kim, D. S., Burt, A. A., Ranchalis, J. E., Wilmot, B., Smith, J. D., Patterson, K. E., & . . . Jarvik, G. P. (2017). Sequencing of sporadic attention-deficit hyperactivity disorder (ADHD) identifies novel and potentially pathogenic de novo variants and excludes overlap with genes associated with autism spectrum disorder. *American Journal of Medical Genetics Part B: Neuropsychiatric Genetics, 174*, 381–389.

Kim, W., & Linan-Thompson, S. L. (2013). The effects of self-regulation on science vocabulary acquisition of English Language Learners with learning difficulties. *Remedial and Special Education, 34*(4), 225–236.

King, D., & Coughlin, P. K. (2016). Looking beyond RtI standard treatment approach: It's not too late to embrace the problem-solving approach. *Preventing School Failure, 60*, 244–251.

King, M. B., & Youngs, P. (2003). *Classroom teachers' views on inclusion (Riser Brief No. 7)*. Madison: University of Wisconsin-Madison, Research Institute on Secondary Education Reform for Youth with Disabilities (RISER). (ERIC Document Reproduction Service No. ED477878)

King-Sears, M. E. (2007). Designing and delivering learning center instruction. *Intervention in School and Clinic, 42*(3), 137–147.

King-Sears, M. E., Burgess, M., & Lawson, T. L. (1999). Applying curriculum-based assessment in inclusive settings. *Teaching Exceptional Children, 32*(1), 30–38.

King-Sears, M. E., Evmenova, A. S., & Johnson, T. M. (2017). Using technology for accessible chemistry homework for high school students with and without disabilities. *Learning Disabilities Research & practice, 32(2)*, 121–131.

Kiuhara, S. A., O'Neill, R. E., Hawken, L. S., & Graham, S. (2012). The effectiveness of teaching 10th grade students STOP, AIMS, and DARE for planning and draftin persuasive text. *Exceptional Children, 78*(3), 335–355.

Klehm, M. (2014). The effects of teacher beliefs on teaching practices and achievement of students with disabilities. *Teacher Education and Special Education, 37*, 216–240.

Kleinert, H., Green, P., Hurte, M., Clayton, J., & Oetinger, C. (2002). Creating and using meaningful alternate assessments. *Teaching Exceptional Children, 34(4),* pp. 40–47.

Kleinhenz, E., & Ingvarson, L. (2004). Teacher accountability in Australia: Current policies and practices and their relationship to the improvement of teaching and learning. *Research Papers in Education, 19*(1), 31–49. Retrieved October 23, 2007, from Academic Search Complete database.

Kluth, P. (2003). *"You're going to love this kid": Teaching students with autism in the inclusive classroom*. Baltimore: Brookes.

Kluth, P., & Causton, J. (2016). *30 days to the co-taught classroom: How to create an amazing, nearly miraculous & frankly earth-shattering partnership in one month or less*. Minneapolis, MN: North Look Books.

Knackendoffel, A., Dettmer, P., & Thurston, L. P. (2018). *Collaborating, consulting, and working in teams for students with special needs* (8th edition). Boston, MA: Pearson.

Knight, J. (2002). Crossing boundaries: What constructivists can teach intensive-explicit instructors and vice versa. *Focus on Exceptional Children, 35*(4), 1–15.

Knight, V., Sartini, E., & Spriggs, A. D. (2015). Evaluating visual activity schedules as evidence-based practice for individuals with autism spectrum disorders. *Journal of Autism and Developmental Disorders, 45*, 157–178.

Knoff, H. M. (2012). *School discipline, classroom management, and student self-management: A PBS implementation guide.* Thousand Oaks, CA: Corwin.

Knopf, A. (2016). CDC: Parent training underutilized in ADHD in young children. *Brown University Child & Adolescent Behavior Letter, 32*, 1–2.

Kode, K. (2002). *Elizabeth Farrell and the history of special education.* Arlington, VA: Council for Exceptional Children.

Koegel, L. K., Vernon, T. W., Koegel, R. L., Koegel, B. L., & Paullin, A. W. (2012). Improving social engagement and initiations between children with autism spectrum disorder and their peers in inclusive settings. *Journal of Positive Behavior Interventions, 14*, 220–227.

Koellner, K., Colsman, M., & Risley, R. (2014). Multidimensional assessment: Guiding Response to Intervention in mathematics. *Teaching Exceptional Children, 47*(2), 103–111.

Kohn, A. (2010). How to create nonreaders: Reflections on motivation, learning, and sharing power. *English Journal, 100*(1), 16–22.

Korinek, L., & deFur, S. H. (2016). Supporting student self-regulation to access the general education curriculum. *Teaching Exceptional Children, 48*(5), 232–242.

Korpershoek, H., Harms, T., de Boer, H., van Kuijk, M., & Doolaard, S. (2014). Effective classroom management strategies and classroom management programs for educational practice: A meta-analysis of the effects of classroom management strategies and classroom management programs on students' academic, behavioural, emotional, and motivational outcomes. Groningen: RUG/GION.

Kozen, A. A., Murray, R. K., & Windell, I. (2006). Increasing all students' chance to achieve: Using and adapting anticipation guides with middle school learners. *Intervention in School and Clinic, 41*(4), 195–200.

Kozik, P., Cooney, B., Vinciguerra, S., Gradel, K., & Black, J. (2009). Promoting inclusion in secondary schools through appreciative inquiry. *American Secondary Education, 38*, 77–91.

Kozleski, E. B., Yu, T., Satter, A. L., Francis, G. L., & Haines, S. J. (2015). A never ending journey: Inclusive education is a principle of practice, not an end game. *Research and Practice for Persons with Severe Disabilities, 40*, 211–226.

Kuchle, L. B., Edmonds, R. Z., Danielson, L. C., Peterson, A., & Riley-Tillman, T. C. (2015). The next big idea: A framework for integrated academic and behavioral intensive intervention. *Learning Disabilities Research & Practice, 30*(4), 150–158.

Kuder, S. J. (2017). Vocabulary instruction for secondary students with reading disabilities: An updated research review. *Learning Disability Quarterly, 40*(3), 155–164.

Kuiper, E., Volman, M., & Terwel, J. (2005). The web as an information resource in K–12 education: Strategies for supporting students in searching and processing information. *Review of Educational Research, 75*(3), 285–328.

Kunsch, C. A., Jitendra, A. K., & Sood, S. (2007). The effects of peer-mediated instruction in mathematics for students with learning problems: A research synthesis. *Learning Disabilities Research & Practice, 22*, 1–12.

Kuriyan, A. B., Pelham, W. R., Molina, B. G., Waschbusch, D. A., Gnagy, E. M., Sibley, M. H., & . . . Kent, K. M. (2013). Young adult educational and vocational outcomes of children diagnosed with ADHD. *Journal of Abnormal Child Psychology, 41*, 27–41.

Kurth, J., & Mastergeorge, A. M. (2012). Impact of setting and instructional context for adolescents with autism. *Journal of Special Education, 46*, 36–48.

Kurz, A., Elliott, S. N., & Roach, A. T. (2015). Addressing the missing instructional data problem: Using a teacher log to document Tier 1 instruction. *Remedial and Special Education, 36*, 361–373.

Kyzar, K. B., Brady, S. E., Summers, J. A., Haines, S. J., & Turnbull, A. P. (2016). Services and supports, partnership, and family quality of life: Focus on deaf-blindness. *Exceptional Children, 83*, 77–91.

Ladson-Billings, G. (1994). *The dreamkeepers: Successful teachers for African American children.* San Francisco: Jossey-Bass.

Lagares, C. L., & Connor, D. J. (2010). Help students prepare for high school examinations. *Intervention in School and Clinic, 45*(1), 63–67.

Lalvani, P. (2012). Parents' participation in special education in the context of implicit educational ideologies and socioeconomic status. *Education and Training in Autism and Developmental Disabilities, 47*, 474–486.

Landis, R. N., & Reschly, A. L. (2013). Reexamining gifted underachievement and dropout through the lens of student engagement. *Journal for the Education of the Gifted, 36*, 220–249.

Landrum, T. J., & McDuffie, K. A. (2010). Learning styles in the age of differentiated instruction. *Exceptionality, 18*(1), 6–17.

Landrum, T. J., Scott, T. M., & Lingo, A. S. (2011). Classroom misbehavior is predictable and preventable. *Phi Delta Kappan, 93*(2), 30–34.

Lane, K. L., Carter, E. W., Pierson, M. R., & Glaeser, B. C. (2006). Academic, social and behavioral characteristics of high school students with emotional disturbances or learning disabilities. *Journal of Emotional and Behavioral Disorders, 14*(2), 106–117.

Lane, K. L., Oakes, W. P., Ennis, R. P., & Eisner, S. (2014). Identifying students for secondary and tertiary prevention efforts: How do we determine which students have Tier 2 and Tier 3 needs? *Preventing School Failure, 58*(3), 171–182.

Lane, K. L., Royer, D. J., Messenger, M. L., Common, E. A., Ennis, R. P., & Swogger, E. D. (2015). Empowering teachers with low-intensity strategies to support academic engagement: Implementation and effects of instructional choice for elementary students in inclusive settings. *Education and Treatment of Children, 38*, 473–504.

Lane, K. L., Wehby, J., & Barton-Arwood, S. M. (2005). Students with and at risk for emotional and behavioral disorders: Meeting their social and academic needs. *Preventing School Failure, 49*(2), 6–9.

Lane, K., Capizzi, A. M., Fisher, M. H., & Ennis, R. (2012). Secondary prevention efforts at the middle school level: An application of the behavior education program. *Education and Treatment of Children, 35*, 51–90.

Lane, K., Menzies, H., Bruhn, A. L., & Crnobori, M. (2010). *Managing challenging behaviors in schools: Research-based strategies that work.* New York, NY: Guilford Publications.

Lane, K., Oakes, W., Menzies, H., Oyer, J., & Jenkins, A. (2013). Working within the context of three-tiered models of prevention: Using school-wide data to identify high school students for targeted supports. *Journal of Applied School Psychology, 29*, 203–229.

Langberg, J. M., Dvorsky, M. R., & Evans, S. W. (2013). What specific facets of executive function are associated with academic functioning in youth with attention-deficit/hyperactivity disorder? *Journal of Abnormal Child Psychology, 41*(7), 1145–1159.

Langberg, J. M., Dvorsky, M. R., Molitor, S. J., Bourchtein, E., Eddy, L. D., Smith, Z., Schultz, B. K., & Evans, S. W. (2015). Longitudinal evaluation of the importance of homework assignment completion for the academic performance of middle school students with ADHD. *Journal of School Psychology, 55*, 27–38.

Langberg, J. M., Epstein, J. N., Urbanowicz, C. M., Simon, J. O., & Graham, A. J. (2008). Efficacy of an organization skills intervention to improve the academic functioning of students with attention-deficit/hyperactivity disorder. *School Psychology Quarterly, 23*(3), 407–417.

Langberg, J. M., Vaughn, A. J., Williamson, P., Epstein, J. N., Girio-Herrera, E., & Becker, S. P. (2011). Refinement of an organizational skills intervention for adolescents with ADHD for implementation by school mental health providers. *School Mental health, 3*(3), 143–155.

Langer, J. (1984). Examining background knowledge and text comprehension. *Reading Research Quarterly, 19,* 468–481.

Langner, I., Garbe, E., Banaschewski, T., & Mikolajczyk, R. T. (2013). Twin and sibling studies using health insurance data: The example of attention deficit/hyperactivity disorder (ADHD). *Plos ONE, 8*(4). doi:10.1371/journal.pone.0062177

Laushey, K. M., Hefflin, L. J., Shippen, M., Alberto, P. A., & Fredrick, L. (2009). Concept mastery routines to teach social skills to elementary children with high functioning autism. *Journal of Autism and Developmental Disorders, 39,* 1435–1448.

Lavoie, R. (1991). *How difficult can this be? Understanding learning disabilities* [Videotape]. Portland, OR: Educational Productions.

Lavoie, R. (2007). *The Motivation breakthrough: 6 secrets to turning on the tuned out child.* New York City, NY: Simon & Schuster.

Lazarus, S. S., Thurlow, M. L., Lail, K. E., & Christensen, L. (2009). Longitudinal analysis of state accommodations policies: Twelve years of change, 1993–2005. *Journal of Special Education, 43,* 67–80.

Leach, D., & Duffy, M. (2009). Supporting students with autism spectrum disorders in inclusive settings. *Intervention in School and Clinic, 45*(1), 31–37.

Leaf, M. L. (2012). Teaching social skills to children with autism using the cool versus not cool procedure. *Education and Training in Autism and Developmental Disabilities, 47,* 165–175.

Learning Disabilities Association of America. (n.d.). Symptoms of learning disabilities. Retrieved from: https://ldaamerica.org/symptoms-of-learning-disabilities/

Lee, D. L., Vostal, B., Lylo, B., & Hua, Y. (2011). Collecting behavioral data in general education settings: A primer for behavioral data collection. *Beyond Behavior, 20*(2), 22–30.

Lee, H., McCullough, C., Heider, F., Hanlon, C., & Kniffin, T. (2016, August). The effectiveness of interventions to address childhood asthma: A scan of the literature and current approaches. New York, NY: MDRC. Retrieved from MDRC http://files.eric.ed.gov/fulltext/ED568392.pdf

Lee, K., Penrod, B., & Price, J. N. (2017). A comparison of cost and reward procedures with interdependent group contingencies. *Behavior Modification, 41,* 21–44.

Lee, O., & Buxton, C. A. (2013). Integrating science learning and English language development for English language learners. *Theory into Practice, 52*(1), 36–42.

Lee, S. (2013). The problem with punishment. *Reclaiming Children and Youth, 21*(4), 51–54.

Lee, S., Olszewski-Kubilius, P., & Thomson, D. (2012). Academically gifted students' perceived interpersonal competence and peer relationships. *Gifted Child Quarterly, 56,* 90–104.

Lee, S., Wehmeyer, M. L., Soukup, J. H., & Palmer, S. B. (2010). Impact of curriculum modifications on access to the general education curriculum for students with disabilities. *Exceptional Children, 76*(2), 213–233.

Lee, Y., Wehmeyer, M. L., Palmer, S. B., Williams-Diehm, K., Davies, D. K., & Stock, S. E. (2012). Examining individual and instruction-related predictors of the self-determination of students with disabilities: Multiple regression analyses. *Remedial and Special Education, 33*(3), 150–161.

LeGray, M. W., Dufrene, B. A., Mercer, S., Olmi, D., & Sterling, H. (2013). Differential reinforcement of alternative behavior in center-based classrooms: Evaluation of pre-teaching the alternative behavior. *Journal of Behavioral Education, 22,* 85–102.

Legutko, R. S. (2015). *One secondary school's subject-area teachers' perspectives on co-teaching students with special needs.* Retrieved from http://www.eric.ed.gov/contentdelivery/servlet/ERICServlet?accno=ED558191

Lehraus, K. (2015). How to integrate cooperative skills training into learning tasks: An illustration with young pupils' writing. *Education 3–13, 43*(1), 55–69.

Leinhardt, G., & Zigmond, N. (1988). The effects of self-questioning and story structure training on the reading comprehension of poor readers. *Learning Disabilities Research, 4*(1), 41–51.

Leko, M. M. (2015). To adapt or not to adapt: Navigating an implementation conundrum. *Teaching Exceptional Children, 48*(2), 80–85.

Lemons, C. (2007). Response to intervention (Rtl): Important aspects of effective implementation. Presentation at 29th International Conference on Learning Disabilities, Myrtle Beach, SC.

Lenz, B. K. (1983). Using the advance organizer. *Pointer, 27,* 11–13.

Lenz, B. K., Ellis, E. S., & Scanlon, D. (1996). *Teaching learning strategies to adolescents and adults with learning disabilities.* Austin, TX: PRO-ED.

Lenz, K. (2006). Creating school-wide conditions for high-quality learning strategy classroom instruction. *Intervention in School and Clinic, 41*(5), 261–266.

Lerna, A., Esposito, D., Conson, M., & Massagli, A. (2014). Long-term effects of PECS on social–communicative skills of children with autism spectrum disorders: A follow-up study. *International Journal of Language & Communication Disorders, 49,* 478–485.

Lerner, J., & Johns, B. (2014). *Learning disabilities and related mild disabilities: Characteristics, teaching strategies and new directions* (13th ed.). Boston, MA: Houghton Mifflin.

Lessen, E., Sommers M., & Bursuck, W. (1987). *Curriculum-based assessment and instructional design.* DeKalb, IL: DeKalb County Special Education Association.

Lewis, T., Jones, S., Horner, R., & Sugai, G. (2010). School-wide positive behavior support and students with emotional/behavioral disorders: Implications for prevention, identification and intervention. *Exceptionality, 18,* 82–93.

Liddon, C. J., Kelley, M. E., & Podlesnik, C. A. (2017). An animal model of differential reinforcement of alternative behavior. *Learning and Motivation, 58,* 48–58.

Lieberman, L. J., Haegele, J. A., Columna, L., & Conroy, P. (2014). How students with visual impairments can learn components of the expanded core curriculum through physical education. *Journal of Visual Impairment & Blindness, 108,* 239–248.

Lilly, M. S. (1971). A training model for special education. *Exceptional Children, 37,* 740–749.

Lindquist, T. (1995). *Seeing the whole through social studies.* Portsmouth, NH: Heinemann.

Lindsey, D. B., & Lindsey, R. B. (2016). Build cultural proficiency to ensure equity. *Journal of Staff Development, 37*(1), 50–56.

Liou, Y. (2016). Tied to the Common Core: Exploring the characteristics of reform advice relationships of educational leaders. *Educational Administration Quarterly, 52,* 793–840.

Litvack, M. S., Ritchie, K. C., & Shore, B. M. (2011). High- and average-achieving students' perceptions of disabilities and of students with disabilities in inclusive classrooms. *Exceptional Children, 77,* 474–487.

Lloyd, B. P., Weaver, E. S., & Staubitz, J. L. (2016). A review of functional analysis methods conducted in public school classroom settings. *Journal of Behavioral Education, 25,* 324–356.

Lo, Y., Correa, V. I., & Anderson, A. L. (2015). Culturally responsive social skill instruction for Latino male students. *Journal of Positive Behavior Interventions, 17*(1), 15–27.

Lo, Y., Mustian, A. L., Brophy, A., & White, R. B. (2011). Peer-mediated social skill instruction for African American males with or at risk for mild disabilities. *Exceptionality, 19*, 191–209.

Lofton, R., & Davis, J. E. (2015). Toward a Black habitus: African Americans navigating systemic inequalities within home, school, and community. *Journal of Negro Education, 84*, 214–230.

Loiacono, V. (2009). Autism: A high-incidence or low-incidence disability. *Journal of International Special Education, 24*(2), 109–114.

Long, N. J., & Newman, R. G. (1971). Managing surface behavior of children in school. In N. J. Long, W. C. Morse, & R. G. Newman (Eds.), *Conflict in the classroom: The education of children with problems* (2nd ed., pp. 442–452). Belmont, CA: Wadsworth.

Lopez, D., Catani, M., Ripolles, P., Dell 'Acqua, F., Rodriguez-Fornells, A., & de Diego-Balaguer, R. (2013). Word meaning is mediated by the left arcuate fasciculus. *Proceedings of the National Academy of Sciences.* Retrieved from http://dx.doi.org/10.1073/pnas.1301696110

Lortie, D. C. (1975). *Schoolteacher: A sociological study.* Chicago: University of Chicago Press.

Lott, B. (2003). Recognizing and welcoming the standpoint of low-income parents in the public schools. *Journal of Educational and Psychological Consultation, 14*, 91–104.

Lovitt, T. C., Rudsit, J., Jenkins, J., Pious, C., & Benedetti, D. (1985). Two methods of adapting science materials for learning disabled and regular seventh graders. *Learning Disability Quarterly, 8*, 275–285.

LRP Publications. (1997). *Grading individuals with disabilities education law report, 25*(4), 381–391.

Luckner, J. L., & Muir, S. (2001). Successful students who are deaf in general education settings. *American Annals of the Deaf, 146*, 450–461.

Luft, P. (2015). Transition services for DHH adolescents and young adults with disabilities: Challenges and theoretical frameworks. *American Annals of the Deaf, 160*, 395–414.

Lum, J. K., Tingstrom, D. H., Dufrene, B. A., Radley, K. C., & Lynne, S. (2017). Effects of tootling on classwide disruptive and academically engaged behavior of general-education high school students. *Psychology in the Schools, 54*, 370–384.

Lundblom, E. G., & Woods, J. J. (2012). Working in the classroom: Improving idiom comprehension through classwide peer tutoring. *Communication Disorders Quarterly, 33*, 202–219.

Luster, J. N., & Durrett, J. (2003, November). Does educational placement matter in the performance of students with disabilities? Paper presented at the annual meeting of the Mid-South Educational Research Association, Biloxi, MS. (ERIC Document Reproduction Service No. ED482518)

Luthar, S. S., & Eisenberg, N. (2017). Resilient adaptation among at-risk children: Harnessing science toward maximizing salutary environments. *Child Development, 88*, 337–349.

Lynch, S. A., & Warner, L. (2012). A new theoretical perspective of cognitive abilities. *Childhood Education, 88*, 347–353.

Lytle, R., & Todd, T. (2009). Stress and the student with autism spectrum disorders: Strategies for stress reduction and enhanced learning. *Teaching Exceptional Children, 41*(4), 36–42.

Maag, J. (2006). Social skills training for students with emotional and behavioral disorders: A review of reviews. *Behavioral Disorders, 32*(1), 5–17.

Maag, J. W. (2001). Management of surface behavior: A new look at an old approach. *Counseling and Human Development, 33*(9), 1–10.

Maag, J. W., & Reid, R. (2006). Depression among students with learning disabilities: Assessing the risk. *Journal of Learning Disabilities, 39*(1), 3–10.

MacArthur, C. A., & Stoddard, B. (1990, April). Teaching learning disabled students to revise: A peer editor strategy. Paper presented at the Annual Meeting of the American Education Research Association, Boston.

MacArthur, C., Schwartz, S., Graham, S., Malloy, D., & Harris, K. R. (1996). Integration of strategy instruction into a whole language classroom: A case study. *Learning Disabilities Research and Practice, 11*, 168–176.

MacSuga, A. S., & Simonsen, B. (2011). Increasing teachers' use of evidence-based classroom management strategies through consultation: Overview and case studies. *Beyond Behavior, 20*(2), 4–12.

Macy, M. G., & Bricker, D. D. (2007). Embedding individualized social goals into routine activities in inclusive early childhood classrooms. *Early Child Development and Care, 177*, 107–120.

Madden, J. A. (2000). Managing asthma at school. *Educational Leadership, 57*(6), 50–52.

Maggin, D. M., Johnson, A. H., Chafouleas, S. M., Ruberto, L. M., & Berggren, M. (2012). A systematic evidence review of school-based group contingency interventions for students with challenging behavior. *Journal of School Psychology, 50*, 625–654.

Maher, J., Burroughs, C., Dietz, L., & Karnbach, A. (2010). From solo to ensemble: Fine arts teachers find a harmonious solution to their isolation. *Journal of Staff Development, 31*(1), 24–29.

Malanchini, M., Wang, Z., Voronin, V. J., Piomin, R., Petrilli, S. A., & Kovas, Y. (2017). Reading self-perceived ability, enjoyment and achievement: A genetically informative study of their reciprocal links over time. *Developmental Psychology, 53*(4), 698–712.

Mallett, C. A. (2016). The school-to-prison pipeline: From school punishment to rehabilitative inclusion. *Preventing School Failure, 60*, 296–304.

Mammarella, I. C., Ghisi, M., Bomba, M., Bottesi, G., Caviola, S., Broggi, F., & Nacinovich, R. (2016). Anxiety and depression in children with nonverbal learning disabilities, reading disabilities, or typical development. *Journal of Learning Disabilities, 49*(2), 130–139.

Mandlebaum, L. H., & Wilson, R. (1989). Teaching listening skills. *LD Forum, 15*(1), 7–9.

Margolis, H. (2005). Resolving struggling learners' homework difficulties: Working with elementary school learners and parents. *Preventing School Failure, 50*(1), 5–12.

Marino, M. T., Marino, E. C., & Shaw, S. F. (2006). Making informed assistive technology decisions for students with high incidence disabilities. *Teaching Exceptional Children, 38*(6), 18–25.

Markelz, A. M., & Taylor, J. C. (2016). Effects of teacher praise on attending behaviors and academic achievement of students with emotional and behavioral disabilities. *Journal of Special Education Apprenticeship, 5*(1). Retrieved from http://www.eric.ed.gov/contentdelivery/servlet/ERICServlet?accno=EJ1127753

Maroney, S. A., Finson, K. D., Beaver, J. B., & Jensen, M. M. (2003). Preparing for successful inquiry in inclusive science classrooms. *Teaching Exceptional Children, 36*(1), 18–25.

Marschark, M., Convertino, C., & LaRock, D. (2006). Optimizing academic performance of deaf students: Access, opportunities, and outcomes. In D. F. Moores, & D. S. Martin (Eds.), *Deaf learners: Developments in curriculum and instruction* (pp. 179–200). Washington, DC: Gallaudet University Press.

Marschark, M., Shaver, D. M., Nagle, K. M., & Newman, L. A. (2015). Predicting the academic achievement of deaf and hard-of-hearing students from individual, household, communication, and educational factors. *Exceptional Children, 81*, 350–369.

Marsh, R. J. (2016). Identifying students with mental health issues: A guide for classroom teachers. *Intervention in School and Clinic, 51*(5), 318–322.

Marston, D. B., Tindal, G., & Deno, S. (1984). Eligibility for learning disability services: A direct and repeated measurement approach. *Exceptional Children, 50*, 554–556.

Marston, D., Muyskens, P., Lau, M., & Canter, A. (2003). Problem-solving model for decision making with high-incidence disabilities: The Minneapolis experience. *Learning Disabilities Research and Practice, 18*(3), 187–200.

Martel, M. M., Roberts, B., & Gremillion, M. L. (2013). Emerging control and disruptive behavior disorders during early childhood. *Developmental Neuropsychology, 38*, 153–166.

Martin, J. E., & Williams-Diehm, K. (2013). Student engagement and leadership of the transition planning process. *Career Development and Transition for Exceptional Individuals, 36*, 43–50.

Martínez, J. F., Schweig, J., & Goldschmidt, P. (2016). Approaches for combining multiple measures of teacher performance: Reliability, validity, and implications for evaluation policy. *Educational Evaluation and Policy Analysis, 38*, 738–756.

Marzano, R. J. (2003). *What works in schools: Translating research into action*. Alexandria, VA: Association for Supervision and Curriculum Development.

Marzano, R. J. (2004). *Building background knowledge for academic achievement*. Alexandria, VA: Association for Supervision and Curriculum Development.

Marzano, R. J. (2010). *Formative Assessment & Standards-Based Grading*. Bloomington, IN: Marzano Research Laboratory.

Marzano, R. J., & Marzano, J. S. (2003). The key to classroom management. *Educational Leadership, 61*(1), 6–13.

Marzano, R. J., & Pickering, D. J. (2007). Special topic/The case for and against homework. *Educational Leadership, 64*(6), 74–79.

Marzano, R. J., Gaddy, B. B., Foseid, M. C., Foseid, M. P., & Marzano, J. S. (2005). *A handbook for classroom management that works,* Alexandria, Va.: ASCD.

Marzano, R.J. (2000). *Transforming Classroom Grading*. Alexandria, VA: ASCD.

Marzola, E. S. (1987). Using manipulatives in math instruction. *Reading, Writing, and Learning Disabilities, 3*, 9–20.

Maskey, M., Warnell, F., Parr, J. R., Le Couteur, A., & McConachie, H. (2013). Emotional and behavioural problems in children with autism spectrum disorder. *Journal of Autism and Developmental Disorders, 43*, 851–859.

Mason, B. A., Gunersel, A. B., & Ney, E. A. (2014). Cultural and ethnic bias in teacher ratings of behavior: A criterion-focused review. *Psychology in the Schools, 51*, 1017–1030.

Mason, L. H., Snyder, K. H., Sukhram, D. P., Kedem, Y. (2006). TWA + PLANS strategies for expository reading and writing: Effects for nine fourth-grade students. *Exceptional Children, 73*(1), 69–89.

Massat, C. (2013). Where do we go from here? *School Social Work Journal, 37*(2), ix–x.

Mastropieri, M. A. (1988). Using the keyword method. *Teaching Exceptional Children, 20*(4), 4–8.

Mastropieri, M., Scruggs, T. E., Cerar, N. I., Guckert, M., Thompson, C., & Bronaugh, D. A. (2015). Strategic persuasive writing instruction for students with emotional and behavioral disabilities. *Exceptionality, 23*(3), 147–169.

Mathieu, J. E., Hollenbeck, J. R., van Knippenberg, D., & Ilgen, D. R. (2017). A century of work teams in the *Journal of Applied Psychology*. *Journal of Applied Psychology, 102*, 452–467.

Matson, J. L., Hess, J. A., & Mahan, S. (2013). Moderating effects of challenging behaviors and communication deficits on social skills in children diagnosed with an autism spectrum disorder. *Research in Autism Spectrum Disorders, 7*, 23–28.

Matuszny, R. M., Banda, D. R., & Coleman, T. J. (2007). A progressive plan for building collaborative relationships with parents from diverse backgrounds. *Teaching Exceptional Children, 39*(4), 24–31.

Matzen, K., Ryndak, D., & Nakao, T. (2010). Middle school teams increasing access to general education for students with significant disabilities: Issues encountered and activities observed across contexts. *Remedial and Special Education, 31*, 287–304.

May, A. (2017, May 15). Stop telling your child they're 'amazing': Instead, say this. *USA Today* [on-line]. Retrieved from https://www.usatoday.com/story/news/nation-now/2017/05/15/why-you-might-not-want-tell-your-child/319605001/

Mazzotti, V. L., Rowe, D. A., Sinclair, J., Poppen, M., Woods, W. E., & Shearer, M. L. (2016). Predictors of post-school success: A systematic review of NLTS2 secondary analyses. *Career Development and Transition for Exceptional Individuals, 39*, 196–215.

McCardle, P., & Chhabra, V. (Eds.). (2004). *The voice of evidence in reading research*. Baltimore, MD: Brookes.

McClanahan, B. (2009). Help! I have kids who can't read in my world history class! *Preventing School Failure, 53*, 105–112.

McComas, J. J., Downwind, I., Klingbeil, D. A., Petersen-Brown, S., Davidson, K. M., & Parker, D. C. (2017). Relations between instructional practices and on-task behavior in classrooms serving American Indian students. *Journal of Applied School Psychology, 33*, 89–108.

McConnellogue, S. (2011). Professional roles and responsibilities in meeting the needs of children with speech, language and communication need: Joint working between educational psychologists and speech and language therapists. *Educational Psychology in Practice, 27*, 53–64.

McCord, K., & Watts, E. (2010). Music educators' involvement in the individual education program process and their knowledge of assistive technology. *Update: Applications of Research in Music Education, 28*(2), 79–85.

McCray, E. D., & McHatton, P. A. (2011). "Less afraid to have them in my classroom": Understanding pre-service general educators' perceptions about inclusion. *Teacher Education Quarterly, 38*, 135–155.

McCurdy, B. L., Thomas, L., Truckenmiller, A., Rich, S. H., Hillis-Clark, P., & Lopez, J. C. (2016). School-wide positive behavioral interventions and supports for students with emotional and behavioral disorders. *Psychology in the Schools, 53*, 375–389.

McGinnis, E., & Goldstein, A. P. (2005). *Skills-streaming: Teaching prosocial skills to the elementary-school child*. Champaign, IL: Research Press.

McGrath, M. Z., Johns, B. H., & Mathur, S. R. (2010). Empowered or overpowered? Strategies for working effectively with paraprofessionals. *Beyond Behavior, 19*(2), 2–6.

McGrath, P. (2007). *The OCD Answer book: Top questions about obsessive compulsive disorder*. Naperville, Illinois: Sourcebook Inc.

McGuire, J. M., Scott, S. S., & Shaw, S. F. (2006). Universal design and its applications in educational environments. *Remedial and Special Education, 27*, 166–175.

McIntosh, K., Filter, K., Bennett, J., Ryan, C., & Sugai, G. (2010). Principles of sustainable prevention: Designing scale-up of school-wide positive behavior support to promote durable systems. *Psychology in the Schools, 47*, 5–21.

McIntosh, K., Kelm, J. L., & Canizal Delabra, A. (2016). In search of how principals change: A qualitative study of events that help and hinder administrator support for school-wide PBIS. *Journal of Positive Behavior Interventions, 18*, 100–110.

McKenna, J. W., Flower, A., & Adamson, R. (2016). A systematic review of function-based replacement behavior interventions for students with and at risk for emotional and behavioral disorders. *Behavior Modification, 40*, 678–712.

McKenna, M. K., & Millen, J. (2013). Look! Listen! Learn! Parent narratives and grounded theory models of parent voice, presence, and engagement in K–12 education. *School Community Journal, 23*(1), 9–48.

McLaughlin, M. J. (2010). Evolving interpretations of educational equity and students with disabilities. *Exceptional Children, 76*, 265–278.

McLaughlin, M. J. (2012, September/October). Access for all. *Principal*, 22–26.

McLaughlin, M.J., Speirs, K.E., & Shenassa, E.D. (2014). Reading disability and adult attained education and income: Evidence from a 30-year longitudinal study of a population-based sample. *Journal of Learning Disabilities, 47(4)*, 374-386.

McLeod, J., Fisher, J., & Hoover, G. (2003). *The Key Elements of Classroom Management*. Alexandria, VA: ASCD.

McLeskey, J., & Waldron, N. L. (2011). Educational programs for elementary students with learning disabilities: Can they be both effective and inclusive? *Learning Disabilities Research & Practice, 26*, 48–57.

McLeskey, J., Waldron, N. L., & So, T. H. (2001). Perspectives of teachers toward inclusive school programs. *Teacher Education and Special Education, 24*, 108–115.

McLester, S. (2012). Rick and Becky DuFour. *District Administration, 48*(8), 61–62.

McMaster, K. L., & Fuchs, D. (2016). Classwide intervention using peer-assisted learning strategies. In S. R. Jimerson, M. K. Burns, A. M. VanDerHeyden, S. R. Jimerson, M. K. Burns, A. M., & VanDerHeyden (Eds.), *Handbook of response to intervention: The science and practice of multi-tiered systems of support (*2nd edition) (pp. 253–268). New York, NY: Springer Science + Business Media.

McMaster, K. L., Du, Z., & Petursdottit, A. (2009). Technical features of curriculum-based measures for beginning writers. *Journal of Learning Disabilities, 42*, 41–60.

McMaster, K. L., Fuchs, D., & Fuchs, L. S. (2006). Research on peer-assisted learning strategies: The promise and limitations of peer-mediated instruction. *Reading & Writing Quarterly, 22*, 5–25.

Meadan, H., & Monda-Amaya, L. (2008). Collaboration to promote social competence for students with mild disabilities in the general classroom: A structure for providing social support. *Intervention in School and Clinic, 43*, 158–167.

Meadows, E. A., Owen Yeates, K., Rubin, K. H., Taylor, H. G., Bigler, E. D., Dennis, M., & . . . Hoskinson, K. R. (2017). Rejection sensitivity as a moderator of psychosocial outcomes following pediatric traumatic brain injury. *Journal of the International Neuropsychological Society*, doi:10.1017/S1355617717000352

Meichenbaum, D. (1977). *Cognitive behavior modification: An integrative approach.* New York: Plenum.

Meinzen-Derr, J., Wiley, S., Grether, S., Phillips, J., Choo, D., Hibner, J., & Barnard, H. (2014). Functional communication of children who are deaf or hard-of-hearing. *Journal of Developmental and Behavioral Pediatrics, 35*, 197–206.

Melby-Lervag, M., & Hulme, C. (2013). Is working memory training effective? A meta-analytic review. *Developmental psychology, 49*, 270–291. doi:10.1037/a0028228

Mellard, D. F., & McKnight, M. A. (2008). *RTI implementation tool: Best practices for grades K–5.* Lawrence, KS: National Center on Response to Intervention.

Mellard, D., & Prewett, S. (2010). *RTI in middle schools* [Electronic version]. Lawrence, KS, and Nashville, TN: National Center on Response to Intervention. Retrieved from http://www.rti4success.org/images/stories/webinar/RTI_in_Middle_Schools_TranscriptFINAL.pdf

Mellard, D., McKnight, M., & Woods, K. (2009). Response to intervention screening and progress-monitoring practices in 41 local schools. *Learning Disabilities Research & Practice, 24*, 186–195.

Menzies, H. M., Lane, K. L., Oakes, W. P., & Ennis, R. P. (2017). Increasing students' opportunities to respond: A strategy for supporting engagement. *Intervention in School and Clinic, 52*(4), 204–209.

Meo, B. (2008). Curriculum planning for all learners: Applying universal design for learning (UDL) to a high school reading comprehension program. *Preventing School Failure, 52*(2), 21–30.

Mercer, C. D., & Pullen, P. C. (2008). *Students with learning disabilities* (7th ed.). Upper Saddle River, NJ: Merrill/Pearson.

Mercer, C. D., Mercer, A. R., & Pullen, P. C. (2010). *Teaching students with learning problems* (8th ed.). Upper Saddle River, NJ: Pearson.

Merrell, K. W., Ervin, R. A., & Gimpel, G. A. (2012). *School psychology for the 21st century: Foundations and practices* (2nd ed.) New York, NY: Guilford.

Meyer, N. K., & Houck, E. C. (2014). The impact of text-to-speech on expository reading for adolescents with LD. *Journal of Special Education Technology, 29*(1), 21–33.

Miller, G., & Hall, T. (2005). *Classroom management.* Wakefield, MA: National Center on Accessing the General Curriculum. Retrieved from http://www.cast.org/publications/ncac/ncac_classroom.html

Miller, K. J. (2014). Trends impacting one public school program for students who are deaf or hard-of-hearing. *Communication Disorders Quarterly, 36*, 35–43.

Miller, R. D. (2016). Contextualizing instruction for English language learners with learning disabilities. *Teaching Exceptional Children, 49*(1), 58–65.

Miller, S. P. (1996), Perspectives on mathematics instruction. In D. D. Deshler, E. S. Ellis, & B. K. Lenz (Eds.), *Teaching adolescents with learning disabilities: Strategies and methods* (2nd ed., pp. 313–367). Denver, CO: Love.

Milsom, A., & Hartley, M. (2005). Assisting students with learning disabilities transitioning to college: What school counselors should know. *Professional School Counseling, 8*, 436–441.

Minahan, J., & Rappaport, N. (2012). Anxiety in students: A hidden culprit in behavior issues. *Phi Delta Kappan, 94*(4), 34–39.

Minskoff, E., & Allsopp, D. (2003). *Academic success strategies for adolescents with learning disabilities and ADHD.* Baltimore, MD: Paul H. Brookes.

Miranda, A., Tárraga, R., Fernández, M. I., Colomer, C., & Pastor, G. (2015). Parenting stress in families of children with autism spectrum disorder and ADHD. *Exceptional Children, 82*, 81–95.

Mitchell, B. B., Deshler, D. D., & Lenz, B. (2012). Examining the role of the special educator in a response to intervention model. *Learning Disabilities: A Contemporary Journal, 10*(2), 53–74.

Mmari, K., Blum, R., & Teufel-Shone, N. (2010). What increases risk and protection for delinquent behaviors among American Indian youth?: Findings from three tribal communities. *Youth & Society, 41*, 382–413.

Moats, L. C. (2007). *Language essentials for teaching of reading and spelling. Module 6: Digging for meaning: Teaching text comprehension.* Boston, MA: Sopris West.

Molina, B. G., Hinshaw, S. P., Arnold, L., Swanson, J. M., Pelham, W. E., Hechtman, L., & . . . Marcus, S. (2013). Adolescent substance use in the Multimodal Treatment Study of Attention-Deficit/Hyperactivity Disorder (ADHD) (MTA) as a function of childhood ADHD, random assignment to childhood treatments, and subsequent medication. *Journal of the American Academy of Child & Adolescent Psychiatry, 52*, 250–263.

Montague, M., Warger, C. L., & Morgan, H. (2000). Solve It! Strategy instruction to improve mathematical problem solving. *Learning Disabilities Research and Practice, 15*, 110–116.

Montgomery, K. (2001). *Authentic assessment: A guide for elementary teachers.* New York: Longman.

Monuteaux, M., Mick, E., Faraone, S., & Biederman, J. (2010). The influence of sex on the course and psychiatric correlates of ADHD from childhood to adolescence: A longitudinal study. *Journal of Child Psychology and Psychiatry, 51*, 233–241.

Morgan, P. L., Farkas, G., & Maczuga, S. (2015). Which instructional practices help first grade students with and without mathematics difficulties? *Educational Analysis and Policy Development, 37(2),* 184–205.

Morgan, P. L., Farkas, G., Cook, M., Strassfeld, N. M., Hillemeier, M. M., Pun, W. H., & Schussler, D. L. (2017). Are black children disproportionately overrepresented in special education? A best evidence synthesis. *Exceptional Children, 83*(2), 181–198.

Morgan, P. L., Farkas, G., Hillenmeier, M. M., Mattison, R., Maczuga, S., Li, H., & Cook, M. (2015). Minorities are disproportionately underrepresented in special education. *Educational Researcher, 44,* 278–292.

Morgan, P. L., Farkas, G., Tufis, P. A., & Sperling, R. A. (2008). Are reading and behavior problems risk factors for each other? *Journal of Learning Dis-abilities, 41*(5), 417–436.

Morgan, P. L., Fuchs, D., Compton, D. L., Cordray, D. S., & Fuchs, L. S. (2008). Does early reading failure decrease children's reading motivation? *Journal of Learning Disabilities, 41* (5), 387–404.

Morin, A. (2017). *Common modifications and accommodations.* New York, NY: Understood. Retrieved from https://www.understood.org/en/learning-attention-issues/treatments-approaches/educational-strategies/common-classroom-accommodations-and-modifications

Mosenthal, P. (1984). The problem of partial specification in translating reading research into practice. *Elementary School Journal, 85,* 199–227.

Mosteller, F., Light, R., & Sachs, J. (1996). Sustained inquiry in education: Lessons from skill grouping and class size. *Harvard Educational Review, 66,* 797–828.

Mueller, T. G. (2015). Litigation and special education: The past, present, and future direction for resolving conflicts between parents and school districts. *Journal of Disability Policy Studies, 26*(3), 135–143.

Mueller, T. G., & Carranza, F. (2011). An examination of special education due process hearings. *Journal of Disability Policy Studies, 22,* 131–139.

Mullen, C. A. (2016). Alternative mentoring types. *Kappa Delta Pi Record, 52,* 132–136.

Mulloy, A., Lang, R., O'Reilly, M., Sigafoos, J., Lancioni, G., & Rispoli, M. (2010). Gluten-free and casein-free diets in the treatment of autism spectrum disorders: A systematic review. *Research in Autism Spectrum Disorders, 4,* 328–339.

Munk, D. (2009). Grading students with disabilities: FAQs. *CEC Today.* Retrieved from: http://www.cec.sped.org/AM/Template.cfm?Section=Home&CONTENTID=12679&TEMPLATE=/CM/ContentDisplay.cfm

Munk, D. D. (2003). *Solving the grading puzzle for students with disabilities.* Whitefish Bay, WI: Knowledge by Design.

Munk, D. D. (2007). *Equitable, effective, and meaningful grading practices for students with disabilities/exceptionalities.* Retrieved from http://icdd.idaho.gov/pdf/Parent%20League/GradingWebinar Mar07Handout.pdf

Munk, D. D., & Bursuck, W. D. (2001). Personalized grading plans: A systematic approach to making the grades of included students more accurate and meaningful. In L. Denti, & P. Tefft-Cousin (Eds.), *Looking at learning disabilities in new ways: Connections to classroom practice* (pp. 111–127). Denver, CO: Love.

Munk, D. D., & Bursuck, W. D. (2003). Grading students with disabilities. *Educational Leadership, 61*(2), 38–43.

Munk, D. D., Bursuck, W. D., Epstein, M. H., Jayanthi, M., Nelson, J., & Polloway, E. A. (2001). Homework communication problems: Perspectives of special and general education parents. *Reading and Writing Quarterly, 17*(3), 189–203.

Munk, J., Gibb, G., & Caldarella, P. (2010). Collaborative preteaching of students at risk for academic failure. *Intervention in School and Clinic, 45,* 177–185.

Murawski, W. W. (2012). 10 tips for using co-planning time more efficiently. *Teaching Exceptional Children, 44*(4), 8–15.

Murawski, W. W., & Bernhardt, P. (2016). An administrator's guide to co-teaching. *Educational Leadership, 73*(4), 30–34.

Murdock, L., Finneran, D., & Theve, K. (2016). Co-teaching to reach every learner. *Educational Leadership, 73*(4), 42–47.

Murillo, M. A. (2017). The art of the reveal: Undocumented high school students, institutional agents, and the disclosure of legal status. *High School Journal, 100,* 88–108.

Murphy, S., & Korinek, L. (2009). It's in the cards: A classwide management system to promote student success. *Intervention in School and Clinic, 44,* 300–306.

Musti-Rao, S., Hawkins, R. O., & Tan, C. (2011). A practitioner's guide to consultation and problem solving in inclusive settings. *Teaching Exceptional Children, 44*(1), 18–26.

Musu-Gilette, L., Zhang, A., Wang, K., Zhang, J., & Ouderekerk, B. A. (2017, May). Indicators of school crime and safety: 2016. Washington, DC: National Center for Education Statistics. Retrieved from https://nces.ed.gov/pubsearch/pubsinfo.asp?pubid=2017064

Myles, B. S., & Adreon, D. (2001). *Asperger syndrome and adolescence: Practical solutions for school success.* Shawnee Mission, KS: Autism Asperger Publishing.

Nag, S., & Snowling (2012). School underachievement and specific learning disabilities. In: *IACAPAP Textbook of Child and Adolescent Psychiatry.* Geneva International Association for Child and Adolescent Psychiatry.

National Association for Down Syndrome. (2013). *History of NADS.* Retrieved from http://www.nads.org/history/index.html

National Association for Down Syndrome. (2016). *History of NADS.* Park Ridge, IL: Author. Retrieved from http://www.nads.org/about-us/history-of-nads/

National Association for Gifted Children and Council of State Directors of Programs for the Gifted. (2015, November). *2014–2015 State of the states in gifted education: Policy and practice data.* Washington, DC: Author. Retrieved from http://www.nagc.org/sites/default/files/key%20reports/2014-2015%20State%20of%20the%20States%20%28final%29.pdf

National Association for Gifted Children. (2008). *Frequently asked questions.* Retrieved from http://www.nagc.org/index2.aspx?id=548

National Association for Gifted Children. (2011). Executive summary of the 2010–2011 State of the States Report: State of the Nation. In *Gifted education—a lack of commitment to talent development.* Retrieved from http://www.nagc.org/uploadedFiles/Information_and_Resources/2010-11_state_of_states/State%20of%20the%20Nation%20%20(final).pdf

National Association for Gifted Children. (2017, June). *Gifted education in the U.S.* Washington, DC: Author. Retrieved from https://www.nagc.org/resources-publications/resources/gifted-education-us

National Center for Education Statistics. (2010). *Indicators of school crime and safety: 2009.* Washington, DC: U.S. Department of Education. Retrieved from http://nces.ed.gov/programs/crimeindicators/crimeindicators2009/index.asp

National Center for Education Statistics. (2012, February). *Indicator 11: Bullying at school and cyber-bullying anywhere.* Washington, DC: Author, Institute of Education Sciences, U.S. Department of Education. Retrieved from http://nces.ed.gov/programs/crimeindicators/crimeindicators2011/ind_11.asp

National Center for Education Statistics. (2013a). *The condition of education: English language learners.* Washington, DC: Author, Institute of Education Sciences, U.S. Department of Education. Retrieved from http://nces.ed.gov/programs/coe/indicator_cgf.asp

National Center for Education Statistics. (2013b). *Status and trends in the education of racial and ethnic minorities* [Indicator 7]. Washington, DC: Author, Institute of Education Sciences, U.S. Department of Education. Retrieved from http://nces.ed.gov/pubs2010/2010015/indicator2_7.asp#1

National Center for Education Statistics. (2017, May). *Indicator 11: Bullying at school and cyber-bullying anywhere* [Indicators of School Crime and Safety]. Washington, DC: Author. Retrieved from https://nces.ed.gov/programs/crimeindicators/ind_11.asp

National Center for Education Statistics. (2017a, March). *English language learners in public schools*. Washington, DC: Institute of Education Sciences, Author. Retrieved from https://nces.ed.gov/programs/coe/indicator_cgf.asp

National Center for Education Statistics. (2017b, May). *Racial/ethnic enrollment in public schools*. Washington, DC: Institute of Education Sciences, Author. Retrieved from https://nces.ed.gov/programs/coe/indicator_cge.asp

National Center for Educational Outcomes (2016). Lessons learned about assessment from inclusion of students with disabilities in college and career-ready assessments. Retrieved from https://nceo.info/standards_and_accountability/college_standards

National Center for Educational Statistics (2015). The nation's report card: *Science 2015*. Washington, DC: US Department of Education. Retrieved from: https://nationsreportcard.gov/science_2015/#?grade=4

National Center on Educational Outcomes (2012). *Alternate assessments for students with disabilities*. Retrieved from http://www.cehd.umn.edu/edu/nceo/

National Center on Secondary Education and Transition. (2002). *Age of majority: Preparing your child for making good choices*. Minneapolis, MN: Author. (ERIC Document Reproduction Service No. ED467248)

National Center on Secondary Education and Transition. (2012, April). *IEP & transition planning: Frequently asked questions*. Minneapolis, MN: Author. Retrieved from http://www.ncset.org/topics/ieptransition/faqs.asp?topic=28

National Coalition for the Homeless. (2011). *Who is homeless?* Washington, DC: Author. Retrieved from http://www.nationalhomeless.org/factsheets/who.html

National Coalition for the Homeless. (2017, June). *Homelessness in America*. Washington, DC: Author. Retrieved from http://national-homeless.org/about-homelessness/

National Council of Teachers of Mathematics. (2000). *Principles and standards for school mathematics*. Reston, VA: Author.

National Dissemination Center for Children with Disabilities (NICHCY). (2013a, March). *Related services*. Retrieved from http://nichcy.org/schoolage/iep/iepcontents/relatedservices

National Dissemination Center for Children with Disabilities (NICHCY). (2013b, March). *Supplementary aids and services*. Washington, DC: Author. Retrieved from http://nichcy.org/schoolage/iep/iepcontents/supplementary

National Dissemination Center for Children with Disabilities (NICHCY). (2013c, March). *Special education*. Retrieved from http://nichcy.org/schoolage/iep/iepcontents/specialeducation#specially

National Dissemination Center for Children with Disabilities. (2010). *Traumatic brain injury*. Retrieved from http://www.nichcy.org/Disabilities/Specific/Pages/TBI.aspx

National Early Literacy Panel. (2008). *Developing early literacy: Report of the National Early Literacy Panel*. Washington, DC: National Institute for Literacy.

National Governors Association & Council of Chief State School Officers (NGA & CCSSO). (2010). *Reaching higher: The Common Core State Standards Validation Committee: A report from the National Governors Association Center for Best Practices & the Council of Chief State School Officers* [Electronic version]. Retrieved from http://www.corestandards.org/assets/CommonCoreReport_6.10.pdf

National High School Center, National Center on Response to Intervention, and Center on Instruction. (2010). *Tiered interventions in high schools: Using preliminary "lessons learned" to guide ongoing discussion*. Washington, DC: American Institutes for Research.

National Information Center for Children with Disabilities. (2012, August). *Response to intervention (RTI)*. Retrieved from http://nichcy.org/schools-administrators/rti

National Institute of Mental Health. (2009, November). *The Multimodal Treatment of Attention Deficit Hyperactivity Disorder Study (MTA): Questions and answers*. Washington, DC: National Institutes of Health. Retrieved from http://www.nimh.nih.gov/health/trials/practical/mta/the-multimodal-treatment-of-attention-deficit-hyperactivity-disorder-study-mta-questions-and-answers.shtml

National Institute of Mental Health. (2013, July). *Attention deficit hyperactivity disorder* (ADHD). Retrieved from http://www.nimh.nih.gov/health/topics/attention-deficit-hyperactivity-disorder-adhd/index.shtml

National Institute of Mental Health. (2016, March). *Attention deficit hyperactivity disorder*. Rockville, MD: Author. Retrieved from https://www.nimh.nih.gov/health/topics/attention-deficit-hyperactivity-disorder-adhd/index.shtml

National Institute of Neurological Disorders and Stroke. (2013, May). *Autism fact sheet*. Bethesda, MD: National Institute of Neurological Disorders and Stroke, National Institutes of Health. Retrieved from http://www.ninds.nih.gov/disorders/autism/detail_autism.htm

National Institute on Drug Abuse. (2010, September). *Co-morbidity: Addiction and other mental illnesses* [NIH Publication No. 10-5771]. Bethesda, MD: National Institutes of Health, Author. Retrieved from https://www.drugabuse.gov/sites/default/files/rrcomorbidity.pdf

National Institute on Drug Abuse. (2011, May). *Drug abuse among pregnant women in the U.S.* Bethesda, MD: Author, National Institutes of Health. Retrieved from http://www.drugabuse.gov/publications/topics-in-brief/prenatal-exposure-to-drugs-abuse

National Institute on Drug Abuse. (2012). *Monitoring the future survey: Overview of findings 2012*. Bethesda, MD: Author, National Institutes of Health. Retrieved from http://www.drugabuse.gov/related-topics/trends-statistics/monitoring-future/monitoring-future-survey-overview-findings-2012

National Institute on Drug Abuse. (2016, December). *Monitoring the future survey: High school and youth trends*. Bethesda, MD: National Institutes of Health, Author. Retrieved from https://www.drugabuse.gov/publications/drugfacts/monitoring-future-survey-high-school-youth-trends

National Institutes of Health. (2010). *What are the signs and symptoms of sickle cell anemia?* Washington, DC: National Heart, Lung, and Blood Institute. Retrieved from http://www.nhlbi.nih.gov/health/dci/Diseases/Sca/SCA_SignsAndSymptoms.html

National Institutes of Health. (2016, August). *What are the signs and symptoms of sickle cell disease?* Washington, DC: National Heart, Lung, and Blood Institute, Author. Retrieved from https://www.nhlbi.nih.gov/health/health-topics/topics/sca/signs

National Institutes of Health. (2017, April). *Childhood cancers*. Bethseda, MD: National Cancer Institute, Author. Retrieved from https://www.cancer.gov/types/childhood-cancers

National Mathematics Advisory Panel. (2008). *Foundations for Success: The final report of the national mathematics advisory panel*. Washington, DC: US Department of Education.

National Reading Panel (2000). *Teaching children to read: An evidence-based assessment of the scientific research literature on reading and its implications for reading instruction*. Washington, DC: National Institute of Child Health and Human Development.

National Spinal Cord Injury Statistical Center. (2013, February). *Spinal cord injury: Facts and figures at a glance.* Birmingham, AL: Author. Retrieved from https://www.nscisc.uab.edu/PublicDocuments/fact_figures_docs/Facts%202013.pdf

National Spinal Cord Injury Statistical Center. (2016). *Spinal cord injuries (SCI): Facts and figures at a glance.* Birmingham, AL: University of Alabama at Birmingham. Retrieved from https://www.nscisc.uab.edu/Public/Facts%202016.pdf

Neal, L. V. I., McCray, A. D., Webb-Johnson, G., & Bridgest, S. T. (2003). The effects of African American movement styles on teachers' perceptions and reactions. *Journal of Special Education, 37,* 49–57.

Neale, M. H., & Test, D. W. (2010). Effects of the "I can use effort" strategy on quality of student verbal contributions and individualized education program participation with third-and fourth-grade students with disabilities. *Remedial and Special Education, 31*(3), 184–194.

Neece, C. L., Baker, B. L., Crnic, K., & Blacher, J. (2013). Examining the validity of ADHD as a diagnosis for adolescents with intellectual disabilities: Clinical presentation. *Journal of Abnormal Child Psychology, 41,* 597–612.

Nelson, J. S., Epstein, M. H., Bursuck, W. D., Jayanthi, M., & Sawyer, V. (1998). The preferences of middle school students for homework adaptations made by general education teachers. *Learning Disabilities: Research and Practice, 13,* 109–117.

Nelson, J., Hurley, K., Synhorst, L., Epstein, M., Stage, S., & Buckley, J. (2009). The child outcomes of a behavior model. *Exceptional Children, 76,* 7–30.

Neuman, S. B. (2016). Opportunities to learn: Give children a fighting chance. *Literacy Research: Theory, Method, and Practice, 65,* 113–123.

Neuman, S., Kefer, T., & Pinkham, A. (2017). Anticipation Guide Reading Rockets. Retrieved from http://www.readingrockets.org/strategies/anticipation_guide.

New Jersey Coalition for Inclusive Education (2013). *Plotting your course: A guide to using the MAPS process for planning inclusive opportunities and facilitating transitions.* Trenton, New Jersey: New Jersey Council on Developmental Disabilities. Retrieved from njcie.org.s160251.gridserver.com/wp.../Plotting-Your-Course-MAPS-Guide.pdf

Newcomer, L. (2009, March). Universal positive behavior support for the classroom. *PBIS Newsletter.* Retrieved from http://www.pbis.org/pbis_newsletter/volume_4/issue4.aspx

Newton, J., Horner, R. H., Todd, A. W., Algozzine, R. F., & Algozzine, K. M. (2012). A pilot study of a problem-solving model for team decision making. *Education and Treatment of Children, 35*(1), 25–49.

Ng, S. J., Hill, M. F., & Rawlinson, C. (2016). Hidden in plain sight: The experiences of three twice-exceptional students during their transfer to high school. *Gifted Child Quarterly, 60,* 296–311.

Nicholson, J., Capitelli, S., Richert, A. E., Bauer, A., & Bonetti, S. (2016). The affordances of using a teacher leadership network to support leadership development: Creating collaborative thinking spaces to strengthen teachers' skills in facilitating productive evidence-informed conversations. *Teacher Education Quarterly, 43,* 29–50.

Niesyn, M. (2009). Strategies for success: Evidence-based instructional practices for students with emotional and behavioral disorders. *Preventing School Failure, 53,* 227–233.

Nieto, S. (2013). Language, literacy, and culture: Aha! Moments in personal and sociopolitical understanding. *Journal of Language and Literacy Education, 9*(1), 8–20.

Nolan, J. D., & Filter, K. J. (2012). A function-based classroom behavior intervention using non-contingent reinforcement plus response cost. *Education and Treatment of Children, 35*(3), 419–430.

Nolan-Spohn, H. (2016). Increasing student involvement in IEPs. *Mid-Western Educational Researcher, 28,* 300–308.

Nolet, V., & McLaughlin, M. J. (2005). *Accessing the general curriculum: Including students with disabilities in standards-based reform* (2nd ed.). Thousand Oaks, CA: Corwin.

Nomi, T. (2010). The effects of within-class ability grouping on academic achievement in early elementary years. *Journal of Research on Educational Effectiveness, 3*(1), 56–92.

Nunez, J.C., Gonzalez-Pienda, J.A., Gonzalez-Pumariega, S., Roces, C., Alvarez, L., Gonzalez, P., Cabanach, R.G., Valle, A., & Rodriguez, S. (2005). Subgroups of attributional profiles in students with learning disabilities and their relation to self-concept and academic goals. *Learning Disabilities Research & Practice, 20(2),* 86–97.

Nunn, G., & Jantz, P. (2009). Factors within response to intervention implementation training associated with teacher efficacy beliefs. *Education, 129,* 599–607.

Nurmi, J. (2012). Students' characteristics and teacher-child relationships in instruction: A meta-analysis. *Educational Research Review, 7,* 177–197.

O'Connor, E. (2010). Teacher-child relationships as dynamic systems. *Journal of School Psychology, 48,* 187–218.

O'Connor, R. E., Beach, K. D., Sanchez, V. M., Bocian, K. M., & Flynn, L. J. (2015). Building bridges: A design experiment to improve reading and United States history knowledge of poor readers in eighth grade. *Exceptional Children, 81*(4), 399–425.

Odegard, T. N., Ring, J., Smith, S., Biggan, J., & Black, J. (2008). Differentiating the neural response to intervention in children with developmental dyslexia. *Annals of Dyslexia, 58,* 1–14.

Office for Civil Rights. (2011, March). *Protecting students with disabilities: Frequently asked questions about section 504 and the education of children with disabilities.* Washington, DC: Author. Retrieved from http://www2.ed.gov/about/offices/list/ocr/504faq.html

Office for Civil Rights. (2012, January). *Questions and answers on the ADA Amendments Act of 2008 for students with disabilities attending public elementary and secondary* schools. Washington, DC: U.S. Department of Education, Author. Retrieved from https://www2.ed.gov/about/offices/list/ocr/docs/dcl-504faq-201109.html

Office of Civil Rights. (2015, October). *Protecting students with disabilities: Frequently asked questions about section 504 and the education of children with disabilities.* Washington, DC: Author. Retrieved from https://www2.ed.gov/about/offices/list/ocr/504faq.html

Office of Juvenile Justice and Delinquency Prevention. (2013, July). *Educational advocacy for youth with disabilities.* Washington, DC: Author. Retrieved from http://www.ojjdp.gov/pubs/walls/sect-03.html

O'Keeffe, S. B., & Medina, C. M. (2016). Nine strategies for helping middle school students weather the perfect storm of disability, diversity, and adolescence. *American Secondary Education, 44*(3), 72–87.

Okolo, C. M. (2000). Features of effective instructional software. In J. Lindsey (Ed.), *Technology and exceptional individuals* (3rd ed.). Austin, TX: PRO-ED.

Okolo, C. M., Ferretti, R. P., & MacArthur, C. A. (2007). Talking about history: Discussions in a middle school inclusive classroom. *Journal of Learning Disabilities, 40*(2), 154–165.

Oldfield, J., Hebron, J., & Humphrey, N. (2016). The role of school level protective factors in overcoming cumulative risk for behavior difficulties in children with special educational needs and disabilities. *Psychology in the Schools, 53,* 831–847.

Olivos, E. (2009). Collaboration with Latino families: A critical perspective of home-school interactions. *Intervention in School and Clinic, 45,* 109–115.

Olivos, E. M., Gallagher, R. J., & Aguilar, J. (2010). Fostering collaboration with culturally and linguistically diverse families of children with moderate to severe disabilities. *Journal of Educational & Psychological Consultation, 20,* 28–40.

Olson, A., Leko, M. M., & Roberts, C. A. (2016). Providing students with severe disabilities access to the general education curriculum. *Research and Practice for Persons with Severe Disabilities, 41,* 143–157.

Olson, J. L., Platt, J. C., & Dieker, L. (2007). *Teaching children and adolescents with special needs* (5th ed.). Upper Saddle River, NJ: Merrill/Prentice Hall.

Olson, R. K., Hulslander, J., Christopher, M., Keenan, J.M., Wadsworth, S.J., Wilcutt, E.G., Pennington, B.F. & DeFries, J.C. (2013). Genetic and environmental influences on writing and their relations to language and reading. *Annals of Dyslexia, 63(1),* 25-43.

Olsson, N. C., Rautio, D., Asztalos, J., Stoetzer, U., & Bölte, S. (2016). Social skills group training in high-functioning autism: A qualitative responder study. *Autism, 20,* 995–1010.

Olulade, O. A., Napoliello, E. M., & Eden, G. F. (2013). Abnormal visual motion processing is not a cause of dyslexia. *Neuron, 79,* 180–190.

Ong-Dean, C., Daly, A. J., & Park, V. (2011). Privileged advocates: Disability and education policy in the USA. *Policy Futures in Education, 9,* 392–405.

Opitz, M. (2007). Back-to-school tips: Learning centers: The first week. Excerpted from Michael Opitz's book *Learning Centers: Getting Them Started, Keeping Them Going.* Retrieved from http://teacher.scholastic.com/professional/backtoschool/learning_center.htm

Oram, L., Owens, S., & Maras, M. (2016). Functional behavior assessments and behavior intervention plans in rural schools: An exploration of the need, barriers, and recommendations. *Preventing School Failure, 60,* 305–310.

Ornstein, A. C., & Lasley, T. J. II. (2004). *Strategies for effective teaching* (4th ed.). New York, NY: McGraw-Hill.

Orosco, M. J. (2014a). Word problem strategy for Latino English language learners at risk for math disabilities. *Learning Disability Quarterly, 37(1),* 45–53.

Orosco, M. J. (2014b). A math intervention for third grade Latino English language learners at risk for math disabilities. *Exceptionality, 22(4),* 205–225.

Orosco, M., & Klingner, J. (2010). One school's implementation of RTI with English language learners: "Referring into RTI." *Journal of Learning Disabilities, 43,* 269–288.

Osborne, A. G., & Russo, C. J. (2014). *Special education and the law: A guide for practitioners* (3rd edition). Thousand Oaks, CA: Corwin.

Osgood, R. L. (2008). *The history of special education: A struggle for equality in American public schools.* Westport, CT: Greenwood-Praeger.

Ostovar-Nameghi, S. A., & Sheikhahmadi, M. (2016). From teacher isolation to teacher collaboration: Theoretical perspectives and empirical findings. *English Language Teaching, 9,* 197–205.

Overton, T. (2015). *Assessing learners with special needs: An applied approach* (8th ed.). Upper Saddle River, NJ: Merrill/Pearson.

Owens, M., & Bergman, A. (2010). Alcohol use and antisocial behavior in late adolescence: Characteristics of a sample attending a GED program. *Journal of Child & Adolescent Substance Abuse, 19,* 78–98.

Owens, R.E., Farinella, K.A., & Metz, D.E. (2015). *Introduction to Communication Disorders.* Boston: Pearson.

Paine, S. C., Radicchi, J., Rosellini, L. C., Deutchman, L., & Darch, C. B. (1983). *Structuring your classroom for academic success.* Champaign, IL: Research Press.

Pajo, B., & Cohen, D. (2013). The problem with ADHD: Researchers' constructions and parents' accounts. *International Journal of Early Childhood, 45(1),* 11–33.

Palawat, M., & May, M. E. (2012). The impact of cultural diversity on special education provision in the United States. *Journal of the International Association of Special Education, 13(1),* 58–63.

Palincsar, A., & Brown, A. (1988). Teaching and practicing thinking skills to promote comprehension in the context of group problem solving. *Remedial and Special Education, 9(1),* 53–59.

Papay, C., Unger, D. D., Williams-Diehm, K., & Mitchell, V. (2015). Begin with the end in mind: Infusing transition planning and instruction into elementary classrooms. *Teaching Exceptional Children, 47(6),* 310–318.

Parette, H. P., Hourcade, J. J., & Huer, M. B. (2003). Using assistive technology focus groups with families across cultures. *Education and Training in Developmental Disabilities, 38,* 429–440.

Parker, R., Hasbrouck, J. E., & Tindal, G. (1992). The maze as a classroom-based reading measure: Construction methods, reliability, and validity. *Journal of Special Education, 26,* 195–218.

Partin, T., Robertson, R., Maggin, D., Oliver, R., & Wehby, J. (2010). Using teacher praise and opportunities to respond to promote appropriate student behavior. *Preventing School Failure, 54,* 172–178.

Patall, E., Cooper, H., & Robinson, J. C. (2008). The effects of choice on intrinsic motivation and related outcomes: A meta-analysis of research findings. *Psychological Bulletin, 134(2),* 270–300.

Patillo, J., & Vaughn, E. (1992). *Learning centers for child-centered classrooms.* Washington, DC: National Education Association.

Patton, J. R. (1994). Practical recommendations for using homework with students with disabilities. *Journal of Learning Disabilities, 27,* 570–578.

Patton, J. R., Payne, J. S., & Beirne-Smith, M. (1986). *Mental retardation* (2nd ed.). Columbus, OH: Merrill.

Pavri, S. (2010). Response to intervention in the social-emotional-behavioral domain: Perspectives from urban schools. *Teaching Exceptional Children Plus, 6(3),* article 4. Retrieved from http://escholarship.bc.edu/education/tecplus

Pavri, S., & Monda-Amaya, L. (2001). Social support in inclusive schools: Student and teacher perspectives. *Exceptional Children, 67,* 391–411.

Pearl, C., Dieker, L., & Kirkpatrick, R. (2012). A five-year retrospective on the Arkansas Department of Education co-teaching project. *Professional Development in Education, 38,* 571–587.

Peck-Peterson, S. M., Derby, K. M., Berg, W. K., & Horner, R. H. (2002). Collaboration with families in the functional behavior assessment of and intervention for severe behavior problems [Electronic version]. *Education and Treatment of Children, 25,* 5–25.

Pederson, S. (2003). Motivational orientation in a problem-based learning environment. *Journal of Interactive Learning Research, 14(1),* 41–77.

Pedrotty-Bryant, D., Bryant, B. R., & Raskind, M. H. (1998). Using assistive technology to enhance the skills of students with learning disabilities. *Intervention in School and Clinic, 34,* 53–58.

Peijnenborgh, J., Hurks, P., Aldenkamp, A., Vles, J., & Hendriksen, J. (2015). Efficacy of working memory training in children and adolescents with learning disabilities: A review study and meta-analysis. *Neuropsychological Rehabilitation, 1,* 1–26. http://dx.doi.org/10.1080/09602011.2015.1026356

Pennington, B., & McComas, J. J. (2017). Effects of the Good Behavior Game across classroom contexts. *Journal of Applied Behavior Analysis, 50(1),* 176–180.

Pennington, R., Courtade, G., Jones Ault, M., & Delano, M. (2016). Five essential features of quality educational programs for students with moderate and severe intellectual disability: A guide for administrators. *Education and Training in Autism and Developmental Disabilities, 51,* 294–306.

Peper, R. J., & Mayer, R. E. (1986). Generative effects of notetaking during science lectures. *Journal of Educational Psychology, 78,* 34–38.

Perrachione, T. K., DelTufo, S. N., Winter, R., Murtagh, J., Cyr, A., Chang, P., Halverson, K., Ghosh, S. S., Christodoulou, J. A., & Gabrieli, J. D. E. (2016). Dysfunction of rapid neural adaptation in dyslexia. *Neuron, 92*(6), 1383–1397.

Pertsch, C. F. (1936). *A comparative study of the progress of subnormal pupils in the grades and in special classes.* New York: Teacher's College, Columbia University, Bureau of Publications.

Peterson, J. S. (2016). Gifted children and bullying. In M. Neihart, S. I. Pfeiffer, & T. L. Cross (Eds.), *The social and emotional development of gifted children: What do we know?* (2nd edition) (pp. 131–141). Waco, TX: Prufrock Press.

Peterson, L.Y., Burden, J. P., Sedaghat, J. M., Gothberg, J. E., Kohler, P. D., & Coyle, J. L. (2013). Triangulated transition goals: Developing relevant and genuine annual goals. *Teaching Exceptional Children, 45*(6), 46–57.

Peverly, S. T., Ramaswamy, V., Brown, C., Sumowski, J., Alidoost, M., & Garner, J. (2007). What predicts skill in lecture note taking? *Journal of Educational Psychology, 99*(1), 167–180.

Pewewardy, C., & Fitzpatrick, M. (2009). Working with American Indian students and families: Disabilities, issues, and interventions. *Intervention in School and Clinic, 45,* 91–98.

Pfannenstiel, K. H., Pedrotty-Bryant, D., Bryant, B. R., & Porterfield, J. A. (2015). Cognitive strategy instruction for teaching word problems to primary-level struggling students. *Intervention in School and Clinic, 50*(5), 291–296.

Pfiffner, L. J., Villodas, M., Kaiser, N., Rooney, M., & McBurnett, K. (2013). Educational outcomes of a collaborative school-home behavioral intervention for ADHD. *School Psychology Quarterly, 28,* 25–36.

Pham, A., Carlson, J., & Kosciulek, J. (2010). Ethnic differences in parental beliefs of attention-deficit/hyperactivity disorder and treatment. *Journal of Attention Disorders, 13,* 584–591.

Phippen, J.W. (2015, July 5). The racial imbalance of special education. *The Atlantic Monthly.* Retrieved from https://www.theatlantic.com/education/archive/2015/07/the-racial-imbalances-of-special-education/397775/

Pillet-Shore, D. (2016). Criticizing another's child: How teachers evaluate students during parent-teacher conferences. *Language in Society, 45*(1), 33–58.

Pinquart, M., & Kauser, R. (2017). Do the associations of parenting styles with behavior problems and academic achievement vary by culture? Results from a meta-analysis. *Cultural Diversity and Ethnic Minority Psychology,* doi:10.1037/cdp0000149

Pinquart, M., & Pfeiffer, J. P. (2015). Solving developmental tasks in adolescents with a chronic physical illness or physical/sensory disability: A meta-analysis. *International Journal of Disability, Development and Education, 62,* 249–264.

Pisha, B. (2003). Assistive technologies: Making a difference. *IDA Perspectives, 29*(4), 1, 4.

Pisha, B., & Coyne, P. (2001). Smart from the start: The promise of universal design for learning. *Remedial and Special Education, 22*(4), 197–203.

Pisha, B., & Stahl, S. (2005). The promise of new learning environments for students with disabilities. *Intervention in School and Clinic, 41*(2), 67–75.

Plotner, A. J., Mazzotti, V. L., Rose, C. A., & Carlson-Britting, K. B. (2016). Factors associated with enhanced knowledge and use of secondary transition evidence-based practices. *Teacher Education and Special Education, 39,* 28–46.

Pogrund, R. L, & Fazzi, D. L. (Eds.). (2002). *Early focus: Working with young blind and visually impaired children and their families* (2nd ed.). New York: American Foundation for the Blind.

Polloway, E. A., Bursuck, W. D., Jayanthi, M., Epstein, M. H., & Nelson, J. S. (1996). Treatment acceptability: Determining appropriate interventions within inclusive classrooms. *Intervention in School and Clinic, 31,* 133–144.

Polloway, E.A., Houck, E. C., Patton, J.R., & Lubin, J. (2017). Intellectual and developmental disabilities. In *Handbook of Special Education* (2nd ed.) In J. M. Kauffman, D. P. Hallahan, & Paige Cullen Pullen (eds.). New York: Routledge.

Poteet, J. A., Choate, J. S., & Stewart, S. C. (1993). Performance assessment and special education: Practices and prospects. *Focus on Exceptional Children, 26*(1), 1–20.

Powell, S. R., Fuchs, L. S., & Fuchs, D. (2013). Reaching the mountaintop: Addressing the common core standards in mathematics for students with mathematics difficulties. *Learning Disabilities Research & Practice, 28*(1), 38–48.

Powell-Smith, K. A., & Shinn, M. R. (2004). *Administration and scoring of Written Expression Curriculum-Based Measurement (WE-CBM) for use in general outcome measurement.* Eden Prairie, MN: EdFormation.

Prater, M. A., Redman, A. S., Anderson, D., Gibb, G. S. (2014). Teaching adolescent students with learning disabilities to self-advocate for accommodations. *Intervention in School and Clinic, 49*(5), 298–305.

Pressley, M. (2000). What should comprehension instruction be the instruction of? In M. Kamil, P. B. Mosenthal, P. D. Pearson, & R. Barr (Eds.), *Handbook of Reading Research* (Vol. 3). Mahwah, NJ: Erlbaum.

Pressley, M., & Hilden, K.R. (2006). Cognitive strategies: Production deficiencies and successful strategy instruction everywhere. In D. Kuhn, & R. Siegler (Eds.), W. Damon, & R. Lerner (Series Eds.), *Handbook of Child Psychology: Vol. 2. Cognition, perception, and language* (6th ed.). Hoboken, NJ: Wiley.

Price, K. M., & Nelson, K. L. (2011). *Planning effective instruction: Diversity responsive methods and management* (4th edition). Belmont, CA: Wadsworth.

Puckett, K., Mathur, S. R., & Zamora, R. (2017). Implementing an Intervention in Special Education to Promote Social Skills in an Inclusive Setting. *Journal of International Special Needs Education, 20*(1), 25–36.

Purcell, M. L., Turnbull, A., & Jackson, C. W. (2006). Linking early childhood inclusion and family quality of life: Current literature and future directions. *Young Exceptional Children, 9*(3), 10–19.

Pyle, D., Pyle, N., Lignugaris/Kraft, B., Duran, L., & Akers, J. (2017). academic effects of peer-mediated interventions with English language learners: A research synthesis. *Review of Educational Research, 87,* 103–133.

Qian, Y., Shuai, L., Chan, R. K., Qian, Q., & Wang, Y. (2013). The developmental trajectories of executive function of children and adolescents with attention deficit hyperactivity disorder. *Research in Developmental Disabilities: A Multidisciplinary Journal, 34,* 1434–1445.

Quigney, T. A., & Studer, J. R. (2016). *Working with students with disabilities: A guide for school counselors.* New York, NY: Routledge/Taylor & Francis Group.

Rafdal, B. H., McMaster, K. L., McConnell, S. R., Fuchs, D., & Fuchs, L. S. (2011). The effectiveness of kindergarten peer-assisted learning strategies for students with disabilities. *Exceptional Children, 77,* 299–316.

Rafferty, Y., Piscitelli, V., & Boettcher, C. (2003). The impact of inclusion on language development and social competence among preschoolers with disabilities. *Exceptional Children, 69,* 467–480.

Rajala, A. Z., Henriques, J. B., & Populin, L. C. (2012). Dissociative effects of methylphenidate in nonhuman primates: Trade-offs between cognitive and behavioral performance. *Journal of Cognitive Neuroscience, 24,* 1371–1381.

Ramsey, W. L., Gabriel, L. A., McGuirk, J. F., Phillips, C. R., & Watenpaugh, T. R. (1983). *General science.* New York: Holt, Rinehart, and Winston.

Rao, K., Ok, M. W., & Bryant, B. R. (2014. A review of research on universal design models. *Remedial and Special Education, 35*(3), 153–166.

Rappaport, J. (1982/1983). Effects of dietary substances in children. *Journal of Psychiatric Research, 17,* 187–191.

Raskin, T. (2013, June). The prevalence of corporal punishment in U.S. schools. *The Nation* (Student Nation). Retrieved from http://www .thenation.com/blog/174664/prevalence-corporal-punishment-us-schools#axzz2dTxdrcGA

Rausch, K., & Skiba, R. (2006). *Discipline, disability, and race: Dispro-portionality in Indiana schools* (Education Policy Brief, vol. 4, no. 10). Bloomington, IN: Center for Evaluation and Education Policy. (ERIC Document Reproduction Service No. ED495751)

Ray, J., Pewitt Kinder, J., & George, S. (2009, September). Partnering with families of children with special needs: One parent's advice. *Young Children.*

Rea, P. J., McLaughlin, V. L., & Walther-Thomas, C. (2002). Outcomes for students with learning disabilities in inclusive and pull-out programs. *Exceptional Children, 68*(2), 203–222.

Read, N. W. (2014). *NDTAC fact sheet: Youth with special education needs in justice settings.* Washington, DC: National Evaluation and Technical Assistance Center for Children and Youth Who Are Neglected, Delinquent, or At-Risk (NDTAC).

Readence, J. E., Moore, D. W., & Rickelman, R. (2000). *Prereading activi-ties for content-area reading and learning* (3rd ed.). Newark, DE: Inter-national Reading Association.

Redl, F. (2007). Rethinking youthful defiance [Reprint]. *Reclaiming Children and Youth: The Journal of Strength-Based Interventions, 16*(1), 33–35.

Reetz, L., & Rasmussen, T. (1988). Arithmetic mind joggers. *Academic Therapy, 24*(1), 79–82.

Reid, R., Lienemann, T. O., & Hagaman, J. L. (2013). *Strategy Instruction for Students with Learning Disabilities* (2nd ed). New York, NT: Guil-ford Press.

Reid, R., Trout, A. L., & Schartz, M. (2005). Self-regulation interventions for children with attention deficit/hyperactivity disorder. *Exceptional Children, 71*(4), 361–377.

Reilly, C., Hughes, C., Harvey, M., Brigham, N., Cosgriff, J., Kaplan, L., & Bernstein, R. (2014). "Let's talk!": Increasing novel peer-directed questions by high school students with autism to their general edu-cation peers. *Education and Training in Autism and Developmental Disabilities, 49,* 214–231.

Reinke, W. M., Herman, K. C., & Stormont, M. (2013). Classroom-level positive behavior supports in schools implementing SW-PBIS: Iden-tifying areas for enhancement. *Journal of Positive Behavior Interven-tions, 15*(1), 39–50.

Reis, S. M., & Renzulli, J. S. (2004a). Current research on the social and emotional development of gifted and talented students: Good news and future possibilities. *Psychology in the Schools, 41*(1), 119–130.

Reis, S. M., & Renzulli, J. S. (2004b). Curriculum compacting: A system-atic procedure for modifying the curriculum for above average ability students. Storrs, CT: National Research Center on the Gifted and Talented. Retrieved from http://www.sp.uconn.edu/~nrcgt/sem/semart08.html

Reis, S. M., & Sullivan, E. E. (2009). Characteristics of gifted learners: Consistently varied, refreshingly diverse. In F. A. Karnes, & S. M. Bean (Eds.), *Methods and materials for teaching the gifted* (3rd ed., pp. 3–35). Waco, TX: Prufrock.

Reis, S. M., McCoach, D., Little, C. A., Muller, L. M., & Kaniskan, R. (2011). The effects of differentiated instruction and enrichment ped-agogy on reading achievement in five elementary schools. *American Educational Research Journal, 48,* 462–501.

Reis, S. M., Westberg, K. L., Kulikowich, J. M., & Purcell, J. H. (2016). Curriculum compacting and achievement test scores: What does the research say? In S. M. Reis (Ed.), *Reflections on gifted education: Critical works by Joseph S. Renzulli and colleagues* (pp. 271–284). Waco, TX: Prufrock Press.

Rentinck, I. M., Ketelaar, M. M., Schuengel, C. C., Stolk, J. J., Lindeman, E. E., Jongmans, M. J., & Gorter, J. W. (2010). Short-term changes in parents' resolution regarding their young child's diagnosis of cerebral palsy. *Child: Care, Health And Development, 36,* 703–708.

Rentner, D. S., Kober, N., & Frizzell, M. (May, 2016). *Listen to us: Teachers' views and voices.* Washington, DC: Center on Education Policy.

Renzulli, J. S., Baum, S. M., Hébert, T. P., & McCluskey, K. W. (2016). Reversing underachievement through enrichment. In S. M. Reis (Ed.), *Reflections on gifted education: Critical works by Joseph S. Ren-zulli and colleagues* (pp. 429–442). Waco, TX: Prufrock Press.

Reschly, D. J. (2007). *Overview document: Teacher quality for multi-tiered interventions.* Washington, DC: National Comprehensive Center for Teacher Quality.

Reutzel, D. R., Child, A., Jones, C. D., & Clark, S. K. (2014). Explicit instruction in core reading programs. *The Elementary School Journal, 114*(3), 406–430.

Reynolds, C. R., & Shaywitz, S. E. (2009). Response to intervention: Ready or not? or, from wait to fail to watch them fail. *School Psychol-ogy Quarterly, 24*(2), 130–145.

Rice, J. (2007). New media resistance: Barriers to implementation of computer video games in the classroom. *Journal of Educational Multi-media and Hypermedia, 16*(3), 249–261.

Richards, H. V., Brown, A. F., & Forde, T. B. (2007). Addressing diversity in schools: Culturally responsive pedagogy. *Teaching Exceptional Chil-dren, 39*(3), 64–68.

Richards-Tutor, C., Baker, D. L., Gersten, R., Baker, S. K., & Smith, J. M. (2016). The effectiveness of reading interventions for Eng-lish learners: A research synthesis. *Exceptional Children, 82*(2), 144–169.

Richmond, A. S., Aberasturi, S., Abernathy, T., Aberasturi, R., & DelVec-chio, T. (2009). One school-district's examination of least-restrictive environments: The effectiveness of pull-out and inclusion instruction. *The Researcher, 2*(1), 53–66. Retrieved from www.nrmera.org/PDF/Researcher/Researcherv22n1Richmond.pdf

Riesz, E. (2004). Loss and transitions: A 30-year perspective on life with a child who has Down syndrome. *Journal of Loss and Trauma, 9,* 371–382.

Rimm-Kaufman, S. E., La Paro, K. M., Downer, J. T., & Pianta, R. C. (2005). The contribution of classroom setting and quality of instruc-tion to children's behavior in kindergarten classrooms. *The Elemen-tary School Journal, 105*(4), 377–394.

Rinn, A. N., & Reynolds, M. J. (2012). Overexcitabilities and ADHD in the gifted: An examination. *Roeper Review, 34*(1), 38–45.

Ritchie, S.J., Della Sala, S., & McIntosh, R.D. (2011). Irlen colored lenses do not alleviate reading difficulties. *Pediatrics, 128*(4), 932–938.

Ritchotte, J., Rubenstein, L., & Murry, F. (2015). Reversing the under-achievement of gifted middle school students: Lessons from another field. *Gifted Child Today, 38,* 103–113.

Roach, A.T., Beddow, P.A., Kurz, A., Kettler, R.J., & Elliott, S.N. (2010). Incorporating student input in developing alternate assessments based on modified academic achievement standards. *Exceptional Children, 77*(1), 61–80.

Roach, V., & Salisbury, C. (2006). Promoting systemic, statewide inclu-sion from the bottom up. *Theory into Practice, 45,* 279–286.

Robers, S., Kemp, J., & Truman, J. (2013). *Indicators of school crime and safety: 2012* (NCES 2013-036/NCJ 241446). Washington, DC:

National Center for Education Statistics, U.S. Department of Education, and Bureau of Justice Statistics, Office of Justice Programs, U.S. Department of Justice. Retrieved from http://nces.ed.gov/pubs2013/2013036.pdf

Robinson, J. P., & Espelage, D. L. (2012). Bullying explains only part of LGBTQ-heterosexual risk disparities: Implications for policy and practice. *Educational Researcher, 41*, 309–319.

Roblyer, M. D. (2017). *Integrating education technology into teaching* (7th ed.). Boston, MA: Pearson.

Rock, M., Gregg, M., Ellis, E., & Gable, R. A. (2008). REACH: A framework for differentiating classroom instruction. *Preventing School Failure, 52*(2), 31–47.

Roditi, B. N., Steinberg, J. L., Bidale, K. R., Taber, S. E., Caron, K. B., & Kniffin, L. (2005). *Strategies for success: Classroom teaching techniques for students with learning differences.* Austin, TX: Pro-Ed.

Rodríguez-Medina, J., Martín-Antón, L. J., Carbonero, M. A., & Ovejero, A. (2016). Peer-mediated intervention for the development of social interaction skills in high-functioning autism spectrum disorder: A pilot study. *Frontiers In Psychology, 7* (Article 1986), 1–14. doi: 10.3389/fpsyg.2016.01986

Roe, B., Smith, S. H., & Burns, P. C. (2011). *Teaching reading in today's elementary schools* (11th ed.). Boston: Houghton Mifflin.

Roeber, E. D. (2002, November). *Appropriate inclusion of students with disabilities in state accountability systems.* Retrieved from Education Commission of the States website, http://www.ecs.org/clearinghouse/40/11/4011.htm

Rojas, N. L., & Chan, E. (2005). Old and new controversies in the alternative treatment of attention-deficit hyperactivity disorder. *Mental Retardation and Developmental Disabilities Research Reviews, 11*(2), 116–130.

Rojewski, J. W., Lee, I. H., & Gregg, N. (2015). Causal effects of inclusion on postsecondary education outcomes of individuals with high-incidence disabilities. *Journal of Disability Policy Studies, 25*, 210–219.

Romig, J.E., Therrien, W.J., & Lloyd, J. (2017). Meta-analysis of criterion validity for curriculum-based measurement in written language. *The Journal of Special Education; Bensalem, 51(2)*, 72–82.

Rommelse, N., van der Kruijs, M., Damhuis, J., Hoek, I., Smeets, S., Antshel, K. M., & . . . Faraone, S. V. (2016). An evidenced-based perspective on the validity of attention-deficit/hyperactivity disorder in the context of high intelligence. *Neuroscience and Biobehavioral Reviews, 7*, 21–47.

Root, J. R., Browder, D. M., Saunders, A. F., & Lo, Ya-yu (2017). Schema-based instruction with concrete and virtual manipulatives to teach problem solving to students with autism. *Remedial and Special Education, 38(1)*, 42–52.

Rose, J., & Norwich, B. (2014). Collective commitment and collective efficacy: A theoretical model for understanding the motivational dynamics of dilemma resolution in inter-professional work. *Cambridge Journal of Education, 44*, 59–74.

Rosenshine, B. (1997). Advances in research on instruction. In E. J. Lloyd, E. J. Kameanui, & D. Chard (Eds.), *Issues in educating students with disabilities* (pp. 197–221). Mahwah, NJ: Lawrence Erlbaum.

Rosenshine, B. (2012, Spring). Principles of instruction: research-based principles that all teachers should know. *The American Educator*, 12–20.

Rosenshine, B., & Meister, C. (1992). The use of scaffolds for teaching higher-level cognitive strategies. *Educational Leadership, 49*, 26–33.

Rosenthal. B. M., & Barned-Smith, St. J. (2016). Denied: Houston schools block disabled kids from special ed. *Houston Chronicle.* Retrieved from http://www.houstonchronicle.com/denied/6/

Ross, E. J., Graham, D. L., Money, K. M., & Stanwood, G. D. (2015). Developmental consequences of fetal exposure to drugs: What we know and what we still must learn. *Neuropsychopharmacology, 40*, 61–87.

Ross, R., & Kurtz, R. (1993). Making manipulatives work: A strategy for success. *Arithmetic Teacher, 40*(5), 254–257.

Ross, S. W., & Sabey, C. V. (2015). Check-in Check out + social skills: Enhancing the effects of Check-in Check-out for students with social skill deficits. *Remedial and Special Education, 36*(4), 246–257.

Rossetti, Z. (2015). Descriptors of friendship between secondary students with and without autism or intellectual and developmental disability. *Remedial and Special Education, 36*, 181–192.

Rueda, R., & Genzuk, M. (2007). Sociocultural scaffolding as a means toward academic self-regulation: Paraeducators as cultural brokers. *Focus on Exceptional Children, 40*(3), 1–7.

Ryan, C., & Quinlan, E. (2017). Whoever shouts the loudest: Listening to parents of children with disabilities. *Journal of Applied Research in Intellectual Disabilities*, doi:10.1111/jar.12354

Ryndak, D. L., & Alper, S. (2003). *Curriculum and instruction for students with significant disabilities in inclusive settings* (2nd ed.). Boston: Allyn & Bacon.

Ryndak, D., Alper, S., Hughes, C., & McDonnell, J. (2012). Documenting impact of educational contexts on long-term outcomes for students with significant disabilities. *Education and Training in Autism and Developmental Disabilities, 47*, 127–138.

Sabornie, E. J., & deBettencourt, L. U. (2009). *Teaching students with mild and high-incidence disabilities at the secondary level* (3rd ed.). Upper Saddle River, NJ: Merrill/Pearson.

Sabornie, E. J., Evans, C., & Cullinan, D. (2006). Comparing characteristics of high-incidence disability groups. *Remedial and Special Education, 27*(2), 95–104.

Sáenz, L. M., Fuchs, L. S., & Fuchs, D. (2005). Peer-assisted learning strategies for English language learners with learning disabilities. *Exceptional Children, 71*, 231–247.

Saggers, B. (2015). Student perceptions: Improving the educational experiences of high school students on the autism spectrum. *Improving Schools, 18*(1), 35–45.

Sahin, A. (2011). Effects of Jigsaw III technique on achievement in written expression. *Asia Pacific Education Review, 12*, 427–435.

Sailor, W. (2015). Advances in schoolwide inclusive school reform. *Remedial and Special Education, 36*, 94–99.

Sale, P., & Carey, D. M. (1995). The sociometric status of students with disabilities in a full-inclusion school. *Exceptional Children, 62,* 6–19.

Salend, S. J. (2005). Report card models that support communication and differentiation of instruction. *TEACHING Exceptional Children, 37*(4), 28–34.

Salend, S. J. (2006). Explaining your inclusion program to families. *Teaching Exceptional Children, 38*(4), 6–11.

Salend, S. J., & Duhaney, L. M. G. (2005). Understanding and addressing the disproportionate representation of students of color in special education. *Intervention in School and Clinic, 40*, 213–221.

Salend, S. J., & Duhaney, L. M. G., (2002). Grading students in inclusive settings. *Teaching Exceptional Children, 34*(3), 8–15.

Salinger, R. L. (2016). Selecting universal screening measures to identify students at risk academically. *Intervention in School and Clinic, 52(2)*, 77–84.

Salvia, J., Ysseldyke, J., & Whitmer, S. (2016). *Assessment in Special and Inclusive Education* (13th ed.). Boston, MA: Houghton-Mifflin.

Sánchez, S. Y. (1999). Learning from the stories of culturally and linguistically diverse families and communities. *Remedial and Special Education, 20*, 351–359.

Sansosti, J. M., & Sansosti, F. J. (2012). Inclusion for students with high-functioning autism spectrum disorders: Definitions and decision making. *Psychology in the Schools, 49,* 917–931.

Santangelo, T. E., Ruhaak, A. E., Kama, M. M., & Cook, B. G. (2013). Constructing effective instructional toolkits: A selective review of evidence-based practices for students with learning disabilities. In B. G. Cook, M. Tankersley, T. J. Landrum, B. G. Cook, M. Tankersley, & T. J. Landrum (Eds.), *Evidence-based practices* (pp. 221–249). Bingley, United Kingdom: Emerald Group Publishing.

Santangelo, T., Novosel, L. C., Cook, B. G., & Gapsis, M. (2015). Using the 6S Pyramid to identify research-based practices for students with learning disabilities. *Learning Disabilities Research & Practice, 30*(2), 91–101.

Sapp, W., & Hatlen, P. (2010). The expanded core curriculum: Where we have been, where we are going, and how we can get there. *Journal of Visual Impairment & Blindness, 104,* 338–348.

Satsangi, R., Bouck, E. C., Taber-Doughty, T., Bofferding, L., Roberts, C. A. (2016). Comparing the effectiveness of virtual and concrete manipulatives to teach algebra to secondary students with learning disabilities. *Learning Disability Quarterly, 39*(4), 240–253.

Sauer, J. S., & Lalvani, P. (2017). From advocacy to activism: Families, communities, and collective change. *Journal of Policy and Practice in Intellectual Disabilities, 14*(1), 51–58.

Saunders, W. M., Foorman, B. R., & Carlson, C. D. (2006). Is a separate block of time for oral English language development in programs for English language learners needed? *The Elementary School Journal, 107*(2), 181–198.

Savage, T.V., Savage, K., & Armstrong, D.C. (2006). *Teaching in the secondary school* (6th ed.). Upper Saddle River, NJ: Merrill/Prentice Hall.

Sayeski, K. (2009). Defining special educators' tools: The building blocks of effective collaboration. *Intervention in School and Clinic, 45,* 38–44.

Scanlon, D., & Baker, D. (2012). An accommodations model for the secondary inclusive classroom. *Learning Disability Quarterly, 35,* 212–224.

Scanlon, D., & Mellard, D. F. (2002). Academic and participation profiles of school-age dropouts with and without disabilities. *Exceptional Children, 68,* 239–258.

Scheerenberger, R. C. (1983). *A history of mental retardation.* Baltimore, MD: Paul H. Brookes.

Schieltz, K. M., Wacker, D. P., & Romani, P. W. (2017). Effects of signaled positive reinforcement on problem behavior maintained by negative reinforcement. *Journal of Behavioral Education, 26,* 137–150.

Schifter, L. A. (2016). Using survival analysis to understand graduation of students with disabilities. *Exceptional Children, 82,* 479–496.

Schilling, E. J., & Getch, Y. Q. (2012). Getting my bearings, returning to school: Issues facing adolescents with traumatic brain injury. *Teaching Exceptional Children, 45*(1), 54–63.

Schmeichel, M. (2012). Good teaching? An examination of culturally relevant pedagogy as an equity practice. *Journal of Curriculum Studies, 44,* 211–231.

Schmitt, A. J., Hale, A. D., McCallum, E., & Mauch, B. (2011). Accommodating remedial readers in the general education setting: Is listening-while-reading sufficient to improve factual and inferential comprehension? *Psychology in the Schools, 48,* 37–45.

Schneider, B. W., Gerdes, A. C., Haack, L. M., & Lawton, K. E. (2013). Predicting treatment dropout in parent training interventions for families of school-aged children with ADHD. *Child & Family Behavior Therapy, 35,* 144–169.

Schoppek, W., & Tullis, M. (2010). Enhancing arithmetic and word-problem solving skills efficiently by individualized computer-assisted practice. *Journal of Educational Research, 103*(4), 239–252.

Schultz, B. K., Evans, S. W., Langberg, J. M., & Schoemann, A. M. (2017). Outcomes for adolescents who comply with long-term psychosocial treatment for ADHD. *Journal of Consulting and Clinical Psychology, 85,* 250–261.

Schumaker, J. B., Deshler, D. D., & Denton, P. (1984). *The learning strategies curriculum: The paraphrasing strategy.* Lawrence: University of Kansas.

Schumaker, J., & Deshler, D. (2006). Teaching adolescents to be strategic learners. In D. Deshler and J. Schumaker (Eds.). *Teaching Adolescents with Disabilities: Accessing the General Education Curriculum* (pp.121–156). New York: Corwin Press.

Schunk, D. (1989). Self-efficacy and cognitive achievement: Implications for students with learning disabilities. *Journal of Learning Disabilities, 22,* 14–22.

Scott, G. A. (2011). *Deaf and hard of hearing children: Federal support for developing language and literacy* [Report to Congressional Requesters, GAO-11-357]. Washington, DC: U.S. Government Accountability Office. Retrieved from http://www.gao.gov/assets/320/318707.pdf

Scott, P. B., & Raborn, D. T. (1996). Realizing the gifts of diversity among students with learning disabilities. *LD Forum, 21*(2), 10–18.

Scott, T. M., Alter, P. J., & McQuillan, K. (2010). Functional behavior assessment in classroom settings: Scaling down to scale up. *Intervention in School and Clinic, 46*(2), 87–94.

Scruggs, T. E., Mastropieri, M. A., & Marshak, L. (2012). Peer-mediated instruction in inclusive secondary social studies learning: Direct and indirect learning effects. *Learning Disabilities Research & Practice, 27,* 12–20.

Scruggs, T., & Mastropieri, M. (1988). Are learning disabled students "test-wise"? A review of recent research. *Learning Disabilities Focus, 3*(2), 87–97.

Scruggs, T., Mastropieri, M., & McDuffie, K. (2007). Co-teaching in inclusive classrooms: A metasynthesis of qualitative research. *Exceptional Children, 73,* 392–416.

Searight, H. R., Robertson, K., Smith, T., Perkins, S., & Searight, B. K. (2012). Complementary and alternative therapies for pediatric attention deficit hyperactivity disorder: A descriptive review. *International Scholarly Research network, ISRN Psychiatry, Volume 2012, Article ID 804127,* 8 pages. doi:10.5402/2012/804127

Sebag, R. (2010). Behavior management through self-advocacy: A strategy for secondary students with learning disabilities. *Teaching Exceptional Children, 42*(6), 22–29.

Seethaler, P. M., Powell, S. R., & Fuchs, L. S. (2010). *Help students solve word problems with "Pirate Math."* [Electronic version]. Reston, Virginia: Council for Exceptional Children CEC Today. Retrieved from http://www.cec.sped.org/AM/Printer1&TEMPLATE=/...

Segall, M. J., & Campbell, J. M. (2012). Factors relating to education professionals' classroom practices for the inclusion of students with autism spectrum disorders. *Research in Autism Spectrum Disorders, 6,* 1156–1167.

Sejnost, R. L. & Thiese, S. M. (2010*). Building content literacy.* Thousand Oaks, CA: Corwin Press.

Sela, I., Izzetoglu, M., Izzetoglu, K., & Onaral, B. (2014). A functional near-infrared spectroscopy study of lexical decision supports and dual route model and the phonological deficit theory of dyslexia. *Journal of Learning Disabilities, 47*(3), 279–288.

Semke, C. A., Garbacz, S., Kwon, K., Sheridan, S. M., & Woods, K. E. (2010). Family involvement for children with disruptive behaviors: The role of parenting stress and motivational beliefs. *Journal of School Psychology, 48,* 293–312.

Seong, Y., Wehmeyer, M. L., Palmer, S. B., & Little, T. D. (2015). Effects of the self-directed individualized education program on self-determination and transition of adolescents with disabilities. *Career Development and Transition for Exceptional Individuals, 38,* 132–141.

Sepiol, C. (2015). *Section 504-A legal guide for educators: Practical applications for essential compliance.* Eau Claire, WI: PESI Publishing and Media.

Sermier Dessemontet, R., & Bless, G. (2013). The impact of including children with intellectual disability in general education classrooms on the academic achievement of their low-, average-, and high-achieving peers. *Journal of Intellectual & Developmental Disability, 38,* 23–30.

Serres, S. A., & Nelson, J. A. (2011). Professional school counselor. In C. G. Simpson, J. P. Bakken, C. G. Simpson, & J. P. Bakken (Eds.), *Collaboration: A multidisciplinary approach to educating students with disabilities* (pp. 237–252). Waco, TX: Prufrock Press.

Servick, R. A., & Romski, M. A. (2019). *AAC: More than three decades of growth and development.* Rockville, MD: American Speech-Language-Hearing Association. Retrieved from http://www.asha.org/public/speech/disorders/AACThreeDecades.htm

Sessions, L., Kang, M., & Womack, S. (2016). The neglected 'R': improving writing instruction through iPad Apps. *Techtrends: Linking Research & Practice to Improve Learning, 60*(3), 218–225. doi:10.1007/s11528-016-0041-8

Severson, H. H., Walker, H. M., & Hope-Doolittle, J. (2007). Proactive, early screening to detect behaviorally at-risk students: Issues, approaches, emerging innovations, and professional practices. *Journal of School Psychology, 45,* 193–223.

Sewell, T. (2012). Are we adequately preparing teachers to partner with families? *Early Childhood Education Journal,* 40, 259–263.

Sgouros, I., & Walsh, K. (2012). Response to intervention within tier 3: A model for data teams. *Communique, 40*(8), 8–9.

Shamaki, T. A. (2015). Influence of learning environment on students' academic achievement in mathematics: A case study of some selected schools in Yobe State–Nigeria. *Journal of Education and Practice, 6*(34), 40–45.

Shapiro, D. R., & Sayers, L. K. (2003). Who does what on the interdisciplinary team regarding physical education for students with disabilities? *Teaching Exceptional Children, 35*(6), 32–38.

Sharma, A. (2015). Perspectives on inclusive education with reference to United Nations. *Universal Journal of Educational Research, 3,* 317–321.

Shaywitz, S. (2005). *Overcoming dyslexia: A new and complete science-based program for reading problems at any level.* New York: Knopf.

Shaywitz, S. E., & Shaywitz, B. A. (2007). What neuroscience really tells us about reading instruction. *Educational Leadership, 64*(5), 74–76.

Shaywitz, S. E., Fletcher, J. M., Holahan, J. M., Schneider, A. E., Marchione, K. E., Stuebing, K. K., Francis, D. J., Pugh, K. R., and Shaywitz, B. A. (1999). Persistence of dyslexia: The Connecticut longitudinal study at adolescence. *Pediatrics, 104*(6), 1351–1359.

Shaywitz, S., Morris, R., & Shaywitz, B. (2008). The education of dyslexic children from childhood to young adulthood. *Annual Review of Psychology, 59,* 451–475.

Sheldon, S. B., Epstein, J. L., Hutchins, D. J., & Thomas, B. G. (2012). *Sampler: Improve student behavior with family and community involvement.* Baltimore, MD: National Network of Partnership Schools, Johns Hopkins University. Retrieved from http://www.csos.jhu.edu/p2000/PPP/Samplers/2012-Behavior-Sampler.pdf

Shen, J., Leslie, J. M., Spybrook, J. K., & Ma, X. (2012). Are principal background and school processes related to teacher job satisfaction? A multilevel study using schools and staffing survey, 2003–04. *American Educational Research Journal, 49,* 200–230.

Shepherd, K. G., Fowler, S., McCormick, J., Wilson, C. L., & Morgan, D. (2016). The search for role clarity: Challenges and implications for special education teacher preparation. *Teacher Education and Special Education, 39,* 83–97.

Sheridan, S. M., Witte, A. L., Holmes, S. R., Coutts, M. J., Dent, A. L., Kunz, G. M., & Wu, C. (2017). A randomized trial examining the effects of conjoint behavioral consultation in rural schools: Student outcomes and the mediating role of the teacher–parent relationship. *Journal of School Psychology, 61,* 33–53.

Sherman, M. C. (2016). The school social worker: A marginalized commodity within the school ecosystem. *Children & Schools, 38,* 147–151.

Shin, J., Deno, S. L., & Espin, C. (2000). Technical adequacy of the maze task for curriculum-based measurement of reading growth. *Journal of Special Education, 34,* 164–172.

Shin, M., & Bryant, D. P. (2015). A synthesis of mathematical and cognitive performances of students with mathematics learning disabilities. *Journal of Learning Disabilities, 48*(1), 96–112.

Shin, M., Bryant, D. P., Bryant, B. R., McKenna, J. W., Hou, F., & Ok, M. W. (2017). Virtual manipulatives: Tools for teaching mathematics to students with learning disabilities. *Intervention in School and Clinic, 52*(3), 148–153.

Shinn, M. R., & Hubbard, D. (1992). Curriculum-based measurement and problem-solving assessment: Basic procedures and outcomes. *Focus on Exceptional Children, 24,* 1–20.

Shogren, K. (2012). Hispanic mothers' perceptions of self-determination. *Research and Practice for Persons with Severe Disabilities, 37,* 170–184.

Shogren, K. A., Villirreal, M. G., Lang, K., & Seo, H. (2017). Mediating role of self-determination constructs in explaining the relationship between school factors and postschool outcomes. *Exceptional Children, 83*(2), 165–180.

Shores, K. (2017). *The Student with Poor Listening Skills, Education World.* Retrieved from: http://www.educationworld.com/a_curr/shore/shore055.shtml

Short, D., & Echevarria, J. (2004/2005). Teacher skills to support English language learners. *Educational Leadership, 62*(4), 8–13.

Shumate, E., & Wills, H. (2010). Classroom-based functional analysis and intervention for disruptive and off-task behaviors. *Education and Treatment of Children, 33,* 23–48.

Sideridis, G. S., & Scanlon, D. (Eds.). (2006). Motivational issues in learning disabilities. *Learning Disability Quarterly, 29*(3), 131–135.

Silberglitt, B., & Hintze, J.M. (2007). How much growth can we expect? A conditional analysis of R-CBM growth rates by level of performance. *Exceptional Children, 74,* 71–84.

Silva, J. M., Langhout, R. D., Kohfeldt, D., & Gurrola, E. (2015). "Good" and "bad" kids? A race and gender analysis of effective behavioral support in an elementary school. *Urban Education, 50,* 787–811.

Silver, L. B. (2010). *The misunderstood child: Understanding and coping with your child's learning disabilities.* (4th ed.). New York: Three Rivers Press.

Silverman, S. K., Hazelwood, C., & Cronin, P. (2009). *Universal education: Principles and practices for advancing achievement of students with disabilities.* Columbus, OH: Ohio Department of Education, Office for Exceptional Children. Retrieved from http://education.ohio.gov/GD/DocumentManagement/DocumentDownload.aspx?DocumentID=73339

Simmons, D. (2015). Instructional engineering principles to frame the future of reading intervention research and practice. *Remedial and Special Education, 36*(1), 45–51.

Simmons, D.C., Coyne, M.D., Hagan-Burke, S., Oi-Man, K., Leslie, S., Caitlin, J., & Yvel, C.C. (2011). Effects of supplemental reading interventions in authentic contexts: A comparison of kindergartners' response. *Exceptional Children, 77*(2), 201–228.

Simos, P. G., Fletcher, J. M., Sarkari, S., Billingsley-Marshall, R. L., Denton, C. A., & Papanicolaou, A. C. (2007). Intensive instruction affects brain magnetic activity associated with oral word reading in children with persistent reading disabilities. *Journal of Learning Disabilities, 40*(1), 37–48.

Simpson, R. L., Peterson, R. L., & Smith, C. R. (2011). Critical educational program components for students with emotional and behavioral disorders: Science, policy, and practice. *Remedial and Special Education, 32*, 230–242.

Singer, E. (2008). Coping with academic failure, a study of Dutch children with dyslexia. *Dyslexia, 14*(4), 314–333.

Singleton, S. M., & Filce, H. G. (2015). Graphic organizers for secondary students with learning disabilities. *Teaching Exceptional Children, 48*(2),110–117.

Skiba, R. J., Poloni-Staudinger, L. P., Simmons, A., Feggins-Assiz, L. R., & Chung, C. (2005). Unproven links: Can poverty explain ethnic disproportionality in special education? *Journal of Special Education, 39,* 130–144.

Skiba, R. J., Simmons, A. B., Ritter, S., Gibb, A. C., Rausch, M. K., Cuadrado, J., & Chung, C. (2008). Achieving equity in special education: History, status, and current challenges. *Exceptional Children, 74,* 264–288.

Skiba, R., Albrecht, S., & Losen, D. (2013). CCBD'S position summary on federal policy on disproportionality in special education. *Behavioral Disorders, 38*, 108–120.

Skilton-Sylvester, E., & Slesaransky-Poe, G. (2009). More than a least restrictive environment: Living up to the civil covenant in building inclusive schools. *Perspectives on Urban Education, 6,* 32–37.

Skinner, C. H., Mccleary, D. F., Skolits, G. L., Poncy, B. C., & Cates, G. L. (2013). Emerging opportunities for school psychologists to enhance our remediation procedure evidence base as we apply response to intervention. *Psychology in the Schools, 50,* 272–289.

Smith, C., & Strick, L. (2010). *Learning Disabilities: A to Z.* New York: Free Press.

Smith, J. M., Doabler, C. T., & Kame'enui, E. J. (2016). Using explicit and systematic instruction across academic domains. *Teaching Exceptional Children, 48*(6), 273–274.

Smith, K. G., Dombek, J. L., Foorman, B. R., Hook, K. S., Lee, L., Cote, A. . . . Stafford, T. (2016). *Self-study guide for implementing high school academic interventions* [REL 2016-218]. Washington, DC: Department of Education, Institute of Education Sciences, National Center for Education Evaluation and Regional Assistance, Regional Educational Laboratory Southeast. Retrieved from http://ies.ed.gov/ncee/edlabs

Smolkowski, K., Girvan, E. J., McIntosh, K., Nese, R. T., & Horner, R. H. (2016). Vulnerable decision points for disproportionate office discipline referrals: Comparisons of discipline for African American and White elementary school students. *Behavioral Disorders, 41,* 178–195.

Snell, M., Chen, L., Allaire, J., & Park, E. (2008). Communication breakdown at home and at school in young children with cerebral palsy and severe disabilities. *Research & Practice for Persons with Severe Disabilities, 33*, 25–36.

Snow, C. E., Burns, M. S., & Griffin, P. C. (1998). *Preventing reading difficulties in young children.* Washington, DC: National Academy Press.

Sobel, D. M., & Taylor, S. V. (2006). Blueprint for the responsive classroom. *Teaching Exceptional Children, 38*(5), 28–35.

Soleas, E. K. (2015). New teacher perceptions of inclusive practices: An examination of contemporary teacher education programs. *Alberta Journal of Educational Research, 61,* 294–313.

Solis, J. M., Shadur, J. M., Burns, A. R., & Hussong, A. M. (2012). Understanding the diverse needs of children whose parents abuse substances. *Current Drug Abuse Reviews, 5,* 135–147.

Solis, M., Vaughn, S., Swanson, E., & Mcculley, L. (2012). Collaborative models of instruction: The empirical foundations of inclusion and co-teaching. *Psychology in the Schools, 49,* 498–510.

Solish, A., Perry, A., & Minnes, P. (2010). Participation of children with and without disabilities in social, recreational and leisure activities. *Journal of Applied Research in Intellectual Disabilities, 23,* 226–236.

Southern Regional Education Board. (2011, November). *Address new, rigorous core state standards through English/language arts, mathematics, science, social studies and career/technical courses: High schools that work.* Atlanta: Author. Retrieved from http://publications.sreb.org/2011/11V20w_BestPractices_Address_New_Rigorous_Standards.pdf

Sparks, N. M. (2000, July). Assistive technology criteria. Paper presented at International Special Education Congress.

Sparks, S. D., & Harwin, A. (2016, August 23). Corporal punishment use found in schools in 21 states. *Education Week.* Retrieved from http://www.edweek.org/ew/articles/2016/08/23/corporal-punishment-use-found-in-schools-in.html

Spaulding, L. S., Mostert, M. P., & Beam, A. P. (2010). Is Brain Gym an effective educational intervention? *Exceptionality, 18,* 18–30.

Spencer, M., Wagner, R. K., Schatschneider, C., Quinn, J. M., Lopez, D., & Petscher, Y. (2014). Incorporating RtI in a hybrid model of reading disability. *Learning Disability Quarterly, 37*(3), 161–171.

Spiel, C. F., Evans, S. W., & Langberg, J. M. (2014). Evaluating the content of individualized education programs and 504 Plans of young adolescents with attention deficit/hyperactivity disorder. *School Psychology Quarterly, 29,* 452–468.

Spiel, C. F., Mixon, C. S., Holdaway, A. S., Evans, S. W., Harrison, J. R., Zoromski, A. K., & Yost, J. S. (2016). Is reading tests aloud an accommodation for youth with or at risk for ADHD? *Remedial and Special Education, 37*(2), 101–112.

Sporer, N., & Brunstein, J. (2009). Fostering the reading comprehension of secondary school students through peer-assisted learning: Effects on strategy knowledge, strategy use, and task performance. *Contemporary Educational Psychology, 34,* 289–297.

Staels, E., & Van den Boeck, W. (2015). Orthographic learning and the role of text-to-speech software in Dutch disabled readers. *Journal of Learning Disabilities, 48*(1), 39–50.

Stahl, R. B. (1994). Using "think-time" and "wait time" skillfully in the classroom. *ERIC Digest.* Bloomington, In.: ERIC Clearinghouse. ED370885.

Stahl, S. A. (1999). Vocabulary development. Cambridge: Brookline.

Stainback, S., & Stainback, W. (1988). Educating students with severe disabilities in regular classes. *Teaching Exceptional Children, 21*(1), 16–19.

Stambaugh, T., & Chandler, K. L. (2012). *Effective curriculum for underserved gifted students: A CEC-TAG educational resource.* Waco, TX: Prufrock.

Stanovich, K., & Siegel, L. S. (1994). Phenotypic performance profile of children with reading disabilities: A regression-based test of the phonological-core variable-difference model. *Journal of Educational Psychology, 86,* 24–53.

State, T. M., Harrison, J. R., Kern, L., & Lewis, T. J. (2017). Feasibility and acceptability of classroom-based interventions for students with emotional/behavioral challenges at the high school level. *Journal of Positive Behavior Interventions, 19*(1), 26–36.

Stecher, B. (2010). *Performance assessment in an era of standards-based educational accountability.* Stanford, CA: Stanford University, Stanford Center for Opportunity Policy in Education.

Stecker, P. M., Fuchs, L. S., & Fuchs, D. (2005). Using curriculum-based measurement to improve student achievement: Review of research. *Psychology in the Schools, 42*(8), 795–819.

Stein, M., Kinder, D., Silbert, J., & Carnine, D. G. (2005). *Designing effective mathematics instruction: A direct instruction approach* (4th ed.). Upper Saddle River, NJ: Prentice Hall.

Stenhoff, D. M., Davey, B. J., & Kraft, B. L. (2008). The effects of choice on assignment completion and percent correct by a high school student with a disability. *Education and Treatment of Children, 31*(2), 203–211.

Stichter, J. P., Conroy, M. A., & Kauffman, J. M. (2007). *An introduction to students with high-incidence disabilities.* Upper Saddle River, NJ: Pearson.

Stichter, J. P., Stormont, M., & Lewis, T. J. (2008). Instructional practices and behavior during reading: A descriptive summary and comparison of practices in Title One and non-Title elementary schools. *Psychology in the Schools, 46,* 172–183.

Stinson, M., Elliot, L., Kelly, R., & Yufang, L. (2009). Deaf and hard-of-hearing students' memory of lectures with speech-to-text and interpreting/note taking services. *Journal of Special Education, 43,* 52–64.

Stoiber, K., & Gettinger, M. (2011). Functional assessment and positive support strategies for promoting resilience: Effects on teachers and high-risk children. *Psychology in the Schools, 48,* 686–706.

Stone, S., & Uretsky, M. (2016). School correlates of academic behaviors and performance among McKinney-Vento identified youth. *Urban Education, 51,* 600–628.

Storey, K., & Post, M. (2012). *Positive behavior supports in classrooms and schools: Effective and practical strategies for teachers and other service providers.* Springfield, IL: Charles C. Thomas.

Storey, K., & Post, M. (2017). *Positive behavior supports in classrooms and schools: Effective and practical strategies for teachers and other service providers* (2nd edition). Springfield, IL: Charles C. Thomas.

Stosich, E. L. (2016). Building teacher and school capacity to teach to ambitious standards in high-poverty schools. *Teaching and Teacher Education, 58,* 43–53.

Stronge, J. H. (2002). *Qualities of effective teachers.* Alexandria, VA: Association of Supervision and Curriculum Development.

Sugai, G., & Horner, R. H. (2008). What we know and need to know about preventing problem behavior in schools. *Exceptionality, 16,* 67–77.

Sullivan, A. L. (2011). Disproportionality in special education identification of English language learners. *Exceptional Children, 77,* 317–334.

Sullivan, A. L., & Bal, A. (2013). Disproportionality in special education: Effects of individual and school variables on disability risk. *Exceptional Children, 79,* 475–494.

Sullivan, A. L., Artiles, A. J., & Hernandez-Saca, D. I. (2015). Addressing special education inequity through systemic change: Contributions of ecologically based organizational consultation. *Journal of Educational & Psychological Consultation, 25,* 129–147.

Sullivan, A.L. (2011). Disproportionality in special education identification and placement of English language learners. *Exceptional Children, 77*(3), 317–334.

Sun, Y. F., Lee, J. S., & Kirby, R. (2010). Brain imaging findings in dyslexia. *Pediatric Neonatal, 51*(2), 89–96.

Sutherland, K. S., Lewis-Palmer, T., Stichter, J., & Morgan, P. L. (2008). Examining the influence of teacher behavior and classroom context on the behavioral and academic outcomes for students with emotional and behavior disorders. *The Journal of Special Education, 41,* 223–233.

Swanson, E. A., & Vaughn, S. (2010). An observation study of reading instruction provided to elementary students with learning disabilities in the resource room. *Psychology in the Schools, 47,* 481–492.

Swanson, E., Hairrell, A., Kent, S., Ciullo, S., Wanzek, J., & Vaughn, S. (2014). A synthesis and meta-analysis of reading interventions using social studies content for students with learning disabilities. *Journal of Learning Disabilities, 47*(2), 178–195.

Swanson, H. L. (2000). What instruction works for students with learning disabilities? Summarizing the results from a meta-analysis of intervention studies. In R. Gersten, E. Schiller, & S. Vaughn (Eds.), *Contemporary special education research: Syntheses of the knowledge based on critical instructional issues* (pp. 1–30). Mahwah, NJ: Lawrence Erlbaum Associates.

Swanson, H. L. (2001). Reading intervention research outcomes and students with learning disabilities: What are the major instructional ingredients for successful outcomes? *Perspectives, 27*(2), 18–20.

Swanson, H. L., & Deshler, D. (2003). Instructing adolescents with learning disabilities: Converting a meta-analysis to practice. *Journal of Learning Disabilities, 36,* 124–135.

Swanson, H.L. (2011). Working memory, attention and mathematical problem solving: A longitudinal study of elementary school children. *Journal of Educational Psychology, 103*(4), 821–837.

Sze, S. (2009). A literature review: Pre-service teachers' attitudes toward students with disabilities. *Education, 130*(1), 53–56.

Tankersley, M., Harjusola-Webb, S., & Landrum, T. (2008). Using single-subject research to establish the evidence base of special education. *Intervention in School and Clinic, 44(2),* 83–90.

Taylor, K. R. (2011). Inclusion and the law: Two laws—IDEA and Section 504—support inclusion in schools. *Education Digest: Essential Readings Condensed for Quick Review, 76*(9), 48–51.

Teasley, M. L. (2016). Related services personnel and evidence-based practice: Past and present challenges. *Children & Schools, 38,* 5–8.

Test, D. W., Fowler, C. H., Brewer, D., & Wood, W. M. (2005). A content and methodological review of self-advocacy intervention studies. *Exceptional Children, 72*(1), 101–125.

Test, D. W., Mason, C., Hughes, C., Konrad, M., Neale, M., & Wood, W. M. (2004). Student involvement in individualized education program meetings. *Exceptional Children, 70,* 391–412.

The ARC. (2016). *History of The ARC.* Washington, DC: Author. Retrieved from http://www.thearc.org/who-we-are/history

The Iris Center (2010). *Assistive Technology: An Overview.* Retrieved from: https://iris.peabody.vanderbilt.edu/module/at/

Theoharis, G., & Causton, J. (2016). "He won't get anything out of this!" Intersections of race, disability, and access. *Journal of Cases in Educational Leadership, 19*(1), 40–50.

Therrien, W. J., Hughes, C., Kapelski, C., & Mokhtari, K. (2009). Effectiveness of a test-taking strategy on achievement in essay tests for students with learning disabilities. *Journal of Learning Disabilities, 41*(1), 14–23.

Theule, J., Wiener, J., Tannock, R., & Jenkins, J. M. (2013). Parenting stress in families of children with ADHD: A meta-analysis. *Journal of Emotional and Behavioral Disorders, 21,* 3–17.

Thompson, S., & Thurlow, M. (2003). *2003 state special education outcomes: Marching on.* Minneapolis, MN: University of Minnesota, National Center on Educational Outcomes. Retrieved from http://education.umn.edu/NCEO/OnlinePubs/2003StateReport.htm

Thompson, S., Thurlow, M., & Moore, M. (2006). *Using computer-based tests with students with disabilities: NCEO policy directions* (Synthesis Report No. 15). Minneapolis: University of Minnesota, National Center for Educational Outcomes.

Thurlow, M. L., Albus, D. A., & Lazarus, S. S. (2015). *Graduation policies for students with disabilities who participate in states' general assessments* (Synthesis Report 98). Minneapolis, MN: University of Minnesota, National Center on Educational Outcomes.

Thurlow, M. L., Elliott, J. L., & Ysseldyke, J. F. (2003). *Testing students with disabilities: Practical strategies for complying with district and state regulations* (2nd ed.). Thousand Oaks, CA: Corwin Press, Inc.

Thurlow, M., & Thompson, S. (2002). Large-scale assessment practices for students with disabilities in urban states. *Urban Perspectives, 7,* 1–13.

Thurlow, M., Lazarus, S. S., Albus, D., & Hodgson, J. (2010). *Computer-based testing: Practices and considerations* (Synthesis Report No. 78). Minneapolis: University of Minnesota, National Center on Educational Outcomes.

Thurlow, M., Test, D., Lazarus, S., Klare, M., & Fowler, C. (2016). *Considerations for developing state-defined alternate diplomas for students with significant cognitive disabilities.* Minneapolis: National Center on Educational Outcomes and the National Technical Assistance Center on Transition.

Thurlow, M. L., Quenmoen, R. F., & Lazarus, S. S. (2011). *Meeting the Needs of Special Education Students: Recommendations for Race to the Top.* Washington, DC: Arabella.

Tindal, G., McDonald, M., Tedesco, M., Glasgow, A., Almond, P., Crawford, L., & Hollenbeck, K. (2003). Alternate assessments in reading and math: Development and validation for students with significant disabilities. *Exceptional Children, 69,* 481–494.

Tomlinson, C. A. (2000). Reconcilable differences? Standards-based teaching and differentiation. *Educational Leadership, 58*(1), 6–11.

Tomlinson, C. A. (2005). Quality curriculum and instruction for highly able students. *Theory into Practice, 44,* 160–166.

Tomlinson, C. A. (2014). *The differentiated classroom: Responding to the needs of all learners.* Alexandria, Va.: ASCD.

Tomlinson, C. A. (2017). *How to differentiate instruction in academically diverse classrooms* (3rd edition). Alexandria, VA: ASCD.

Tomlinson, C. A., & Jarvis, J. (2006). Teaching beyond the book. *Educational Leadership, 64*(1), 16–21.

Toney, L. P., Kelley, M. L., & Lanclos, N. F. (2003). Self- and parental monitoring of homework in adolescents: Comparative effects on parents' perceptions of homework behavior problems [Electronic version]. *Child and Family Behavior Therapy, 25,* 35–51.

Topping, K., Buchs, C., Duran, D., & van Keer, H. (2017). *Effective peer learning: From principles to practical implementation.* New York, NY: Routledge.

Torgesen, J. (1991). Learning disabilities: Historical and conceptual issues. In B. Wong (Ed.), *Learning about learning disabilities* (pp. 3–39). San Diego, CA: Academic Press.

Torres, C., Farley, C. A., & Cook, B. G. (2014). A special educator's guide to successfully implementing evidence-based practices. *Teaching Exceptional Children, 47*(2), 85–93.

Toth, K., Munson, J., Meltzoff, A. N., & Dawson, G. (2006). Early predictors of communication development in young children with autism spectrum disorder: Joint attention, imitation, and toy play. *Journal of Autism and Developmental Disorders, 36,* 993–1005.

Towles-Reeves, E., Kleinert, H., & Muhomba, M. (2009). Alternate assessment: Have we learned anything new? *Exceptional Children, 75,* 233–252.

Treble-Barna, A., Zang, H., Zhang, N., Taylor, H. G., Stancin, T., Yeates, K. O., & Wade, S. L. (2016). Observed parent behaviors as time-varying moderators of problem behaviors following traumatic brain injury in young children. *Developmental Psychology, 52,* 1777–1792.

Trembath, D., Germano, C., Johanson, G., & Dissanayake, C. (2012). The experience of anxiety in young adults with autism spectrum disorders. *Focus on Autism and Other Developmental Disabilities, 27,* 213–224.

Tremblay, P. (2013). Comparative outcomes of two instructional models for students with learning disabilities: Inclusion with co-teaching and solo-taught special education. *Journal of Research in Special Educational Needs, 13,* 251–258.

Trenholm, S. (2011). *Thinking through communication: An introduction to the study of human communication* (6th ed.). Upper Saddle River, NJ: Pearson/Allyn & Bacon.

Treptow, M. A., Burns, M. K., & McComas, J. J. (2007). Reading at the frustration, instructional, and independent levels: Effects on student time on task and comprehension. *School Psychology Review, 36,* 159–166.

Trevisan, D. A., & Birmingham, E. (2016). Are emotion recognition abilities related to everyday social functioning in ASD? A meta-analysis. *Research in Autism Spectrum Disorders, 32,* 24–42.

Trexler, M. J. (2015). A case study analysis about the use of digital transition portfolio for secondary students with mild to moderate disabilities in an urban inclusive high school classroom. Baltimore, MD: Johns Hopkins University.

Trumbull, E., & Pacheco, M. (2005). Leading with diversity: Cultural competencies for teacher preparation and professional development. Providence, RI: Brown University. (ERIC Document Reproduction Service No. ED494221)

Trussell, R. (2008). Classroom universals to prevent problem behaviors. *Intervention in School and Clinic, 43,* 179–185.

Trute, B., Benzies, K. M., & Worthington, C. (2012). Mother positivity and family adjustment in households with children with a serious disability. *Journal of Child and Family Studies, 21,* 411–417.

Tucker, V., & Schwartz, I. (2013). Parents' perspectives of collaboration with school professionals: Barriers and facilitators to successful partnerships in planning for students with ASD. *School Mental Health, 5*(1), 3–14.

Turnbull, A., Turnbull, R., Erwin, E. J., Soodak, L. C., & Shogren, K. A. (2011). *Families, professionals, and exceptionality: Positive outcomes through partnerships and trust* (6th ed.). Upper Saddle River, NJ: Merrill/Pearson.

Turnbull, B. J., & Arcaira, E. R. (2012). Implementation of turnaround strategies in chronically low-performing schools. Evanston, IL: Society for Research on Educational Effectiveness. Retrieved from http://www.eric.ed.gov/contentdelivery/servlet/ERICServlet?accno=ED535511

Tyler, K. A., Hagewen, K. J., & Melander, L. A. (2011). Risk factors for running away among a general population sample of males and females. *Youth & Society, 43,* 583–608.

U.S. Department of Education (2008, October). Questions and Answers on Report Cards and Transcripts for Students with Disabilities Attending Public Elementary and Secondary Schools. Retrieved from https://www2.ed.gov/about/offices/list/ocr/letters/colleague-qa-20081017.html

U.S. Department of Education (2010). *National Education Technology Plan.* Washington, DC: Author. Retrieved from: http://www.ed.gov/technology/netp-2010/

U.S. Department of Education. (2007). *Final regulations on modified academic achievement standards.* Retrieved from Special Education and Rehabilitative Services website, http://www.ed.gov/policy/speced/guid/modachieve-summary.html

U.S. Department of Education. (2010). *Thirty-five years of progress in educating children with disabilities through "IDEA."* Washington, DC: U.S. Department of Education, Office of Special Education and Rehabilitative Services.

U.S. Department of Education. (2010, August). *Free appropriate public education for students with disabilities: Requirements under Section 504 of The Rehabilitation Act of 1973.* Washington, DC: Author. Retrieved from https://www2.ed.gov/about/offices/list/ocr/docs/edlite-FAPE504.html

U.S. Department of Education. (2011). *Thirtieth annual report to Congress on the implementation of Individuals with Disabilities Education Act, 2011.* Washington, DC: Author.

U.S. Department of Education. (2012). *ESEA flexibility.* Retrieved from http://www2.ed.gov/policy/elsec/guid/esea-flexibility/index.html

U.S. Department of Education. (2013). *OSEP Center on positive behavioral interventions & supports: Effective schoolwide interventions.* Washington, DC: Author, Office of Special Education Programs. Retrieved from http://www.pbis.org/

U.S. Department of Education. (2016). *38th annual report to Congress on the implementation of the Individuals with Disabilities Education Act*. Washington, DC: Author. Retrieved from https://www2.ed.gov/about/reports/annual/osep/2016/parts-b-c/38th-arc-for-idea.pdf

U.S. Department of Education. (2016). *EDFacts data warehouse (EDW): IDEA Part B child count and educational environments collection, 2015–16* (Data extracted as of July 14, 2016, from file specifications 002 and 089). Washington, DC: Author. Retrieved from https://www2.ed.gov/programs/osepidea/618-data/static-tables/index.html#partb-cc

U.S. Department of Education. (2016, July). *The state of racial diversity in the educator workforce*. Washington, DC: Office of Planning, Evaluation and Policy Development; Policy and Program Studies Service, Author. Retrieved from https://www2.ed.gov/rschstat/eval/higher/racial-diversity/state-racial-diversity-workforce.pdf

U.S. Department of Education. (2017). *Positive behavioral interventions & supports* [website]. Washington, DC: OSEP Technical Assistance Center on Positive Behavioral Interventions and Support. Retrieved from https://www.pbis.org/

U.S. Department of Education. (2017a, January). Number of students ages 6 through 21 served under IDEA, Part B, by disability and state. *IDEA Section 618 data products: State tables.* Washington, DC: Author. Retrieved from https://www2.ed.gov/programs/osepidea/618-data/static-tables/index.html#partb-cc

U.S. Department of Education. (2017b, January). Students ages 6 through 21 served under IDEA, Part B, as a percentage of the population, by disability category and state. *IDEA Section 618 data products: State tables.* Washington, DC: Author. Retrieved from https://www2.ed.gov/programs/osepidea/618-data/static-tables/index.html#partb-cc

U.S. Department of Education, Office of Special Education and Rehabilitative Services, Office of Special Education Programs. (2016, October). *38th annual report to Congress on the implementation of the Individuals with Disabilities Education Act*. Washington, DC: Author. Retrieved from https://www2.ed.gov/about/reports/annual/osep/2016/parts-b-c/38th-arc-for-idea.pdf

U.S. Department of Health & Human Services. (2017). *Child maltreatment 2015*. Washington, DC: Administration for Children and Families, Administration on Children, Youth and Families, Children's Bureau. Retrieved from http://www.acfhhs.gov/programs/ cb/research-data-technology/statistics-research/child-maltreatment

U.S. Department of Health and Human Services. (2007, April). *Results from the 2005 national survey on drug use and health: National findings.* Washington, DC: Author. Retrieved August 2, 2007, from www.oas.samhsa.gov/NSDUH/2k5NSDUH/2k5results.htm#Ch2

U.S. Department of Health and Human Services, Administration for Children and Families, Administration on Children, Youth and Families, Children's Bureau. (2012). *Child maltreatment 2011.* Washington, DC: Author. Retrieved from http://www.acf.hhs.gov/programs/cb/research-data-technology/statistics-research/child-maltreatment

Uberti, H. Z., Mastropieri, M. A., & Scruggs, T. E. (2004). Check it off: Individualizing a math algorithm for students with disabilities via self-monitoring checklists. *Intervention in School and Clinic*, 39(5), 269–275.

Uberti, H.Z., Scruggs, T.E., & Mastropieri, M. A. (2003). Keywords make the difference! Mnemonic instruction in inclusive classrooms. *Teaching Exceptional Children, 10(3),* 56–61.

Umansky, I. M. (2016). Leveled and exclusionary tracking: English learners' access to academic content in middle school. *American Educational Research Journal*, 53, 1792–1833.

Umansky, I. M., Valentino, R. A., & Reardon, S. F. (2016). The promise of two-language education. *Helping ELLs Excel, 73*(5), 10–17.

United Cerebral Palsy. (2013). Cerebral palsy fact sheet. Washington, DC: Author. Retrieved from http://www.ucp.org/uploads/media_items/cp-fact-sheet.original.pdf

United Cerebral Palsy. (2013). *History of UCP*. Retrieved from http://www.ucp.org/about/history

United Cerebral Palsy. (2015). *History of UCP*. Washington, DC: Author. Retrieved from http://www.ucp.org/about/history

United Federation of Teachers. (2007, August). *Child abuse: Questions and answers for New York City's educators* (7th ed.). New York: Author. Retrieved from http://www.uft.org/member/education/development/brochure/article3

Urban-Woldron, H (2009). Interactive simulations for the effective learning of physics. *Journal of Computers in Mathematics and Science Teaching, 28*(2), 163–176.

Vacca, R. T., & Vacca, J. L., & Mraz, M.E.(2013). *Content area reading: Literacy and learning across the curriculum* (11th ed.) Boston: Little Brown.

Valente, J. M., & Danforth, S. (2016). *Life in inclusive classrooms: Storytelling with disability studies in education* (occasional paper series 36). New York, NY: Bank Street College of Education. Retrieved from https://d2mguk73h8xisw.cloudfront.net/media/filer_public/filer_public/2016/11/15/ops_36_4_1021.pdf

Valle, J. W., & Conner, D. J. (2011). *Rethinking disability: A disability studies approach to inclusive practices*. New York: McGraw-Hill.

van Ginkel, G., Oolbekkink, H., Meijer, P. C., & Verloop, N. (2016). Adapting mentoring to individual differences in novice teacher learning: The mentor's viewpoint. *Teachers and Teaching: Theory and Practice*, 22, 198–218.

Van Laarhoven-Myers, T. E., Van Laarhoven, T. R., Smith, T. J., Johnson, H., & Olson, J. (2016). Promoting self-determination and transition planning using technology: Student and parent perspectives. *Career Development and Transition for Exceptional Individuals*, 39, 99–110.

Vandercook, T., York, J., & Forest, M. (1989). The McGill Action Planning System (MAPS): A strategy for building the vision. *Journal of the Association for Persons with Severe Handicaps (JASH), 14*(3), 205–218.

VanDerHyden, A., Burns, M., Brown, R., Shinn, M. R., Kukic, S., Gibbons, K., Batsche, G., & Tilly, W. D. (2016). Four steps to implement RTI correctly. Retrived from http//www.edweek.org/ew/articles/2016/01/06/four-steps-to-implement-rti-correctly.html

Vannest, K.J., Parker, R., & Dyer, N. (2011). Progress monitoring in grade 5 science for low achievers. *The Journal of Special Education, 44*(4), 221–233.

VanTassel-Baska, J. (2003). *Curriculum planning and instructional design for gifted learners*. Denver, CO: Love.

VanTassel-Baska, J. L., Cross, T., & Olenchak, F. R. (Eds.). (2009). *Social-emotional curriculum with gifted and talented students*. Waco, TX: Prufrock.

VanTassel-Baska, J., Feng, A., Swanson, J., Chandler, K., & Quek, C. (2009). *Patterns of development to the special needs of gifted learners*. Denver: Love.

Vaughn, B. S., Roberts, H. J., & Needelman, H. (2009). Current medications for the treatment of attention-deficit/hyperactivity disorder. *Psychology in the Schools, 46*, 846–856.

Vaughn, S., & Bos, C. S. (2014). *Strategies for teaching students with learning and behavior problems* (9th ed.). Upper Saddle River, NJ.: Merrill/Pearson.

Vaughn, S., & Fletcher, J. M. (2012). Response to intervention with secondary school students with reading difficulties. *Journal of Learning Disabilities, 45*, 244–256.

Vaughn, S., Cirino, P., Tolar, T., Fletcher, J., Cardenas-Hagan, E., Carlson, C., et al. (2008). Long-term follow-up of Spanish and English interventions for first-grade English language learners at risk for reading problems. *Journal of Research on Educational Effectiveness, 1*, 179–214.

Vaughn, S., Hughes, M. T., Moody, S. W., & and Elbaum, B. (2001). Instructional grouping for reading for students with LD: Implications for practice. *Intervention in School and Clinic, 36*(3), 131–137

Vaughn, S., Linan-Thompson, S., Kouzekanani, K., Pedrotty-Bryant, D., Dickson, S., & Blozis, S.A. Reading instruction grouping for students with reading difficulties. *Remedial and Special Education, 24*(5), 301–315.

Vaughn, S., Wanzek, J., Murray, C. S., Scamacca, N., Linan-Thompson, S., & Woodruff, A. L. (2009). Response to early reading interventions: Examining higher responders and lower responders. *Exceptional Children, 75,* 165–183.

Vaughn, S., Wanzek, J., Wexler, J., Barth, A., Cirono, P.T., Fletcher, J., Romain, M., Denton, C. A., Roberts, G., & Francis, D. (2010). The relative effects of group size on reading progress of older students with reading difficulties. *Reading and Writing, 23*(8), 931–956.

Vaughn, S., Wexler, J., Leroux, A., Roberts, G., Denton, C., Barth, A., & Fletcher, J. (2013). Effects of intensive reading intervention for eighth-grade students with persistently inadequate response to intervention. *Journal of Learning Disabilities, 45*(6), 515–525.

Verill, O H., & Rinaldi, C. (2011, May). *Research brief: Multi-tier system of supports (MTSS).* Waltham, MA: Urban Special Education Leadership Collaborative. Retrieved from https://www.urbancollaborative.org/sites/urbancollaborative.org/files/mtss_brief_final.modified_1.pdf

Vincent, C. G., Randall, C., Cartledge, G., Tobin, T. J., & Swain-Bradway, J. (2011). Toward a conceptual integration of cultural responsiveness and schoolwide positive behavior support. *Journal of Positive Behavior Interventions, 13,* 219–229.

Vinoski, E., Graybill, E., & Roach, A. (2016). Building self-determination through inclusive extracurricular programs. *Teaching Exceptional Children, 48*(5), 258–265.

Vogel-Walcutt, J. J., Schatschneider, C., & Bowers, C. (2011). Social-emotional functioning of elementary-age deaf children: A profile analysis. *American Annals of the Deaf, 156*(1), 6–22.

Voix, R. G. (1968). *Evaluating reading and study skills in the secondary classroom: A guide for content teachers.* Newark, DE: International Reading Association.

Volpe, R. J., DuPaul, G. J., Jitendra, A. K., & Tresco, K. E. (2009). Consultation-based academic interventions for children with attention deficit hyperactivity disorder: Effects on reading and mathematics outcomes at 1-year follow-up. *School Psychology Review, 38,* 5–13.

von Ravensberg, H., & Blakely, A. (2014). *When to use functional behavioral assessment? Best practice vs. legal guidance* [website]. Retrieved from https://www.pbis.org/evaluation/evaluation-briefs/when-to-use-fba

Vossekuil, B., Fein, R. A., Reddy, M., Borum, R., & Modzeleski, W. (2004, July). *The final report and findings of the safe school initiative: Implications for the prevention of school attacks in the United States.* Washington, DC: U. S. Department of Education and U.S. Secret Service. Retrieved from http://www2.ed.gov/admins/lead/safety/preventingattacksreport.pdf

Vu, J. A., Babikian, T., & Asarnow, R. (2011). Academic and language outcomes in children after traumatic brain injury: A meta-analysis. *Exceptional Children, 77,* 263–281.

Vue, G., Hall, T. E., Robinson, K., Ganley, P., Elizalde, E., & Graham, S. (2016). Informing understanding of young students' writing challenges and opportunities: Insights from the development of a digital writing tool that supports students with learning disabilities. *Learning Disability Quarterly, 39*(2), 83–94. doi:10.1177/0731948715604571

Vujnovic, R. K., Fabiano, G. A., Morris, K. L., Norman, K., Hallmark, C., & Hartley, C. (2014). Examining school psychologists' and teachers' application of approaches within a response to intervention framework. *Exceptionality, 22,* 129–140.

Wade, J. L., & Reeve, R. E. (2014). Autism spectrum disorder and intellectual giftedness. In J. A. Plucker, C. M. Callahan, J. A. Plucker, C. M. Callahan (Eds.), *Critical issues and practices in gifted education: What the research says (*2nd edition), (pp. 77–93). Waco, TX: Prufrock Press.

Wade, S., Carey, J., & Wolfe, C. (2006). An online family intervention to reduce parental distress following pediatric brain injury. *Journal of Consulting and Clinical Psychology, 74,* 445–454.

Waitoller, F. R., Artiles, A. J., & Cheney, D. A. (2010). The miner's canary: A review of overrepresentation research and explanations. *Journal of Special Education, 44*(1), 29–49. doi:10.1177/0022466908329226

Waldron, N. L., & McLeskey, J. (2010). Establishing a collaborative school culture through comprehensive school reform. *Journal of Educational and Psychological Consultation, 20,* 58–74.

Walker, A. R., & Test, D. W. (2010). Using a self-advocacy intervention on African American college students' ability to request academic accommodations. *Learning Disabilities Research & Practice, 26*(3), 134–144.

Walker-Dalhouse, D., Risko, V., Esworthy, C., Grasley, E., Kaisler, G., McIlvain, D., Stephan, M. (2009). Crossing boundaries and initiating conversations about RTI: Understanding and applying differentiated classroom instruction. *Reading Teacher, 63,* 84–87.

Walser, K., Ayres, K., & Foote, E. (2012). Effects of a video model to teach students with moderate intellectual disability to use key features of an iPhone. *Education and Training in Autism and Developmental Disabilities, 47,* 319–331.

Walsh, J. M. (2012). Co-teaching as a school system strategy for continuous improvement. *Preventing School Failure, 56*(1), 29–36.

Walsh, M. (2013, April). Court upholds school's use of "timeout room." *Education Week.* Retrieved from http://blogs.edweek.org/edweek/school_law/2013/04/court_upholds_schools_use_of_t.html

Walton, K. M., & Ingersoll, B. R. (2013). Improving social skills in adolescents and adults with autism and severe to profound intellectual disability: A review of the literature. *Journal of Autism and Developmental Disorders, 43,* 594–615.

Wannarka, R., & Ruhl, K. (2008). Seating arrangements that promote positive academic outcomes: A review of the empirical research. *Support for Learning, 23*(2), 89–93. Retrived from www.corelearn.com/files/Archer/Seating-Arrangements.pdf

Wanzek, J., Vaughn, S., Wexler, J., Swanson, E., Edmonds, M., & Kim, A. (2006). A synthesis of spelling and reading interventions and their effects on the spelling outcomes of students with LD. *Journal of Learning Disabilities, 39*(6), 528–543.

Warger, C. (2017). *Five homework strategies for teaching students with learning disabilities.* Retrieved from http://www.ldonline.org/article/Five_Homework_Strategies_for_Students_With_Learning_Disabilities

Warren, J. S., Bohanon-Edmonson, H. M., Turnbull, A. P., Sailor, W., Wickham. D., Griggs, P., et al. (2006). School-wide positive behavior support: Addressing behavior problems that impede student learning. *Educational Psychology Review, 18,* 187–198.

Warren, S., Thurlow, M., Christensen, L., Lazarus, S., & Moen, R., Davis, K., & Rieke, R. (2011). *Forum on accommodations in the 21st century: Critical considerations for students with disabilities.* Minneapolis, MN: University of Minnesota, National Center on Educational Outcomes and Washington, DC: Council of Chief State School Officers, Assessing Special Education Students State Collaborative on Assessment and Student Standards.

Wasburn-Moses, L., Chun, E., & Kaldenberg, E. (2013). Paraprofessional roles in an adolescent reading program: Lessons learned. *American Secondary Education, 41*(3), 34–49.

Watson, S. (2004). Open the science doorway: Strategies and suggestions for incorporating English language learners in the science classroom. *Science Teacher, 71*(2), 32–35.

Wayman, M. M., McMaster, K. L., Sáenz, L. M., & Watson, J. A. (2010). Using curriculum-based measurement to monitor secondary English language learners' responsiveness to peer-mediated reading instruction. *Reading & Writing Quarterly: Overcoming Learning Difficulties, 26,* 308–332.

Wayman, M., McMaster, K. L., Saenz, L. M., & Watson, J. A. (2010). Using curriculum-based measurement to monitor secondary English language learners' responsiveness to peer-mediated reading instruction. *Reading & Writing Quarterly, 26*, 308–332.

Webb, C. E., Coleman, P. T., Rossignac-Milon, M., Tomasulo, S. J., & Higgins, E. T. (2017). Moving on or digging deeper: Regulatory mode and interpersonal conflict resolution. *Journal of Personality and Social Psychology, 112*, 621–641.

Webb, M., Lederberg, A. R., Branum-Martin, L., & McDonald Connor, C. (2015). Evaluating the structure of early English literacy skills in deaf and hard-of-hearing children. *Journal of Deaf Studies and Deaf Education, 20*, 343–355.

Wehmeyer, M. L., Palmer, S. B., Shogren, K., Williams-Diehm, K., & Soukup, J. H. (2013). Establishing a causal relationship between intervention to promote self-determination and enhanced student self-determination. *Journal of Special Education, 46*, 195–210.

Wehmeyer, M. L., Shogren, K. A., Toste, J. R., & Mahal, S. (2017). Self-determined learning to motivate struggling learners in reading and writing. *Intervention in School and Clinic, 52*(5), 295–303.

Weiser, B. (2014). *Academic diversity: Ways to motivate and engage students with learning disabilities.* Austin, Tx.: Council for Learning Disabilities. Retrieved from http://www.council-for-learning-disabilities.org/wp-content/uploads/2014/07/Weiser_Motaching Exceptional Children, Vol. 42, No.

Weisz, J. R., Kuppens, S., Ng, M. Y., Eckshtain, D., Ugueto, A. M., Vaughn-Coaxum, R., & . . . Fordwood, S. R. (2017). What five decades of research tells us about the effects of youth psychological therapy: A multilevel meta-analysis and implications for science and practice. *American Psychologist, 72*, 79–117.

Welch, A. B. (2000). Responding to student concerns about fairness. *Teaching Exceptional Children, 33*(2), 36–40.

Wellner, L. (2012). Building parent trust in the special education setting. *Leadership, 41*(4), 16–19.

Welsh, M. E., & D'Agostino, J. V. (2009). Fostering consistency between standards-based grades and large-scale assessment results. In T. R. Guskey (Ed.), *Practical solutions for serious problems in standards-based grading* (pp. 75–104). Thousand Oaks, CA: Corwin.

Wery, J. J., & Niefeld, J. L. (2010). Supporting self-regulated learning with exceptional children. *Teaching Exceptional Children, 42*(4), 70–78.

Wery, J., & Thomson, M. M. (2013). Motivational strategies to enhance effective learn- ing in teaching struggling students. *Support for Learning, 28*(3), 103–108.

Westling, D. (2010). Teachers and challenging behavior: Knowledge, views, and practices. *Remedial and Special Education, 31*, 48–63.

Wexler, J., Reed, D. K., Mitchell, M., Doyle, B., & Clancy, E. (2015). Implementing an evidence-based instructional routine to enhance comprehension of expository text. *Intervention in School and Clinic, 50*(3), 142–149.

Wexler, J., Reed, D. K., Pyle, N., Mitchell, M., & Barton, E. E. (2015). A synthesis of peer-mediated academic interventions for secondary struggling learners. *Journal of Learning Disabilities, 48*, 451–470.

What Works Clearinghouse. (2013). *Peer-assisted learning strategies. What Works Clearinghouse intervention report.* Washington, DC: What Works Clearinghouse, Institute of Education Sciences, U.S. Department of Education. Retrieved from http://files.eric.ed.gov/fulltext/ED539064.pdf

Wheatley, R., West, R., Charlton, C., Sanders, R., Smith, T., & Taylor, M. (2009). Improving behavior through differential reinforcement: A praise note system for elementary school students. *Education and Treatment of Children, 32*, 551–571.

Wheeler, J. J., & Richey, D. D. (2005). *Behavior management: Principles and practices of positive behavior supports.* Upper Saddle River, NJ: Merrill/Prentice Hall.

Whitaker Sena, J. D., Lowe, P. A., & Lee, S. W. (2007). Significant predictors of test anxiety among students with and without learning disabilities. *Journal of Learning Disabilities, 40*, 360–376.

White, R. B., Polly, D., & Audette, R. H. (2012). A case analysis of an elementary school's implementation of response to intervention. *Journal of Research In Childhood Education, 26*, 73–90.

Whiting-MacKinnon, C., & Roberts, J. (2012). The school experiences of children with epilepsy: A phenomenological study. *Physical Disabilities: Education and Related Services, 31*(2), 18–34.

WIDA. (2017, June). *WIDA performance definitions—Speaking and writing grades K–12.* Madison, WI: Author. Retrieved from https://www.wida.us/get.aspx?id=543

Wiek, A., Xiong, A., Brundiers, K., & van der Leeuw, S. (2014). *International Journal of Sustainability, 15*(4), 431–449.

Wilen, W. W., Ishler, M., Hutchinson, J., & Kindsvatter, R. (1999). *Dynamics of effective teaching* (4th ed.). Boston: Allyn & Bacon.

Williams, G. J., & Reisberg, L. (2003). Successful inclusion: Teaching social skills through curriculum integration. *Intervention in School and Clinic, 38*, 205–210.

Williamson, P., & McLeskey, J. (2011). An investigation into the nature of inclusion problem-solving teams. *Teacher Educator, 46*, 316–334.

Wills, H. P., & Mason, B. A. (2014). Implementation of a self-monitoring application to improve on-task behavior: A high school pilot study. *Journal of Behavioral Education, 23*(4), 421–434.

Wilson, G. L. (2016). Revisiting classroom routines. *Educational Leadership, 73*(4), 50–55.

Wilson, G. L., & Bladnick, J. (2011). *Teaching in tandem: Effective co-teaching in the inclusive classroom.* Alexandria, VA: ASCD.

Wilson, J., Fang, C., Rollins, J., & Valadez, D. (2016). An urgent challenge: Enhancing academic speaking opportunities for English learners. *Multicultural Education, 23*(2), 52–54.

Winkler, J. L., Walsh, M. E., de Blois, M., Maré, J., & Carvajal, S. C. (2017). Kind discipline: Developing a conceptual model of a promising school discipline approach. *Evaluation and Program Planning, 62*, 15–24.

Winter-Messiers, M. A., & Herr, C. M. (2010). Dinosaurs 24/7: Understanding the special interests of children with Asperger's. Baltimore, MD: Interactive Autism Network of the Kennedy Kreiger Institute. Retrieved from https://iancommunity.org/cs/about_asds/the_special_interests_of_children_with_aspergers

Winter-Messiers, M. A., Herr, C. M., Wood, C. E., Brooks, A. P., Gates, M. A. M., Houston, T. L., & Tingstad, K. I. (2007). How far can Brian ride the Daylight 4449 Express? A strength-based model of Asperger syndrome based on special interest areas. *Focus on Autism and Other Developmental Disabilities, 22*, 67–79.

Winters, K., Lee, S., Botzet, A., Fahnhorst, T., Realmuto, G., & August, G. (2011). A prospective examination of the association of stimulant medication history and drug use outcomes among community samples of ADHD youths. *Journal of Child & Adolescent Substance Abuse, 20*, 314–329.

Winzer, M. A. (1993). *The history of special education: From isolation to integration.* Washington, DC: Gallaudet University Press.

Wodrich, D., & Spencer, M. (2007). The other health-impairment category and health-based classroom accommodations: School psychologists' perceptions and practices. *Journal of Applied School Psychology, 24*, 109–125.

Wood, J. W., Miederhoff, J. W., & Ulschmid, B. (1989). Adapting test construction for mainstreamed social studies students. *Social Education, 53*(1), 46–49.

Wood, K. D., Lapp, D., Flood, J., & Taylor, D. B. (2008). *Guiding Reading Through Text: Strategy Guides for New Times* (2nd ed.). Newark, DE: International Reading Association.

Worley, C. (2015). The perfect girl syndrome: Perfectionism and self-esteem in gifted girls. *Parenting for High Potential, 5*(1), 6–7.

Wormeli, R. (2006). *Fair isn't always equal: Assessing and grading in the differentiated classroom*. Portland, ME: Stenhouse Publishers.

Wormeli, R. (2007). *Differentiation: From planning to practice: Grades 6–12*. Portland, ME: Stenhouse Publishers.

Wright, P. W. D., Wright, P. D., & O'Connor, S. W. (2010). *Wrightslaw: All about IEPs*. Hartfield, VA: Harbor House Law Press.

Wright, P. W. D., & Wright, P. D. (2006). *IDEA 2004*. Hartfield, VA: Harbor House Law Press.

Wright-Gallo, G. L., Higbee, T. S., & Reagon, K. A. (2006). Classroom-based functional analysis and intervention for students with emotional/behavioral disorders. *Education and Treatment of Children, 29*, 421–434.

Wu, E. H. (2013). The path leading to differentiation: An interview with Carol Tomlinson. *Journal of Advanced Academics, 24*, 125–133.

Xenofontos, C. (2016). Teaching mathematics in culturally and linguistically-diverse classrooms: Greek-Cypriot elementary teachers reported practices and professional needs. *Journal of Urban Mathematics Education, 9*(1), 94–116 ©JUME. Retrieved from http://education.gsu.edu/JUME

Xu, Z. X. (2016). Just do it! Reducing academic procrastination of secondary students. *Intervention in School and Clinic, 5*(4), 212–219.

Yakimowski, M. E., Faggella-Luby, M., Kim, Y., & Wei, Y. (2016). Reading achievement in the middle school years: A study investigating growth patterns by high incidence disability. *Journal of Education for Students Placed at Risk, 21*, 118–128.

Yakubova, G., & Taber-Doughty, T. (2017). Improving problem-solving performance of students with autism spectrum disorders. *Focus on Autism and Other Developmental Disabilities, 32*(1), 3–17.

Yang, Y. F. (2002). Reassessing readers comprehension monitoring. *Reading in a Foreign Language, 14*, 18–42.

Yell, M. L. (2006). *The law and special education* (2nd ed.). Upper Saddle River, NJ: Merrill/Pearson.

Yell, M. L. (2012). *The law and special education* (3d edition). Boston, MA: Pearson.

Yell, M. L., & Gatti, S. (2012). Legal issues and teachers of students with emotional and behavioral disorders. In J. P. Bakken, F. E. Obiakor, & A. F. Rotatori (Eds.), *Behavioral disorders: Identification, assessment, and instruction of students with EBD* [Advances in Special Education, Volume 22] (pp. 1–29). Cambridge, MA: Emerald Group.

Yell, M. L., Katsiyannis, A., Ennis, R. P., Losinski, M., & Christle, C. A. (2016). Avoiding substantive errors in individualized education program development. *Teaching Exceptional Children, 49*(1), 31–40.

Yell, M. L., Katsiyannis, A., Losinski, M., & Marshall, K. (2016). Peer-reviewed research and the IEP: Implications of "Ridley School District v. M.R. and J.R. ex rel. E.R." (2012). *Intervention in School and Clinic, 51*, 253–257.

Yell, M. L., Rogers, D., & Rogers, E. L. (1998). The legal history of special education: What a long, strange trip it's been! *Remedial and Special Education, 19*, 219–228.

Yell, M., Ryan, J., Rozalski, M., & Katsiyannis, A. (2009). The U.S. Supreme Court and special education: 2005 to 2007. *Teaching Exceptional Children, 41*(3), 68–75.

Yoder, P., & Lieberman, R. (2010). Brief report: Randomized test of the efficacy of picture exchange communication system on highly generalized picture exchanges in children with ASD. *Journal of Autism and Developmental Disorders, 40*, 629–632.

Yoon, I. H. (2016). Trading stories: Middle-class White women teachers and the creation of collective narratives about students and families in a diverse elementary school. *Teachers College Record, 118*(2), 1–54.

Young, H. L., & Gaughan, E. (2010). A multiple method longitudinal investigation of pre-referral intervention team functioning: Four years in rural schools. *Journal of Educational & Psychological Consultation, 20*, 106–138.

Young, S., & Amarasinghe, J. (2010). Practitioner review: Non-pharmacological treatments for ADHD: A lifespan approach. *Journal of Child Psychology and Psychiatry, 51*, 116–133.

Ysseldyke, J., Burns, M. K., Scholin, S. E., & Parker, D. C. (2010). Instructionally valid assessment within response to intervention. *Teaching Exceptional Children, 42*(4), 54–61.

Ysseldyke, J., Dennison, A., & Nelson, R. (2003). Large-scale assessment and accountability systems: Positive consequences for students with disabilities (Synthesis Report 51). Minneapolis, MN: University of Minnesota, National Center on Educational Outcomes. Retrieved from http://education.umn.edu/NCEO/OnlinePubs/Synthesis51.html Google Scholar

Zablotsky, B., Boswell, K., & Smith, C. (2012). An evaluation of school involvement and satisfaction of parents of children with autism spectrum disorders. *American Journal on Intellectual and Developmental Disabilities, 117*, 316–330.

Zarger M., & Rich, B. (2016, December). Predictors of treatment utilization among adolescents with social anxiety disorder. *Children and Youth Services Review, 71*, 191–198.

Zascavage, V. & Winterman, K. G. (2009). What middle school educators should know about assistive technology and universal design for learning. *Middle School Journal, 40*(4), 46–52.

Zebehazy, K. T., & Smith, T. J. (2011). An examination of characteristics related to the social skills of youths with visual impairments. *Journal of Visual Impairment & Blindness, 105*, 84–95.

Zeitlin, V. M., & Curcic, S. (2014). Parental voices on individualized education programs: 'Oh, IEP meeting tomorrow? Rum tonight!' *Disability & Society, 29*, 373–387.

Zirkel, P. (2009a). Section 504: Student eligibility update. *Clearing House: A Journal of Educational Strategies, Issues, Ideas, 82*, 209–211.

Zirkel, P. (2009b). What does the law say? *Teaching Exceptional Children, 42*, 73–75.

Zirkel, P. A. (2011). Legal currency in special education law. *Principal Leadership, 12*(3), 50–54.

Zirkel, P. A. (2012). Section 504 for special education leaders: Persisting and emerging issues. *Journal of Special Education Leadership, 25*, 99–105.

Zirkel, P. A. (2013). The legal meaning of specific learning disability for IDEA eligibility: The latest case law. *Communique, 41*(5), 10–12.

Zirkel, P. A. (2015). Special education law: Illustrative basics and nuances of key IDEA components. *Teacher Education and Special Education, 38*, 263–275.

Zirkel, P. A., & McGuire, B. L. (2010). A roadmap to legal dispute resolution for students with disabilities. *Journal of Special Education Leadership, 23*, 100–112.

Zirkel, P. A., & Thomas, L. B. (2010). State laws for RTI: An updated snapshot. *Teaching Exceptional Children, 42*(3), 56–63.

Zirkel, P. A., & Weathers, J. M. (2015). Section 504-only students: National incidence data. *Journal of Disability Policy Studies, 26*, 184–193.

Zirkel, P. A., & Weathers, J. M. (2016). K–12 students eligible solely under section 504: Updated national incidence data. *Journal of Disability Policy Studies, 27*, 67–75.

Zirkel, P., & Krohn, N. (2008). RTI after IDEA: A survey of state laws. *Teaching Exceptional Children, 40*(3), 71–73.

Zirkel, S. (2008). The influence of multicultural educational practices on student outcomes and intergroup relations. *Teachers College Record, 110*, 1147–1181.

Zirpoli, T. J. (2016). *Behavior management: Positive applications for teachers* (7th edition). Boston, MA: Pearson.

Zumeta, R. O. (2015). Implementing intensive intervention: How do we get there from here? *Remedial and Special Education, 36*(2), 83–88.

NAME INDEX